Communication at a Distance

The Influence of
Print on Sociocultural
Organization and Change

COMMUNICATION

A series of volumes edited by
Dolf Zillmann and Jennings Bryant

Barton • Ties That Blind in Canadian/American Relations: Politics of News Discourse

Becker/Schoenbach • Audience Responses to Media Diversification: Coping With Plenty

Beville • Audience Ratings: Radio, Television, Cable, Revised Edition

Biocca • Television and Political Advertising, Volume 1: Psychological Processes

Biocca • Television and Political Advertising, Volume 2: Signs, Codes, and Images

Botan/Hazleton • Public Relations Theory

Brown • Television "Critical Viewing Skills" Education: Major Media Literacy Projects in the United States and Selected Countries

Bryant • Television and the American Family

Bryant/Zillmann • Perspectives on Media Effects

Bryant/Zillmann • Responding to the Screen: Reception and Reaction Processes

Cahn • Intimates in Conflict: A Communication Perspective

Dobrow • Social and Cultural Aspects of VCR Use

Donohew/Sypher/Bukoski • Persuasive Communication and Drug Abuse Prevention

Donohew/Sypher/Higgins • Communication, Social Cognition, and Affect

Edgar/Fitzpatrick/Freimuth • AIDS: A Communication Perspective

Ellis/Donohue • Contemporary Issues in Language and Discourse Processes

Flagg • Formative Evaluation for Educational Technologies

Gunter • Poor Reception: Misunderstanding and Forgetting Broadcast News

Hunter/Narula • New Communication Technologies in Developing Countries

Huesmann/Eron • Television and the Aggressive Child: A Cross-National Comparison

Johnson-Cartee/Copeland • Negative Political Advertising: Coming of Age

Kaufer/Carley • Communication at a Distance: The Influence of Print on Sociocultural Organization and Change.

Communication at a Distance

The Influence of Print on Sociocultural Organization and Change

David S. Kaufer
Kathleen M. Carley
Carnegie Mellon University

LEA LAWRENCE ERLBAUM ASSOCIATES, PUBLISHERS
1993 Hillsdale, New Jersey   Hove and London

White (1984) is reprinted by permission on pages 4, 21, 165, 166, and 174 of this volume, © 1984 by The University of Chicago Press.

The University of Chicago Press, Chicago 60637
The University of Chicago Press, Ltd., London
© 1984 by The University of Chicago
All rights reserved. Published 1984
Printed in the United States of America
93 92 91 90 89 88 87 86 85   5432

Lawrence Erlbaum Associates, Inc., Publishers
365 Broadway
Hillsdale, New Jersey 07642

Library of Congress Cataloging-in-Publication Data

Kaufer, David S.
   Communication at a distance : the influence of print on sociocultural organization and change / David S. Kaufer, Kathleen M. Carley.
      p.   cm.
   Includes bibliographical references and index.
   ISBN 0-8058-1238-5 (c). — ISBN 0-8058-1273-3 (p).
   1. Communication—Social aspects.   2. Printing—Social aspects.
3. Communication and culture.   I. Carley, Kathleen M.   II. Title.
III. Series: Communication (Hillsdale, N.J.)
HM258.K318   1993
302.2—dc20   92-17793
                                                    CIP

Books published by Lawrence Erlbaum Associates are printed on acid-free paper, and their bindings are chosen for strength and durability.

Printed in the United States of America
10 9 8 7 6 5 4 3 2 1

To our Parents

Harry L. and Beverly S. Kaufer
Wilber W. and Birdie L. Parker

Contents

Preface

The title *Communication at a Distance* might first suggest a book about talking, writing, reading, browsing, or learning about the latest communication technologies: text, voice, or video links. Communication at a distance suggests the very latest technologies—so much so that we tend to forget that more primitive technologies also served the purposes of communication at a distance: language, alphabets, and writing (Bolter, 1991). The subject of this book represents an important milestone between these primitive modes of communication at a distance and the computer-based modes of this century. The milestone we explore is the advent of print and, especially, the mechanization of print during the Industrial Revolution. In many ways, our present society has surpassed a world whose most sophisticated technology is writing. Nevertheless, our society has yet to completely embrace, much less comprehend, a world that universally supports electronic communication with well agreed-upon conventions. The world of communication we currently inhabit remains one very much shaped by industrialized print. Curiously, the impact of the Industrial Revolution on print has been overlooked by many commentators. One can appreciate this fact by considering that more people associate print with Gutenberg and the moveable type of the 15th century than with Nicholson and Konig's steam press of the early 19th century or Hoe's rotary press of the mid-19th century. Yet these latter inventions were perhaps more important in shaping the world as we know it today.

Industrialized printing proliferated the contexts for writing, thus bringing to a head key issues about the dimensions of literacy, the nature of genres, and the authoritative status of texts that are debated to this day in legal and literary theory. Furthermore, the proliferation of print contexts made it possible not only to communicate over longer distances, but to use communication to build and maintain organizations, including professional and academic organizations, whose members were themselves geographically dispersed. Our aim is to understand the extent and limit of the social and cultural consequences of giving members of a society a new communication technology, in this case print. We develop this understanding systematically, using both formal modeling and historical analysis. Using a formal model of communication and its role in social and cultural change, we systematically explore specific features of the communication technology and their possible effects on sociocultural change. By examining specific historical events in which print played a role, such as the development of the Royal Society, we gain insight into the effects of communication technology on sociocultural change. The phoenix that hopefully emerges from the conflagration of historical and formal analysis is a more robust theory of interaction and sociocultural change, particularly as it is impacted by communication technology.

ACKNOWLEDGMENTS

Like all projects, this one has a history that is important in understanding the project's scope. David Kaufer is a rhetorical theorist with an interest in written information, the written communication of innovative information, and the relationship between writing conventions and social conventions. With his colleagues, he spent the last few years developing a theory of academic writing and software tools to support the practice of such writing (Geisler & Kaufer, 1989; Kaufer & Geisler, 1989, 1990, 1991; Kaufer, Geisler, & Neuwirth, 1989; Kaufer, Neuwirth, Chandhok, & Morris, in press; Neuwirth & Kaufer, in press; Neuwirth, Kaufer, Chandhok, & Morris, 1990). As he tried to understand conventions of academic writing and how they could be supported electronically and at a distance, it became clear to him that such conventions were incomprehensible if applied to single acts of writing, and only became meaningful when analyzed within a dynamic system of ongoing transactions over time. He began to appreciate that conventions of academic writing depend, in part, on the dynamics of professional organizations which, in turn, embed various dynamic and over-time assumptions of print communication. The way to understand the engagements of even a single writer or reader of academic discourse, Kaufer came to believe, was to understand the individual's decision to move to print; to replay this move within an enveloping professional context; and to replay it once more in a professional context dedicated to the formulation and diffusion of new ideas, that is, within an academic milieu. He found Carley's theoretical framework, con- structuralism, useful for exploring and learning a variety of surprising things about the replay of these scenarios within a dynamic model.

Kathleen Carley is a mathematical sociologist with an interest in un- derstanding and modeling sociocultural systems as they evolve in response to individual action and adaptation. Much of her work is in the area of organizational design and learning, and the diffusion of innovative in- formation within science. In Carley's original model, based on construc- tural theory, sociocultural systems change as a consequence of the actions (or interactions and communications) of the individuals within it, with the individuals typically interacting face-to-face or one-to-one. After a few brief discussions, it became clear to us that texts, no less than per- sons, function as interaction partners and, no less than persons, can change the course of societies and cultures. The challenge was to extend the constructural model to mass communication, including print com- munication, by enumerating the properties that relate and distinguish texts from people as interaction partners, and then to formalize these proper- ties into an expanded model.

The promise of meeting this challenge was significant. For Kaufer, it meant providing theoretical foundations for the effects of written infor- mation on social systems. For Carley, it meant expanding her theory and models of social systems to include a world of written texts in tandem with live or face-to-face interaction. We hope that in creating meaning for ourselves, we have managed to create something of meaning for gener- al and specialist readers in the humanities and social sciences.

This book represents a true blending of humanist inquiry and mathe- matical sociology. In large part, it is the product of the interdisciplinary environment fostered at Carnegie Mellon University, the College of Hu- manities and Social Sciences, and within our respective departments of English and Social and Decision Sciences. Even given this supportive en- vironment, this book would not have been written had it not been for a single fateful lunch, at which our far-sighted colleague, Lois Fowler, introduced us. From that lunch, a long collaboration and friendship began.

Within our home institution and outside, there are many individuals, from a variety of disciplines, who have helped to formulate the ideas here- in and who have given us a sense of the diverse audiences we want and need to address. We especially thank our many colleagues and students who provided moral support, patiently letting us bounce ideas off them, and often agreeing to read draft chapters, including Alan Kennedy, Richard Young, Erwin Steinberg, Cheryl Geisler, Chris Haas, Mike Palm- quist, Ann Blakeslee, Patti Dunmire, James Hirsch, Stuart Greene, Mike Leff, John Lyne, Randy Collins, David Banks, John Modell, Sara Kiesler,

Doug Wholey, and Ev Rogers. We would also like to thank members of the PREP editor group (Chris Neuwirth, Ravinder Chandok, Jim Morris, Dale Miller, and Paul Erion) for their feedback. Special thanks go to Hollis Heimbouch, our editor at Lawrence Erlbaum Associates, who supported this project from the start and has made the editorial process a rare pleasure. Kathryn M. Scornavacca did a masterful job on the production side. Valerie McKay helped with editing and indexing. Separate grants from the National Science Foundation made it possible to develop and run the simulations in Part II, as well as to think about and work on communication technologies from a historical as well as a technical perspective.

Most importantly, our families played a very major role. Our spouses, Barb and Rick, managed to provide the late night snacks, Chinese food, and patience that enabled this work to be completed. The children, Aaron, Mollie, and Cassandra, provided the antics and questions that only the very young can, and so kept up our laughter and our spirits. Without such familial support, and without being able to compare notes on what the kids were up to, this project would have been no less stimulating, but certainly less entertaining.

—*David S. Kaufer*
—*Kathleen M. Carley*

CHAPTER ONE

Approaches to Communication Research

"Communication" is a single word but not a single idea. This simple truth explains, among other things, why the world has room for communication experts with marvelously different talents. Consider some uses of communication in business. Market researchers spend years learning how to locate the right audiences for a product or service, but may spend comparatively little time learning how to design the copy needed to make sales. Advertisers trained in writing and graphics know how to produce that copy, but may have no expertise in evaluating whether their copy actually works, a skill often left to evaluation consultants. The division of labor among communication experts is real but not absolute. Market researchers could not locate target audiences as easily if the researchers were entirely innocent of the messages needed to rouse consumers. The advertisers could not sculpt these messages into rhetorical masterpieces if they were not also sensitive to the message's prospects for persuading. The evaluation consultants could not improve these prospects without insight into both how demographics are broken down and how messages will play to different audiences in the breakdown.

Within academe, no less than within the marketplace, communication researchers vary widely in the aspect of communication that they study. Despite the differences in the approach or aspects of communication they study, researchers tend to work from a common implicit scenario about communication. According to this scenario, every communicative transaction depends on a communicator locating or making contact with partners, nearby or from a distance, and crafting and exchanging communications with them. The partners then carry the effect of their communication, however slight or subtle, however shared or private, with them as they separate and go on to other pursuits, including further communicative transactions. The process of locating partners, exchanging information, and continuing on are regularities of all communicative transactions. All communication researchers touch on all of these regularities, more or less, explicitly or implicitly, in their investigations.

Despite the common scenario, communication researchers rarely pay equal attention to each of these regularities. The empirical tradition in communication research has focused on the demographic selection of communications and their diffusion to audiences (in the case of mass communication), as well as the effects of specific communications aimed at audiences in controlled settings. The humanistic tradition in rhetoric and communication has focused on the specific communication (and negotiation) of information between speakers and audiences, as played out through ordinary conversation, speeches, or written texts, and in settings of assumed sociocultural importance. These generalizations are not to suggest that the empirical tradition in communication neglects outright the production and reception of culturally complex communications; nor that the humanistic tradition focuses only on the meaning of communications apart from their demographics, diffusion, and effect. We note only a difference in emphasis across these traditions.

There are occasions, however, when even a slight emphasis in either direction can impede inquiry, both for the humanist and the social scientist. Suppose we ask, "What are the consequences for a community that conducts its communicative transactions in a particular way?" This question lies outside the bounds of traditional humanistic questions about the conditions and terms under which speakers produce and hearers interpret a specific communication. The question also lies outside the bounds of traditional social science inquiry about the demographics, diffusion rates, or effects of a specific communication, and does not make reference to a specific message, audience, or effect at all. Rather it refers to a particular type of community and a particular way, or a particular set of ways, that the community chooses to structure its communicative transactions. The question inquires about the consequences, on the community, of structuring its transactions as it does. Furthermore, it presupposes the entire interaction cycle, and not a particular component, as the integral unit of analysis for research.

This shift in presupposition has implications for the way the researcher frames an inquiry. Although traditional research tends to make the specific communicator, the audience, the communication, the communication technology, or the effect into the object of inquiry, the effect of the shift—making the interaction cycle the integral unit of analysis—is to bundle all these elements into a single ecology and to allow for a certain degree of arbitrariness in some of the elements. For example, given this shift, the researcher may choose to study the implications of a specific type of communication technology as it alters the types of communicative transactions available to a population across any audience or any communication. The arbitrary element assures that the implications studied result directly from the nature of the interaction cycle and do not depend upon a particular set of individuals engaged in the transaction or a specific content being communicated during the transaction.

This arbitrariness may seem like a reductive step—and it is. But it is no different from the idealizations made in humanistic inquiry when a critic makes a credible argument for a specific interpretation of a culturally complex communication generalized from an "ideal" reader's putative reading. Nor is it different from the standard idealizations made in any scientific model. Furthermore, given this shift, the researcher need not be fixed on a single transaction, but can pursue the short- and long-term implications that multiple, ongoing, and over-time transactions of a particular type or of mixed types have on a community. The approach to communication under these shifted presuppositions applies well beyond "one-shot" interaction and can be used to study the concurrent and over-time transactions that constitute the social life of a community.

Focusing on the interaction cycle allows us to break down a number of distinctions that often attend (and, in our opinion, restrict) traditional communication research. These distinctions tend to suppress opportunities to see and explore continuities between the content and context of a transaction; between the information communicated within a particular transaction and the path of diffusion through which it comes to influence later transactions; and between the microactions of communicators participating in these transactions and the macrostructures that result as these transactions aggregate across time (Alexander, Giesen, Munch, & Smelzer, 1987). Traditional research focuses on all these aspects of interaction, but without focusing on the continuities that tie them together into a single ecology.

This book is an example of research conducted with these continuities foremost in mind. We proceed from the premise that there are integral units, called communicative transactions, that can help us explore continuities of social and cultural organization arising from the circulation of information through concurrent transactions unfolding over time. This focus is particularly useful in comparing and projecting the aggregate and over-time implications of different communication technologies. This is our interest and hence our focus. We compare print-based and face-to-face conditions for their aggregate and over-time implications for sociocultural organization and change. Setting up the terms of comparison between these conditions is nontrivial, however, and problems abound in the existing research that tries to compare the consequences of different media in social, historical, and cultural terms.

We can illustrate these problems by enumerating some ostensible facts about print. Print enables communication to take place at a distance. The author, through the vehicle of a text, can be indirectly involved in transactions in which the communication of information is one-way (author to reader). The physical separation—in time, space, or culture—between the author and reader in print transactions is potentially much greater than in oral transactions. In print transactions, the interaction partners can be serendipitous strangers (some long dead) living in remote times and places. The potential distance in many relationships tends to make print interaction a more reflective medium than face-to-face interaction. There is simply too much work in writing, and deciding what to write, for the author to be casual or unmindful of the separation from the reader; too much work in reading, and deciding what to read, for the reader to overlook the "absences, gaps, silences, and opacity" in the author's context (Ong, 1980, p. 1132). A text, in part, can be engineered to overcome this separation.

A single archived text can survive generations, and individuals in a contemporary generation can rely on such texts to replenish memories of their cultural inheritance. White (1984) observed that archived texts can be important purveyors of culture and community:

> The written "text" has a unique place in the history of culture, for it reduces to permanence a process that is otherwise ephemeral and renders public, through the multiplication of readings, what is in the first instance essentially private. Unlike any other conversation, it has an unlimited number of anonymous but necessarily individual partners, located in an unlimited set of cultural contexts. It offers its reader an experience of cultural reconstitution that can be repeated in the imagination at any place or time. In this sense it is a part of the culture that transcends its own immediate location in space, time, and social context. (p. 280)

The unlimited number of anonymous readers that White attributes to the written text is an exaggeration; nonetheless it is an exaggeration first made possible through the potential of print. To be sure, communication at a distance was not an idea born with the mechanical reproduction of the written word; it occurs whenever space, time, or culture separate producers of information from recipients. Separations in culture always presuppose separations in space and often separations in time. Separations in time presuppose separations in space. When space is the only important factor of separation (and time is only incidentally relevant because it takes time to travel physically from one site to another), communication at a distance is a rather banal notion and has been with us since time immemorial, carried out through a variety of stock roles and occupations: gossips, nomads, wandering minstrels, merchants, war correspondents, town criers, royal emissaries.

Long before print, moreover, there was a remarkable technology supporting separations in space but also important separations in time—writing. Goody (1986) argued that the economy, commerce, law, and civic organizations of the ancient world relied on certain abstractions made possible only through the distancing assumptions of writing—the fact that texts could function as a proxy for (and reminder of) agreements that had been made at sites removed in space (e.g., bills of sale, deeds, court records, licenses, tax records) and, even more importantly, in time (e.g., constitutions, histories, decrees). The capacity of writing to organize urban life required that texts be a durable proxy for enacted social agreements. One could not organize the life of a community if each new generation had to renegotiate all its social agreements anew. Writing made it possible to preserve these agreements across generations, perhaps in a more fixed fashion than was possible in a purely oral environment.

Print, better than writing, overcame the more challenging author–reader separation of time and culture. The natural competitor to writing was human memory. Print also competed (well) with human memory because it shared with writing the property of archivability. But, unlike writing, print was reproducible and no longer held a text hostage to the material fate of a single physical surface. Print proliferated the life of a text into copies and editions, and this proliferation increased the chances that a text (some copies, some editions) would survive into different cultural epochs. Despite its important ties to long-term archiving, print's most important contribution was the way it helped to physically redefine social interaction. Specifically, print altered the relationship between communicators, communications, and the communicative transaction as that relationship had been understood in ordinary face-to-face interaction. In speech and writing systems lacking a sophisticated system for copying—unlike the sophisticated copying systems of the monastic scribes—a single communication presupposes the travel of at least one human communicator. Either the listener must travel to the speaker, or the speaker to the listener; either the reader must travel (or find a courier to travel) to the site of the writer's text, or the writer must work out a parallel set of logistics to bring a text to the site of the reader. This dynamic changes profoundly with print. Because of the mechanical reproducibility of the printed word, a single communicator, distributing copies, could be responsible for multiple sites of reading; the communicator need not be physically present during the communicative transaction. The ratio of communications to communicators dramatically increased, furthermore, with the introduction of the steam press in the mid-19th century. After the telegraph, print transactions attained the speed of electronics and no longer required a human communicator to travel at all. Through its reproducibility and speed, print conferred an unprecedented sociocultural presence to communication at a distance, making it possible to maintain, through fast-circulating texts, various macroinstitutions of the society—government, corporate, professional, and academic—beyond the bounds of spatio–temporal and even cultural proximity.

These are the facts about print. Why do we hint at some distrust for them? Our story has naively proceeded as if oral, written, and print transactions were simply evolutionary replacements for one another. The story disguises the fact that new media coexist with, rather than replace, established media. Ong (1971) noted: "When men learned to write, they continued to talk. When they learned letterpress printing, they continued both to talk and write. Since they have invented radio and television, they have continued to talk and write and print" (p. 25).

It is one thing to acknowledge the complication of coexisting media; it is quite another to make this coexistence a starting point for theory. Eminent theorists who rightfully recognized the complication of coexisting media, such as McLuhan (1962), Ong (1971), and Eisenstein (1979), nonetheless retained, in basic outline, rather unbroken accounts of how newer media came to dominate older ones. Although the various accounts offered by these theorists are full of rich detail and valuable insight, their overall direction charted the dominating effects of the newer media. Their stories indicate how writing came to dominate speaking as the culturally powerful modality; how print came to dominate speaking and writing; and more recently, how electronic communication came to overtake print. Stories of the dominance of new media are simple and elegant but they often leave embarrassing holes, (e.g. that newer media often increase the contexts of use for the older media). Writing did not squelch speaking but created new contexts for speech; print created new contexts for writing; electronic communication proliferated the contexts for paper and printing.

In light of the limitations of the dominance story, one must be careful not to set up contrasts assuming that media are independent of one another. A contrast between any two media must instead be set up between the older media and the older media in conjunction with the newer. In other words, we do not need to set up oral communication in direct conflict with writing, but rather to ask what new possibilities were opened up to speakers when they could also take advantage of writing? We need to avoid pitting orality and writing directly against print but instead to ask what additional possibilities became available to speakers and writers when they could also rely on print? This is the central question raised in this book. To answer it, we need to formalize a notion of how various technological conditions—face-to-face, writing, and print—affect the communicative transaction and the surrounding context, and then to compare the aggregate and over-time implications of (a) societies with only face-to-face and written technologies against (b) societies where individuals have these technologies and also a printing press.

Part I is designed to provide historical background and to present our formalization of different technologies, mainly face-to-face interaction and print. In chapter 2, we stress the interdependence of writing and print by discussing the myriad of new writing contexts that opened up during the industrialization of print. In chapter 3, we discuss the web of new social (in many cases, face-to-face) contexts that developed before the industrial revolution, and especially after, to sustain print. In the course of this largely historical discussion, we tease out a host of features needed for modeling oral, written, and print technologies. In chapter 4, we lay out these features more explicitly as a set of definitions and axioms underlying a constructuralist (Carley, 1990b, 1991b) perspective toward the interaction cycle and communicative transactions. These definitions and axioms are often motivated from the perspective of print transactions, but are applicable to other modalities of communication as well. In chapter 5, we discuss the role that language plays in a theory of the interaction cycle since it is, after all, language that diffuses, regardless of technology, across transactions and that changes as the individuals who use it change. In chapter 6, we present an extended formal model based on constructural theory. This model allows us to distinguish oral (face-to-face) and print-based technologies and their impact on sociocultural organization and change.

In Part II, we employ this formal model in an examination of four idealized print-based settings or, as we sometimes call them, *societies*. These analyses employ both computer simulations and historical discussions. These settings represent four distinct environments, marking major historical milestones in the transition to industrialized print: (a) societies with only scattered printing presses, roughly resembling the preindustrialized print societies of Europe and America—although we extend inferences from these societies to aspects of the industrialized print market as well (chapter 7); (b) societies that include professional groups, resembling the acceleration of specialization in the print market at the end of the 19th century (chapter 8); (c) societies that include academic groups, resembling the growth of the knowledge industry since World War II (chapter 9); and (d) societies with intellectual migrants, academics who circulate texts across diverse academic communities (chapter 10). Chapter 10 is not strictly anchored in an approximate historical period but reflects a long held belief—perhaps myth—that associates innovation and migration.

In the course of these investigations, we offer preliminary answers to the following questions: To what extent does print alone influence the internal organization of a community? To what extent are professional and academic organizations facilitated by print? How does intellectual migrancy work; and what role, if any, does print play in its functioning? We show in each of these domains that print dominated oral interaction in some respects and failed, at least in relative terms, to dominate in others. These results suggest the serious limitations of any treatment that makes print's (or any newer technology's) dominance over oral interaction (or any older modality) monolithic and total. On the other hand, we show that by expanding the individual's reach, print proved itself an important factor in determining the patterns of interaction that could be most effective in promoting rapid sociocultural change.

It is important to make it clear that the print contexts we explore in Part II are abstracted societies, motivated by a good deal of historical data, but based on models far simpler in their structure than the historical record. Throughout Part II, we intermingle formal models of such societies and historical data; we use one set of information to constrain our reasoning about the other. This style of presentation and argument is likely to be unfamiliar to most readers and it deserves some explanation. We share Giere's (1988) understanding of theory development as the framing of high-level historical accounts and the operationalizing of these accounts into a set of models that furnish insight into how the accounts need to be elaborated and revised. The models capture minute detail that the historical account cannot capture on its own. The historical account, in turn, confers a unity, coherence, historical texture, depth and, one hopes, a consistent background commentary on the models. The historical account is always richer, more detailed, and, in the end, more interesting than the abstracted models. These models function in turn as focal points for the history, helping us to distill the information in the historical record that has theoretical relevance and importance. The abstracted models also function as reality checks for the historical account, insuring that the generalizations we make can claim some logical rigor that follows upon a set of clearly stated and explicit assumptions. The reader should keep in mind from the outset that our results are not intended as definitive and require further investigation and confirmation. Our aim throughout is hypothesis generation and clarification rather than confirmation. Given the Gordian knots attaching communication, technology, and sociocultural organization and change, our aim is to make some surgical cuts through the tangle, and to prepare a path for sharper, more focused, and more definitive cuts.

PRECURSORS

This book takes a different perspective on communication from most accounts, but it is not without intellectual precursors. Our precursors share a starting point that reveals a deeper interest in the communicative transaction and in the aggregations of transactions across a community than in the nature of the individuals, audiences, and local effects that constitute and arise from a single transaction. Work that indicates this interest sees deeper continuities than divisions between the nature of transactions in a community and its evolving sociocultural organization, deeper continuities than divisions between issues of meaning and diffusion, between language as an embodiment of an inherited self or culture and language as a plastic resource for changing either or both.

On these criteria, we see ourselves continuing a set of inquiries into print initiated by cultural historians such as Ong (1958, 1971), McLuhan (1962), Yates (1966), and Eisenstein (1979). These authors affirmed that print changed the basic cognitive and cultural organization for understanding information, from units organized by the oral/aural senses to units organized by the visual senses. The effect of this reorganization codified in visual format many of the conventions of culture that had only heretofore been preserved through mnemonic formulas. The codifications of print required their own conventions, including paragraphs, headings, tables, diagrams, outlines, and so on. And these conventions, these cultural histories affirmed, not only preserved information from oral culture but, in the process, changed it. Ong (1971) noted:

> [T]he use of printing moved the word away from its original association with sound and treated it more and more as a "thing" in space. . . . [T]he emphasis on visual layout ushered in by the Gutenberg era made older texts seem less well organized. (pp. 184–185)

A common assumption of authors in this tradition is one we have already mentioned and criticized: Newer media came to dominate the meaning, relevance, and terms in which the older media were understood. For example, Ong (1971, p. 167) implied that the very idea of the dissemination potential of writing did not crystallize until the printer's art of typography: "Typography did more than merely 'spread' ideas. It gave urgency to the very metaphor that ideas were items which could be 'spread.' " Both Ong (1958, 1971) and Yates (1966) focused on how literacy steadily eroded the essentially oral/aural mindsets of ancient cultures. Yates implicated the role of print in eroding oral memory; Ong implicated its role in altering mindsets away from living sounds and toward fixed Cartesian spaces that he believed were more scientific but less social. McLuhan (1962) and Eisenstein (1975) were somewhat less nostalgic about the changes wrought by literacy and print but their focus also targeted the dominance of the printed word over earlier information media (and, in McLuhan's case, the rising dominance of the newer electronic media over print).

Despite its many rich insights and its differences in emphasis, the thrust of this intellectual tradition shows how newer media dominate the terms in which the older is understood and received. Although there is value in this emphasis, it fails to explain why new media often raise, not lower, the demand for the old. Furthermore, the emphasis on media dominance in this tradition eclipses the legitimate competition that can take place across coexisting media. After all, when one lives in a society with a choice between media, one needs to become more circumspect about which to use. Office managers who want everyone in the organization to know a hot piece of news can write a memo or let word of mouth make its way around. The memo will not compete with word of mouth but will fuel it. Thus, the office manager who decides to rely on word of mouth without the memo is really only deciding not to give word of mouth an additional boost. What are the consequences of granting or refusing to give word of mouth this boost? The answer depends on many factors, among them how fast word of mouth is traveling, who would read the memo (were one composed), and whether readers of the memo would be inclined to pass on their information to nonreaders. These factors point out the real complexities involved when asking questions about the contrastive role of media in structuring sociocultural organization and change. Yet the same factors get lost or shunted aside when a theorist stands on high and proclaims "print dominates."

We further build on the work of some composition, educational, and rhetorical theorists who have investigated the nature of author–reader separations over space, time, or culture. We have found the works of Brandt (1989, 1990), Nystrand (1986, 1989), White (1983), and Mailloux (1989) helpful in this regard. These theorists, some more directly than others, provide a corrective to the seeds of technological determinism in the writings of many of the media theorists cited earlier. Conflating principles of external storage and retrieval with principles of human cognition, technological determinism assumes that the technologizing of society inevitably led to a technologizing of mind. Because of its reproducibility and archivability print undoubtedly established new standards of precision for information storage and retrieval. Yet technological determinists go further by assuming that with the growth of methods to store and retrieve information precisely came the growth of (literate) mentalities that could deal with precise information more ably than the preliterate mind. Proponents of this determinism also claim (or appear to claim) that print technology taught literate readers how to fashion the mind into a computer that could decontextualize meaning into a set of abstracted symbols, that could engage texts apart from the involvements of ordinary social interaction.

The work of Brandt, Nystrand, White, and Mailloux is poised against technologically deterministic views, views that see print as a medium abstracting mind and meaning from a concrete world of face-to-face interaction. Rather, these investigators assume that print transactions are deeply contextualized, continuous with, and not disengaged from the passions and involvements of an ongoing face-to-face social world. They further assume that the reader's challenge is not to abstract context from the text but rather to find and fill in the context that confers meaning to its signs. Brandt specifically showed how print communication requires interpersonal involvements no less—and often more—intense than face-to-face communication. Nystrand's approach, what he called a "social-interaction" theory of writing, studied how writers and readers learn their roles by learning to adjust (in their own time and place) to one another. Nystrand's basic principle of literate interaction is reciprocity, the notion that writing–reading is an ongoing fiduciary act in which writer and reader seek to coordinate perspectives and are willing to make adjustments, when necessary, to maintain a coordinated perspective. Brandt and Nystrand analyzed the microdetails of individual texts written by contemporary authors for contemporary (often student) readers. They studied communication at a distance between authors and readers separated in space but not separated, in any problematic way, in time or culture.

White (1983) and Mailloux (1989) discussed author–reader separations involving time and culture as well as space. Both are interested, but for different reasons, in the problem of interpreting texts that endure across generations. White showed how his reading of enduring texts separated in time and culture—Homer, Thucydides, Plato, Johnson, Swift, Burke—yields insight into the boundedness of language within any cultural epoch. White maintained that these great authors, who addressed the foundational issues of their culture, also addressed this boundedness and, in the process, escaped their bounds by investing their culture and language with new meanings. White proposed that the reciprocally detached and invested relations that these authors achieved with their culture and language are case studies of the reciprocity required of any literate writer or reader. White, it should be clear, relied on a notion of reciprocity that differs from Nystrand's. For Nystrand, reciprocity explains how writers and readers learn to coordinate meanings across space. White, on the other hand, treats reciprocity not as a coordination principle but as a reflective principle underlying literacy which one can learn, in part, by learning to read authors and texts removed in time and culture. This reflective principle of reciprocity, pursued by White, states that individuals cannot be truly literate in the language of their inherited culture without learning to see meanings beyond those that their language and culture make immediately visible. This is why, in White's estimation, the reading of culturally "long-distance" texts can play such an important role in the development of literacy.

The ability that White considers so crucial—to reflect on language and its invested meanings beyond the immediate possibilities of the culture—presupposes a certain elasticity in the nature of language itself. This elasticity is possible because language users are continually learning about the world. They bring this learning to their new communicative transactions and to the language invested within them. This elasticity is necessary because the world being learned is also changing, and language users must continue to address these changes in new transactions. Mailloux focused on both the possibility and necessity of linguistic elasticity in author–reader relationships separated by time and culture. He showed, in a number of case studies, how authors and readers interpret cross-generational texts as rhetorical resources adapted to their own time and place. For example, he investigated how advocates on many sides of the racial argument in late 19th-century America used *Huckleberry Finn* to advance their specific interests; how Twain's book also figured in many cultural definitions, debates, and reworkings of the meaning of juvenile delinquency in the late 19th century; how the language in the ABM treaty of the Carter years was stretched in the 1980s to meet the local (and opposing) goals of the Reagan defense policy.

Taken together, this tradition of theory says a great many interesting things about the reading, writing, and interpretation of texts removed in space, time, and culture. But, in each case, researchers in this tradition start with the supposition that individuals are already engaged in transactions with texts, either as writers or readers. These researchers drop in on individuals only after they have decided to engage a text as readers or writers and after the only outstanding issue (a large and important issue, to be sure) has become what they will get out of a text (as readers) or put into it (as writers). This is, in many respects, a perfectly reasonable circumscription of boundaries, and not at all peculiar to the above theorists. As we mentioned at the outset, many, if not most, researchers in communication, oral or written, tend to associate theories of communication with theories of how information from texts or spoken discourse is engaged and communicated in single acts of production or interpretation, without going on to consider the preconditions and consequences of those engagements as they recur in a dynamic system unfolding over time.

For us, however, it is important to start earlier in this process, when individuals are in a suspended state of social interaction and have made no firm decisions about interacting with anyone, much less a text. For us, it is important that a theory of the communicative transaction try to explain how individuals ever decide to engage a partner (a person or a text) in the first place. For example, an individual may enter a large room poised for social interaction and see a dozen people busily engaged and a hundred books on the shelf. With whom or what will that individual make a first encounter and how will that encounter and the effects of all the other ongoing encounters lead to a second? An understanding of the communicative transaction and the aggregate and over-time effects of such transactions must include some account of the decision making that goes into the selection of a partner (person or text) at any point in time. Because this decision making is so important to the overtime dynamics of interactions, our emphasis is on principles that underlie it. Instead of involvement or reciprocity in the communication of information, principles that emphasize either author–reader coordination (Nystrand) or a reader's reflections on new possibilities of coordination (White), our focus is on principles that help communicators decide with whom (or what) to enter transactions and the dynamic consequences of these transactions on evolving patterns of interaction. One of our chief axioms (chapter 4) also employs a type of reciprocity between interaction and cognition that determines the trajectory of communicative transactions. The observation of language's elasticity, so crucial to Mailloux's work, is also crucial to ours. For, within any theory of a communicative transaction, one must explain how language can both endure across transactions and yet be changed in the process. We discuss the elasticity of language in terms of the symbols that can come into play during communicative transactions (chapter 5).

Our methods differ from those of this tradition of theorists as well. We rely less on textual analysis than Nystrand and Brandt; less on historical exegesis than White and Mailloux. Our method is drawn in part from history, in part from the social sciences. For us, history and the analysis of specific texts provide an indispensable backdrop for a theory of the communicative transaction; but alone it does not tell the whole story. We try to explore regularities of communicative transactions (both oral and print-based) and do not let the phenomenon of the single classic or blockbuster tell the story for us, or rob us of the story we want to tell. Our story is not about specific communicators in specific circumstances but about specific types of transactions (speech, writing, print) and their aggregate effects within institutions that, for the most part, emerged with print. In the postmodern tradition of Derrida (1976) Foucault (1977), and Barthes (1981, 1982a), we take a systemic view of writers and readers as roles with important and measurable consequences on the social world, whether or not their individual impact, or even their identity, is perceptible or stands apart from the individual impacts of others. Clearly, there is no strict incompatibility between a systemic interest in communicators and the traditional literary focus on authors of renown. Were our interests in a specific world historical author—a Rushdie, Eco, or Stowe— we could easily devote an entire book to a reconstruction of the systemic factors that defined the roles of single print authors (see, e.g., Rodden, 1989, on Orwell) and those of their readers, both in their contemporary setting and over time. With the exception of chapter 5, where we consider a single transaction based on a single text, our focus in this book is not on individual transactions or texts but on the morphologies of certain writing and reading roles—the print, professional, academic, and the migrant intellectual author/reader—and the role that print may have played in their evolution.

This focus moves us away from composition, rhetorical, educational, and historical inquiry, and into the social science literature on social systems: how they are organized and how they change. Our precursors here fall within the specialties of social theory and information diffusion. In social theory, we rely on the work of Collins (1981), Giddens (1984), Archer (1988), and Turner (1988), all of whom seek a middle ground or "mesostructure" between the microinteractions of individuals and the macrostructures of society. Turner's synthesis of social interaction theory showed how researchers in social interaction focused on one or another of the components that we identify with the communicative transaction—either (a) how social actors find their communication partner; (b) how information is communicated once a partner is found; or (c) the short- and long-term consequences of this communication on sociocultural organization and change. Turner's account implied that social interaction theory lacks operational accounts and methods for combining each of these phases of social interaction into a single unified theory. Theorists seeking a mesotheory to unite microinteraction and macrostructure are now working to provide one.

None of these theorists has seen that such a unified theory needs to take the form of a communication theory—and, specifically, a theory of the interaction cycle—as directly or explicitly as Carley (1990b, 1991b). We rely on Carley's framework, what she called "constructuralism," to model communicative transactions and to trace the aggregate effect of such transactions on sociocultural organization and change. Carley's work involves a theory and a formal model that describe, at a somewhat abstract level, how social and cultural life is constituted through the interaction cycle. The original model, based on the more general constructural theory, reflected only transactions that took place face-to-face or one-to-one. In this book, we have extended the model to accommodate print and other mass media (viz., one-to-many) transactions as well. It is nontrivial to make this extension, and much of Part I is designed to motivate the theoretical and methodological assumptions needed to understand how we represent face-to-face and print transactions.

Researchers in the diffusion of information (Katz, 1961; Rogers, 1982) are concerned with the movement of information over time, not "one-shot" communication. Consequently, such researchers tend to take the communicative transaction as a basic unit of analysis, one that aggregates and unfolds over time. At the same time, standard diffusion models fail to accommodate a number of assumptions that are essential for our purposes. For example, the majority of models do not represent the changing meaning of a communication as it moves from one transaction to another. There is no formal attempt to represent a communication as decomposable into many components, any of which can be lost or newly elaborated from one transaction to another, and so change in meaning. Carley's (1990b, 1991b) approach to diffusion, on the other hand, includes a representation system for the communications that diffuse, one that accommodates the capacity of a communication to consist of multiple pieces of information, each of which can be communicated and understood separately. This system of representation captures the reality that the information negotiated in transactions is more than a single undifferentiated transmission passing intact from one communicator to the next.

The majority of diffusion models do not try to draw out the relationships between the information that moves across transactions and the evolving states of knowledge and beliefs of the individuals who interact or their movements in and out of these transactions themselves. In most diffusion models, in other words, the tracing of a communication ignores the underlying network of people and knowledge that constitute the integrated sociocultural system through which the communication diffuses. Carley's theory makes specific assumptions about these relationships and, as a result, one can apply this as a diffusion theory, as we do in Part II, to study not simply the movement of information but the possible dependencies between the way it moves (e.g., face-to-face or print) and the social and cultural organization of the society in which these movements take place.

Most diffusion models follow a single trail of diffusion where only one communication is diffusing at a time. This approach makes it impossible to study the competition between communications for a person's attention. Carley's model, on the other hand, does make it possible for the investigator to study multiple communications diffusing simultaneously and competing for the attention of listeners or readers. In addition, most diffusion models consider communication only as it occurs in one-to-one transactions. With the exception of some contagion models, formalized diffusion models do not handle assumptions of mass communication within their formal frameworks. A feature new to this book is the extension of Carley's model to one-to-many as well as one-to-one interactions. This extension makes it possible for us to study, though at a somewhat abstract level, the competition between speech and writing alone and speech and writing augmented by print.

Recently, there has been a growing concentration of attention on the effect of new communication technologies, such as electronic mail, bulletin boards, and networks, on sociocultural organization and change (see, e.g., Hiltz, 1984; Hiltz & Turoff, 1978; Kerr & Hiltz, 1982; Kiesler & Sproull, 1987; Kraut, Egido, & Galegher, 1990; Rice, 1980, 1984, 1987; Sproull & Kiesler, 1986; Schatz, 1991). We make reference to this work throughout this book, and we apply important research findings about computer and video-based communication technologies, retrospectively, to the analysis of 19th century print technology. For example, Kraut and his associates (Kraut et al., 1990) documented current technologies that are used most successfully to support cooperative work at a distance when the communicators have already built a fund of mutual knowledge and understandings through proximate, face-to-face contact. They found that the same technologies are used less frequently and, by implication, work less effectively when they are used to support communicators trying to build this base of mutual knowledge from scratch. One may generalize from this finding that either proximity (i.e., having face-to-face access), or shared knowledge (i.e., sharing mutual understandings based on prior contact or simply sharing many parallel experiences), or both are important determinants of whether a communication technology will be used and the extent to which its use will be successful or satisfying for the participants. Moreover, for participants operating in the absence of proximity, their prior shared knowledge and mutual understandings will be the dominant factors controlling the extent to which they entrust their communications to advanced technology. These are exactly the terms within which we formulate how people came to entrust more of their communications to print technology in the absence of proximity assumptions in the 19th century.

We stalk what was the "hot" technology in the 19th century—mechanized printing—using some of the same assumptions and approaches that one might use to stalk the hot technologies of communication in our own century. We have three main reasons for sustaining a historical focus on print in particular:

1. We have found there is more than ample material relating to print, and applying our methods to newer technologies would require another book in its own right.

2. We believe that lessons learned from our analysis of print can, should be, and are often not applied to the newer technologies. For example, the historical literature is sometimes guilty of making print the simple causal agent of much sociocultural change without taking into account other sociocultural factors that were, at the very least, accessories to the effects of the technology itself. Analogously, investigators of the newer technologies are sometimes guilty of pronouncing their effects without paying sufficient attention to other sociocultural variables that may play a vital accessory role. To be fair, it is much harder to give the newer technologies the same kind of analysis we can give for print, because we are still living at the beginning of the computer revolution and do not have the hindsight of history on our side. At the same time, the hindsight of history often helps us get our bearings on the present. This is a key strategy of Bolter's (1991) excellent study and it is, to a certain extent, a strategy of ours. While we reference but do not focus on the electronic technologies of communication in this book, we believe that researchers interested in these technologies might learn something by analogy with our treatment of print. Much of the current research in telecommunications and collaborative technology uses face-to-face interaction as a comparison condition for advanced information systems in controlled experiments (Galegher, 1990). We also use face-to-face interaction as a comparison condition for print (and in some cases as a specific augmentation of face-to-face interaction). Our comparisons are not controlled experiments, and we have less to say than the above research about the empirical confirmation of hypotheses. At the same time, by interleaving historical and formal analysis, we have more to say about general processes of interaction and how technology and sociocultural variables may affect the aggregate and over-time outcomes of these processes. We generate, in other words, a set of hypotheses rich enough to accommodate interactions between technology and sociocultural variables that are also mathematically precise and logically consistent.

3. We believe there is an unfortunate "futurist" bias that impels many to assume qualitative differences between older and newer communication technologies before first exploring whether their differences might lie on common quantitative continua. The result of this tendency is to think of new technologies as a rupture from the past and to cluster the technology immediately superseded closer to the technologies it itself superseded. Writing must have seemed a gigantic and strange leap from speech for humans first experimenting with it. To the Renaissance printer, enticed by the possibilities of print, writing probably seemed more like speech, with print standing apart from both. In our electronic age, print is often scorned as the outmoded technology that only a curmudgeon can love because it remains reminiscent of a familiar world of speech and

writing. But many, if not most, important dimensions of communication technologies we credit as first opening up with computer networks were already opened up, though less visibly, in print and even in writing. For example, it is a commonplace to think that an artifact of today's communication networks is the "virtual" group, the capacity of groups to form under no constraint of proximity. Yet such a virtual organization was a requirement for the establishment of government and organized urban life in the ancient city-states supplied by writing (Goody, 1968). In chapter 8, we consider, within a strictly quantitative model, how much more virtual organization print, as an augmentation of speech and writing, was able to supply in the 19th century, so that professions could maintain themselves across a geographically dispersed membership. To ignore historical continuities across technologies is to reveal more than a historical ignorance of what came before. It is to remain primarily ignorant of the technologies we now take for granted.

PART ONE

THEORY

CHAPTER TWO

Written Content as Emergent Phenomena

Burke's central perception [is] that the relation between self and culture is not instrumental but reciprocal. In his view we are in large measure constituted by the very culture it is our task to maintain and improve. Therefore, the kind of "ownership" that this text seeks to establish in its reader is not the mere claiming of title or the assertion of a right to possession, as of an object; rather, it is an engagement in a process by which both the individual and the culture are continually remade.
—James Boyd White (1984, p. 209)

Edmund Burke's 18th-century experiments in constitution making were, for White, an important moment in understanding the fluid possibilities of texts. For to understand the nature of a living constitution was to understand texts as more than type, binding, and glue dispatching information one time only, and then used up. What breathed life into the modern constitutional documents was the understanding that they could be rescinded but not depleted. As long as they were operative, they would have to be responsive to many future readers and their reading contexts. Yet to be responsive and accountable, they had to be responsible—like a person. Texts, like people, can have future accountabilities; texts, like people, can remain open for indefinite interaction; texts, like people, can be partners in communication and not just the props of communicators. These observations are difficult not because they are abstractions but because we try to make them so. We read sentences associating texts with interaction partners and we assume we are being struck by a metaphor that requires deep thinking to unpack. Texts, so the educated among us are wont to say, live in a different, more abstract world than people.

The bias has been to think of informal speech in terms of living transactions, but to think of texts in a quite different way, as revealed in the
following statement: "Perhaps more than any other topic in sociology,
the process of interaction among individuals is considered to involve
spontaneity and indeterminacy." Turner (1988, p. 12) wrote these words
in his opus on social interaction theory. Turner's comment is telling, for
our purposes, because it reflects the bias of social theorists towards identifying social interaction exclusively with face-to-face communication.
Spontaneity, after all, is a factor few would use to describe the transactions of authors and readers. The following factors have conspired, it
seems, to make written interaction into something different in kind from
ordinary transactions: (a) the hardened belief in the "autonomous" text
as ultimate authority; (b) the association of literate culture with schooling, prestige, sophistication, status, and truth; and (c) the coupling of literacy with economic mobility and power. These factors have so come to
distinguish written interaction that "twentieth-century readers tend to
assume that written documents and written communication will automatically be more important than verbal exchanges" (Houston, 1988, p.
24); they have so come to distinguish writing that Ong (1980) was led
to pronounce reading an activity fundamentally different from listening:

> Reading is a special activity and can not be understood as simply an activi-
> ty parallel to listening . . . faced with a text, the reader finds that both the
> author and original context are absent . . . in this situation the text is al-
> ways marked by absences, gaps, silences, and opacity. (p. 1132)

The inference accepted by many is that cultural objects, like texts, command a sweep that makes them stand apart from the microdetails of
person-to-person interaction. Giddens (1987) distinguished ordinary talk
from texts, with only the latter vying for status as a cultural object. To
be a true cultural object, Giddens suggests, the artifact must be consumed
at a distance from the source of its production. In Gidden's terms, the
producer and consumer of written communication are typically not "copresent" with one another:

> In ordinary talk, individuals routinely employ a diversity of aspects of set-
> ting in order to understand others and to "gear" what they themselves say
> to such a process of understanding. The interpretation of cultural objects
> occurs without certain elements of the mutual knowledge involved in co-
> presence within a setting, and without the coordinated monitoring which
> co-present individuals carry out as part of ongoing talk. (p. 216)

Randall Collins (1979) acknowledged that culture can be produced in
face-to-face settings as well as through interactions with artifacts that cir-

culate widely across time and space. Yet he designates only this latter type of production as formal and he claims that formally produced culture, associated with writing, paper, or book-printing is: "not only more innovative than indigenous culture, but also allows the creation of much larger and more self-conscious communities composed of more abstract concepts and symbols and more generalized references" (p. 63).

The "strong text" tradition of Goody (1986), Ong (1971), and Olson (1977), as characterized by Brandt (1990, p. 57), associated the rise of literacy with people's growing comfort with working in the abstract and decontextualized world of texts. Brandt called these theorists strong text because, for them, to be literate is to fashion the mind after a text, with the capacity to turn signs on the page into fixed digitized bits of meaning, abstracted from the "noise" of the world of living speech. The Russian linguist Bakhtin (1986), though a strong advocate of the importance of "social context" in speaking and writing, did not miss an opportunity to draw a fundamental difference between "simple" genres, based in speech, and "complex" genres, based in writing. Simple genres involve rejoinders to everyday speech as well as letters contained in a novel. Complex genres consist of novels, dramas, science, and commentary. Bakhtin suggested that complex genres both incorporate and transform simple genres, abstracting the simple genres from "their immediate relationship to actual reality and to the real utterances of others" (pp. 60–62).

The scholarship (Eisenstein, 1979; Houston, 1988; Ong, 1982) discussing the rise of literacy in post-Renaissance Europe suggested that the perceived autonomy of written interaction grew with the assumption that the pace of information was no longer constrained by the pace of personal travel. This assumption is very recent. It was not until the invention of the telegraph in the 1840s that communications began to travel faster than the communicator, that communication could outpace the physical limits of transportation. Before that time, written and oral communication were necessarily intertwined. Readings were public events as much as private experiences. Folklore, tales, news, and knowledge were items of interest transmitted indifferently between texts and the carriers who transported them. Bibles could spread the gospel, but seldom without the voices of the clergy. Pamphlets and broadsides could sway public opinion, but seldom without the supporting word of mouth from the taverns and meeting halls. (See the volume on orality vs. written modes of communication by Enos, 1990.)

At some point between this past and our own electronic age, the status of written communication has been transmogrified beyond social interaction. Brandt (1989, p. 36) suggested (citing Ong) that the writer's "separation" from the reader has become "the most salient shaper of literate experience" and that the focus on the author–reader relationship has in fact been a focus on its "(non)-relationship." Because their interaction is distant and mostly one directional, authors and readers are not seen as "persons interacting." Readers can talk back to a text, but the author is not immediately present or even alive to hear and respond. Authors can use texts to influence readers, but readers are not afforded the reciprocal privilege. Their only opportunity for influencing authors lies in channels of correspondence outside the text. Thus, to think of the engagement of authors and readers as "social interaction" is, seemingly, to stretch concepts and strain terminology.

This strain was, of course, felt early on when writing systems were first beginning to compete with oral channels of transmission. In the *Phaedrus* (275a, 278a), for example, Plato objected to writing because, as he saw it, writing made a farce of social interaction as authors were not present to elaborate or defend their statements, and because writing "divorced verbal communication from the original efforts and intentions implicit in face-to-face speech" (Harris, 1986, p. 24). Because of the tendency to equate systems of social interaction with systems of synchronous interaction, one may initially resist labeling the written relationship, one that is radically asynchronous and one-directional, as "interactive."

However, in the end, it seems easier to concede than to deny the label interactive to authors and readers—especially if we go on to qualify this type of interaction as specifically one way and mediated at many institutional levels. To be sure, there is no lack of mediation in face-to-face interaction, as belief, ethnic, gender, and cultural factors intrude themselves even among the most proximate of communicators (Goffman, 1974; Tannen, 1990). Nevertheless, since the advent of print, the mediation between authors and readers has been institutionalized through formal organizations (e.g., church, governments, courts, publishing houses). To interact with a reader, for example, an author must interact often with a publisher and not infrequently with a literary agent. The publisher, who has a history of government interaction via regulations and court rulings, must bring the content of these interactions to bear in dealings with the author. The reader, in turn, claiming a different-interactive history, is likely to learn about the author through a review, citation, advertisement (Altick, 1957), and, not least, word of mouth.

Classifying reading as social interaction is less problematic when the author enjoys unusual visibility. For example, when one thinks of authors and readers engaged in meaningful social interaction, one usually thinks of extraordinary interactive events. One thinks of political intrigue—Islamic hit squads hunting down Salman Rushdie. One thinks of the improbable blockbuster (what Alexander Stille called the "Eco phenomenon"), so named because Umberto Eco first sold 9 million copies in 24 languages of a detective story, *The Name of the Rose*, that he claims to have originally intended for 1,000 cognoscenti (Stille, 1989, p. 21).

One thinks, above all perhaps, of precedent-setting social reach and influence, like that of Harriet Beecher Stowe. In the early 1860s, Stowe visited Lincoln at the White House, and Lincoln is alleged to have said, "So this is the little lady who made the big war." Reflecting on *Uncle Tom's Cabin* some 40 years after publication, Kirk Monroe mused that Stowe's influence was "probably greater than that of any other individual." Charles Sumner dared to speculate that if *Uncle Tom's Cabin* had not been written, "Lincoln could not have been elected president" (Altick, 1988, p. 145; Gossett, 1985, pp. 164–167; Reynolds, 1985, p. 149). When authors rise significantly above the ordinary course of political, economic or cultural interaction with their readers, investigators take the time to notice and, occasionally, to try to explain the event. Once biographers acknowledge Stowe's achievement, for example, they are led to seek the roots of her success. And after digging into the situation further, they often find that it depended on many converging factors, such as the recent innovation of serial publishing, steam printing, northern industrialization, an expanding literate population, the telegraph, England's decision on the slavery issue some 20 years earlier, and so on. Like Stowe's identity, an authorial identity becomes especially visible when the author's influence lies "off the chart," and the author's potential reach gets lost in the mystique of the authorial persona. Some of the mystique separating texts from their authorial roots may rest with biases in the traditional schools of textual criticism that equate literature with universalizing experiences transcending time and place. According to some of these schools, literature deals "with the human why of the story and the human meaning. This humanizing of the facts is one feature that distinguishes any literary account" (Brooks, Purser, & Warren, 1967, p. 3).

For many traditional critics of literature, the "humanness" of the literary text furnished a reason for taking literary content as universal. Because the literary content was considered larger than history, literary accounts following this perspective diminished the role of the historical reader. The authors' readers became fictionalized (Ong, 1975) and the traditional literary historian often spoke of the author's implied readers, those addressed or evoked through images of the text. The focus of the text's content was removed from the readings of in situ readers. Even though various critical traditions welcomed the ambiguity of interpretation, there was, given the putative universality of literary meaning, no reason for these traditions to accept its inevitability. There was no reason, in other words, to suppose a priori that literary meanings could not survive intact across readers and readings. The importance of the literary text in these traditions—particularly in some of its pedagogical implications—rested not in its extensional possibilities across communicative transactions but in its message or morale. The word "message" implies a meaning that we typically expect will remain stable across transactions. We generally use the word message in indirect reporting of a previous transaction (e.g., the message I was asked to give you is . . .). For some literary traditions, in some of its pedagogical practices if not its theory, the meaning of the literary text was its message—the morale was passed down from teacher to student unchanged. Traditional criticism left us in the dark about how sensitive the meaning of the literary text was to variations in communicative transactions as it was read over time—or why such an obvious possibility might be more than a matter of error but one of intense theoretical interest.

More recent scholars sought to relate the content or genre of a text to a wider analysis based on its history of transactions. The focus of these investigations has been on discrete studies tracing the over-time influence of specific authors and texts (DeGrazia, 1991; Rosenthal, 1991; also see Ong, 1958, on the diffusion of Ramus; Rodden, 1989, on the diffusion of Orwell) or on the historical analysis of single genres (e.g., Bazerman's 1988 study of the experimental report over 200 years; see also Bazerman & Paradis, 1991). What is missing from discrete studies, however, is a sense of how much continuous change, growth, and specialization in our understanding of written content can happen merely with the quantitative proliferation of texts. We have never been at a loss for informal speech communication partners, for they are easy to access and as close as our nearest neighbor. But texts, as communication partners, are more rare and expensive and, in the scheme of history, a scarce resource.

This changed dramatically with the industrial revolution of the 19th century. Although printing techniques were available in China since the 3rd century B.C. and movable type in the West since 1440, the speed of print changed little between 1440 and the last quarter of the 18th century. As late as the 18th century in Europe, the production of paper and print remained handicrafts (Innis, 1951). Paper remained, in many cases, more fragile, rougher, and harder to ink and illuminate than parchment (Reynolds & Wilson, 1968). Printing was dominated by the wooden hand press. Not until the late 18th and 19th centuries were the basic mechanisms for industrializing printing and paper making developed.

In 1790, Nicholson patented the concept of the steam-powered cylinder press and in 1810 Konig received a patent for the first implementation of a steam-driven hand press. In 1814 the introduction of the cylinder steam press with self-inking rollers increased printing speed from 300 copies per day to 1,100 per hour (McGarry, 1981, p. 47). In 1814, the *Times* of London put out the first newspaper from Konig's machine with a production capacity of 1,100 impressions per hour. In 1817, Konig invented a double cylinder press with a production capacity of 1,500 impressions. The next year, the *Times* commissioned two engineers, Applegath and Cowper, to make further improvements in Konig's invention, and by 1827, they had a double cylinder press that could produce up to 5,000 impressions per hour. By the 1830s, improvements in the steam press made possible serial fiction (publishing a book in affordable installments). It also made possible increased runs of editions. For example, runs of Dickens' *Pickwick Papers* grew, over the century, from 400 to 40,000, and eventually to 100,000. Steam printing increased the production of, and reduced the price of, books in England throughout the 1830s and 1840s. The number of titles rose from 580 in the 1820s to more than 2,600 by mid-century and the average price of new books fell from 16 shillings to just over 8 shillings (Williams, 1961, pp. 158–168).

In the 1840s, a new revolution in printing speed dawned with the rotary press, which linked eight or more cylinders rotating in contact with a central cylindrical print surface. An American, Richard Hoe, patented the first rotary press in 1845, and in 1847 it was used to print the *Philadelphia Public Ledger*. Applegath, working on a different rotary design in England, patented his new rotary machine in 1846. The rotary presses of the 1840s could handle 8,000 impressions per hour; by the 1860s, this rate had increased to 25,000 impressions. The process of creating paper by mixing wood and rag pulp was patented in 1844. Major applications for the rotary press of the 19th century were for letterpress (printed matter) rather than for lithography, required for illustrations. In 1860, newspapers began to replace rags with straw, allowing for the lighter, cheaper, and thicker Sunday paper (Innis, 1951, pp. 25–26). In 1905, the first offset lithography presses went into production, which combined lithographic and rotary printing, sometimes called offset rotary. Today, modern newspapers handle upwards of 30,000 impressions per hour using offset rotary presses (Forkert, 1933; McMurtrie, 1937; Moran, 1973; Oswald, 1928; Winship, 1968). In Fig. 2.1, we illustrate the rapid growth of print technology from the 19th century onward.

The proliferation of texts gave rise to a stream of ideas that were unprecedented in their availability. Many of these ideas had no source in a reader's local context and no bearing on his or her material existence. Viewed on a macroscale, as a commodity distributed across a social system conferring social status and privileged membership, the content of widely circulating texts constituted what industrial societies in Europe and America since the industrial revolution came to call "culture" (Williams, 1976, pp. 151–154). Authors within this time span have been perceived at the vanguard of cultural shaping and production. This perception developed with the awareness that the aggregate content com-

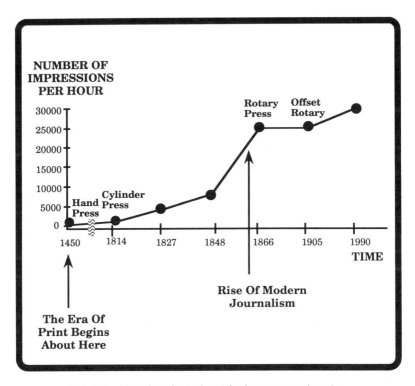

FIG. 2.1. Time line for industrial advancements in print.

municated between authors and readers as they interacted—because of the fast rate of these interactions and the distances they can span—exerted a disproportionate impact on the leading ideas in the culture. Unlike other industries, the book industry produced more than capital wealth. It produced cultural capital, symbolic wealth. As Fred Melcher observed in a 1937 *Publisher's Weekly* editorial (cited in Tebbel, 1968, Vol. III, p. 3): "[W]hen the history of today's publishing and bookselling is written, its high spots will not be its statistics nor the graphs of deficits or profits, but the story of great books and of publishing vision and of books made vital to our communities."

Technological innovations from the 19th century on made the content of written interaction an increasingly important factor in the shaping of culture. The increased speed and availability of print made the words of a relative few available to the minds of the masses, making "culture" itself a mass-produced product of the industrial revolution (Williams, 1961). The industrialization of letters became an important watershed in our thinking about written content because it stretched what was heretofore an individual artifact into a mass-produced commodity, turning what had previously been essentially elite or private information into a salable public stock. Print became a watershed because it subverted many hardened assumptions about the nature of textual content and the transactional contexts in which texts could serve as interaction partners. The relative scarcity of texts, for example, had engendered an association between texts and durable content: When something is scarce, make sure it does not become dated. The relative scarcity of texts had engendered an association between texts and imaginative or sublime content: When something is scarce, consider it beyond the mundane. The relative scarcity of texts had engendered an association between texts and ritual: When something is scarce, do not jeopardize it with the unknown.

The industrial revolution helped to uproot these assumptions and, in a sense, subvert them by exposing previously concealed possibilities for texts in contexts that required content that was timely, practical, and original (over and above the shifts and corruptions incurred from one ritualistic communicative transaction to another). Brandt (1990, p. 57) astutely observed that the printed text is more than an archivable object, separate and distinct from the world of action. She points out that it is not the nature of texts to confer meaning to acts of reading and writing. It is rather the nature of the contexts of reading and writing to breathe meaning into texts as sites for these writer–reader contexts to unfold. From a process perspective, in other words, the printed text is the site of writers and readers working to coordinate themselves in an action-centered context. To become literate is not to learn how to deal with texts out of context but to understand the context of action for which the text provides a site: "Learning to read and write is not learning how texts stick together but how people stick together through literate means" (Brandt, 1990, p. 42).

Brandt's useful understanding of literacy explains both why the industrial revolution was so important in the history of literacy and why its importance is so often overlooked. The industrial revolution proliferated potential contexts of action for print. This in turn proliferated the need to define new types of content—new genres—for authors and readers to actualize and work through these contexts. In the following sections, we examine in more detail the restrictive assumptions about the content of texts prior to the industrial revolution and the dramatic loosening of these restrictions afterward.

EMERGENT DIMENSIONS OF WRITTEN CONTENT SINCE THE INDUSTRIAL REVOLUTION

We consider three dimensions of content (a) the durable or the timely (b) the imaginative or the practical, and (c) the assimilated or the original. Prior to the industrial revolution texts occupied a narrower position on these dimensions than they did afterward.

Durability and Timeliness

Durability is the number of time periods, measured in days, years, centuries, millenia, that a content is available for interaction. Since the invention of writing systems (Harris, 1986), the written text has been set apart and distinguished from speech for its relative durability. As Brandt (1989) observed, the durability of writing put additional pressure on the written content to meet standards of particularity and uniqueness unknown to speech:

> The permanence of writing gives it a high degree of particularity and uniqueness. Each text, even someone's encyclopedia entry, is one of a kind; it would be hard to imagine two writers ever spontaneously composing identical texts, even mundane ones. In conversation, on the other hand, we all recycle familiar topics and anonymous cliches, repeating the same familiar morning greetings, for instance, as we move from street to elevator to hallway. (p. 37)

The Monastics, prior to print, and textual critics, after print, often defined their role as curators, valuing texts as timeless cultural artifacts. A common boast of critics was that while authors had to suffer the vagaries of their local context, critics got to work with immortal works (West, 1988, p. 4). Throughout the history of letters, the durability of the textual product has been associated with the privileged term "literature." However, literature itself is not a stable concept and has undergone important changes from late medieval to contemporary society. The word literature in manuscript culture and throughout the age of the hand press designated a highly valued type of text, but it also implied the productive or perceptual capacities reflecting on the writer or reader's class, cultivation, and breeding. Literary texts were more broadly associated with enduring intellectual capacities and cultural standing. This broad understanding of literature was a throwback to manuscript cultures, where the costs and logistics of textual dissemination and procurement made it prohibitive for all but the most powerful organs of the state to produce or procure texts with societal reach (Williams, 1961). In manuscript cultures, it was a sign of economic, educational and class standing merely to have access to a text (Curran, 1979; Febvre & Martin, 1976; Kernan, 1987; Levine, 1986; McGarry, 1981). Prior to the 18th century, a primary purpose of constitutions was to legitimate discrepancies in the rights of those who had access to property (and to literacy itself) and to those who did not.

These privileged images of literature survived the industrialization of print in the late 18th and 19th centuries, but eventually splintered into competing images as print made the distribution and procurement of texts

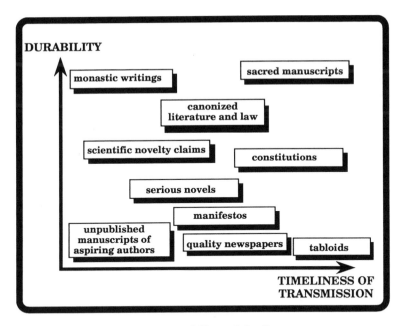

FIG. 2.2.   Durability and timeliness.

less salient milestones, shifting the salience to the consequences and out-comes of reading (Williams, 1961, pp. 151–154). Mechanizing print made it increasingly easy for printers to blanket a society with texts without the sanction of an authoritative body, leaving judgments of validity and durability up to the reading market. One consequence was that timeli-ness competed with durability in determining a text's value. Figure 2.2 plots a variety of genres relative to their durability and timeliness.

Durability is perhaps the oldest measure for valuing a text. The texts with roots in oral and scribal traditions (e.g., sacred texts, canonized liter-ature, and constitutions) were considered durable for interaction across generations of readers. They were not considered timely. Monastic writ-ings designed to preserve learning, for example, were valued for their durability. The impetus for a market in timely ephemeral print did not begin in England until after 1695. In that year print was deregulated and printers, losing their monopoly of copyright over classic books, found themselves having to make a living by supplying the reading public with contemporary authors and texts (Laurenson & Swingewood, 1971; Smith, 1979) that could not claim to provide truth and wisdom for the ages. In the years and decades following deregulation, there was a gradual in-crease of new genres, stressing timeliness and the sense of intimacy made possible by an author sharing the contemporary context of readers. These genres were all christened with names emphasizing their dependence on journeys, time, novelty, intimate experience, and periodicity: war *jour*-*n*als, *news*books, *dailies, news*papers, *period*icals, and *novels*, all earning their reputation on the timely and intimate transmission of detail (Hughes, 1989). The scientific periodical of the 17th century proved an interesting hybrid between the older value of durability and the newer value of timeliness (chap. 9). Scientific discoveries were typically considered less durable than sacred truth and less timely than the nightly news. On the other hand, the tabloids making their debut in the 19th century penny press offered timeliness as their singular selling point.

We have more to say about the print market (chap. 3, 7), but in the present context it is important to appreciate the mounting challenge of defining a text's qualifications for enduring interaction when the hand press and, especially, automated presses had the capacity to make yesterday's text stale overnight. The same challenge, of course, is felt today, but it must have been especially keen in the early history of print when readers, aghast, found the cherished styles and seals of the ancient masters mechanically reproduced on advertisements, handbills, posters, pornography, and other throwaway literature. In an era when print and later the industrial revolution made an increasing value of timeliness, what could be done to protect the idea that some texts are worth keeping?

One answer, dating from the 15th century, was to insist that some texts (e.g., the Bible) are simply too valuable for mechanical copying and need to remain under the care of the scribes and their manual art (Reynolds & Wilson, 1968, chap. 6). A second answer, dating from the late 18th century, was to insist on canon making, on establishing corpora of texts whose content was considered too valuable to leave hostage to the market of timely print. The first answer did little to discourage mechanical copying, and the scribal arts have now been relegated to an exotic craft. The second answer did much to protect certain works from the vagaries of timely print and merits further scrutiny.

The canon, advocates claims, includes what is worth remembering for all time (Mueller, 1989). However, there is arguably nothing in the content of a text that justifies (without controversy) its permanent value. Arguments for canonicity flow in the opposite direction: The critic starts with the premise that the canonical work "must be read across generations" and then leaves it to readers to come to this same conclusion. Literary texts are seldom, if ever, agreed upon as durable as a result of resolving specialist debates about their durability. Rather it is the fact of their inclusion in the specialist debate, arguably, that confers durability.

A slightly different move toward canonicity has issued from reformist attempts, like those of Matthew Arnold and, more recently, Hirsch (1987), to standardize an educational curriculum and the "culture" on which it is founded. The argument for standardization, however, is ambiguous.

Educational programs stressing the reading of canonical works perennially waver between a prospective and a retrospective interpretation. Prospectively, the canon as platform is invoked—plausibly—to propose a standard set of texts around which a "common culture" of learning can be formed. Retrospectively—and on more dubious grounds—the canon is invoked as if the durable texts it includes are already gainfully employed as cultural pillars, turning the prospect of their not being read into an ominous threat of cultural collapse (Kennedy, 1989). It is this retrospective interpretation of standardization that tumbles into hopelessly muddled inferences. We are told that Western standards are at risk because Stanford freshmen do not read Shakespeare—as if the balance of Western civilization teeters on what Stanford freshmen do.

In an even less flattering light, canon making has issued from the petty ambitions of critics. One critic can cede to another's assessments so long as the second critic cedes in kind. As long as critics get some of their authors and titles included under their criteria for durability, they are guaranteed a reference point in the history of letters by which they can define themselves and accept definition from peers. In the 1920s, for example, Eliot was instrumental in rediscovering the metaphysical poets and the genius of Donne. By the late 1920s, it was common for Eliot's fellow critics to use the metaphysical poets and Donne to explain Eliot's genius. The critic of Shakespeare finds new details about the bard and hopes, in turn, to acquire some of the bard's weight in critical circles (see Booth, 1979, p. 277, on the "career authors" who provide critics with texts as vehicles for their own career mobility). Graff (1987) reported that critics are reluctant to find anything but coherence in their career author lest a diminished judgment decrease their own career stock (pp. 228–229).

Arguments against the intellectual justification of a canon cannot fail to acknowledge the commonplace fact that some texts are durable—especially when someone can command $1.4 million for an original copy of the American Declaration of Independence! Opponents of the canon, however, insist that canonicity is often used as a blanket justification for the durability of a corpus of texts over generations. A more scholarly approach to canonicity is to adopt a jurisprudential model in which criteria for enshrinement in a canon are applied on a text-by-text basis. Literary scholars under this rubric choose "minor" authors and texts and make a detailed brief that they should be promoted to "major" status. However, as advocates of "politically correct" curricula have observed, the criteria for enshrinement into a canon, no matter how dispassionate, are never independent of the sociocultural biases of the persons who nominate themselves as selectors. Discussions about which authors and texts are durable across generations have, for this reason, turned away from the criteria of choice to the question of who gets to choose. Aside from the pernicious assumption that one group can decide the reading for everyone else,[1] there is nothing untoward about thinking that choices for reading are determined by the reader's perceptions of similarity with the author. White European male authors who like to spoof middle-class culture are the most likely choices of White European male readers who like to see it spoofed, and so on. We argue in later chapters that a fundamental dynamic underlying written interaction is perceived relative similarity. Deprived of the opportunity to explore initially perceived similarity between their own acquisitive interests—the content of a text and the cognition of the author partially encapsulated in it—readers would lack, arguably, the most important incentive to engage a text.

Current discussions about politically correct readings sometimes clarify but sometimes confuse these issues. The discussions clarify when they point out that not all ways of engaging a text should be deemed equally appropriate or enlightened. There is, for example, legitimate cause for concern when the similarity that attracts readers to texts is found to harbor a narrow ethnocentricity bred by uninformed cultural biases. Teachers are chagrined for good reason when they find students accepting the racist statements in *Huckleberry Finn* without grasping the irony Twain intended for them. The discussions confuse when they collapse the reader's perception of similarity with an author (a natural mechanism of reader selection and engagement) with ethnocentric reading (a negative judgment about a reader's particular reading). Those who preach stocking the classroom with more culturally diverse (and so politically correct) texts undermine their cause when they try to enforce diversity as an alternative to similarity. What diversity can sensibly mean is an approach for enlarging a student's sense of similarity, for helping to give students common interests and empathies with texts and authors in whom they would normally not find such interests and empathies.[2] Diversity falls into incoherency, on the other hand, when it is principally offered as a method of impugning, without further seeking to enlarge upon, the very

---

[1]This assumption admittedly seems less pernicious to those who believe that if the content of reading is left to individual choice, cultural commonality will dissolve. Those who express this view frequently confuse the "common culture" with their opinion about which elements of the culture should command everyone's attention. As a result of this confusion, cultural doomsayers direct cultural attention to targets (King Lear, King Kong, King Friday) without justifying why precious attention should be expended in that direction. Given the shared social and even biological histories of individuals, it is not likely that a "common culture" is ever an object under serious jeopardy. The more realistic danger is the common incapacity of persons to argue rationally about what our priorities should be in expending cultural attention (see Booth, 1970, 1974).

[2]In chapter 4, we discuss how principles of relative, similarity based interaction do not preclude interaction between persons with diverse sociohistorical backgrounds.

subjective interests that keep a culturally situated reader engaged. To ask students to read native American literature only because it is "good for them" betokens the same paternalism and portends the same failed efforts of the 19th-century Methodists who preached the reading of "moral" literature for its intrinsic value.

A less cynical defense for "great texts" is White's (1984) suggestion that such texts provide opportunities for learning not found in lesser texts or artifacts. According to this view, we simply learn more about self and community by engaging Homer, Thucydides, and Burke than King Kong and Superman. This is to provide a truly cognitive, not merely political, justification for such texts. On this defense, it is acknowledged that the classics are elaborated on, imitated, and popularized in every generation. Some of these elaborations may become dominant enough to obscure the original. Since the 1930s, for example, the dominant image of Boris Karloff in Universal Studio's *Frankenstein* has eclipsed Shelly's monster and the novel that introduced it. But the proponent of the classic novel will argue that the reach of the original should (and can) never be stolen because it, more than any imitation or popularization, leads to the richest supply of cultural elaborations.

Inasmuch as this cognitive argument for the classics has merit, however, it still becomes entangled in a political morass. For as a text (on cognitive merit) gains durability, it also increases in sociocultural distance from the generations of readers who have yet to engage it for themselves. This distance makes it necessary to increase the "motivators" required for a new reader to want to engage it. As White insists there is much the contemporary reader needs to know about the world of the epic, the fall of Athens, and 18th-century England in order to "plumb" the treasures of Homer, Thucydides, and Burke, respectively. Critics of canons can object that these motivators are but timely political instruments to keep a text durable. The more durable across generations an advocate aspires a text to be, the more politically timely—and intrusive— the advocates must become to make good on their aspirations to bring new generations of readers to the text. Politics, in short, necessarily intrude even on strictly cognitive arguments for the legitimacy of a durable text. In addition, the same arguments can be turned around to defend the cognitive legitimacy of works with no claim to greatness. For the motivators to a text are themselves cognitively rich sources of learning. And the canon critic can argue that these motivators supply a rich source of learning, even for artifacts admitted to be, on first glance, superficial. The learning source of a music video may be negligible on passive viewing. But if motivated by a history of the technologies, corporate decision making, assumptions of youth and gender feeding into this form, there is much to learn. In this way, King Kong and Superman can become representative for the culture enveloping them no less than Homer, Thucydides, and Burke proved representative of their distant cultures. Canonical arguments tend to be oversimplified by making a clean separation between cognitive and political arguments. Politics and cognition are not so easy to split.

In an age of timely print, efforts to claim durability for a text, as well as efforts to counter such claims, rest on elusive ground. The need to maintain arguments for durable texts—however founded—suggests that the value of durability has never been fully eclipsed by, and has in fact come to depend more than ever on, the newer value of timeliness. To maintain the value of traditional artifacts, one must work even harder to make arguments for their relevance. Artifacts that are transparently seen as relevant need no explicit defense on such grounds. Students of the 1960s who argued for more ''relevance'' in their reading were not so much making an argument for relevance as such (they did not have to, because there was no issue about the relevance of what they wanted to read). They were simply making a statement about their lack of participation in decisions about what one needs to read to make one an educated person. Although they often labeled the issues as *relevance*, the issue for them was inclusion more than relevance: They wanted to be included in the decision making about the texts they were required to read. As far as authentic arguments for relevance are concerned, there is no opposition but mutual implication between arguments for tradition and relevance. For traditions to endure, arguments on why they remain ''living'' traditions become all the more pressing. Understandably, then, in her effort to defend the enduring traditions of the liberal arts, Chicago's Gray (1981, p. 20) pointed out that it fell upon the university to ''create a higher relevance of the unfashionable and unpopular.'' The relationship between durability and timeliness, between tradition and relevance, is one of symbiotic tensions. We monitor, in various guises, the subtle dependencies and tensions between these two values in Part II.

Imaginative and Occupational

The early book market had been devoted to religious tracts, Greek and Roman classics, histories, and other high-minded subjects stimulating the sublime imagination. Books were expensive trophies only affordable by a leisure class who let others provide for the mundane aspects of their lives. Consequently, there was no reason for the content of books to enter the world of the practical in order to help persons negotiate mundane life. As the industrialized print trade grew, printed matter became cheaper, increasing its potential to address life's drudgeries. Eventually, print penetrated every sector of mundane life: self-help guides, cookbooks, travel guides, cheap romance novels. The growing banality of the print market became the explicit issue for the post-industrial movement known as Romanticism. A literary, artistic, and philosophical movement of the late 18th and early 19th century, Romanticism was a response to the widening penetration of the print market and the growing industrialized society it served. Romantic writers focused on the antithesis of occupational commerce: on nature, on the emotions, on the primitive, on the mysterious and other-worldly. Ong (1971) argued for a relationship between the Romantic interest in mystery and a new confidence spawned by technology. He speculated that a movement celebrating the more occult sides of life could only have developed after the technologies of print and retrieval were sufficiently developed to make the unknown less threatening than it had heretofore been: "With knowledge fastened down in visually processed space, man acquired an intellectual security never known before" (p. 279).

Endowed with the capacity to enter practical life, the print trade became an issue for the Romantic writers. Authors like Lamb and Coleridge, under contract to the London publishing house of Taylor and Hessy, attacked the public for its interest in practical reading. Explaining their own universalism, Keats and Wordsworth complained that they wrote not for "men" but for "man" (Chilcott, 1972, pp. 203–204). In league with this universalism, the Romantics avowed an aesthetics of antioccupationalism (Saunders, 1964; West, 1988).[3] They rejected the notion that the composition of texts had anything to do with "manufacturing" (Young, 1970, p. 12). They discouraged the association of "sincere" or "authentic" writing with labor, and associated it instead with intense and personal suffering. Flaubert is known for spending a day on a word and a week on a page, a precious "devotion" abstracted from the deadlines of occupational time.[4] The occupational author labored, but only true authors under the Romantic definition, were heroes (Carlyle, 1899) who suffered in the netherworld of the imagination. The Romantics rejected the idea of purpose and intent in writing, for intent was both too slow for inspiration and too simple for the poetic imagination. Intent was also too client-centered, since written intents could be negotiated from the outside, beyond the writer's private purposes. The Romantics claimed that the writer's only legitimate employer was the language itself, that reaping the beauties of language was the only master driving the author (Ruthven,

---

[3]Saunders (1964) represents the contemporary Romantic aesthetic. Ruthven (1979) did much to unpack the antioccupational assumptions of Romanticism. We are indebted to both their accounts in this section.

[4]Barthes (1982b, pp. 305–316) called this literary toil the "Flaubertization" of writing and claimed that it issues from the need for authors to justify their devotion.

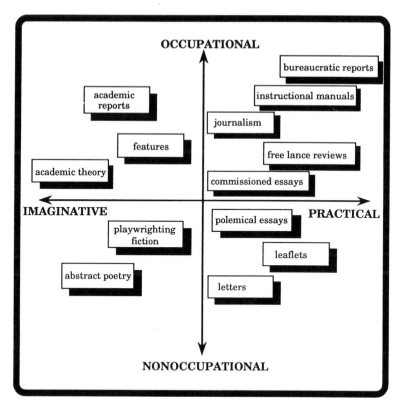

FIG. 2.3. Imaginative and practical.

1979, p. 52). Finally, the Romantics lionized the literature of the "creative imagination" and affirmed that the textual genres most important for cultural production are imaginative and nonoccupational, genres like playwrighting, fiction, and especially poetry—genres falling into the lower left quadrant of Fig. 2.3.

These dimensions remain relevant today in understanding tensions between the language most privileged in English departments (imaginative/non-occupational) and the functional language most relied upon in the professions and the world of work. In some cases, these biases run in unexpected directions, where professions—in restricted venues—continue to revere the language of leisure over the functional language of work. Conley (1990), for example, carefully documented a bias in the law of copyright and fair use that assessed genres in the imaginative/non-occupational quadrant as "creative" and those in the occupational/practical quadrant "derivative" and "parasitic." She cited recent rulings that have denied biographers (in the court's view, a type of scavenger journalist) the right to publish the previously unpublished and private writings of the biographical subject.

Assimilation and Novelty

A text is ritualized when it is only engaged as a communication partner in transactions where meanings are well assimilated, familiar, repeated, and relatively self-contained. The author intending to compose a ritualized text has no interest in conveying as yet unheard of or unknown meanings. Originality is the degree to which a communication contains such ideas and meanings. More specifically, an original text contains information that is nonredundant with any other piece of information available in the culture. A content can be original in a strong sense because it offers new ideas or, in a weaker sense, because it offers new treatments, emphases, or presentation of known ideas to novitiates. It is not uncommon for texts to be original in at least a weak sense. It is much less common, however, for a text to gain far-reaching public recognition for its originality. Given this disparity, it is useful to distinguish the originality of a text (as we mean it here) and an authorized, official, or public record of originality, as publicly credited to a writer in a text. The first notion of originality is a cognitive construct, a statement about the cognition underlying the production of the text. The second notion is a sociohistorical construct, based upon how a text comes, over time, to be socially classified. No doubt there are continuities between the first notion and the second. But there are also disjunctures. Brannigan (1981, pp. 128–141) documented many such discontinuities, showing how the public accounts of the discovery (originality in the second sense) are often just prospective and retrospective interpretations that do not match the cognitive state of the discoverer while preparing the report of discovery (originality in the first). Columbus' logs, widely copied and translated throughout Europe within months of his first voyage, were instrumental in eventually making him "the discoverer of America"—even though his logs reveal that he utterly misunderstood what he was later credited for discovering. Priestly and Lavoisier's experimental write-ups made them the official "discoverers of oxygen," although their documents reveal a very incomplete understanding of what is now known as oxygen. In such cases, official records of discovery are fashioned in spite of the fact that they do not exactly match the original ideas of the texts used as evidence for the public record.

In other cases, less favorable to the discoverer, official records of discovery are rescinded because inadequacies come to light in the original work of the discovery. In 1912, Woodward and Dawson reported on their paleontological finds on the missing link earlier predicted by Darwin.

The importance of this find was later reversed (even considered fraudulent) when Darwin's original prediction was called into question. The line between discovery and the social recognition of discovery is not smooth and is fraught with contingency (Simonton, 1988). We address this line more directly in chapter 9, when we discuss print in academic settings. For now, it suffices to say that the difficulty involved in naming or socially classifying the originality in texts need not deter us from assigning originality as a fundamental property of texts (and, more specifically, of the cognition of the writers who produce them).

Original content becomes increasingly important as a community becomes more self-aware of the value of expanding its culture, of making its capacity for new ideas a measure of its productivity and no less a productivity index than its capacity for the quantity of goods and services it can generate. Communities that fashion themselves into production centers for ideas come to place less value on ritualistic information and cast it in a supportive role, like the cup of coffee needed to begin each new day. Written content becomes valued to the extent it explores the unknown. Readers agree to engage it on the premise that they will know more by the end of the text than they knew at the beginning. Cultural expansion does not arise because an author ignores all that has been assimilated. It works because writers are able to take previously assimilated information and find a way to say more (Kaufer & Geisler, 1989). The dependency between original and assimilated information is functional because readers cannot be expected to pick out what is new from a text unless they can relate it to what they already know. This is the principle of immediate comprehension (Carley, 1986b, 1988, 1989b) that we develop later (chap. 4). Because of this principle, we must understand originality in two dimensions—assimilated knowledge and new knowledge. A text high in assimilated knowledge contains much information that is already widely known in the culture. Texts inevitably contain elements of both assimilated and new information—something to tie it to other texts and something to set it apart.[5] But textual genres differ profoundly in their ratio of old to new information.

These ratio differences, furthermore, have much to do with the relation of authority within which a text operates to exert change. Authority is the degree to which a person or text can effect sociocultural change.[6] Although there are many types of authority (chap. 4), one important source of authority, particularly for texts, is their originality. The capacity of a text to disseminate new ideas is one and the same with its capacity to increase the culture of a community (i.e., the number of ideas),

---

[5]Whether the differences that set a text apart from others are copyrightable is the subject of over 200 years of copyright law. See chapter 3.

[6]We define authorial authority at greater length in chapter 4.

as well as the capacity to alter its culture by altering the distribution of ideas (i.e., who knows what). Altering the distribution of ideas, in turn, can change patterns of social interaction (an effect discussed in later chapters of Part I) to create social as well as cultural change. In this way, the issue of the originality of a text invariably raises an issue of its authority.

However, the authority linked to a text's originality is always a matter of degree because, as indicated, every unique text is invariably a mix of assimilated as well as new information. The question of a text's authority becomes a matter of the degree to which it is engineered to reach certain individuals and produce change and the degree to which it happens to reach certain individuals and produce change. Since the industrial revolution, the potential for communicative transactions involving texts to produce change has grown; but, so too has their potential for ritual. The sheer proliferation of printed texts has increased their availability as communication partners, whether they serve as ritualized instruments or resources for change. These continuums of assimilated novel content allow for a variety of authority relationships. Figure 2.4 plots a variety of genres as they position themselves along the dimensions of assimilation and novelty. The figure also clusters these points within relations of authority.

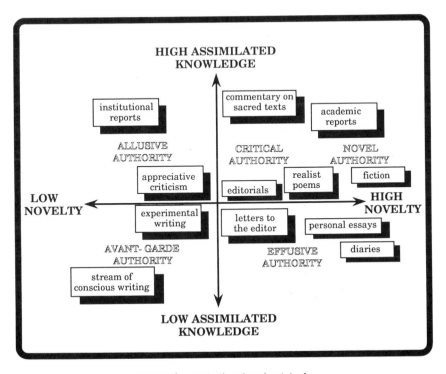

FIG. 2.4. Assimilated and original.

Much belletristic[7] and all scientific writings fall in the high assimilated/high novelty quadrant. Poems and fiction are not without cultural antecedents. Their borrowings, however, are not official coinage of the content itself—a marked contrast to scientific writing and the scientific text, which is expected to announce its borrowings explicitly, in a review of literature section. Conley's (1990) remarks on the similarities between the novel and biography ring true for belletristic and science writing as well:

> The difference between the novel and biography is not that one genre is more creative than another, or that one uses [i.e., reworks existing material] and the other does not. The difference between them—and this has great significance for copyright law—is that biography uses [i.e., reworks] more overtly than the novel and its uses [rather than invents] language. A novel's plot may be a reworking of the plots of earlier works, its characters may be drawn from well-established types, and even its individual scenes may be based on those created by other writers. [But these reworkings are indirect and covert.] Biography, on the other hand, uses earlier works directly and overtly. (pp. 21–22)

Borrowings in scientific writing, as well as in biography, must be specific and direct. Personal essays and letters, on the other hand, are expected to be highly novel but low on the assimilated dimension. The needs for assimilation are less stringent in a personal essay because the writer needs only to assimilate to the knowledge of a single addressee, not to an anonymous community of peers or a wider public. Institutional reports, textbooks, manuals, and commentaries, on the other hand, should have a higher ratio of assimilated to new knowledge. They are designed to rehearse the knowledgeable and initiate the newcomer. In neither case does the author need to be identified as the source of this insider knowledge. Avant-garde writers in the modernist tradition of Joyce and the postmodernist traditions of Barthes (1981) and Derrida (1976) tend deliberately to push on and against the assumptions of a text being systematically partitioned into known and new knowledge. Rather than segmenting a text into figure (what is given to be understood) and ground (what is taken to be understood), experimental texts of the avant-garde tend to emphasize collages, evocative associations, and other nonlinear patternings that spotlight the hundreds of decisions about the writer's status, tone, and attitude, as well as the writer's rights and obligations in managing figure/ground that conventions of writing (i.e., writing genres) automate and take below the writer's conscious decision making.

---

[7]A belletristic writing is one of literary art, a writing that is esthetic rather than informational.

As a result of inheriting, as defaults, so many decisions when investing in a genre, the avant-garde writer sees the writer trapped within the conventions of print. Furthermore, many commentators, regardless of their sympathies with the avant-garde, believe our parallel struggle to find our way into conventions for electronic communication has slowly been making us more aware of our entrapment in print and the terms under which we will eventually find our way out of its limiting assumptions (Bolter, 1991; Kernan, 1990; see Lanham, 1992, for a review; Ulmer, 1989). The genres (or antigenres) of the avant-garde tend to fall in the quadrant of being low in both assimilated and new information only in the sense that the dimensions themselves in these genres lose their efficacy of demarcation.

Authority depends on the capacity to produce change but this capacity is not linearly related to originality alone. This is because persons or texts enact the most change, not by ignoring assimilated information, but by incorporating it and saying much more. A text's capacity for effecting change, therefore, is a function of containing high degrees of both assimilated and original information. The capacity for change, of course, is further enhanced by putting into constant circulation multitudes of texts, high in both assimilated and newsworthy content. The effect of this huge capacity for change since the industrial revolution has been the rise of the knowledge industry, an industry which, at the moment, can induce what often feels like a turnover of knowledge in a very short amount of time. This capacity for change, restricted to specialized professionals, lies within a system of authority we call *novel* for reasons discussed later. But as Fig. 2.4 indicates, novel authority is but one element of a system of authority (viz., texts with a content with a potential for enacting change) that has proliferated since the industrial revolution, and we need to mention others as well.

Systems of allusive authority predate both print and the time when originality was associated with a cognitive endowment of individuals (Woodmansee, 1984). The function of originality in the allusive sense has medieval roots (Williams, 1976, p. 193) and is tied to assumptions of restoration more than to creation. The scribal culture prized the discovery and perpetuation of those texts expressing widely accepted truths as a more original (i.e., back to the source) and fundamental undertaking than those texts with no proven cultural worth or power of assimilation. Authors who seek originality through allusion reinforce these priorities by creating texts that are high on the assimilated dimension and low on the novelty dimension. Their originality stems less from the new information in the text—which in allusive texts is minimal—than from the timely re-presentation of important borrowings. Allusive authors leave their own text in the shadow of the prior landmarks they recall. The author after allusion, in the words of Mallon, has no mind for "an Emersonian call to 'thrust thyself' " but only for an "Horatian exhortation" (Mallon, 1989, p. 3). Textual contents containing allusion are consumed with the "patrimony" of earlier texts (Ruthven, 1979, pp. 108–109) and, in particular, the communicative transactions between earlier readers and their readings. In trying to define the possibilities of literary theory, Wellek and Warren (1956) contrasted their understanding of original literature with an older, allusive literary culture:

> In earlier periods there was a sounder understanding of the nature of literary creation, a recognition that the artistic value of a merely original plot or subject matter was small. The renaissance and neo-classicism rightly ascribed importance to translations . . . [to] commonplaces, recurrent themes and images handed down from antiquity to modern literatures. No author felt inferior or unoriginal because he used, adapted, and modified themes and images inherited from tradition and sanctioned by antiquity. To work with a given tradition and adopt its devices are perfectly compatible with emotional power and artistic value. (p. 249)

The focus of the alluding author is not on making progress from the source but on initiating a return to it. Consider the words of Mueller (1989), who favored an allusive foundation for literary scholarship:

> A work of literary scholarship at its best typically invites us to return to its object of enquiry. I recently read Pocock's *Machiavellian Moment*, a magisterial work of scholarship if ever there was one. . . . I came away from my reading of this book with a strong desire to read the treatises of Guicciardini, a slightly younger contemporary of Machiavelli. My desire to read Guicciardini does not point to some failure of exposition on Pocock's part, as if I would no longer have the desire to read Guicciardini if Pocock had done his job a little better. On the contrary, I am confident in saying that Pocock intended to persuade his readers that Guicciardini, Machiavelli, and his other authors are thinkers and writers to be reckoned with. (p. 24)

This "return to" the text, according to Mueller, need not be literal repetition; rather it can mean repetition with interpretive distance, the rehearsal of old themes adapted to new readers and contexts (p. 25). Pope recognized allusion as taking this subtle middle ground between routine and innovation, a device that allowed the author to re-present in artful ways "what oft' was thought, but ne'er so well expressed." To be creative is to learn to seize the past with fresh eyes, to revitalize it even as one invokes it.

Despite this element of creativity in allusion, the alluding author never fails to weight the referenced text (and the transactions in which it rests) more than the text being composed and the enveloping transaction in which the reference is currently being issued. The merit of the alluding text is often judged by the density of alluded-to texts that make up its content. Studying the rhetoric of a literary criticism with vestiges of this allusive habit, for example, Fahenstock and Secor (1991, p. 91) observed that the "ethos" of the critic is often conveyed by the "allusive density" of the criticism, the "casualness that reaches out to a wide range of knowledge and pulls it into significance, creating the ethos of an alert and well-stocked mind." The capacity for change (hence authority) of the allusive author rests in the degree to which readers have assimilated the knowledge activated by the allusion. For that originality and authority, allusive authors are restricted to an audience of approving insiders. We have more to say about allusion in a slightly different context (chap. 5).

Systems of critical authority cover genres that are high on assimilated knowledge but low overall on the novelty dimension. The author exercising originality through critical authority relies on the representation of borrowings but additionally on new ideas about how to evaluate and classify them. Authors working from critical authority remain bound to a universe of assimilated knowledge, one that remains in need of constant monitoring and active structuring. A traditional critic who writes criticism to keep the canon up to date writes with critical authority, preserving the past by appending new categories to it; so does the writer within an organization who must keep routines up to date in memoranda and organizational reports. In literary criticism, Wellek and Warren (1956) suggested that critical authority is the first step toward writing the history of literature:

> The real critical problems in [theorizing about literature] arise when we reach the stage of weighing and comparing and showing how one artist utilizes the achievements of another artist, when we watch the transforming power. The establishment of the exact position of each work in a tradition is the first task of literary history. (p. 249)

According to Kernan (1987, p. 159), the role of the authoritative critic was fashioned by Samuel Johnson in the expanding but still preindustrialized print market of the mid-18th century—when there was a growing need to impose a "systematizing logic" on the "continuous surge of new ever accumulating print products." Like the alluding author, the critic fashioned after Johnson maintained a deferential attitude toward the referenced texts and to the previous communicative transactions involving them. Johnson's model of the authoritative critic remains, in other words, essentially subordinate to what Kernan called the "primary writings" of a "text-centered institution" (p. 159). Yet the critic in Johnson's mold exercised a prerogative that would be deemed unfathomable to the alluding author: the right to judge and to include or exclude texts according to standards defined by the critic:

> Johnson's vigorous canon-making shows an activity proceeding by exclusion as well as inclusion: Pope is a true poet but the metaphysicals, being obscure, are not; Percy's border ballads are acceptable but Ossian is spurious. Richardson is superior to Fielding because he knew the human heart; Sterne is transitory because novelty pleases only briefly, but Shakespeare will endure because he depicts the eternal truth. (p. 159)

Johnson's critic has the right and obligation to both include and omit authors and texts from a literary canon. The authoritative critic can compare his or her own written criticism favorably against the texts that will be rejected; but must give it a lower ranking relative to the landmarks that will be accepted. There is originality in such criticism insofar as the critic must be a judge on the scene, vigilant and active. Indeed, cultivating an active mind is one of the postmedieval renderings of being an "original" (Woodmansee, 1984, pp. 425–448). Yet the creative moment at issue in critical authority still operates, for the most part, in the service of restoration, of keeping a tradition whole. And this fact puts serious limits on the capacity for change (authority) of the critic who seeks to be authoritative. Authors exercising critical authority, with their balance of interest in borrowed and new, are likely to attract a like-minded readership, one primarily interested in borrowings but also in a certain amount of new information about how best to tie them together with the fewest loose ends.

Systems of novel authority provide an authoritative base for genres that are high in both assimilated and new knowledge. The author seeking originality through novelty rivals authors under earlier authority systems in an interest in recalling the past, in reviewing, and (in the case of science) citing a standing archive. But the author transacting business from assumptions of novel authority wants to make history and not simply to recall or adjudicate it; wants to add to a literature and not just to invoke or referee it. Novel authority can be defined both in terms of and in opposition to originality as it was understood in 19th-century Romanticism. In Romantic originality, an original was a mind or an artifact that was not only active but "unfamiliar," "striking" and shimmering with signs of "genius." To be original in Romantic terms was to avoid falling under an outside system of rules (Pearsall Smith, 1971, p. 16–17). Novel authority resembles Romanticism in highlighting new information that is striking enough to make a difference (i.e., for future writers to find worth citing); yet it also contrasts with Romanticism in insisting upon an external system of rules and regulations governing what it means to be new. Academic writers must systematically work from the borrowings of the past in order to claim a new advance on them (Garvey, 1979; Kaufer & Geisler, 1989; Meadows, 1973). While novelty describes originality within academic conventions (chap. 9), it also describes a standard of originality for texts in the marketplace, texts over which authors claim ownership and copyright protection (Mallon, 1989, chap. 3).[8] Whether in academe or the free market, the author relying on novelty seeks to reach readers who are centrally interested in the new information within the text. Yet it is an interest deeply whetted by the author's deliberate inclusion of much culturally assimilated information that readers already know and want to learn more about.

Avant-garde is our term for the experimental genres that fall in the low assimilated, low novelty quadrant. To position such genres in this quadrant is not to deny their claim to originality or difference—that, precisely, is what the avant-garde claims for itself. It is rather to indicate that the avant-garde often denies the very boundaries between assimilated and new that makes the "novel" easy to classify and comprehend. Writers interested in this experimentation have, in one way or another, sought to question the assumptions underlying other systems of authority in other quadrants, systems that make a clearer division between the assimilative and the novel dimensions of written discourse. Tensions between systems of avant-garde authority and more conventional systems have been the basis of much recent public debate. For example, a debate receiving a great deal of media play is one between the experimentalist approaches to texts taken by some postmodernists and the allusive and critical authority assumptions brought to texts by traditional literary scholars (e.g., Should we teach Shakespeare reverentially or experimentally?).

Another debate, perhaps even more fundamental, is that between avant-garde and novel systems of authority. Postmodernists interested in both experimentation and politics question the individualism implicit in systems of novel authority—the idea that authors can act autonomously by leveraging themselves against a compliant past. They sometimes criticize what they see as the implicit positivism in the assumption that writing projects logically proceed from "what's there" in the current literature to "what's new." They attack what they consider to be the folly of treating authors, texts, ideas, and periods as discrete nodes tied together through links of progress. They question whether the authors of previous texts now constituting the past were themselves anything but opportunistic in the construction of their past. They suggest that previous texts are simply conveniences, rather than logical warrants, of current

---

[8]See chapter 3 for a more complete discussion of copyright.

texts. While avant-garde and politically minded postmodernists are somewhat united in the authorial orientations they reject, there is no consensus about the shape of the postmodern text (Sprinker, 1989). Despite these schisms, much of the work in the avant-garde is driven by an eagerness to experiment with new discursive forms that do not carry the baggage of clearly circumscribed assimilative or novelty assumptions about authority, history, individuality, and property (Said, 1983). Insofar as these experiments produce texts with a low yield in both assimilated and new knowledge, the texts themselves can be expected to claim a very negligible reach outside their inner circles. The paradox of the avant-garde, one its practitioners often accept, is that to be too new is to preclude ever being too important.

Effusive authority describes the genres that are low in assimilative knowledge but high in novel knowledge, the lower right quadrant of Fig. 2.4. Writers seeking originality through the authority of effusion leave only the authorial ego at centerstage. They create an environment for change that is only as deep and extensive as the lived experience of the writer. Effusive texts are unsurprising when they are used to write personal letters or to keep diaries. Yet effusive models of writing, surprisingly, have come to dominate American composition classrooms, which tend to emphasize personal expression at the expense of prior imitative models, writing strategies, and historical traditions. In their 1989 study of classroom practices in American writing courses, Faigley (1989) found that teaching writing as personal expression is the dominant model for writing education in the American college classroom. In *Cultural Literacy*, Hirsch (1987) argued that American students are not being taught enough cultural content, and, as a result, they lack the knowledge base needed for performing basic acts of reading and writing. As a solution to this problem, Hirsch proposed and subsequently published dictionaries of cultural facts for students at the primary and secondary levels. Many have criticized Hirsch for appearing to resurrect the environment of clubby and genteel English departments. Yet Hirsch's program must also be understood as seeking to replace the effusion culture that reading and writing classrooms in America have sometimes become with a more traditional allusion culture. Whatever one thinks of Hirsch's efforts on behalf of reform, he is perhaps not off the mark in his critique of the effusive (content-free) authority underlying much of today's education in reading and writing. Effusive authority derives its power purely from the writer's self-manufactured insight, an insight that is necessary for self-reflection, but altogether too weak an engine to produce, on its own power, substantive change outside one's own range of personal experience.

LITERACY DEBATES:
WHICH CONTENT TO BE LITERATE ON?

With what content must an author or reader interact, toward mastery, to be literate? The many dimensions on which content can be understood help to explain the diverse and diffuse nature of literacy debates. Should the content be enduring or ephemeral? Imaginative or practical? Should the writer forfeit his or her claim of novelty to the past, dispense with the past to tout a new idea, or try to carry forward the text and the past as an undifferentiated blend of ideas? For a century, American English departments have been entrusted to teach literacy, and for that long, the conceptions of the content chosen as a measure of literacy, in such departments have been almost as diverse as the society at large (Graff, 1987; Graff & Warner, 1989). The Arnoldian belief in landmark texts for building character—a culture of allusive and critical authority—has perennially competed with the research university's interest in new knowledge, in cultivating cultures of novelty. Postmodernism, further, has called into question the fundamental assumptions of texts that fall within the range of allusive, critical, and novel authority. The debate is further complicated, at least in America, because many in English departments hold multiple allegiances. One and the same individual may elect novelty as an image for one paper (saying something new about Shakespeare by answering a question that arises from the literature) and allusion for another (rehearsing common touchstones about Shakespeare with wit and vigor). The novelist or short story writer often insists that permitting students "to emote" is necessary but not without models of the masters to read and imitate. Postmodernists often see standard literary conventions and standard models of academic writing as necessary foils to help students appreciate why the conventions underlying them must be unearthed and questioned for their political as well as semantic assumptions. Teachers of written composition are distributed across all these orientations. A student taking a reading or writing class purported to teach literacy can be presented with almost any content under any number of assumptions about its durability, practicality, and originality (Young, 1978), leaving the work of English departments, as far as defining literacy is concerned, ill defined (Herron, 1988). Further adding to the confusion, the meaning of literacy is now often extended to include many everyday cultural activities (e.g., watching television or film) as well as work-related activities for the marginally employed (e.g., working a cash register) that do not involve significant interaction with written information. The double consequence of this extension has been to metaphorize reading and writing beyond traditionally recognizable bounds and, at the same time, to associate instruction in reading and writing as a curative for most of the nation's social and economic ills. Moreover, even when they are well focused, debates about literacy tend to miss the mark when the debaters try to represent their own vantage as a discrete position wholly noncontinuous with and ideologically incompatible with others, when their position is in fact just that—a position fixed in a multidimensional space of communication transactions, one position deeply entangled with the next.

IMPLICATIONS

The general impoverishment of debates about literacy and the incapacity to coherently define, much less address, the issues involved in them, represents, in our view, an instructive failure from which we can learn. The failure is symptomatic of a more general failure to address the theoretical implications of the communicative transaction. The matter of textual content was not an issue when a text was construed as a physical artifact to be kept in a glass case; nor was it an issue when it was a message—a meaning stabilized and enforced by a royal or religious authority and transferred in tact under the aegis of that authority. Prior to the industrial revolution, this was the lot of most of the entities known as texts, especially for the mass culture. Texts were then, as now, situated in communicative transactions, but the transactions were relatively well delineated and culturally circumscribed. The industrial revolution broke through the barrier of the "appropriate" cultural placement for texts, making it difficult to eliminate texts as a potential medium for virtually any communicative transaction currently supported by speech.

The potential of texts to be anywhere engendered deep uncertainties about where texts should properly be. The uncertainties involved were probably not unlike those faced by ancient rhetoricians when they first became aware of the potential to support mass communication through formal speech—and then pondered the occasions for which it was appropriate to write a rhetoric. For the descendent of the industrial revolution, however, the issue was not one between informal and formal speech. The issue was primarily one between informal (face-to-face) speech plus writing and informal speech/writing augmented by print. Because of its reproducibility and speed, print in combination with speech and writing evinces prima facie advantages over speech and writing alone. But speaking and writing absent print have advantages that should not be overlooked. Speaking and writing allow for richer and less ambiguous interaction because the participants are not importantly separated in time and place. Moreover, speaking and writing avoid the work of composing a mass circulation document. A mass circulation document, it should be noted, is not the only way that information can diffuse to a larger audience dispersed in time and space. There is also word of mouth. A speaker or writer can tap the shoulder of a passerby, can continue to find new passersby to tap, and can leave it to those already tapped to start tapping those near them. Informal speaking and writing in this sense can begin to emulate the reach of a mass circulation document. The capacity of word of mouth to pass information across long distances is not infinite, however; there comes a breaking point when a community, institution, or organization becomes internally too large or complex to be sustained through informal speech and writing alone. The issue underlying the choice between print, on the one hand, and speaking and writing, on the other, involves these break points. Under what conditions in the life of a collective will speaking and writing work as well as print for maintaining social cohesion, consensus, and structured change? At what point does print become a necessity? These questions are of vital importance to the life of institutions investing heavily in print, for such institutions want to enjoy the advantages of print without also losing the attendant advantages of proximate speech and writing. (Similar issues are now playing themselves out with electronic media, though that is beyond the scope of this study.)

As an important aside, we note that the issues played themselves out differently in the competition between print and public address or oratory. Oratory is formal speech designed for a relatively small audience. As a device of mass communication, oratory had (and has) some important advantages over print. Oratory is premised on the assumption that what moves audiences is not simply the orator's words but the orator's presence, along with the presence of the audience. People and the assembly of people are important accessories to the oratorical art. But the price of this assembly is to endure the logistical problems that any mass assemblage presents. Print, on the other hand, was a way of assembling a mass audience while avoiding the physical assembly of people. Print thus solved many of the logistical problems of oratory, but with a loss of the electricity of oratory's physical immediacy and with a new incredibly large burden imposed on the text. In oratory, the crowd was gathered before the speech. In print, the text had to be up front and reviewed before an anonymous market would begin to move toward it, one reader at a time. The tradeoffs between print and oratory denied neither a place in the arena of mass communication. Oratory was mass communication for relatively small concentrated gatherings; print was mass communication for larger, more widely dispersed, audiences.

More fundamental tensions surfaced between these two arts, however, when oratory started being supported by print—that is, when the contents of speeches were printed and distributed to audiences well beyond the orator's immediate audience.[9] An orator, playing to a local gathering, could be long winded and passionate, playing to the specific biases of the audience to good effect. When mass media began to cover oratory, words and meanings intended and interpreted in a small space were now carried to the larger, more anonymous, space of print. By covering public speeches meant to play to different audiences, print journalists had the power to expose a speaker's local prejudices, inconsistencies, and hypocrisies. Because the political orator had to curry the favor of a broad constituency to build coalitions, media-savvy speakers had to start attending less to what was in their speeches than to how the print media would cover them. Orators learned that they had to compose their speeches to be taken in context by their immediate audience; but also that they should not say anything that could jeopardize their being taken out of context (to their detriment) by the anonymous print audience. Long-winded, passionate, and audience pleasing, but parochial, speeches were easy to turn into damaging news bites (and later sound and video bites). The news bite was itself concise, dry, and nonregionalized; political speakers learned that they could better control the media by composing public discourse in the very news bites the media would report (Bennett, 1977; Jamieson, 1988). Public address, as a result, came increasingly to mold itself into the very news bites of press reporting. The tendency was to recast the organization of speeches into tight and short packets of quotable statements. Evidence suggests that in the last 25 years, the length of sound bites reported on the airwaves has increasingly shortened. In an often cited content analysis of major news coverage of the 1968 and 1988 elections, Adatto (1990) found that the average sound bite, or block of uninterrupted speech from a candidate, dropped from 42.3 seconds in 1968 to only 9.8 seconds in 1988. Whether candidates have shortened their quotable statements to accommodate this shortening air time remains an interesting empirical question.

To return to our larger point, the industrial revolution proved that texts circulating across the mass culture can be timely as well as durable; practical as well as high minded; original as well as ritualistic. It proved, in other words, that texts can vary in content and engage in a spectrum of transactions with partners drawn from the whole of society. But the response to this development was not—as it should have been—to investigate the comparative advantages of texts for certain classes of trans-

---

[9]According to Zarefsky (1990, p. 54), the Lincoln/Douglass debates of 1858 probably represent the first time the press covered campaign speeches verbatim. The content of the speeches was telegraphed to newspapers across America. Zarefsky also noted (pp. 214–215) that newspapers tended to give more complete coverage to the candidate they endorsed.

actions when the competition between print and speech was consequential. The response, rather, was to politicize some classes of transactions against others; to fashion a caste system between "high" and "low" texts; to accept the proliferation of texts and then to create a ranking of contents according to their capacity to be partners in revered communicative transactions.

The politicization of content is naive, however, because of the complex interdependencies between ostensibly opposed types of content. If our educational system supports the reading of only durable texts, it is because contemporary speakers and writers are willing to make timely, impassioned, and often ephemeral arguments to keep them durable. Writers of the avant-garde must still depend on the paperwork of the lowest bureaucrats following the most common routine for support. Writers who want to facilitate change need to submit themselves to the humblest rituals of editorial review to get their breakthrough ideas into wide circulation.

The outcome of the industrial revolution was to help us see how the proliferation of print throughout the society proliferated new contexts for writing. There were far more cultural contexts for writing than there were classifications of genres for which printed texts had been traditionally used. But there was also a fundamental problem of knowing how many genres to create; that is, a problem of knowing where to use print to bolster speaking and writing when there was no place in principle that print could not be used. Publishers, for example, had to know how much print advertising was necessary before word of mouth would do its part. Employers had to know how to coordinate the flow of paper in their firms so that it neither duplicated word of mouth nor stifled it. Professionals had to know how geographically dispersed their organizations could reliably become when they knew that it would increasingly fall to paper to hold together an ever widening, ever dispersed membership. Academics had to know when their interest groups had become large enough to justify a journal or diversified enough to break into different groups supported by different journals. The industrial revolution legitimately raised such problems about texts without formulating the theories needed to address them. The rest of our route through Part I embarks on the formulation of such a theory.

Contexts Sustaining
Print Transactions

The author–function is tied to the legal and institutional systems that circumscribe, determine, and articulate the realm of discourses.
                                   —Michael Foucault (1977, p. 130)

The removal of the Author . . . is not merely an historical fact or an act of writing; it utterly transforms the modern text.
                                   —Roland Barthes (1981, p. 210)

Writing is sometimes portrayed as though texts wrote themselves; the relegation of the author to the role of a shadowy adjunct to writing is manifestly unsatisfactory . . .
                                   —Anthony Giddens (1987, p. 211)

In light of our efforts in chapter 2 to herald the importance of the communicative transaction in understanding print, the work of postmodernists would seem a welcome alternative. To a large extent the alternative *is* welcome, especially in its understanding of the problem. The problem is that traditional literary theory ignored (or is widely reputed to have ignored) the role of historical transactions in understanding the nature of written content over time. In view of this problem, an appropriate path would be to trace back to the historical transactions of which printed texts are a part—particularly since the industrial revolution—and to isolate some of the features from which a theory of the communicative transaction, crossing modalities, might begin. Generally speaking, this was not the approach of postmodernists in the tradition of Foucault (1977) and Barthes (1981). Instead the path they took pursues an abstracted notion of context that does not point back to concrete historical transactions as much as it theorizes across them. In the process, they strip authors and readers of their cognitive identities in communicative transactions. This is the basis of Gidden's (1987) critique of postmodernism—accusing many postmodernists of making the author (not to mention every other element of the historical transaction) a "shadowy adjunct"—and the basis of ours.[1]

Authors and readers are sociocognitive agents who remain limited in their information processing capacities and who are inundated by information made available through their interaction with others. The others with whom they interact and from whom they acquire information form a constrained set, codetermined by knowledge and sociocultural positions (explored more fully in chap. 6). In spite of the sociocognitive grounding of authors and readers, many postmodernist writers express a preference for "social" accounts of author–reader interaction over "cognitive" accounts. To be fair, this expression of preference seems at times more attached to the flair of their argumentation than to their actual beliefs or practice, because avowedly social accounts of author–reader interaction cannot get off the ground without a supplementary cognitive account. Take the insights of Bakhtin (1981), a theorist widely embraced by postmodernists for being in the social camp and whose approach to language resembles the approach we take (chap. 5):

> The word in language is half someone else's. It becomes "one's own" only when the speaker populates it with his own intention, his own accents, when he appropriates the word, adapting it to his own semantic and expressive intention. . . . Language is not a neutral medium that passes freely and easily into the private property of the speaker's intentions; it is populated—overpopulated—with the intentions of others. Expropriating it, forcing it to submit to one's own intentions and accents, is a difficult and complicated process. (p. 294)

Language may be a social possession but it requires nonetheless a cognitive machinery to make it one's own. By denying (in their exposition, if not their actual theory) the bottlenecks authors face in making their cognitive representations public, and the public representations of the

---

[1]Our objection to certain strands of postmodernism is directed at the postmodernist's tendency to strip individuals of a cognitive architecture, thereby reformulating individuals as undifferentiated elements of a social world. Despite this departure from postmodernist thought, we find ourselves sympathetic with many specific tenets of postmodernism and, in particular, postmodernism's focus on the constructed nature of knowledge. (See Carley, in press-a, chap. 4; Kaufer & Geisler, 1990.)

culture in which they dwell personally invested, postmodernists in the tradition of Barthes (1981) and Foucault (1977) collapse all the variation of author–reader interaction on the shoulders of a single feature—social context[2]—which wants more explanation than it offers.

One can, however, sympathize with both the importance and difficulty of developing a theory of context useful for explicating print transactions. The notion of context is primarily associated with communication at small distances. We think we know what "context" means when we are talking about speaking and simple writing occasions. Context, however, turns into a black box when we apply it to interactions across vast distances, like those connected to print. Print enables interaction across significant separations of space, time, and culture. Because of the range of these separations, we like to think that print makes possible contexts, not a (singular) context. But establishing context as a plurality does not, by that act alone, render it less enigmatic. Postmodern writers have rightly been fascinated by the conundra of context when the communication is temporally, geographically, and culturally dispersed.

Nonetheless, the enigma of context is made more elusive than necessary through the conflation of distance with the plurality of context. Although it is true that contexts have plurality when communications are dispersed spatially, temporally, and culturally, it is, at the very least, misleading to associate a singular proximate context with the absence of distance in a communicative transaction. The work of Garfinkel (1968), Goffman (1974), and Tannen (1990) shows how great a cultural divide can separate speakers even when they are practically standing on top of

---

[2]The tendency to seek social foundations of all knowledge is not peculiar to postmodernism but belongs to a larger intellectual movement known as social construction. This movement is an approach to language and knowledge employed by theorists in multiple disciplines who have attempted to challenge the traditional cognitive foundations of knowledge and to replace these foundations with social premises. For example, Kuhn (1970, p. 201) stated that scientific knowledge is "the common property of a group or nothing at all." Geertz (1973, p. 360) argued that so-called cognitive universals (e.g., motivation, perception, imagination, and memory) are fundamentally social in their origin; Rorty (1979, p. 170) projected a social basis for the whole of knowledge.

The advent of social construction has opened up and legitimated socially rich accounts of the authoring role and of the author's interactions with readers (Foucault, 1977). Among its virtues for fostering the study of author–reader interaction, social construction has freed theorists from the romantic assumptions of the author as the lone (cognitive) genius and has helped to situate the authoring role in a more realistically complex social system rife with friends, collaborators, competitors, editors, publishers, reviewers, and markets (Bruffee, 1986). It has also liberated histories from the individualist assumptions of the traditional literary historian who tended to divorce context from content by reducing the author's context to mere stage setting for a more universal content. Rather than view the author as an isolated site of cultural production, social construction focuses on the author (and reader for that matter) as roles constructed by an ongoing and ever changing social system. We have many sympathies with social construction (see chapter 4). Our departure from it, like our departure from postmodernism, is explained in footnote 1.

one another in space and time. The work of Labov and Fanshel (1977) reveals that the trained therapist cannot understand even the simplest face-to-face statement of the psychiatric patient without months of interactive history. We tend to collapse speech, small distances, and singular contexts into one bundle; to associate print, large distances, and multiple contexts into another. But we should recognize that these tendencies are not foolproof.

Postmodernists following Derrida (1976) made a distinction between speech and writing on the assumption that writing (and print) confront us with complexities of context well beyond speech. But if the complexities of print are seen to exceed those of speech, this perception owes to the simple fact that it is easier to overlook the complexities of context in speech. In face-to-face interaction, the myth of a seamless context enveloping speakers and hearers persists only because it has remained a plausible fiction, a veneer that we are able to lace with politeness (Brown & Levinson, 1987) and interaction rituals (Collins, 1981), but one that nonetheless masks the complexities of splintered backgrounds and that all too easily lulls interlocutors into thinking that they are engaged in seamless communication.

The myth of seamlessness is harder to maintain for print because disjunctures across contexts become increasingly visible as separations in time, space and culture increase. The author–reader encounter mediated by print is achieved in the face of such separation. But it is not an accomplishment completely unheard of in the oral medium. Our purpose for establishing a level playing field between the oral and print mediums is to question the notion that communicative transactions are straightforward for theoretical purposes when the distances are small and become problematic only for large distances. Indeed, there are reasons for thinking that the very opposite is true, that a theory of the communicative transaction crossing modalities best starts with print. Because of our deep familiarity with speaking contexts, where distance is often minimized, it is very hard to x-ray such contexts for the features needed for a transactional theory extendible to print. Yet, as the postmodernists have made us aware, print extended across vast distances remains a very strange and unfamiliar type of communicative transaction. There must be deliberateness just in thinking through these contexts; an impressive scholarly literature has amassed to describe these transactions in various historical periods.[3] It is from these careful descriptions that we are most

---

[3]The historical systems examined include: (a) systems of scribal authoring (Reynolds & Wilson, 1968); (b) the uses of official manuscripts in 12th-century England (Clanchy, 1978); (c) middle class authors and readers in prerevolutionary France (Darnton, 1979); (d) 18th-century Europe (Belanger, 1982; Speck, 1982; Wiles, 1976); (e) working and middle-class authors and readers in 19th-century urban England or America (Reder, 1966; Hepburn, 1968; Webb, 1955; Wilson, 1985); and so on.

likely to abstract the features required for a theory of the ecology of communicative transactions.

In the rest of this chapter, we work backward from a historical survey documenting the context of communicative transactions in the rise of the print industry. We isolate from these contexts a set of contextual features that are independent of print and that are necessary components of a theory of the communicative transaction. As the reader will learn from our survey, print transactions depend on a host of complex institutions, including government, publishing, and patronage. The institutions grew in number and complexity with the industrial revolution but many (like patronage) were in place long before that watershed. We filter from this institutional history a relatively small set of features.

Our attempt to isolate features from history for a theory that transcends time and place requires some defense. Some theorists who believe in the importance of viewing author–reader interaction as historical transaction also take a holistic position on these transactions. They argue that historical transactions of author–reader communication cannot be decomposed further for theory construction. They contend that the very most we should expect is writing good histories of these transactions (Mailloux, 1989, p. 134). The holistic position in this context seems a bit naive, as there is no escaping the problem of abstraction, even for the historian. Every description of the author and reader's transactional context is necessarily a selection of certain details and an omission of others. Even as historians of that transaction, we cannot escape theorizing about the very context we describe and, in many cases, we find common abstractions across contexts. Certain details of author–reader interaction will survive one context and, when abstracted, show themselves in many others. If we do not make these transcontext or even transperiod abstractions, we lose the opportunity to develop a theory of the communicative transaction that can be applied and tested in multiple contexts and extended to modalities other than print.

To anticipate our discussion a bit, these common, albeit abstract, features include, but are not limited to, such entities as the cognitive similarity relationships between authors and readers, reach, sociocultural opportunities to interact, cultural integration, and population size. In chapter 4, we discuss the communicative transaction and provide formal definitions of some of these features. In this chapter, we motivate these definitions using information on actual historical periods involving print, particularly during the industrial revolution. Before we begin our survey, we mention two features that have dominated the context of communication between authors and readers since the industrial revolution and that were crucial in determining what we have chosen to include in our present survey or to defer to a later chapter: print and professions.

TWO CONTEXTUAL FEATURES DOMINATING
AUTHOR–READER TRANSACTIONS
SINCE THE INDUSTRIAL REVOLUTION

Two features have dominated the historical context of author–reader transactions and demand single chapters in their own right: print and professions. Although print is exclusively a feature of context (imposing no hard and fast restrictions on content as we saw in chapter 2), professionalization is primarily a feature of context that imposes some general restrictions on the relationship of the content to the context (e.g., that the content of information circulating within a professional group be more elaborated and shared within than outside the group). In the following paragraphs, we mention enough about these features to indicate why their influence on the context of author–reader interaction has been profound. More specific details, however, are deferred (chapters 7, 8).

Print

Print allegedly contributed much to the modern condition of author–reader interaction. Eisenstein (1979) showed that print brought writers out of scriptoria and into urban shops where their words could be mechanically reproduced. It made words timely as well as authoritative; it put newspapers, novels, and cultural cliches into circulation and made possible the development of slogans and propaganda on an unprecedented social scale (Hughes, 1989). Bledstein (1976) claimed that print gave an impetus, more or less, to professional culture and to the knowledge industries requiring regular contact across distant sites.

Given the scope of these claims, many controversies, freighted with much overstatement, have swirled about print. It is easy to ridicule the overstatement but much harder to extract the nagging grains of truth such debate always leaves behind. For example, some say that print "defined" the author. Although authors undoubtedly existed before print, there is no doubt that print redefined in profound ways the context of author–reader interaction. The question is how. Some say that print gave us modern science and rationality. Although scientific mentalities were clearly not hostage to printing presses, there is little doubt that modern science and the organizational structures within which it is practiced would not be what they are today without the platform of print. But what is the connection? These are questions we cannot pretend to answer in full, but in Part II, we cut through some of these thicket-ridden issues.

Professions

Professions have no strict definition, but they usually describe an organization entrusted by the public to apply specialized knowledge to some client base for the common welfare (Abbott, 1988). Doctors and lawyers are prototypes of a professional class. Car salesmen and Mafia lieutenants stray from the prototype but nonetheless qualify as professionals on many criteria. Professions have common standards for training, licensing, and policing their members, and lobbies to secure legislative recognition for their services (West, 1988). They have their own meetings and their own channels for internal communication. In the corporate world where so much writing is done in professionalized settings, the role of the author has come to intersect at many junctures with the role of professional, and many authors now see themselves as addressing readers exclusively within a professional context.

Indeed, since World War I, the largest sector of the book publishing business has been devoted to professional markets, books dealing in education, business, science, technology, and reference (Tebbel, 1968, Vol. 4), written by specialized experts and usually for them. In channeling written communication within special knowledge groups with high cognitive similarity, professionalism has had a radical impact on the context of author–reader interaction, imposing a level of homogeneity on author and reader profiles, making common assumptions about their level of literacy, educational background, and their opportunities to meet face-to-face (in classrooms, lectures, and conferences).

Contexts of author–reader interaction that are "professional" (where the author writes for his or her group) need to be distinguished from those that are "occupational" (where the author simply writes for pay). In his classic 1897 study of Dryden, Addison, and Pope, Beljame (1948) traced the rise of authorial occupationalism in late 17th- and early 18th-century England. The mid-18th-century English writer Samuel Johnson, who wrote essays, criticism, dictionaries, and calendars for clients—anything for a price—became the prototype of the preprofessional occupationalist (Fussell, 1971). In contrast to the occupational author, a lone gun, the new class of author as professional was identified with a group's special knowledge and was a creature of the late 19th century, a time when all sectors of American and European life were being divvied up into territories for professionals to claim as their own (Bledstein, 1976, chap. 8). In the remainder of this chapter, we ignore professional contexts in favor of contexts in which authors write for readers in general markets. These latter contexts sustained the growth of the print industry.

CONTEXTS OF COMMUNICATIVE TRANSACTIONS
IN THE PRINT INDUSTRY

Author–reader transactions as mediated by print have emerged within a variety of institutional relationships, including that between government and publishing, publishing and the courts, authors and government, authors and patrons, authors and publishers, authors and agents, authors and reviewers, and even authors and other authors (Golding, 1974). The strengthening or weakening of these relationships has a decided impact on strengthening or weakening the ties between authors and readers.

These ties are often inherited from other ongoing relationships. An important theoretical feature underlying these ties is reach (chap. 4). Some institutional relationships enhance the author's reach, others restrict it, and some do both. For example, an author's readers are derived in part by: (a) a publisher who has assessed the author's reach through independent readers; (b) a government and a court system responsible for balancing the author's claim to property against society's claim to benefit from the free communication of information (Boyle, 1991); (c) literary agents who negotiated the terms under which the author agreed to contract with the publisher; and (d) reviewers hired by editors of independent publications to mobilize or dampen the author's reach once the manuscript is published. The ties between author and readers in an open market, in brief, depend on many other ongoing ties, each influencing on an author's reach.

The institutional relations influencing authorial reach have changed over the history of print in western Europe and America. The functions of some institutional relationships have been taken over by others; other institutional relationships have co-evolved, and still others have grown or diminished in influence, depending on the circumstances. Publishers, for example, displaced patrons to a large extent; patrons in turn displaced political parties as the primary mechanism for underwriting the distribution of texts, thus affecting an author's reach. Literary agents co-evolved with court rulings that increased the author's legal autonomy and ability to negotiate economic terms based on estimates of reach. Economic conditions gave some institutional relationships more leverage than others and gave some individuals more leverage to assume certain roles within these relationships. In hard times, an average but market-proven author had an advantage over an unknown upstart with more promise. In a competitive buyer's market, reviewers have an inordinate say over which authors and publishers will flourish. Some of these interactive relationships, both synchronic and temporal, are depicted in Fig. 3.1, resembling what Darnton (1983, p. 6) called the "communication circuit" in the post-

print world of books. The relationships represented by bold lines in Fig.
3.1 are discussed in the rest of this chapter. The shaded ovals—authors
and readers—are the components that we focus on throughout this book.

For these relationships, we describe the various links that comprise
them, their historical development, and the theoretical features that were
at issue in their development. Our discussion only scratches the surface
but indicates how these components have worked as a web of interaction patterns, more or less lasting, more or less successful, and always
evolving. More importantly, it is detailed enough to help us abstract the
contextual features needed for the systematic analysis we carry out in
Part II.

Authors–Readers

Readers are, of course, the destination point of author–reader interaction. The contextual terms of that interaction as we know them today—at
least in England and America—were laid in the 19th century. One of the
more important theoretical features for influencing author–reader interaction is the sociocultural opportunity to read. Such opportunities result
from the convergence of many independent factors: the price of books,
the rate of literacy, the nature of work, and the rise of income and leisure.
Data that are relevant to these sociocultural opportunities are partially
available for England (Altick, 1957; Williams, 1961). The 19th century
saw an enormous increase in population. In England, no decade in that
century had a rate of growth less than 11%, and between 1811 and 1821,
the population increased 18% (Altick, 1957, p. 81). Edmund Burke estimated the number of committed readers in England in 1790 at about
80,000. In 1894, the *Author's Society* conservatively placed that figure
at about 240,000 (Altick, 1957, p. 312). In the middle decades of that
century, there was a steep growth in a professional class—physicians,
teachers, civil servants, and other white collar workers—whose members relied on the reading habit. Altick (1957, p. 306) estimated that this
professional class grew from 357,000 in 1851 to 647,000 by 1881. He
also estimated that the percentage of English workers involved in commerce rose from 39% in 1841 to 68% by 1891. The percentage of workers in agriculture dropped from 19% to 10% over the same time span.
The number of regular newspaper readers also steadily increased. In 1820,
the percentage of the public reading daily newspapers was about 1%;
Sunday newspapers, just over 1%; and magazines, 3%. By 1860 the readers of daily newspapers had risen to 3%; of Sunday newspapers, 12%.
However, newspapers did not reach a majority of the public until World
War I (Williams, 1961). The real income for buying books also rose stead-

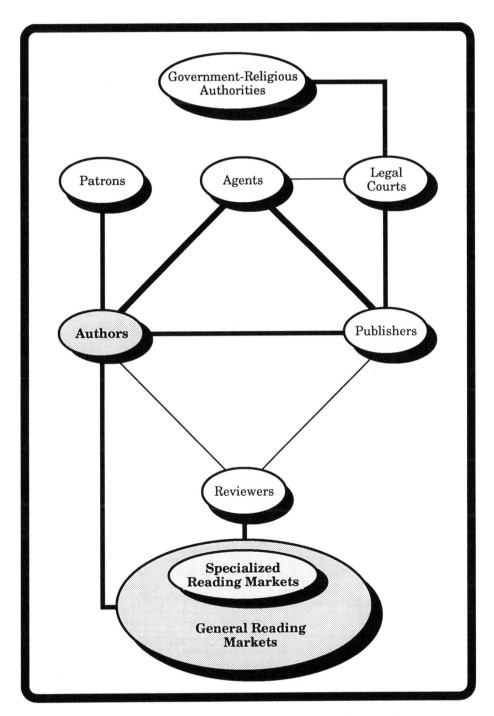

FIG. 3.1. Postprint landscape of contextual features affecting author–reader interaction.

ily over the decade as the real cost of producing them dropped. In 1850, 83,300 English families had an income of over 150 pounds. That number rose to 285,000 by 1880. During approximately the same period, the average annual English middle-class income rose from 90 to 110 pounds. Given improvements in the technology of book making, the price of books steadily dropped from the 1860s onward (Altick, 1957). These statistics are tabulated in Table 3.1.[4]

The figures in Table 3.1 reflect a steady expansion in literacy from as far back as the Renaissance. Cressy (1981, p. 105) estimated that the literacy rate in England in the 1500s ranged somewhere between 1% and 50%. By 1850, the literacy rate had climbed to 60%, higher than it had ever been (Schofield, 1981). Literacy figures, however, are inconclusive because literacy was typically measured in ways that did not require meaningful interaction with a text (e.g., by the ability to sign a legal document; see Graff, 1987). Furthermore, as we saw in chapter 2, literacy is not a unidimensional nor a strictly monotonic skill. In spite of the realistic difficulties of defining what literacy means, the state had vested interests in imposing definitions (Laqueur, 1980). For example, the state often defined the literate public on the basis of social, political, and economic requirements designed for the workplace and not intended to accommodate a person's general capacity to interact with texts, to reason critically, or to question authority (Resnick & Resnick, 1977). The state has perennially been concerned that training in literacy remain compatible with obedient citizenship (Coser, 1965; Williams, 1961).

Given the suspicion that a literate public can be harder to control than an illiterate one, it is not surprising that methods of schooling in reading were as restricted as the conceptions of literacy they were meant to further. Altick (1957) chronicled England's many movements attempting to stir the reading habit from 1800 on: elementary education, the Sunday School movement, the Mechanics Institutes, Methodist instruction in reading, the Chartist movement. Most of these movements had limited success because they assumed that reading could be taught as something less than open-ended interaction with a text. The case is even plausible that schooling and the incentive to read had little to do with one another. Resnick and Resnick (1977, p. 371) contended that the relationship between reading and social interaction—that is, using reading to comprehend an unfamiliar content offered by another human being—has been a universal goal of schooling for at most, [only] three generations. Prior to our own century, according to the Resnicks, practice in this form of reading was confined to elitist technical schools. Instruction in reading for the masses concerned itself with oral recitation, recall, or the

---

[4]Sources for these statistics are Altick (1957); Williams (1961).

TABLE 3.1
Statistics on the Rise of Sociocultural Opportunities to Read
in 19th-Century England

Year	Population	Number of Committed Readers	Number of Workers in Middle-Class Professions	Percentage of Workers Engaged in Commerce	Percentage of Population Who Read Newspapers	Number of Families with Income over 150 Pounds
1700	5 million					
1750	7.5 million					
1800	11 million	80,000			1	
1840			357,000	39		
1850	21 million				3	83,300
1880			647,000			
1890		240,000		68		
1900	37 million				<40%?	280,100

application of textual content with which the reader was already familiar. Consequently, the image of reading perpetuated in mass education until only recently was quite distinct from the rewards of social interaction, the opportunity to acquire information one does not already have. In sum, we can see that literacy rates may have risen with sociocultural opportunities to read. But we must also inspect very closely the nature of these opportunities in order to understand the nature of the literacies they were promoting.

The development of author–reader interaction has been most qualitatively fruitful, it seems, when it arises from opportunities that play off the individual motivation of the reader, opportunities that do not restrict the reader from experiencing reading as an open form of social interaction with all the pleasures, payoffs, and surprises of face-to-face interaction. With this cardinal principle in hand, all that is needed to develop the reading habit are the cultural opportunities to ''get hooked'' on reading, until the intrinsic rewards of the dependency become self-evident. There is some evidence that this is how reading developed among the underschooled. According to Cruse's study of working class readers of the late 18th century, a typical workman of the new reading class dropped out early in his teens, had a poor reading education, but nonetheless did learn the rudiments of reading:

a typical workman of the new reading class was Francis Place . . . born in 1771, went to school from 4–14 . . . [his] education was poor but [he] did learn how to read . . . at 14 was apprenticed to a leather breeches maker and education was finished . . . [there were] no books in his father's house but he had the desire to read . . . no money to buy books . . . visited book-stalls and was able to take out books from reasonable bookowners who would charge nominal borrowing rates . . . read histories of Greece and Rome, Hume, Smollett, Fielding, geography, anatomy, surgery. . . . (Cruse, n.d., pp. 150–152)

If there was an incentive for reading beyond schooling, politics, and economics, it was surely the world opened to the reader by including texts as an interaction partner, by having enough of these interaction part-ners in circulation (Williams, 1961) and by having enough supporting so-cial mechanisms to keep the interaction from becoming overly tedious or expensive (e.g., book clubs, literary societies, and circulating libraries; see Klancher, 1987). In the 18th century the number of people with this incentive and sufficient leisure time grew steadily. Wiles (1976) called the evidence of reading habits in 18th-century England "fragmentary and statistically inconclusive." Nonetheless, he concluded that:

so many towns had local newspapers with extensive circulation, so many books and pamphlets and magazines were offered for sale, so many lend-ing libraries sprang up and flourished, that it would be denying the obvi-ous to insist that the century which began with *A Tale of the Tub* (1704) and ended with *Lyrical Ballads* (1798) was a period when illiteracy predominated. (p. 88)

Having the opportunity to read is only part of the story. Prior to read-ing the text, the potential reader needs to know that the text exists. This knowledge can come through the text itself, through reviews, and through word of mouth. Such knowledge channeled through word of mouth is probably the least discussed and yet the most influential. We see in chapter 7 that word of mouth can play an important role in diffusing a text to readers. Enough people can interact with a text to make it a (sometimes mandatory) topic of conversation even among those who have not. The more widespread the knowledge of the text, that is, the greater the author's potential reach, even among individuals who are nonreaders. Even nonreaders can positively register at social gatherings that they "know of" the book without actually having seen or read it first hand. We might call this phenomenon *reverse vicariousness*, because we nor-mally think of immediate viewing or reading as vicarious experiences for face-to-face interaction. But, in this case, a viewer or reader uses face-to-face interaction to experience the viewer or reader role vicariously.

The phenomenon of reverse vicariousness is fundamental, widespread, and too often misidentified with the stigma of "low culture"—a phenome-non that schooled adults may scoff at and the Cliff Note industry is ac-cused of creating. It rears its head every time an educator complains that students receive most of their information from a less rather than a more demanding medium: from television and radio rather than quality newspapers; from movies rather than books; from word of mouth rather than reading. However, reverse vicariousness is not so much an issue of reading skills and literacy as an issue of belonging, usually with peers. To keep up with the vogue information of culture is to maintain one's ties to it and to the others who are doing their part to keep up as well. The hows of keeping up are a less important consideration than the fact of doing so. One of the effects of stigmatizing reverse vicariousness, to misidentify it as a sign of cultural decay, is to lead us to exaggerate the status of prestige media (i.e., printed texts) as autonomous objects whose cultural influence somehow projects outside of routine channels of social interaction.

Sociocultural opportunities to read, the formal capacity to read, and the readers' knowledge that texts exist are still not a sufficient raison d'etre for author–reader interaction. In addition there must be some "cognitive"[5] similarity between the text and the reader. A reader must perceive that the text (and the author behind it) shares enough information with the reader to make the text interesting. Only this recognition of cognitive similarity represents a worthwhile invitation for interaction from the reader's point of view. The more readers who are cognitively similar to the text, in turn, the more complete will be the author's potential reach. In summary, then, we need: (a) the theoretical features of sociocultural opportunities to read; (b) knowledge that the text exists; and (c) the cognitive similarity between the text and the reader in order to explain contingencies in author–reader interaction. Yet these features do not exist in a vacuum and are themselves manipulated by the institutions used to regulate author–reader interaction. Such institutions manipulate interactions by controlling the opportunities for interaction and by controlling who knows what. For texts, such controls affect the opportunities to read, which potential readers know of which texts, and, to a certain extent, what potential readers know in general, determining their relative similarity with available texts. Institutional life can thus exert a profound influence on author–reader relationships. In the following sections, we consider some of these institutions and how they interact with the theoretical features we have already described, as well as with other features we have yet to consider.

---

[5]We are not suggesting that texts are cognitive entities. Rather they are external representations or encapsulations of some portion of the mental models or knowledge held by the author at the time the text was composed (chapter 4). Unlike individuals with a cognitive system, a text cannot learn; and so the knowledge base it encapsulates remains fixed over time. This difference has, as we see in Part II, important implications for the ability of texts to change society.

Government–Publishers

In the early history of print, the government and the church controlled the resources required to underwrite the production of mass circulation documents and so had almost total say in regulating an author's reach. By controlling authorial reach, government and the church also controlled author–reader interaction. They accomplished this by financing publishers whose political interests meshed with their own and by withholding copyright, censuring, taxing, and prosecuting publishers they considered wayward.[6] Government control over printing in England remained unshaken until the lapse of the licensing act in 1694, at which point it began to decline slowly (Barnes, 1964; Febvre & Martin, 1976; Innis, 1951; Mumby, 1956).

Government control over print was often designed for prescriptive as well as prohibitive purposes. It was designed to put "right-thinking" reading material in the hands of readers as well as to prevent "wrong-thinking" reading from reaching them. Consequently, its influence has been more successful as a prohibitive force than as a prescriptive force. The reasons for this are deeper than economics and even first amendment issues. They speak to the inherent nature of reading as an affective and cognitive activity. There is a noticeable difference between making texts available to readers and insuring that they are read. Authors can be prevented from putting a text into circulation, but reading remains a voluntary habit that cannot be easily controlled or monitored from the outside. A reader can be forced to look at and even "mouth" a text but not to comprehend it in any strong sense—or care to. Yet government and religious authorities seeking control of print have consistently tended to miss this point, mistakenly reasoning that to coerce interaction between publishers and authors would equally control reading.

---

[6]Records of government control over texts date as far back as the Roman book trade, when emperors exercised strict censorship over literary property. Augustus, for example, decreed that Greek and Latin copies of the Sibylline prophecies be burned, and another Roman leader, Domitian, had the historian Hermogenes executed for including passages in a book he considered objectionable (Mumby, 1956, pp. 19–20). Church censorship of texts became an organized institution during the Reformation. Government censorship of print in English history dates back to the early 1500s, when Caxton had only recently imported printing techniques from the continent. Although publishers enjoyed more independence under the rule of Elizabeth in the mid 1500s and James I in the early 1600s, as late as 1663, Roger L'Estrange, an agent for the monarchy after the Restoration, wrote *Considerations and Proposals in order to the Regulation of the Press*, in which he argued that treasonous printers should be forced, for a period of time, to wear a badge as a "mark of ignominy." He further proposed that this punishment be lifted earlier if the printer was able to turn in another treasonous author, printer, or stationer (Mumby, 1956, p. 115).

There is a long history of failed social programs based on this mistaken reasoning. Efforts by Methodists and Bethamites in 19th-century England to place only right-minded literature in the hands of the working class failed. Social reformers like Hanna Moore found, to her dismay, that "good books" cannot be fed to the public like bad-tasting medicine. Even in our own time, the failure of paternalistic literature (e.g., no-smoking campaigns targeted to the young) reminds us that the reading habit comes only when readers are allowed to choose what to read for their own purposes (Altick, 1957, pp. 40–100), that social structures binding authors and readers cannot be imposed from without, but must develop from culturally similar interests. All this suggests that the ability to influence authorial reach may not, in the end, be sufficient for influencing author–reader interaction, if readers are left with the same cultural opportunities to read and their same perceptions of which texts are most cognitively similar to them. Unless outside authorities seek to build upon, rather than resist, the natural cognitive affinities between authors and readers, even powerful institutions commanding large resources may exert a surprisingly small effect on reader habits.

Patrons–Authors

Patronage was another institution influencing authorial reach. Patrons are individuals who, through their class, wealth, power, or connections, underwrote the publication of an author's work. Patrons representing political parties commissioned authors to write a piece with a particular theme or for a particular rhetorical purpose. Authors solicited wealthy patrons by seeking payment for an acknowledgment or dedication (Mumby, 1956).[7] Although patronage has a longer history in science, politics, and the arts than print, patronage practices were reflected in print conventions as early as the 16th century. Printers left space at the beginning or end of a book for laudatory verses to the patron. In patronage, cultural and economic relationships commingle. Viewed in cold economic terms, patrons imposed a common culture and social structure on authors because they were paying for the work. Viewed culturally, patrons underwrote the author because they saw, in the author's work, a person

---

[7]Patronage predates print by many centuries. In ancient Rome, Augustus commissioned Virgil, Horace, Livy, and others to write favorably of his reign and to promote the social harmony of the old republic (Laurenson, 1969, pp. 101–105). Laurenson distinguished the old patronage of late feudalism from a newer, more mercantilist patronage relationship that came to dominate Elizabethan Europe around 1600. Under the older patronage, writers remained part of aristocratic cliques, bound by social ties and political affiliation to the patron and honored as a loyal and steadfast member of the patron's extended household.

with similar cultural ties and taste. Under either view, patronage generally restricted the reach of an author's text to a circle whose social interests, class, and tastes were aligned with those of the author and the patron.

Despite the fidelity relationships it implied, social patronage was often a cold business ruled by an anonymous market with fixed rates.[8] In Milton's time, a dedication for a drama had a going rate of 40 shillings (Mumby, 1956). Authors sent unsolicited copies of their manuscripts to the well-to-do with a flattering dedication, for which they expected payment. Payment was not automatic, but authors would publicize their unhappiness when they felt it was not adequate (Beljame, 1948; Clark & Clark, 1980; Collins, 1929; Febvre & Martin, 1976). Patronage survived into the late 18th century, well past the rise of commercial publishing. Though the free market promised the author greater potential reach, it also offered more uncertainty. Patronage remained a secure and personal net under the tightrope of the free market, which offered only potential readers whose anonymity left them difficult to cultivate. Publishers, staring into the same uncertainty, were averse to gambling too much on a single author and would hedge their bets. Authors often hedged their bets by working in both free and patronage markets at once. A common refrain was, "When an author [can] not get enough of an audience in the reading market, a patron [is] no shame" (Collins, 1929, p. 115). In the late 16th century, it was possible for an author to contract with a publisher; but this did not become an acceptable practice until the 18th century nor, in comparison to patronage, a tasteful practice until the 19th (Beljame, 1948; Febvre & Martin, 1976; Kernan, 1987).

The slowness with which patronage declined corresponds to the slowness with which the free market developed. Because a reading public remained an unknown quantity both to publishers and authors, the literary market remained small, and the potential for publishers and authors to form alliances, limited. Until the early 18th century, writers had few commercial outlets for their work. English newspapers did not begin to carry belles lettres or crafted products until 1695. It was not until the 1790s that England first became a society with a commercial basis in print

---

[8]The anonymity of patronage under the new "mercantile temper" of 17th-century England (Laurenson & Swingewood, 1971, p. 109) closed off opportunities for authors. The emphasis in letters moved away from the aesthetics of a national literature and toward the utility of international commerce. Translators were more prized than authors; the gentry class saw that the money they invested in translators yielded a higher return than the money they might invest in an author. Moreover, translation, being the coin of international commerce, was a subject studied by and for members of the monied classes. Patrons and translators were often linked by class interest and even family ties, and these sociocultural ties tended to be stronger than patron–author ties.

(Belanger, 1982). Only when a reading market began to crystallize and author–publisher interaction became an economic possibility for a steady class of authors did patronage start to decline (Laurenson & Swingewood, 1971). By the 19th century, attitudes about patronage had dramatically reversed in Europe. In the 18th century, Voltaire remained aloof from his publishers because he did not need their money. In the next century, Zola understood the writer's independence as the savvy to hold out for the best contractual terms (Darnton, 1983, p. 15). Patronage declined as a force in the 19th century when the class of "ordinary reader" attained enough size, economic clout, and leisure to sustain publishing (see Table 3.1).

Publishers–Authors

By the 1830s, the reading public was large enough to make free market publishing a worthwhile form of economic speculation, fulfilling Defoe's prediction that writing would someday become a "considerable branch of English commerce" (Williams, 1961, p. 168). Altick (1988) offered the date 1850 as a milestone after which the phrase "literature for the millions" could be more than hyperbole (p. 142). For in 1852, the unprecedented success of *Uncle Tom's Cabin* taught the publishing industry that the reach of the book-buying public could swell to readers counted in the millions (Altick, 1988).

By the 19th century, publishers came to dominate the terms of author–reader interaction. Publishers discerned a steady reading market, requiring constant nourishment from a stable class of authors. Education and leisure expanded cultural opportunities to read, and individuals with the wherewithal to take advantage of these opportunities began to discern a market of texts with which they wanted to engage. Industrialization brought oppressive work to people migrating into the cities, but it also imposed leisure, a rise in real income, and a desire for escapist experiences that could be satisfied through an ever expanding and ever cheapening print market (Altick, 1957; Patten, 1978).

Publishers and authors began to form powerful business alliances, such as those between Johnson and Boswell, Scott and Constable, and Dickens with Chapman and Hall (Mumby, 1956). They also recognized how marketing strategies could make a difference in the sale of books. For example, the introduction of serial publishing in the 1830s allowed the reader to pay in installments and made it possible for the lower end of the retail market to purchase books, a factor behind Dickens' unprecedented success.

Publishers were not of one mind when it came to taking on authors, but they tended to fall into predictable categories. There were those who went after quality first, those who went after profit first, and those who were interested in acquiring anything that could increase their turnover (Swinnerton, 1932). Different publishing houses were known for the different statements they wanted to make through their cultivation of authors. For example, from the 1830s the Harper brothers were known among New York publishers for quality, both in design and literary content. They were the first American publishers to use cloth over boards as a binding, the first to use stereotypes[9] in their printing system, the first to market a library series and use literary advisers for reviewers (Tebbel, 1968, Vol. 1). No matter what reputation they wished to cultivate, all publishers wanted to turn a profit, and authors and publishers often found themselves with conflicting bottom-line priorities. Authors typically wanted to maximize their actual reach (i.e., the number of readers), because they assumed that increased circulation would increase their reputation and sociocultural influence, as well as their profit. Publishers typically wanted to maximize their profit and, commonly, this was accomplished by limiting production, restricting the market, and inflating price—factors that limited the author's reach by limiting circulation in absolute terms. Publishers often turned a larger profit when they sold high-priced books to a small but reliable "quality" market than when they tried to push cheap books intended for a wider circulation. Their immediate response to Walter Scott's phenomenal success in the 1820s, for example, was to raise, not lower, prices based on rising demand (Altick, 1957). Consequently, authors interested in reaching large numbers at cheap prices often could not find a publisher (West, 1988). In brief, it was commonplace for authors to link profit with production and for publishers to be more wary about the risks of overproduction. In the economic dealings between authors and publishers, authors usually got the short end of the stick. For every Dickens, Trollope, or William Dean Howells who could have their way with publishers, there were hundreds of "grub streeters" who had no leverage. In his 1840 essay, "On Heroes, Hero-Worship, and the Heroic in History," Thomas Carlyle bitterly lamented that the man of letters remained unrecognized by the state, living in a garret, famous in death but impoverished in life. The expanding markets of readers in 18th-century England did not guarantee pay from publishers. Unless an author was a "name" in the book trade or a regular and popular contributor to a widely circulating periodical, he or she often did not expect to be paid. And when an author could expect payment, the expectations were usually based not on the work's potential reach, but on the work's proven earning power through sub-

---

[9]In printing, stereotypes are matrix casts that allowed a page to be printed without requiring individual letters to be punched.

scription sales or on a lump sum sale of copyright (Belanger, 1982, p. 6; Speck, 1982).

In almost every case, the payment systems that evolved in the 19th century were designed for the publisher's advantage. As Hepburn (1968, pp. 4–5) put it, "No system had developed in which the rewards of authorship came as certainly to the author as to others." Before the time of the literary agent, payment to authors was rather simple and did not require contracts but could be accomplished with "blurred handwritten letters drowned in the water of the copying press" (Hepburn, 1968, p. 5). Throughout the 18th century, for example, the usual form of payment to the author was a lump sum for the copyright or nothing at all. Swinnerton (1932) described the innocence of the young author in these transactions:

> a young author, in those days, was often tempted by the sight of a cheque made out in his name by one of these doubtful firms and parted lightly with his literary property as if it were something he was selling to an old clothes man. (p. 41)

A later form of payment to the author was the commission. The author paid for a small run with the understanding that the publisher would receive a commission on sales. The cut for the publisher was so low that no publisher would enter it with the thought of making a big sale. This system provided the best cut for the author and the worst for the publisher only if the work became a top seller. But in practice publishers only agreed to commission payment for untalented authors who wanted a vanity press. Interestingly, as late as 1890, the Society of Authors favored commission publishing as most advantageous to the author, but the Society also conceded that the author needed a name to make it pay off.

Still another payment arrangement was the half-profit system. In this system, the author and publisher agree to split the profits down the middle, but there is no advance to the author. Needy authors could not afford to participate because if the book lost money the author had to compensate the publisher for lost expenses. The half-profit system proved a no win situation for the author, in any case, because the publisher kept the accounting books and could underreport profits and overreport expenses. In 1867, a New York publishing firm, Hurd and Houghton, instituted the royalty system. This system distributed risk more equitably and objectively across publisher and author. Under the royalty system, publishers estimated costs, surcharges, probable sales, and profit margins. Without divulging their calculations, they quoted the author a percentage of sales for each edition. The author was then free to take the offer or turn it down (Hepburn, 1968, pp. 13–14).

While publishing had always been ruled by a bottom line, demographic changes between the World Wars began to change the priorities of the industry toward large scale profitability. In America alone, the population increased 64% from 1910 to 1950, and the illiteracy rate decreased from 7.7% in 1910 to 2.9% in 1940. In those same years, the rate of urbanization went from less than 50% to almost 60%, as over 10 million new immigrants entered American urban life. The number of university presses grew from 8 to 70 (Tebbel, 1968, Vol. 3).

These trends from the "golden age" between the Wars convinced the industry that the reading public could be targeted as any mass consumer group (Tebbel, 1968, Vol. 4, p. 347). Publishers began to market authors as media stars with cross-over potential to other media. The industrialization of publishing also changed the profile of publishers. By 1950, the ownership of nearly all major American publishing houses had fallen into the hands of conglomerates run by businesspersons and bean counters (Reynolds, 1955; Tebbel, 1968, Vol. 4; West, 1988). Even though only a fraction of authors commanded large advances for memoirs, movie rights, and serialization, the publicity of big money deals put them at the center of the public conception of publishing, making the publishing industry more sensitive to the bottom line in all its transactions.

The typical author—one with a manuscript to sell but no commercial bonanza to promise—has also becoming increasingly displaced to an earlier era of subscription publishing, when the author had to assume the preponderance of risk in creating a market for a text. For example, on Labor Day, 1990, *The New York Times* reported on the growing trend for publishers to postpone investing money in advertising until a book has proven itself. This trend, the story continued, has forced authors to finance their own publicity tours and promotional material, a contemporary version of 18th century subscription publishing, leaving the risk of delivering readers to the selling skills of the author. Perhaps this is a portent of the brave new world of Christopher Whittle, who has created a publishing house that first seeks corporate sponsorship and then uses these corporate funds to retain "name" authors.

While publisher–author interaction continues to dominate author–reader interaction, it is clear that this interaction is in a state of flux, and variations on the existing model or completely new models are likely to supersede it. Whatever its future, it is clear that as publishing has become more sensitive to accounting ledgers, it has also become increasingly interested in promoting authorial reach only when that reach can be directly translated into profits. In brief, the author, tending to see the reader as the primary constituency, wants to remain a cultural force, a shaper of culture and social structure—of context. Corporate publishers tend to see investors as their primary constituents, and have come to deal with the author increasingly as a corporate employee, expecting the author to settle for the combination of costs, distribution, and pricing that maximizes profit.

Thus, like the government seeking to dictate the content of reading, publishers often seek to impose artificial limits on authorial reach as a matter of good economics. Tensions between authors and publishers have arisen over the question of how to balance the publisher's interests in costs and profits against the author's interest in attracting the largest readership.

Courts–Publishers

Legal issues surrounding authoring often focus on clarifying the nature of the author's signature and handle. We save formal definitions of these terms for chapter 4, but they both deal, directly or indirectly, with the author's claim as a property holder. The disposition of these claims, further, influences the author's reach inasmuch as the owner of the text has greater say in making decisions that affect the reach of the text, and so the reach of its author.

In England and the United States, the interaction between the courts and the publishing industry has exerted a profound influence on author–reader interaction. The courts were left to interpret government prerogatives on publishing and, indirectly, the terms of publisher–author interaction. In England, from the 16th century on, the cartel of publishers that dictated publishing—known as the Congers—enjoyed both a regulatory and a commercial monopoly. They could impose censorship by denying a freelance publisher the license to publish, and they could assure their own profits by maintaining fixed copyright fees, imposing sanctions against pirating, and enforcing their claims to perpetual copyright. It is important that prior to 1709, the author's signature and handle—the author's claims as property holder to the text—carried no legal acknowledgement, direct or implied.

With the lapse of the licensing act in 1694, both the regulatory and commercial monopolies were broken. Publishing entered a chaotic and uncertain phase and, throughout the 18th century, publishing cartels worked through the courts to have their previous protections restored. An early judicial result was a 1709 ruling widely known as the Statute of Anne. This statute restored the publishers' regulatory monopoly but not their commercial monopoly. From perpetual copyright, the ownership of copyright was reduced to 21 years. The court ruled that only the author could claim a perpetual copyright, though the term "author" in the Statute was used interchangeably with anyone who held legal title (Bowker, 1912; Patterson, 1968). This ruling gave no direct legal acknowledgment of the author as property holder, but it left room for the interpretation of an implicit legal acknowledgment of the special relationship of the author to the text.

For decades after the 1709 ruling, publishers conspired to use the court's special ruling on the author as a loophole to maintain perpetual copyright. They required authors, or trustees of the estates of authors, to surrender their perpetual copyright as a condition for publishing (Patterson, 1968). Authors who refused did not get published. Outraged at these heavy-handed tactics, many advocates of public education argued that authors could not claim a transferable perpetual copyright—a copyright surrenderable to publishers—because authors had an inalienable and nontransferable right to their work. These same intellectuals claimed that to believe otherwise was an egregious misinterpretation of the Statute of Anne. This last claim was directly tested in the 1774 case of Donaldson v. Beckett. The ruling of Donaldson v. Beckett denied an author's natural right to a work but did strengthen the author's economic hand vis-à-vis the publisher (Yen, 1990). From 1774, an author held complete control over the work until the time of publication, and was protected thereafter by whatever prevailing copyright laws were in effect (Pforzheimer, 1964). The practical force of the ruling clarified for authors their political and economic divisions with publishers, especially because it was a ruling that publishers denounced and authors hailed (Patterson, 1968).

Donaldson v. Beckett (1774) was a landmark in shaping some of the basic interaction patterns between authors and publishers as we know them today. With that ruling, the perception of copyright as a publisher's right slowly gave way to the perception of copyright as an author's right—and with that transformation, the author was increasingly seen as a person to be dealt with over the long haul. Rose (1988) declared Donaldson v. Beckett a landmark in the genealogy of authorship and copyright because it laid the groundwork for associating the author with the chief legal holder of textual property. This legacy describes British more than American law.

The legacy of American law centered less on the author as property holder and more on seeking a utilitarian balance between the author's natural rights to a text and society's welfare in having unrestricted access to it (Barnes, 1974; McGill, 1991). American law, more than British, has discouraged wide interpretations of copyright that extend an author's property claims and, in turn, restrict public accessibility to a text (Litman, 1990). In their 1909 report on copyright laws, the American House Committee on Patents said, "Not primarily for the benefit of the author, but primarily for the benefit of the public, such [copyright] rights are given" (Pforzheimer, 1964, p. 29). Even within the area of copyrightable material, the notion of copyright has been tempered by that of "fair use," what Shaw (cited in Pforzheimer, 1964, p. 30) defined as "what the author must dedicate to society in return for his statutory copyright." Fair use gives readers the right to paraphrase, quote, critique, and comment on portions of a text without violating the author's copyright. The boundaries between fair use and copyright infringement resist precise definition, as the law must make a delicate negotiation between the right of the current author to claim literary property against the rights of subsequent authors to use that property in pursuit of their own literary property. As fact finders for copyright infringement, the courts, in a tradition from Donaldson v. Beckett (1774) have relied on two tests to establish the infringement of copyright: evidence of "copying" and evidence that the copied material was "improperly appropriated." These two tests reflect the tensions between assimilated and new information inherent in such fact finding. Evidence of copying, for example, establishes that the defendant's work shares a striking likeness to the original. This evidence is necessary, but not sufficient, for the finding of copyright infringement. Further evidence of improper appropriation is required, establishing that the defendant's work bears a substantial likeness to the original work and has no redeeming new information beyond that borrowed from the original. In light of these traditional tests,[10] Barry (1987) argued that the appropriate model for copyright infringement must be one that seeks to maximize the accumulation of new information (and the accumulation of wealth based on ownership of that information) across all authors—present and future. As a republican principle designed to foster the free exchange of ideas required for cultural growth, this principle seems unimpeachable. Yet Yen (1990) questioned whether laws of utility maximization, economic or otherwise, can lead to legally unambiguous copyright rulings.

For our purposes, legal arguments over authorship and copyright are interesting to a theory of print interaction because they demarcate two radically different routes through which an author's ideas can become assimilated into the culture. One route is for texts that bear the author's

---

[10]Since 1946, other copyright infringement tests have been devised, which tend to collapse these two criteria into one. One test is to assume every "striking likeness" is a substantive one. This is an unreliable test because it restricts the possibility of a work's being truly original simply because it relies heavily on (and so has a striking likeness to) borrowings. See Barry (1987) and Litman (1991) for implausibilities in this test. A second test is the distinction between ideas (which cannot be copyrighted) and expression (which can)—a distinction without an empirical difference in many contexts. For an interesting ideological analysis of the idea/expression dichotomy and why it is maintained in spite of its ineffectiveness, see Boyle (1991) who argued that the distinction has provided an appealing, if impractical, mask for the contradiction in Anglican law between the public sphere and the entitlements of private property holding.

name to disseminate. In this case, the extent to which the author's ideas diffuse is a direct reflection of a text's circulation. A second route is for the author's ideas to seep (Litman, 1990) into the public domain before the author has a chance to copyright them. In this case, authors become influential (though without acknowledgment or recognition) because the ideas in their texts are picked up by influential readers whose collective reach may extend well beyond the reach of the original text. The author's ideas gain influence not so much from the singular influence of the text but from the singular influence of its many readers on even more non-readers. Some legal scholars imply that the limits of authorial copyright depend on which diffusion path an author's ideas happen to travel (Litman, 1990, 1991; Yen, 1990). Unfortunately, this is not likely to be a helpful test because, for many texts, diffusion occurs through both paths. This last observation notwithstanding, fundamental questions about what is copyrightable, in sum, may hinge on issues about the diffusion of new ideas, their timing, and their trajectory—issues that dominate Part II of this book.

Authors–Agents–Publishers

The literary agent emerged historically as an arbiter between the publisher and the author in deciding matters of ownership and reach. Authors perennially complained that they got short shrift from publishers. But without legal and organizational backing to give them serious economic resources to protect, they could do little about it. By the late 19th century in England and America, they were beginning to feel that backing. Moreover, the royalty system made it increasingly important to formalize author–publisher agreements in legally binding written documents. And, as written contracts and payment arrangements became more complex and required savvy about the market, the need for specialists who could bring this savvy to the author's side of the bargaining table became more pronounced. The literary agent became that specialist.

Agents typically started as authors who became interested in the publisher's perspective or publishers who became interested in the author's. Both authors and publishers often saw them as double agents, working for the other side more than for their own, and authors were as likely to have relations as tense with their agent as they had with their publisher (Hepburn, 1968). Yet authors tolerated and even befriended their agents as long as they seemed effective in negotiations. Moreover, they knew that to be effective, their agent had to think like the publisher across the bargaining table—and to know which publisher to bring to the bargaining table. For example, the agent had to know which publishers would pay top dollar for proven work, which would absorb the most loss for unproven work, which would give the best terms, do the best marketing, or give the best going advances and royalty rates (Swinnerton, 1932).

Until the era of the blockbuster, the agent's work was to adjust royalty rates, get advances, and, in many cases, establish a close editorial relationship with an author. Many agents continue in this fashion. But with publishing contracts containing complicated clauses for subsidiary rights—paperback rights, movie rights, video rights, television rights—the era of the superagent has emerged, with agents who, like lawyers (and who often are lawyers!), organize themselves into corporate firms, have become specialists in media law and legal negotiation, and have become less directly involved in manuscript preparation. The economics of the superagent, like the economics of publishing in general, tend to restrict author–reader interaction because authors without a manuscript with cross-over potential across various media often cannot get an agent, and authors who cannot get an agent cannot get a publisher.

The agent functions as a representative of the legal system, seeking to adjudicate disputes about the authorial signature and handle, in terms favorable to the author. The agent tries to promote the author's interest in maintaining the text as authorial property and maximizing the author's financial gain as the holder of title. The agent further functions as a representative of the author and the reading public if the agent perceives that the publisher is misreading that relationship. Knowing that fame is the author's best capital asset, the agent tries to convince the publisher that maximizing the author's reach (through advances, production, promotion, advertising) is compatible with extending the publisher's bottom line. The agent implicitly understands that the publisher's advertising (along with reviews and word of mouth) are intermediate forms that can promote the reader's cognitive similarity with the text. The agent, acting as a bridge between author, publisher, and readers, tries to represent all these constituencies to maximize the author's advantage.

Reviewers–Readers

Reviewers evaluate a text for cognitive similarities with their clients, the reading public. Reviewers are filters between the vast number of texts put out by the publishing industry and the reading public. Such filters are necessary because reading drains the scarce resources of a reader's time and money, and because the publishing industry makes more available to read than there is time or money to read. So what texts should be read? Reviewers help readers answer this question. Reviews are texts of relatively low cost requiring low reader investment that help the reading public monitor their prospective similarity with texts that are of higher cost and that demand higher reading investments than do the reviews. The author fashions a text while keeping in mind its similarities with a reading market. But, without reviews, the author's (and publisher's) projections of similarity with potential readers would remain trapped in the author's (and publisher's) head, never publicized or tested by "advanced scouts" representing the reading market. Like gossips, reviewers serve as a central node in the web of interactors, disseminating sufficient information to expose readers' similarity with (or lack of similarity with, as the case may be) the text as a motivation for interacting with (i.e., reading) it.

Reviewing has a history that is as old as the early news trade. Reviews regularly appeared in the quarto newsbooks as early as 1641. Book notices and the periodical reviews of books were available in the early 1700s. In 1712, Addison's critical essays on Milton in the *Spectator* suggest an emerging audience for the longer review. England's long established *Gentleman's Magazine* carried reviews. Samuel Johnson distinguished between those reviewers who tended to be long and critical and didn't seem to read the books all the way through and those "duller men" who were more concise and seemed glad just to say what the book was about (Walford, 1986, pp. 14–16).

Only a small fraction of published books are reviewed. So merely the decision to review a work, even if only to register its existence in print, is an act of selecting it from others (Harvey, 1986). These preferential implications were well understood in the history of English journalism; newspapers would charge publishers for reviews as they would for any advertising space and publishers. Like advertisers, publishers would be charged according to the length of the review. In the late 19th century, newspaper editors in England and America decided that books were not news and they cut back on long reviews (Swinnerton, 1932, p. 114). Today, newspaper reviews compete with radio and television, and all are shorter and less critical than the press reviews in the 19th century and the reviews published in current literary periodicals. Nevertheless, because of the circulation of these reviews to a wider reading public, they can have more impact on the author's reach than a more critical review designed for a more discriminating, but much smaller, audience. The more popular the review, the greater the number of readers who can potentially see themselves with enough affinities with the book to interact with it.

We should distinguish the roles of the advance reader retained by the publisher from the reviewer. As Swinnerton (pp. 110–115) said, the publisher's reader "must have his stethoscope pressed close to the heart of the public," must stand in for the reader, assessing the potential reach of the work, long before it becomes a clean manuscript. On the other hand, the reviewer makes a personal judgment on the final product independent of the publisher's estimate of the work's reach. According to Swinnerton, it is a common misconception to think that the publisher's advertising sells books. Reviews sell books. Advertising mainly reinforces the image left by reviews and, ultimately, word of mouth. According to Harvey, publishers use advertising mainly to stroke their current stable of authors and to recruit new authors to their stable by showing the lengths to which they will go to showcase them (Dyer, 1982; Harvey, 1986).

In learned societies (which we cover in depth in chapter 9), the priorities differ between blind reviews that play a gatekeeping function and signed reviews that play the kind of postpublication assessment function that reviews play in the general market. The extent to which a learned society relies upon prepublication blind reviews or retrospective signed reviews depends on the medium through which it chiefly disseminates new knowledge—books or journals. For highly technical fields that disseminate through journals more than books, very little and often no journal space is allotted to retrospective reviews. The primary responsibilities for reviewers are associated with blind reviews for journal entry or for the funding of grant proposals. By contrast, a journal like the *American Historical Review* devotes over 50% of its text to book reviews (Harvey, 1986).

Authors–Authors

Another important theoretical feature is group similarity (or homogeneity) and interaction, the shared knowledge and patterns of interaction between individuals that constitute them as a group. Group similarity and interaction is an essential characteristic for understanding author–reader interaction within professional contexts (chapter 8). We consider the role of group interaction among authors who had nothing more in common than an interest in addressing the general market reader.

The interaction among authors provides a useful barometer for comparing authors as a group with prototypical trades and professions whose shared knowledge and interaction are high. Author interactions in the early print trade are hard to measure because, outside the book market (see Altick, 1962, and Laurenson, 1969, for related studies of the class background of 19th- and early 20th-century authors in this market), authors were not known as a class apart from printers, publishers, artists, bookbinders, and booksellers. These roles formed a loose knit and overlapping set of occupations within publishing. One's occupation could easily combine writing, printing, and selling to the itinerant vendors

(Belanger, 1982). In addition, writing was often seen as the least specialized skill in printing, and for job protection writers often tried to perform in other roles as well. For example, Mackie, one of the leading
journalism educators in America in the 1890s, argued that the reporter
should also be well versed in compositing, proofing, Pitman's shorthand,
and bookkeeping (Lee, 1978).

From the late 1700s and throughout the 1800s, English writers who
did not want to compromise their role status comprised either a select
group of successful writers—for example, Trollope or Dickens—or a
much larger underclass of bohemians living hand to mouth (Cross, 1985).
During this same time period, this group of writers made an assortment
of attempts to organize themselves. There was much disagreement,
however, about the appropriate model under which to organize, resulting from a disagreement about what authors had most in common: Writing talent? Poverty? A need for charity? Recognition? Antagonism toward
publishers? An interest in mobilizing for better contractual terms with
publishers? An interest in rewarding proven talent? An interest in sub-
sidizing young, promising talent? An interest in more favorable legal interpretations of copyright? We saw earlier that a key issue uniting authors
and readers was similarity. But what similarities did authors have with
one another? The issue has never been settled, other than that they write.

A variety of organizations came and went with one or another similarity
assumption as a founding principle.[11] On the assumption that what
writers shared most was a need for charity, David Williams organized
the Royal Literary Fund in 1790. However, because some 40% of the
Fund's expenses went into the cost of administration, it did not last (Cross,
1985; Hepburn, 1968). On the assumption that what writers most shared
was the need for recognition, the Royal Society of Literature was founded in 1820, which awarded authors on merit. That, too, did not last. On
the assumption that what writers most desired were better terms with
publishers, an organization was founded in 1825, called the Society for the
Encouragement of Literature, whose purpose was to increase the cut taken
by authors—and that, too, did not last. Insisting that material incentives
and competitive instincts were preferable to welfare for organizing authors,
Dickens, with Bulwer Lytton, founded the Guild of Literature and Art in
1850. The Guild paid a salary and housing for acclaimed writers of literature, but eventually lost its appropriations from Parliament (Cross, 1985).

The Society of Authors, founded in 1884, proved more successful than
its predecessors for two reasons:

---

[11]Victor Bonham-Carter's (1978) two-volume history of the authoring profession, commissioned by the Society of Authors, is the most definitive account to date of the various
efforts of authors to organize since 1800.

1. It was able to coax the best authors of the day to administer it. Its first president was Tennyson and its members included Arnold, Huxley, Collins, and Reade.
2. The society started with limited and focused goals, mainly to help authors understand the publishing industry, deal with agents, read contracts, and have the half-profit system of payment outlawed as unfair.

In 1978, the Society declared itself an independent union for authors in Britain. American organizations for authors have never been quite as successful. In 1892, American writers formed the Association of American Authors (later called the American Authors Guild), but it proved to be more a social club than a political or literary organization (Tebbel, 1968, Vol. 2). A more important and lasting organization was formed in 1912; the Author's League of America is the major organization of American authors to this day (Tebbel, 1982, Vol. 2).

On balance, coalitions of authors have been more successful in making gains on the legal than the economic front. In a 1980 survey of 2,241 American authors—their definition of "author" being any person with at least one book published, whether for general or specialized markets—Kingston and Cole (1980) concluded that outside the professional or blockbuster context, the economics of authoring today are not vastly different from those of the 18th century: few authors can live on their writing-related income. In 1979, the year Kingston and Cole conducted their survey, the median income from writing for all authors in the survey—generated from book royalties, magazine and newspaper fees, and motion picture and television options—was only $4,475; half of the authors earned less than this amount and one fourth earned less than $1.000 per year from writing. Only one tenth of the authors in the survey earned more than $45,000 from writing, and only one twentieth, more than $80,000. Broken down into hourly wages, the median income came to $4.90 an hour for writing. Dillard (1989) was on the mark when, in trying to describe the "writing life" to aspiring authors, she compared the market advantage of the shoe seller to the author:

A shoe salesman—who is doing others' tasks, who must answer to two or three bosses, who must do his job their way, and must put himself in their hands—is nevertheless working usefully. Further, if the shoe salesman fails to appear one morning, someone will notice and miss him. Your manuscript, on which you lavish such care, has no needs or wishes; it knows you not. Nor does anyone need your manuscript; everyone needs shoes more . . . Why not shoot yourself, actually, rather than finish one more excellent manuscript on which to gag the world? (pp. 11–12)

More to our own purposes, Kingston and Cole (1980) studied the number of contact hours authors shared with their fellow authors. They found the level of contact, for authors who did not write in a professional or academic context, quite low. Of the authors surveyed, 30% met socially with other authors at least once a month. The rest, only "every few months" or "rarely." More telling, perhaps, only 20% "always" or "usually" discussed ideas for books or work in progress with other authors. The rest "sometimes" or "never" did. Virtually 20% of all authors counted no fellow authors as a "good friend." And virtually 60% had only three or fewer "good author friends" (pp. 9, 134). Although more than half (53%) of academic writers talked regularly with at least three colleagues about their work, only 27% of the general market writers conversed with three other writers about theirs. Kingston and Cole (1980, pp. 112–113) concluded that authors without a professional or academic affiliation have no strong disposition to "talk writing" with their fellow authors and that for authors without these affiliations, the organization life is "thin" and "disconnected."

The organizational life of a writer can remain thin and disconnected even when the writer is occupationally affiliated with an organization and has dense social ties within it. The creative writer with university affiliations, according to many self-reports, tends to feel isolated despite these affiliations. To George Garrett, writers in universities are something like "freelance cavaliers" who drift in and out of the ivory tower according to their "current rating on the board of the literary stockmarket" (cited in Siegal, 1989, pp. 9–35). Weiss (1989, p. 53) likened the university patronage of the writer to the earlier church patronage of the poet: "As the clergy once accommodated poets in 17th and 18th century England, so now the university provides refuge to an always increasing population of writers." Ragan (1989, p. 65) thought that the large migration of writers into universities in the last decade was spawned by the yuppie leisure class who believed that writing programs were an "in" subject for their career preparation. Madden (1989) reported that the university promotes a professional careerism that distracts from the writer's true calling. Bellow (1980, p. 181) lamented that within the culture of expertise of the university, creative writers "have no independent ground to stand on."

Individuals who have taken the career path defined only in the last 20 years—that of the corporate writer—feel the same displacement in their settings. Until recently, these occupational roles were staffed by people with little formal training in writing (business and human resource majors who found their job required full-time writing) or little training in the corporate culture (majors in the liberal arts who needed to enter the work force). In either case, the role of corporate writer has been learned primarily on the job and honed in an ad hoc fashion to meet the changing demands of the local worksite. Often the primary skills emphasized in corporate writing—clarity, conciseness, organization, mechanical correctness (Anderson, 1985), retrieving and archiving information (Paradis, Dobrin, & Miller, 1985)—are too generic to give the corporate writer a strong sense of affiliation with either corporate culture or an outside culture of writers. Programs in professional writing are expanding in American universities and, with them, the role identities of the corporate writer are likely to change as well.

An alternative to feeling a sense of isolation from both the culture of writers and the culture of the worksite is to accept a kind of hybrid status that allows a writer to maintain a strong sense of affiliation in one culture and to "go through the motions" in the other (Christian, 1980; Eliot, 1978). In his study of the Scottish newspaper, Tremayne (1980, pp. 122–129) reported on these hybrids. He isolated one group of writers who had retained an identity affiliation as "writers who happened to be employed in the newspaper industry." He isolated a second group who had clung to a reverse identity affiliation, that of "newspaper people who happened to write." The first group consisted of writers working in advertising, management, accounts, personnel, and public relations, who retained strong ties with writers in other industries; they saw themselves as mobile for work in these other industries and they saw their writing skills as highly transferable to them. Their attitude toward the newspaper was, "I enjoy working here though I would readily move elsewhere if I were offered a better job with more pay. I don't know whether I like working here because it's a newspaper or because it's a good company" (p. 125). The second group consisted of reporters, editors, and the production staff who had abandoned their ties to writers in other industries, who now saw their skills as specialized to newspaper work and who questioned the loyalty of the writers in the first group: "Some of the people in departments upstairs have never seen a press. They're not newspapermen like us" (p. 127).

Until the explosion of professional groups in the mid-19th century (chapter 8), authors (or readers, for that matter) did not have a well-established culture or social structure within which to relate. Group similarity or interaction was not decisive among general market authors. There was, as a result, little to predict why authors or readers would interact among themselves more than with the general population.

SUMMARY AND IMPLICATIONS

We surveyed the expansive literature on the various contexts associated with the print industry in which communicative transactions occur. We have appealed to historical detail and showed that beneath the detail there are relatively few features—authorial reach, population size, number of authors, sociocultural opportunities to read, cognitive similarity, signature, handle, group similarity, and interaction—that can explain many interesting communicative regularities. We organized this literature not around institutional histories in specific periods but around a set of recurring and overlapping theoretical features that have evolved over time. A theory of the communicative transaction requires abstracting such features from the history of that interaction, without being needlessly reductive. Henceforth, our account of context will deal exclusively with these theoretical features, leaving behind the chronology of the institutional history. This path sacrifices many of the interesting details about the institutions bringing authors to readers and creating readers in a mold immediately accessible to authors. But this path also enables us to close the loop between the content and context of print (and, ultimately, oral) interaction at a sufficiently detailed yet general level to make formal modeling possible.

Communicative Transactions
and Their Ecology

*Given the protean nature of culture, human agents can elaborate
culture in an infinite number of ways.*
—Lesley Johnson (1987)

Johnson echoed a point often made by Raymond Williams (1961, 1962,
1976, 1977, 1980, 1981, 1982) throughout his illustrious career—cultural
theories must view the content and context of human action as part of
a working sociocultural ecology. Without a cultural content—handed
down from histories and texts—from which to draw, human agents would
have no materials for describing their world. Yet without a context for
shaping, they would have no circumstances through which to change the
objects of culture. Scenarios couched in language of this sort seem abstract and Olympian, reserved for the great persons of the culture. But
to believe Williams and a more recent generation of social theorists like
Collins, Giddens, and Archer is to believe that agents, through the inter-
mingling of content and context, can influence social organization and
culture in the humblest of circumstances. Content and context affect
everyday communicative transactions and through such transactions social organization and culture are altered. These observations describe the
insights of social theorists as well as those of ethnomethodologists (Garfin-
kle, 1968; Heritage, 1984) and sociologists with an interest in cognition
(Cicourel, 1974; Goffman, 1959, 1963, 1974; Mead, 1962). Despite the
contributions of these scholars, what is missing from their analyses is a
systematic account of the communicative transaction, the site at which
content and context coverage to effect social and cultural change. The

communicative transaction, we submit, has been the missing cornerstone integrating agents, content, and context as components of a single ecology. Though most scholars allude to its existence, the communicative transaction itself has remained a black box. As Cicourel (1974) noted:

> It is commonplace in sociology for writers to acknowledge the ultimate importance of the interacting situation between two or more actors. The assumed relationship between structure and process, however, is often no more than an expression of faith rather than the integration of social process with social structure. . . . (p. 11)

When the communicative transaction is treated as a black box, it is difficult to see how agents, content, and context fit into a single ecology, and even more difficult still to model rigorously how that ecology evolves. Without a systematic ecological perspective, furthermore, the impact of communication technologies, such as print, is often misunderstood.

Content, context, agents, and the communicative transaction are inextricably bound into a single ecological system such that affecting one ultimately affects all (see Fig. 4.1). The components of this ecology will be described in greater detail as we continue through this chapter. Figure 4.1, and the following brief discussion, illustrate the many dependencies between content, context, agents, and communicative transactions. Agents, for example, have a language and history beyond any single communicative transaction that they bring to each transaction; this language and history help to determine and define the transactions in which they engage. During the course of a communicative transaction, an agent constructs a communication whose content is transmitted to the partner or partners. During the course of interaction, agents are exposed to some of the partner's language and history through the content of the communication proffered by the partner during the transaction. Through communicative transactions, the language and histories of the agents can be continually constructed. As a consequence of such transactions, agents can change, and their language and history may evolve with irrevocable consequences for the content of future communications. Acquiring information leads to the construction of meaning (Fauconnier, 1985) and the evolution of language (Whorf, 1956, chap. 5, for more discussion on the role of language within communicative transactions).

From the standpoint of any single agent and any one transaction, the effect of such construction or evolution may be too slight, too unremarkable, to achieve notice. The important business of the transaction, from the agent's perspective, will be what it accomplishes for the agent's local purposes and not its over-time social, cultural, and historical consequences. Yet if we aggregate all the transactions going on in a society, both concurrently and over time, we see that what the agents have collectively constructed through multiple communicative transactions is the community's history and sociocultural change. The change at the social and cultural level occurs as a by-product of all concurrent transactions, and typically overwhelms the accomplishment of any single transaction. Collectively, and regardless of whether or not they had conscious intent, the agents have wrought change to the context and their position within it. There is thus an ongoing dynamic in which individuals, through the content of the communications they tender during communicative transactions, construct self and context, and so alter the ecology of the communicative transaction. We think of this story as the constructural story.

The topography of social structure and culture within a society emerge

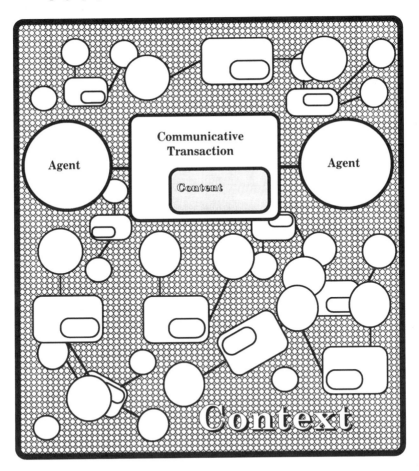

FIG. 4.1. The ecology of the communicative transaction: A constructural framework.

as the contingent byproduct of individuals trying, concurrently, to manage their local environment, to learn, rehearse, and share information from their particular sociocultural position in the landscape. Because the social world is a cooperative enterprise of individuals, no individual has complete control in determining its shape. This fact, of course, has become the signature slogan of social construction theory. Yet, constructuralism differs from social construction. Social construction abstracts away from individual cognition; constructuralism makes individual cognition (specifically, individual information; the ability to learn and to choose interaction partners with whom to learn) the central showpiece. According to constructuralism, the slightest change in what an individual knows can, in principle, affect the entire sociocultural landscape.

Portions of the constructural story have become increasingly popular with social theorists who tell about the creation and recreation of culture through communicative acts. Portions of this story have become increasingly popular with organizational and cognitive theorists who explain how individual action is socially and culturally constrained. Despite its popularity, the details of this story are rarely developed formally, and the formal detail, insofar as it exists, never focuses on a model of the communicative transaction itself. Furthermore, this story has not been used to investigate the potential impact of the communication technology (such as print) employed by interacting agents. The details of the story may depend on the available communication technology, but the story in its entirety applies, and is meant to apply, regardless of the technology. Because the story is relatively uniform across technological conditions, we must first understand the story and its generic detail prior to focusing on the role of communication technology (and specifically print) within the story (the focus of Part II).

This general ecological perspective underlies our interest in grounding print transactions in a more fundamental theory of the communicative transaction. In chapter 3, we focused on the history of print transactions in order to isolate features that seemed theoretically relevant to print transaction and yet generalizable to other modalities. We isolated features such as cognitive similarity, reach, signature, sociocultural opportunities to read, and so forth. Although we extracted these features from surveying print, many of these features, we believe, are generalizable, mutatis mutandis, to face-to-face transactions and writing. Chapter 3 allowed us to glimpse these features, though still entangled in historical detail. This chapter lays bare these features in the form of definitions and axioms, so that we can examine them more closely and in greater depth. Most of our discussion is from the perspective of print and author–reader transactions, though the reader should bear in mind that the axioms and definitions apply to communicative transactions in general, their context and content, and the agents involved in them. These definitions and axioms are building blocks for the constructural story. In chapter 6, we elaborate many of these definitions and axioms into a formal model which we apply in Part II to explore the logical consequences of print.

Before presenting the definitions and axioms underlying the constructural story, we describe an alternative view—individualism. This view conceives of print authors as different in kind from ordinary agents and the context of texts as different in kind from ordinary communications. Individualism focuses on the print-based author as an agent of cultural change and resists an ecological view of communications that spans different technological conditions. By considering the individual sans the larger ecology, proponents of individualism have inhibited the search for a general theory of the communicative transaction, and so have indirectly inhibited our understanding of the role of print.

INDIVIDUALISM

Individualism views people (including authors, readers, etc.) as isolated units of activity, creativity, and influence. This view toward individuals (mainly toward authors) has been taken by traditional literary theorists. Individualist approaches to the author focus less on the authoring role than on the individual who happens to have authored. Much work in the study of canonized literature, for example, is devoted to the "period author"—the thematic study of an individual named Milton, Chaucer, or Shakespeare. When an individualist methodology is taken, the authoring role is seldom addressed *sui generis*, as a datum deserving special abstraction from life events.

Instead, individualism collapses historical statements about the individual author and about the individual in the role of author. To be sure, the collapse is never absolute, because even individualist critics understand that the worth of historical information about single authors is redeemed when it can be linked to information about the role they play against a backdrop of other authorial roles.

Imagine a scholar who had just unearthed the following first-person entry from Upton Sinclair:

> For seven years I have borne poverty . . . sickness, heat, cold, toil—that I might make myself an artist. The indignities, the degradations—I could not tell them, if I spent all the time I have in writing a journal. I have lived in garrets—among dirty people—vulgar people—vile people. I have worn rags and unclean things . . . But I have said, "I will be an artist." (cited in Wilson, 1985, p. 126)

Or one who retrieved the following journal from David Graham Phillips, another Progressive Era writer:

> I write every night, from about eleven until about four or five or six in the morning. Sometimes seven or eight. You can work in the day time. Let me urge you to work the same hours every day and never, never, never to let anything or anyone interfere between you and working at those hours. (cited in Wilson, 1985, p. 156)

Taken as historical information about individual writers, these statements are unremarkable. They suggest two writers speaking of the determination (in Sinclair's case) and the discipline (in Phillips' case) required for writing. The same statements are uttered regularly by thousands of writing teachers every term and at least mouthed by their students. What makes these statements interesting as data is that both Sinclair and Phillips exemplified the role of author in culturally potent ways; the critic is teased with the promise that this historical information can be made to say something about the larger roles the two authors came to fill.

A similar kind of juxtaposition between the individual and the role can be found in individualist treatments of authorial biographies. An individualist's interest in Defoe appears in the following excerpt adapted from the *American Academic Encyclopedia* (1989):

> Defoe was born in 1660 and died in 1731. In his youth, he flirted with a career in the ministry but went into business instead. He did not begin writing under his own name until 1692 when he declared bankruptcy. He wrote social criticism, satire, and novels and did not begin his novels until he was well into his 50s. He was a supporter of William III and in 1701 wrote *The True-Born Englishman, A Satyr* a popular poem on William's behalf. After William's death in 1702, Defoe was arrested for publishing *The Shortest Way with Dissenters* and was released with the help of Robert Harley. He edited a periodical called *The Review* from 1704–1713 and wrote about politics and economics for that periodical as well as others. He wrote a ghost story in 1706 that displayed his talent for reporting and narrative that he was to use in his later adventure fiction *Robinson Crusoe* (1719), "Captain Singleton" (1720), *Moll Flanders* (1722), *Colonel Jack* (1722). *Robinson Crusoe* was . . . the first successful English novel; Defoe is one of the originators of realistic fiction. (database file)

Note the mix of historical information about the individual (mileposts, events, compositions) and the role (first at a successful novel; an originator of realism). The first type of information can be witnessed by chronicling an individual through life. The second can only be chronicled by situating Defoe in an environment of other authors, readers, genres, conventions, and precedents. The gap separating these classes of information does not stand out as a gulf—an irresolvable discrepancy. Perhaps this is because we—all individualists in our common sense world—never miss the challenge of trying to link them, of trying to comb the secrets of what led Defoe to the role he was to assume in letters.

Thus, individualism—contrary to some charges against it—cannot be faulted with overlooking social information entirely. But because individualism is unconcerned about representing, in explicitly systematic ways, the information that can inform the authorial role, the individualist takes notice of the authorial role only when the role commands notice, is culturally visible, or has achieved standing and acclaim. This state of affairs leaves the individualist with a skewed understanding of the authorial role—detailing the basic principles of authoring by examining the culturally visible author, somewhat like detailing the fundamentals of retailing by touring megamalls. It also leaves the individualist with an underappreciation of the reader as a determinant of the author, for as the cultural visibility of an author increases, the tendency also increases to make over the author's role into a self-sufficient persona. There are, as we have indicated, practical difficulties in trying to learn about the operation of author roles from extreme cases. Nevertheless, this is the perspective into which one is firmly locked by individualism.

When we look at the authoring role with fresh eyes, we see that much goes into the role beyond success, and that success describes only a tiny fraction of such roles. We see that any historical information about the individual author is potentially ripe for informing the authorial role and, with it, a theory of print interaction. From our discussion of the various features of content and context that can shape print interaction, we understand that attributes like "lived in London in 1830," "sued a New York publisher at age 26," "wrote short fiction before joining a newspaper," or "attended a grammar school up to age 12" can all be features determinative of the author (and reader) role and are no less important in their own way than features like "first to have a successful novel."

In contrast to individualism, our approach views people as situated actors, whose actions and influence are a function of their position in a sociocultural landscape. We focus on the structure of the individual's relations to other people in the society, relative to all other ongoing relations. Hence, any and all historical information, both about the individual and about the society, are important in understanding a specific author and the more general role of authoring. We think of our approach as situated individualism. As we shall see, social constructionists and postmodernists also embrace the approach of situated individualism, and we distinguish ourselves from various strands of these schools.

AUTHORSHIP AS AN HONORIFIC NOTION

A close offshoot of the individualist approach to the author defines the authorial role in honorific terms, as a term signifying high cultural stature and standing. In this view, the words "author" and "authorship" are reserved only for those individuals whose texts have achieved some level of cultural visibility and acclaim, even canonization. The individualist can cite an etymological basis for elevating the author (in this favored sense) above ordinary writers. More specifically, the individualist can cite the fact that the *Oxford English Dictionary* traces writer to the manual crafts of painting (*rizari*) and tracing (*reisser*), whereas author is the authority and originator (*auteur*) behind making and creating. The author is literally the force, authority, and mover behind the hand that writes.

By and large, theorists who reject individualism in favor of situated individualism also reject honorific definitions of the author and the a priori distinction between the designation author and ordinary writers. This is certainly the case for us, but it is not always the case for postmodernists. For example, Barthes abandoned individualist premises about authors, yet maintained, for his own purposes, the honorific distinction between authors and writers. In his 1982 essay, "Authors and Writers," Barthes observed that the writer uses language for a controlled purpose in a controlled situation (the "clerk," in Barthes' terms, was an unflattering reference to the occupational author) without appreciating the culture-defining properties of language that are rehearsed in the writer's practice, but usually outside the writer's deliberate control (e.g., the ideological struggles at issue in the use or avoidance of sexist language). The author, by contrast, is a person who knowingly understands himself or herself as both a reflection of the language system and an instrument through which the system changes. Barthes' author thus attains a certain cultural reflectiveness that is missed by the ordinary writer. Barthes' program—like that of many postmodernists—is aimed to defeat individualism, to bring a level of heightened awareness about the author as an active creator of culture. Yet, to bring that about through honorific distinctions (viz., author-/writer) is to replicate individualism, not to make an advance beyond it.

THE ECOLOGY OF COMMUNICATIVE TRANSACTIONS: A CONSTRUCTURAL PERSPECTIVE

An advance beyond individualism comes with an ecological perspective that considers the individual as a dynamic component within a dynamic environment. An ecological perspective goes beyond most open system theories familiar to students of organizations (Scott, 1981).[1] In an open system, the agent (or organization) is viewed in terms of its inputs and outputs with the larger environment. An open system approach to communication emphasizes the agent, the context (environment), and the content of the transactions (inputs and outputs). Yet, often, only the content (inputs, outputs) is seen as changeable; everything else in the environment is considered static. Moreover, the communicative transaction is an unproblematic black box that exists but is irrelevant to understanding the flow of inputs and outputs. An ecological perspective, such as constructuralism, differs from an open systems perspective because it perceives all the components of communication—the agent, content, context, and communicative transaction—as mutually defining, coadaptive, and coevolving components of a single ecology (Fig. 4.1). The communication transaction is not left implicit or taken for granted, but is the centerpiece of all the other components of communication, requiring a higher level of formal explication. To understand the dynamics of these components of communication, one must begin by breaking out the dynamics of the communication transaction itself.

In Fig. 4.1, we see a snapshot of the interrelationship between agents, communicative transactions, content, and context. In this snapshot, agents are concurrently engaged in communicative transactions. During these transactions, there is a communication with a particular information content from at least one of the agents to one or more others. Agents adapt in response to these communications which alter the context (i.e., their position in the sociocultural landscape and the landscape itself). If we could animate this snapshot, we would see the agents alter position, select new partners, and engage in new transactions; we would see agents come and go as the population changes; and we would see the content of the communications change as the culture shifts in response to earlier transactions. This figure, and the story we have told so far, are couched at an extremely general level of detail, too general to be of value for adequate prediction and explanation. To make the story more complete, we provide a series of definitions and axioms to fill in much of the detail left out of Fig. 4.1. Still further elaboration will occur in chapters 5 and 6.

DEFINITIONS

We present a series of definitions concerning the context (society), the agent (especially the author), the text (including its content), and the communicative transaction. Many of the concepts we define are familiar,

---

[1]Constructuralism is closer in style and intent to resource dependency theory (Pfeffer & Salancik, 1978); under both theories, the environment affects the agent (organization) and the agent affects the environment.

though within the general literature they often lack standard definitions precise enough for a formal model. We define these concepts to characterize the extent, limits, and focus of our analysis, and to establish a common framework from which we can proceed. The length of our discussion for various definitions varies depending on the degree to which the definition we offer is controversial or is meant to supersede better known alternatives. As a further caveat, many of the concepts defined are not peculiar to print and authors, although print-based communication is the dominant orientation of this book. In most cases, what we say about authors applies generally to all individual communicators.

Context: Society

Communicative transactions take place within a context. As we saw in chapter 3, such contexts have historical affects on communicative transactions, as different contexts facilitate different transactions. The context of the communication is described locally as the immediate factors surrounding a particular transaction, or is described more generally in terms of the general factors surrounding all concurrent transactions occurring in a given time and place. We refer to the general description of context as society. Strictly speaking, a society consists of both the sociocultural landscape (defined later) and the technological conditions (defined later) that facilitate communication. For the society, the technological condition, in conjunction with the sociocultural landscape, define the context for all communicative transactions.

Sociocultural Landscape

The sociocultural landscape is the social, cultural, historical, and political context in which communicative transactions occur. The sociocultural landscape is not a static context, but a dynamic, evolving environment whose existence, maintenance, construction, reconstruction, and evolution is dependent on changes within and between the individuals in the society.

Population. Every society is composed of a collection of individuals (i.e., a population). This population is itself dynamic. Demographic processes, such as birth and death, integration, and mobility, determine the extant population. The size of the population in and of itself limits sociocultural outcomes and individual communicative transactions. Within a tribal culture, there are fewer individuals with whom to interact than within a modern technological society. Seventeenth-century England had a significantly smaller literate population than 18th-century England, a fact affecting the reach and authority of the authors living within each society: fewer people, fewer potential readers.

Groups. Within the society, there are groups. There are multiple ways of characterizing groups—by function, purpose, name, level of interaction, sociometric or demographic trait, and so on—but, for our purposes, how the group is characterized is less important than the fact of its existence. Indeed there is extensive literature on groups—how they form, dissolve, and function; their nature; how to locate them analytically; how their membership changes; and so forth—portions of which will seep into the analysis in later chapters. Our current interest is simply to note that groups exist, that they can be named, and that while some individuals in the society are members, others are not. Group characteristics and behavior are inherited from the characteristics and behaviors of individual group members (Carley, 1991b). As noted by Carley, "groups form and endure because of discrepancies in who knows what. Groups typically are in flux simply because members are continually acquiring new information and communicating it to each other" (p. 332).

Social Structure. The individuals within the society differ in terms of those with whom they are most likely to interact and in terms of their membership in groups. By affecting opportunities for interaction, membership in a group can affect how likely individuals are to interact (i.e., their probabilities of interaction). Collectively, we refer to the distribution of these interaction probabilities as social structure.

Viewed in this light, social structure encompasses and is defined by all the interaction probabilities between individuals (and, consequently, by all the relations between individuals). Social structure changes as any of these probabilities change (however, in many contexts, this change may be microscopic). There are alternate views of social structure, such as those emphasizing the pattern of relations or subgroups within social networks (Lorrain & White, 1971; White, Boorman, & Breiger, 1976); those emphasizing sociometric and demographic conditions (Blau, 1977; McPherson & Smith-Lovin, 1987); and those emphasizing institutions, their memberships, and the distribution of tasks within them (Cohen, March, & Olsen, 1972; Pfeffer & Salancik, 1978). In contrast to these views, the representation of social structure as the distribution of interaction probabilities emphasizes the communicative transaction as the dynamic bond linking individuals to each other and to society.

Culture. Individuals differ in what they know and believe, their norms, values, superstitions, and conceptions. Culture is the distribution of information across the individuals in the society. Similar characterizations of culture appear in the work of symbolic interactionists (Stryker, 1980), cultural theorists (Archer, 1988; Namenwirth & Weber, 1987), organizational theorists (Krackhardt & Kilduff, 1990), and anthropologists (Romney, Batchelder, & Weller, 1987; Romney, Weller, & Batchelder, 1986). Such characterizations are predicated on the assumption that information can be characterized as discrete separable pieces or symbols, separately learned and communicated. This assumption is shared by a wide range of research traditions including, but not limited to, cultural dynamics (Melischek, Rosengren, & Stappers, 1984; Namenwirth & Weber, 1987), attitude and belief formation (Ajzen & Fishbein, 1980; Anderson, 1971; Hunter, Danes, & Cohen, 1984), diffusion (Coleman, Katz, & Menzel, 1966; Rapoport, 1953), and individual learning (Bush & Mosteller, 1955). We discuss the implications of this assumption later. Like the definition of social structure as the distribution of interaction, the definition of culture as the distribution of knowledge emphasizes the communicative transaction and the social and cultural evolution that occurs in response to the communicative actions and adaptations taken by individuals in the society.

Integration.   Integration is the degree to which individuals within the society, or group, share information and culture. In a completely integrated society—utopia—the culture is uniform and everyone knows everything that anyone knows. That is, all share the same ideas, facts, findings, beliefs, norms, and values. In a completely nonintegrated society—anarchy—cultural differentiation is complete and no individual shares any knowledge with any other. In such a society, there are no norms and each person has an individual set of beliefs and values. Completely integrated and nonintegrated societies represent hypothetical extremes. Nonetheless, they are useful in illustrating how varying levels of integration can affect society.

Such variation is often characterized in terms of the homogeneity and heterogeneity of a society's population. Social structuralists, such as Blau (1977), argued that the degree of homogeneity and heterogeneity within a society is a primary determinant of individual action. However, particularly within sociology, homogeneity and heterogeneity are often characterized in terms of sociometric and demographic conditions, such as the breakdown of old and young, Blacks and Whites, women and men, within a population. In contrast, we recast homogeneity and heterogeneity in terms of integration, and we recast sociometric and demographic conditions in terms of information. Under constructuralism, different sociometric and demographic dimensions are associated with different sets of information and affect individual behavior only insofar as individuals know information that is characteristic of a certain dimension (e.g., people know certain characteristic things because they are doctors or because they are on welfare). Knowledge thus mediates the impact of sociometric and demographic dimensions on individuals and further conditions their communicative transactions.

Technological Condition

Every society has a technological condition. We define this condition as a set of available technologies and their distribution across individuals in the society. The technological condition is the technological context in which communicative transactions take place. Technologies can enhance or degrade the number of individuals who simultaneously engage in a single communicative transaction, and it can affect the physical properties of the content of the communication. For example, print increases an author's opportunities to communicate to the masses. Technology can be used to create artificial agents,[2] themselves capable of information processing. An extreme case, familiar within both manufacturing contexts and science fiction, is the robot, an agent with a limited capability to understand and to carry out instructions. Another artificial agent, one with which we are particularly concerned, is the text. The author writes a text and encapsulates, in an essentially unchanging fashion, knowledge at the point of composing (a point in time to which we return in a moment). The text, as agent (and particularly as enhanced by print), can engage in multiple simultaneous communicative transactions (as multiple individuals read different copies). The text, as agent, lays claim to a distinctive set of information-processing capabilities. For example, a text cannot select a partner for interaction, but must be selected by a reader. Moreover, a text can communicate or impart information, but it can neither receive nor learn new information.

To say that technologies can enhance or limit individual behavior within the communicative transaction is not to commit ourselves to technological determinism. According to technological determinism, sociocultural change is a direct outcome of technological change (Eisenstein, 1979; Goody, 1986; Olsen, 1977). In contrast, we argue simply that technologies exist, that their use can effect sociocultural change and the rate of change, but that the mere existence of a new technology does not guarantee change. More importantly, as we make clear in this book, technologies—particularly communication technologies—have specific properties that can affect the communicative transaction and the physical properties of the content of the communication; through these properties artificial agents which engage in communicative transactions can be

---

[2]Such agents, like texts, are artificial in the sense that they are created by humans (Simon, 1981).

created. Through these artificial agents and their properties, communication technologies can effect sociocultural change. Yet this is not to imply, as determinists are wont to imply, that technologies effect change by changing the human cognitive system itself.

Communication technologies differ in their characteristics and, consequently, in their impact on the communicative transaction. We do not intend to belabor this point or to provide an extensive analysis of such characteristics and impacts. Rather, we focus on those characteristics that are important in understanding the impact of print and which typify the differences between oral and written modes of communication. These include synchronicity, fixity, durability, and multiplicity. Each characteristic affects the possible distance between communication partners.

Synchronicity. Synchronicity occurs when the communication technology requires the communication partners to be co-temporal. To be co-temporal, communication partners are not necessarily sending their communications at the same time; rather, they are simply involved at the same time in a single transaction. There is, in other words, no temporal distance to speak of in their communication. Face-to-face communication, oration, and telephone conversations have this feature. Asynchronicity frees communication partners from this constraint and enables communication partners to be involved with the same communicative transaction but at different times. The written word made it possible for individuals to engage in communicative transactions, if not at their leisure, at least not at exactly the same time. When a technology affords asynchronicity, communication partners can be, though they need not be, temporally distant. Asynchronicity breaks the temporal and therefore proximal tie between the original communicating agent (the author) and the communication. Consequently, the communication becomes an artificial agent capable of engaging in communicative transactions without its originator (the author). For the originator (the author), the creation of this artificial agent facilitates reach across greater temporal and spatial distances.

Fixity. Fixity is the degree to which communication technology enables the communication to be retransmitted without change. By recreating a communication in mechanical reproducible type, print increased the fixity of a communication. The fixity of the printed word is not the same as its fidelity. Fixity is a property of a communication technology; fidelity, as we see later, is a property of a communication. Fixity is an important precondition for fidelity because once information is in a text, barring corruptions in printing, translation, or the untoward motives of speakers, the information should have higher fidelity as a result of its higher fixity in print. Information that is highly fixed, furthermore, should be easier to pass on with intact meanings as it moves, within communications, from transaction to transaction. Eisenstein (1979) and Ong (1971, 1982) argued that print increased the fidelity of cultural information by stabilizing its fixity, even as it diffused across time and space. According to Ong (1971):

> With print, the possibility of exactly reproducing complicated spatial arrangements of words or other symbols (far harder to transcribe in manuscript than a text) was spectacularly improved, since the most complicated display, once it is locked up in a form, is just as easy to multiply typographically as straight discursive material. Dichotomized tables such as those of the Ramists can of course be seen in manuscripts, but print gave them ready currency on paper and in the mind to a degree never remotely approximated in a manuscript culture. (p. 111)

Eisenstein (1979) argued that the increased fidelity of information conferred by print paved the way for a more standardized collective memory and more standardized ways to change that memory through scientific inquiry. Eisenstein and Ong suggested that the standardizing effects of print were consistent with its intellectual, detached, and decontextualized presentation of meanings. Brandt (1989) agreed that fixity enhances fidelity but for entirely different reasons. She argued that the fixity of print only increased the subjective and local involvements of agents; increased the work they had to invest in order to maintain fidelity; increased their attention to fidelity by entrusting more culturally valuable information to print and by making the trust increasingly exclusive; that is, by leaving increasingly more important cultural information only to the thin bandwidth of text to disseminate. According to Brandt (1990) the fixed lexicalized form of print has become the precarious channel on which literate cultures rely to sustain some of their most important intersubjective understandings:

> Writing does not make involvement less relevant; it makes it most precarious. Involvement must be fanned at every moment or the writing becomes meaningless. The lexical channel is obviously the sole means of involvement—all aspects of text work to keep a reader involved. . . . The fixity of the text rather than "fixing out" the relationships of participants actually raises awareness of that developing involvement, which influences the possibilities that writers have for preceding. (pp. 38–41)

A very similar insight about fixity lies behind Bakhtin's (1981, pp. xix, 288) concept of "heteroglossia," a concept expressing the two-headed principle that a communication system needs a fixed and repeatable system of symbols in order to blossom into an unbounded variability of high fidelity social meaning when refracted by context. The fixity of print is considered a crowning achievement of Western technology, often because of its implications for fidelity.

Some futurists are already beginning to dismiss, as an anachronism of print, both fixity and its consequences for fidelity. Computers can effect the fixity of electronic texts in a variety of ways. In contrast to users of printed texts, users of electronic texts have increased control over the verbal and visual layout and can navigate the text in nonlinear ways, according to their purposes, not the author's (Bolter, 1991). They also have the ability to rewrite, zoom, color, and annotate a text, to interleave text with graphics and, in general, to customize text to their own preferences and purposes, making the text unique for them. The ability for readers of electronic texts to tamper with fixity holds obvious implications for their capacity and willingness to tamper with fidelity. There is no doubt that issues of fixity and fidelity become a matter of concern for electronic text. Whether the concern will be legitimate, and how author–reader relationships will be affected by electronic media over the long haul, are empirical issues that need to be examined.

Durability.   Durability is the length of time the communication is available for communicative transactions (chap. 2). Print made communications more durable and hence includable in multiple communicative transactions. Unless it is part of an oral tradition handed down from one generation to the next, the content of talk lacks durability. The content dies as soon as it is uttered. Isolated manuscripts also lack durability, as the paper conveying the communication can disintegrate and the bindings holding it can corrode and collapse. An important property of written texts and, especially, printed texts has been their durability. With the advent of print, texts could have a life that extended well beyond the physical life of the author. Texts could continue interacting with readers long after their author could not. Durability increased the number of communicative transactions in which the communication could be involved; fixity increased the accuracy with which the communication was reproduced in these transactions. Durability and fixity increase distance and so increase the author's potential and actual reach.

Durability also enables communications to diffuse faster. If a communication is nondurable, those individuals who receive it initially may learn the information within it (primary communication or diffusion), but the future diffusion of the information in that communication will require that the original communicator (the author) or these primary receivers fashion new communications to pass that information (secondary communication or diffusion). However, a durable communication can be received by different individuals at different times without composing secondary, tertiary, and n-level mediating communications. A durable text can continue to diffuse information through primary communication with readers even while some of these readers (e.g., reviewers, scholars, etc.) are composing secondary communications to sustain the content of the primary communication.

Durability, as a property of the technology, is concerned with the length of time a textual content is preserved as a result of the material actions taken to preserve it (e.g., printing it on durable paper, careful archiving, new editions). Print technologies employing acid-free paper, india ink, and leather bindings confer greater durability on a text than one employing more degradable materials. Such physical durability can effect the length of time a textual content is considered valuable for interaction (chapter 2). The technological support given to preserve a textual content often corresponds with the cultural value the communication is perceived to have. While the "Great Books of Western Civilization" are published in editions using "quality" materials, the latest in a line of cookbooks is unlikely to receive the same attention. Communication technologies differ in their durability and the longevity they provide to the communication. As a consequence, communication technologies can effect the ultimate reach of the author or authors responsible for the communication.

Multiplicity. Multiplicity is measured by the number of partners with whom one can communicate at the same time. In face-to-face oral transactions, multiplicity is low—there is only a single other communication partner. In contrast, the one-to-many nature of both the written mode and the oration grant the communication greater multiplicity. Mass communication technologies all have high multiplicity.

Multiplicity guarantees greater spatial distance than that which is needed for one-to-one communication. For example, the spatial distance between the orator and audience is generally greater than that existing between two individuals having a discussion. In general, the greater the multiplicity allowed by the communication technology, the greater the potential spatial distance between communication partners. Multiplicity also provides the agent with another advantage—speed; if one can communicate with multiple people at once, then the information communicated to them spreads faster.

Although multiplicity is often considered a distinctive property of print, face-to-face interaction and multiplicity (one-to-many) are not, strictly speaking, incompatible. The ancient poet and orator, the medieval minstrel, bard, vagabond, and story teller engaged in interactions that were typically one-to-many. Historically, print facilitated one-to-many communication, but not necessarily because it increased the number of receivers. An amphitheater could hold more persons (in the thousands) than the number (in the hundreds) needed to buy all the copies of most early single edition books. Print facilitated one-to-many communication by allowing for the temporal and geographical dispersal of the many. The impact of print over oration is attributable not just to its multiplicity, but also to its asynchronicity, fixity, and durability.

Content: Text—The Author Encapsulated

The communicative transaction has a content—that which is communicated from one agent to another. In written communication, we think of this content as a text.[3] This content (the author's text) is an encapsulation of a sample of a socially, culturally, and historically situated agent's (author) mental models within a particular physical form. The author's text encapsulates aspects of the author's knowledge at the time the text was created, within a time capsule whose physical form is defined by the communication technology. As a text diffuses, readers may generate a plethora of further elaborations (including interpretations and readings). In literary theory, a good deal of work has empirically distinguished aspects of the author's cognition from the social elaborations of readers (i.e., what is in the text from what is read into it; see Hirsch, 1972). While these distinctions can be notoriously difficult to make in specific cases, the analytic primacy of the distinction does not disappear. At the same time, we bear in mind that it is perfectly possible for much of the original cognition that went into the production of a text to be obliterated as it travels across time, space, and culture.

A reader who only knows that Homer's texts are myths about ancient Greeks can claim little understanding of Homer's context of production; for, surely Homer did not see himself producing myths (in our modern sense) and surely he did not consider himself an ancient Greek (White, 1983). Those who want to efface, by fiat, the cognition of the original author cannot easily explain how the author's cognition might continue to be involved in historical transactions with the text. Those who want to save, by fiat, the cognition of the original author cannot easily explain

---

[3]In this section, we discuss aspects of the text as content. But texts can act as artificial agents and serve, like humans, as interaction partners. Both texts and humans have "mental models" that we can think of as the information "within" or "known by" them. When interacting, both the text and the human can tender a communication. For the text, this communication is its entire mental model. For the human, this communication is only a portion of the mental model. For the text in each communicative transaction in which it engages, exactly the same communication is tendered. For the human, different communications may be tendered in different communicative transactions.

the real possibility that readers, after time, rely only on their elaborations and eventually lose most or all traces of the original context of production. Whether the production context of the original author, including his or her cognitive state, is saved or lost in historical transactions with a text is an empirical question resolvable on a case-by-case basis, not a blanket theoretical assumption.

The term "text" itself is ambiguous. It has been used within the literature for a variety of factors ranging from context to physical presence, from artifact to message (and so meaning). In the next three definitions—communication, code, and meaning—we disambiguate these factors.

The Communication

The communication is the content of a physical utterance or text. In a literal sense, it is the string of symbols or concepts created by the agent. For an author and a text, this is the set of sentences that comprise the written work. As such, barring factors such as translation and physical deterioration, the communication remains unchanged through space and time. For a text, the words are immutable. Shakespeare's *Romeo and Juliet* retains a certain number of words in a certain order. In this sense, the words of the bard are immortal.

The communication qua communication can be analyzed. For example, one can count the number of words, or identify the syntactical style. In author attribution studies, researchers study the communication to ascertain an authorial signature (e.g., Was this text written by Shakespeare or Bacon?) The statistical techniques used in author attribution studies are designed on the premise that the communication can be a reliable fingerprint of an author even when the historical attribution of authorship is a contested point (see Erdman & Fogel, 1966, for a bibliography).

Importantly, from a transactional perspective, the communication is divisible into pieces of information. Each piece of information can be communicated and understood separately. Consequently, the text may diffuse not in total, but only in part. Readers interact with a whole text, but typically come away with only portions of it. For any given text, more individuals will know pieces of information within it than will know the entire text. While many readers of *Romeo and Juliet* may know that Juliet asks, "Wherefore art thou Romeo?" fewer may know that the question begins a soliloquy on the nature of names. In Shakespeare's case, the difference between what individuals have "learned" and what "is" within the text has served as the basis for many comedic take-offs on this tragedy with the heroine of the comedy calling for a lost Romeo.

Code

Although the communication is the conceptual content of the text, the code is the physical reality. Whether the original context of production remains part of the historical transactions with a text or not, there is a physical text availing itself for further transactions. We apply the term "code" to the text participating in these transactions, independent of how it is elaborated in any single transaction. The code is the text's material structure as embodied in its visual design and typography. Readers rely on the code in order to sense and, consequently, read a text. For a given text, the communication can remain unchanged across a number of codes. *Romeo and Juliet* remains *Romeo and Juliet*, whether it appears in a hand-tooled leather bound volume or on a computer screen.

Meaning

Meaning is the result of local interpretation. We can talk about the meaning of the text itself. By this we mean the text's lexicon—the set of concepts within the text and the links between them (see chap. 5 for additional detail). More commonly, we think of meaning in terms of that ascribed by the reader. Such ascribed meaning is the result of individual cognition and is dependent on the information in the text and the information known by the individual reader at the time of the reading. A full discussion of meaning is beyond the scope of this book; however, we attempt to provide readers with enough detail to distinguish meaning from communication.

To understand meaning, we need to consider the nature of human cognition and information. An individual's cognition includes a knowledge base (i.e., a set of information known to the individual). Such knowledge bases have been referred to as mental models (Carley & Palmquist, 1992; Johnson-Laird, 1983; Sowa, 1984). The information within them can include facts, beliefs, norms, conceptions, procedures, and so on. This information can be thought of as a set of interlinked but separable or discrete pieces of information. Discreteness of information does not imply that all such information appears in chunks of equal grain size, nor does it imply that the pieces of information are self-contained in terms of their meaning. Discreteness does imply that each piece of information, though related to other pieces, can be communicated, learned, counted, and analyzed separately from the other pieces of information. Meaning derives from the relationships between the discrete pieces of information (chapter 5). Meaning is built out of what pieces are known and how they are interlinked. Consequently, the same piece of information can have multiple meanings. The same individual may attribute a different meaning to the same information at different points in time, depending upon what the individual is currently doing. Different individuals may attribute different meanings to the same information, depending on their personal histories and on what information they have linked to the original piece of information in question. Meanings can change over time, even within an individual, as the individual learns and as the individual's linkages between information change.

The communication is the set of information the author composed into the text. In this way the communication encapsulates a fixed portion of the author's cognition at the time of composition. The author had, at the time of composing, a meaning relating the various pieces of information in the communication. The communication has a fixed meaning because it represents the author's meaning at a fixed point (a span of points in time). The author, however, continues to learn. Consequently, if asked later about the meaning of a text, the author may provide a meaning that has little to do with the meaning that was operative at the time of the text's composition.

At the time the text is read, the reader's knowledge base will have a specific set of information that will facilitate (as we discuss in more detail later) how the reader learns some of the information in the communication. Each piece of information within the communication can be learned by the reader separately, and the reader relates this learned information to a pre-existing set of interlinked information. Meaning is dynamically created during this process. The reader creates a "reading," which is the interpreted reconstruction of the text, based on both what the reader knew prior to engaging the text and what the reader learns during the transaction. A reading, therefore, involves the meaning ascribed by the reader.

The code and the communication travel from one transactional context to another; a reading marks the site of a single transaction. The code and the communication, unlike readings, are not shackled to any single transaction; it is the code and communication to which White (1984, p. 19) referred when he claimed that a text has an "actual identity," that it is "too complex [as a predigested stimuli for cultural elaboration] ever to be completely known" and "too alive to be fixed in a single interpretation forever." Outside graphic design contexts, the code (e.g., typographic and spatial layout) seldom surfaces as an isolated component of textual interpretation because readers associate the meaning of a text with the readings or social elaborations they bring to the text and less with its actual physical form.

Information, and hence meanings, can be shared by multiple members of a society. To the extent that two (or more) individuals share not only the same information but also the same interactions between them, they share the same meaning(s). Thus we can talk about social shared meanings as the set of information and linkages between them that are shared by a set of individuals in the society. Such sharing can be tacit (i.e., the individuals do not need to consciously know that they share the information),[4] but it need not be. Indeed an "authorized" reading can be thought of as a socially shared and, therefore, accepted reading for which the sharing happens to be explicit. An authorized reading conveys a message (chap. 2) when there are social norms to pass it along, intact, as a prescribed way of reading a text.

Signature

The signature is an abstraction linking the communication to the agent who produced it. For a printed text, a signature is more abstract than the proper name of the author—though the author's proper name is the most common way of referencing a signature. A kidnapper's ransom note will try to conceal all traces of a signature but the police will look for one anyway. Whether seeking anonymity or not, an author leaves a signature, a trace of a distinctive intelligence, up front or behind the scenes. In an age when signed texts are taken for granted, it is difficult to appreciate the authorial signature for the abstraction it is. In preprint writing systems, the abstractness of the signature was likely to be overlooked because writing retained many of the characteristics of oral communication. The scribe's signature, after all, retained a physical embodiment in the style of handwriting, in the slant of the script, and in other identifying features that distinguished the writer from all other individuals (Vachek, 1989, p. 10). Print obliterated these physical embodiments of the writer's signature and also helped transform that signature into a commodity of cultural value and exchange (Mallon, 1989, p. 4). Both outcomes made the latent abstractness of the author's signature more evident. Derrida (1976, pp. 97–99) credited Rousseau as the first author with a modern signature, an author who was self-conscious about the abstraction that "Rousseau" had become as a result of his corpus of circulating texts (see also Kamuf, 1988, on the development of the modern authorial signature).

The author's signature is often linked with knowledge that newly originates or is at least singularly identified with the person of the author

---

[4]The idea that tacit agreement may be sufficient for social agreement, and perhaps even cultural truth, is fairly widespread in the social sciences. Polanyi (1962) argued that such tacit consensus arises if the individuals in question both went through the same experience (such as two women in different cities giving birth or a set of students sitting through the same lecture course though perhaps during different years). Similar conceptions of consensus through tacitly shared knowledge include Whorf's shared culture (1956), Bar-Hillel's universal encyclopedia (1960), Sowa's background knowledge (1984), and Romney's cultural truth (Romney, Batchelder, & Weller, 1987; Romney, Weller, & Batchelder, 1986).

as its source. Nonetheless, to have a distinctive signature, an author need not be responsible for new knowledge, for innovation. The author's signature, for example, is often linked to a distinctive style (e.g., the frequency with which first person or passive voice is used). Popularizers, adapters, expositors, and translators can fashion a signature even when their ideas are not, strictly speaking, new. This last observation is contestable, however, as the empirical boundaries between new and assimilated ideas are seldom clear cut. Legal tests used in copyright cases to help make the discrimination are barely workable (chap. 3). These difficulties notwithstanding, we often assume, throughout this book, that an author's signature is a mark of new ideas, as opposed to those ideas in a text that the author has borrowed.

Handle

A handle consists of the descriptions used to index or reference an author's signature. The handle comprises the various descriptions used to instantiate the signatorial abstraction (e.g., *Rousseau, writer of Emile, propounder of social contract theory,* etc.). The author's proper name (via a signed text) is now the most common of handles, but this was not always so. The bibliographical practice of using the author's name as the primary key for indexing texts was practiced in Greece, but the practice did not gain wide acceptance until the 1500s. Before that time, the title, not the author, was the primary index for the work (McInnis & Symes, 1988, p. 391). Studying print interactions in the latter Middle Ages, Allen (1971, p. 59) concluded that authors were typically "content to remain anonymous" and that readers (or hearers), no less typically, were content to hear stories they already loved. Until the 18th century, it was customary in polite letters to use anon., pseudonyms, and other evasive tricks to disguise the proper name (Kernan, 1987, pp. 71–72). The development of the author's name as the primary handle was evident in the examples of Dante, Petrarch, and Chaucer, who were among the first authors to sign their texts with their real names. As printed matter became more abundant and potentially more subversive, the English government saw an independent political advantage in insisting on the name as legal signature. They came to recognize that a signed text could hold the author to greater accountability. In 1641, the English House of Commons tried to reduce seditious writings by ordering the Company of Stationers, "Neither print, nor reprint anything without the name and consent of the Author" (Kernan, 1987, pp. 71–72).

Requiring the author to use a proper name had important regulatory functions; it also came to have more positive functions with the Renaissance and the emerging (innovative) cultures of science and literature that turned texts into property (Bowker, 1912, chap. 1). The handle became elevated beyond tangible property to the less tangible capital of reputation. For example, Mallon (1989) wrote that:

> from the lyric poem to the scientific footnote, the printed word is the writer's means of proving and perpetuating his existence. The identity of self and work and the prospect for continuation, are more precious to him than the promiscuous coin of the realm. (p. 237)

When the author is not known, the most informative handles are descriptions (e.g., *Dead Sea Scrolls*), and a handle can vacillate between a name and a description based on the latest scholarship on author attribution. For generations, ancient scholars attributed the authorship of a first century B.C. treatise, *Rhetoric Ad Herrenium*, to Cicero. However, through dating and style analysis (i.e., a comparison of signatures), they later concluded that Cicero was not the author and, thus, the authorial handle for that document reverted to a description. Studying authorial handles beyond proper names has become a passion among literary theorists who wish to "problematize" the author. Some critical circles theorize about authorial handles in philosophically stylized ways. For example, French criticism of consciousness makes the author incarnate in the text and rejects characterizations of the author's handle that imply "the person who wrote the work." Rather they propose handles like "the scriptor born simultaneously with the text." Consider Barthes (1981) on the author versus the scriptor:

> The Author is thought to nourish the book, which is to say that he exists before it, thinks, suffers, lives for it, is in the same relation of antecedence to his work as a father to his child. In complete contrast, the modern scriptor is born simultaneously with the text, is in no way equipped with a being preceding or exceeding the writing, is not the subject with the book as predicate; there is no other time than that of the enunciation and every text is eternally written here and now. (pp. 208–213)

Other critical circles equate the pleasure of the literary text with having an appropriately elaborated handle for the author. Ruthven (1979, p. 95), for example, made the remarkable claim that "readers like to feel the presence of a known poet behind a poem and therefore find anonymous poems much less appealing than those with known authors." One wonders whether Ruthven really means to link pleasure with having a name for the author or whether he means (more sensibly, it seems) that we derive more pleasure from works whose context of origin is known to us—a condition more likely (but far from guaranteed) when we can refer to the authorial handle with a proper name. Knowing that Milton wrote a work, but knowing nothing else of its context of origin, would hardly seem to augment reader's pleasure in reading a poem.

Authors can control their own handles to some extent through the text they create. That is, they can use the text to portray a representation of self. Cherry (1988, p. 2611) worked out a useful continuum of how an author's self-representations can inform a handle:

historical author → ethos → implied author → persona

According to Cherry, an author's ethos represents, through the text, the credibility of the historical author, the person writing in the actual social, cultural, and historical situation. Cherry (crediting Booth) associated the implied author with the constructed writer, behind the scenes, making reasoned choices about the authorial persona, the image or personality of the author as projected through the text. Distinguishing these layers of self-representation, Cherry suggested, allows us to explain discriminations in our critical judgments. Among other things, it explains how we can credit some authors as credible people pursuing a credible purpose, but with something nonetheless phony or off-putting about the person in the writing; or how we can call into question the moral purposes of an author, despite acknowledging the appeal of the authorial persona. In the first case, we accept the author's ethos and would suggest reworking the authorial persona; in the second case, we reject the author's ethos in spite of the cover of the persona.

Although authors can manipulate a handle through the art of self-representation in their texts, there are many aspects of the authorial handle that are conferred less through the text than through the author's social position and institutional affiliations. A writer working for Exxon produces documents that have only the Exxon name as handle. Such contexts provide another reason behind the distinction between authors (the source of authority) and writers (the functionary). In institutional settings, writers often prepare documents that are intended to retain the handle and authority of the institution. Bills of sale, contracts, deeds, manuals, tax pamphlets, and insurance forms are examples. Foucault (1977, pp. 125–130) had such institutional contexts in mind when he wrote that a "contract can have an underwriter, but not an author."

The printed word diminishes traces of the individual that remain visible in the immediacy of speech, but some authors manage, even in a diffuse and distant print market, to project their handle through a distinctive signature or style. Authors can forge signatures out of elements in the language which reverberate with their presence, even after the type has been set, the ink has dried, and the official name on the manuscript has been removed (i.e., independent of the code). Even under these circumstances, the author's identity may still be given away by a distinctive vocabulary, an interesting pattern of word choice, an uncommon syntax, or an unmistakable attitude. The ability of authors to give away their identity through their signatures presents problems for editors who seek to preserve the integrity of peer review. Commonly, authors with signature styles become famous for that alone, and their style or signature becomes intimately tied to their handle—giving these authors a double handle of a sort. That is to say, the author's handle will seem just a verbal reinforcement for a set of auditory sounds, meters, words, and rhythms; the author's signature, an acoustic or informational reinforcement of the handle. Such double handles apply to authors as diverse as Hemingway and Hegel.

Reference to the author can oscillate between individual descriptions and the cultural handle. Foucault (1977) developed this point in his celebrated discussion of the authoring role—what his translators sometimes call the "authoring function." He noted, for example, that the disclosure that Shakespeare was not born in the house that tourists now visit would not modify the functioning of the author's name. Yet suppose it were proved that Shakespeare had not written the sonnets that we attribute to him or had written Bacon's *Organon*. These discoveries, according to Foucault, would stir an important cultural change and alter the way in which Shakespeare's name functions as a term of reference. Foucault concluded that the name of an author is unlike that of other proper names; the author's name need not constitute a rigid reference to a specific individual but rather a fluctuating set of references to diverse cultural artifacts (e.g., the Globe Theater, *Hamlet*, etc.). In contrast, our account of language (chap. 5) maintains that all proper names (indeed all concepts) act like the author's name insofar as they have connections to a fluctuating set of diverse cultural artifacts.

If the author's name does not work exactly as a proper name, neither does it work strictly as a cultural designation. After all, Foucault reasoned, the capacity of "Rimbaud" to refer to Rimbaud does not disappear just because we discover that he did not write *La Chasse spirtuelle*. Foucault (1977) concluded that the author's name is neither a fixed individual reference nor a fixed cultural designation. The authoring role rather "oscillate[s] between the poles of [individual] description and [cultural] designation, and [the author] is not totally determined" by either one (Foucault, 1977, p. 121). The author's name is thus not exactly a flesh and blood reference nor exactly a set of key words at the mercy of indexers. The author's name, according to Foucault, is both; moreover he suggested that the only way to hold these images in juxtaposition is to appreciate the author as having a malleable status defined within a system. Within assumptions about language we endorse, this point is true for all individuals and not just authors. Moreover, we argue that the authorial role does not oscillate between individual and cultural roles but is always comprised of both.

Authorial handles in organizational environments are often used to help the power structure maintain its power.[5] The leader becomes "larger than life" by having a name singularly associated with documents that enjoy the leverage of the group. A corporate CEO becomes the handle for a document written by staff. A screenwriter's single name appears on a screenplay that actually passed across the desk of many writers. A professor's name becomes the handle for a document written by graduate students or members of a lab. The authorial handle is shaped by interactive power and communicative relationships, as well as by descriptive realities.

At the same time, authorial handles are fluid enough to allow for the occasional redefinition of power relationships. Some bureaucratic writers remain effaced in organizational handles, but others break through the shield of organizational anonymity and emerge with their own name as handle. In his early fiction, Joseph Wambaugh's handle was "a real L.A. cop"; Carl Sagan's, "an astronomer from Cornell." At some point, every new PhD's authorial handle is "that student who trained with so-and-so." And, at some point, that PhD is reviewed to find out how much the authorial handle has changed. The recent genre of the CEO book (a John Scully or Lee Iacocca detailing a rise to fame) offers readers the chance to learn, through retellings, how an executive made his (*sic*) name synonymous with the company.

Handles do not exist in isolation but in the minds of readers as part of an expansive network of information (chap. 5). The handle is a quick index, or pointer, into a reader's mental model of the text, which can include portions of the communication, representations of the code, and the reader's sociocultural elaborations of the text. Through handles and the mental models they reference, cultural knowledge becomes linked to texts in a sticky but not sedimented way. As this knowledge changes over time or regionalizes, so do handles. Readers in the South may have a range of mental models for Stowe different from readers in the North. Readers in Islamic countries may have a range of mental models for Rushdie different from readers in the West. Handles evoke different images depending upon the readers and their mental models. As previously noted, these models are dynamic and change over time.

Although handles are subject to many contingencies, there are sociocultural environments organized to control these vagaries. One such environment is academia. In academic societies, authors are regularly assessed

---

[5]In this book, we use power to mean either epistemic or nonepistemic authority. See chapter 7 for more details.

and rewarded on the social constitution of the mental models associated with their handles—the extent to which their handles are associated with new and socially accepted discoveries (chap. 9).

Fidelity

Fidelity means veridicality of representation, the property that the communication (content) transmitted by the sender will remain relatively complete and intact as it enters the environment of the receiver. A story that changes in major ways every time it is told lacks fidelity. We discussed earlier the closely perceived relationship between fixity and fidelity. Ideas diffusing across a sociocultural landscape would have no reliability were they to become corrupted beyond recognition as they moved. A communication with perfect fidelity is one in which the set of information remains unchanged across communicative transactions. The idea is not whether all readers grasp exactly the intent of the author or meaning the author attributes to the text—which is a function of comprehension as well as fidelity. Rather fidelity is concerned with, "Does the information as presented remain unchanged?" Rumors have low fidelity not because those who hear them receive different information but because they tend to pass on different information to others. Texts, on the other hand, are expected to have high fidelity, as the set of information within the communication is fixed, unalterably and durably, in code.

Complexity

Complexity is the quantity of information contained in a single communication. Many messages—graffiti, cereal boxes, roadsigns—impact the sociocultural landscape in short bursts of energy and contain only a limited content. The more content a communication can carry, the greater the potential impact (i.e., reach, authority, power) of the agent and the more interesting it may become to study the completeness of the agent's ultimate reach. It has been alleged that print had much to do with increasing the complexity of communications on a regular basis, making it routine to transmit volumes of information—hundreds of thousands of statements based on years of the author's interaction and reflection—in single bound manuscripts (Reynolds & Wilson, 1968). We argue that complexity is a property of the communication and is a function of the agent who creates the communication. Complexity is not a property of the communication technology; although the technology may enhance or inhibit the level of complexity chosen by the agent, the technology does not determine whether or not the communication will be complex.

A thick text is more complex than a short conversational turn because it can encode hundreds of thousands of statements. The thick text will take longer (i.e., more time periods) to decode because it has more pieces of information to be decoded. Notice that there is no a priori reason to believe that a reader's rate of comprehension (i.e., the amount of information in the communication that is acquired by the individual per time period) will speed up or slow down on a thick text as opposed to a shorter one. For simplicity, we assume throughout this book that the rate of information processing is constant, whether an individual is deciphering a simple sentence or a daunting manuscript. We are assuming, that is, that it takes 3 times as long to decipher 3 sentences as it takes to decipher 1; 100 times longer to read 100 pages than 1. We assume these rates of processing remain constant regardless of whether one is reading a 10-sentence children's book or *War and Peace*. This assumption may be false, but it simplifies the model we introduce in a later chapter and does not distort what we try to conclude from that model. Because of these assumed constancies in processing, furthermore, to the extent that the complexity of a text has bearing on the author's reach, it bears on the text's ultimate (i.e., over-time), not immediate, reach and, further, on the speed with which completeness of reach can be achieved.

Complexity is being reconsidered in the age of computer-based text. CD-ROM, with a storage capacity of some 550,000 pages of text, can store quantities of text too large to be conceivably packaged for a human's sustained reading. Although few single texts (other than phone books and encyclopedias) are that long, large computer companies are now packaging documentation for their workstations on ROM disks that approach 30,000 pages of text. Such documentation can remain one text in physical terms, though users often need to reorient themselves to work with it. Individuals typically think of large scale texts, such as manuals and encyclopedias (and such texts are usually logically organized), as a database of multiple texts, with separate portions of text or entries accessible on a need-to-know basis.

Agent: Individual

The communicative transaction links agents together. Typically, we think of these agents as individuals, human in makeup and form, and with particular information processing capabilities. And indeed in this section, where we lay out the basic capabilities of the actor and the consequent properties, the discussion focuses on the actor as human individual. However, as we previously noted, the agents involved in a communicative transaction need not be human, as communication technologies can make artificial agents a party to such transactions. We take up the issue of texts as artificial agents in chapter 6. For now it is sufficient to consider the basic properties of the human agent.

Situated Individualism

Situated individualism is the view that individuals are situated within a context, are integral components of a sociocultural landscape, and can only be understood by their relationships to other individuals within that system. Situated individualism does not deny the agency of individual cognition, but argues that such cognition is affected by the position of the individual within the sociocultural landscape.[6] According to this view, our understanding of an individual is dependent on an understanding of other individuals connected with the first individual. Similarly, our understanding of authors is dependent on an understanding of the readers and the bonds of knowledge that unite and separate all from the others. By dint of viewing agents in terms of their relations to others, situated individualism marks an important advance on individualism. Individuals are recognized as components of a larger sociocultural system.

A theory of the author based on the principle of situated individualism views the author in many other ongoing roles and communicative relationships (chap. 3). Moreover, a theory based on this principle is concerned not with the capacity of a very few authors to stand apart from the rest of the social world in some mythic sense but rather with the capacity of any author to integrate with that world. A systemic approach to the author as a situated individual seeks a way of describing the effects of authoring irrespective of extreme cases (i.e., cases that produce self-reflectiveness, visibility, and high social reward). From the perspective of situated individualism, there is a huge difference between understanding a system and understanding successful cases within it—the difference between understanding the American economy and obtaining a list of millionaires; the difference between understanding the electoral system and surveying the candidates who win in November. The assumption of situated individualism forces us to specify parameters of time and perspective when we discuss print interaction. Unlike the individualist who often talks about the author's meaning and influence without specifying for whom and for when that meaning and influence are meant, it is incumbent on systemic theories of the author to make these specifications.

Such a theory must specify characteristics of the sociocultural landscape. Constructuralism is such a systemic theory (Carley, 1990b, 1991b).

---

[6]Readers familiar with organization theory will recognize in situated individualism the information processing perspective of Simon (1976), March and Simon (1958), and Galbraith (1973). This perspective means that the organization limits what information is available to whom and affects the individual's behaviors and decisions. Individuals in different positions in the organizations perforce have access to different information and act differently. Thus, individual actions are affected by their relations to other individuals. Similarly, within situated individualism, the sociocultural landscape limits what information is available to whom.

When an analyst discusses an agent's meaning and influence using a constructural perspective, a variety of factors must be specified. These include, though need not be limited to: (a) the number of actors in the society under investigation; (b) the knowledge available to members of the society and the distribution of this knowledge across actors (and hence how much information any two actors share); and (c) the opportunities available for actors to interact. Given such information, the analyst can apply the theory to engage in historical reconstruction and measure the hypothetical diffusion of the agent's communication as the agent uses either oral or print technology. By tracing through the diffusion of a communication under print conditions, for example, the influence of the author can be traced. Such analyses can be done to explore the reach of a single author or the joint impact of a collection of authors. Further, this same approach can be used to examine the change in impact afforded an individual or group when different communication technologies become available.

Sociocultural Position

Every agent has a sociocultural position. At a very general level this can be considered the pattern of similarity between the agent and all other agents in the society. Sociocultural position can be measured either in terms of the set of interaction probabilities with all others in the society or the set of knowledge shared with those others. In both cases, similarity to self (the probability of interacting with self and the total amount the individual knows) also needs to be considered so that an agent knows how similar or different he or she is from all others.

Distance

Distance is a measure of the difference between communication partners. Distance has three dimensions: spatial, temporal, and sociocultural.[7] It might be measured as the number of geographic miles between the author's location and the reader's. The more geographically dispersed a population, the greater the average sociocultural distance. Temporal distance is the time span beginning when the agent (or the publisher in the case of print) first circulates the communication and ending when the receiver first accepts it. By "accept," we mean that the receiver notes that a communication has arrived, and not that the receiver acquires (i.e., learns) the information in the communication. Temporal distance might

---

[7]We see this aspect of distance as encompassing political and epistemological differences as well as other knowledge or beliefs based on differences that follow from differences in sociocultural landscapes.

be measured as the years between the time an author creates a text and a reader reads it. Sociocultural distance is the difference between the communication partners' sociocultural positions. This might be measured in a number of ways, including, but not limited to, the difference in individuals' groups, the difference in individuals' mental models, and the inverse of the degree of sociocultural overlap between individuals. The more diverse the populations represented by author and reader and the more diverse the systems of beliefs and norms those populations represent, the greater the average sociocultural distance between the author and the readership.

Mental Models

Mental models are the internal systems used by individuals to represent information and to construct meanings. All individuals have mental models. Furthermore, the existence and nature of these models (though not their content), as well as the processes by which they motivate, constrain, and adapt to actions, are endemic to the human cognitive system. Individuals use their cognition to model the world outside themselves, and on the basis of such models they engage in actions (including innovation, discovery, and communication). These models can constrain human action (e.g., they enable individuals to estimate their relative similarity with potential interaction partners in their environment). The notion of human agents using and relying on mental models to negotiate an external world permeates much of cognitive and social science. One of the most formal treatments appears in the work of Johnson-Laird (1983, p. 10), who wrote that "[H]un an beings understand the world by constructing working models of it in their minds."

Although the architecture of mental models is hotly debated among cognitive scientists, there is wide agreement that mental models rely on some type of symbolic representation scheme (see, e.g., Carley & Palmquist, 1992). Typically, within such schemes, symbols function as ideational kernels whose meaning is conferred through their association with other symbols. This is true whether the symbol happens to represent a proper name (e.g., "Shakespeare") or more general concepts or ideas (e.g., "white," "passive action," or "creates"). Such associated sets of concepts take the form of propositions in some schemes; in others, associational networks. In most characterizations, mental models are themselves discrete pieces of information (of differing size and internal complexity) that contain other pieces of information within them and that can be linked to other discrete pieces of information. Pieces of information, which comprise and contain mental models, are discrete and separable. Consequently, each piece of information, no matter how tightly linked to others in the individual's mental representation, can nonetheless be communicated separately, learned separately, lost separately, and "understood"[8] in contexts other than, and relative to, contents other than those in which the individual originally acquired it.

Mental models adapt in response to actions taken during a communicative transaction, and such adaptation in turn alters the motivation for future actions. As previously noted, mental models, their nature, and the processes surrounding them, are a feature of cognitive agents (Carley & Newell, 1990).[9] Implicit within this assumption is yet another argument against technological determinism in its strongest formulations. Proponents of such determinism (Eisenstein, 1979; McLuhan, 1962; Ong, 1958, 1971) argued that communication technologies, in particular print, changed the fundamental way in which information was understood by individuals. Supposedly, the change to print gradually moved the human cognitive system from units organized through the oral and aural senses to units organized through the visual senses. In contrast, we suggest that the basic structure of mind as a collection of mental models is part of a human condition that is not so plastic. Rather, communication technologies affect human behavior only by altering the content and rate of information supplying an agent's mental models, not by changing the architecture of the mental models themselves.

This understanding of mental models and the decomposability of the information they contain distinguishes our approach to communication from many theorists who study information diffusion. Diffusion models typically trace the movement of information across transactions but they do not capture the human decision making that regulates the trajectory of these transactions. Furthermore, diffusion theorists, typically interested in the spread of information about a very simple and undifferentiated communication (e.g., the existence of a disease, a vaccine, or a technology), tend to represent the meaning of a communication as unchanging as it moves from one transaction context to another. The mathematical models typically specified by diffusion theorists offer no formalisms for representing the reality that a communication (spoken or written) is decomposable into many components, any of which can be (and typically are) lost or newly elaborated across transactions (Katz, Levin, & Hamil-

---

[8]We place the term *understood* in quotes to bring to the reader's attention that we are not here presenting a theory of meaning and understanding. Rather we use this term as a placeholder to indicate that there is a process going on whereby others (listeners or readers) access the communication and learn at least some of the information it contains. This in turn alters their mental models. We are making no claims about the accuracy or completeness of this process.

[9]For a more detailed discussion of the cognitive agent and a process model of such an agent, see Newell (1990) and Laird, Newell, and Rosenbloom (1987).

ton, 1963; Rogers, 1982). Nor are the standard methods of diffusion theorists well suited to studying how the selective loss or inattention to pieces of information in a communication can have major public effects. On January 29, 1992, Alan Greenspan, chairman of the Federal Reserve, announced that the economy, mired in recession, seemed headed for an upswing, and so it would not be necessary to lower interest rates further. He immediately went on to reassure investors that if the economy did not pick up, interest rates would be lowered as needed. After Greenspan's announcement, the stock market suffered a precipitous drop and the newswires, trying to explain the event, reported that investors had heard the first part of Greenspan's announcement and missed the second. Diffusion theorists seldom formally address the issue of how information can be lost in the manner of Greenspan's communication. They study the adaptive effects of communication, but often at the expense of abstracting away important regularities in the decision-making and action phases of communication.

Local Consistency

Local consistency means that two individuals with identical content information will perceive their environment in identical ways, and the probability of any action will be the same for both individuals. Local consistency also means that a single individual will continue to perceive the environment in the same way and will not alter the probability of any action directed at that environment without changes in information. Because of these characteristics, local consistency precludes irrational or entirely idiosyncratic behavior.

Action Set

For each task or problem that must be resolved, every agent has an action set. This is the set of actions an individual associates with the mental model(s) relevant to the task. In this sense, action sets are the repertoires of known and relevant actions that agents associate with various tasks and situations. For example, an American classroom, a student may assume that the kinds of actions that can be engaged in are taking notes, asking questions, listening, reading, taking tests, passing notes, falling asleep, and chewing gum. This would be the student's action set. Within the same classroom, the teacher might assume that other kinds of actions can be engaged in, such as lecturing, showing films, asking questions, giving exams, and writing on a black or white board. More relevant to our purposes, an author's action set may include writing, editing, rewriting, typing, and calling editors; similarly a reader's action set may include purchasing texts, borrowing texts, and reading.

Role

A role, such as that of author or reader, is defined in terms of characteristics of a sociocultural position and action sets. This definition of role combines two features similar to sociologists and organizational theorists. Role as social position is a familiar concept to those who take a structural perspective on social systems (Blau, 1977). Role as action set is a familiar concept to those who take an institutional perspective (Skvoretz & Fararo, in press; Skvoretz, Fararo, & Axten, 1980). Role is a task-based concept integrating both position and action. Consequently, shifting tasks may lead to shifts in role. Shifts in sociocultural position, even for the same task, may lead to shifts in role.

Similarity

Similarity is a knowledge-based notion. Agents are more or less similar, according to the extent to which they share information. We use the term "information" in its broadest sense to include facts, beliefs, norms, conceptualizations, definitions, and so forth—anything that can be represented symbolically.

Relative Similarity

Relative similarity is the ratio comparing (a) the degree to which one individual is similar to another; to (b) the degree to which that same individual is similar to everyone in the social system, including him or herself (Carley, 1990b, 1991b). Judgments of similarity require very little information about the larger environment in which such judgments are made. Regardless of their differences, any two individuals can be similar to each another in a variety of respects. Judgments of relative similarity, however, do require information about the larger environment in which the judgment is made. Consequently, as the environment changes, so do perceptions of relative similarity. On a neighborhood block, Smith and Jones may perceive themselves to have a high level of relative similarity, since they are the two most interested in physical fitness. But in the local health club, Smith and Jones may perceive themselves poles apart, since Smith is a runner and Jones, a weightlifter.

Similarity, specifically relative similarity, is a fundamental basis for interaction and a central tenet of constructuralism. Applied to print, authors create opportunities to interact with readers because they show themselves, through their texts, to be similar to classes of readers; readers are able to relate their own interests to the interests addressed by the author in the text. Readers rely on judgments of relative similarity with a text when deciding to interact with (i.e., read) it. Syndicated newspaper columnists and their readers interact on the basis of relative similarities in the issues and the positions they mutually consider worth exchanging. The same is true for literary clubs and academic communities. In science, problem-oriented specialties arise as scientists find their work similar enough to one another, relative to others, to become writers and readers for each other in an invisible college (Crane, 1971). In brief, the author's claim to authority rests on an ethos of similarity, the capacity of an author to be like the reader. Since there is competition among authors for readers, at least tacitly, the extent of the author's actual authority is dependent not on just being similar to readers but in (a) the readers' perceiving the author more similar to them than other possible agents (authors, speakers), and (b) the readers having opportunities to read the text. The claim to authority rests on similarity; the actualization of authority rests on relative similarity and opportunity.

Authors do not need to specifically target their readers apart from investing their text with a set of knowledge and interests to which readers can relate. Their texts circumscribe a potential class of readers, based on mutual knowledge and interest and the availability for interaction. Viewed in this light, authors are less likely (than speakers) to address their audiences (i.e., as a discrete target with faces and names) than to circulate texts that are similar to them (i.e., entering a more anonymous marketplace). As Nystrand (1990, p. 8) aptly observed, "In describing writers and their readers, we do better to think of them less as 'addressing these readers' than as fashioning texts that do not exclude certain kinds of readers.''

Local Autonomy

Individuals have local autonomy because they act on a course determined by their own state of information and by their own unique position in the sociocultural landscape. This position, in turn, is determined by the position of many other individuals in the sociocultural landscape, itself a result of concurrent patterns of information communication and interaction. Consequently, no individual lives entirely under the thumb of any other. No individual's change of information will necessarily affect another's. No individual's shift in patterns of interaction will necessarily affect another's interaction. In this regard, individuals are loosely constrained by everyone in the society, but rarely by any one person in particular. The assumption of local autonomy is consistent with a society where no one behaves like someone else's puppet.

The principle of autonomy does not deny the existence of power hierarchies and puppet relationships, where individuals can live under the thumb of others. Yet the existence of these relationships at most suspends, rather than rescinds for all time, the general point of autonomy. To appreciate this fact, we need to distinguish epistemic from non-epistemic authority (or power). Epistemic authority is the capacity of an agent to influence the distribution of information and interaction patterns in a of society through information. This is the kind of authority (defined later) generally granted to authors in a liberal culture. An individual with an advantage of information is also likely to have an advantage of social position, which are both explicable through the ecology of information and interaction that we have been developing. Non-epistemic power is the capacity to influence these distributions in spite of, or apart from, what one knows. Non-epistemic power thus includes the capacity to effect patterns of interaction in a society (e.g., wars, invasions, occupations, corporate intrigue, takeovers) without waiting for relative similarity as a constraining mechanism.

The identification of power with non-epistemic power is a common theme of liberal political theory in the tradition of Locke and Mill. So, too, is the idea that non-epistemic power is not a primitive of society but an unhappy consequence of concentrating too much arbitrary control in the hands of too few without a system of checks and balances. Constructuralism assumes an orientation toward non-epistemic authority or power that is compatible with Lockean or Millean liberalism. Non-epistemic power relationships are assumed to be second-order modulations that act upon the more primitive social regularities rooted in the cycle of information and interaction. Non-epistemic power relationships can temporarily disrupt the assumption of autonomy guaranteed through relative-similarity-based interaction; but such relationships can never rescind the assumption altogether. Individuals can be artificially restrained from their pursuit of a self- and a cultural identity (since the two co-evolve), but they cannot be permanently wrested from their basic human nature (i.e., their tendency to pursue an identity by interacting and acquiring information about the world).[10]

---

[10]A standard criticism is that liberals represent power as a discrete relationship between individuals (e.g., a sovereign and a subject). Critics then show that power is in fact an intrinsic and continuous feature of social systems, affecting the lives of individuals in intricate and often unanticipated ways (Foucault, 1980; Lukes, 1974; Rouse, 1987). But liberalism is not bound to a discrete view of power. Indeed, once we take seriously the idea of concurrency (i.e., individuals acting in parallel, with consequences that intersect), then either epistemic power (similarity-based interaction) or nonepistemic power (interaction without the constraint of similarity) interlocks the lives of individuals in unforeseen and intricate ways. More basic to liberalism than the discreteness of power relationships is the prioritizing of epistemic over nonepistemic power, the idea that epistemic hierarchies are necessary and part of the continuous stream of social life, whereas nonepistemic—or arbitrary—hierarchies may be necessary but only as isolated disruptions from that continuity (e.g., a President who suspends habeas corpus in war time).

Constructuralism rejects, as a primitive, the notion of a hegemonic power buried deeply in the interstices of society that routinely—and seemingly without reason—obstructs people from their pursuit of a self- and a cultural identity. But to say this is not to reject the less metaphysical notion of "structural power," the idea that some individuals enjoy structural advantages over others in choosing their ideal interaction partners from the standpoint of relative similarity. Structural power falls out readily from the primitives of constructuralism: Individuals who are seeking their self- and cultural identities through interaction are in competition with all other individuals who are concurrently seeking their identities. The supply of interaction partners at any given time can be scarce and an individual's ability to compete for an interaction partner depends largely on current sociocultural position. For example, according to the principle of relative similarity, an individual who is relatively isolated in information has a higher probability of remaining isolated than one who is already well connected. Or an individual who is centrally connected to a large group in the society has a higher probability of maintaining "in group" interactions than an individual belonging to a minority group, who will find it necessary, based on the laws of numbers alone, to regularly interact with majority groups. Individuals with an advantage in information or interaction ties over others have a competitive edge to maintain that advantage. These results fall out mechanistically from principles of relative-similarity-based interaction but they also exemplify the basic features of structural power.

The fact that individual autonomy does not preclude but often results in relationships of structural power illustrates how autonomy departs from the notion of individualism. This notion overlooks the effects of social structure and concurrency on individual choice and supposes that individuals can fully determine their sociocultural position with resources they control—a refrain of the Horatio Alger myth. The assumption of autonomy, on the other hand, is much weaker than individualism because it merely denies that individuals are fully determined in their actions based on the actions of specific others. In constructuralism, autonomy and social determinism are fully compatible, for individuals are determined by the concurrent actions of individuals in the whole society, but "the whole" in this case includes the individual. Individualism says that all persons live under some one person's thumb—namely, their own. Autonomy, under the assumption of the situated individual, says that no person lives completely under one person's thumb—not even his or her own.

Immediate Comprehension

Immediate comprehension is the constraint that individuals are able to acquire new information only if they can relate the new idea to one or more ideas already present in one or more of their mental models

(Carley, 1986b, 1988, in press a, in press b).[11] Immediate comprehension guarantees that individuals learn in an incremental fashion linking new information to old. In relation to reach, immediate comprehension explains why some readers can be counted, in the long term, as members of an author's audience even when, in the short term, they are not. During some time periods, readers will not have the mental preparation to acquire the information in the author's text. But readers may fill in this background over time and find themselves receptive to ideas to which they were not previously receptive. Immediate comprehension explains how elementary students who are not ready for Shakespeare in 1980 may be ready for him in 1990; how a generation of critics who were not ready for Donne in the 19th century may "rediscover" him in the early 20th. Immediate comprehension is also used, implicitly, by some social psychologists to explain the gradual acceptance of scientific theories, especially when there is a temporal lag between the time of the theory's discovery and the time at which it commands wide cultural acceptance. According to Simonton (1988), the scientific world was not ready for a mathematical theory of heredity in 1865, but embraced Mandel in the next century. Simonton referred, implicitly, to immediate comprehension as the reason for such lags:

> [the] implications [of their discoveries] can't be connected to existing knowledge and if it can't be connected, it will be seen as undermining the current cognitive order and thereby provoke [other members of the field], at worst, to attack or, at best, to ignore the obtrusive intellectual challenge. (p. 144)

Diffusion and Reach

Diffusion is the process by which a communication is transmitted and received; reach is the result of this process, the trail of people that have been touched by the communication. Reach is thus closely allied to the concept of diffusion. The communication diffuses; people are reached. Texts diffuse; an author has reach. Individuals who are able to extend their signature within the mental models of other individuals are able to reach (or have reach) with those individuals.

It is important to recognize that reach is a concept general to all agents, their communications, and their audiences and is not unique to the

---

[11]Immediate comprehension bears some resemblance to Chafe's (1970, pp. 210–232) notion of new and old information in language. Chafe observed that every language has ways of signaling whether information in a sentence is old (assumed to have been assimilated by listener or reader) or new. Immediate comprehension is a more basic principle about textual comprehension and learning, namely that individuals cannot acquire concepts that are not tied to concepts they already know.

authorial role.[12] All individuals who can communicate have reach. The shut-in and the isolate are known for having very little reach but they have some nonetheless. Gossips or rumormongers are known for their great reach within interpersonal circles. Ancient orators with loud voices, long memories, and an amphitheater are known for their great reach as well. However, reach is particularly relevant to the author because authors are known for their extended reach, the dissemination of their ideas through mass circulation texts that can exist and circulate well past the author's lifetime. When speaking of the author's reach, we usually mean the reach of the author's text, which is an encapsulation of only a fraction of an author's knowledge at a particular point in time.

An author's reach and handle, though related, are nonetheless distinct. Consider the subtle differences between the crimes of forgery and plagiarism. Forgers steal the handle of a more public (in the context) writer in order to boost their own reach, influence, and authority. Plagiarists steal the reach of a less public (in the context) author in order to enhance their own handle (cf. Mallon, 1989, pp. 144–193).

Communication technology does not affect whether the individual has reach, but it can affect the degree of reach that can be achieved. There are various factors that can systemically restrict or extend reach. Psychological, economic, and political forces can interfere with the production of a communication, its transmission, and/or reception. As Williams (1962) insisted throughout his career, the history of communication and the advance of communication technologies does not paint an optimistic picture of a democratic increase in either the average citizen's reach or the citizen's access to information (see Smith, 1978, 1979; Seaton & Curran, 1985).

Characteristics of Reach

Reach is a property of the agent relative to a communication or a set of communications. More specifically, reach is defined as the number of people within a society who potentially or actually receive the agent's communication (or set of communications).[13] The key term here is "receive." There are multiple types of reach, both conceptually and methodologically, depending on how one defines receives. Consequently, there is no single technical definition of reach, but a family of related

---

[12]Although we can average across individuals and talk about the average reach of a message within a social system.

[13]As previously noted, the communication may contain multiple pieces of information. A text's communication potentially contains hundreds of thousands of such pieces of information.

definitions. These definitions can be viewed as variations on a theme and differ only because reach can be subclassified according to a variety of factors.

Reach varies in degree both socially—who and how many are reached by the communication—and cognitively—how much of the information in the communication is grasped by whom. For example, a gossip or rumormonger with a wide circle of friends has more social reach in terms of the sheer number of people touched by the communication than does the social isolate with few friends; however, the cognitive reach of the gossip in terms of the quality or accuracy of the communication as received by others may not effectively extend beyond that of the isolate. Shakespeare has extensive social reach—many readers in North America and Europe have some conception of Shakespeare (or, in the terms used earlier, a mental model concerning who is Shakespeare), but these readers vary in the extent of their understanding of Shakespeare (how much of the information in one of his plays) is in each of these individual's mental model concerning Shakespeare). While the social aspect of reach involves the completeness of reach (i.e., how many of the relevant individuals are reached), the cognitive aspect of reach involves the comprehensiveness of reach (i.e., how much of the information in the communication has been acquired by individuals and is now part of their mental models). Reach can be complete without being comprehensive, and comprehensive without being complete.

Distinguishing completeness and comprehensiveness is particularly important because texts typically do not contain a single idea that can be selectively grasped or ignored as a ball in flight. Rather, they can contain thousands and even hundreds of thousands of pieces of information, each of which can be noted or lost. Comprehensiveness of reach is the fraction of a communication that is understood or known by a reader (i.e., becomes part of the reader's mental model). We define the degree of cultural comprehension as the fraction of the communication known by the average individual in the society. For example, imagine a society with three readers and a text with 1,000 ideas. If the three readers, Aaron, Cassi, and Mollie, each acquire 800, 500, and 200 ideas in the communication, respectively, then their comprehension, respectively, is 80%, 50%, and 20%, and the degree of cultural comprehension is 50%. Significantly, this does not imply that all readers grasp 50%, nor that all readers who do grasp 50% grasp the same 50% of the communication. In this hypothetical society, the author has complete reach since each of the individuals in the society has read the text and knows at least one piece of information in it.

Completeness and comprehensiveness allow us to discriminate broad versus deep understanding of a text across a population of readers. Many readers in North America and Europe may be able to identify Leopold Bloom as the central character of *Ulysses*. But only a smattering of scholars across the world have an in-depth or "expert" understanding of that work. Completeness and comprehensiveness of reach can also be applied across an author's corpus of texts. Measuring the completeness and comprehensiveness of an author's reach given a corpus of works not only yields numerical scores, but further provides an authorial portrait or persona of the author as an effective cultural producer.

Reach can be considered from a potential, actual, or expected perspective depending on whether the individual's ideas can, actually do, or are expected to diffuse through and across sociocultural landscapes. Having a printing press, for example, always increases an agent's potential reach and expected reach. But if all the printed flyers ended up in a desk drawer, that potential is never actualized and the expectation never met. Potential reach is concerned with physical realities; expected reach is concerned with perceptions. Expected reach involves an individual's mental projection of the agent's reach. Expected reach is thus a subjective estimate of actual reach, an expectation that can have both a social aspect (expected number of readers) and a cognitive aspect (expected grasp of the readers).

Reach also varies in terms of whether it is immediate or ultimate. Immediate reach relies exclusively on just those primary communicative transactions—such as those that occur between an author and readers when the reader reads the author's text—that occur within the same sociocultural landscape. An orator, for example, speaking to a full house has greater immediate reach than the member of the audience who whispers comments to the person sitting in the next seat. Ultimate reach relies on both primary and secondary communication—such as those that occur when the reader hears about the author's text from another, reads a critic's review, or goes to the movie—and spans multiple contexts or sociocultural landscapes. While the orator's immediate reach is constrained to the local audience, ultimate reach depends on the network of interactions through which the communication is passed by the audience (and their audiences) after the oration is finished.

In the foregoing discussion we identified a number of properties or aspects of reach: social (which can vary in completeness), cognitive (which can vary in comprehensiveness), potential, actual or expected, immediate or ultimate. Given these properties, a set of specific types of reach can be defined based on combinations of these properties. Let us now consider some of the subclassifications of reach that are of specific interest to print-based interaction.

Immediate Actual Comprehensive Reach. This refers to the number of individuals in the agent's sociocultural environment who acquire (either because they already know or because they learn) all of the information in the communication, such that the learned information is acquired from the communication.

Immediate Actual Reach. This refers to the number of individuals in the agent's sociocultural environment who acquire (either because they already know or because they learn) at least some of the information in the communication, such that the learned information is acquired from the communication. We talk about the degree with which individuals are reached, or the extent to which the individual's communication has permeated others' cognitions and hence the culture.

Immediate Potential Comprehensive Reach. This refers to the number of individuals in the agent's sociocultural environment who can interact with the communication and can acquire (either because they already know or because they learn) all of the information in the communication.

Immediate Potential Reach. This refers to the number of individuals in the agent's sociocultural environment who can interact with the communication and can acquire (either because they already know or because they learn) at least some of the information in the communication.

Corresponding to these four definitions we create another set in terms of ultimate reach. The term *ultimate* refers here to the individual's long-term influence across the multiple sociocultural environments that result as the sociocultural landscape evolves. From the point of view of pure theory, ultimate reach occurs at the end of time or at the limit of some theoretically defined temporal process. In practice, ultimate reach can be associated with the cumulative reach of a text at the end of some temporal period of interest (making it practically indistinguishable from intermediate reach). For example, if we are concerned with the ultimate actual reach of X's work across Y years, then this is measured as the sum of readers of X's work after Y years. Yet were we concerned with the immediate actual reach of X's work, we would measure this as the number of readers who had accumulated during the first year of its publication. In this case, we have chosen "years" as our temporal units designating immediate and ultimate periods of time. The temporal units chosen for studying reach and authority need to be drawn from the specific context of authoring being investigated. For a classic work, relevant temporal units might be decades and centuries. For a trendy potboiler riding the crest of an isolated good review, the relevant unit might be days. That said, let us consider these four types of ultimate reach.

Ultimate Actual Comprehensive Reach.   This refers to the number of individuals across all sociocultural environments[14] who acquire (either because they already know or because they learn) all of the information in the communication. For ultimate reach, the receivers may receive the information in the communication either directly from the agent (primary diffusion) or indirectly, from a communication from someone else (other than the original agent) who has received that information from either a primary or secondary source (secondary diffusion). Moreover, for ultimate actual comprehensive reach, eventually all of the information in the communication is added to the individual's mental model. The individual might learn this information piecemeal over the course of many transactions involving the same communication.

Ultimate Actual Reach.   This refers to the number of individuals across all sociocultural environments who eventually acquire (either because they already know or because they learn) at least some of the information in the communication. For print, the notion of ultimate actual reach captures an author's total number of readers, both over time and across sociocultural landscapes. Ultimate actual reach, in other words, is a measure of the author's over-time interaction with readers.

Ultimate Potential Comprehensive Reach.   This refers to the number of individuals across all sociocultural environments who can eventually acquire (either because they already know or because they learn) all of the information in the communication. An author's ultimate potential comprehensive reach is the number of readers who are able to grasp all of the pieces of information in the communication, as counted across all sociocultural landscapes and all time periods. It is a measure of the author's over-time potential interaction with readers vis-à-vis a particular text. Depending on the social system of interest, this measure may include both over-time interaction with the same readers as well as over-time interaction with a changing set of readers as generations die and new generations become available for interaction. For print transactions, the author's ultimate potential reach sums across readers who are prepared to grasp the author's ideas within the current time period, as well as readers (the same or a changing set) who will be prepared to do so during later periods.

---

[14]When using the term "all sociocultural environments," we are speaking hypothetically. In practice, the researcher would define ultimate reach in terms of reach at time "x," which is clearly not the same as reach across all time and all geographic locations.

Ultimate Potential Reach.   This refers to the number of individuals across all sociocultural environments who can eventually acquire (either because they already know or because they learn) at least some of the information in the communication. In the case of immediate reach, all receivers acquire information from the original communication during the first transactions involving this communication. In a society where the only communication technology is oral or face-to-face communication, acquisition of information from the communication occurs immediately when the receiver interacts with the agent. Under oral conditions, immediate potential reach depends on the network of people who have the opportunity to interact with the agent (ego network) and are prepared to grasp the individual's ideas as contained within the communication at the time they first become available. Immediate reach is a measure of the agent's short-term actual or potential authority. The strength of that authority depends on both the number of individuals who are prepared to grasp some of the ideas and the fraction of ideas that they are prepared to grasp. Viewed in these terms, immediate potential reach is a measure of the agent's current "market," a measure of the individual's short-term sphere of potential influence.

Print technology transfers immediate potential reach from a dependency on the author's social network to a dependency on a text's social network. For an author in a print-based society, immediate reach is a measure of the agent's short-term actual or potential authority as exercised through the text, a measure of the network of readers who have the opportunity to interact with the text and who are prepared to grasp the ideas in it when they first interact with it. Viewed in these terms, immediate potential reach is a measure of the text's current market, a market influenced not only by the content of the text but by the author's handle. Because print technology makes possible interaction with a text sans human agent, authors can exert a reach and authority over readers that is not immediate but that evolves over time.

Authors, of course, differ in their immediate reach. Typically, well known authors, such as Danielle Steel, Robert A. Heinlein, and Tom Clancy, have greater immediate reach, both potentially and actually, than first-time novelists. Similarly, in academic circles, the eminent scholar has greater immediate reach than the new PhD. An author's immediate reach can change from text to text and can depend on the content of the text as well as its context.

Publishers who contract with authors naturally take into account the author's reach. Conflict between publishers and authors may arise due to differences in the type of reach in which they are interested. Publishers are rarely concerned with the comprehensiveness of the reach, simply the number of readers (i.e., the number of unit sales) who will be reached. In this sense, publishers are concerned with how many purchase the text and not how many read it or the depth with which they read it. Authors, on the other hand, have a vested interest in the comprehensiveness of their reach. Publishers, particularly when they are oriented to a bottom line, may be more concerned with immediate reach, while authors may be more concerned with their ultimate reach.

Economic and institutional factors may affect the type of reach with which publishers are concerned. When publishers are bottom-line oriented, they demand evidence of the author's immediate actual reach (i.e., what is the assured market now?). Subscription publishing in the 18th century (chap. 3) was a mechanism for having authors demonstrate their immediate actual reach prior to publication. In the 1880s, when advertising began to account for half of the newspaper's revenue and filled over half its space, advertisers in England and America became more exacting in their concerns about a newspaper's immediate actual reach and editors became responsive to their concerns. In England, Northcliffe initiated the practice of publishing his own circulation figures for the benefit of advertisers, and he challenged other newspaper editors to follow suit (Williams, 1962, p. 30–33). In America, Pulitzer started selling advertising based on circulation numbers (Schudson, 1978) and inaugurated the practice common in all media today of "metering" immediate actual reach. Despite many publishers' interest in the short-term payoff, however, those who can husband greater patience and deeper pockets for long-term planning will also support authors or publications on the basis of their ultimate potential reach (i.e., what market might this book create over the long term?).

Ultimate reach, whether potential or actual, can vary, in theory, like immediate reach, for the same author from text to text. The authority of an author and the impact of a text are often adjudicated on the basis of ultimate rather than immediate reach. The "classics" are defended precisely on these grounds—for their ultimate potential reach rather than their immediate potential reach, for their sphere of potential influence over the long run, both for a society and for an individual reader. High school students who sleepwalk through *Lear* or *Ulysses* the first time around are never dismissed from being counted within the ultimate potential reach of Shakespeare or Joyce. Bakhtin (1986) relied upon the principle of ultimate reach when he accepted an invitation from the editorial staff of *Novy Mir*, a Soviet journal, to evaluate the current state of literature. He suggested that great literature offers semantic possibilities that unfold not only across the lives of individuals but generations:

> Great literary works are prepared for by centuries, and in the epoch of their creation it is merely a matter of picking the fruit that is ripe after a lengthy

and complex process of maturation. Trying to understand and explain a work solely in terms of the conditions of its epoch alone, solely in terms of the most immediate time, will never enable us to penetrate into its semantic depths. (p. 4)

Communication technologies affect the agent's reach by affecting the communication's circulation. For example, technologies that enhance a communication's durability allow it to circulate longer. However, there is not necessarily a linear relationship between the durability of a communication and the reach of the original agent. The longer a communication circulates, the more likely it is that new audiences will never directly interact with the original author's signature and handle, but with a signature and handle that belongs to certain dominant elaborators down the chain. These elaborators may explain the original communication (or an elaboration of the original, and so on) in a way that controls word of mouth communication on the original topic. When a dominant elaboration can control word of mouth, it can potentially control the mental model of anyone who claims to have any passing social knowledge about the subject. Dominant elaborations can literally steal the reach of an original communication. For moviegoers from the 1930s, the dominant image of Boris Karloff and the Universal production of *Frankenstein* stole the reach of Shelly's monster and the classic novel that introduced it. For a generation of moviegoers who saw Oliver Stone's *JFK*, it may be that Kevin Costner will steal the reach, relative to the Kennedy assassination, once held by Earl Warren and Gerald Ford.

A defense of classic texts, we noted in chapter 2, is that many attempts are made in every generation to steal their reach (so profound is their cultural timeliness), but the thievery is never (and, it is argued, can never be) complete because the original dominates any adaptation in its capacity to help elaborate the culture further. Significant cultural producers are often characterized as agents who generate communications that resemble the classics in the extent of their reach. Such cultural producers are persons who are able to have reach well beyond the bounds of personal proximity, to have significant ultimate reach. Such individuals are able, given the appropriate communication technology, to reach well beyond their personal social networks. For many proponents of individualism, the designation "author" is employed as an honorific to denote just these significant cultural producers. It is clear from the foregoing discussion, however, that these significant cultural producers differ only in the extent of their reach. They differ from other individuals only in degree, not in kind.

Even this brief discussion illustrates that reach is a fairly rich and complex concept and that, when used, it must be qualified to indicate the type of reach under examination. Indeed, there may be aspects of reach that we have not discussed. Reach is a property of all individuals in all sociocultural systems. Reach is important, in large part, because there is a pervasive and important relation between reach and authority: the greater the individual's reach, the greater the individual's communicative authority. Communication technologies, finally, can affect an individual's potential reach. Print, for example, increases the asynchronicity, fixity, durability, and multiplicity of a communication, and therefore its reach.

Rate of Reach

The rate of reach is the rate at which an agent's ideas move through a social system. Rate equals change per unit time (e.g., 60 miles per hour). Under print conditions, the rate of an author's reach can be thought of as the number of new readers per time period (e.g., 100 copies sold per day) for a given text. Exactly how the rate of reach is measured depends on the type of reach being considered. An author may have a slower rate of reach if one is concerned with monitoring complete comprehension more than lower levels of comprehension. Shakespeare's rate of reach relative to readers who have heard of him and, perhaps, read *Hamlet* is assuredly faster than it is relative to readers who have memorized significant passages of his plays. The rate of reach often varies over the lifetime of a text and can continue to change after the author's death. In diffusion studies of scientific texts (Price, 1963), it has been repeatedly shown that the rate of reach of most scientific texts escalates slowly at first, then more sharply, and then finally tails off, forming the familiar s-shaped adoption curve illustrated in Fig. 4.2.

Authority

Agents have authority to the degree that they can potentially bring about change in the sociocultural landscape, either immediately or over time. For authors, authority is tied to the diffusion of a text and the sociocultural change that can occur in response to that diffusion. Print made it apparent that authorial authority, like diffusion, was a matter of degree and not kind, a matter of "more or less" not "all or none." Even very insignificant authors—those whose texts produce little change within a social system—still have some authority. The authority they command may produce change that remains invisible from the perspective of the system overall but is there nonetheless. An agent's authority is assigned by an observer looking in on a social system and measuring the change produced by an agent's communication within the system. Different observers may bring different assumptions and instruments of measurement

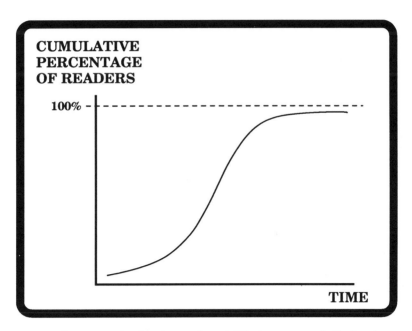

FIG. 4.2.   Example of ojivle or s-shaped diffusion curve typically found
in studies of information and technological diffusion.

to bear, which means that claims about authority can be highly disputed. Relative similarity as a basis for interaction is likewise a basis for
authority. Authors acquire and lose authority as their relative similarity
with members of the reading public changes.

We need to distinguish relative similarity, which provides the author
with the fundamental basis for achieving authority, with other individual and social mechanisms through which authors can exercise their
authority. Without similarity, the channels for authors exercising authority probably would not have actual or longstanding effect. Yet without
channels for exercising authority, the author's relative similarity with
readers might remain a hidden and so, ineffective, fact. Much of the sociological literature has focused on the channels for exercising authority, leaving implicit the basis for achieving it through relative similarity.

For example, Weber (1968) discussed disparate channels for exercising authority by classifying authority into charismatic, traditional, and
rational–legal authority. According to Weber, individuals exercise charismatic authority when they are able to identify themselves with the central problems, concerns, and hopes of people's lives. Charismatic
authority is at the root of the Greek notion of *rhetor* and the Roman notion of *orator*. Burke's (1969, p. 19) name for charismatic authority is

"identification," the capacity of a speaker to identify interests, concerns, and goals with an audience. In charismatic authority, the exercise and achievement of authority is close knit because the agent exercises authority by calling attention to standing similarities with others (i.e., to the relative similarity that binds the agent to others). Traditional authority, for Weber, is founded in the sanctity of age-old rituals and powers. Rational–legal authority is founded in the authority vested in laws and constitutions conferred by natural or divine law. As with charismatic authority, traditions and constitutions are attempts to exercise the authority of similarity, but they do so by appealing to a similarity with readers that is broader than the personage of the author and extends to the similarity of heritage.

   Giddens (1984, 1987, pp. 195–223) also discussed channels for exercising authority in terms of two types of resources—what he calls "allocative" and "authoritative"—that agents use to exercise authority. Allocative resources are raw materials and other material goods; they include the means of production including, but not limited to, information and communication technology. Allocative resources include the goods produced through the interaction of these raw materials and technologies. In the history of authoring, allocative resources include reed and papyrus rolls, the alphabet, the caravans that escorted a scribe to the library at Alexandria, codex tablets, steam presses, card catalogues, automatic indexing systems, word processors, and railway paperbacks (Giddens, 1987, pp. 258–259). Authoritative resources are, for Giddens, an agent's capacity to organize the social world, to bring others, and the allocative resources they control, under the agent's will. Authors, for example, must have enough authoritative resources to convince a publisher, with allocative resources, to commit to their work. And they must command enough authoritative resources within the text itself to attract a larger audience, and the various resources under their control, to it.

   Giddens maintained that it is the interaction of authoritative and allocative resources that allows for human agents to expand their influence on social structures. Allocative resources in particular—print and other technologies for storing and transmitting information—have allowed individual agents to spread their influence at ever greater distances across time and space (Giddens, 1987, p. 260). To Giddens, the augmenting of allocative resources, especially writing and print, has been fundamental to the expansion of cultural production. At the same time, Giddens claimed, authoritative resources have themselves changed with changes in allocative resources. For example, before print, the role of the individual author did not become visible unless a text was found to be a transgression of church or government interests. After print, the author became visible as a property holder. This is an effect that an evolving allocative resource like print can have on the evolving authoritative resources of the author. From our perspective, allocative resources are technological conditions external to the individual that affect the nature of the communicative transaction. Hence, allocative resources define potential and actual changes in the nature of the communicative transaction and can influence sociocultural organization and change. The allocative resource of print and its implications for sociocultural organization and change dominate the focus of Part II.

The author's authoritative resources consist of knowledge and position in the sociocultural landscape, the sociocultural inheritance with which the author is currently vested and brings to any current transaction. Although the literature has remained focused on the channels for exercising authority, these channels are, from our vantage, second-order factors that extend or limit the natural authority the author can summon through similarity with readers. For example, while authors ultimately rest their authority over readers (i.e., the authority of their text) in relative similarity, they can be described, in different circumstances, as exercising their authority through de facto, coercive, arbitrary, contractual, or paternalistic means. For example, authorial authority may not be coercive (Airaksinen, 1988), but can still be exercised under coercion (e.g., decreeing the writings of chairman Mao). Authorial authority is not necessarily de facto, but can certainly be exercised under de facto conditions (e.g., a teacher assigning a reading). Authorial authority need not be whimsical nor arbitrary but is regularly channeled through markets that seek to exploit whim and arbitrariness (e.g., the exercise and diet book market). Authorial authority may not be rooted in paternalism toward the reader "for the reader's own good," but, as we saw in chapter 3, 19th-century Methodists and Bethamites sought to have authors exercise authority over readers with the reader's own good in mind.

In the genealogy of the author, print was an important watershed for augmenting the level of authority potentially available to the author. Prior to print, a manuscript reflected the sovereign authority of the institution controlling its production and dissemination. By controlling the text's diffusion, the institution controlled the author's potential authority. This point lies at the heart of Eco's *The Name of the Rose*, in which the church could forbid monks from copying texts and so could prevent authors, such as Aristotle, from achieving much reach or authority. Throughout written history prior to print, institutions could define the author's authority by controlling the reproduction and dissemination of texts. Cheaper forms of mechanized printing eventually mitigated this institutional control by making it easier to put unauthorized texts into the hands of the public. Through print, the power of the free market to limit authorial authority began to grow beyond the power of the government and the church (chap. 3).

The basis for authorial authority has been greatly debated in literary circles. For example, traditional literary critics—individualists in their perspective—typically gauge authority purely as a cognitive phenomenon, a judgment about the quality of a text and, by implication, the quality of the mind that produced it. Yet such a cognitive interpretation of authority is counterintuitive because it allows an author with negligible social impact to claim non-negligible authority. Recluse authors with brilliant but unread manuscripts could, on the cognitive account, be designated the most authoritative of their day. Nevertheless, traditional literary scholars (Brooks & Warren, 1959) viewed an encapsulation of the author's cognition—the textual content and a particular reading derivable from it—as the basis of authorial authority. They considered (or at least alleged to consider) certain readings of canonical texts as universal time capsules, more or less impervious to the contextual maelstrom surrounding them. They translated authorial authority to mean the authorized reading of a literary work.

Many postmodernists have subsequently argued that authorized readings cannot be the basis of authorial authority because of the sheer divergence of readings (Derrida, 1978). Other critics, seeking to avoid the relativist implications of some currents in postmodernism, claim that there are too few reading conventions to establish whose context—the author's or some reader's—should be given more weight during the interpretive process. They thus sought to establish weighting norms for interpretation—norms that gave inordinate weight either to the author's context (Booth, 1979, pp. 272–275, 1988; Hirsch, 1972, 1982, pp. 48–52; Tully & Skinner, 1989, pp. 57–63) or the reader's (the early Fish, 1980, for a historical review; Larmarque, 1991, for a more analytic review). Unlike the more radical implications of postmodernism, these efforts did not question the efficacy of authorized readings but only the reliability of current hermeneutic methods (or rhetorics, as Fish, 1980, would say; see also Harris, 1989; Merod, 1987; Weber, 1987, p. 36) to establish them.

For Derrida (1988), however, authorial authority cannot be reduced to authorized reading because of the inherent uncertainties of interpretation, uncertainties which reading necessarily pulls from the past and writing necessarily projects into the future. An example of this Derridean uncertainty arises on a recurring basis in the interpretation of case law. Relying on assumptions of indeterminacy, Dworkin (1982) noticed that interpreting case law depends upon previous cases "reaching" across time and space to "fit" present and future ones. However, Dworkin noted, since the contexts extending the reach of the legal principle are themselves not fully commensurable, neither are the criteria defining fit across these contexts:

Suppose the Supreme Court of Illinois decided, several years ago, that a negligent driver who ran down a child was liable for the emotional damage suffered by the child's mother who was standing next to the child on the road. Now an aunt sues another careless driver for emotional damage suffered when she heard, on the telephone many miles from the accident, that her niece had been hit. Does the aunt have a right to recover from that damage? (p. 263)

Does the decision about the mother on the road cover the aunt on the telephone? Without a retrospective projection of the authority of historical intent, a judge would not understand the law that is there to be used. Yet without a forward projection of an authoritative political theory— answering how the world should be shaped—the judge would not know how to use the law that is there to be understood. The judge is faced with the uncertainty of deciding which past to project into the present and which future to let the past reverberate toward. The judge cannot resolve the uncertainty but can only respond to it, and the judge's response will become part of the historical legacy of the principle, the story of the law's authority.

Dworkin's insight is important because it helps us trace the open-textured social and political dimensions of interpretations that often purport to be deduced from closed-form interpretive rules. These disjunctions across cases are typically suppressed in the styles of literate behavior, which permit the writer—in this case, the judge—to relate distant cases through a continuous historical present tense—as if they occupied the same universe of co-temporal reference (Geisler, 1990). Thus, the judge can write as if the rulings for Case A and B (indeed, the entire literature of statue law) occupy a single series of proximate conversational moves (e.g., "Case A affirms the right of the mother to sue and, with Case B, we are faced with whether this right extends to the aunt").

Authors cannot rely for their authority on the basis of so-called authoritative (temporally static) readings. Efforts to make this reduction land us in a number of quagmires; we would then need to doubt whether the authors of the Bible or Shakespeare have attained authority! The authority of many prize-winning authors would have to be dismissed in light of their results being interpreted diffusely, without the benefit of an official reading. In their pathbreaking book on scientific work, Gilbert and Mulkay (1984, chap. 5) reported on a Nobel prize winner in biochemistry whose contributions are still a matter of debate among peers occupying the same specialty. In this case, the authority of the Nobel-winning text cannot be explained as a result of an authorized reading and other factors need to be identified.

The point is not to deny authorized readings nor the capacity to manufacture such readings by appealing to coarse-grained descriptions about a textual content. Indeed, if we settle for a large enough grain size of description, we can always manufacture an authorized reading (e.g., *Romeo and Juliet* is a tragedy). The point is rather to claim that such readings are too tenuous a soil on which to plant the judgment of authorial authority. Efforts to determine authorized readings abstract from, and hence overlook, the reader's own construction of the purposes for reading and the author's for writing (Flower, 1988). The idea of an authorized reading further assumes that the author's text can be understood relative to a single transaction site, a single reading. Such an assumption, ironically, actually denies the canonical author authority in other contexts of reading and among readers who insist on reading against the party line.

Pappas (1989, p. 331) likened the healthy relationship between writer and reader to that of a healthy relationship between therapist and patient. The therapy will not work if the therapist does not exert some authority over the interaction; but neither will it work if both allow or assume that the therapist's authority will not at some point be transformed by the patient's own initiatives. An author's authority, in any case, is not jeopardized merely with the dissolution of certain authoritative readings of the text, as Shakespeare's cultural presence is not reduced simply because he elicits divergent readings. Clearly, authorial authority, though distinct from the readings, is nonetheless related to, and dependent on, being read.

Seeking to correct the conflation of authorial authority and authorized readings, postmodernists generally argue that cultural artifacts (including texts) occupy multiple sites of interpretation within sociocultural landscapes with both the sites and structures changing over time. The multiple positions of interpretive sites make it futile to base the authority of the artifact in a single authorized interpretation. For example, since the 1950s, Sundays in America have arguably moved from a religious image to one that includes the football ritual as much as the church ritual. Since the 1940s, Frankenstein and Dracula have gradually moved from straight horror to camp, from Boris Karloff to Herman Munster and from Bela Lugosi to George Hamilton. While the literal references to Sundays, Frankenstein, and Dracula may not have changed over time, their elaborative histories, their connections with other concepts, and the reach of these changing connections, have.

At the same time, some politically minded postmodernists (Kessler, 1987; Merod, 1987; Said, 1983; Williams, 1962, 1981) contend that just because the meaning of an artifact (or text) can become widely distributed over time does not imply that meanings disperse democratically. Quite the contrary. Individuals with uncommon authority, controlling the dominant outlets of dissemination, hold an unfair advantage in extending the reach of their particular meanings beyond the reach achieved by less authoritative agents working through less visible forums.

Since we have already raised Frankenstein, consider the plethora of meanings associated with that symbol. Glut (1984) catalogued over 2,800 cultural artifacts depicting the character since Shelley's 1818 novel, including series, poems, articles, critiques, plays, films, comics, satires, cartoon strips, and television programs. Nonetheless, of this enormous number, Glut suggested that only three in particular have had a truly disproportionate influence in shaping the symbol's definition into what we know of it today: (a) Shelly's original novel; (b) the 1931 Universal film directed by James Whale; and (c) Peggy Webling's stage play from which the film was adapted. Would the cultural domination of Shelly, Whale, and Webling over the image of Frankenstein be an argument for the unusual quality of their work and a reason for making them (a book, a play, and a movie) required reading (or viewing) for future generations? For many postmodernists, this question ridicules—but still does justice to—the dubious reasoning behind reading the classics for their quality. For Williams (1961), authors exhibit authority just by controlling the institutions that keep their work in circulation: It is the fact of interaction with readers, not the specific terms of that interaction, that are decisive for authority. In summary, postmodernists have recognized, by and large, a social basis to authorial authority, one going well beyond the text.

Some postmodernists err, however, when they make the social world (or context) the sole basis of authorial authority—at the expense of the author's cognition and textual content. While certain postmodernists approach the author from the assumption of situated individualism, they also deny the integrity of individuals within that very system (see Smith, 1988, for a critique of the diminished role of the individual in many strains of postmodern thought). They assume instead that individual cognition is itself a social construct made possible through language; thus, they seek to associate authority not with the individual author but with the social system of language. For example, for Foucault (1977), the individual presence filling the authorial role was an entirely dispensable commodity—authority resides in the social system of meaning that gives the author visibility. For Barthes (1981), language was the authoritative resource required for configuring and reconfiguring texts into new combinations. Barthes employed the term *writing* to indicate these protean properties of language, and he asserted that ''a text is made of multiple writings, drawn from many cultures and entering into mutual relations of dialogue, parody, contestation.'' In Barthes' view, a theory of the author must address itself to the basic question of what writing is—What is it that gets extended when texts are extended through time and space? What is the special malleability of ''writing'' that tolerates this extensionality while still anchoring local meaning? Rather than the individuals who author, Barthes envisioned writing as the authoritative agent of social change. He assumed that the authorial role is an artifact of writing and that to trace authority back to the individual author is not to trace it back far enough. Authority resides in the distributional potential of writing itself and "to give a text an Author" is only to "impose a limit on that text" and "to close the writing" (1981, pp. 211–212). Derrida (1976) similarly positioned authority in what he called the "iterability" of language and the property of language to "graft" itself into new forms across writing events (see also Culler, 1982, pp. 135 ff.; Schilb, 1989, p. 433).

We reject the anti-individualism in these strains of postmodernism and, with it, the attempt to wrest individuals from any cognitive basis for authority. The Barthian view of the author as the localized site of culturally diffuse writings is useful for tracking the influences of a text, but it fails entirely to account for the author's perceived agency and authority. At the other pole, we reject individualism and its attempt to wrest individuals from any social basis for authority. Situated individualism, along with the simultaneous construction of the self and society, corrects many of the simplifications inherent in individualism without forcing us to abandon (as certain postmodernists abandon) the agency of historical individuals. For us, a theory of the author and authorial authority is still a theory about individuals (albeit individuals situated in a social system) and not about the various languages and writings that happen to converge, for a historical moment, in the personage of the author. The postmodern impulse to deny the primacy of individuals within social systems stems from an overreaction to the naive individualist's Horatio Alger stories, linking the effort of single authors (the Shakespeares and Stowes) to profound cultural and (in Stowe's case) social change. These individualist stories explain the author's authority solely through the cognitive traits of the author and the content of the author's text. They do not take into account the further reliance of authorial authority on the underlying sociocultural landscape in which the author and the text are situated. Some traditionalist literary critics err in undervaluing the social basis for authority; some postmodernists err in undervaluing the cognitive basis for authority. Authorial authority, however, has both a cognitive and a social foundation. The story of an author's authority must include information about the author's cognition, the textual content, and the enveloping and evolving sociocultural landscape. To deny cognition is to deny the individual agency. To deny content is to deny the individual action. And to deny the evolving sociocultural landscape is to deny the dynamics whereby authority increases and erodes over time.

Communicative Transaction: The Cornerstone

The communicative transaction is the cornerstone of the ecology whose components we have described. Through the communicative transaction, individuals interact, communicate, adapt, and reposition themselves in the sociocultural landscape. The communicative transaction is a cyclic process in which the full cycle is repeated each time period. Through each cycle of the transaction, social structure and culture co-evolve. Within each cycle, individuals go through three distinct phases (Fig. 4.3): (a) they are motivated through considerations of relative similarity to decide on an interaction partner; (b) they act to communicate information to the partner; and (c) they adapt their position in the landscape given their own changes in knowledge, even as the landscape adapts itself to the totality of changes that have taken place across the entire population. This is the sense in which the life of individuals and society as a whole co-evolve. These phrases are called, respectively, motivation, action, and adaptation (see Carley, 1991b, for a general orientation relating each of these phases to Turner's (1988) comprehensive theory of social interaction).[15] These three phases—motivation, action, and adaptation—follow each other in a never-ending cycle. In Fig. 4.3, the movement in time is indicated by lines growing darker with each new cycle. Throughout these phases, individuals act concurrently.

Briefly stated, motivation concerns the cognitive and affective decision making that informs the choice of an interaction partner. Action involves the communication of information once an interaction partner has been located. Adaptation involves collectively updating everyone's new state of knowledge in conjunction with the information received during exchanges. During every subsequent time period, the three phases are repeated and the cycle remains unbroken. The ordering of the three phases within each time period is irrelevant within constructural theory. Motivation can precondition social communication and adaptation. But social communication and adaptation can also precondition motivation. This flexible ordering marks an important departure between constructural theory and Turner's (1988) theory, which makes cognitive factors (concerned with the agent's knowledge and motivation) the driving force behind social effects (exchanges and adaptation). In contrast, in construc-

---

[15]These phases are similar in spirit to those of Turner's (1988) social interaction theory. The motivation phase corresponds with Turner's motivation phase of social interaction, the considerations that induce individuals into an interaction. The action phase corresponds with Turner's interactional process, what actually happens during an interaction. The adaptation phase corresponds to Turner's structuring phase, the results of an interaction on the individuals interacting and the larger social units in which the interaction takes place.

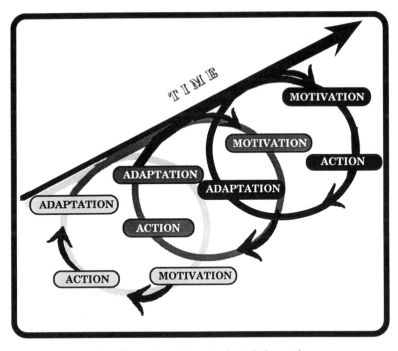

FIG. 4.3.   The interaction–knowledge cycle.

tural theory, social factors are as likely to drive cognitive events as the other way around.[16] An individual's goal-directed cognition can contribute to the planning of social effects; yet cognition can also result from individuals falling into social situations, unplanned. From the point of view of author–reader interaction, this means that finding a text to read can result from a calculated literature review (i.e., cognition conditioning a social interaction with a text) or from a chance meeting with a person making a book recommendation (i.e., a social communication conditioning cognition). A robust theory of social interaction, including the interaction of readers and texts, cannot afford to put cognitive variables exclusively in charge of social ones or social variables exclusively in charge of cognitive ones. The influence between cognitive and social parameters is two-way, and neither set of parameters occupies the driver's seat at all times.

---

[16]In constructural theory, social factors can drive cognitive factors. Yet social and cognitive phenomena maintain their integrity as autonomous realities, derived from the different primitives of interaction and knowledge. This is different from social construction, which seeks to reduce cognitive entities to social ones.

Concurrency

Individuals act concurrently when they act more or less at the same time, with the results of their actions having interdependent consequences for each other's future actions. Concurrency is a fundamental feature of social systems where multiple agents compete for interaction partners more or less at the same time. The outcome of such concurrent action shapes the sociocultural landscape and affects the competition and decision making that will go on during later time periods. Concurrency makes compatible two ideas that are often mistaken as incompatible, namely, that individuals can exert historical agency and that the societal consequences of any single individual's actions are constrained by others. Individuals can make a difference, in other words, but the difference they make is not independent of the difference other agents are trying to make.

Concurrency, though tacitly acknowledged, is rarely considered an explanation of social phenomena. Yet the very basis for change in the sociocultural landscape is the concurrent actions and adaptations of the individuals that comprise a society. Authors do not sit idle waiting for readers; readers do not sit idle awaiting new texts to read. Each individual, author and reader, continually acts, adapts, learns, and seeks interaction partners based on these dynamic states. An interesting consequence of such concurrent action, adaptation, and learning is that individuals can be "out of sync" with one another. Their memories, however historically accurate, may not reflect the true current state of the world. The author who started an epic on the "red menace" prior to *perestroika* will likely find the actual reach of the text disappointing compared to authors who have been timely enough to come to market with texts describing a balkanized former power plagued by an ailing economy. In a concurrent world, where well-laid plans can be nullified in the process of trying to execute them, discrepancies often emerge between perception and reality as well as expected and actual reach.

Individuals live their reality in the microworld of interaction. Yet they can effect macrostructures insofar as they are part of all the concurrent interactions that affect it. Individuals thus have control over the composition of the sociocultural world but it is limited control, constrained by the control exerted by all other individuals. However, individuals maintain their integrity as agents due to their local consistency and autonomy. In chapter 9 we return to these assumptions as they relate to the Renaissance assumptions of progress and rationality.

Motivation

Motivation covers the considerations that bring individuals who hold different sociocultural positions to attempt interaction with one another. In this phase, individuals rely on relative similarity judgements to decide on a possible interaction partner within the sociocultural landscape. That partner can be another individual, including him or herself,[17] or an artificial agent, such as a text.

Action

There are a variety of actions in which an agent can engage, and this variety is defined by the agent's current action set. Among those actions most relevant to our purposes are: communicative actions, the choice of a partner, the choice of information to communicate, the creation, transmission, and receiving of the communication.

Like Blumer's (1969) symbolic interactionism and Turner's social interaction theory (1988), constructuralism assumes that interaction and communication are the basic social actions in which individuals engage. This does not suggest that all actions are fundamentally or even usefully conceived as exclusively information-based interactions—washing the car and jogging are actions which are not on their face symbolic interactions. What is suggested, rather, is that to the extent an action can provide input to the constitution of the social world, the action can be expressed in terms of information-based interaction. This is not news to cultural theorists and semioticians, who often seek the cultural meaning in seemingly pure actions like washing the car and jogging. To do so, they routinely re-represent these activities as having a content that can be communicated and used to shape culture and social structure. This step of re-representation is what the symbolic interactionists had in mind when they claimed that, without information-based interaction, the texture of social life with its institutions, roles, religions, rituals, and so forth would have no vehicle for development.

For constructuralism, principles of interaction function at the microlevel of social organization and do not imply—as American functionalism (Parsons, 1937, 1949) implied—the immediate achievement of stability or consensus at the macrolevel of social structure. We should not confuse a social world built from microacts of interaction and communication with a social world free of conflict or instability. The mere fact of communicating information need not lead, in the short term, to improved interpersonal understanding. A little bit of interaction can actually exacerbate conflict by increasing miscommunication—"I think you understand the communication in the same way I do" (but you do not)—and false consensus—"Given what you've just said, I think you would agree with me on this point" (but you do not). Furthermore, in the short term, there is nothing necessarily stabilizing or consensus-producing about

---

[17]This is an example of internal communication or reflection.

genuine understanding. In many cases, conflict will arise from genuine understanding (e.g., understanding the statements of the bigot). Often our interactions teach us with whom we would rather not be dealing in the long term. In summary, then, combining the micro-organization of the social world into interactions does not impose any unrealistic short-run assumptions of stability, consensus, or the absence of conflict at either the micro or macrolevel of society.

Adaptation at the Individual Level

Individuals adapt in response to the actions of their communication partners. Such adaptation can take the form of learning any or all of the information in the communication that was not previously known. Immediate comprehension limits this process. As individuals adapt, their mental models change. Consequently, they change their sociocultural position (and their motivation) for future interactions. Such individual adaptation, inasmuch as it occurs across many individuals, has social and cultural repercussions in terms of the diffusion of information, social stability, and the consensus that is reached across individuals.

Co-Evolution of Self and Society

Because multiple individuals interact and adapt concurrently, their mental models and consequent patterns of interaction co-evolve. As a consequence, the distribution of knowledge in the society changes and, with it, the culture; as a further consequence, the pattern of interaction in the society changes and, with it, the social structure. Through the concurrency of multiple over-time changes in both knowledge and interaction at the individual level, changes at the social level ensue and result in a modification of the sociocultural landscape. In a phrase, self and society co-evolve.

The relationship between situated individuals (including situated authors) and society is one of symbiotic mutual influence. The co-evolution that marks this relationship is to be contrasted with the "great person" impact attributed to the (canonical) author under individualism. It is further to be distinguished from the "socially determined" impact attributed to authors by many postmodernists. Led by heroic stories of greatness, individualists tend to overlook situatedness and social position as determinants of an author's impact. Led by the thesis of cultural determination, postmodernists tend to overlook the author's own mental models and text, working in conjunction with the sociocultural landscape, as co-determinants of authorial impact.

Measures of Adaptation at the Social Level

Social and cultural change can be measured in a variety of ways. Three of these measures are of particular interest to the study of the communicative transaction: diffusion, stability, and consensus.

Diffusion. When people receive new information (i.e., content they did not previously know), we say that the information has diffused to them. The level of diffusion is the fraction of the population to which the information has diffused. Over-time measures of diffusion involve the number of time periods before some fraction of information in a communication reaches some fraction of readers. When 100% of the communication has reached 100% of the population, we say that the communication has completely diffused throughout the society (and has also achieved complete ultimate actual comprehensive reach). Suppose an author issues a communication within a sociocultural system and we want to ask the following types of questions: How long (i.e., how many time periods) will it take before everyone in the social system knows everything in the communication? How long will it take before 90% of the individuals in the social system know at least 20% of the communication? How long before 5% of the individuals know 1% of the communication? Questions of this kind inquire into the over-time characteristics of a communication's diffusion.

Stability. Stability is the degree to which the sociocultural environment can not shift. Stability can be measured in terms of the fraction of available information shared by any two individuals, as averaged across all dyads in the society (see Carley, 1990a, 1991b, for an extended discussion of stability). The more available information the average dyad shares, the less new information there is to communicate and learn. The less new information exchanged and learned, the less opportunity there is for their belief, opinions, and interaction probabilities to change. The fewer such changes, the more stable the society. Consequently, the more available information the average dyad shares, the more stable the society. A society whose members share, on average, 5% of the available knowledge is thus more stable than one whose members share just 1% of cultural knowledge. In the extreme (typically unreal) case when individuals within a society share 100% of their knowledge, we say that the society has reached a state of complete stability. In a completely stable society, nothing can change because no one has new or unfamiliar information that can disrupt existing patterns of interaction. In principle, with enough time, any social system that is both demographically closed (i.e., maintains the same set of individuals without emigrants or immigrants) and culturally closed (i.e., no new ideas are discovered) will reach complete stability.

Consensus. Consensus is the degree to which the individuals in the sociocultural environment share the same belief about some focal idea or decision point (Carley, 1989a). Consensus can be measured as the fraction of interaction partners in a society who share, either at the same time period or over time, the same belief about some focal idea or decision point. A belief is formed by evaluating known information in terms of its pros and cons vis-à-vis the decision to be made. Whether a piece of information is pro or con can be thought of as a fixed weight, true for all individuals. Consider a belief like "Washington was a good president." This belief can be thought of as the result of having examined many individual pieces of knowledge, each of which either positively or negatively disposes one toward this belief. It is entirely conceivable that interaction partners will share beliefs even when they do not share knowledge. Two people can agree that Washington was a good president although they each make this judgment on the weight of different knowledge (e.g., some will make this judgment based on the myth of his honesty; others, on his role in the American Revolution). Over time, agreements based on different and incomplete knowledge easily dissolve, especially as people interact further and acquire new knowledge with different weights. Consensus in a society does not fully stabilize until the society itself has reached a high state of stability.

AXIOMS

We now relate some definitions from the previous section to the axioms or orientating assumptions of constructuralism. These definitions contain many implicit axioms but we highlight several additional axioms that seem most pertinent to understanding the communicative transaction, and that may not be immediately obvious from the foregoing definitions. Some of these axioms are not new and have precursors in prior literature; however, their mobilization for a unified theory of the communicative transaction is new. Clearly, additional axioms exist, and we make no claims that the brief discussion to follow represents a complete axiomatic system. Rather, we present only a few key axioms to introduce the reader to the processes that underlie the dynamic system we use in later chapters to examine the impact of print. Despite their incompleteness, these axioms, in conjunction with the foregoing definitions, make it possible to deduce a number of theorems about interaction, communication technology, and sociocultural change.

Axiom: Individuals are Situated Within Sociocultural Systems

We take a situated individualistic perspective, and take it as axiomatic that individuals are situated within sociocultural systems. As such, individuals can only be understood by considering the system of which they are a part. It follows that authors, being individuals who happen at a particular time to fill an authoring role, can only be understood by considering the readers and the bonds of knowledge and interaction that unite them within a single mutually adjusting system.

Axiom: Individuals Have Mental Models That Limit Behavior

In addition, we take a cognitive perspective and take it as axiomatic that individuals have mental models that limit their behavior. Though living in an information rich environment, individuals are limited in what information they know and their ability to process information (Simon, 1983). A cognitive perspective encompasses and adds precision to the perspective of humans as boundedly rational and limited information processors (Carley & Newell, 1990). As we discussed, the cognition of individuals is comprised of a set of mental models, themselves comprised of separable and discrete pieces of information. Such information limits all behaviors, including choices regarding interaction partners, actions in which to engage, information to be communicated, information to be acquired, and perceptions and meanings to be altered. Such information also limits the individual's ability to produce new information. Mental models thus affect all three phases of the communicative transaction: motivation, action, and adaptation.

Let us consider for a moment the effect of such constraints on agents. In any communicative action, agents can only generate or attend to one communication at a time. Every text an author allocates time to write defines a time when other possible texts never get composed and other noncomposing activities (talking, sleeping, washing the car) never get done; in turn, every text a reader allocates time to read defines a time in which other texts forego a potential reader and other nonreading activities get tabled. These temporal choices, moreover, reverberate to and structure later choices, as choosing to attend to a communication or not can become a habit increasingly strengthened or extinguished. The cognitive constraints on communication are important because they mean that the social world built through communicative transactions will involve competition for attention and decision making about how to spend one's time.[18]

Axiom: Individuals' Mental Models Adapt

From a cognitive perspective, mental models are dynamic entities that continuously adapt. An invariant of human behavior is that individuals learn. Put individuals in any situation and they will learn. They may not learn what someone wants them to learn. They may not learn what they want to learn. They may not learn something that will improve their performance or ability to make future decisions. They may not learn quickly. Their learning may be undetectable, both to observers and even to themselves. Still, they will learn. Engagement in a communicative transaction will lead either to adaptation (the individuals will learn, their mental models will change) or to ritual (the individuals will reacquire information they already know). Such continual and automatic adaptation means that at a particular point in time the individual's behavior is a function of his or her knowledge at that time; but the individual's rationale for that behavior, at a later point in time, will be based on the individual's knowledge at that later time (an example of why retrospective accounts of the past are often error prone). Furthermore, having mental models that are dynamic means that it may not be possible for an individual placed in an almost identical context to engage in exactly the same behavior (same choice of communication partner, same choice of information to communicate). As Greek Hereclitus argued, you cannot step into the same river twice. For Hereclitus, the mutation was on the part of the river (or sociocultural landscape); for the cognitivist, regardless of whether the river mutates, the individual's perception of the river does.

Axiom: Individuals Continuously Engage in Communicative Transactions

Individuals are continuously engaged in choosing interaction partners (motivation), communicating information (action), and adjusting themselves to the effects of that information (adaptation). Such activities recur

---

[18]In fixing processing constraints on authors and readers in this way, we are implicitly limiting our discussion to cases in which only individuals, not institutions, fill the author and reader role. Were institutions allowed to fill these roles, the information processing capacities of readers and writers might need to be less constrained. It is certainly possible for institutions (e.g., the state department) to offer official readings and to issue official documents, but the issue of institutionalized readers and writers is beyond the scope of this book.

over time. Authoring and reading, and communication activities in general, are not "one-shot" activities. Authors do not typically compose just one text; readers do not typically read just one. Authors are multiple producers; readers, multiple consumers. Communicative transactions in general, reading and writing in particular, are recurring options for structuring social life.

The ability to participate in this structuring of social life is a property common to everyone. All individuals, whether authors or readers, are situated within a sociocultural system, have mental models which influence behavior, and engage in communicative transactions. Adaptation in mental models may move individuals between tasks, add actions to their action sets, and alter their sociocultural position. As a consequence, their roles, their action sets, and their sociocultural position may change. It follows that authors and readers are potentially interchangeable roles.

Theorem: Authors and Readers are Potentially Interchangeable Roles. To be an author, an individual must be able to acquire information available in the culture system and communicate it to others. But these capacities are true of readers as well. Authors typically differ from (ordinary) readers in terms of their accomplished reach—the number of individuals to whom they have communicated some of their communications. Nonetheless, the similarities between authors and readers in their cognitive and social capacities are much greater than their differences. Authors and readers are potentially interchangeable roles. Authors are often readers; readers, occasionally authors. The potential interchangeability of authors and readers is important because it means that there is no class of individuals innately born to author and a separate class born to read; it means that we can expect a fluidity in the shaping of culture and social structure that would be difficult to expect were authors and readers born to the role; it means that we can make inferences about the structure of authority and power in a society should we find, over certain time periods, that the authorial role is overrepresented by a particular class of individuals in a society, such as the finding that English authors of the 19th century were disproportionately Oxbridge trained, middle to upper-middle class, and male (Altick, 1962; Laurenson, 1969).

Axiom: Communicative Transactions Occur Concurrently

Communicative transactions occur concurrently. This means that multiple motivations, actions, and adaptations may occur more or less at the same time. With the concurrency of communicative transactions, the interactions of one set of individuals may have consequences for others who are not directly involved. The consequent assessment of relative similarity also occurs concurrently, which can often make individuals misjudge their similarity to others as they rely on dated information. For example, not being aware of someone's last interaction with someone else, one might assume that a person thinks "x" when in actuality that person thinks "y."

An alternative to concurrency sees communication carried out in a serial fashion. Serial interaction hardly seems like a realistic possibility for describing the social world. When individuals interact in a local context, others in the society do not hold their breath, waiting to pick up where the first set of agents left off. No less importantly, the assumption of serial interaction distorts the relationship between local interaction and the larger social world. Specifically, it exaggerates the importance of local interaction to the shaping of a larger social structure and, in turn, diminishes how ongoing events can change the nature of local interaction. Concurrency, by contrast, corrects the naivete in pure individualism. Contrary to the Horatio Alger myth, individuals are not completely self-determined agents who can achieve any local or distant goal merely by willing it. Individuals are not fully self-determined because we live in a world of other interacting agents whose goals compete with our own. How an individual fares in achieving a goal often depends on how well the totality of other agents fare in achieving theirs.

Knorr-Cetina (1981, pp. 35–48) observed how historians have turned from serial to concurrent assumptions about the sociocultural world to explain the influence of seemingly remote events on the local representations of historical actors. She specifically referred to Wedgwood's historical account of the Thirty Years War—a war, according to Wedgwood, that was the product of many countries' collective representations, yet a war each country wanted to avoid. Despite each country's intention to avoid conflict, each was myopic about most things outside their immediate context, and the impact of the collective environment pushed it inexorably toward military action (compare Simon, 1983, pp. 18–20, on bounded rationality).

When considering print, a serial conceptualization of reading and writing would make the author–reader pairing a static interaction devoid of the parameters of time and simultaneous learning. A concurrent conceptualization of author–reader transactions, on the other hand, is inherently dynamic and competitive. Under assumptions of concurrency, readers are continually learning about their environment (including other authors and readers) and adjusting their interests (mental models); authors are constantly learning about their environment (including other authors and readers), adjusting their interests, and creating new texts. Whether we prefer to think of an author targeting a reader or a reader selecting an author, we should not envision their interaction as one static target fixing on another. It is rather, at least within the author's lifetime, one moving target engaging another, via a set of communications (texts) which, once created, remain unchanging while affording variable readings at every localized site of reading. Concurrency, and the ability of individuals to learn and continue to create communications, mean that there is a certain reciprocity among communication partners insofar as they continue over time to adapt to one another. At a social level, adaptations appear as trends and fads. In the case of authors and readers, this adaptation can be seen as trends in topics, changing writing styles, and in varying levels of readership. For the author, such adaptation ends with the last text produced. Readers, on the other hand, can live in times different from the author and adapt to an author who is no longer adapting. In consequence, the reciprocity is not complete. This analysis is complementary to Nystrand's (1986, 1989) social interaction theory in which he argued, using the principle of reciprocity, that writers and readers learn their roles by learning to adjust to one another. We suggest that such reciprocity is a byproduct of the social interaction process and the nature of communications and individual cognition, making it endemic to all individuals whether or not they are writers or readers.

Concurrency is a strong argument against individualism in its strong formulation. It also provides a representation of interaction that is more intuitive than serial representations. As they learn more and interact more, individuals can grow together and may interact even more frequently, depending on whether or not they and others in the society continue to learn on a convergent course. For the author, continued interaction depends, in some sense, on the author's ability to stay a workhorse, like Dickens, and maintain the supply and quality of texts. But author and reader can also grow further apart. Readers can learn that they should really be reading other authors. For example, readers of secondary accounts routinely have their appetite whetted to read the original works. Readers of scholarly works often hunt for the one or two citations they are really looking for. Through negative feedback or poor sales, writers can also learn from readers that they should really be writing for other readers. We cannot assume that authors and readers are locked in an eternal embrace.

Understanding author–reader transactions as concurrent also brings to light, partly, why interaction is competitive. Because individual agents try to interact concurrently and because everyone cannot physically interact with everyone at once, the availability of an interaction partner becomes an important issue. Concurrency transforms interaction partners into potentially scarce resources. As we see in chapter 6 and throughout Part II, print mitigates this problem somewhat by creating artificial agents (texts) whose availability for interaction is much less problematic than the availability of a human agent.

Axiom: The More Relatively Similar an Individual Perceives Him or Herself to Another, the More Likely the Individual is to Attempt Interaction With That Other

Individuals are more likely to interact with each other at a particular time if they perceive themselves as being more like each other than they are with others. Readers are more likely to interact with a text at a particular time if their interests are more similar to the ones addressed in that text at that time than they are to all the other persons and texts with which they might interact. We have already laid out much of the rationale for this axiom when defining authority, similarity, and relative similarity.

There are many important aspects of this axiom that merit further comment.

1. This axiom is a statement about the likelihood of interaction and not a deterministic statement about who interacts with whom.

2. This axiom does not imply that relative similarity is the only motivation for interaction, merely that it is an important one. We return to this point later.

3. This axiom makes use of perceived relative similarity and not actual relative similarity. An individual cannot perceive him or herself as similar to another unless the other is known to the individual.

4. Interaction based on relative similarity may be asymmetric. For example, just because an author targets a reader as being the most relatively similar (given other readers) does not mean that those readers will also target the author as the most relatively similar. A related point is that relative similarity makes possible nonreciprocal relationships.

5. Relative-similarity-based interaction is relative to time and task. A reader can have high relative similarity to a text in terms of timely learning interests but have little in common with it in some absolute or enduring sense. Imagine you have just been given a wok as a gift and have a new-found interest in oriental cooking. Your next trip to the bookstore will take you to the section on cookbooks and you are likely to choose an oriental cookbook that meets your taste, the kind of ingredients you are willing to keep around, your commitment to preparation, and so forth. Let us say you select Madame Wong because she satisfies the criterion of relative similarity—being more what you are now after than any other cookbook on the shelf. But in terms of satisfying that criterion, nothing

can be said about your similarity to Madame Wong and her recipes in any absolute or long-term sense.

6. Relative-similarity-based interaction is not a forced or parochial view of communication that keeps "like to like" and thus denies difference or diversity. It is rather a natural mechanism for how social interactors—including authors and readers—acquire and express information about their world. Authors, as the saying goes, must write what they know. Yet they are not gods who enter the world omniscient. They must learn what they know. And then, through the instrument of a written document, they interact with readers at a distance, through the text, to communicate what they have learned. Authors follow a trail of acquiring and expressing knowledge that satisfies their curiosity to learn about the world. Readers for their part follow a parallel trail of knowledge acquisition and expression. Readers are not, to use Garfinkel's (1968) term, "cultural dopes" thrown about like puppets obliging any author whose work passes by (Heritage, 1984, pp. 23–33). Like authors, readers are also driven by a learning interest, and they will be moved to interact at a distance with some author (through a text) when resource barriers (e.g., time, money) do not stand in the way and when they perceive a sufficient degree of relative similarity between the text and themselves.

7. Aside from shifting interests and contexts, one might ask: Does not relative-similarity-based interaction still assume that readers will lock in an eternal embrace with whatever authors and texts win the contest of relative similarity? If an author and text are most relatively similar now and the task—and topic—do not change, will not the author and text continue to keep the reader occupied? The answer to both questions is no. Authors are not the same as the texts they write. Authors are people who learn and from whom others can learn. Texts are artifacts (and artificial agents) that can be learned from but cannot learn. Madame Wong's cookbook is not changing because a text has no acquisitive interests. It can neither learn nor change (i.e., it has 100% fidelity). This is an essential difference between texts and people and a reason why people make better lifelong companions than individual books. Since they can learn, readers are bound to loosen ties with any given text simply because they are changing and eventually becoming less similar to the text. This simple difference has profound implications for the diffusion of the author's ideas, as we see in Part II.

Authors and readers live in a dynamic world in which new information is continually being acquired, forcing authors and readers to constantly recompute their degree of relative similarity to one another. Madame Wong is certainly changing and so are you, and your mutual changes can mean continued interaction with her (via other texts) or none at all. Whether you continue to interact with Madame Wong depends on whether you and she are becoming more alike faster than you or she are becoming like other potential authors (in your case) or readers (in hers). One of the most important lessons readers learn from texts is what other texts they should really be reading—texts are thus stepping stones to others.

8. Relative-similarity-based interaction does not deny the reality of interaction among people who are not like minded. Relative-similarity-based interaction is only one factor affecting the probability of interaction. Other factors, such as proximity and availability, also affect the actual course of interaction. We interact with many people simply because they are around and willing. While these factors are usually too loose to determine social interaction in the long term, they can promote interaction in the short term when the persons (or texts) who are the ideal interaction partners (the most relatively similar) are unavailable for interaction, or are available but too distant to make their similarity and availability matter. Similarly, relative-similarity-based interaction is not the only motivation for communicative transactions. Other motivations include, but are not limited to, coercion and difference. For example, authors can be coerced toward readers they would normally not reach (writing propaganda for the enemy) and readers can be coerced toward authors they would rather not read (a student reading an assigned text). And, for a second example, listeners and readers may seek out speakers and authors they expect will provide them with information that they did not previously know. In this case, it is the difference between the individuals that brings them to interact. Our point is not that relative similarity is the only motivation for interaction, but simply that it is an important mechanism whose implications have important consequences for the communication of the written text. Not least importantly, an analysis of communicative transactions based on relative similarity will enable us to examine some fundamental over-time consequences of print on sociocultural organization and change.

9. Concurrency, along with relative similarity, explains why print interaction is so difficult to predict in simple linear terms: Individual agents are typically myopic about anything outside their immediate context and yet their immediate context is constantly being affected by what's happening in these remote contexts (Knorr-Cetina, 1981, pp. 35–48; Simon, 1983, pp. 18–20). Given both concurrency and relative similarity, it is the totality of all other ongoing interactions that can potentially affect the individual. This is important because it suggests that seemingly remote events can impact one's immediate environment in unpredictable ways. Imagine that on August 1, 1990, a publisher put out four books on the savings and loan scandal, projecting all to be bestsellers. This strategy seemed like a perfectly good marketing decision because on that par-

ticular date the savings and loan scandal was the hottest item in the American press. On August 2, the Persian Gulf erupted into turmoil and the savings and loan scandal was all but obliterated from the news. Overnight, the savings and loan books began to get edged out via relative similarity by a flurry of new books on the Persian Gulf. Readers were still keenly interested in the savings and loan scandal, but they were becoming more interested at a faster rate in the Persian Gulf.

Being affected by the totality of all other communicative transactions implies a certain level of tacit competition. Individuals are naturally in a competitive situation, although they need not view it in this light. Authors and readers are both in a competitive situation, but the competition runs at parallel levels. To continue an earlier example, Madame Wong is trying to maintain her leverage in the cookbook market against other authors and you the reader are trying to maintain your leverage as a reader with a say in the books that publishers are eager to rush to market. Madame Wong can suffer by losing the contest of relative similarity when compared to many other cookbooks. You can lose the same contest if the market turns in a direction that no longer publishes books that meet your needs. The market will leave you behind just as it left behind those still interested in the savings and loan scandal after August 2, 1990. There is, of course, an explanation of this axiom in purely economic terms—as a story about supply and demand—and we do not mean to question the cogency or relevance of the economic explanation. We suggest, however, that to miss the explanation in terms of relative similarity is to miss the sociocultural factors that may drive the economic ones. For additional discussion of relative similarity and its sociocultural consequences, see Carley (1990b, 1991b).

Axiom: Interactive–Cognitive Reciprocity

What individuals know affects with whom they are likely to interact. Whom they interact with, furthermore, will likely make a difference about what they know. Knowledge and interaction are reciprocally related to one another. Changes in knowledge both condition and are conditioned by changes in interaction and vice versa. At any moment in time, individuals can consider either in terms of cognition (shared information) or interaction. Social interaction is derived, in part, from the individual's cognition, and cognition is required for an individual to retain a memory of what is learned in social interaction. Notice that this axiom of reciprocity is markedly different, yet still complementary, to that of Nystrand's (1986, 1989). Nystrand showed that reciprocity is an ongoing fiduciary act in which writers and readers coordinate perspectives with one another and make adjustments in their assumptions, in Grice-like fashion, when their assumptions of coordination are ostensibly violated. Nystrand's principle of reciprocity applies just to the action phase of communication. In contrast, interactive–cognitive reciprocity applies to all three stages of the communicative transaction. As part of the motivation phase, relative similarity (cognition) determines individuals' probabilities of interaction with each other (interaction). As part of the action phase, interactions (interaction) predicated on these probabilities are put into action (interaction), and the individuals (cognition) impart and receive information from their mental models (cognition). As part of the adaptation phase, individuals acquire new information with which they augment their mental models, thereby altering their relative similarity (cognition).

Interactive–cognitive reciprocity at the individual level has important consequences at the sociocultural level. Recall that social structure has been defined as the distribution of interaction probabilities; culture has been defined as the distribution of information across the society's population. When interactions change in response to cognition at the individual or microlevel, social structure changes at the sociocultural or macrolevel. When cognition changes in response to changes in response to interactions at the microlevel, culture changes at the macrolevel. Interactive–cognitive reciprocity lead to sociocultural reciprocity, a co-evolution of social structure and culture. Microlevel changes, however small, have macro repercussions. However, because such micro changes occur concurrently, the overall macro change may not be small. Moreover, since individuals respond on the basis of relative similarity, changes at the macrolevel have repercussions for the microlevel. Interactive–cognitive reciprocity leads to social–individual (or macro–micro) reciprocity.

Axiom: Individuals Exert Communicative Authority by Effecting Change in the Mental Models of Others Through Communications

Any communication can potentially effect change in the mental models of those individuals who receive it. The greater the change, both in terms of the completeness and comprehensiveness of the communication's reach, the greater the communication's authority. Whether this authority becomes associated with the agent depends on the presence or absence of a signature. In oral face-to-face communication, in which it is difficult to separate the agent from the communication, the communication comes with an obvious attached signature. The authority of the communication is often perceived as the authority of the agent. Print-based technologies impose distance between the human agent (the author) and the communication. If the text is designed to appear sans signature, the authority of the communication and the agent become distinct. Under print conditions, texts without signatures simply call attention to the authority invested in the communication, the force of the words. The greater the reach of a nonsignatured communication, the greater its authority. Texts with signatures, however, enable both the author and the communication to have recognizable authority.

The greater the reach of the signatured communication, the greater its and the author's authority. For print contexts, this distinction helps us understand the difference between authorial authority and an authorized reading. An authorized reading is a message (chap. 2) imposed and stabilized by an external authority with the intent to pass it intact across transactional contexts. The more complete and comprehensive the reach of the message, the greater the communicative authority of the authorities who want it sent. Authorial authority, on the other hand, is based on the reach of the communication carrying the author's signature. Furthermore, unlike a message, whose authority depends upon remaining intact, the authority of an authorial communication is based more in the completeness than in the comprehensiveness of its reach. That is, Shakespeare's authority as an author does not diminish because he has no single message for readers. In fact, for the purposes of an author's authority, the extent to which the authorial communication needs to reflect the historical author's mental model seems quite minimal, involving simple rules of categorization. For example, suppose the accepted word of mouth—our "social knowledge"—about Shakespeare came to associate that concept only with a type of English accent or the name of a famous theater; then Shakespeare's (historical) reach and authority would be largely decimated. To maintain authority, the communications (plays) through which Shakespeare achieved his reach cannot be eclipsed or dominated by artifacts (accents, theaters) or communications (comic books) that mask the categories of the original communications (cf. Foucault's, 1977, discussion of the author function is relevant here).

Axiom: The Greater the Average Potential Distance, the Greater the Potential Reach

As previously noted, the technological condition, what communication technologies are present and their distribution, affects the potential distance between communication partners. The technology of print endowed communications with greater synchronicity, fixity, durability, and multiplicity. These factors increased the potential distance between communication partners. Foucault and Giddens both recognized the unusual extensionality of the writer in contrast to the speaker. Giddens (1987, pp. 199–206) drew a quantitative relationship between the reach of writing and print: "[P]rinting is for the most part a quantitative extension of [writing]." Giddens (1988) argued that as the author became a voice of the church, government, and commercial institutions, the author's written expression changed qualitatively. It had to pull up its moorings from the situated references of talk and become less dependent on specific contexts of utterance:

> Since language as "carried" by cultural objects is no longer talk, it loses its saturation in the referential properties which language-use has in the contexts of day to day action. As a visible or recoverable trace, separated from the immediacy of contexts of talk, the signifier becomes of peculiar significance. (p. 200)

Giddens painted a picture in which the development of writing, print, and formal organization placed stresses on language that caused it to change from within. We suggest that the order of causation is more likely the other way around: Writing and, in particular, print increased the reach of the author sufficiently to make interaction at a distance possible and to foster the sociocultural development of more geographically and temporally dispersed organizations (chap. 8, 9). Written communication is not distinctive, as Giddens and strong text theorists (Goody, 1986; Olsen, 1977; Ong, 1982) suggested, because it fostered a new kind of language that could survive without context, but because it allowed traces of the everyday language to survive across greater temporal, spatial, and sociocultural distance.

SUMMARY AND IMPLICATIONS

The basic constructural story has been presented in this chapter. According to this story, the communicative transaction takes place within an ecology consisting of not only concurrent transactions, but their content, context, and agents. Individuals adapt during a transaction, and because of the reciprocity between interaction and cognition, such adaptation leads not only to new mental models but to new sociocultural positions (and hence roles). Through concurrent and recurrent transactions, changes at the level of the individual collectively construct social and cultural changes. In response to interactive–cognitive reciprocity at the individual level, social structure and culture co-evolve. We provided details for this in the form of definitions and axioms. A formal model, consistent with these definitions and axioms, is presented in chapter 6 and used thereafter to examine the impact of print.

The purist will note that there are many additional axioms embedded within the definitions we provided. We highlighted only those axioms necessary to the skeleton of the constructural story that may be less obvious and perhaps most contentious. There is, however, an important constituent of the communicative transactions and individual's mental models that we have ignored in this chapter—language. In fact, language is arguably the resource whose existence permits portions of mental models to become encapsulated in communications, and information within the communication to alter mental models, making language itself another component of a co-evolving social structure and culture. As this chapter demonstrates, it is possible to build up the logic of sociocultural and individual change, the logic of constructuralism, without resorting to the details of language. Much of the impact of print can be explored without considering the details of language or developments and changes in meaning affected by print. Indeed, in later chapters we employ a model that abstracts away from more fine-grained analyses of language. Nevertheless, an interlude on language (chap. 5), particularly as it relates to meaning, permits a more informed discussion.

The Role of Language in the Communicative Transaction

> *Advanced literacy depends on a large volume of available materi-*
> *al which is clearly printed. . . . Widespread literacy cannot be*
> *based on inscriptions, since there are not enough of them; and*
> *rolls of parchment are awkward to consult. [Havelock] argues*
> *that rapid reading, and hence full literacy in the sense in which*
> *we understand the term, would have been difficult to achieve . . .*
> *without large volumes of materials to practice on. . . . A major*
> *factor in the development of effective and full-scale literacy is*
> *therefore the development of machine printing.*
> —Michael Stubbs (1980, p. 77)

Stubbs, like many writers, associated mechanical print with a literacy that is widespread, rapid, effective, and full scale. So pervasive is our modern association of literacy to print that we tend to think of language without print as necessarily regional, slow, ineffective, and remote. In some respects, these associations may be justified. But, in other respects, they overlook the insights of people like Tully and Skinner (1989):

> Our social practices bestow meaning on our social vocabulary, but it is equal-
> ly true that our social vocabulary helps to constitute the character of those
> practices. To see the role of our evaluative language in helping to legiti-
> mate social action is to see the point at which our social vocabulary and
> our social fabric mutually prop each other up. (p. 132)

Austin-Broos (1987, p. xxv) wrote that language is the basis of social forms that are at once "insightful and reified; visionary and cliche; formless and sedimented." These and other writers maintain that the capacity of individuals to use language remains the primary force behind the emergence and decay of social forms. The author may have greater potential reach than the speaker (thanks to print or other mass communication technologies), but if there is nothing in the language from which the author can draw that can influence the larger society and culture, then owning a printing press (an electronic mail address or a television station for that matter!) may not make an interesting difference to the individual's reach.

Although the story of sociocultural co-evolution in response to individual, interactive, and cognitive changes holds together without considering language in any great detail (as we saw in chapter 4), language has a place in the story of cognitive adaptation, the construction, reception, and interpretation of communications, the co-evolution of self and society, and the co-evolution of social structure and culture. This chapter explores that place and, in doing so, marks a departure from both previous chapters and those to follow. In previous chapters, we laid out an approach to the communicative transaction, but from a macroperspective that paid little attention to the specific details of any single transaction. In this chapter, we consider, from a constructuralist perspective, the role language plays within communicative transactions. For various reasons, it is difficult to tell an interesting or detailed story about this role without focusing closely on a single transaction, on a single author addressing a fairly circumscribed set of readers through a single text. This microfocus takes up much of the exposition of this chapter. Much of our preliminary discussion prepares the way for analyzing a single text by Terrence Rafferty, the film critic for the *New Yorker*.

Before we turn to that microfocus, we need to understand why a theory of the communication transaction, even if its primary focus (as ours) is to compare transactions under different technological conditions, needs to address a theory of the role of language in these transactions:

1. Communicative transactions are noncontinuous and recurrent episodes. Individuals survive them and enter more. But, along with persons, symbols survive transactions from the past and recycle into current ones. A theory of the communicative transaction thus requires some notion of a symbol set whose evolution must be counted as part of the co-evolution of the individual and the society. As it turns out, we do not discuss language at length in this book because most of the over-time questions we ask about print (in Part II) can be studied adequately within very impoverished assumptions about language. But that is not to say that investigators who want to study communicative transactions will always want to ask questions that permit such impoverished assumptions. Sometimes, questions we want to ask about communicative transactions and their over-time trajectory require us to open up the details of a single

transaction or a small set of transactions, and opening up this detail usually involves looking at the symbols agents communicate at a finer grain.

2. One of the key assumptions of certain technological determinists (Eisenstein, 1979; Goody, 1986; Ong, 1971) is that writing and print technology were sufficient unto themselves to alter our basic orientation to language. A useful way to explore this determinist assumption is to ask: What is the nature of language such that a technology might change it? What could a technology possibly change about language? It is difficult to pursue these questions with a theory of the communicative transaction that begins with an impoverished representation of language. Thus, by opening up, in this chapter, the issue of language in the communicative transaction, we can respond to the question of what language makes available for technology to change.

Agents bring their language and history to bear in every transaction, and any transaction may thus effect not only the agent's language and history, but also the society's. The effect of any single transaction may be negligible, but the sum of such transactions across the society can have monumental effects on the language and culture of the community (Cicourel, 1970). White (1984) linked language to the development of society and culture in general, and to the communicative transaction in particular. He recognized that the language we speak and write is a repository of the meanings determined from previous transactions within the culture:

> the language, after all, is the repository of the kinds of meaning and relation that make a culture what it is. In it, as I have suggested, one can find the terms by which the natural world is classified and represented, those by which the social universe is constituted, and those terms of motive and value by which action is directed and judged. In a sense we literally are the language we speak, for the particular culture that makes us a "we"— that defines and connects us, that differentiates us from others—is enacted and embedded in our language. (p. 20)

White further recognized that speakers and writers inherit meanings from this repository as they enter into new transactions:

> whenever a person wishes to speak to another, he must speak a language that has its existence outside himself, in the world he inhabits. If he is to be understood, he must use the language of his audience. This language gives him his terms of social and natural description, his words of value, and his materials for reasoning; it establishes the moves by which he can persuade another, or threaten or placate or inform or tease him, or establish terms of cooperation or intimacy; it defines his starting places and stop-

ping places and the ways he may intelligibly proceed from one to the other. Sometimes, of course, he can use words in new ways—can cast new sentences and make new moves—for the user of the language is also its maker; but for the most part his resources are determined by others. (1984, p. 6)

According to White, speakers and writers have the power to change this repository as a byproduct of these transactions:

> to learn a language is also to change it, for one constantly makes new gestures and sentences of one's own, new patterns of combinations of meaning. Language is in part a system of invention, an organized way of making new meaning in new circumstances. Some of these inventions are shared with others and become common property; others remain personal, part of the process by which the individual within a culture is differentiated from others who are similarly situated. Culture and the individual self are in this view to be understood not in isolation, as independent systems of structures, but in their reciprocal relations one with the other: the only way they ever exist in the world. (1984, p. 8)

White's observations bear some resemblance to the story we presented in chapter 4. In this chapter, we flesh out these observations by showing, at a finer grain of detail, how language fits within the constructuralist framework. Language is a representation of information as symbols and the links between those symbols. At the individual level, language exists as a mental construct dependent on an individual's mental models. At the social level, language exists as a set of tacit agreements across the population about what symbols exist and how symbols are to be elaborated in relation to one another. As individuals interact and learn more about the world, they adapt their mental models, causing the system of agreements that bind language together at the social level to adapt. In this respect, the communicative transaction becomes the vehicle for learning and practicing the language as a personal resource, and for helping, in indirect and remote ways, to modify the language as a social resource.

The basic capacity of language to accommodate sociocultural organization and change is an endowment of language, regardless of the technological conditions present in society. This is why we insisted in chapter 3 on a level playing field for the oral and print medium. Describing how language works in the oral medium is not trivial; describing how it works in the print medium is not impossible. both descriptions present a challenge. But our immediate point is that the account of language underlying either technology must be the same account. Brandt (1990) made much the same point:

> while the move from the oral to the literate does require a new level of symbolic reflectiveness, it does not require a renunciation or reformula-

tion among context, language, and meaning that pertains in oral language use. (p. 103)

In light of these commonalities, it is instructive to begin by considering the general relationship between language and society, putting aside for the moment considerations of modality (oral, writing, print).

LANGUAGE AND SOCIETY: PRE- AND POSTPRINT

In the West, the relationship between language and society was studied long before print and the role of the author became an issue. In the classical rhetorical tradition, the cultural definition of the ancient equivalent of the author—the *orator*—was being formulated as were primary understandings of the relationship between language and society. The influence of the rhetorical tradition and its underpinnings in the oral arts remained dominant for centuries. For example, with the exception of the medieval art of letterwriting (*ars dictaminis*), the dominant modes of expression taught in the schools until well into the 19th century remained oral (Ong, 1971). Classical theorists of rhetoric distinguished between private and public communication and classified the art of rhetoric or oratory as public. For the major theorists—Aristotle, Cicero, and Quintilian—rhetoric involved only public discourse used in public forums, such as the legislature, the courts, and official celebratory events. The major theorists acknowledged that private communication relied on language in order to convey meaning, but they saw public communication as the proper domain of rhetoric. They believed that rhetoric, or the use of language for public persuasion, could maintain or change levels of social cohesion and consensus across the population of decision makers. Language, in this capacity, was considered essential for maintaining social stability and fostering change.

Burke (1969) criticized the ancients' rigid distinction between public and private discourse but admired their perception that rhetorical discourse could work seamlessly between the individual and the society, a perception suggesting at least a partial isomorphism in the structure of language and aspects of the society (Bitzer, 1968). The ancient rhetoricians classified language into types and suggested that this partial isomorphism did not apply to all types of language. For example, Aristotle distinguished rhetoric from propositional logic and did not believe that the extended reasoning so useful for analytic reasoning was of central importance to the truncated and elliptical reasoning so common in public discourse. A similar sentiment, with respect to computer languages, might be shared by formal logicians and computer scientists today. The fully elaborated syllogism was useful for disciplining inferences but not for inspiring crowds or mobilizing them to action. The ancient theorists, particularly in the Isocratean tradition,[1] were more inclined to believe that the language useful for culture building was rooted in more efficient chunks—symbols—packed with associations that did not need to be spelled out for their audiences to feel their effect (Jaeger, 1965). Despite this recognition, the ancient rhetoricians never developed a comprehensive theory of the symbol. They were more interested in giving students of oratory examples of the kinds of language—the metaphor, the trope, the slogan, the turn of phrase—that were most likely to function symbolically on audiences. They recognized the rhetorical potency of symbolic language in relation to ordinary linguistic expression, yet they did not seek to characterize what made symbolic language symbolic.

Interest in symbolic language never abated from the classical period, although it seemed to have a new revival with print. Print is a different kind of mass-communication technology from oratory, and this difference sparked a new interest in symbols. The symbols of the orator gave cohesiveness to the social sphere but the orator's words were ephemeral and needed to be reinforced in repeat performances. The symbols of the print author, because of the durability and fixity of print, were less ephemeral. They had a lasting resonance in printed texts, and readers could reinforce these symbols merely by turning to their shelves. In light of the new resonance of the symbol with print, symbols themselves became a more visible and talked about entity of academic and mass culture. As language became a more visible and fixed object of study, vocabularies developed to talk about the effects of the printed word. Terms that once would have remained within the technical argot of the rhetorician entered the vernacular of the mass audience.[2]

For example, only after print, in 1513, did the slogan, a type of enthymematic expression intended to create solidarity and mobilize action, receive its modern name. According to the OED, the slogan became the name for an Irish war cry, and later came to signify any concise rallying language whose power was a function of its repetition. During the industrial revolution, moreover, the durability and fixity of print led to

---

[1]Isocrates stressed the symbolic use of language to promote themes of national unity— and Isocratean schools of rhetoric dominated the classical world despite Aristotle's greater ultimate reach. Aristotelian scholarship focused on Book 1 of the *Rhetoric*, in which Aristotle related rhetoric to dialectic and the truncated syllogism or enthymeme. More recent scholarship has given added importance to Book III—which Aristotle wrote after the *Poetics*— where Aristotle addressed the interaction of language and style on persuasion (Enos, personal communication).

[2]In contrast, few of the hundreds of Latin tropes codified in ancient rhetoric have entered the public vernacular.

other symbols whose names, as well as effects, were indebted to the print trade. In the late 18th century, Didot developed techniques to cast and duplicate whole pages in fixed form without having to retypeset individual letters. The English name for this case was "stereotype." The French, "cliche." Through relentless repetition (via durability, multiplicity, fixity) of the symbol, print made it possible to freeze the visible language, making approximately fixed and powerful cliched formulae (Zijderveld, 1980). These innovations in print technology were eventually extended into names for symbols as people came to recognize their rhetorical power. Ironically, even as new symbols were created in response to the technology, thus extending language, the fixity (made possible by print) of the code came increasingly to be misidentified with language per se. The fixity of print spawned a longstanding historical confusion between the living language of societies and the frozen language of printed texts.

The oral tradition of rhetoric emphasized the enthymematic relationship between language and the beliefs of the audience addressed. For the rhetorician, the language did not create the beliefs of the audience; yet it needed to accommodate those beliefs as a premise for steering them further. Analogously, neither print nor any communication technology could directly create the beliefs of the reading audience, but they could sufficiently influence the context in which language was circulated to exert at least a potential impact, however indirect or remote, on belief.

Lippman (1922) was one of the first intellectuals to argue for the indirect, potentially disturbing associations between language and belief that mass media such as print could influence. He argued that the beliefs of the mass audience could easily be shaped by what is printed in the newspapers. To attract the widest readership, he observed, most newspapers had to address the lowest common denominator, to smooth over subtleties and ethnic differentiation, and to frame a mass reader with the stereotypical beliefs of a civic booster and the intellectual curiosity of a carnival huckster. In actual fact, the extent to which print can create such a mass reader remains even now an open question. It is plausible that because of its multiplicity and fixity, print can forward exactly the same code and communication (though not the same meaning) to members of a mass audience. Print, moreover, can extend the potential reach of the writer and the potential size of the audience. On these grounds, there is little doubt that media moguls, with the resources to channel a pointed message to the masses for days, weeks, or years at a time, have a huge potential to condition an audience. To move from this observation, however, to the argument that the press created an audience with stereotypes for beliefs requires additional assumptions and remains an open historical question for the press of Lippman's day and an open empirical question for the press of today.

The larger point in all this is the heightened visibility of the symbol conferred by print and the renewed intellectual interest in the study of symbols, especially since the industrialization of letters in 19th-century Europe and America. Since that time and extending into our own, Cassirer (1953) and a line of theorists following his lead (Alexander, 1988; Bennett, 1980, 1985; Boulding, 1956; Burke, 1966; Duncan, 1968; Durkheim, 1965; Edelman, 1977; Graber, 1976; Hudson, 1978; Langer, 1957; Lippman, 1922; McGee, 1980; Pocock, 1971; Richards, 1936) have pursued explicit theories of symbolic language and how it functions. A loose consensus has evolved that symbolic language is highly compacted and typically conveys a web of social meaning under the cloak of a simple word or phrase (e.g., democracy, social progress, imperialism, and freedom fighters). Inferences moving across the web are so fast that the potency of symbolic language is often measured in terms of how much social information can be conveyed for the smallest amount said. The greater the amount conveyed relative to the amount said, the higher the potency of language. As Graber (1976, p. 289) observed, the lightning efficiency of symbolic inference can be attributed to the capacity of a symbol to "stir . . . vivid impressions involving the listener's most basic values." A term of art that has evolved to express these features of the symbol is the *condensation symbol* (Graber, 1976), so named because the symbol seems to compress a network of social meaning into common words and phrases.

Hudson (1978, p. 66) noted, that only a member of the British communist party would, in an official capacity, characterize the land speculator's profit as the money made by the slick operator of land speculation working in a plush office. The strategic deployment of "slick" and "plush" evokes a network of implications about the "profligate capitalist" seen from the eyes of Marxism and redirects any narrow instrumental point being made into a more intense rallying cry. Hudson called the socializing function of condensation symbols "group-cement" because the speaker issuing them seeks to identify with emergent or actual groups in the culture who are willing to give a sympathetic ear to the network of meaning condensed in the message.

The implicit web of social belief associated with the condensation symbol implies that such symbols have a distinctive internal structure. McGee (1980) made two useful points about this structure:[3]

1. He noted that the structure of condensation symbols is not strictly propositional because "such terms as property, religion, right of priva-

---

[3]McGee used the term *ideograph* rather than "condensation symbol," but the difference is only in naming.

cy, freedom of speech, rule of law, and liberty are more than propositions ever could be.''

2. He observed that condensation symbols have both a diachronic (what he also calls "vertical") and a synchronic (what he also calls "horizontal" or "situation-specific") significance.

Condensation symbols are vertically structured according to their history of usage over time. A symbol like "rule of law" has a history of variant usages, each held together by common threads in the legal tradition. Yet they are also horizontally structured, he noted, according to the social impact they are expected to exert in the immediate context of utterance. He concluded that the meaning of the condensation symbol is some intersection between its vertical and horizontal associations.

The body of literature on the symbol, often insightful, is sometimes subject to the same criticism we levied at the body of individualistic literature on the author in chapter 4. The authorial role has been elevated into an honorific standing apart from ordinary agents; the symbol has been elevated into an honorific standing apart from ordinary words. Some of the same arguments that we used in chapter 4 to return authors to the everyday world of situated individuals can apply to returning symbols to the everyday world of situated meaning. Even as authors differ from other individuals, symbols (specifically, condensation symbols) differ in degree, not in kind, from the role they play in specific contexts of communication. If some agents have more reach than others, it is because of their situatedness in the sociocultural landscape. Analogously, if some words have more connectivity than others, it is because of their sociocultural-historical situatedness in a web of situated meaning.

SYMBOLS AND WORDS

Despite the impressive body of literature on symbolic language, the word "symbol" has remained rather vague. Yet it is often precisely distinguished from ordinary words. As entries in the lexicon of a language, ordinary words are part of the grammar that participates in the syntax of spoken and written sentences. Symbols, on the other hand, are built from social beliefs and they participate in a "grammar" of motive leading to social cohesion and division (Burke, 1966, 1969). Bakhtin urged an understanding of language more as a pastiche of the hustle and bustle of social life than as a uniform axiomatic structure. In the essay *Discourse in the Novel* (1981) he wrote:

> language has been completely taken over, shot through with intentions and accents; For any individual consciousness living in it, language is not an

abstract system of normative forms but rather a concrete heteroglot conception of the world. All words have the "taste" of a profession, a genre, a tendency, a party, the day and hour. Each word tastes of the context and contexts in which it has lived its socially charged life; all words and forms are populated by intentions. Contextual overtones (generic, tendentious, individualistic) are inevitable in the word. (1981, p. 293)

Our own assumptions about language resonate closely with Bakhtin's. All words, as concepts, have the same fundamental properties. Every word or concept in a language to some extent connects to other concepts, thereby creating a network of social meaning and belief. Words that we call ordinary have this status only because they are low in their achieved connectivity. Words we call symbolic are high or at least higher in their connectivity.

The connectivity relationships of a word need to be described at various levels: (a) at the level of a single speaker; (b) at the level of two or more speakers; and (c) at the level of a whole society. We must be careful to indicate the level at which we are speaking when we speak of a word's symbolic status. For a lawyer, the term *rule of law* is a highly connected symbol, rife with historical and social meaning. Yet if that same lawyer mentions rule of law to a 10-year-old, it is likely to be processed as an ordinary (and probably inscrutable) phrase. One person's symbol can thus be another's ordinary word. Furthermore, one person's symbol can have a very different symbolic meaning from another's. Lawyers with different political ideologies may elaborate rule of law very differently. They may disagree about its appropriate history of usage and its implications for future policy. In essence, symbols can be (and usually are) richly ambiguous, even among those for whom they are symbols.

CONSTRUCTURALISM AND INTENTIONAL COMMUNICATION

Let us consider how these observations about symbols fit into the constructural story. According to that story, agents bring their personal language and history to each new transaction. They bring their symbols and the connections between these symbols—their lexicons, as it were, and the social and historical meanings with which they have invested their words.[4] According to the constructural story, agents then engage in in-

---

[4]For ease of exposition, we sometimes use the terms *symbol, word,* and *concept* interchangeably, and this usage is acceptable insofar as their meanings overlap. Nonetheless, there are some important shades of difference between these terms that the reader should understand and that we maintain throughout, especially in contexts where one term is not an adequate substitute for another. Symbols and concepts can be words, but only concepts

teraction, communicating symbols, language and narratives with one another. This action leads, potentially, to the construction of meaning. By bringing their symbols to the transaction, some of the social and historical ties of one agent's concepts will be picked up by the other. Some of Agent A's social and historical elaborations of concepts will impact B's; some of B's, A's.

At the semantic level, such evolution is seldom, if ever, a planned or intended event. As agents, we are rarely so reflective as to inspect our entire network of internal meaning, nor so perceptive to inspect the receiver's network. We thus engage in communicative transactions, but the terms of the transactions—the actual meanings that are communicated, that slip across agents or that fail to slip across—are never fully in the control of either agent. Not knowing in detail the extent of the other's mental models, we cannot know in complete detail what he or she actually takes from the communication. This is not to deny that individuals exercise some control over the transaction. From the perspective of the agent's intentions and purposes, aspects of the communicative content can function as a message whose meanings are stabilized in time and place, often for limited and recurring instrumental purposes. No doubt, our communications work at this instrumental level frequently enough to convince us of the instrumental value of language. Furthermore, there is no evil demon to ensure that the meanings embedded in our communications and the meanings derived by others are unrelated to the meanings under our intentional control. It would be perverse to assume that information an agent takes from a communication has nothing to do with what an agent puts into it. Constructuralism and intentionality are not necessarily at odds (see chap. 9 on engineered reach). Intentionality alone, however, is far too weak a factor, in and of itself, to explain the construction of meaning—that is, to predict or explain which meanings will evolve as communications move across speakers. How much intentionality matters to constructuralism is an open question, probably depending on the beliefs and the sociocultural distance between the

---

(not words) and the relationships between them configure symbols. Symbols and concepts consist not only of single words but phrases as well (e.g., rule of law). When we describe an agent's lexicon, we really think of it as a lexicon of concepts (i.e., ideational kernels expressed as words and phrases) and not words. Unlike word or concept, furthermore, symbol expressly captures the idea that, in a communicator's lexicon, symbols are connected to one another in historically relevant clusters, called meanings. When we refer to symbol, therefore, we are always referring not only to a single word or atomistic concept but to a network of concepts and relationships that have been related through historical use. The meaning of a lexical entry includes its connections with other entries. These meanings, in turn, are derived through the communicator's history of interactions. As a result, meanings for a single communicator depend on personal history; social meanings depend on shared histories.

communication partners, the goals of the agents, the level of attention each is willing to give to the other's communication, the level of care each is willing to put into the design of a communication to try to control others' attention, and so on. Although these factors may affect the relationship of intentionality to constructuralism, the construction of meaning occurs regardless of the extent to which intentionality is part of the story.

Within the constructural story, agents, through contact, begin to share not simply concepts, but meanings (i.e., connected concepts) and aspects of their sociocultural histories and heritage. They coordinate pockets of the internal network of meaning embodying their knowledge of the sociocultural landscape. They become more similar (even if this increased similarity makes them aware that they are less relatively similar to one another than to others and so discourages them from further interaction). The meanings of their concepts become windows into the sociocultural landscape they see themselves inhabiting; yet these rich and continuously evolving windows cannot be flattened into instrumental intentions couched in superficial paraphrases. As White (1984) observed:

> When we look at particular words, it is not their translation into statements of equivalence that we should seek but an understanding of the possibilities they represent for making and changing the world. This can be done only by giving attention to the shape and working of the language itself. Think of such terms in our own language as "honor," "dignity," "privacy," "property," "liberty," "friend," "teacher," "family," "marriage," "child," "university," or "school." Such words do not operate in ordinary speech as restatable concepts but as words with a life and force of their own. They cannot be replaced with definitions, as though they were parts of a closed system, for they constitute unique resources, of mixed fact and value, and their translation into other terms would destroy their nature. Their meaning resides not in their reducibility to other terms but in their irreducibility; it resides in the particular ways each can be combined with other words in a wide variety of contexts. They operate indeed as gestures, with a meaning that cannot be restated. Words normally acquire this sort of complexity and richness gradually, as the incremental effect of many uses by many speakers and writers. (pp. 11–12)

Agents are able, incrementally, to share their histories through their language as they engage in communicative transactions. This sharing irrevocably alters one another's histories, language, and meaning. This does not imply that meaning evolves in a uniform fashion for all members of the population, nor that all pairs of individuals have equal effect on each other. According to the axiom of relative-similarity-based interaction (chap. 4), agents are more likely to interact with those whose language is already more similar, relative to all other potential interaction partners. The co-construction of meaning is thus most likely to occur among agents whose language and history already converge to a great extent relative to others with whom they might have been interacting. It is in this sense that groups that manage to keep both their members and their ideas relatively intact also manage to develop their own localized language and meanings. Intentions in single transactions play an unsure role in this co-evolution (especially as the co-evolution of meaning aggregates across transactions). For this reason, we can often make the idealizing assumption that although it is not random which agents interact in a given group or society at a given time, it is random which meanings will evolve in response to the communicative transaction. These assumptions are further formalized in chapter 6.

An important implication of the constructural story is that the single transaction plays a role, albeit possibly an imperceptible role, in the development of sociohistorical and cultural meaning. To glimpse the socially visible effects of co-evolution, one must not limit oneself to the single transaction but must study the aggregation of many ongoing concurrent transactions over time. The information that comes to the surface and is at issue in any single transaction is only the tip of the iceberg for an individual's network of meaning. No single transaction may produce much change in either party. Indeed, in the constructural story, a single transaction may have the same importance as a millenium in a theory of continental drift. Without understanding what is happening every 1,000 or 10,000 years, one could not predict continental movement. Containing one's analysis within a relatively short span, such as one day, the scientist would be hard put to discover any noticeable, much less significant, change. Similarly, the theorist's focus on the visible author (or speaker) engaged in a single transaction in a single rhetorical situation holds little interest when the issue is sociocultural organization and change. To address that issue, one needs to understand the communicative transaction as a unit that can aggregate over time. Accordingly, the theory of meaning applied to the single transaction ultimately needs to be embedded in a theory of how to aggregate concurrent and recurrent transactions (chap. 6).

The foregoing discussion anticipates where we are headed and does not describe the immediate business at hand, which is to understand the symbol in enough operational detail to fit within an operational theory of the communicative transaction, a theory of the symbol. A symbol at any level of description (i.e., individual, interpersonal, societal) is simply a concept whose meaning depends on establishing connections to other concepts in the language, thereby creating social and historical elaborations. The objects that participate in the co-construction of meaning during communicative transactions are not only the concepts but the connective ties between them. To understand a symbol at an operational level within the context of the co-construction of meaning, we need to understand more about the nature and range of these connections between concepts.

VARIABILITY IN THE FOUNDATIONS
OF SYMBOLIC CONNECTIONS

There has been some progress operationalizing the idea of symbol in terms of connectivity. Because much theorizing since the 19th century has focused on the relationship of the symbol to literary meaning, especially the metaphor, analyses of the symbol have tended to focus on the dimension of density. The literary text is often distinguished from other text types because of its reputed density of meaning, its wide reliance on allusion, metaphor, and allegory. To say that a word is dense means that it is attached to a bundle of statements and inferences (e.g., the world is a stage) far too numerous and far too continuous in shading to be easily sliced apart, like bologna, one discrete meaning after another, in the manner of an ambiguous sentence. Because of their reputed density, we sometimes call symbols "rich" in meaning, with richness not explicable as simple ambiguity. Density descriptions apply to the literary text, and analyses of the literary text tend, in the tradition of Cassirer, to dominate our common understandings of symbols. To make language dense with meaning was also a common prescription in manuals written to train newspaper ad writers (Surrey, 1930).

Density, however, is not the only fundamental connective dimension that can be used to describe symbols. A second independent dimension is consensus. In chapter 4, we defined consensus as a measure of the fraction of interaction partners in a society who share, at the same time or over time, the same beliefs about some focal idea or decision. This is a somewhat specialized definition of consensus (the one we use throughout Part II). Alternate definitions of consensus exist and all retain the intuitive idea that individuals hold a consensus to the extent that they share knowledge, ideas, beliefs, inferences, and so on.[5] Consensus occurs by

---

[5]One of the central issues in discussions of consensus is whether the agreement or sharing involved in a consensus must be consciously recognized or whether it can be tacit. In this book, we take the latter position. That is, we assume that individuals can agree (have a consensus) without being aware of it. Consensus can thus occur because individuals tacitly share the same information, knowledge, beliefs, values, norms, and so forth. The association of consensus with tacitly shared knowledge is widespread in the literature. Polanyi (1962) noted, for example, that a tacit consensus can arise if the individuals in question

degree, a matter of more or less, not all or none. The more beliefs and inferences individuals share, the more likely they are to concur. From the standpoint of language and the connectivity of concepts, consensus is a function of the number of individuals who, within their mental models, have the same connection between the same two concepts. For a particular concept, consensus, much as reach for the author, varies both in completeness and comprehensiveness, in how many people share a connection and in how many of the connections are shared.

Consensus is independent of density. Symbols can have both a highly consented to meaning and a meaning that is dense (e.g., *rule of law* among lawyers of the same political leaning). A symbol can also be an object of wide consensus without being dense. For example, an expression like *1492* has relatively low density for a grammar school student but nonetheless draws on a set of conceptual relationships that are almost universally shared among the population. Grammar students elaborate 1492 in only a few ways, but they all elaborate it with the discovery of America.

There is a third connective dimension underlying symbolic expression—conductivity.[6] This is the capacity of a symbol to act as both a source and a destination for social and historical elaboration. The basic intuition about conductive symbols is that they are neither starting nor stopping points for the ideas with which they are associated. Rather they lie at the hub of such elaborations and act as conduits linking together sets of meanings. The importance of such highly conductive words is that they are known as much, if not more, for the ideas they can stimulate than for the ideas they are actually understood to mean. The primary example of a purely conductive symbol is the *buzzword*.

Conductivity is the least well-documented dimension of symbolic expression, and this fact is reflected in the absence of detailed historical documentation for the buzzword. The term *buzzword* is itself a neologism, having been coined in the 1960s (Random House 2nd Unabridged). The term is often omitted from prestigious dictionaries. For example, neither the *2nd Unabridged Edition of the Oxford English Dictionary* (1989) nor *Webster's 3rd New Unabridged Dictionary* (1981) includes an entry for it. Where documentation on buzzwords is available, it is typi-

---

both went through the same experience (such as two women in different cities giving birth or a set of students sitting through the same lecture course though perhaps during different years). Whorf's shared culture (1956), Bar-Hillel's universal encyclopedia (1960), Sowa's background knowledge (1984), Romney, Weller, & Batchelder (1986), and Romney, Batchelder, & Weller's (1987) cultural truth are similar conceptions of consensus through tacitly shared knowledge.

[6]Carley (1984) initially used the term *transitivity* to refer to this property. We employ the term *conductive* to emphasize that information is flowing through, being conducted by, the concept.

cally misleading, if not altogether off the mark. For example, Random House offers that a buzzword is "a word or phrase, often . . . authoritative or technical, that is a vogue term in a particular profession, field of study, [or] popular culture." This definition, not without merit, essentially collapses buzzwords into jargon or argot. "Jargon" is a medieval word meaning gibberish. "Argot" is a word of unknown origin, meaning the language of rogues and thieves. In our century, both terms have retained their pejorative meaning and are invoked[7] to criticize the seemingly excessive and secret codes of particular groups, especially the professions. *Newsweek* magazine strengthened the linkage of buzzwords to argot by running a regular feature, "Buzzwords," in which the inside codes of various professions are exposed for ridicule. Exploring the so-called buzzwords of bus drivers, for example, *Newsweek* (August 19, 1991) pointed out that their common term for passengers is *freight*. This usage is clearly a piece of secret code; certainly a neologism as far as popular culture is concerned; perhaps a consensual emblem shared by bus drivers; perhaps even a metaphoric (and so dense) symbol for them; and, yes, a piece of argot, dense or otherwise; but it is not, in terms of conductivity, a buzzword, either for the bus drivers or for the popular culture.

Unlike argot, buzzwords typically cannot provide detailed elaborations of what the buzzword strictly means. A buzzword, unlike argot, is never a dense reference. A buzzword functions rather as an instrumental reference to topics that are only loosely connected to it. A good example of a buzzword is "mips and megs." Few individuals, other than computer engineers and high-powered computer users, can provide great detail about this term's meaning. Nonetheless, the term provides a speedy gateway for computer purchasers and sellers who want to talk about how certain computers will perform under certain conditions. Argot represents the reality of specialized subcultures; buzzwords represent the reality of a specialized group's impact on the larger culture. Buzzwords result when the words of an inside community are heard to "hum" with implications for a larger community of outsiders, even when the outsiders cannot fully access the precise meanings of the words that hum for them. The remote implications of a buzzword overwhelm its direct or immediate meaning, a trait characteristic of purely conductive symbols.

Buzzwords come under public attack with the recognition that a person may be trying to pass off for substance or meat the hum of a buzzword's remote implications. For example, just before the 1992 Demo-

---

[7]We need to distinguish between using jargon and argot and invoking the words "jargon" and "argot" to attack a linguistic practice. Those who use jargon and argot are often involved in an efficient form of symbolic expression, one that relies on standard symbols and stereotypes.

cratic New Hampshire primary race, Mark Stamaty (1992), an editorial cartoonist for *The Village Voice* lampooned Bill Clinton for trying to pass off his buzzwords in this fashion (reprinted in Fig. 5.1). Stamaty portrayed an image of a confident Clinton who distinguished himself from other presidential hopefuls with his specific multipointed "plan" for the future that he deposited in public libraries across America. Stamaty showed Clinton "elaborating" his plan in front of a throng of New Hampshirites gaping in admiration. Clinton's plan oozed out in a mosaic of connected but nonetheless unelaborated (i.e., nondense) words like "change," "middle class," and "responsibility," and a man in the front row is remarking "I LOVE his specificity."[8] Buzzwords are examples of symbols with only conductivity going for them. There are, however, other symbols that combine conductivity with density and consensus.

This discussion of buzzwords suggests a relationship between the strength of a symbol's connective properties and the influence an agent can exert on the sociocultural landscape by using that symbol. Further, were there not a fundamental relationship between a symbol's connectivity and the solidarities between individuals in the society, symbols could not be used to exert influence on the sociocultural world. According to the constructural story, the co-evolving relationship of language and solidarities is built in and through the communicative transaction and aggregations of these transactions extending over time and space. Return for a moment to the group of computer users who find mips and megs a useful term to guide their purchase of computers; and to the group of New Hampshire voters who find Bill Clinton's plan a conduit for further discussion about the candidate. Individuals in each group have acquired a buzzword. Their acquisition of mips and megs and plan as buzzwords indicates a history of transactions that is not only co-evolving but creating solidarities between them. Admittedly, the level of solidarity attained for sharing a buzzword is minimal because the only agreement required is that the word in question has remote implications that are somehow "electric."

Levels of solidarity become even more consequential at the group level, when the agents share a more extended transactional history. For example, we can talk about conservative Republicans as a group, in part because they are likely to have very similar social orientations to words like *free market*, and *liberal*. Symbols create solidarity among those who share them. To share a symbol is to share more than a lexicon; it is to share a specific social orientation, a history, a way of dealing with and describing the world. Different agents in the same community can use

---

[8]Syndicated editorial cartoon. Published in the *Pittsburgh Post-Gazette*, January 18, 1992.

FIG. 5.1. © 1992 Mark Alan Stamaty. Reprinted with permission.

the same words with very different social orientations to them. In that case, agents have the same concepts but different symbols. For the consumer, mips and megs is a buzzword. For the computer engineer, it is a term of art. The word mips and megs, in this case, does not create solidarity between these populations but rather emphasizes the different lives they lead.

A TYPOLOGY OF SYMBOLS

Symbols vary on the three connective dimensions discussed above: density, consensus, and conductivity. On each dimension, symbols can be either *low* or *high* and, as a consequence, they can be categorized into a typology. Each type is determined according to whether the symbol is high or low in density, consensus, and conductivity, respectively. Dividing each of the three dimensions into the values of high and low yields eight (2^3) types of symbolic expression. These types (adapted from Carley 1984, 1986c; see also Carley & Kaufer, in press; Kaufer & Carley, in press) are presented in Fig. 5.2.

These types are ordered around the cube in Fig. 5.2. Ordinary words have low connectivity on all three dimensions of connectivity and are least likely to indicate or exploit significant solidarities when individuals employ them in a communicative transaction. Standard symbols, on the other hand, are highly connected on all three dimensions and are most likely to indicate or exploit solidarities when used in a communicative transaction. A useful way to illustrate the entire typology is to watch a skilled author manipulate each symbol type in a single writing—a single transaction with readers. Studying a single transaction does not tell us how symbols are distributed across a particular community. It does not supply us with the empirical methods we require to extract social maps from a community of agents. Yet it does illustrate the distribution of symbols within the encapsulated mental model of one writer, and it further suggests how an author can seek to exert authority over a community of readers by altering their mental models. To do so, the author needs to exploit concepts considered high in connectivity in a social mapping of the targeted readership.

The author we examine for illustration is Terrence Rafferty, film critic of the *New Yorker*, and the writing we look at is his scathing critique ("Smoke and Mirrors," January 13, 1992) of Oliver Stone's heralded but controversial film *JFK*. Rafferty's (1992) piece is an uncommonly good example to study because, like many critics writing about *JFK*, he gives relatively little space to the film and its merits as a piece of filmmaking. Critics most offended by the film, like Rafferty, often admitted it was

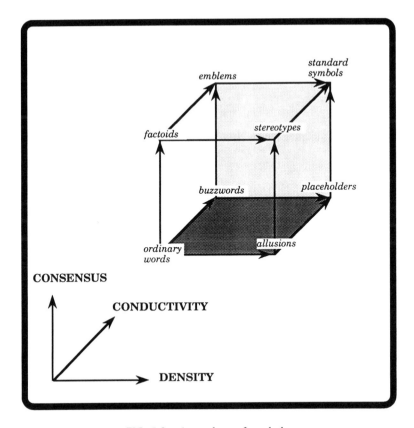

FIG. 5.2.   A typology of symbols.

an example of magnificent film making. Their essential problem with the film, like Rafferty's, is based on Stone's claim to have made a film that very plausibly, if not accurately, depicts the events of the Kennedy assassination. Rafferty's target in the critique is not so much *JFK* itself, but Stone and the legion of conspiracy buffs who would be taken in by Stone's allegedly visual propaganda. Rafferty's piece established two communities of interest relative to *JFK*. The first community consists of those who have doggedly sifted through the reams of conflicting evidence that have come out about the assassination for a quarter century. Members of this community are presumably responsible, thoughtful, and driven by logic. They are thus exasperated by all the loose ends and contradictions the evidence has left behind. They do not totally believe the Warren Commission; nor do they totally believe anyone else. This community is held together only by its weary skepticism about the whole subject. This is the community to which Rafferty and, presumably, most readers of the

New Yorker belong. The second community consists of Stone and those he might persuade. This community, in Rafferty's view, consists of passionate true believers who mistake buzzwords for substantive beliefs. Most of Rafferty's critique is designed to establish the credibility of the first community and to impugn that of the second.

Let us consider one of the hundreds of ordinary words[9] in Rafferty's text. These ordinary words have standard, but narrow, dictionary meanings and little historical presence. They are concepts that dominate our everyday vocabularies but have, because of their low connectivity, only a weak presence in our communicative lexicons and maps. Examples of such ordinary words are *the*, *even*, and *and*. Because of both their low connectivity and the relationship we noted earlier between connectivity and solidarity, ordinary words are the least potent symbols for solidarity. They almost never distinguish the histories of different groups. Although it is tempting to limit ordinary words to simple function words in English, ordinary words can convey substantial content and even sharp attitudes. Consider Rafferty's use of the ordinary word *maddeningly*, as in: "Even the forensic data are maddeningly inconclusive. . . ."

The entire sentence to which this fragment belongs describes a belief of Rafferty and his like-minded readers. But the belief applies across many positions on the issue, and by no means distinguishes Rafferty and the readers who think like him. After all, even Stone's community could not deny or disagree with the meaning of maddeningly in this fragment as a statement about the perplexity of the case and the frustration all have suffered in trying to get to the bottom of it. Maddeningly, like other ordinary words, is low in conductivity, density, and consensus. Ordinary words are relatively inert concepts that hold their dictionary meaning but do not unite with many other words to form a much larger pattern of sociohistorical meaning. Were agents to rely exclusively on ordinary words, the information they communicate with others would be deprived of sociohistorical depth and continuity, and the content and evoked meaning of sentences would vary as a direct function of their length. Language would be neither an effective nor efficient vehicle for community building.

Ordinary words acquire more sociohistorical significance and continuity when they become objects of widespread or detailed sociohistorical consensus. Rafferty could not speak to either his own community or to Stone's in an efficient way about the assassination were the following words not objects of some minimal historical consensus, carrying an overt historical dimension to their meaning not attributable to ordinary words: *Zapruder Film, Dealy Plaza, November 22, 1963*. Some words, such

---

[9]This type was originally called *prostista* in Carley (1984, 1986c).

as "factoids,"[10] have agreed-upon meanings that are neither conductive nor dense but are high in consensus. Factoids function as uncontroversial reference points for communities of speakers and Rafferty uses them as such. Through factoidal reference, he is able to tap into his readers' knowledge of the Kennedy assassination. Use of these words does not allow him to build solidarity with his projected community against Stone's. An important function of factoids is to create a veneer of a shared culture when the beliefs shared remain shallow and, in some sense, superficial. Factoids remind us, but only in the thinnest way, that we share a common culture every time we play a trivia game, watch a TV quiz show, or take an IQ test.

Words can move beyond the ordinary not only by increasing their consensus but also by increasing their conductivity or density. Lacking a consensus among language users, symbols that are nonetheless highly conductive or dense do not so much build solidarity within the group as they name issues for which a consensus is sought. Such concepts can still build common orientations toward points of salience within an issue. In Rafferty's text, such a symbol is *Kennedy assassination*. The phrase Kennedy assassination is a placeholder[11] for the issues raised by the events of November 22, 1963. These placeholders give individuals with very different orientations on an issue the sense, nonetheless, of a common vocabulary with which to discuss it. They allow Rafferty, in many places, the appearance of addressing readers with whom he vigorously disagrees about the assassination. Placeholders may serve to focus or to mask a conflict by identifying those issues for which there is general concern but little agreement.

In contrast, symbols that are highly conductive but neither dense nor highly consented to are, as we have seen, buzzwords.[12] Being low in consensus, buzzwords are not objects of consensus; being low in density, they may lead to or from only a few other concepts. Nonetheless, buzzwords activate a bevy of remotely related concepts whose content and whose relationships to the buzzword, for many language users, are not well thought through. Rafferty associates the Kennedy assassination with a rat-a-tat-tat of buzzwords: *right-wing conspiracy, intelligence community, defense establishment, coup d'état, military brass, covert-action cowboys, the assassinations of Robert Kennedy and Martin Luther King, Jr., Watergate, Iran–Contra, the October Surprise*. These buzzwords pervade the community Rafferty projects and the community he sees Stone projecting. However, there is, to Rafferty's way of thinking,

---

[10]This type was originally called *measures* in Carley (1984, 1986c).
[11]This type was originally called *place holders* in Carley (1984, 1986c).
[12]This type was originally called *buzzwords* in Carley (1984, 1986c).

one key difference in how they pervade each of these communities. For Rafferty's community, the concepts are recognized for the buzzwords they are. They are understood to be sparsely elaborated, poorly specified, vague, and wishful. For Stone's community, in Rafferty's thinking, these concepts have been mistakenly elevated to the status of standard symbol (dense, highly consented to, and conductive) and have clouded Stone's (and his community's) capacity to discriminate the plausible from the implausible: "It's a thick gumbo of truths, half-truths, unverifiable hypotheses, and pure rant, and Stone ladles it out indiscriminately."

Through irony directed at Stone's expense, Rafferty calls attention to the significant difference between focused evidence and the spiraling tide of remote inference aided by buzzwords treated as standard symbols.

Rafferty is less interested in attacking Stone's film than in describing the audience who can be expected to buy into its basic premises. The draw of *JFK* is not based on the prior beliefs of the American public but on their prior cynicism, which renders them, in Rafferty's view, incapable of knowing what to believe. Cynicism against the government runs so deep for the audience of 1992, Rafferty conjectures, that it will run with any anti-establishment diatribe.

Emblems[13] are concepts high in conductivity and consensus but low in density. In view of their low density, emblems are often proper names that have come to achieve a relatively thin but nonetheless agreed-upon sociohistorical meaning within the collective memory of groups. Of course, since emblems rely on consensus, an emblem for one group may not be an emblem for another, or at least a very different kind of emblem. One can view Rafferty's argument in part as a clash of different group's emblems. For Rafferty and his projected community, the historical Jim Garrison as emblem represents a character of questionable moral and legal judgment; for Stone and his community, as Rafferty presents them, Garrison, with cinematic magic and sleight of hand, has become an emblem of "good guy" decency.

Among serious students of history, Rafferty maintains, the historical Garrison was a flawed character who pursued an irresponsible case against Clay Shaw.

Yet Stone chose actor Kevin Costner to play Jim Garrison and the hero of *JFK*. Rafferty observed that Costner has become an object of admiration for the American audience of moviegoers, whatever their stand on the Kennedy assassination. There is thus a conspicuous mismatch between Costner's status as emblem and the historical Garrison's.

The mismatch is so sorely apparent that, in Rafferty's view, Stone could only have made it deliberately, in an attempt to blur presidential history

---

[13]This type was originally called *emblems* in Carley (1984, 1986c).

with Hollywood history. Such directional and casting choices for a film that claims documentary realism call into question Stone's own ethos, and Rafferty emblematizes Stone as an impetuous and irresponsible visual historian.

Now let us turn our attention to allusions,[14] symbols high only in their density. Rafferty acknowledged the allusive qualities of the *Grassy Knoll*, especially among conspiracy theorists, in a passing reference to its fame. On the strength of being dense yet low in consensus, allusions are especially useful for making contact with the backgrounds of diverse audiences in order to build solidarity with them in the absence of strong agreement. For example, conspiracy theorists of the assassination tend to elaborate the role of the Grassy Knoll in different ways, but they can all wink at the density of the reference given its presumed role in the assassination plot. Although conspiracy theorists cannot agree on the meaning of the Grassy Knoll, they can at least agree—not because of consensus but because of the sheer density of connections—on the importance of its presence and the implications of its importance in rendering the findings of the Warren Commission incorrect.

In contrast to the allusion, stereotypes[15] are concepts that are dense and highly consented to. They form the basis for a broad sociohistorical consensus within groups. Stereotypes are low in conductivity, however, and are unlikely to be "vogue" terms on the tip of everyone's tongue. They are more likely to be symbols left just below the surface, called upon only in passing to imbue a focal subject with a wealth of implied attributes. For example, Rafferty observed that Costner made Garrison appealing not simply because of Costner's emblematic appeal to moviegoers but because Stone had Costner's character play a stereotypical Hollywood figure—the *Capra-style hero*, an understated hero playing the underdog who eventually triumphs over more powerful forces, a hero that American audiences since the 1930s have grown to love. The Capra-style hero, an image for a leading man across an entire genre of American films, television shows, and Saturday morning cartoons, is a much denser reference than the person of a single actor—which is why Rafferty asked *New Yorker* readers to view Costner's performance in terms of this stereotype rather than the other way around.

Rafferty also relied on stereotypes at Stone's expense and repeatedly associated the director with two unflattering stereotypical motifs. The first, less frequent, motif is that of Stone as the purveyor of tabloid information, playing out like an installment of "America's Most Wanted." The

---

[14]This type was originally called *prototypes* in Carley (1984, 1986c).
[15]This type was originally called *stereotypes* in Carley (1984, 1986c).

second, more frequent, stereotype is that of Stone as an out-of-control military commando, still shell shocked from Vietnam, still thinking he is on a combat mission and still trying to direct *Platoon*, with a different cast of characters. Viewed from the vantage of this stereotype, Stone's film does not establish a relationship with the audience but rather ambushes it: "platoon-leader Stone carries out his mission here."

Finally, we turn our attention to standard symbols.[16] These are words high in density, conductivity, and consensus. Standard symbols are the purest examples of what Cassirer (1953) and Burke had in mind when they thought of symbolic language and its ties to group identification, the type of symbols most likely to "induce cooperation in beings that by nature respond to symbols" (Burke, 1969, p. 43). In professional communities, standard symbols take the form of terms of art—another name for the conceptual (not merely gratuitous) jargon and argot that a profession uses to furnish its own interior in a decor that outsiders do not know how to reproduce. The term *standard symbol* was coined by the anthropologist Leach (1976). He defined standard symbols as those symbols reflecting societal or group consensus and maintained that such symbols are particularly essential for the growth of a common culture through language. Leach's notion of standard symbol is not far afield from Small's (1978) notion of *concept symbol* in science. Small maintained that concept symbols are inferences shared by members of a scientific specialty about what a scientific text (and citations to that text) mean. Small tied the notion of concept symbol explicitly to scientific citation, yet it is clear that he believes concept symbols are standard symbols (in Leach's sense) and underlie the growth of a common culture within scientific specialties.

In civic communities, like those that wage verbal battle over the Kennedy assassination, standard symbols reduce a group's stance on the issues to its essentials. They are the shibboleths of a group's identity, logos in verbal form that carry the baggage of the group's experiences forward into new transactions. Concepts referring to well-known roles carrying the weight of agreed-upon sociocultural experiences and norms, such as president, conspiracist, assassin, actor, and so forth, are examples of standard symbols. Significantly, standard symbols are not always easy to compress into single words or phrases plucked from a group's public utterance. They often need to be summarized from a network of meaning inferred from a group's recurring discourse. From the following passages, for example, we gather that Rafferty projects as standards within his community the concepts of *wearied individual* and *satisfactory solution*. The first of these concepts identifies the role Rafferty wants to

---

[16]This type was originally called *symbols* in Carley (1984, 1986c).

legitimate relative to the Kennedy assassination and the role he wants his community to accept for themselves. The second identifies the implicit statements of proof and evidence that Rafferty expects readers of the *New Yorker* to demand, which has not been forthcoming.

From a constructural point of view, agents who share standard symbols already share, to a large extent, a language and a history. The greater the number of standard symbols within a community, the more extensive its common history, and the more embedded or implicit the meaning of any communication within any of its transactions. On the other hand, the fewer the number of standard symbols, the more openly explicit and elaborate communications must be in order to coordinate meanings successfully. An agent who mistakes as a standard symbol a concept that only functions within a communicative transaction as a placeholder will fail to communicate adequately and will be surprised at the alternative meanings that listeners or readers will extract. Legal communications are explicitly documented, in part, because the law takes as its burden the laying bare of the trusts and agreements that are taken for granted in social life. One final point is worth making about standard symbols and communication. Merely because a community shares a great many standard symbols does not imply that their sharing or solidarity will continue. If individuals in such communities continue to engage one another, they will continue to co-construct meanings and so continue to co-construct their language and history. In some cases, this continued co-construction will increase their solidarity; in other cases, it will reduce it as they find their relative similarity with outside partners increasing faster than the relative similarity that has fueled their own interaction.

Despite the obvious importance of standard symbols to the life of communities, we bear in mind that symbols play a significant role in communicative transactions and in the life of communities, even when they are low in consensus. There may be little consensus on what *military establishment* means in reference to the Kennedy assassination, yet the mere mention of the word, because of its conductivity, can generate much heated debate and commentary. There may be little consensus in what Grassy Knoll means among conspiracy theorists, yet the mere mention of the word, because of its density, is enough to pull them together. There may be little sociohistorical consensus about what maddeningly means in a statement about the Kennedy assassination but there is nonetheless a social consensus about its meaning as a discrete dictionary entry. In each case, individual networks of symbolic meaning cross over into social networks of meaning in the absence of deeply rooted consensus.

QUANTIFYING QUALITATIVE INTUITIONS
ABOUT SYMBOLS

Exploring a typology of symbols within the confines of a single text allows us to compare different types of symbols working in close proximity. However, restricting this analysis to single texts (or single artifacts in general) does not allow us to track the co-construction of meanings that take place when agents communicate information in concurrent or recurrent transactions. The example of Rafferty only shows us a writer attempting to construct social meanings from but one side of a communicative transaction. Furthermore, our rhetorical analysis of the symbols in Rafferty's text has been notoriously qualitative and subjective. We have offered no supporting evidence for our classification of Grassy Knoll as an allusion, Kennedy assassination as a placeholder, and so on. We relied on the license of the critic to make these classifications and hoped that you, the reader, shared our intuitions and at least found them plausible.

However, if we want to embed this analysis of language into the constructural framework of chapter 4, we need a more objective way of measuring the connectivity of symbols that exist in the utterances or texts that an agent brings to actual transactions. In much the way Chomsky sought a logical theory and model (called grammar) that can be used to generate and analyze all and only the grammatical sentences of a language, a more scientific approach to the communicative transaction seeks a theory and model that can be used to encode, generate, and analyze communications as encapsulations of mental models. The theory must fit into the larger story of the communicative transaction of chapter 4, but must remain consistent with the details of language, communication, and solidarity we have included in this chapter.

Thus far, we have indicated what the dimensions of density, conductivity, and consensus mean, but we have yet to consider how these dimensions might be measured or computed from verbal or textual data. We have also divided each dimension into high and low values, shown both how this division leads to a typology of symbols and how the critic might usefully apply this typology. But we have yet to indicate methods for dividing dimensions of connectivity into high or low values and computing, for any particular concept, where it falls within the typology of symbol classes. Simply put, we have yet to operationalize the dimensions of symbolic connectivity and the typology following from it. To seek operationalizations of these judgments is to seek an essentially quantitative basis for what we have been treating as essentially qualitative judgments. It is to seek a social science that can begin to account for and explain what we have been treating as a sociorhetorical theory of the symbol.

To help us in the search, let us return briefly to the Rafferty article, no longer as a rhetorical critic but as a social scientist inquiring into the actual effect of Rafferty's article on readers of the *New Yorker*. We might determine the effect of Rafferty's article on the internal symbol systems of *New Yorker* readers in this way:

1. We would identify a corpus of concepts from the Rafferty article whose symbolic function we are interested in measuring. We would want, in other words, a way to represent the communication itself as a network of symbols.

2. We would require a way to analyze the network which would measure the level of density, conductivity, and consensus for any symbol within the network. We would also need to establish cutpoints to allow us to determine whether a particular level of density, conductivity, or consensus is high or low. We need these cutpoints to subclassify any symbol in the network into one of the eight types (ordinary word, factoid, etc.).

3. We would want to find a subject pool of regular *New Yorker* readers who had not yet read Rafferty's article.

4. We would want to use these same reliable network extraction and analysis procedures to see how these readers connect the concepts in the communication into their own network of elaborations. Because the readers have not yet read Rafferty, we would expect the conceptual network for Rafferty's text and for *New Yorker* readers to be somewhat different, although somewhat alike (since Rafferty, after all, is writing for these readers). The extent of these similarities and differences needs to be empirically determined. Rafferty's text, for example, will elaborate *Lee Harvey Oswald* in certain ways, and readers who had not been influenced by Rafferty might elaborate the same concept in certain overlapping but nonetheless distinct ways. Based on the network derived from the *New Yorker* article, for example, Lee Harvey Oswald might have the connective properties of an allusion; based on the network derived from *New Yorker* readers (or at least some readers), Oswald might have the connective properties of an emblem or stereotype.

5. We would invite the *New Yorker* readers to read Rafferty.

6. We would again encode and analyze the conceptual networks of the readers after they had read Rafferty.

7. We would compare the pre- and postnetworks of these readers to determine whether change has occurred. Were readers at all influenced by Rafferty, we would expect their networks to change in consonance with the network of meaning established by his text. If it is the case that authors can persuade through the use of highly connected symbols, we

would expect that any changes occurring in the reader's networks would be related to the type of symbols employed by Rafferty and the differences in types between those Rafferty assigned and those initially assigned by readers.

In any case, our analysis should tell us something about Rafferty's lexicon as an individual language user discussing the Kennedy assassination; it should tell us something about the social lexicon of the typical *New Yorker* reader; and it should assess Rafferty's transaction with these readers (and their over-time trajectory) as an instance of individual lexicons co-evolving with pockets of shared or social lexicons.

To summarize, a more quantitative approach to the qualitative notions of language, symbols, and community building involves the following steps:

1. Extracting conceptual networks from communications or persons.
2. Determining the connectivity of the symbol (viz., density, conductivity, consensus), given one or more extracted networks.
3. Setting empirical cutpoints for distinguishing high and low values for each dimension, dividing a conceptual network into one of the eight types.
4. Constructing social maps of language in order to measure the lexicons of individual language users and their co-evolution with social lexicons.

In the following paragraphs, we describe some progress made on each of these steps.

Extracting Networks From Texts and Persons

Recently, researchers have reported techniques for extracting connectivity relations among the concepts elicited in situated discourse (Alexander & Danowski, 1990; Carley, 1986a; Carley & Palmquist, 1992; Danowski, 1988; Palmquist, 1990). Indeed, a variety of techniques from a variety of approaches exist for extracting conceptual frameworks from transcribed interview data or from texts (see, e.g., Carley, 1988; Carley & Palmquist, 1992; Danowski, 1982). These techniques all offer reliable methods for transforming raw linguistic data into a conceptual network in which concepts (i.e., words and phrases) are the nodes, and the relationships between concepts, the links.[17] It is beyond our purposes to

---

[17]These techniques vary in how they locate relationships and, consequently, what they admit as being a relationship (see Carley, in press-c, for more discussion).

review each of these methods here as they are adequately detailed in the literature just cited. Moreover, to perform the kind of social science study on the symbol that we are advocating, one can be rather eclectic about the extraction procedure used to build the network. This is because the techniques for analyzing a conceptual network for connectivity relations do not depend on the details of the network's original construction.

It is important that a vocabulary of concepts be developed for their theoretical interest prior to studying them in particular communications. The communications must be examined to determine whether the concepts are present in the vocabulary and to trace the frequency of their occurrence (as is the case for standard content analysis). In addition, the communication should also be examined to determine the relationships between concepts. A relationship links two concepts and can stand for any type of association, not necessarily causation or implication. Relationships are also directed, meaning that the concepts in a relationship need to be distinguished according to whether they occupy the anterior (subject) or the posterior (predicate) position. One way to code a communication for concepts and relationships is to code it statement by statement. A statement consists of two concepts and the relationship between them.

Analyzing Networks for Connectivity

The resultant conceptual network can then be analyzed and the connectivity of each symbol in the network measured. A numerical score for density, conductivity, and consensus can be computed. For clarity and precision, let us define a concept as any ideational kernel that is devoid of meaning, except as it is connected to other concepts. A focal concept is one whose connective properties one is specifically interested in discussing or measuring.

The density of a focal concept is defined as the number of concepts to which the focal concept is directly linked. A direct link begins or ends at the focal concept and does not intersect any intermediate concepts. In Fig. 5.3, Focal Concept A has a density of 4 because it is directly linked to four other concepts (B,C,D,E).

The conductivity of a focal concept is defined as the product that results when the number of concepts linked directly into the focal concept is multiplied by the number of concepts linked directly out from it. For example, in Fig. 5.3, the conductivity of Focal Concept A is 9, as three concepts (C,D,E) link into it and three (B,C,E) out. Because conductivity represents the capacity of a symbol to function as a nonterminating gateway for concepts beyond itself, a focal concept will have zero conductivity if it is a launching point (out links but no in links) or a sink-hole (in links but no out links).

The consensus of a focal concept can be defined as the number of links that meet or exceed some threshold of agreement for some population of language users. Imagine a community of 50 language users. The numbers on the links in Fig. 5.3 represent the number of language users in this community who agree to the link. Of the 50 users, 20 share a link between A and B, one between A and C, five between A and D, and 32 between A and E. Let us suppose that 30 (a majority in our community of 50) is our threshold value, the number of people who must agree to the link before we say it has become incorporated into the community's social knowledge.

Researchers may disagree about where to set the threshold value, but threshold values are easy to set and reset and many thresholds can be explored for a particular community before one is settled on. For purposes of illustration, let us assume that 30 remains a reasonable threshold. We can then say that in view of the fact that Concept A has two links that meet or exceed this threshold, A has a consensus value of 2. Notice that this measure of consensus refers to a dormant consensus, social knowledge that agents may not be aware of or exploit for rhetorical purposes. For more on social knowledge, see Polanyi (1962) and Carley (1986b).

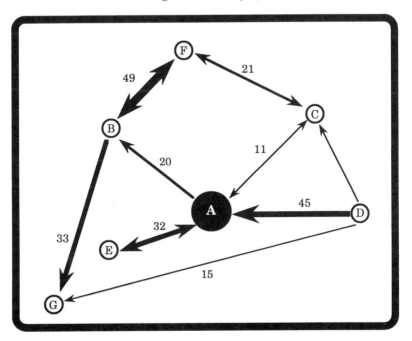

FIG. 5.3. Stylized conceptual network or map.

Setting Cutpoints to Classify Symbols Into Types

As we have seen, any focal concept in a network can be assigned a density, conductivity, or consensus score. To further assign a focal concept into one of the eight types, we need a way to establish whether a particular score on each dimension constitutes a high or low value. There are various ways to establish these cutpoints, and the best way depends on the researcher's purposes. For example, the median makes a good cutpoint when we want to cut a sample corpus in half. On this strategy, we calculate the median density, conductivity, and consensus for all the focal concepts in the network. We then assign all the concepts (half the corpus) that fall below, say, the medium density a low on density. All the concepts that fall at or above the medium receive a score of high. The use of quartiles is a good cutpoint when the focus is on extremes, words of either extremely low or extremely high connectivity in a corpus. The statistical mean makes a reasonable cutpoint when we want to quantify the intuition that words low in connectivity are just "below average" in their connectivity and words high in connectivity are "above average."

Employing the statistical mean as the cutpoint, suppose we find that a sample of 50 *New Yorker* readers assigned to read Rafferty's text employed 100 symbols with an average density of 7 elaborations, and average conductivity of 15, and an average consensus of 3. This means that in the social lexicon of these readers, whether a word is classified as an ordinary word, factoid, buzzword, or emblem (low density), or as a placeholder, allusion, stereotype, or standard symbol (high density) depends on whether its density is above or below 7 elaborations.

The notion of a social lexicon is important to a theory of language as community building and deserves a more precise definition. Strictly speaking, a social lexicon consists of the set of concepts such that: (a) each concept is known by at least one individual in a social grouping of interest (e.g., readers of the *New Yorker*); and (b) each of these concepts is associated just with elaborations that everyone in the social grouping agrees (tacitly) to be elaborations. A social lexicon consists, then, of the minimal premise about the connectivity of symbols that enables a group (readers of the *New Yorker*) to exist as a group, that enables an author (Rafferty) to address the group persuasively, and that enables analysts of an author (like us) to access the author's probable strategies in doing so.

Although social lexicons can be quantitatively measured, it is important to appreciate that our intuitions of social lexicons are already driven by quantitative principles. For example, our analysis of Rafferty's text was purely qualitative and subjective. Nonetheless, what guided our assessments was an image of the average judgments of the *New Yorker* reader. We used no explicit calculations to classify Kevin Costner as an emblem and Capra style as a stereotype. Yet our classification was based on a quantitatively relevant intuition about readers of the *New Yorker*. We assumed that such readers would know a good deal about Frank Capra's influence on American cinema—more, on average, than other symbols in Rafferty's text. We also assumed that the same readers would know that Costner was a "hot" actor and they would share some basic knowledge that he was hot. This would be sufficient knowledge for readers of the *New Yorker* to discern Costner's emblematic status. Being an actor of relatively recent vintage, Costner, we assumed, would not be as well known, on average, to the *New Yorker* reader as other symbols in Rafferty's text. Whether we are ultimately right in our subjective assessments is not important. The point is that our judgments about what appear to be extremely hazy and elusive qualitative data were not without some implicit quantitative cutpoints. Moreover, a detailed quantitative analysis of Rafferty's text could be done given the foregoing measures. Such an analysis would differ in detail, though not in intent, from the qualitative exemplar we provided.

Constructing Social Maps of Language

A set of statements with overlapping concepts form a map or network. Consequently, an individual's lexicon relative to a specific topic (e.g., the Kennedy assassination), elicited as a series of statements with overlapping concepts, can be represented as a map or concept network. Furthermore, a researcher can represent a community's social lexicon on a topic by combining the maps representing individual lexicons. In such a social map, the strength of the relationship linking any two concepts can be considered a measure of the degree of agreement across the members of the society that the two concepts are linked. If we found, for example, that 25 of 50 *New Yorker* readers associate Kevin Costner and Capra style, then a social map of these readers would have a value of 25 on the link between these concepts. Carley (1984, 1988, 1990a, in press-d) developed a battery of computer programs to code transcripts of any communication (e.g., utterances, dialogue, texts) into statements and to extract individual and social maps from these coded statements (Carley, 1986a, 1988, in press-d; Carley & Palmquist, 1992). These programs were put to use in a variety of contexts to study the co-evolution of individual and social lexicons within and across particular communicative transactions (Carley, 1984; Carley, in press-a, b, & c; Carley & Kaufer, in press; Carley & Palmquist, 1992; Palmquist, 1990).[18]

---

[18]These programs are part of a software package, the MECA system, for coding and analyzing textual material. Readers may write to Carley for more information on these programs.

NETWORKED REPRESENTATIONS OF SYMBOLS

For a more rigorous understanding of the eight symbol types and a deeper appreciation of how one type may evolve into another, it is useful to consider their distinctive network representations; that is, the way each symbol type is distinctively expressed as a concept network within a larger network representing an individual or social lexicon. We close this chapter by illustrating each symbol type in terms of its particular network characteristics.

Ordinary Words

Earlier, we suggested that the symbol maddeningly had the characteristics of an ordinary word in Rafferty's text. Rafferty used maddeningly in its normal dictionary definition, to indicate the sense of frustration and exasperation that a person may feel in sorting through the contradictory evidence of the Kennedy assassination. Rafferty's meaning applied across different social orientations to the Kennedy assassination. That is to say, as Rafferty saw it, the symbol's meaning described an attitude reflective of many positions on the assassination and provided no point of solidarity for any one position. And, despite the wide application of the word's meaning, it has very little implicit or socially embedded meaning (Fig. 5.4).

Factoids

Factoids, unlike ordinary words, have achieved greater consensus in what little embedded meaning they have. Factoids may also result from erstwhile emblems that have lost the timeliness that once made them conductive (e.g., the 1904 World's Fair), or stereotypes that, through time, space, or cultural distance, have lost their density and sedimented into historical curiosities (e.g., 19th-century beliefs associating the education of minorities with seditious activity). We saw in Rafferty's text that focal concepts like Zapruder Film, Dealy Plaza, and November 22, 1963 seem to function as factoids (Fig. 5.5).

Placeholders

The network representation of a placeholder like Kennedy assassination is indicated in Fig. 5.6. As a placeholder, that concept is both dense and conductive but low in consensus, a hot area of intense but nonconver

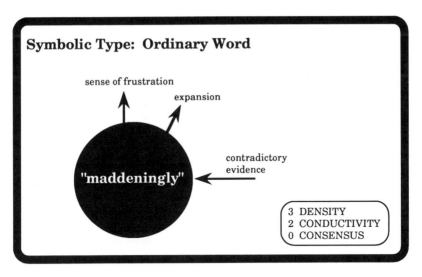

FIG. 5.4.   An example of an ordinary word.

gent discussion. Notice that although low in consensus overall, a placeholder can still reflect the site of a broad but very thin consensus. For example, most *New Yorker* readers might associate Kennedy assassination with concepts like Oswald and presidential assassinations. Placeholders can be the center of some agreement but, on average, they attract fewer agreements than other available symbols in the sociolinguistic community.

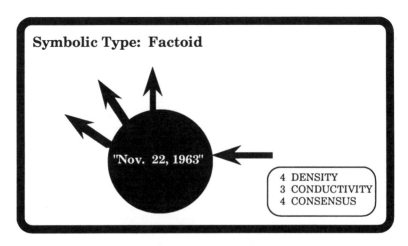

FIG. 5.5.   An example of a factoid.

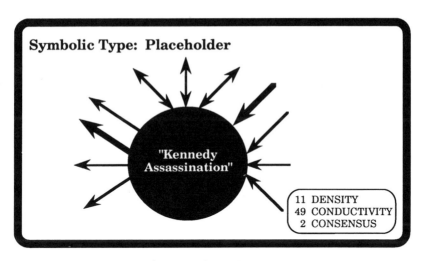

FIG. 5.6.   An example of a placeholder.

Buzzwords

Buzzwords are high only in conductivity. They may emerge when ordinary words become above average in their conductivity but remain low in density and consensus. In his critique, Rafferty spoke of Stone's allegations of a right-wing conspiracy to kill Kennedy, which Stone turned into a gateway to other terms: the escalation of the Vietnam War under L.B.J., the assassinations of Robert Kennedy and Martin Luther King, Jr., Watergate, Iran–Contra. Stone's audience, to Rafferty, agrees that connections exist between the assassination conspiracy and this slew of other developments. Yet the conspiracy itself, Rafferty noted, remains curiously underspecified, only sparsely tied to all the harm it has supposedly continued to wreak. Many of these later developments, it turns out, are more dense and better specified than the Kennedy right-wing conspiracy. This fact is reflected in Fig. 5.7. Thematic issues, such as Vietnam, the assassinations of RFK and King, Watergate, and Iran–Contra, are all more dense and better specified than right-wing conspiracy, each linked to 10 other concepts. Yet right-wing conspiracy is the only word falling on a high number of paths. The other thematic words have more out links (10), but fewer in links (1) than right-wing conspiracy and so lie on only 10 paths. Right-wing conspiracy has 4 in links and 4 out links and lies on 16 paths. Although less dense and defined than the other themes, right-wing conspiracy is the best concept to spark recognition of all the other issues—which is the kind of spark a buzzword is supposed to ignite.

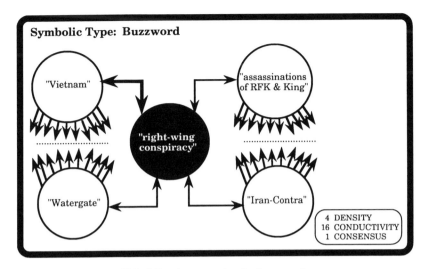

FIG. 5.7.   An example of a buzzword.

Allusions

Allusions are words lying in a dense network of meaning, with low conductivity and consensus. Conspiracy theorists are united in assigning density to what Rafferty called the famous Grassy Knoll, even though they do not converge on its role in the assassination and take little common meaning from it.

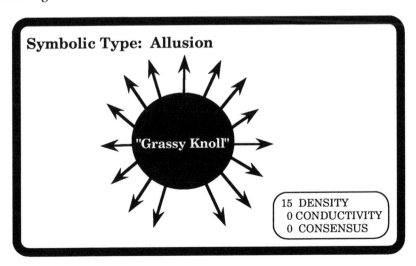

FIG. 5.8.   An example of an allusion.

Emblems

An emblem involves high consensus and conductivity but low density. In many respects, emblems are the direct opposite of allusions in their symbolic functioning. Allusions are heavily elaborated but nonconvergent and nonfluid aspects of a social lexicon. Emblems, on the other hand, are agreed upon and fluid but also light and fleeting aspects of that lexicon. These disparate functions distinguish the roles of Grassy Knoll and Kevin Costner in Rafferty's text (Fig. 5.8).

Stereotypes

Stereotypes are concepts that are high in density and consensus but not conductivity. They may be allusions whose links have become widely agreed upon over time, at least within a group. It is worth noting that a symbol with an above average number of highly agreed upon elaborations can still have many elaborations that are not agreed to. Thus Capra style can still function as a stereotype in the social lexicon of a *New Yorker* reader even if some *New Yorker* readers elaborate Capra style in a purely idiosyncratic way and even if some are clueless about who Capra was. The network representation of this stereotype is illustrated in Fig. 5.9.

Standard Symbols

Standard symbols are high on all connectivity dimensions. Symbols that have become standard may include terms of art and role names. For Rafferty and his audience, *president* and *assassin* function as standard symbols. But so do the terms which describe the norms and criteria (e.g., *judicious*, *cautious*) Rafferty would have us use when investigating the Kennedy assassination or any other historical event, for that matter (Fig. 5.10).

SUMMARY AND IMPLICATIONS FOR PRINT

The constructural story of the communicative transaction can be told by making minimal assumptions about language, by abstracting language into a simple symbol set consisting of information in mental models that can be encapsulated and externalized in communications. These were the minimalist assumptions of language that we accepted in chapter 4 and that continue to operate for the duration of this book. Nonetheless, at

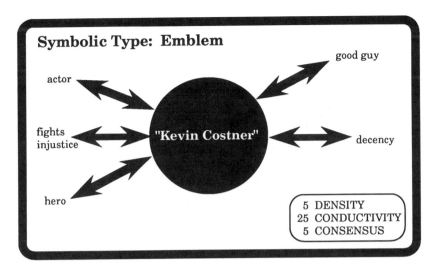

FIG. 5.9. An example of an emblem.

the beginning of the chapter, we pointed out two reasons for exploring the role of language beyond these minimalist assumptions:

1. Some questions that can legitimately be asked about a single communicative transaction benefit from a more extended treatment of language.
2. If there is any merit to the claim that communication technologies change the nature of language, then we can scarcely understand,

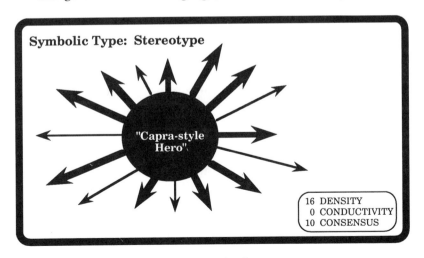

FIG. 5.10. An example of a stereotype.

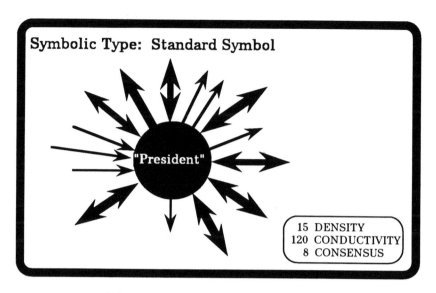

FIG. 5.11.   An example of a standard symbol.

much less test, such claims without a fairly rich understanding of the role of language in the communicative transaction.

Although an interlude for the purposes of this book, this chapter suggests that language can play a central role in the constructural story. We have described dimensions of linguistic connectivity (density, consensus, conductivity) that define the limits through which communicative transactions can affect language and meaning. The greater an agent's reach, the more likely the agent is to increase the connectivity (density, consensus, conductivity) of symbols utilized in a communication and to decrease the connectivity of symbols that fail to be utilized or reinforced.

It remains to draw out the larger implications of this discussion of language for print. Hypotheses about the impact of print often imply that the high connectivity of meaning was an achievement of print technology, that only when print technology (and the social organizations associated with it) came upon the scene, did sociolinguistic phenomena like buzzwords, slogans, cliches, professional knowledge, and the terms of art required for professional scientific consensus appear. From the perch of our current exploration, we see that these generalizations, left unqualified, are nonsense. The high connectivity of our sociolinguistic world can be accounted for without entering the realm of mass communication technologies. Although we noted that studies of the symbol were rejuvenated at the time of industrialized print, we should not confuse bringing a phenomenon to visibility with bringing it to existence. Innovations and new technologies often lead to the proliferation of new words. But the naming of a thing should not imply that the thing did not previously exist; merely that no one paid attention to it.

The strongest case one can make for the relationship between print technology and language is that print may have changed the quantity of symbols of specific types or the rate at which symbols of one type metamorphorized into symbols of another. For example, print did not create buzzwords but, because of its durability, fixity, asynchronicity, and multiplicity, print may have put many more buzzwords (or more of any connected symbol) into circulation at once than is possible in an oral society. Furthermore, language communities did not need print to see ordinary words crystallize into placeholders or stereotypes, or to see placeholders or stereotypes dissolve into ordinary words. But because it made possible more comprehensive and complete reach, print also made possible greater consensus, density, and conductivity for the symbols in the communication. Because it gave greater speed and mobility to words across longer distances, print could increase the rate at which words could change their connectivity relations across populations of language users who were increasingly geographically dispersed.

In some respects, these conjectures about print and language follow from analytic considerations alone. Because of print's multiplicity—the ability of a single author to engage in hundreds, even thousands, of concurrent text-based transactions—it follows that print produced a quantitative increase in the number of communicative transactions that took place within a given community. To claim that print increased the potential number of highly connective symbols circulating at once in a language community is not all that magical when we assume that print does this simply by increasing the overall number of transactions and symbols in circulation. Nor is it magical to say that print increased the rate at which a symbol could undergo changes in connectivity (from one symbol type to another), were we to find that print simply speeded the diffusion of information overall, a hypothesis we explore in chapter 7.

To say that hypotheses about print and print's influence on language are not magical is not to say they are not interesting or deserving of further attention. In later chapters, we make reference to these hypotheses. But the model we introduce in chapter 6 does not equip us to address issues of language formally. As previously noted, the constructural story stands without any additional details of language. To be sure, language, in the form of abstracted symbol sets is part of the formalism developed in chapter 6. But the network representation of language, as described in this chapter, is not part of that formalism. Ultimately, one would like to develop a theory that encompasses both the first order factors described previously and in chapter 6 and the underlying factors of language laid out in this chapter.

The Dynamics of the Communicative Transaction

Compared with the normative conception of order [in Parsonian sociology], the cognitive turn . . . is marked by a shift of interest towards language use and cognitive processes. . . . In a sense, the problem of social order is redefined by turning the traditional approach to social order on its head. Social order is not that which holds society together by somehow controlling individual wills, but that which comes about in the mundane but relentless transactions of these wills. The problem of social order has not only turned into a problem of cognitive order; it has also turned from a macro-level problem to a micro-problem of social action.

—Karin Knorr-Cetina (1981, p. 3)

The new orientation in sociology of which Knorr-Cetina wrote emerged from an attempt to focus on the "mundane but relentless" transactions (of wills) that bridge the reality of individuals to the reality of social and cultural life. This orientation is a reaction to an older sociology that had subsumed the individual and the collective within grand analytic schemes, masking the nature of the transactions linking together the micro and the macro. Rather than specify the dynamics of these transactions, classical theorists of sociology employed mediating concepts to bridge the gap between individual agents at the microlevel and sociocultural organization and change at the macrolevel. For example, Parsons (1937) related individual agency and structure through the mediating concept of *value*; Homans (1961) relied on the economic notion of *exchange*. Blumer (1969) proposed the *role* as the mediator between individuals and the structures of society they can influence.

By the 1980s, social theorists began to realize that the linking concepts presupposed in classical theory were too thin to handle the intricate connections between the microactions of individuals and the macrostructures of society (Knorr-Cetina & Cicourel, 1981; Munch & Smelser, 1987). That same decade produced an impressive output of social theory undertaken to describe micro–macro connections in greater detail and to propose mechanisms to relate them. For example, Collins (1981) described individual actions as "aggregating" to form macrostructures; he identified one aggregation mechanism with interaction-ritual chains. Cicourel (1981) focused his attention on the filtering mechanisms—what he called "summarizing procedures"—required to determine which aspects of the microlevel will survive to the macrolevel. Callon and Latour (1981) probed the agent's capacity to accumulate the human and material resources needed to become a "larger than life" projection at the macrolevel. Giddens (1984) propounded a theory of *structuration*, by which agents influence the macrolevel through a similar husbanding of resources (see chap. 4). Archer (1988) formulated what she called a *morphogenesis* theory, in which macrostructures are formed by combining ideas (the cultural influence) and social relations (the social influence). These theories, uniformly, have useful and insightful things to say about micro–macro connections. All of these social theorists imply, and sometimes state, that these micro–macro connections are rooted in communication, in the dynamics of interactions (or transactions) and the process whereby such transactions aggregate across individuals and over time. Turner (1988) synthesized large portions of this research in his theory of social interaction. Yet none of these theoretical statements provides an operational model of the actual dynamics whereby individuals create macrolevel structures through microlevel transactions. At least, none provides an operational model of communication that is sufficiently detailed or precise enough to permit formal analysis. And, despite a growing acceptance in the literature that individuals, social structure, culture, technology, and language are somehow related as mutually defining elements, the literature has mainly been silent on positing specific mechanisms tying them together.

The silence is not total. A few social scientists have developed more precise quantitative models, intended to describe how individuals integrate themselves within a social structure. As noted by Carley (1990b):

Recent advances in both cognitive science and network theory have engendered the belief that it should be possible to develop analytical models of the relationships between individuals that would enable quantitative predictions of changes in interaction that take into account both the self and the society, the individual and the group, the cognitive and the social. These advances have rekindled the dream, originally seen in social comparison theory (Festinger, 1954), cognitive dissonance theory (Festinger, 1957), and balance theory (Heider, 1958), that it is possible to build a mathematics of group change as a function of individual change. (p. 2)

Nevertheless, these advances are limited in that: (a) They leave out at least one aspect of concern—individuals, social structure, culture, technology, or language; and (b) they tend to describe micro–macro dependencies under asymmetric and often static conditions. To say that a model treats micro–macro connections asymmetrically is to say that it treats the social world merely as a constraint for an essentially individualist theory. Examples of such models are structural symbolic interactionism (Stryker, 1980, 1987) and affect control theory (Heise, 1977; Smith-Lovin, 1988). As representations of social processes, these models are somewhat impoverished, in part, because they ignore the factor of multiple individuals acting concurrently and the specification of mechanisms through which multiple microevents aggregate to form macrolevel phenomena.

Alternatively, to say that a model treats micro–macro connections asymmetrically means that it treats individual cognition only as a constraint for what are essentially theories of group dynamics (Burt, 1982; Chase, 1974; Fararo & Skvoretz, 1986; Krackhardt & Porter, 1986). These group models incorporate a stronger notion of concurrency and aggregation, and they define group behavior in terms of the concurrent aggregation of individual behavior. Yet, such models rely on an impoverished notion of the individual, culture, and language; they do not differentiate individual representations or show how the slightest changes in the knowledge or actions of a single individual can reverberate to the overall behavioral and structural dynamics of the group. In brief, because of either omissions or assumptions of asymmetry (or both), previous social scientific models relating individual and social level behavior fall short of detailing the process by which individual and sociocultural organization and change can co-evolve.

In contrast, constructuralism is specifically tailored to model the interplay between the knowledge of individuals and the interactive ties on which individuals rely in co-constructing a sociocultural world. In a way, constructuralism is a structural theory of diffusion (Burt, 1973; Granovetter, 1973; Merton, 1949; Pool & Kochen, 1978; Price, 1965; Rogers, 1979). Unlike purely structural theories, constructuralism contains a more cognitive perspective on diffusion and the use of information (Feldman & March, 1981; Festinger, 1950; Festinger et al., 1948). Constructuralism is not as fine grained about individuals as standard cognitive theories. Nor is it as rich in historical detail as many theories within sociology. But, in return for abstracting both the realms of the individual and the social, a constructural model can be developed in which the cognitive structure of individuals and the sociocultural environment they cohabit with others are linked in a symmetric fashion. Such a model makes each realm explicable and accountable to the other in explicitly processual and dynamic terms.

FORMALIZING THE DYNAMICS
OF THE COMMUNICATIVE TRANSACTION:
A CONSTRUCTURAL MODEL

Constructuralism, as a theory of the interaction cycle, manages to capture some interesting assumptions about motivation, action, and adaptation as they surround a single communicative transaction. In addition, it fits the single transaction as an integral unit into the larger dynamic of the interaction cycle, relating individual change to sociocultural change. We discussed constructuralism in chapter 4 and provided baseline definitions and axioms. In this chapter, we describe a formal model based on the theory's central tenets. The basic model, limited to human agents who engage only in one-to-one interaction, was presented previously and used to examine social and group stability (Carley, 1990b, 1991b). Herein, we extend the basic model so that the consequences of print technology can be examined. Thus, in addition to the limited one-to-one human agent, we describe the artificial agent—a text or book. We also describe what we call the *enhanced human agent*, who has access to both oral (one-to-one) and print (one-to-many) technology.

The process of defining a formal model requires both additional specification of the theory (providing details previously overlooked) and additional abstraction (eliminating second order factors that, though important, have only secondary effects from the perspective of the formal model). The extended model is presented in this chapter in an incremental or building-block fashion. That is, the model contains the central components of constructuralism (chap. 4) but captures these elements in a purer, more abstracted, and more error-free form. Such abstraction is often a necessary aspect of scientific idealization, but it also represents a way of prioritizing the most fundamental elements in the dynamics relating human communication to sociocultural organization and change. Once we describe this basic model, we add blocks to it, such as artificial agents and print, that result when we alter the technological conditions. This incremental, or building-block, approach makes it possible to explore the fundamental results affecting sociocultural organization and change that occur when new technologies appear on the scene.

The promise of such formalized, yet abstract, dynamic models is legion (see Carley, 1989b). With respect to the language analysis of chapter 5, this type of model allows us to study changes in the language of a society as individuals with different histories interact and co-alter one another's meaning. From the perspective of individuals, this model enables us to examine their reach and the rate at which their ideas diffuse to impact the society and culture at large. From the perspective of groups, such a model allows us to predict and examine a group's co-evolution, its social and cultural trajectory over time. From the perspective of societies, such a model makes it possible to examine the gross impacts of new communication technologies.

By adding the building block of print to the basic model, we engage in historical reconstruction to examine and predict, through a kind of "what if" analysis, which factors are important, indeed necessary, for particular sociocultural change and how other factors would have effected different results. Employing what if analysis, for example, helps us determine how the semantic histories of particular literary figures or artifacts (e.g., Frankenstein) might have differed if the topology of the sociocultural landscape had been different. It can help us make predictions about different elaborative histories tied to a particular author or text based on regionalized patterns of reach (Stowe in the North vs. Stowe in the South). Through a series of computer-aided gedanken experiments, we examine the logical effects of print technologies on rates of diffusion, stability, and consensus at the group and societal level. The results of such analyses provide insight into actual historical events. This last route is the actual path we follow throughout Part II.

BASIC MODEL

We describe the basic model that abstracts from, but is consistent with, the central tenets of constructuralism. In doing so, we first describe the society (the sociocultural landscape and the technological condition), and then the process by which the society and the individuals within it co-evolve (the dynamic of the communicative transaction). After that, we describe some of the empirical results that corroborate the basic model.

Describing the Sociocultural Landscape

The sociocultural landscape is defined in terms of the society's social structure, culture, and population. The number of individuals in a society, its population, is denoted by I. Individuals in a society can interact and they all have a certain probability of doing so. The distribution of these interaction probabilities across the population is the social structure. Each individual knows things, and the number of things they can know (i.e., possible knowledge or information) is denoted by K. The more things there are to know (i.e., the greater K is), the more complex the culture. The distribution of information across the population is the culture. The sociocultural landscape is the social structure plus the culture, the codistribution of interaction probabilities and information across the population. Both the social structure and the culture have a temporal quality because they change as the interaction probabilities and the distribution of information changes.

In Fig. 6.1, a particular sociocultural landscape is illustrated. This landscape can be described in summative terms. The population size is 7; the cultural complexity is 8 (i.e., there are eight pieces of information available). There are two groups, and each group is relatively specialized in its information, as there is little overlap in what individuals in each group know. Individuals share more information within their groups than without; the only piece of information known by members of both groups is E and only one individual within each group (Individuals 3 and 4) shares it. In Fig. 6.1, each idea or piece of information is represented by a circle. The lines connecting a person to a piece of information indicate that the person knows that piece of information. The lines connecting people to each other indicate their probability of interaction. The darker the line, the higher the probability. As individuals share relatively more or fewer pieces of information, their probability of interaction strengthens or weakens correspondingly. In this sense, culture and social structure (i.e., the basic elements of context) co-evolve. The individuals shown in Fig. 6.1 belong to two groups, and only one pair of individuals (3 and 4) interact across the group boundary. Unlike other group members, these two individuals can interact because they share a single piece of information (E). Nevertheless, they are more likely to interact with members of their own groups because they share even more information with fellow members than they do with one another.

Agents

In constructuralism, agents are tied by information and interaction to other agents in the society. Individuals, by which we mean human agents, are a special class of agents—they are intelligent and capable of learning and taking action. Individuals lead lives in which they learn, rehearse, and communicate information. They are discriminating about their interaction partners and they choose these partners based on the criteria of relative similarity and availability. These processes are described in formal terms later, but first we need a more formal characterization of the individual than we provide in chapter 4.

The individual has a set of mental models which are represented as

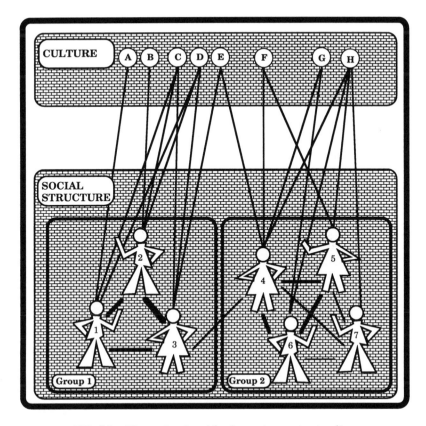

FIG. 6.1.   The sociocultural landscape in constructuralism.

a set of discrete information. Each individual's information, at any point in time, is a subset of all the information available to the current generation of individuals. The individual's knowledge, at a particular point in time (t), can be described by querying for each piece of information (k) available in the culture, whether that individual knows k at time t. This query can be represented as $F_{ik}(t)$, such that:

$$F_{ik}(t) = \begin{cases} 1 \ \textit{iff} \text{ individual } i \text{ knows the piece of information } k \\ 0 \ \textit{iff} \text{ individual } i \text{ does not know the piece of information } k. \end{cases}$$

Referring to Fig. 6.1, we see that for individual 3, initially (time $t = $ *),

- $F_{3a}(^*) = 0$
- $F_{3b}(^*) = 0$
- $F_{3c}(^*) = 1$
- $F_{3d}(^*) = 1$

- $F_{3e}(*) = 1$
- $F_{3f}(*) = 0$
- $F_{3g}(*) = 0$
- $F_{3b}(*) = 0$

Results of this query determine patterns of shared information or knowledge across a society of individuals. Two individuals can share information simply by knowing it at the same time, even if they are not explicitly aware of their mutually knowing it (i.e., their knowledge is tacitly shared). Let us define shared information as the fraction of possible information known by two individuals at a particular point in time. Shared knowledge can be represented as $SK_{ij}(t)$, with i and j representing two individuals in the society and b representing a piece of information. The shared information between i and j can be expressed as the sum of all pieces of information that both i and j know, divided by the total number of pieces of information in the culture, as indicated in Equation 6.1:[1]

$$SK_{ij}(t) = \frac{\sum_{b=1}^{K} F_{ib}(t) \wedge F_{jb}(t)}{K}. \tag{6.1}$$

Shared knowledge changes as individuals learn new information and adapt their mental models.

This formalization of shared knowledge abstracts away from many of the factors of mental models we discuss in chapter 4 and language we discuss in chapter 5. For example, the pieces of information in this formalization are not distinguishable. As a result, the formalization does not discriminate even contradictory pieces of information, such as *the sky is blue* and *the sky is green*. Furthermore, the formalization does not indicate how pieces of information are related to one another. Finally, the formalization does not discriminate the valence (positive or negative) of the information (i.e., levels of dissociation as well as association, as in *the sky is NOT green*) or the degrees of strength (as indicated by the analysis of consensus in chap. 5). These more complex representations of knowledge and language form part of the constructural story, but they are not elements that survive the formalization of the model used to address the issues of Part II. To address the basic issues of print in Part II, we do not require a model that captures this complexity. We do require a model that retains, from the constructural story, the fundamental notion that ideas are separable pieces of information that can be communicated and learned separately (chap. 4).

---

[1]The symbol $\wedge$ used in Equation 6.1 is the mathematical symbol for the logical "and."

We need this fundamental notion to rigorously describe the position of any individual within a sociocultural landscape and to describe the basic communication and learning processes. Each individual has a particular position in the sociocultural landscape. By understanding the position of each individual, we can determine the social structure, culture, and groups within the landscape. The individual's position can be described by noting, for each other individual in the landscape, the probability that the first individual will choose that other as an interaction partner. The probability for individual i interacting with individual j at a particular time (t) can be represented as $P_{ij}(t)$.

Social Structure

Social structure is the distribution of interaction probabilities across the population. The social structure can be thought of as the set of constraints on the free flow of information in the society. We say that there is a tie between two individuals in case they have a nonzero probability of interaction. The social structure is thus composed of a specific number of ties between individuals that vary in strength. The more complex the social structure, the less uniform the distribution of ties and their strengths. Various factors affect the social structure, one of which is the size of the population. Within real societies, the population is hardly constant, except in the short run, because individuals migrate, are born, and die. However, within our analyses we abstract away from these population dynamics and treat the population as a fixed and closed set. We assume that the same set of individuals endures across time periods. Strictly speaking, population dynamics can be incorporated into the larger constructural story, but they are not a part of the model used in this book.

Culture

Culture is the distribution of information across the individuals in the society. It is the ultimate repository of what is known, knowable, and the degree to which it is known, and it is composed of a specific number of cultural ideas or pieces of information. The more complex the culture, the larger the number of information pieces there are to know. The culture in Fig. 6.1 can be described by the matrix:

$$F(^*) = \begin{matrix} 1 & 0 & 1 & 1 & 0 & 0 & 0 & 0 \\ 0 & 1 & 1 & 1 & 0 & 0 & 0 & 0 \\ 0 & 0 & 1 & 1 & 1 & 0 & 0 & 0 \\ 0 & 0 & 0 & 0 & 1 & 1 & 1 & 1 \\ 0 & 0 & 0 & 0 & 0 & 1 & 0 & 1 \\ 0 & 0 & 0 & 0 & 0 & 0 & 1 & 1 \\ 0 & 0 & 0 & 0 & 0 & 0 & 0 & 1 \end{matrix}$$

From the look of Fig. 6.1, it may at first appear that culture is a Platonic form of abstract ideas hovering above and indifferent to human affairs. This is not at all the case. In constructuralism, culture is a nominalist rather than a Platonistic entity, meaning that cultural knowledge does not endure across generations unless someone in the current generation holds that piece of information. Culture is temporally situated, a historical rather than an abstract entity. On the assumption that discovery has a random element of contingency associated with it (Simonton, 1988), a cultural idea that has been lost for generations can nonetheless be randomly "rediscovered" by an individual in a later generation.

In principle, culture as a repository of information is not a closed set, for individuals can discover new information and add it to the repository. Moreover, culture can "degrade" as information is lost. Our analyses, however, abstract away from this point and treat culture as a fixed and closed set (i.e., no discovery). The complexity of the culture (K, the number of pieces of information) is set as an initial condition, and remains constant over time. Thus individuals do not discover[2] information nor do they forget it. Our treatment of print thus has nothing to say about how printing may have mattered to the discovery of new ideas. We have much to say, however, about how print may have mattered to the diffusion of newly discovered ideas.

It is a short step from the idea of culture as repository to the idea of cultural integration, that is, the extent to which individuals in the society share the culture. Societies can vary in how culturally integrated they are, either initially or over time. Cultural integration is defined as the average, across all dyads in the population, of the fraction of possible information shared by a dyad. This can be represented as:

$$\frac{\sum_{i=1}^{I} \sum_{j=1, j \neq i}^{I} SK_{ij}(t)}{I^2 - I}.$$

Cultural integration changes over time, and in analyzing various societies the initial level of cultural integration must be specified.

---

[2]In chapters 9 and 10, we investigate academic writing as discovery writing in which authors have new things to say with texts. We pursue academic writing without resorting, specifically, to simulation models incorporating discovery in the sense intended in this passage. In these later chapters we restrict our focus to the dissemination of ideas that start in the mind of a single author and move outward. Embodying a formal mechanism of discovery into the simulation model would become important were our goals to elaborate a cognitive theory of discovery or to study the direct effects of authorial cognition on cultural expansion. We address topics related to both of these subject areas (particularly the latter); however, these subjects are beyond the scope of the formal model used in this book.

Groups

Societies can typically be subdivided into groups. The constructural theory makes no *a priori* claim about what groups are or how their nominal characteristics arise. Given an initial group description, the model can be used to examine the over-time trajectory of a group, whether it will remain stable, dissolve in favor of other group formations, reconstitute itself, or change fundamentally with the addition of new members or pieces of information (Carley, 1990b, 1991b). In Fig. 6.1, the seven individuals shown comprise two groups. As part of the initial description of the sociocultural landscape, who is in which group, and the degree of cultural integration within and between groups, are specified. Any depiction of a sociocultural landscape is a sparse abstraction of the living society. Thus, how the landscape is represented—including the assignment of individuals to groups—depends entirely on the theoretical goals of the researcher. In the analyses in Part II we examine societies comprised of both one and two groups.

Describing the Technological Condition

The technological condition is the set of available technologies and their distribution across the population. We are concerned here with communication technologies. In the base model, there is only a single technology available and all individuals have access to it—oral, face-to-face, one-to-one communication. This technology limits the communicative transaction to two individuals who have essentially no spatial or temporal distance between them (i.e., they must be copresent and cotemporal at the time of the communicative transaction). Under this technology, each agent engaged in a communicative transaction tenders a communication which contains a single piece of information. Communications in oral face-to-face settings have little durability or fixity, and are not extended beyond the communicative transaction through artificial agents (e.g., texts).

Process: The Interaction/Knowledge Cycle

Having reviewed the basic components of the sociocultural landscape in constructuralism, we now turn to the dynamics that alter these landscapes over time. Interaction occurs as part of a cyclic communicative process, with the full cycle repeated each time period. Within each cycle, individuals go through three distinct phases—motivation, action, and adaptation.

Motivation

The axiom of relative similarity (chap. 4) states that the more relatively similar an individual perceives him or herself to another, the more likely
the individual is to attempt interaction with that other, *ceteris paribus*.
In chapter 4, we indicated how relative-similarity-based interaction is
more flexible as a principle of author–reader interaction than it may at
first seem. Before further specifying how relative similarity serves as a
motivation for action, we offer three additional points of clarification
as to how relative-similarity judgments work as a component of communicative transactions in general. These points are not explicit components of the mathematical model we use to describe the motivation,
action, and adaptation phases of a communicative transaction, but they
are part of constructural theory and should be included, as additional
building blocks, in future models.

Motivation and Task. Relative-similarity judgments are constrained
by task. Constructural theory assumes that interaction is focused and task
specific. Individuals are not idle but work on specific tasks. The motivation for interaction depends on the fact that the individuals involved are
focused on tasks and are making judgments of relative similarity on information made especially salient by those tasks. Imagine Mary in her
garden trying to do battle with defiant weeds. What is salient to Mary
are the gardening tips her green-thumbed neighbor has given her. At this
brief moment, Mary thinks she and her neighbor stand against the world,
and from Mary's vantage (though not necessarily her neighbor's), her relative similarity—and her probability to interact—with her neighbor in comparison to everyone else is extremely high. The urgency of similarity and
salience, however, can shift instantaneously as the tasks shift and individuals readjust those focal concepts which are the most central. Should Mary's
attention suddenly get diverted to a leaky sink, so will her assessments
of relative similarity and salience. In brief, the motivation for interaction needs to include the salience of task in directing relative-similarity
judgments.

Motivation and Opportunities for Contact. Relative-similarity
judgments and hence the motivation for interaction depend on judgments
of opportunity (Carley, 1987). We cannot entertain the possibility of interacting with an individual if the opportunity to do so cannot exist. Even
if Shakespeare were our cognitive twin relative to everyone else, we could
not interact with him (face-to-face) because he lived at a different time.
The greater the distance between individuals, the less likely they are to
interact (face-to-face), and some distances may be so great as to preclude

such interaction. Communication technologies can affect this situation by effectively collapsing distances through artificial agents. Print, for example, made it possible for individuals to communicate at a distance. Nevertheless, availability and opportunities for contact still play a key role. Even if Shakespeare were our cognitive twin relative to everyone else, and even if, through print, Shakespeare is technically available to us as contemporary readers, we would still need his text to complete the interaction. Without a Shakespearean text, we lose our opportunities to interact with Shakespeare.

The opportunities for contact can be thought of in terms of the copresence of agents at events. Events are discrete situations, such as a church gathering, a department meeting, a subway ride, or a computer linked to another network site. We can divide up any temporal unit, such as a day, into a series of events, many of which may occur simultaneously. An individual, i, has the opportunity to contact individual j (i.e., an interaction partner, including a text) according to the number of events, s, at which i and j are copresent and according to the duration and importance of these events. A normalized measure of opportunities for contact, OC_{ij}, that takes these factors into account is presented in Equation 6.2:

$$OC_{ij} = \frac{\sum_{s=1}^{all\ events} \dfrac{length\ of\ event_s \times copresence_{ijs}}{number\ of\ people\ present\ at\ event_s}}{\sum_{s=1}^{all\ events} length\ of\ event_s} \qquad (6.2)$$

This measure is highly general and holds for both individuals interacting with each other and individuals interacting with artificial agents such as texts. Texts, which are highly portable and capable of moving from event to event with an individual, should have high opportunities for contact. It is easy to confuse opportunities for contact with availability, so we need to distinguish them. Opportunities for contact involve copresence (i.e., individuals sharing a context) but do not involve what individuals are doing while copresent. By contrast, availability focuses on what individuals are doing in the shared context that makes them open or not open for interaction. If Aaron, Cassi, and Mollie are in a library and Cassi and Aaron are occupied talking to each other, then, though all three individuals and all the library holdings have opportunities to contact one another, from Mollie's perspective, only the books remain available for interaction. Aaron and Cassi remain part of Mollie's possible contacts, but are not, for the moment at least, available to her.

Motivation and Perceptual Error.   Individuals may make perceptual errors when they are making relative-similarity judgments. They may
forget, become distracted, lose sight of, or simply not know all the information they need to make reliable assessments of relative similarity.
The motivation phase must be understood to accommodate the possibility of errors such as these. Consequently, to assume that individuals are
motivated to select interaction partners (people or texts) that are most
relatively similar to themselves does not mean they will be successful at
doing so. Individuals often choose suboptimal interaction partners because of limited information about who is available for interaction or because of their limited information about the cognitive profile of the
potential interaction partner. Nevertheless, the fact of these limitations
does not undermine the coherence of relative similarity as much as it raises
the need for two caveats: (a) There is "noise" in the system for making
judgments of relative similarity, though these errors may have random
sources that balance out across a population; and (b) making these judgments often requires trial and error and a certain amount of "social canniness" learned by experience (Carley, 1991a, 1991b). Over time,
individuals build up their views of whom they are most like through both
direct and indirect interaction, through talking to or about the person,
through reading and word of mouth. The same canniness applies to readers in search of texts. As anyone who goes to parties or libraries well
knows, it often takes meeting the wrong people (and texts) to figure out
who the right ones are likely to be.

Motivation Equation.   The model abstracts away from the compli-
cations just discussed by employing a set of idealizing assumptions: (a)
All information is equally salient; (b) all individuals behave as though they
have equal opportunities to contact all other agents (people or texts); and
(c) all individuals make "correct"[3] estimates of their relative similarity
to other agents (both people and texts). In spite of these idealizations,
the model captures the fundamental motivation for interaction as characterized in constructuralism—relative similarity.[4]
    Referring back to Fig. 6.1, we see that slanted lines link information
to individuals. These lines indicate which individuals know which pieces
of information. They also indicate information ties (or cognitive similar-

---

[3]Exact accuracy is not at issue here, but bias is. It is necessary that the individual's estimates of relative similarity are not systematically biased. A systematic bias might occur,
for example, if individuals consistently overestimated their relative similarity to members
of their group and underestimated their relative similarity to members of other groups.
    [4]Most formal descriptions of the relation between interaction and similarity focus on
similarity (Davis, 1966; Fararo & Skvoretz, 1987; Homans, 1950) rather than on relative
similarity.

ity) between pairs of individuals. For example, Individuals 1 and 2 are similar in both knowing C and so share an information tie. In constructuralism, information ties are dynamically related to interaction ties, as the more information shared by two individuals relative to what they share with all others, the stronger their probability of interacting. For example, Individuals 2 and 3 share more information with each other (C,D,E) than either shares with Individual 1. The higher cognitive similarity of 2 to 3 relative to all others results in 2 having a higher probability of interacting with 3 than with any other individual in Group 1 (as indicated by the thicker line between this pair).

This idea is represented mathematically in Equation 6.3.[5] According to this equation, the probability of individual i choosing j as an interaction partner at time t, $P_{ij}(t)$, is a function of the amount of information that i shares with j relative to what i shares with everyone else in the society:

$$P_{ij}(t) = \frac{SK_{ij}(t)}{\sum_{b=1}^{I} SK_{ib}(t)} \qquad (6.3)$$

The numerator of this equation expresses i's cognitive similarity to j. The denominator expresses i's cumulative cognitive similarity to all other interaction partners, including him- or herself. The shared information between i and j thus influences i's decision to interact with j. Yet shared information is not enough to weight this decision fully. The key weight is on i's relative similarity to j. How much is i like j—*relative to i's be-*

---

[5]If opportunities for contact were incorporated in Equation 6.3, then the reformulation would be:

$$P_{ij}(t) = \frac{OC_{ij}(1 + SK_{ib}(t))}{\sum_{b=1}^{I} oc_{ib}(1 + SK_{ij}(t))} \cdot$$

Given this reformulation, constant and uniform opportunities for contact would reduce this equation to:

$$P_{ij}(t) = \frac{(1 + SK_{ij}(t))}{\sum_{b=1}^{I} (1 + SK_{ib}(t))} \cdot$$

This represents an offset relative to Equation 6.3. This formulation, as opposed to Equation 6.3, guarantees that, regardless of the distribution of information, the society is fully connected and oscillations in consensus are somewhat dampened. Otherwise, the behavior is similar to that observed under Equation 6.3.

ing like everyone else? The denominator emphasizes the italicized part of the last sentence, with *h* standing for all other interaction partners in the society.

Examining Equation 6.3, we see that interaction probabilities are not symmetric. That is, *i*'s probability of interacting with *j* need not be equal to *j*'s probability of interacting with *i*. Asymmetries arise easily, just in case the two individuals differ in the amount of information they share with others (including themselves). Thus, differences in levels of education (e.g., the number of pieces of information known) between individuals are sufficient to result in differences in their probabilities of interacting with each other. Returning to our earlier example, in desperate straits with her weeds, Mary shares a great deal with her green-thumbed neighbor relative to everyone else and her probability of interacting with the neighbor is very high. But her green-thumbed neighbor, at the same time, may share even more information with Gloria (information on both tennis and gardening) and so has a lower probability of interacting with Mary than Mary with her. The neighbor has not lost a bond with Mary. Rather, the neighbor's lower probability to interact with Mary arises simply because there are other people in the society with whom she shares more information than she does with Mary.

Action

Having the motivation to interact does not guarantee interaction will occur nor does the motivation fully determine what actions will take place. Given the motivation, actions occur; in the basic model these are the actual interaction and the communication of information during that interaction. Actual interaction involves the pairing up of agents. Communication involves the selection and transmittal of information.

Actual Interaction. Even though *i* may be highly likely to choose *j* as an interaction partner, *i* may not actually interact with *j*. There are several reasons for this:

1. The interaction partner has to be available. Mary will seek out her neighbor for interaction but her neighbor may have already left for the tennis courts. To be available to Mary, the neighbor must be without an interaction partner at the time Mary seeks her out. Availability limits interaction. Actual interaction is determined by both the selecting individual's probability of interacting with other agents and the availability of the selected agent, as noted in Equation 6.5. This equation says that whether *i* and *j* actually interact at time *t* is a function of *i*'s probability

of interacting with j at time t and j's availability for interaction at that same time.[6]

$$A_{ij}(t) = f(P_{ij}(t), \text{Availability}_j(t)) \qquad (6.4)$$

In one-to-one oral interaction, availability is an important limiting factor for actual interaction. This is decidedly not the case for person–text interaction, a point we take up later.

2. The individual may never get to select an interaction partner because the individual's choice may be co-opted by a more aggressive partner who has sought him or her out prior to the first individual's having the opportunity to seek out the most preferred partner. Larry may call Mary before she ever has a chance to seek out her neighbor.

3. Interaction is stochastic. Even though Mary has the highest probability of contacting her neighbor, she may, for whatever reason, choose to contact someone for whom she has a lower interaction probability. Chance and whim thus play a role in converting preferences into actualities. These factors are incorporated into the model through the procedure which pairs up interaction partners.

This pairing up process, illustrated in Fig. 6.2, occurs as follows. For every time period, one individual is randomly chosen to initiate the pairing up process. In Fig. 6.2 this happens to be individual A (all individuals are represented as ovals and the oval with the dark rim is the one selected to choose an interaction partner). At this point, all other individuals—and for the moment we ignore the differences between people and texts and think of all agents as individuals—are available for interaction. The individual selected to initiate interactions (A) randomly selects an interaction partner from the set of available individuals, such that the probability of selecting a specific partner is defined in Equation 6.4 (and displayed at the top right of Fig. 6.2). In Fig. 6.2 we see that the selected partner is B. The selected individual (B) and the selecting individual (A) are paired up; thus, they become unavailable for interaction with others for the remainder of that time period (in Fig. 6.2, their unavailability is illustrated with ovals that become lighter in the next step). From the remaining individuals, another is selected at random, and the process repeats with the newly selected individual's interaction probabilities being adjusted relative to just those individuals who remain uncoupled. The interaction partner may be another individual or the selecting individual may choose to interact with him- or herself (people always have a probability of interacting with themselves by spending time

---

[6]There are a variety of ways to define this function (see Carley, 1990b).

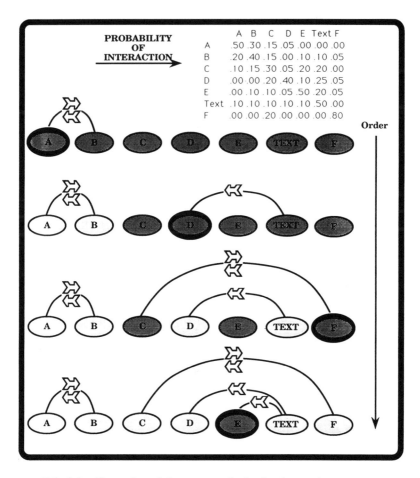

FIG. 6.2.   Illustration of the process of selecting interaction partners.

alone).[7] In Fig. 6.2, we see that D is the next individual chosen at random to select a partner. D can choose among C, D, E, F, and a text. D chooses the text. Then F is randomly chosen to select a partner, and finally E.

___

[7]Everyone is more cognitively similar to him- or herself than to anyone else. So why doesn't everyone interact only with him- or herself and forget about interpersonal interaction? The answer is simple. People may have a greater probability of interacting with themselves than with any single individual. But they are not likely to have a greater probability of interacting with themselves than with all other individuals combined. For example, one may have a 5% probability of interacting with him- or herself and less than a 1% probability of interacting with any other individual. But this still means that one's chances of interacting with someone other than oneself are still 95%.

Communication. Once all individuals have paired up, either with another human partner, themselves, or a text, they can engage in another action—the choice of information to communicate and the communication of that information to the partner. Right now, we consider only the simplest form of communication, namely that which occurs on the spot when individuals are paired with individuals. Communication is abstracted to its simplest, most error-free form. The interacting individual will choose one piece of information from the set of information known at that time and will communicate that piece of information. This piece of information is chosen at random, so all of the information known by the individual is equally likely to be chosen.[8] This assumption of randomness is a justified idealization because in Part II we do not focus on a single transaction context involving the strategic selection of information (e.g., Rafferty on *JFK*). Rather we focus on the aggregation of many such contexts and the effects of print technology on them. Whether individual *j* communicates idea *k* to individual *i* at time (*t*) can be represented as:

$$C_{jik}(t) = \begin{cases} 1 \; \textit{iff } j \text{ communicates } k \text{ to } i \\ 0 \; \textit{iff } j \text{ does not communicate } k \text{ to } i \end{cases} \quad (6.5)$$

The final result of the pairing up and communication process (the action phase) for a single time period is shown in Fig. 6.3. In this figure, we see that individuals can be engaged in a communicative transaction with a single other or they can be alone. Furthermore, individuals engaged in a transaction with another individual both send and receive a communication, a piece of information.

Adaptation

In response to action, both the individuals and the sociocultural landscape they inhabit adapt. Individuals engaged in an interaction learn information communicated to them, thus altering their mental models and their probabilities of interacting with others in the society. During the next time period, what an individual knows depends on what was previously known and what is communicated. More specifically, as represented in Equation 6.6, whether an individual *i* knows a piece of information *k* during the next time period (*t* + 1) depends on whether the individual previously knew that piece of information or whether someone in the society communicated it to him or her:

$$F_{ik}(t + 1) = F_{ik}(t) \lor C_{1ik}(t) \lor C_{2ik}(t) \lor C_{3ik}(t) \ldots \lor C_{Iik}(t) \quad (6.6)$$

The difference between $F_{ik}(t + 1)$ and $F_{ik}(t)$ is what the individual has learned. Since each individual can interact with only one other individual

---

[8]A variety of algorithms can be used for locating which piece of information to communicate. For the algorithm used in this book, see Carley (1990b).

FIG. 6.3.   The result of the action phase in the basic model.

at a time, at most one of these Cs will be 1 and the rest will be zeroes. This equation is, of course, a simplification of reality, for it assumes that the learning process is error free, that individuals immediately comprehend any information communicated to them, and that they never forget anything.

Within the broader constructural story, immediate comprehension limits the learning process (chap. 4). According to the principle of immediate comprehension, an individual who receives a communication will only be able to learn the information within it if it relates to information already known by the individual. Using the network representation of information presented in chapter 5, this means that the individual will not assimilate new meanings or alter extant meanings unless at least one of the concepts in the communication also currently exists within the individual's mental model(s). Suppose the information one individual communicates is the proposition "Shakespeare was the Bard." According to the principle of immediate comprehension, the interaction partner will not assimilate this information unless he or she already has a concept for "Shakespeare" or a concept for the "Bard." Lacking both concepts, the interaction partner will have no background against which to assimilate the new information; instead, the new information will be processed as noise and the mental model of the partner will remain unchanged.

Now, within the basic model, the subtleties of immediate comprehension are lost because concepts and the information conveying them remain unconnected. There is thus no strict sense of information communicated to an interaction partner linking or failing to link to what already exists in the partner's mental model. In the basic model, all information is assimilated when it is communicated. This simplification results in all individuals acting as though they have the requisite base of knowledge to assimilate any incoming communication. In the basic model, in other words, the principle of immediate comprehension can never be violated.

Simply because individuals can learn (or adapt to) every piece of information that comes their way does not imply that every interaction in which they engage will result in adaptation. This is because there is no guarantee that every piece of information that comes their way is new, information that they do not yet know. Individuals, after all, may receive information already known to them. Such interactions in which known information is recommunicated are in a sense ritualistic—the retelling, restating, or reinforcement of previously assimilated information (chap. 2).

When interactions are not ritualistic and involve the communication of new information, the action phase results in individuals increasing their shared information ($SK_{ij}(t + 1)$). Significantly, the extent to which individuals share information can increase even if they do not directly interact. Two individuals can increase their amount of shared knowledge just by interacting with others who are communicating common information to them. Furthermore, even when two individuals interact, the amount of information they share may not increase significantly or at all unless they sustain their interaction over time. Since the basic model puts limits on the amount of information that can be proffered or processed in a single transaction (i.e., one idea per time period), interaction partners may not increase their shared knowledge through direct communication unless their transactions span multiple time periods. This further implies that the better educated the interaction partner (i.e., the more ideas he or she knows), the more interactions (and time periods) it will take to learn what the partner has to offer by way of communication.

In constructuralism, adaptation does not end with the individual. Individuals adapt to the sociocultural landscape as they learn more about their culture through communication with other agents. As individuals concurrently acquire new (though not necessarily the same) information, the distribution of known information changes and, by definition, culture changes. This redistribution of information leads to changes in the relative similarity of individuals and their probabilities of interaction, thereby affecting changes in the social structure as well. The sociocultural landscape is reconstructed automatically in response to the changing distribution of information and interaction probabilities. Reconstruction thus occurs more automatically and with less overt coercion than when sanctions or rituals are employed (for the alternative view see Collins, 1975; Durkheim, 1965; Garfinkel, Lynch, & Livingston, 1981; Giddens, 1984; Goode, 1960).

Given the number of communications that can take place within any one time period, changes may or may not occur rapidly from one time period to the next. An individual's favorite interaction partners in one time period may not be favorites—perhaps even the least favorite—in the next. It is in this collective and distributed sense that the microactions of individuals can, over time, exert agency over the macrostructure of society. During the adaptation phase, the sociocultural landscape registers all the changes in individual information that have taken place during the action phase, and this information is dynamically reconfigured to set the stage for the next round of transactions. During the next time period, this reconfigured landscape affects the next cycle of motivation, action, and adaptation. In the new time period, individuals once again decide on interaction partners, based on a set of relative-similarity relations. But, as a consequence of the previous adaptation phase, these decisions and the patterns of information and communication that follow from them are now "inherited" from a sociocultural landscape that is different from the landscape that had structured motivations and actions at previous times. Individuals change in their preferences for communication in part because the society in which they communicate is changing out from under them.

Empirical Grounding of The Basic Model

A variety of studies have provided some empirical grounding for the constructural theory, even in the simplified form of the basic model. For example, Carley (1991b) observed that an assumption of the basic model, specifically relative similarity and the reciprocity between shared knowledge and social interaction (chap. 4), is consistent with the findings of Shulman (1975) and Lowenthal, Thurnher, and Chiriboga (1975). Their findings suggest that social interaction ties strengthen as dyads come to share more in common. These researchers found, for example, that interaction ties are stronger for married couples compared to unmarried couples, for couples with children compared to couples without children, and for older couples compared to younger couples (Carley, 1991b, p. 340).

In an early study testing the relative-similarity and reciprocity principles, Carley (1984) interviewed undergraduate dorm residents as they were going through the process of selecting a new graduate resident (tutor) for their living group. She also collected interaction data. She found that dorm residents who interacted with one another most frequently developed more shared information over time and appeared to develop shared information at a faster rate.

In a later study testing the relative-similarity and reciprocity principles, Palmquist (1990) interviewed students about research writing at different intervals during a semester-long course they were taking in that subject. He had students keep weekly logs of their interaction with other members of the class (including the teacher). He found that as the class evolved from the 1st to the 12th week, pockets of consensus formed among students around central concepts related to research writing. He also found a statistical correlation between the emergence of these pockets of shared meaning and patterns of interaction. Specifically, students who interacted with one another more (relative to others) over the term also came to share more elaborations (relative to others) about the concept of research writing. Palmquist thus found indirect evidence for a dynamic relationship between culture and social structure in the classroom.

Carley and Krackhardt (1992) examined the nature of the reciprocity between interaction and cognition, using data drawn from an organizational study of work relationships between employees in a small distribution firm. Using these data and the employees' mental models of who interacted with whom (sociocognitive structures), they were able to show that relative similarities among employees did predict their pattern of social interaction. More specifically, they found that relative proximity and relative shared information were correlated with social interaction. Moreover, they found that asymmetries in who interacted with whom, who initiated interactions, and who recalled interactions were all related to differences in relative proximity and shared information.

Using the basic model, Carley (1991b) explained a long-noted anomaly in sociology that had been lacking a clear explanation. Blau (1977) and previous social researchers (Glick, 1960; Kennedy, 1944; Yinger, 1968) noted that, despite being a smaller minority than Catholics in the United States, Jews have a lower intermarriage rate. Blau's structural theory predicted that minorities, because of their small numbers, would be forced to interact with members of the majority culture more than the other way around. But Blau's theory, incorporating parameters of size alone, could not explain how a smaller minority (Jews) could be more resistant to interaction with the majority culture than a larger minority (Catholics). Size parameters would predict just the reverse. Applying the basic model, Carley showed how a smaller minority with few cultural ties to the majority will interact less with the majority than a larger minority with more cultural ties to the majority culture. Carley thus showed how an apparent anomaly of interaction could be explained with a model that took into account the cultural ties of members within and across groups as well as the relative size of the groups.

In another study, Carley (1990b) found that the basic model was a better predictor of change in interaction over time than either balance theory (Heider, 1958) or exchange theory (Blau, 1967; Kapferer, 1972). Using anthropological data on the interaction and shared information patterns of workers in a tailor shop (Kapferer, 1972), Carley employed the basic model to predict the interaction patterns within and across groups of workers and managers prior to both an abortive and a successful strike. In that study, she showed how friendship and conflict relationships can be described in terms of knowledge and interaction patterns. She further showed how conflict between the managers and the workers heightened when there was enough interaction between the two groups for the workers to notice their salient differences from the managers, yet enough within-group interaction among the workers to make these differences a point of internal solidarity for them.

In still another study, Carley (1991a) employed a version of the basic model to develop a theory of the formation and change of intergenerational tension (the generation gap). The basic model predicts that the impact of parental attitudes on children's attitudes changes over the lifecourse. More specifically, it predicts that as children grow older, the impact of what parents say on their children's attitudes remains strong only if what the parents say is reinforced by the children's interactions with peers and other persons outside the immediate family (e.g., daycare workers, teachers). Glass, Bengston, and Dunham (1986) provided empirical evidence that this, in fact, is the case. They reported that the impact of parents' attitudes on their children's attitudes changes over the developmental span of the child. The hypothesis of changing parental influence over the child's lifespan provides an interpretation that can account for discrepant findings when researchers have studied parental influence on children at a particular stage or in a particular locale (see, e.g., the different results found by Bengston, 1975; Bengston & Troll, 1978; Hoge, Petrillo, & Smith, 1982; Jennings & Niemi, 1982; McBroom, Reed, Burns, Hargraves, & Trankel, 1985; Thomas & Stankiewicz, 1974).

EXTENDED MODEL: INCORPORATING PRINT
AS A BUILDING BLOCK

We now turn from the basic constructural model to describe what we call the extended constructural model. The extended model, original to this book, is the basic model plus a building block for print. The extended model is a first step toward acknowledging that an important aspect of modern society is that there are multiple communication technologies available. The properties of the communication technology will determine how it alters the communicative transaction and whether it enables an artificial agent (and, if so, the properties of such an agent). Such changes may have far reaching repercussions for the sociocultural landscape, the subject of Part II. In contrast to oral, one-to-one, face-to-face interaction, print has, as we saw in chapter 4, four important properties—asynchronicity, durability, fixity, and multiplicity. Print shares some of these properties with other technological conditions of communication. Oratory shares multiplicity with print; the written manuscript shares asynchronicity, fixity, and, in rarer cases, durability.

Each of the four properties characteristic of print has different systematic effects. Asynchronicity ensures that the human agent, by creating an artificial agent, a text, can communicate with others without being physically present at the site of the transaction. Durability ensures that the artificial agent continues through time, longer than the agent who created it. Fixity ensures that the artificial agent's content remains unchanged across all communicative transactions, further implying that the artificial agent cannot learn. Multiplicity ensures that the communicative transaction can involve more than two human agents, even though (because of asynchronicity) they may be spread across time and space. Combinations of these properties also have distinctive effects. Coupled with durability, fixity ensures that the artificial agent tenders the same communication (though not the same meaning; see chap. 4) over and over again. Coupled with asynchronicity, fixity ensures that the artificial agent's content can be an encapsulation of at least a portion of its creator's mental model at the time it was composed.

Artificial Print Agents

Although we have been doing so informally, let us more formally refer to the artificial agent, the disembodied communication created by print, the text, or the text-based agent, mathematically as p. Adding artificial print agents to the basic model simply increases the number of communicating agents in any population of size I to I plus the number of texts, T. Since the basic model treats the population (of persons) as constant, and since we do not change this assumption for the extended model's population (of persons and texts), durability has no direct effect within the extended model. Once a person or a text is in the society, each is there for the duration. An implication of this assumption is that the extended model used in Part II differs most from the basic model in allowing multiplicity, fixity, and asynchronicity of communication through texts.

If there are no dominant elaborators or elaborations (chap. 4), we assume that the text as artificial agent has a content that is a subset of the information known by the author at the time of the text's composition. The text's content, like the individual's mental model, can be represented by indicating for the set of possible information, K (the culture), which pieces are contained within the text. For a single text p, this can be represented as:

$$F_{pk}(t) = \begin{cases} 1 \; \textit{iff} \text{ text } p \text{ contains the piece of information } k \\ 0 \; \textit{iff} \text{ text } p \text{ does not contain the piece of information } k. \end{cases}$$

The society can be described in the terms previously identified with the basic model. But now, in addition, we need to describe how many texts there are, who their authors are (i.e., existing individuals in the society), and their content. In addition, we need to specify in formal terms the communicative properties of texts.

Motivation

The text as artificial agent is a passive recipient of interactions and cannot initiate interactions. In this sense, texts have no motivations to speak of. Nonetheless, texts do have a relative similarity to, and a probability of interacting with, human agents (i.e., readers). And human agents have a relative similarity to, and a probability of interacting with, texts. In keeping with the basic model, an individual's motivation to interact with the text is dependent on how relatively similar a mental model is to the content of the text. For individual i and text p, this can be represented as:

$$P_{ip}(t) = \frac{SK_{ip}(t)}{\sum_{b=1}^{I} SK_{ib}(t) + \sum_{x=1}^{T} SK_{ix}(t)}$$

(6.7)

Equation 6.7 is the motivation equation of the basic model (Equation 6.3), adapted to the extended model. According to this formula, an individual's probability of selecting a text as a partner, assuming all individuals and texts are available, is dependent on how much information the individual shares with the text, relative to how much information the individual shares with all other individuals (including him or herself) and all other texts.

Action

Whether an individual actually interacts with a text depends in part on whether the selected partner is available. Because of their multiplicity, texts, unlike individuals, are always available for interaction. We make the simplifying assumption that print makes possible a sufficient number of copies of the text within any one time period to accommodate all the members of the society who want to read it. The extended model assumes the open availability of texts, idealizing away secondary factors such as price. When we model texts throughout Part II, the reader should think of us as modeling cheap pulp for the masses, not coffee-table books for the well-to-do. This assumption of the perfect availability of any text affects the pairing up process of the basic model in dramatic ways, as we see throughout Part II. In the extended print model, texts always remain in the set of possible partners; multiple individuals (readers) may select the same text for interaction during the same time period.

In Fig. 6.2 we see that the text is selected by two different individuals, D and E. An individual selecting a text as an interaction partner, unlike one selecting another individual, will never be disappointed to find the text unavailable for interaction. Failing to be selected by any reader during any time period, a text has no option but to grow moldy on a shelf. Inanimate as they are, texts are only passive partners, perennial wallflowers. They can be chosen for interaction but can never choose. Instead of active choice, they must rely on favorable word of mouth (and referencing by other texts) in order for readers to locate them. Since the age of print, we have grown accustomed to locating texts by associating them with fixed places. We have come to "regard each book as a little person with a name, a place (the library) and a bibliographic life of its own" (Bolter, 1991, p. 86). The extended model incorporating print cannot reproduce the complex history of bibliographic indexing, but it can mimic the passivity of texts by assuring that only people get to decide with which texts to interact and that texts are not making reciprocal decisions.

Through multiplicity, texts can become interaction partners of choice even when their relative similarity to the reader is not as high as the reader's relative similarity to a human (but socially occupied) partner. Unlike people, texts are portable, compliant, easy to smuggle, and impossible to kidnap. We do not hesitate to drag a text on a bus or into bed. In brief, texts enjoy great advantages of availability over human agents as interaction partners. As a historical footnote, the enhanced availability of texts as interaction partners became acutely apparent to the "captive" American and English reading audience traveling by rail in the late 19th century. Readers found themselves with hours to kill, and reading was increasingly accepted as a good way to kill time. The publishing industry came out with lines of pulp reading matter, cheap and in large volumes, designed specifically for rail posts (Altick, 1957, pp. 300–320).

Once the pairing up process has been completed, communication begins. Texts are passive agents and cannot select what information in their content to tender. Rather, the choice is up to the reader. When individuals engage in an interaction with a text, they select information from the set of all the information the text has to surrender. All pieces of information in the text are equally likely to be read. This means that when we model reading in Part II, the reader may be helped to think of us as modeling readers who are doing random lookup of information within texts rather than line-by-line readings.

The final result of the pairing up and communication process (the action phase for a single time period) with both human and artificial print agents is shown in Fig. 6.4. In this figure, we see that individuals can be engaged in a communicative transaction with a single other individual, a text, or they can be alone. Contrastively, texts can be simultaneously engaged in a single communicative transaction with multiple individuals (through the existence of multiple copies of the text). Furthermore, a human agent engaged in a transaction with another human agent can both send and receive a communication, can exchange pieces of information from their mental models. Contrastively, individuals engaged in a transaction with a text only receive information. They do not send it.

Adaptation

For individuals paired to texts, the communication is, as we have seen, only one-way. Texts have no capacity to learn or to acquire new information (i.e., for the text p, $[F_{pk}(t + 1) = F_{pk}(t)]$, for all t). Texts can only provide information. Individuals acquire information from the text, but

FIG. 6.4.   The result of the action phase when artificial print agents are added.

no matter how much information they tender, the text does not change. In a world with texts, individual i knows an idea k just in case i previously knew the idea or someone in the society (with I individuals) communicated that idea in the previous time period, or i learned that information previously while reading a text (in a society with T texts). This can be represented in Equation 6.8, which is a modification of Equation 6.6:

$$F_{ik}(t+1) = F_{ik}(t) \vee C_{1ik}(t) \ldots \vee C_{lik}(t) \vee C_{p1ik}(t) \ldots \vee C_{Tik}(t) \quad (6.8)$$

Human agents can get smarter interacting with a text, but the text will not be enriched by rubbing shoulders with the person. This is simply another way of saying that texts come with all the information they will ever have. There is an upper bound on how much information texts can impart and this bound is set when the text is composed. This is not to say, however, that there is a bound on how much a person can elaborate from a text (although such elaborations are beyond the scope of the basic or elaborated model). People are open learning systems and texts are not learning systems at all.

Enhanced Individuals

Let us now consider the enhanced individual, the human agent who can move back and forth across modalities during the course of communication. Such an individual can engage in either one-to-one or one-to-many interactions, whether they are oral, written, or print, and in an environment in which all communications are equally durable. Such a society could be described in the summative terms used in the basic model. Relative to the basic model, the motivation and adaptation phase would remain unchanged. The only phase affected is the action phase.

During the action phase, each individual can select any other individual, including him or herself, for interaction. And individuals always remain available to be selected by others, at least as artificial agents, as texts representing their mental models at the time of composing. Thus, while each individual can learn only one new piece of information each time period, enhanced individuals have the potential, each time period, to communicate new information to many others.

The final result of the pairing up and communication process (the action phase) when all agents are enhanced, for a single time period, is shown in Fig. 6.5. In this figure, we see that individuals can be engaged in a communicative transaction with a single other, many others, or they can be alone. Further, individuals can receive information from only one other individual but can, through the medium of multiple copies of their text or through oration, send information to many other individuals at once.

On first blush, a society described under the extended model may seem strange. Within such a society, for every time period, any individual has the potential to be an author, to create a new text, or to read information from a text. At other times, such individuals are talking to one another informally, over coffee at conferences and as public speakers giving conference papers. Such a society bears some resemblance to an academic community, where all individuals write for and read each other's work through the medium of journal articles. Such a society also bears some resemblance to our modern society, where television news and news-

FIG. 6.5.   The result of the action phase when all agents are enhanced.

papers bring information into the homes of the millions while the content of that news changes rapidly.

USING SIMULATION TO EXPLORE
THE ISSUE OF PRINT: SOME COMPUTER-AIDED
GEDANKEN EXPERIMENTS

The extended model can be used to examine the social and cultural consequences of different technological conditions within and between various sociocultural landscapes. In Part II, we use this model to explore the contrastive implications of communicative modes without multiplicity (speech and writing) and modes with it (speech, writing, print). Despite the simplicity of the extended model, it is still complex enough to require simulation to address interesting questions about sociocultural organization and change (see Carley, 1990b, for rationale). Our modus operandi throughout Part II specifies a set of initial starting conditions (initial sociocultural landscape) for the extended model and then employs simulation to trace the trajectory of change in such landscapes under different technological conditions. Such simulation experiments do not by themselves constitute an empirical test of a theory but they do provide a way of assuring that a theory has logical plausibility and enough precision to be fashioned as a model capable of generating logically consistent yet testable implications (Carley, 1991b). Moreover, the insights gained from such analyses will foster a better understanding of historical periods in which the society was similar in kind to the artificial society examined using the model. We now describe the general value of a simulation approach, the basic design of the simulation experiments we employ in Part II, and the fundamental behavior of the extended model.

Simulation as Methodology

As a general technique, simulation offers a variety of advantages to the researcher interested in theory development. The first advantage, theoretical precision, holds for any formal modeling technique, including simulation. The discipline of creating a formal model forces the researcher to be precise about the theoretical entities to which one is committed, as well as the relationships between them. Formal modeling also forces the investigator to make implicit assumptions explicit, and to describe in detail the mechanisms by which entities and relationships change. The difference between a formal model and a verbal model can be seen, in part, by contrasting chapter 4 and this chapter. Chapter 4 lays out the constructural theory at a fairly general level. In this chapter, we turn this theory into a formal model by adding precision and abstracting from some of the general concerns discussed in chapter 4. In building a formal model, the researcher must make precise choices about how various mechanisms work, such as the pairing up process, communication, and learning. Although such precision often limits the scope of the model and forces the theorist to abstract away much rich detail, it also allows for location of primitive mechanisms that are sufficient to generate complex behavior. The complexities of converting such eloquent and detailed theories of social behavior as Turner's social interaction theory (1988) or Blau's social differentiation theory (1977) into mathematical equations, logical statements, or code demonstrates how underspecified these theories are (in spite of the length and richness of their verbal formulation!). No less importantly, the effort to model these verbal theories yields much insight into what needs to be done to further specify them.

A particular advantage of simulation is predictive accuracy. Dynamic models that trace a process over time capture more of the reality of a social situation than static equations, but are often insoluble using conventional mathematical techniques and require techniques of simulation and numerical estimation. And if, as is often the case in social science, the question is not "Where does the system end up?" but "How did it get there?" or "How fast did it get there?", then simulation and numerical techniques are often the method of choice. Further, even in the case of a model as simple as that described in this chapter, it is extremely difficult for the researcher to think through the process implications and to extract reliable inferences about the trajectories of behavior without making mistakes. As statistical packages help researchers derive multiple-regression results without error, simulation and numerical techniques help researchers derive predictions from their models without error.

Another advantage is that simulation enables the theorist to reason rigorously about processes of social change. Using simulation, a theorist can examine alternative hypothetical societies and learn what might need to change in a particular society to produce a different outcome. The value of such "what if" exercises goes beyond isolating the factors most responsible for making a particular society change as it does. More importantly, these exercises provide us with a way of reasoning about societies and their transformation. Simulation allows us to reconstruct history by "replaying" alternative transactions and allowing us to explore critical determining factors that are easy to overlook when we study actual history without editing, playing back, or formulating alternative branching scenarios. As a result of "rewinding," "fast-forwarding," and "re-editing" actual history, we are often able to produce better informed explanations of actual history, with better informed predictions for the future and clearer empirical implications.

The final advantage of simulation is that it facilitates the development of mechanism- or process-oriented theories. Mechanism-oriented theories, prevalent in cognitive psychology, characterize the individual through a set of mechanisms that process information and perform tasks. Predictions and explanations derive from characterizing the process and observing the behavior produced. Using simulation, predictions can be made about the relative effects of alternate mechanisms and initial conditions. Modeling dynamic social phenomena at the microlevel requires proposing models of social agents. Although social agents can be characterized as bundles of attributes, as actors it is perhaps more revealing to treat them as sets of mechanisms or processes whose attributes are explicitly coordinated (Carley & Newell, 1990). Thus, mechanism- or process-oriented theories seem particularly well suited for work seeking to lay the foundations of dynamic social theory.

In sum, simulation can be a tool for theory construction, helping the theorist increase the specificity of theory, think through the theoretical implications, explain the past, generate testable predictions, and reason about sociocultural processes.

Experimental Design

In each chapter in Part II, we describe the specific simulation experiments used to address the theoretical and historical questions at issue in that chapter. The experimental design consists of describing, in summative terms, the sociocultural landscapes whose behavior is examined and the technological conditions explored. In each case, a certain number of sociocultural landscapes are explored across a set of different technological conditions. A society is simply a particular sociocultural landscape and a technological condition. If we let the number of landscapes explored in a particular experiment be L and the number of technological conditions be C, then the number of societies explored overall will be $L \times C$. Each society is simulated using a Monte Carlo approach. By systematically varying the technological conditions of a society, we can explore how various factors associated with print affect sociocultural organization and change.

Monte Carlo Analysis

Monte Carlo analysis is a numerical procedure for estimating expected behavior by examining a distribution of sample outcomes as the input parameters are randomly varied across their possible range. This procedure is employed when the mathematical model is intractable and it is not feasible to calculate all possible outcomes, given all possible inputs. This procedure, when employed with the foregoing model, gives one confidence that the predicted behavior is typical. It insures that the over-time behavior observed for each society reflects a "mean" behavior for societies with that type of sociocultural landscape and technological condition. It also shows that the over-time behavior observed has not resulted from a particular pathological history of interaction. Because the societies we simulate in Part II have stochastic elements, such as which individuals know which pieces of information, with whom individuals actually interact, and what piece of information an individual actually communicates during a transaction, each society is resimulated 100 times. By averaging 100 such resimulations of societies with the same sociocultural landscape and technological condition, the average behavior of such a society can be observed.

Each society is also simulated for 500 time periods. This length of time ensures that the vast majority of societies examined will have achieved their ultimate condition. In other words, they will have reached a final steady state, one in which every individual knows everything that any individual or text knows (see Carley, 1990b, for details on the nature of this ultimate state).

Technological Conditions

Our purpose here is not to describe the specific technological conditions that are examined in Part II. These specific conditions are described in chapter 7. Rather, we describe the theoretical and historical considerations that led us to select the specific technological conditions we choose in Part II. In Part II we consider the ability of a print author with an innovative idea to impact society. As such, three factors, related to print, stand out and have variations we manipulate throughout the simulations of Part II. These factors are multiplicity, complexity, and competition.

Multiplicity.   Multiplicity becomes an important factor when one suspects that the author will be able to diffuse a new idea faster as the number of individuals with whom to interact, either face-to-face or through a text, increases. As we already indicated, one of the major distinguishing features of print, and indeed any mass media, relative to one-to-one, face-to-face communication, is multiplicity. To examine the impact of multiplicity in the simulation experiments in Part II, we consider societies where no one has access to print (i.e., all interactions are one-to-one) and where one or more individuals have access to print (i.e., some, though not necessarily all, interactions are one-to-many). Such print societies inherit all the communicative characteristics of societies under oral conditions, but in addition they contain at least one enhanced individual who can speak or write one-to-one or one-to-many. In the simulated life of a literate society, when individuals have to make principled choices about how to occupy their social time, their choice often becomes what it is in an actual society of literates—a choice between people and texts. Naturally, as interaction partners, texts have properties different from people, which we described earlier, and may evoke different outcomes.

Content and Complexity.   Complexity becomes an important factor when one suspects that the author will be able to diffuse a new idea faster the less the idea competes with other information in a text. That is to say, the more ideas in a text that can be communicated, the longer it may take any single new idea (or any single set of new ideas) to spread and influence the society.[9] Off the cuff, one might hypothesize that simple texts, such as pithy and sloganistic campaign writing, might be more influential than long-winded exegeses whose potentially new or arresting information is likely to remain buried in dense passages and labored footnotes. One might turn around and hypothesize just the reverse, namely that complex texts will spread new information faster because such texts will contain lots of assimilated information; thereby drawing many readers to it through immediate comprehension and relative similarity; causing many readers to discuss the text, including its new ideas. Whether complexity is harmful or advantageous for the rapid diffusion of new ideas is an open question that we can use simulation to explore.

Competition. Competition becomes an important factor when one suspects that the rate at which an author will be able to diffuse a new idea will depend on the extent to which the author must compete with other authors who are trying to do the same thing. Whether competition speeds or retards the diffusion of new ideas is also an open question. Some liberal views of the press claim that print tends to "democratize," by potentially extending the reach of all individuals from all sociocultural strata. According to some strains of liberal theory, competition can speed the dissemination of new ideas. Other considerations indicate that the liberal's positive association between competition and diffusion may be too optimistic. One such consideration is that the more different texts in circulation, the more likely it is for any single text to be ignored. For all its apparent advantages, according to this consideration, print increased the number of texts in society that readers were compelled to overlook. Kernan (1987) pointed out this same disadvantage for an author entering the increasingly competitive print trade in 18th-century England. And Bloom (1973) pointed it out for contemporary writers under pressure to compose something new under the weight of all that has come before. These anxieties of writing in competitive markets, so well documented in the literature, speak of a negative relationship between diffusion and competition. Again, the issue seems to cut both ways and simulation may yield insight in which ways the issue cuts and under what conditions.

---

[9]Texts with essentially the same story line can have very different levels of complexity (e.g., *War and Peace* written by Tolstoy and *War and Peace* condensed for *Reader's Digest*).

Measures for the Social Influence of Texts Over Time

The dynamics of social life are interesting to track because no social structure—either at the societal or group level—remains constant over time. Similarly, no culture remains constant. Whether a social structure remains stable depends on whether individuals within it remain constant in their interactions and whether they maintain the same pattern of relative similarity over time. Whether a culture remains stable, moreover, depends on whether the distribution of information across individuals remains constant over time. Individuals who interact a great deal with one another relative to all others have the opportunity to acquire common representations of information and language—and to nurse their investment. Conversely, individuals who interact intermittently or occasionally will lack this opportunity, time, or commitment. Individuals who once interacted regularly but now invest more in other partners may find that the group level social structure and culture they had previously co-constructed are now losing their definition and perhaps, in the long term, will dissolve as they come to have increasingly less in common.

Using the constructural theory and the extended model described in this chapter, Part II explores the influence of print on sociocultural organization and change. We measure organization and change by considering the effects of print on diffusion, stability, and consensus. We define these measures in informal terms in chapter 4. In this chapter, we offer formal definitions of these measures as they are used in the extended model.

Diffusion and Time-to-Diffusion. Diffusion—or more precisely the extent of diffusion—is measured as the fraction of people in the society who have acquired the innovative or new information. Let I be the number of people in a society and K the total number of cultural ideas available in the society. Let x and y be the new ideas known initially only to the innovator and to no one else. Then, the (partial) diffusion of a communication at a particular time is simply the sum of people who now know x or y, divided by the total number of individuals, or

$$\frac{\sum_{i=0}^{I} F_{ix}(t) \vee F_{iy}(t)}{I}.$$

The complete diffusion of this communication is the fraction of the populace who know everything in the communication, or

$$\frac{\sum\limits_{i=0}^{I} F_{ix}(t) \lor F_{iy}(t)}{I}$$

The level of diffusion is only concerned with how many individuals have learned the information, and not with how or from whom (or what) they received it. As one can infer by inspecting these equations, as a communication contains more new information, there are more opportunities to take something new from the communication, decreasing the constraints on that new information's partial diffusion. At the same time, there is more information to take from the communication before one can claim to have taken all that is new, thus increasing the constraints on its complete diffusion.

The time-to-diffusion of a communication (e.g., face-to-face or print) is the number of time periods required before the new information in the communication is known by everyone (chap. 4). Intuitively, time-to-diffusion has to do with the speed with which a communication diffuses to the population. For a motor vehicle, speed is measured by distance traveled per time period (e.g., 100 miles per hour). So the larger the number, the faster the vehicle is moving. In the case of time-to-diffusion, however, the lower the number (of time periods), the faster the communication is traveling. The lower the number, the faster the information reaches everyone.

In the simulations we employ in Part II, for every society simulated, a communication's (e.g., oral or print) time-to-diffusion is calculated at each of 500 time periods and averaged across 100 runs. By the 500th time period, the diffusion rate is virtually 100%. This means that for the vast majority of societies examined, the ideas in the communication will have disseminated to 100% of the individuals in the society. The question of interest is how fast did the society reach this ultimate condition under different communication technologies (including print) within different technological conditions?

In examining the results, a pre-equilibrium measure of the time-to-diffusion is used. The time to 90% of that condition is used for diffusion. Specifically, time-to-diffusion is defined as the number of time periods required for the diffusion level (averaged across all 100 societies of that type) to reach 90% of the average diffusion level that occurs at the last (500th) time period. We rely on this pre-equilibrium measure because, for some pathological cases, 500 time periods may be insufficient to reach these ultimate conditions. Measuring behavior at 90% of the final value effectively mitigates this problem and makes the measures less sensitive to the particular interaction patterns that take place within a pathological society.

Stability and Time-to-Stability.   Stability is the fraction of ideas shared, on average, by any two individuals. Stability in a society for any time period is computed as the sum of the shared information of all interacting individuals divided by the number of dyads:

$$\frac{\sum\limits_{i=0}^{I} \sum\limits_{j=i,j\neq i}^{I} SK_{ij}(t)}{\binom{I}{2}} \ .$$

This yields the average fraction (of the total culture) shared by any two individuals. Stability provides a rough approximation of the level of cultural integration in a society. It allows us to say that any two individuals, on average, share 2% of the total culture, or 20%, or more. However, because stability is an aggregate average, we can make no hard inferences about the actual shared information of any two individuals based on a stability figure. That is, a society whose stability is 5% is one whose members, on average, share 5% of the culture. However, this does not mean that they share the same 5% of the culture. Nor does it mean that if we sample specific individuals, they will overlap 5% in their information. Some dyads will overlap more, some less. Across all dyads, however, the overlap will average out to 5%.

The alert reader may note that the equation for stability is also the equation for cultural integration (provided previously). We refer to this measure in the analyses in Part II as stability (not cultural integration) for several reasons. First, we save the expression cultural integration in Part II to refer to initial levels of shared knowledge, the level of shared knowledge, on average, of individuals in the initial life course (the initial time periods) of a society. We use the expression stability, on the other hand, to refer to the level of cultural integration during the very last stages of a society's life course (converging on the last or 500th time period). We restrict stability to the last meaning because we want the reader to remain aware that stability is the apt description for a society reaching its ultimate condition. In its ultimate condition, after all, every individual knows everything and, by the principle of reciprocity between knowledge and interaction (chap. 4), all interaction will stabilize.[10]

A society's time-to-stability is the number of time periods required for the average society of a particular type to reach perfect stability. As for diffusion, the question is how fast does a society reach this ultimate condition under different communication technologies within different technological conditions? And, like diffusion, a pre-equilibrium measure of

---

[10]This ultimate stabilization will take place as long as we assume no discovery, forgetting, or population dynamics in the model.

the time-to-stability is used, set at 90% of the average level of shared knowledge that occurs at the last (500th) time period averaged across 100 societies of that type.

Consensus and Time-to-Consensus. Consensus is the fraction of the dyads in the population that share the same belief. A belief can be thought of as an answer to a question formed by weighting and combining component pieces of information. Such answers can have valence (i.e., they can be positive, negative, or neutral). For example, consider the question *Can you get AIDS from giving blood?* The answer to this question can be considered a belief that is dependent upon information known about giving blood, about AIDS, and about human biochemistry. Within both the base and extended model, it is assumed that there is a single belief for which the level of consensus is an issue. Each piece of information in the culture is assumed to have a weight of -1 (negative), 1 (positive), or 0 (neutral), relative to the belief in question (see Carley, 1989a, for additional details). The weighting scheme is assumed to be constant over time and across the population. That is, different pieces of information do not have a positive weight at one point and a negative weight later on. Moreover, the same piece of information has the same weight for every individual in the society.

We illustrate this model of beliefs by considering a group of four senators debating the Persian Gulf War. Assume the following question is being debated: *Is the Gulf War justified?* Assume further that there are, overall, six pieces of information (i.e., evidence) that the senators use to debate this belief. Each of these pieces of information is weighted either positively, negatively, or neutrally to the belief. Let us say that the weights of the information for the belief are as follows: 1, -1, 1, -1, 0, 1. That is, the first piece of information supports the belief, the second does not support it, the third supports it, the fourth does not support it, the fifth is neutral (neither supports nor fails to support it), and the sixth piece of evidence supports the belief. These weights are fixed across the four senators. Thus, if they all know all the evidence, they would converge on their belief toward the war. But they have different beliefs because there is, at least initially, no uniformity in what they know.

The distribution of information across senators for all six pieces of evidence is shown in Table 6.1. A 1 in a senator's row indicates that the senator knows that piece of information. A 0 indicates that the senator does not know that information. Thus, as shown in Table 6.1, Senator A knows E1, E3, and E4, but not E2, E5, or E6. Since most of this evidence is weighted in favor of the Gulf War, Senator A believes that the Gulf War is justified. Senator B's information is also weighted in favor of the Gulf War, so Senators A and B agree on the belief, even though

TABLE 6.1
Illustration of Consensus

INFORMATION	E1	E2	E3	E4	E5	E6	
WEIGHT	1*	– 1	1	– 1	0	1	
AGENTS							BELIEF
Senator A	1**	0	1	1	0	0	Aye
Senator B	1	0	0	0	1	1	Aye
Senator C	1	1	1	0	1	0	Aye
Senator D	0	0	0	1	0	0	Nay

Comment: This table illustrates a consensus across Senators A, B, and C, despite their different knowledge.

*A weight of 1 indicates that the evidence supports the belief; 0 indicates the evidence is neutral. A weight of – 1 indicates that the evidence does not support the belief.
**A 1 indicates that the senator knows the piece of evidence; 0 indicates that this evidence is not known.

their information of the evidence is very different. Senator C also agrees that the Gulf War is justified, though C's information differs from both A and B. Senator D disagrees with A, B, and C because the information known by D (namely, E4) is negatively weighted and impels the conclusion that the war is unjustified.

Two individuals are said to concur if they share the same belief. For the society as a whole, consensus is the fraction of dyads (from the total possible) that concur. In a society with I individuals, there are $\binom{I}{2}$ possible dyads, ignoring self–self interaction. Consensus is measured as:

$$\frac{\sum_{i=1}^{I} \sum_{j=i, i \neq j}^{I} belief_i = belief_j}{\binom{I}{2}} .$$

In this example, there are two instances of agreement in six possible unique dyads, so consensus is about 33%. It is worth noting that the level of consensus in a society can fluctuate very quickly, since an agreement between two individuals can be formed or undermined with the communication of a single piece of information. For example, given their current state of information, Senators A and C agree about the war. But if A divulges E4 to C in the action phase and C divulges E1 (which A already knows), then C will become neutral while A's belief remains unchanged. As a consequence, A and C will no longer concur. Assuming nothing else changes, the overall level of consensus in the society will go down to 1/6, or 16%. Although increases in shared information over time always correspond to increases in the diffusion of information and the stability of a society, they do not necessarily correspond to increases in the level of consensus. As empirical support for distinguishing shared knowledge (stability) and consensus, Carley (1984) found that although interaction led to the development of shared information across dorm residents, it did not always lead to consensus about the appropriate selection of a tutor, because individuals favored or were opposed to the same candidate (i.e., held a consensus) on the basis of critical differences in knowledge.

A society's time-to-consensus is the number of time periods required for the average society of a particular type to reach perfect consensus (chap. 4). As for diffusion and stability, the question of interest is how fast societies of particular types reach an ultimate condition of consensus under different communication technologies and technological conditions. Employing the same pre-equilibrium measure as before, the time-to-consensus is defined as the number of time periods required for the level of consensus (averaged across all 100 societies of that type) to reach 90% of the average level that occurs at the last (500th) time period.

Over-Time Implications: Regularities in Diffusion, Stability, and Consensus Curves

There are certain regularities in the over-time trajectories of diffusion, stability, and consensus that hold regardless of the specific technological condition or the characteristics of the sociocultural landscape. For any fully connected society (i.e., a society in which there is a direct or indirect path linking all individuals or individuals and texts in a society), the society will eventually reach a perfect condition of perfect stability, consensus, and complete diffusion. Ultimately, all individuals will know everything that is known by any other individual or text in the society. Given this complete sharing of information, the culture will be uniform, as will the social structure. There will be no further changes in the distribution of information and no further changes in the probabilities of interaction, in who knows what or in who holds what belief. Ultimately all individuals will share the same belief.

Despite the wide variation in the sociocultural landscapes and technological conditions examined, all societies will end up in the same place, but they will vary in how fast they get there. Moreover, if we examine the curves representing the level of diffusion, stability, or consensus over time, we see that, regardless of the society, the curves have the same functional form. These basic forms are shown in Fig. 6.6. For example, over the long run, the diffusion curve characteristically takes on the form of

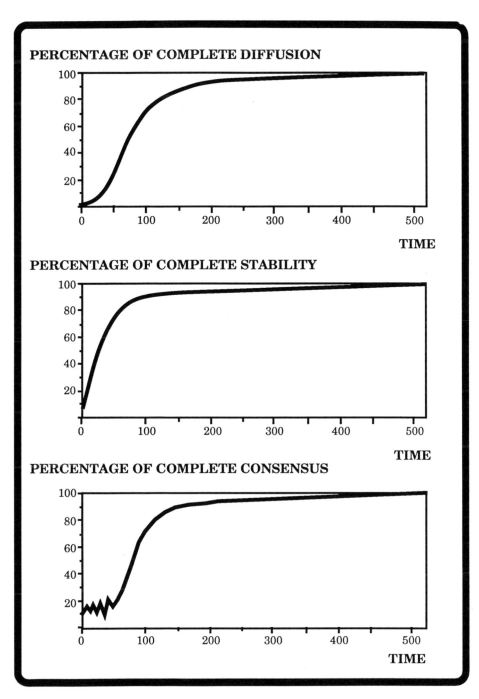

FIG. 6.6. Over-time behavior.

an elongated s (the ojival curve described in chap. 4). Regardless of the society, if we trace the diffusion of a specific piece of information using the extended model, the level of diffusion increases slowly at first, then more rapidly, and then tapers off gradually as every individual, eventually, comes to learn this specific piece of information. The level of stability (i.e., cultural integration) increases sharply at first and then levels out as every individual comes to know everything there is to know.[11] Both the diffusion and the stability curves are monotonic increasing functions (i.e., at each point in time the level is equal to or greater than it was the time before). Consensus, unlike stability and diffusion, is not monotonic. Finally, the level of consensus tends to oscillate in the short run (see the blips at the early phases), as shared beliefs are initially highly volatile (particularly when they are based on different information). Then consensus increases, slowly at first and then more rapidly, as every individual comes to know everything (i.e., the same things), assuring complete concurrence.

The reader should not be misled by the fact that diffusion, stability, and consensus curves, after 500 time periods, all lead to a utopia of complete dissemination of information, complete information, and complete agreement. The focus of interest is the effect of a specific society on these curves in the short and middle run, well before they converge on their final values. The short and middle run represent, in theory, the closest approximations to how these societies would play out as historical contingencies. In addition, our interest is in what type of sociocultural landscapes or technological conditions reach these ultimate conditions the fastest. Such comparisons provide insight into the advantages and disadvantages of the different conditions.[12]

By the short run, we mean the first 5% to 10% of the time periods examined. For runs of length 500, this is approximately the first 50 time periods. During these opening time periods, diffusion, stability, and consensus curves in our data approached 50% of their final values, a high enough percentage to get a sense of what happens to each of these measures when interaction first gets underway and has had a chance to sustain itself for a while. What we call the middle run typically lasts from the first 10% of the time periods to the time when each society reaches 90% of its final values for diffusion, stability, and consensus. In our data, the middle run tends to last from around time period 50 to about time

---

[11]Figure 6.3 shows the over-time behavior of a typical society. Although these figures describe a single society, the patterns conveyed are typical of all societies examined in this book.

[12]This comparative analysis is referred to as comparative statics.

period 100, just at the point when the curve starts to ascend toward its ultimate value. These time periods are crucial for providing a sense of what happens to diffusion, stability, and consensus after a certain mass of information has been circulated and shared, with agreements made, but before that mass has become too large to remain interesting.

SUMMARY AND IMPLICATIONS

We re-presented the basic model based on the constructural theory. In addition, we added a few new building blocks in the form of new technological conditions that make up what we call the extended model. These additional building blocks extend the basic model so that it is more descriptive of print interaction as well as the one-to-one interaction described by the basic model. Within the extended model, texts become artificial agents and potential interaction partners within a sociocultural landscape. Texts have some similarities to human agents and interaction partners but many differences as well. Unlike a person in the role of interaction partner, a text cannot learn, but can only impart, new information. A text, unlike a human partner, can be a source but never a friend. On the positive side, a text, unlike a person, can continue to interact past the life span of a person and can communicate at a distance from the source of the original author. Proximity, an essential feature of oral, face-to-face communicative transactions, becomes a less decisive factor for print interaction because texts are artificial agents that can travel to the site of the reader. Availability, also a constraint on communicative transactions between persons, becomes less decisive in a print society only because texts tend to be more universally available for interaction than persons.

Finally, we identified three factors—multiplicity, complexity, and competition—whose effects in a print environment seem controversial and of theoretical interest. We also identified three measures—diffusion, stability, and consensus—that can be used to examine the over-time behavior of societies with different landscapes and technological conditions. For each measure, we illustrated the basic pattern of behavior that emerges given both the basic and the extended model. We then pointed out that the interesting questions involve not where a society ends up, but how fast it gets there, and the effect of different communication technologies in helping it to get there.

Throughout the applied chapters of Part II, we employ the extended model to investigate in greater depth morphologies of author–reader interaction involving print, professionalism, academia, and intellectual migration. Our chief questions concern the impact of communication technologies in shaping these sociocultural institutions by tracing the effect of print on diffusion, stability, and consensus within each of the historical milieus surrounding these institutions.

APPLICATIONS

CHAPTER SEVEN

Print

Once upon a time there were identical twin brothers Aesop and Damian. From birth on they were inseparable and so identical in every respect that when interacting with others, they would ask and respond to questions in unison, tell the same moral fables in unison, and so on. So Aesop learned just what Damian learned. And Aesop expressed exactly the learning that Damian expressed. One night, Zeus came down from Olympus and delivered a printing press to Aesop and ordered him, on pain of death, not to let anyone else use it—not even Damian. Aesop used the press and, to this day, we remember Aesop's fables and not Damian's.

This spurious myth highlights some of the lore about print and its influence on the context of author–reader interaction (chap. 3). Print is widely heralded for both universalizing and standardizing communications across geographical regions and national boundaries (McGarry, 1981, pp. 40–46). Print's complex interaction with the new empirical sciences remains an open question whose importance few doubt. The interaction is challenging to track, in part, because although print seems to have given a boost to the sciences of direct observation, these sciences also sought to diminish the authority of the written word in favor of the arts of observation. The tension seems resolvable when we consider that print extended a text's circulation and, as a result, enhanced individuals' confidence that they could universalize what they observed in their local environments. Moreover, empiricism, with its emphasis on direct observation and replication, implicitly relies on this kind of communicative confidence, the confidence that attempted replications can be spread from

253

one local site to another in a timely fashion. Print thus played an important role in promoting and helping to proliferate a language about nature—even if that language seemed to diminish the importance of the written word. Even here, the tension between the science of observation and the language of observation seemed to be addressed in the promotion of new stylistic standards for reporting on nature. According to these standards, a language about nature calls attention to itself and distorts what it seeks to report unless it also resembles nature. In post-Baconian Europe, the rhetoric of the new inductive science endorsed a written style that sought to reproduce natural experience in the mind of the reader (Dear, 1985).

These are credible, albeit very incomplete, considerations of what print did for science (and science for print). Such considerations follow upon the premise that print, because it enabled asynchronous, durable, fixed, and multiple communications, played an important role in standardizing and universalizing archives of knowledge. Grains of truth extend into lore, however, when it is claimed (or suggested) that print was the initial, singular, or even dominant force behind the very aspiration toward this standardization and universalization. We risk making a huge conflation, in other words, when, instead of seeing print as instrumental to the development of an existing mental model of universally disseminated knowledge, we envision print as the determining inspiration of the model itself. Let us call the aspiration toward standard and universalized knowledge the aspiration of societal reach. Fundamental to the collective lore about print—what we might call the Strong Print Hypothesis—are a loose array of assumptions:

1. Print extended the author's immediate reach beyond what was possible in oral communication.
2. Print increased the author's rate of reach beyond what was possible in an oral community.
3. Print originated the awareness and actuality of societal reach.
4. Encoding information into print creates an immediate consensus greater than that attainable through oral interaction.
5. Encoding information into print creates an immediate social stability greater than that attainable through oral interaction.
6. From a societal perspective, the more extant information encoded into print, the more consensus and social homogeneity there is likely to be in a society.

Inspection reveals that none of these assumptions holds.

A counterexample to Assumptions 1 and 2 comes to play in the ancient practice of rhetoric, which relied on an orator communicating en masse to citizens of the city–state. The orator, who could address throngs assembled in the tens of thousands in an amphitheater, had an immediate actual reach far greater than the immediate (and often ultimate) potential of a printer living in 1500, disseminating editions that ran under 500 copies and took up to a decade to sell (Kernan, 1987). The industry of print, moreover, would not see editions regularly running into the tens of thousands and selling out in timely fashion until the 19th-century penny press (Altick, 1957). We would thus be in error to assume that print, at least in its preindustrialized history, increased the author's immediate reach or rate of reach (chap. 4). The defender of the Strong Print Hypothesis might remain unconvinced by this quantitative argument for a couple of reasons:

1. The defender might say the Strong Print Hypothesis applies only to the proliferation of print after the industrial revolution (chap. 2); thus, arguments about the early print trade would not apply.
2. The defender might retort that quantitative arguments miss the point altogether and that one must turn instead to qualitative arguments to tease out the subtleties of print.

The first retort is potentially very convincing and we ourselves have made much of the industrial revolution's watershed influence on the print trade. Nonetheless, it is unlikely that most proponents of the Strong Print Hypothesis have this watershed in mind since the hypothesis tends consistently to be formulated around Gutenberg, the disputed inventor of movable type, and not around Nicholson, Konig, and Hoethe, giants of mechanical printing.

The second retort is the more likely. The idea here is that to equate the power of print with the sheer size of the audience is to miss the main point about print and its rupture from orality. Print's main ability, according to this retort, is its capacity to break the bounds of proximity in time, space, and culture, to admit distance. Ancient rhetoric could perhaps outperform early print in the size of the audience amassed. Yet ancient rhetoric's conception of mass communication remained a conception tightly wrapped within assumptions of physical proximity. By making it possible for information to be communicated asynchronously and somewhat more durably, writing systems managed modest gains in affording a kind of communication that could break the bounds of proximity in time and space. But it was not until print, not until the durability of written information could be enhanced through the multiplicity of copies, that proximity diminished as a major constraint on communication. This qualitative argument is not without merit, for print, even as Gutenberg knew it, eroded the constraint of proximity on communication. However, historical evidence suggests that the erosion made possible by Gutenberg occurred in the midst of a long procession of erosions and was not sudden. In the West, the idea of communication at a distance and communication aspiring toward a societal reach existed centuries before print (Clanchy, 1978; Houston, 1988; Innis, 1951; Kittay, 1986; Levine, 1986). The advent of print was not so much the inspiration for communication at a distance but rather the result of a long anticipation. Print was not the unexpected answer to the needs of a medieval world that became increasingly reliant on written records having to survive changes in time, space, and culture. Print, in Resnick's (1983, p. 1) words, was rather "assured" in light of these needs.

COMMUNICATION AT A DISTANCE PRIOR TO THE INDUSTRIAL REVOLUTION

Since print anticipated and responded to the historically perceived need for communication without proximity, it is instructive to position it within a series of prior technological developments that anticipated and responded to the same need. Figure 7.1 sketches a time line of some of the major technological milestones that advanced the reach of the written word up to the industrial revolution.

In conjunction with the development of these technologies, ordinary writers had to make a series of cognitive and affective adjustments in order to commit to these technologies and to entrust information to them. Moreover, they had to assume that their readers would make parallel adjustments and commitments. These cognitive and affective adjustments are not unlike those that individuals have to make now, relative to the new electronic technologies (Sproull & Kiesler, 1986). In the following paragraphs, we review some of the technological, cultural, and psychological developments that had to emerge in the West so that individuals could adjust to the idea of communication at a distance.

The Alphabet and Writing Systems

Pictorial and phonetic writing systems predate alphabetic writing systems (but cf. Harris, 1986).[1] Yet it is widely maintained that writing could not have developed into a significant medium of cultural exchange until the

---

[1]According to Harris, it is the "tyranny" of alphabetic thinking and the alphabetic bias that makes us say "A is for Archer" rather than the more natural "Archer is for A" (1986, pp. 8, 27ff). He claimed writing has a history in drawing as much as speech.

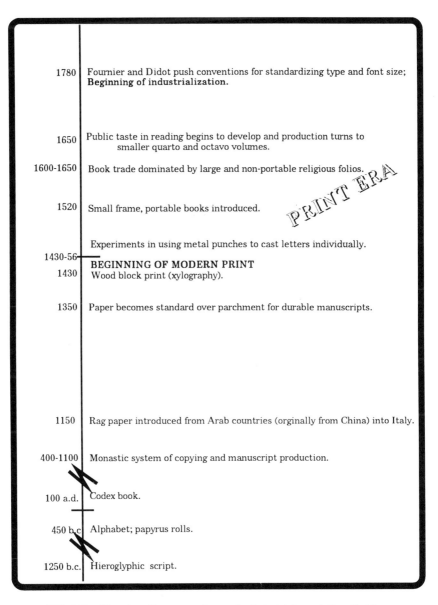

FIG. 7.1. Historic milestones prior to the industrial revolution that increased the societal reach of the written word. *Note.* From Harris, 1986; Reynolds and Wilson, 1968; Febvre and Martin, 1976.

formation of an alphabet, one flexible enough (like pictures and phonetic systems) to encode oral information and yet sufficiently abstract to maintain fidelity across speakers. The achievement of the alphabet, in terms of reach, was its unprecedented mix of fidelity and portability, features attributable to the fact that language users, distanced in time, place, or culture from the writer, could retrieve the meaning of an alphabetic script without having to infer extra information in the slant of the writer's hand (required of a pictograph) or having to reproduce a physical sound (required of phonetic writing; Bolter, 1991; Enos, 1990). The Sumerians and Phoenicians had an alphabet but it was not until the Greeks that the alphabet became an instrument flexible enough to support a rich oral tradition and, after 403 B.C. when Athens adopted the Ionian alphabet, standard enough for leaders to introduce written documents into the official conduct of statecraft. By the end of the Roman republic in the 1st century A.D., written documents had penetrated every aspect of bureaucratic life. These documents, according to Goody (1986), led to an increasing differentiation among the tasks that required writing. The ancient city–states relied on writing to identify merchandise, to hold elections, to record types and quantities of goods, grain purchases, tax revenues, census information, contracts, decrees and laws, and to regulate bureaucracy at all levels. As the Roman empire expanded, writing became increasingly important in transmitting information to peoples outside the city–state. In the 4th century, librarians agreed on the Ionian alphabet as the scholarly standard and began the massive undertaking of translating ancient manuscripts originally written in Attic into the Ionian alphabet.

Coordination of Writing Activities Among Scribes

Official documents could not insinuate themselves into the life of society without an efficient mechanism for mass circulation. Before the 19th century, information could move only at the rate and in the quantity that people could move it. In the absence of mechanical reproduction, trying to bring documents into mass circulation was identified as a logistical problem of human organization. The ancient world, relying on the labor of scribes, experimented with mass-production techniques for documents. In Rome, scribes would be seated in a large room and given simultaneous dictation. This technique could—for a short manuscript—produce an "edition" of hundreds of copies within a day (Williams, 1961). Similar mass-production methods were used not only in the scriptoria of the monasteries but also among medieval booksellers working in university towns. Original texts were maintained as exemplars that copyists were expected to duplicate exactly. Exemplars were then segmented into sections called *quires* or *peciae* and loaned out, one section at a time, to copiers (or to a student hiring a copier) for a fixed fee set by the university (Febvre & Martin, 1976). A student could thus have 10 sections of a manuscript copied concurrently by 10 different scribes—a primitive forerunner of today's distributive computer systems that support conflict-free" concurrent writing (Olson, Olson, Mack, & Wellner, 1990). The distributed techniques of scribal copying remained slow by modern standards and, in many ways, exploitative of human time and labor, but nonetheless they involved an ingenious system of mass production (though manual) that could increase the speed with which manuscripts could be launched into mass circulation. Such techniques explain how the preprint world was able to place hundreds and thousands of manuscript copies into religious, secular, and personal libraries and, by the 14th and 15th centuries, into the inventories of peddlers, urban shopkeepers, and vendors at fairs (Williams, 1961).

It is tempting to think that, after print, the production and publishing of documents no longer required the same massive coordination of human labor. Certainly print changed the nature of coordination activities around documents but neither it nor any subsequent technology has eliminated or even significantly diminished problems of human coordination. Generally speaking, technology has never eliminated the problems of human coordination but only redistributed and redefined them. In the era of the computer, for example, which supports synchronous and collaborative composing at a distance, problems of human coordination among writers are being made visible in a way they were never made visible before (Kaufer, Neuwirth, Chandhok, & Morris, in press). We mention these developments to suggest that human coordination is a fundamental factor in systems of communication and systems that rely on communication, and that the viability of any communication technology depends in large measure on how it addresses that factor (Malone & Crowston, 1991).

Trust in Writing

Another important link in stabilizing the notion of communication at a distance was to regard language in written form as a trusted medium of communication. Before the 12th century, citizens of England, who had no history with the Roman notary system for systematically dating and signing documents, did not recognize written documents as legal instruments. Lacking a coherent system to insure against forgeries, the English courts admitted written documents as admissible evidence only when used to corroborate oral oaths and testimonies. It was only since the 12th century that medieval England gradually—over a 200-year period—began to build the infrastructure required to entrust their societal transactions to written records (Clanchy, 1978). A similar ebb and flow of trust and suspicion is evident in the passing of electronic communications. Electronic mail is still considered an untrustworthy, unsecured, and legally questionable channel of communication. Some research indicates that individuals are often reluctant to use electronic mail to convey highly sensitive information, such as pay raises and announcements of major discoveries (Carley with Wendt, 1991).

In a separate study, Kittay (1986) argued that English medievals had to make what was for them a conceptual leap of faith before they could take written documents at their word. He documented that medievals had a difficult time envisioning writing as anything but frozen speech.[2] Written documents were customarily used as reminders of annual speaking events associated with the seasons. Libraries would lend very few books and those they did lend were almost always anchored to the spoken rituals of the current season. Medievals could not easily envision how writing could have a meaning unto itself, disembodied from the ritualized transactions of voices situated in physical proximity. To perceive writing as more than a reproduction of proximate speech required a leap of faith, and to make it, medievals had to convince themselves that texts could be self-contained objects in their own right. They began to show signs of taking this leap of faith, according to Kittay, when they started to invent content devices for texts to indicate their status as self-contained packets of information. These devices included signatures, seals, dates, locales, tables of contents, indices, and abstracts. The importance of these devices was to organize ideas according to the logic of the text (and the needs of the reader of the text), rather than according to the narrative flow of the spoken events on which these ideas might be reporting. Kittay believes that this leap occurred by the 13th century. By that time, Kittay reported, medieval libraries began to lend books in greater quantities, based on reader demand rather than the time of season.[3] In our

---

[2]The medievals' text as frozen speech is not to be confused with our notion of communication as an encapsulated mental model. Text as frozen speech centers on the content of the communication existing originally as speech and simply being transferred to a different medium, replete with many of the idiosyncrasies and styles imbued by the original medium. In contrast, comunication as an encapsulation of mental models centers not on the transfer of content between technologies but on the transfer of information (and the web of meaning involved in that transfer, see chap. 5) from the communicator to the communication.

[3]In *Orality and Literacy*, Ong (1982, p. 119) offered a related account of the ancient and medieval lack of trust in written expression. He argued that manuscript cultures remained oral–aural in their orientation and retained much of this orientation even in the design of their manuscripts. He observed that manuscripts were not typographically easy to read and not well suited, generally, for retrieving information. What readers discovered in manuscripts, they either memorized or forgot. He contended that written texts retained the oral mnemonic patterning, formulas, schemes, and cadences that promoted ready recall. Moreover, readers vocalized and read aloud even when alone (p. 133).

own day, it remains an open question how electronic communication will evolve should we start seeing beyond our current biases for linear print (Bolter, 1991).

The Development of Literate Culture

Communication at a distance requires perceiving reach from the receiver's as well as the communicator's point of view. An agent must believe in the worth of the information to pass it on and in the existence of an audience (perhaps out of sight) relatively similar enough that they can choose to receive the information. In the case of writing, an author's literacy requires a parallel confidence that a literate culture to reach does exist.

The development of this culture was a long time in the making but it was well in place before print. Before the 6th century B.C., everything handed down from one generation to the next was handed down orally. In the 6th century, single copies of Greek epics, drama, and other literary works were maintained and recited at seasonal occasions. In the 4th century, many Athenian households contained a few written documents, and the Athenian educational system offered noncompulsory education in reading and writing for the elite (Levine, 1986). Science and education flourished and academic institutions with libraries were formed. In the 3rd century, the library in the museum at Alexandria was reputed to carry between 200,000 and 490,000 rolls (Reynolds & Wilson, 1968). By the middle of the 2nd century, Rome had a body of literature of its own but few conventions for handling the distribution of texts.

Authors like Cicero regularly distributed manuscripts to friends, who could make their own copies and distribute them further. Should authors wish to alter a text, they could contact those who had a copy and brief them on the changes. Yet as other copies would remain unaltered, it was common to have many versions of a manuscript in circulation, with no one knowing which version other readers had. Cicero was in the process of revising his *Academica* when his friend and publisher (Atticus) was distributing multiple copies of a previous version. Both versions of Cicero's manuscript remained in circulation, with readers given neither a warning of the other manuscript's existence nor an advisory as to which manuscript was the most trustworthy (Reynolds & Wilson, 1968).

By the early medieval period, the church exercised jurisdiction over education and the care of books. From 550 to 750, the monastic libraries and scriptoria started to shape the idea that trustworthy manuscripts, stockpiled in the same location, were the basis for a literate culture, as they could preserve knowledge across time and culture as well as space (Reynolds & Wilson, 1968). By the 9th century, Alcuin was arguing for minimal standards of education to enable less scholarly citizens to join this literate culture as readers. The most tangible result of his efforts, perhaps, was the development (which he oversaw) of a new script, called "Carolingian minuscule," which rounded, separated, and regularized lettering and made reading an easier and more palatable experience for the scholar and nonscholar alike (Reynolds & Wilson, 1968). With more readers feeding into the literate culture, the demand for copies grew. In the late 11th and early 12th centuries, scribes produced documents from the scriptoria at a record pace, often increasing by a factor of 4 or 5 the manuscripts of a classical author—such as Ovid and Seneca—that had been in existence in all the prior centuries combined. By the 12th century, intellectuals could associate literate culture with a sizable corpus of Latin texts, and many pushed for their translation into the vernacular languages of Europe (Febvre & Martin, 1976). This history, all too brief and sketchy, is enough to indicate the growing confidence among writers and particularly copyists, even before print, that when they put a manuscript into circulation, there would be readers for it on the other end.

Paper

No writing surface can remain a serious candidate for extending the reach of information without being durable. Until the 14th century, there was no more durable writing surface than parchment or vellum. Parchment, however, was expensive and required a scale of animal sacrifice that had stiff economic consequences then and would raise moral and ecological objections today. A single small book might exhaust a dozen or so sheepskins but a large book could consume up to two hundred skins. Febvre and Martin (1976) estimated that one hundred copies of the Gutenberg Bible, produced with vellum, would have used up 15,000 skins. Paper was introduced into Europe in the 12th century as a new kind of "parchment" by Italians who traded with Arabs. This early paper was no match for parchment in durability. It was fragile, tore easily, and had the consistency of cotton. Because of its fragility, no one in the 12th century would have thought to use paper for important documents or charters. In 1145, Roger of Sicily decreed that all official documents be written on parchment. In the 14th century, animal glues were substituted for vegetable glues in paper making, increasing paper's adhesive properties and making it a competitor with parchment for durability. By the end of the 14th century, paper was becoming the standard writing surface. It was still much harder to illuminate and ink than parchment, but it went through hand presses with less resistance and was more affordable to mass produce. Paper making remained pretty much unchanged from the 14th to the 19th century, when it had to be reinvented to work with the steam press and other newer technologies (chap. 2). But had paper not come as far as it did in the 14th century, the invention of movable type in the 15th century would not have been the radical innovation it turned out to be.

Linking Written Text to Rhetorical Invention

For written information to become associated with societal reach, the loop between the roles of writer and reader within a literate culture had to be closed. It was not enough to participate in literate culture merely as a reader. There also had to be a mechanism that enabled participation from the writer's side as well. This meant tying the written document to the resources of the would-be writer who is looking for something to say. It meant, more simply, tying the written document to the essentially oral art of rhetorical invention. In medieval Europe, the arts of invention and writing were noninteractive. The art of composing remained an art of speaking, not writing. The art of writing was considered an art of copying precomposed texts from dictation, an art of fidelity rather than originality or ingenuity (Levine, 1986). Cicero often reworked his speeches into written texts to spread among the literati of Rome. His talent for oral invention was well known to his contemporaries. Yet his talent for written invention did not become widely appreciated until the 15th century. In the medieval world, invention remained an art of the oral register, of the speech and the public sermon, reaching as far as collective earshot allowed (McGarry, 1981). The integration of invention with systems of writing seems to have been the product of Renaissance and especially Enlightenment thinking, themes we return to in chapter 9.

With the standardization of written information through the alphabet, the emergence of organizations to produce and disseminate texts, increased trust in the written word, the perception of a literate culture, the durability and affordability of paper, and the closing of the loop between authoring and reading texts, the notion of communication at a distance was undergoing a systematic process of instantiation long before print. Print, at best, furthered these ideas rather than inspired them. So what relationship did print have to communication at a distance? What did print do? This is the question we pursue, in some respects more conclusively than in others, for the remainder of this chapter.

POLITICS AND PRINT

Despite the caution that seems necessary in concluding what print did, some of the historical scholarship has not been hesitant to draw rather broad conclusions. Some writers, like Williams (1962, p. 22), acknowledged that print can accelerate the movement of information in a society and leaves the politics of print up to the politics of the printer (or whoever owns the presses). Others tried to associate print with more definitive social and political outcomes. The best thinkers in this second group are careful to observe that if print is to be implicated in politics, its alliances are, at the very least, ambiguous. For example, Innis (1951, p. 129) argued, on one page, that print has had ties to political censorship and the control of information: "The vested interests of the printing industry [have] tended to check the flow of ideas and to contribute to the building up of monopolies." On the next page (p. 130), he discussed print's ties to the open exchange of information and its function as a democratic vehicle through which liberating information can gain a universal voice: "The increasing influence of print has been reflected in republicanism with the bias toward constitutions and documents and guarantees of freedom of the press and of the right of individuals."

The politics of print are ambiguous because of the ambiguities of who is printing what for whom and for whose benefit. Early in this century, Beard (1914) wrote that by the late 19th century, print had begun the formation of a national culture that was more inclusive than exclusive. But Innis (1951) later countered that the industrialization of print had only meant a growing monopoly of the few controlling the information for the growing majority forced to consume it. Carey (1988, p. 163), in his tribute to Innis, agreed: "For the right of people to speak to one another and to inform themselves . . . the Constitution substituted the more abstract right to be spoken to and to be informed by other, especially specialist, professional classes."

A further point of contention on the politics of print is whether print and other mass media have proven powerful enough to envelop citizens in an artificial reality. In 1931, Phillpotts (cited in Carey, 1988) contended not. He argued, instead, that because the mass media miss the common experiences of citizens and the commonality of their lives they are unlikely to be agents of influence or change. This view cuts against the widespread belief that the media exert unusual and undue influence precisely because they can bring to us experiences so different from those we regard as common. The only agreement across these contradictory positions is that the media (including print) can transport information across great distances (in time, space, culture) and do so relatively quickly. It is not likely that we can extract a definitive moral dimension to these factors of distance and speed. The history of people living in proximate contexts without print shows a mixed moral and political record. There is no reason to think that introducing a printing press or some other mass-communication technology will change that record decisively in either direction. In brief, despite the inclinations of some proponents of the Strong Print Hypothesis who would wed print to a certain politics, print seems to have no decisive connections to one kind of politics or another. Technology does not determine the politics of communication though it certainly can facilitate the politics of a communicator (Martin, 1981).

COGNITION AND PRINT

Yet another variant of the Strong Print Hypothesis is often used to associate print with a new cognitive orientation toward information. Brandt (1990) called this variant the "strong text" hypothesis and its proponents the "strong text" theorists. According to this hypothesis, print increased societal consensus and the granularity at which consensus could be formed—particularly within scientific groups—by increasing the fixity and consequently the fidelity of information across transactions. According to this hypothesis, print technology and its logic of discreteness and fixity helped to transform the human cognitive system into a more discrete, logical, and fixed representational system of symbols. According to this view, further, the acquisition of literacy required a level of abstract and decontextualized reasoning uncommon to spoken communication. Goody (1986), Ong (1971), Olson (1977), and Eisenstein (1979) are frequently identified with this argument because all assume that writing and print required the mind to draw upon previously untapped logical resources when moving from orality to literacy. Commenting specifically about the cognitive transformations implied by print, Eisenstein argued that, through the fixity of typesetting, scholars increased their sensitivity for detecting errors and corruptions across copies. This increased sensitivity, she maintained, led scholars to approach texts with greater precision, leading eventually to the development of more precise secondary genres (tables of contents, indices, abstracts, bibliographies, catalogues, written commentaries) to index this detail. Eisenstein contended that without the awareness of a text's potential to convey precise and standardized detail, various scientific genres—including cartographies, geographies, navigational charts, and medical texts—would never have developed with the accuracy and resolution that we now take for granted. Similarly, Ong (1982, pp. 117–138) argued that print afforded a stable enclosure for containing information, for repeating it exactly, verbally, or visually. Like Eisenstein, he saw the emergent scientific mentalities as the ultimate benefactor of this repetition. In a passage also linking the fidelity of print to the cognitive mindsets of a new scientific era, McGarry (1981) wrote:

printing increased [the] growth of scientific method. Print helped root errors out of editions rather than propagate errors. . . . . Copernicus stimulat-
ed a revolution in astronomical thinking by comparing Ptolemy, Aristotle,
and other writers on astronomy and mathematics, noting their errors and
inconsistencies and working out a new and more satisfactory synthesis. (pp.
45–46)

What is unconvincing about the strong text argument is the implicit
assumption that an external technology can fundamentally change the
fundamental processes of human cognition. The strong text theorists tend
to be technological determinists who assume that characteristics of people's minds and modes of thinking inevitably shape themselves to the con-
tours of the technologies they happen to use. From chapter 4, we have
been suggesting something quite different—that the basic structure of
mind as a collection of mental models (Johnson-Laird, 1983) is part of the
human condition. Technologies can change minds and modes of reasoning by changing the content of these internal models. But whether they
do so or not must be empirically determined. One cannot infer a change
of mind or mode of reasoning simply because a technology is in existence and in use. Otherwise, on the same quality of evidence we could
just as well claim our minds resemble a toaster, a microwave, or any other
technology in common use. An argument we find more persuasive, weaker than the strong text thesis but nonetheless compatible with Eisenstein's
and Ong's observations, is that the durable and fixed archive left by print
made it easier for multiple readers to share and correct detailed elaborations (i.e., complex networks of content; chap. 5) across greater distances.
In chapter 9, we revisit the features of durability and fixity in the context of the Enlightenment and the modern origins of academic writing.

THREE LOGICALLY TESTABLE CONJECTURES
ABOUT PRINT

Despite the implausibility of the Strong Print Hypothesis, there are conjectures implicit in the literature that can be logically examined within
the constructuralist framework. Because print adds multiplicity to speech
and writing, which increases the potential number of simultaneous
receivers of a communication without increasing the time it takes to reach
them, the most visible advantage of print over one-to-one oral communication and writing should be speed. The three conjectures below are
formal elaborations of this prediction with respect to the three measures
of interest—diffusion, stability, and consensus:

Conjecture 1: Print decreases a communication's time-to-diffusion.

Conjecture 2: Print decreases a society's time-to-stability.

Conjecture 3: Print decreases a society's time-to-consensus.

These conjectures suggest that print facilitated the rapid flow and penetration of specific information (diffusion) and expedited the development of structures of shared knowledge (stability) and belief (consensus) across the individuals in a society. Insofar as these conjectures might have logical plausibility (much less empirical truth), their plausibility is no doubt conditioned by other variables in the society. For example, we know from the literature (Altick, 1957; Barnes, 1964; Collins, 1929; Coser, 1965; Cress, 1980; Febvre & Martin, 1976; Golding, 1974; Houston, 1988; Kernan, 1987; Levine, 1986; Martin, 1981; Schofield, 1981; Williams, 1961, 1962, 1982) that the societal influence of print depended on a host of factors that go well beyond the scope of the formal model but which we have considered informally in this and earlier chapters. These factors include, but are not exhausted by, the cost of paper and production, government policy, government strength, pricing, occupational structure, income, taxes, social class, genre, ease of borrowing or buying books, leisure time to read them, and the sociocultural support given to reading time (chap. 3). The formal model described in chapter 6 does not try to capture all of this rich detail and is therefore limited. However, the challenge in making logical sense of these conjectures, through simulation, is to get a sense of the extent to which these conjectures can be logically supported, refined, and qualified through the interaction of a few selected sociocultural variables.

FORMAL ANALYSIS OF PRINT

We now turn to some simulation experiments designed to explore these conjectures about print. Within these experiments, we vary the makeup of the society by examining both different technological conditions and sociocultural landscapes.

Technological Conditions

We examine five distinct technological conditions—oral, simple print, complex print, competitive simple print, and competitive complex print. These conditions enable us to examine not only the difference between an oral and a written culture, but how two important factors—competition and communicative complexity—affect the benefits of print. To return to our fable, we consider imaginary worlds where (a) neither Aesop nor Damian have a printing press; (b) only Aesop does and he uses it to print his novel insight (the new information); (c) only Aesop has the press and he uses it to print the entire fable; (d) both Aesop and Damian have printing presses but use them only to print their insights; and (e) both Aesop and Damian have printing presses and use them to print the fables in their entirety.

Oral Technological Condition

Under the oral condition, a society has no texts and supports only face-to-face communicative transactions. The historical analog is the preprint world.

Simple Print Technological Condition

This simple print condition builds on the oral condition above and is meant to simulate a society in which one individual has a printing press and has produced a text that circulates a single piece of new information in an otherwise oral society. The content of print information in such a predominantly oral society remains, literally, a "novelty" mode of communication, one that carries avant-garde (low assimilated and new) information. Under conditions of simple print—conditions in effect for the average citizen of Europe until industrialization and the migration of print communication beyond elite circles in the late 18th century (Belanger, 1982)—print is not entrusted to carry the beliefs and knowledge considered most assimilated, ritualized, and important to the mass culture.

Complex Print Technological Condition

The complex print condition is meant to simulate a society in which one individual has a printing press and has produced a text that circulates not only the single piece of new information but also highly assimilated information in an otherwise oral society. Historical analogs might be the circulation of religious and scientific texts by elite religious and science enclaves before the industrialization of print and mass circulating texts after industrialization. Under this condition, individuals continue to interact face-to-face just as they can in the oral and simple print conditions. In this condition, as in the simple print condition, one individual has a printing press and has produced a text that circulates with other interaction partners. But unlike the simple print condition, the content of the text in this condition contains information that is part of the mass culture. The text carries a new piece of information as well as assimilated information. Under the complex print condition, print is no longer a novelty technology but is more embedded in the everyday work of the society, in the histories of its population, and in the complex connections of the language through which members of the society come to share their histories.

Competitive Simple Print Technological Condition

The competitive simple print condition is meant to simulate a society in which multiple individuals (in this case, two) have access to a printing press and have each produced a text containing only the single piece of new information in an otherwise oral society. The previous print conditions did not vary access to the technology but only the kind of written content individuals entrusted to it. Under this technological condition, there are two printing presses, two authors, and two different simple texts (i.e., texts with only one piece of information and that piece of information is new, initially known only by the author) circulating as potential interaction partners. For individuals within this condition who want to spend their social time engaging texts as readers, the two different texts will compete for their reading time and the individuals must make a decision (based on relative similarity) about which text to read.

Competitive Complex Print Technological Condition

The competitive complex print condition is meant to simulate a society in which multiple individuals (in this case two) have access to a printing press and have each produced a text that contains not only the single piece of new information but also highly assimilated information in an otherwise oral society. This condition adds another printing press and another complex text to a society working with a complex print technology. Under this condition, an individual looking for an interaction partner can choose among two different texts, each of which contains assimilated as well as new information.

Discussion of Technological Conditions

Before moving on to discuss the sociocultural landscapes, it is essential to reinforce a point we made in chapter 1: Different technological conditions seldom if ever function as evolutionary replacements for each other. This is true even if some technologies are considered more advanced than others. Rather than evolutionary replacements, different technologies tend to coexist within the same society at the same time. So when asking about the effect of a particular communication technology, we are never posing a zero-sum competition between two technologies. Rather, we are considering what happens when one technology is suddenly augmented by another, making access to the new technology uneven across the population.

This consideration is important to understand because the technological conditions we explore in our simulations overlap in the technologies they make available to individuals as they engage in communicative transactions. We simulate oral societies with only face-to-face interaction partners and no texts. We also simulate print societies where texts become viable partners of interaction. But the print societies continue to accommodate face-to-face transactions. Not all individuals in the print societies employ texts or employ them on every interaction. Furthermore, no individual in the print societies abandons face-to-face transactions or becomes effaced into an anonymous reader necessarily distant from the source of the communication about the culture. Rather, even in the print societies, the predominant mode of communication is face-to-face. The print societies we investigate in this chapter are distinguished only by the fact that some (at least one and at most two) individuals are enhanced, have become bold enough to get their hands on a printing press, and use a single text as an always available alternative to themselves as a partner for social interaction for every time period of interaction.

The questions we pose in comparing oral to print conditions do not involve inquiries about how one technological condition might be preferable to another. Rather, our questions follow paths such as these: Suppose only one individual, perhaps two, had access to a printing press in an otherwise oral society. What could the society of speakers then do— and further what kind of society could they then make—that they could not have done or made previously? One answer to this question might be "not much." Another answer might be "quite a lot." A third answer might be "it depends." The simulations designed for this chapter involve five technological conditions spanning oral and print modalities. Studying the effects of these conditions, we make use of, at one point or another, all of these responses.

By varying access to the printing press we can begin to gauge the effect of competition for the scarce resource—the reader's time. By varying the content of the communication we begin to gauge the effect of immediate comprehension. Although the formal model described in chapter 6 does not specifically embed the theory of language described in chapter 5, texts under the complex print conditions, because of their reliance on assimilated knowledge, mimic some of the properties of texts composed of symbols with high connectivity, density, conductivity, and/or consensus.

Sociocultural Landscapes

To ensure that the results we are seeing across our technological conditions are not due to the idiosyncratic details of a particular sociocultural landscape, we systematically vary features (viz., population size, cultural complexity, level of initial integration) of the landscape. We consider three levels for each of these variables. These three variables taken at three levels define 27 (3^3) different sociocultural landscapes. The three landscape variables are more fully described in the following paragraphs.

Population Size

The sociocultural landscape can be partially characterized by the size of the population. Conceivably, the effects of different technological conditions on the speed of diffusion, stability, and consensus within a society will depend, to a certain extent, upon the number of people in the society. In our simulations, accordingly, we vary the number of individuals in the society as a whole. Some societies contain 6, some 12, and some 18 individuals, respectively.

Cultural Complexity

The sociocultural landscape can be further characterized by how much there is to know in a society (i.e., the size of its culture). A simple culture has relatively few things to know or to learn; a culture becomes more complex as there are more things for individuals to know before they can claim to know everything that the society, as an aggregate of individuals, knows. Conceivably, the effects of different technological conditions on diffusion, stability, and consensus depends to some extent on the number of ideas known by the aggregate that are available for any single individual to learn as a result of interaction. In our simulations, we vary the cultural complexity, the amount of knowledge in the society to know or to be potentially learned. In some societies, there are 10 ideas overall, in others, 20 ideas, and in still others, 40.

Level of Initial Cultural Integration

The sociocultural landscape can finally be characterized by the initial overlap of knowledge between individuals in a society. This initial level of knowledge overlap is called initial cultural integration (or simply cultural integration). Technically, initial cultural integration is the average fraction of knowledge shared by any two individuals at the beginning of the simulation, relative to what the aggregate collectively knows. In a society of high initial cultural integration, each individual knows much of the information there is to know, and any two individuals share a great deal of the available knowledge. In a less culturally integrated society, individuals both know and share less of the available knowledge. Conceivably, the effects of different technological conditions depend on assumptions about the level of initial integration within a society. Accordingly, we vary the level of initial cultural integration across our societies. In some of the simulated societies, each individual was initially assigned 25% of all the ideas in the society; in other societies, 50%; in still others, 75%. Because these percentages are normalized to what the aggregate

TABLE 7.1
Example Societies

Simple Oral Society (e.g., Tribal Society)	
Technological Condition	Sociocultural Landscape
oral society	small population
simple communications	simple culture
noncompetitive conditions	high initial cultural integration
Complex Print Society (e.g., 20th-Century America)	
Technological Condition	Sociocultural Landscape
print society	large population
complex communications	complex culture
competitive conditions	medium initial cultural integration

collectively knows, every pair of individuals, on average, started out sharing 6%, 25%, or 56%, respectively, of all the available information.[4]

Societies

A single technological condition and sociocultural landscape pairing defines a single society whose over-time trajectory can be compared and contrasted with other societies. We examined the impact of each of the five technological conditions against each of the 27 landscapes, for a total of 135 different societies to compare and contrast. Two of these 135 possible societies, representing conceptually quite different contexts, are shown in Table 7.1.

PRINT AND ITS BASIC CONSEQUENCES

Print in the Short and Middle Run

Let us now consider the effect of print in the short and middle run (Fig. 7.2). We can immediately see ways in which we can refine and qualify our initial conjectures about print and its effects on diffusion, stability, and consensus. For example, the communication modality seems to make little difference to stability. Yet it does make a visible difference to diffusion and consensus because print has decisive benefits compared to oral technologies. But even here, it is apparent from Fig. 7.2 that the effect of print as a way of augmenting face-to-face interaction depends on the

---

[4]Under the uniform random assignment of knowledge, individuals who know x% of cultural knowledge have a probability of sharing x^2%. Thus individuals who are randomly assigned 25% of cultural knowledge (i.e., the total number of ideas) have a probability of sharing 25% × 25%, or approximately 6% of these ideas, and so on.

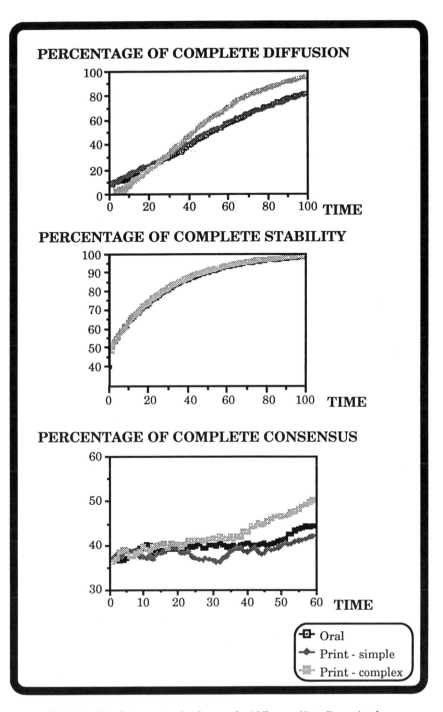

FIG. 7.2.   Print's impact in the short and middle run. *Note*. From simulation results reported in Appendix A.

content of the text that circulates within a print society. In the short run, for example, there is no remarkable difference between oral (one-to-one) interaction and simple print (i.e., one-to-many communications that contain texts with new but unassimilated information). In fact, when print is allowed to carry only unassimilated information (i.e., highly avant-garde information), consensus actually forms slightly more slowly than it does in an oral society when people have no texts on which to rely. This is because an avant-garde text (the only kind of text allowed under the simple print condition) is, in the short run, doing nothing to integrate people into the existing knowledge and beliefs of the society. And, in the short run, the time individuals spend reading such texts is actually consuming time they could have taken (and the time they are taking in the oral societies) to become more integrated into the aggregate culture. In contrast, we do see appreciable differences between oral interaction and print across those print societies that are allowed to circulate complex texts (i.e., texts that contain assimilated as well as new information). Indeed, as Fig. 7.2 indicates, the circulation of texts with complex (i.e., new and assimilated) content affords faster diffusion and consensus in the short run than any alternative technological condition. We also see from Fig. 7.2 that the advantages of complex print become increasingly decisive over any other technological condition—relative to diffusion and consensus—as a society enters the middle phase of sociocultural development, just following the 50th time period. This suggests that whatever advantage complex print accrues in the short run relative to diffusion and consensus, that advantage grows in the middle run. As a final point, Fig. 7.2 shows the behavior of a single prototypical sociocultural landscape under three technological conditions: oral, simple print, complex print. The pattern of short and middle run behavior is typical of all sociocultural landscapes examined under these technological conditions. This is not to say that the exact shapes of the curves are the same, but they are qualitatively similar.

Different Technological Conditions

We now consider the long-term effect of each technological condition when the variations in the sociocultural landscape variables are averaged out. We consider the number of time periods it took for different societies, relying on different technological conditions, to attain 90% of the final diffusion, stability, and consensus values they attained at the last (500th) time period. More simply put, we compare the effect of technological condition on a society's time-to-diffusion, time-to-stability, and time-to-consensus. The fewer the number of time periods required to achieve this 90% value for a particular type of society, the faster and more effective the technological condition associated with it. We plot comparative data about technological conditions in Fig. 7.3. Each point represents the average final value for 2,700 societies (i.e., 100 replications of 27 distinct sociocultural landscapes).

These results underscore the importance of textual content (simple or complex) in the performance of print, especially in relation to consensus and diffusion. In general, the four technological conditions involving print in a competitive or noncompetitive environment perform better on all three measures (consensus, diffusion, stability) than oral interaction, primarily when print can carry complex (assimilated as well as new) content. This analysis suggests that it is neither print per se nor the multiplicity of mass communication alone that speeds diffusion, consensus, and stability. Rather, it seems to be the multiplicity of mass communication utilized to spread information of a particular sort. A tentative generalization here is perhaps obvious in hindsight but escapes the foresight of many theorists of technology: the power of mass communication technologies is limited by the allure of the content being distributed to the masses. For a textual content with little assimilative value—and little allure for readers—technology may not make a noticeable difference. Much can be done to assist the packaging of a text, of course, but its reach continues to depend upon what lies within the binding and readers' demand for it. In his excellent history of journalism, Stephens (1988, p. 56) grasped the need for technology to ally with content when he mixed his images

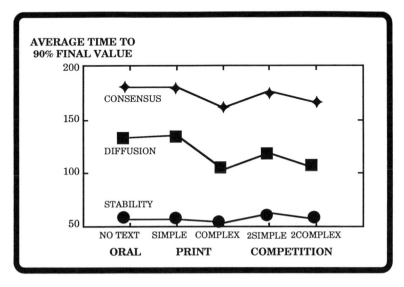

FIG. 7.3. Technological condition and time-to-consensus, diffusion, and stability. *Note.* From simulation results reported in Appendix A.

about print, equating the "blizzard" of print with the converging force of "a thousand handwritten letters." Texts that reflect what readers already know, care about, and want to learn more about have a decided advantage in how technology can make use of them. The words of White are appropriate here: "The true center of value of a text, its most important meaning, is to be found in the community that it establishes with its reader" (1984, p. 17).

Technologies can speed the development of communities that people, through voices and paper, would otherwise create; though they cannot fashion communities through speed alone. Before leaving this point, we remind the reader that our simulations do not allow individuals to forget any of the information they have learned. We mention this point because the influence of complex texts we see in our simulations—and that we sense in history—depends on their archivability as much as their complexity. Print, through its durability and archivability, allows individuals to take more cultural advantage of the complexity of texts.

Competition

Figure 7.3 also plots the effects of technological conditions involving competition. As we hinted earlier, in some respects the effect of competition seems controlled by the effect of simple and complex texts. Complex texts speed consensus and diffusion over simple texts and oral transmissions. Similarly, a society configured with two competing complex texts will hasten the speed of its consensus and diffusion over a society that contains two competing but simple (unassimilated) texts. Competition, in this sense, seems less important than the content of the texts being circulated. At the same time, there are effects for competition that do not directly follow from the effects of textual content. For example, for consensus and diffusion, societies in which there is competition even between two simple texts perform better, relative to consensus and diffusion, than oral societies. Yet it is not at all obvious why competition alone, apart from textual content, should expedite consensus and diffusion within a society. It is all too easy, and in the end incorrect, to simply say, "Ah hah, people are getting into the habit of reading."

The idea of competition is itself rich, with various strains of meaning, many of which are beyond the scope of these simulations. Consequently, it is easy to misinterpret what these simulation results are and are not saying about competition. It is also easy to confuse a set of simulation results about competition by reading into them a meaning that does not apply. For this reason, we need to get our bearings on the notion of competition itself and the relationship of this notion to the kind of competition at issue in these simulations. We describe two general meanings for competition:

1. What we call "opposition-based" competition conforms to many of our rhetorical intuitions about competition. It is a meaning, though, that goes beyond the strict power of these simulations. It is not beyond the scope of constructural theory to discuss and speculate about opposition-based competition in terms of the implications of print.

2. What we call "scarcity-based" competition conforms to many economic intuitions about competition. Scarcity-based competition can be studied within these simulations.

In the following sections, we look more closely at each of these meanings of competition.

Opposition-Based Competition

One way in which texts can compete is in their content. That is, two texts can promote different and even opposing values and beliefs and thus compete to determine the value and priority system of the audiences to whom they potentially circulate. Critics early in this century who called *Ulysses* blasphemous to the Catholic Church and wanted the work banned saw Joyce's text in direct competition with more sacred texts. Notions of opposition-based competition have also figured largely in debates about the first amendment and statecraft. Jurists of first amendment principles and civil libertarians, in their efforts to define "free expression," often rely on abstract arguments that weigh the merits that accrue when tolerating the circulation of printed information that may be abhorrent to the majority. Such jurists often reason that any limits on free expression—and the competition between communications, some espousing even repugnant values—would destroy the natural checks and balances that keep any one value system from ascending to total dominance. Viewed from constructural premises, this argument appears quite unrealistic. Readers come to the marketplace of texts with a value system intact and, for most, the availability of competing texts does not represent a true competition. Since readers choose a text on the basis of their relative similarity to it and not only on the happenstance of a text's mere availability, most readers feel no moral dilemma while spying, on the same bookshelves, such diverse texts as the *Bible,* Joyce, Shakespeare, Marx, and third world writers. As readers, we tend to focus on the fraction of texts we care about and ignore the rest. How then, one may rightfully wonder, can this competition possibly be the inspiration of classical liberalism and the ideals of free expression?

Part of the answer lies in the fact that the free expression argument is an argument about the limit, similar to some of our own limiting arguments about diffusion, consensus, and stability. The free expression argument is more specifically based on a projection of the stability of society, carried out over an indefinite number of time periods that would result as a consequence of mentally simulating certain technological conditions playing themselves out to the limit. Some of these simulated conditions would tolerate any kind of conceivable opposition-based competition; others would restrict it in various ways. But in any case, the argument attempts to project the over-time consequences on stability of a particular type of communicative transaction played out over and over. Civil libertarians, for example, commonly rebut attempts to ban an author by responding, "A society that can ban Joyce (who is hated by the majority) can also ban the Bible (which the majority reveres)." The force of this argument is more than a statement of historical contingency—for, trivially, a society can ban anything. The force of this argument is to call attention to a subtle, ultimate interconnection between banning anything of one value system and banning something else from another. How can the two events be logically related? The following narrative tries to capture the logic of this interconnection:

Imagine a society in the 1930s with two groups, the Christians and the Joyceans. Each group publishes a signature text—the *Bible* and *Ulysses.* The Christians are a much larger group and they believe it will be corrupting for their children to have any contact with *Ulysses.* The Christians thus try to get an impartial body to ban the distribution of *Ulysses.* The civil libertarians in this august body, who are also utopians, rule that the society will never have a change of becoming "stable" (i.e., predictable in its interaction because of the uniform sharing of the total culture) until the Christians and the Joyceans know the same things. Granted, this may take tens, hundreds of years but it will happen (in the limit), and it will never happen if we deprive the society of the very diverse sources of knowledge it eventually needs to share in common—or discard in common. We thus cannot afford to ban information, no matter how presently distasteful to the majority because, in the end, it is all "raw material" for an improved society.

To make a stable society out of Christians and Joyceans in the long run, so the civil libertarian argues, we should not and cannot decide a priori what will eventually make up the elements of their common culture. In the long run, a stable society formed from these groups may commonly celebrate Easter. Yet, for all we know, such a society may decide to transform Leopold Bloom into a Christian icon. According to the civil libertarian, every idea must have its day in court in the marketplace of ideas. Such reasoning is commonly followed by first amendment jurists who maintain that justice must be socially blind. But this reasoning is not impeccable and carries certain fantastical idealizations. In addition to minimizing the bias of cultural and historical practice, it minimizes the size differences between the majority and minority when, in fact, that difference is crucial. Without social intervention, the Christians can win a long-term war of attrition. There being many Christians for every Joycean, Christians are easy interaction partners for other Christians to find. Yet Christians are inevitable partners for many Joyceans, whose numbers are more scarce. Further, Christians, dominating the norms and rituals of the culture, may share more knowledge with one another than Joyceans do, further enhancing their stability as a group over the Joyceans. Consequently, even after generations of living together under seemingly socially blind conditions, the cross fertilization between the Christians and Joyceans is likely to be asymmetrical, and may work to the advantage of the larger group over the smaller. Despite the liberal abstraction of its being possible to leave it to the majority culture and the minority culture to pursue their happiness under socially blind conditions, the size advantage of the majority is not a blind consideration, nor is the cultural cohesiveness of the two groups. Such factors may tend to perpetuate the cultural dominance of the majority.[5]

The movement for "political correctness," coming to the attention of the popular media in the 1990s, must be viewed in part as a response to the limitations of liberal-egalitarian reasoning that fancies the study of texts and the subcultures that support them—for example, the texts of dead Europeans who are white and male—as somehow politically neutral. In fights to dislodge the dominance of canonical authors from American classrooms, advocates of political correctness reject the abstractions of classical liberalism that flatten the hierarchical distinctions between majority and minority subcultures. They assume that the only way to combat "unfair" competition from the literature of the majority (i.e., the literature of an allegedly racist, sexist culture) is through willful resistance. Unfair competition can be destroyed, they believe, by making the reading of canonical and other opposition-based literature "politically incorrect." The reasoning of the political correctness advocate is potentially subtle, yet it often gets filtered through the popular media as crude authoritarianism, even McCarthyism. The issues between the civil liber-

---

[5]The relative impact of group size and culture on social stability is examined in Carley (1991b).

tarian and the proponents of political correctness have yet to be fully sorted out, in part because of certain ambiguities in classical liberalism, as formulated by social philosophers like Locke and Mill.

Advocates of political correctness tend to critique classical liberalism on the grounds that its chief abstractions—among them, personal freedom, autonomy, equality—are socially blind and do not take into explicit account the specific social position of the individuals living within a society. For example, political correctness advocates commonly point out that an individual with a superior social position (in terms of knowledge and interaction potential) have different opportunities for freedom and autonomy than one living in a depressed social position. They go on to complain that classical liberalism, being socially blind, abstracts across these differences and implicitly defends existing stratifications of power. Whether or not notions of social blindness are necessarily implied in formulations of classical liberalism, however, is a debatable point (see Douglass, Mara, & Richardson, 1990, for essays discussing the concept of social blindness in formulations of classical liberalism). Indeed, our argument in chapter 6, suggests that, viewed from constructural assumptions, a central abstraction of classical liberalism, namely autonomy, is not a socially blind concept and that considerations of an individual's specific social position can be deeply factored into it. Future work should go deeper into these premises to explore the relationship between print and contrasting systems of political reasoning.

Scarcity-Based Competition

A second sense of competition is competition for the scarce resources of a reader's attention. Texts and individuals compete for the attention of readers and interaction partners. Fundamentally, a reader cannot read two texts at exactly the same time; nor can an individual read and listen at the same time. Two editions of the New Testament, while highly similar in content, can nonetheless compete insofar as interaction with one strictly prevents (during the same time period) interaction with the other. The texts compete for the cognitive resources of any single reader for a single time period. Yet in a broader sociocultural sense, of course, the texts may or may not compete (oppositionally) at all. They may even reinforce a common set of beliefs and values. For example, the audiences for one New Testament edition (Christians) are likely to be the audiences for the other. The competition is thus not based in opposition but scarcity, and is related to the fact that no reader can assimilate different textual contents at once, no matter how slight the differences in their content might be. What are the effects of competition for the attention of readers on diffusion, consensus, and stability?

By putting two texts in circulation as possible interaction partners, these simulations speak directly to this question. As Fig. 7.3 indicates, scarcity-based competition (i.e., the existence of two texts) can speed up consensus and diffusion relative to an oral society.[6] Putting multiple texts in print, even when the texts are different, can benefit the diffusion of new information, particularly when the texts are similar enough to create a population of readers with an overlapping set of information. That is, if the texts are complementary and overlapping in content, then becoming a reader of one text will increase the probability of becoming a reader of the other. Because of the widening body of shared knowledge that multiple (but similar) texts in circulation can create, scarcity-based competition can also speed consensus. Political campaigners and advertisers adhere to these principles when they shoot multiple commercials with the same underlying message. They do not see the variations in their commercials as "competition" that will dilute the message. Rather, they understand that these variations will help to reinforce and widen the audience of the underlying message (e.g., Vote for X; Buy X). Imagine Frank Baum's original *The Wizard of Oz,* and then an abridged version written for children. The original and abridged version convey much of the same textual content and so can widen the audience, allowing more people in a shorter amount of time to get information about Oz, at least in part (diffusion), and to share beliefs about the basic elements of the story (consensus). In sum then, for highly similar texts, competition for a reader's attention can promote more rapid diffusion and consensus building than would take place were we to rely only on face-to-face interaction. These considerations help to explain why, regardless of whether the textual content is complex, competition speeds up consensus and diffusion in relation to oral conditions (Fig. 7.3).

These results further indicate that competition facilitates diffusion and consensus even when the textual content is simple, when each text contains a single unassimilated piece of information, initially unknown to anyone but the author. In the case of complex texts, it is relatively straightforward to trace how competition facilitates more rapid diffusion and consensus. Readers of either text can acquire not only the new information of the text but information within it that is already culturally assimilated. Because complex texts circulate some information already assimilated into the culture, readers will be drawn to these texts as a consequence of relative similarity more than they will be drawn to simple texts. And the reading of a complex text will tend to make readers more relatively similar to other complex texts in circulation through the recommunication of assimilated information.

---

[6]Whether this result holds as the number of texts in completion increases beyond two is a matter for future research.

Two other mechanisms are implicated in explaining how competition even between simple (i.e., avant-garde) texts can speed diffusion and consensus. The first such mechanism is availability. People will read an avant-garde text simply because, like any print text, its availability is less an issue than the availability of a human partner. The second mechanism is the continuing existence of the author of the avant-garde text. Authors, even of the avant-garde, do not produce a text and then keep themselves sequestered from further face-to-face interaction about their text. Through word of mouth, an author can work behind the scenes (i.e., behind the text, as it were) to increase a reading audience's relative similarity to the text. Individuals who come into contact with the author will be more likely to read the text if they have not already done so on grounds of the text's availability. And once they engage the author or read the text, they are likely to become more relatively similar to others who have the same interactive history. In a competitive situation, these others will include the author of the competing text. Eventually, interacting with or reading one author will decrease the time it takes to interact with or read the other.

Scarcity-Based Competition and Stability

The first amendment arguments we consider above inquire into the effect of opposition-based competition on societal stability. These simulations allow us to consider the effect of scarcity-based competition on stability. As Fig. 7.3 indicates, putting texts into circulation to compete for the reader's attention does not speed up societal stability relative to an oral society. And if the texts are simple (i.e., avant-garde), competition can actually increase the time it takes to achieve stability in relation to face-to-face interaction. Why does scarcity-based competition between texts have negligible or negative effects on stability? Stability grows at the rate that knowledge is shared, on average, across individuals, and inversely with the overall amount of knowledge there is to know. The introduction of a new text can play havoc with stability, as any new text, no matter how similar it is to others, still has some new information that makes it distinct from the others. The introduction of any new text thus increases the complexity of the culture, the amount of information there is to know.[7] Furthermore, the new information introduced by a new text is bound to produce asymmetries of knowledge simply because some individuals will have received this information and some have yet to

---

[7]These simulations assume, in other words, that no texts are completely ritualized performances, conveying (at least initially) only what is known. Initially, some print and oral transactions can (though need not) be ritualized. Eventually, all transactions will be ritualized.

receive it; the result is a degradation in social stability (homogeneity). In this way, the mere introduction of a new text (and ideas) by an author into a society can delay stability. The delay is negligible in the case of complex texts because complex texts also speed the circulation of partially assimilated ideas and increase the rate at which individuals come to share knowledge. Since stability is a ratio between how much knowledge individuals, on average, share and the amount there is to share, putting two complex texts in competition helps stability on the first count and hurts it on the second. Adding a second simple text to the society only hurts and offers no help. At this point, we cannot say what the effects on stability are when scarcity-based competition between complex texts increases beyond the level of two texts. But even at this level of analysis, there are interesting questions to address. For example, although the original and abridged versions of *The Wizard of Oz* are similar, they also contain many differences in storyline, treatment of characters, and social purposes. The introduction of an abridged version adds new information that readers of the original work do not share. Generations of children who read only the abridged work (or saw only the 1939 MGM movie) may never know of Baum's original satire—creating further schisms of knowledge, which should retard the ability of various fans of the story (in whatever form) to think of themselves as part of a single group. The question of how groups can congeal or hold together when their involvement is based on a variety of different but similar documents is a general issue raised by the relationship between scarcity-based competition and stability. Can members of an AIDS awareness group coalesce when they are recruited on the basis of having read very different literature, with different motivations, about why they should become active? Can members of a graphic design team agree on how to approach a problem when they have to sift through hundreds of the client's documents, each of which illustrates, albeit in very different ways, the nature of the problem? These are only a few of the questions that can be addressed by studying the relationship between scarcity-based competition and stability.

Initial Cultural Integration

Let us now explore how variations in the sociocultural landscape may effect social organization and change. In doing so, we are able to ascertain how the various trends we have discussed may depend on features of the sociocultural landscape in which a particular type of communicative transaction is being carried out. The first landscape variable we consider is initial cultural integration. Because we found that most of the difference between oral and print societies depend on the complexity of the information within the text (Fig. 7.3), we restrict the analysis of initial cultural integration to the two technological conditions that vary the most—the oral condition and the single complex text condition. For convenience, we refer to this last technological condition simply as "print." Let us now examine the effect of different levels of initial cultural integration on consensus, diffusion, and stability. In Fig. 7.4, each point represents the average final value of 900 societies (i.e., 100 replications

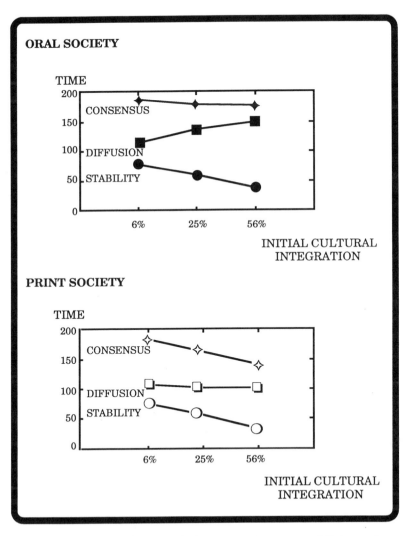

FIG. 7.4. Initial cultural integration and time-to-consensus, diffusion, and stability by technological condition. *Note*. From simulation results reported in Appendix A.

of 9 sociocultural landscapes varying in population and cultural complexity but not integration).

Stability and consensus increase with shared knowledge. Consequently, we would expect that the higher the level of initial cultural integration within a society (i.e., the higher the amount of shared knowledge a society starts off with in some initial phase of interaction), the sooner the society will reach consensus and stability. This is indeed the case, as Fig. 7.4 indicates. Print enhances this process. For the same level of initial cultural integration, diffusion, stability, and consensus occur faster in societies that employ print than they do in face-to-face communication. Furthermore, the more initially culturally integrated a society, the greater the impact of print. The synergistic relationship between print and high initial levels of cultural integration is evidenced in many historical situations. For example, highly integrated societies, such as fundamentalist Islamic and Christian sects and Nazi Germany are known to attain, or to have attained, rapid consensus on the authority of single texts such as the *Koran,* the *Bible,* and *Mein Kampf.* Less integrated societies, like 18th-century India, were far more resistant to the introduction of the *New Testament* as a basis for rapid consensus. As a populace becomes less well integrated, the printed information designed to give it an identity may need to become differentiated to reflect its own cultural differentiation.

Figure 7.4 further indicates that in an oral society relying only on one-to-one communication, the higher the initial level of cultural integration, the longer it takes information to diffuse, though at a decreasing rate. In contrast, print mitigates and may even reverse the relationship between initial cultural integration and diffusion. Individuals who share little information with each other relative to what they share with all others in the society are said to be weakly tied. Individuals with high relative similarity are said to have a strong tie. Oral or face-to-face interaction relies on low integration or weak ties within the society to move information. This is Granovetter's (1973, 1974) strength of weak ties argument. Print, through its multiplicity, decreases the reliance on specific ties between individuals to spread information and makes strong and weak ties equally valuable for the movement of information.

Another explanation centers on the fixity of the communication in contrast to the human mind. Persons, unlike texts, have a memory limited only by their previous history; this memory or set of mental models grows as the individual continues to engage in communicative transactions. When persons engage in a face-to-face communicative transaction within a sociocultural landscape that is highly integrated, they not only have many ideas to draw from but many of these ideas will be shared. Much interaction time will thus be spent exchanging information that is already known by the interaction partner, so the communication will be ritualistic. Ritualistic communication will delay the time it takes for new information to diffuse through the society. In a society augmented with print, there may be proportionally less ritualistic communication. Lacking the capacity to learn, a text is more bounded in its knowledge than people. The communication contains all the information it will ever contain at the time it is composed. The fraction of interactions involving ritual, as opposed to those imparting new ideas, is related to the proportion of assimilated versus new information. Fixed in their content and incapable of increasing their stock of information, texts involve readers in ritual interaction less than human interaction partners can. For texts, unlike humans, there is an upper bound on how much assimilated information they can ever contain. Historically, texts have been used for ritualistic communication (chap. 2). But that is not the issue. The point is that texts, unlike people, cannot learn, so their ability to convey new information (i.e., information their authors represent as new) does not degrade with time. For this reason, texts are efficiently designed for conveying news.[8] As individuals, we all work out strategies in our conversation to acquire new information from our partners. But texts,[9] more easily than people, can be specifically tailored to highlight what an author wants to represent as new information so that less extensive probing or search is required. A relatively highly integrated face-to-face society requiring the rapid diffusion of new information to maintain its organization would be well advised to turn to print and to seek conventions for demarcating new from assimilated information (chap. 2). The best known historical exemplar for this observation is the ascendance of the academic text, described at length in chapter 9. The Royal Society of London, the first modern academic enclave, founded in 1660, sustained itself for only 5 years before inaugurating a journal (Bazerman, 1988).

Cultural Complexity

Let us now focus on how another landscape variable, cultural complexity, matters to diffusion, stability, and consensus across oral and print transactions. These comparisons are plotted in Fig. 7.5. We see that as the cultural complexity, or the number of overall ideas in the society, increases, the time required to reach 90% of the final values for diffusion, stability, and consensus also increases. In this figure each point is the average of 900 societies (nine sociocultural landscapes each simulated 100 times). This trend is intuitive because (a) the more there is to know,

---

[8]We develop this point when we discuss authoring in academic specialties, chapter 9.
[9]This applies to formally planned speech as well.

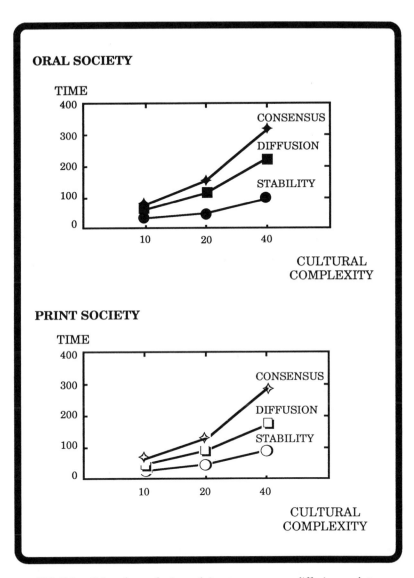

FIG. 7.5. Cultural complexity and time-to-consensus, diffusion, and stability by technological condition. *Note.* From simulation results reported in Appendix A.

the longer it should take, on average, to disseminate a specific piece of information; (b) the longer it should take for individuals to share this information; and (c) the longer it should take for individuals to achieve consensus based on shared information. This trend, however, is significantly attenuated in societies augmented by print. (Notice that the slope of the lines are flatter in print societies than in oral societies as cultural complexity increases.) Consequently, print has the effect of offsetting the price to society, relative to diffusion, consensus, and stability, that greater cultural complexity typically charges.

The fact that print mitigates the effect of cultural complexity underscores an important difference between simple writing systems and print. Writing allows for the archivability of information and, in principle, can accommodate societies of indefinitely expanding complexity. To this end, Merton (1938, p. 27) suggested that forgetting, in the face of increasing cultural complexity, was one of the chief reasons for the scientific periodical: "The scientific journal appeared in the 17th century in order to disseminate findings, not [substantial] enough for a book, but which would otherwise be lost."

Merton's point has much merit. But if a safeguard against forgetting were the main concern of 17th-century scientists, a journal would not have been necessary. Written lab notes carefully documented and protected would have sufficed, as they could have claimed the necessary fixity, durability, and asynchronocity. Science would only have needed a better way of documenting writing, not print. But science may have needed more than writing; it may have needed print. The problem faced by the scientist of the 17th century was not simply maintaining an expanding archive of scientific knowledge. The problem was using it throughout the scientific community, which meant diffusing it, sharing it, and formulating agreements based on it. Lacking multiplicity, the ability to reproduce information en masse, simple writing systems could not meet these requirements. Yet in part because of its multiplicity, print enables a group to maintain an expanding archive (i.e., increasing cultural complexity), still allowing enough concurrent interaction to keep the enlarging archive in timely circulation.

Population Size

Finally, we examine how our third landscape variable, population size effects diffusion, consensus, and stability, given both oral and print conditions (Fig. 7.6). Regardless of the technological condition, the more individuals there are to interact, the less time it takes for the society to reach stability and consensus; but the more time it takes for information to diffuse, because there are more individuals to whom it can diffuse. As we

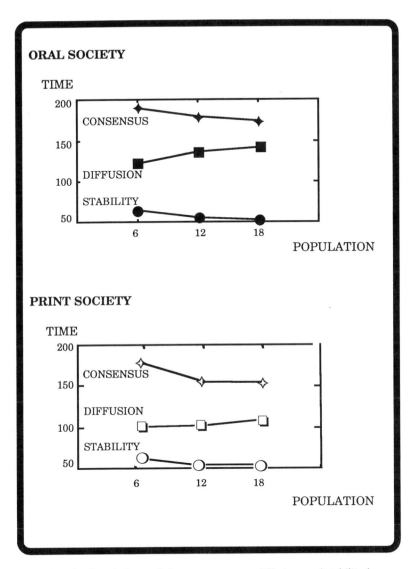

FIG. 7.6.   Population and time-to-consensus, diffusion, and stability by technological condition. *Note.* From simulation results reported in Appendix A.

see in Fig. 7.6, print fosters faster diffusion and consensus, but has little effect on stability. In Fig. 7.6, each dot is the average of 900 societies (nine sociocultural landscapes each simulated 100 times). Overall, the more individuals in a society, the more they collectively benefit when print is available. Because of its multiplicity, print decreases the importance of population size for diffusion. When a communication can reach many at once, the size of the many no longer matters. This point applies centrally to any single piece of information (diffusion), but does not apply to stability. Stability depends on all individuals eventually learning everything. The number of individuals has little effect on that, for even if print offers more individuals the capacity to move information faster, print does not allow them to learn information faster. Regardless of the population size, each person can learn only one piece of information at a time, and this cognitive constraint does not change with print. Thus print, relative to population size, has little effect on stability.

The dynamic between print and an expanding population of individuals was an important issue in early science, and there are some historical analogs to these simulation results. In 1665, Oldenburg moved science from a society of individual correspondents to one with a central journal. This move reflected, in part, growing membership rolls—from an original plan of 55 members situated in London to hundreds of correspondents spread across Europe. It also reflected, in part, a growing interest among Europeans, including nonscientists, to participate in decisions about how science should be promoted and organized (Hunter, 1989). What these simulation results say is that through print, greater numbers could be reached and their input included for consensus building and diffusion without a linear investment in time. By establishing a central journal, Oldenburg not only facilitated the rapid communication of scientific discoveries but encouraged a consensus about how science should be done (see also Meadows, 1973, pp. 32–33).

We note that print may have had many side effects (perhaps major benefits or drawbacks) that are beyond the scope of these simulations. Through multiplicity, for example, it seems that print afforded logistical and coordination advantages that would have been the envy of a correspondence network. In a correspondence network, much like a face-to-face society (but allowed to use writing), every member has to update a mailing list in order to maintain the same relative level of diffusion among an ever expanding collective of scientists. In a society with a central journal, only one member—Oldenburg, the central editor—had to maintain updated lists, making diffusion far more manageable in the face of increasing subscribers. Thus, centralization provided a coordination benefit over and above the one-to-many benefit automatically provided by going to print.

Summary of Results

Collectively, these results suggest that print can, under the right conditions, speed diffusion, stability, and consensus. Unlike the Strong Print Hypotheses, which maintain that print has whatever effects it has unconditionally, these results suggest further conditions and qualifications. In contrast to the Strong Print Hypotheses that print leads to immediate diffusion, consensus, and stability, these results suggest that print only speeds things up. We have seen that print speeds diffusion and consensus, but only when it circulates texts that are assimilated with the knowledge and norms of readers. These results do not rely on, but do underscore, the importance of our analysis of language in chapter 5. The results suggest that for any technology supporting communication at a distance to be more than a "novelty" medium, it must be capable of accommodating assimilated information and facilitate the solidarity- and community-building aspects of language. We have seen how the scarcity-based competition between printed texts can accelerate diffusion and consensus, but also retard stability. We have seen how print takes better advantage of high cultural integration, high cultural complexity, and large populations than oral transactions. This is not to say, categorically, that having the option to add print to augment face-to-face communication should always be a clear preference. For in a context where there are relatively few people, few things shared, or few things to learn, the option to move to print may make little sense and have little effect. In answer, then, to our original question—What can print add?—there is room for all three of our answers: "not much," "quite a lot, " and "it depends."

INTEGRATING PRIOR LITERATURE

Let us now step back and try to fit these results into a larger speculative literature with some further notions about what these results might mean.

The Individuating Power of Print

Some interesting parallels exist between these results and observations in the literature about print's ability to help the words of an individual attain societal reach. These observations are sometimes expressed in a misleading way by saying that the age of print ushered in the age of the individual. This idea, while too facile, may nonetheless contain some mechanistic grains of truth that these simulations invite us to explore.

It is understood that oral societies pass on information that is perceived as belonging to the culture as a whole, rather than to private individuals

(Houston, 1988; Ong, 1982). At the very least, this perception makes reach in ancient societies appear less a property of individuals than of the society at large. Given this diminished sense of communications based on individuals, oral societies can rely on many anonymous speakers—emissaries—to keep a prized piece of cultural information in circulation. They can rely on an intricate set of cognitive, linguistic, and institutional resources for transmitting cultural information concurrently and recurrently through time. These resources include extensive training in memory, storytelling, mnemonics, aphorisms, rhymes, and tropes, as well as a battery of social institutions and occasions, to keep information in wide circulation (Houston, 1988; Yates, 1966).

The results of this chapter invite speculation about how print could enable writers to associate reach with the properties of individuals. The idea is troubling, in part, because we have acknowledged since chapter 2 that oratory has some of the same mass communication potential as print. Why would not the practice of oratory be sufficient to forge a perceived relationship between individuals and societal reach? Some logistical and coordination arguments seem pertinent here:

1. Texts are physical and discrete artifacts. Lacking technology for recording, indexing, and retrieving voice, the ancients—and most of us to this day, even with recording equipment—found it easier to individuate and archive texts than speech.

2. With print, audiences could interact with an individual's text without being physically assembled. Unlike orations, which are synchronous and force audiences to be proximate to the speaking event, texts reduced the logistical burden by remaining always available to the reader's context. (We have made this comparison between oratory and print before (chap. 2) but we did not at that point underscore the importance of this comparison to the perceived association between reach and individuals.)

Because of their durability, texts can remain available and interact with readers without the intervention of emissaries or third party interpreters. To duplicate conditions perceived in an oral society while maintaining the same levels of reach over time, the orator would have to be immortal and (if that were not enough) function as a Broadway performer, giving daily performances and matinees on Sunday.

It is significant that by giving the printing press to Aesop, Zeus also cleared Aesop's calendar. Aesop no longer had to give repeat performances in person, so he had time to compose new fables. The logistical advantages of print, moreover, only increased with the complexity of the information communicated. Orators could go on for hours but, owing to the ephemeral nature of attention, a speech of any length required a good deal of internal repetition if listeners were to assimilate it. Because of their durability, texts can be read and reread; they do not tax memory in the same way as an oration. And, as the technology of paper and print developed,[10] texts could carry tens and hundreds of thousands of statements with the possibility of much less internal repetition than that required by a speech. Moreover, because texts are an encapsulation of a portion of a mental model that, fixed, remains inviolate in content, the content could be diffused in a more rapid, reliable, and distributed mode than the utterances of the orator.[11] These reasons provide a prima facie case for print's expediting the reclassification of communicative reach (in the minds of writers in the arts and sciences seeking a societal reach for their words) from a property of a society or culture to a property of individuals. These speculations go well beyond a strict interpretation of the simulations. But they are all, in one way or another, held together by the premise that print lessened the time it took for single individuals to circulate information with a wide societal penetration—which follows as a result of these simulations along with the logical consequences of print (i.e., durability, fixity, asynchronicity, and multiplicity).

The Speed of Print

The simulation results allow us to assess, in fairly precise ways, what might be meant by the common locution "speed of print." But we can also extend these results into the literature that has also speculated about this speed. A more recent and detailed linguistic argument developed to make sense of the notion of speed in phrases like speed of print was proposed by Hughes (1989). Proceeding through careful lexicographic research into the evolutionary nature of words, Hughes suggested that print made words more mobile, that it allowed the language to change without having to rely on gradual change as it takes place within a static speech community or as it is fostered by migrating peoples. He further observed that whereas spoken language has always been more or less rooted in its time and place, print allowed, in some sense demanded, authors to experiment with meanings because they were to be uprooted anyway as they circulated to audiences across time, space, and culture. The vast circulation

---

[10]Such capacities do not occur overnight, and the technology to bring out numerous thick texts at an affordable rate is relatively recent. See chapter 2.

[11]We should not ignore some disadvantages of textual comprehension. The linearity of texts and the difficulty of looking things up often promote the need for internal repetition as well. Electronic hypertext has been proposed as a way of relieving some of the difficulties believed inherent in linear text (Bolter, 1991).

of printed language, according to Hughes, brought conflict to meanings that were tied to competing local language practices and to the disparate histories and interests of local language users (chap. 5). Among Hughes' more interesting contentions is the idea that print made language itself more conflictual and engendered increased and accelerated societal conflict among groups: "Traveling across continents, print could plead the causes of the reformation, of nationalism, of mercantilism, and of commercialism and at the same time stir the language in which those and other causes were debated" (1989, p. 92).

To support these claims, Hughes showed that before print, words like *errors, heresies, enormity*, and *abuse* were located only within the authority and perogative of the Papacy to define and judge. Yet [after print] the reformist writers appropriated these words for their own uses, questioning not only their prior elaborations but the authority on which these associations historically rested (1989, p. 93). Henry VIII himself penned the "Act of Supremacy" in which he bestowed upon the Church of England the right to correct religious "errors, heresies and other enormities and abuses" (p. 114). He further observed that written genres such as *tract, pamphlet*, and *broadside* had no identification with controversial discourse until print (p. 93). And he suggested that, but for print, the Inkhorn controversy would not have arisen. The Inkhorn controversy was an attempt to translate the classics into the vernacular. Translators discovered that they could not express Greek or Latin meanings in English without adding new words to English or adding new elaborations to old words (p. 102). Purists like Thomas Wilson and Edmund Spencer argued that English should not be changed to accommodate translations. Neologizers, often citing Shakespeare who added some 10% of the new words to Elizabethan English in his writings, argued that English would become a richer language for these borrowings (pp. 103–105). According to Hughes, the Inkhorn debate indicates how print accelerated people's consciousness of the contradictions that language accommodated.

Hughes further indicated that print increased the complexity of culture by adding new meanings through complex texts. On this intepretation, Hughes contends that print itself made people more creative, allowed individuals to devise meanings they could not have devised in speech or writing. However this interpretation—like the cognitive arguments attached to print we criticized earlier—seems implausible insofar as creativity is predominantly an internal variable of individuals, and print is an external technology. There is little reason to believe that oral communication must lack the complexity of the written word (even though it often does). Nevertheless, what the ancients did lack were ways of archiving this complexity. Thus, a more plausible interpretation of Hughes' argument is that print did spread the prevailing cultural diversity in Europe with an unprecedented rapidity. According to this interpretation, concepts, with a set of locally diverse but underpublicized meanings at the societal level, already existed in Europe. As these simulations show, print can spread information from a complex text en masse and can do so efficiently, even in the face of a growing population becoming increasingly diverse in its culture and beliefs. Thus, print could conceivably increase the societal visibility and hence the awareness of conflict between local symbols that were complex and contradictory. Print (like the national media today) could make local symbols more globally visible; but print alone could not cause the wholesale development or dissolution of societally recognized symbols (chap. 5). The emergence or decay of these forms depends on many features of the sociocultural landscape and the content disseminated as well as the technology. But, all things being equal, print could conceivably have accelerated their emergence or decay.

IMPLICATIONS

Print enables the information in a communication to get to more readers faster by getting to many at once. Whether its potential rapidity makes a significant difference depends on the other co-evolving elements of society. Our results provide a small window through which we can view these dependencies and their implications. As a consequence, we see that print appears to alter seemingly inviolate social behaviors. For example, in an oral society, strong ties (i.e., high integration) slow diffusion because of a preponderance of ritualized communication. But print eliminates this relationship. Print has this effect not because it alters the fundamental nature of human beings (as technological determinists would contend) but because print enhances other factors that can mitigate or offset what happens under oral conditions. These simulations both enforce and stimulate a logical framework for thinking through some of the key issues surrounding print. The fresh insight allows us (a) to establish some firm logical relationships between print and a host of sociocultural variables and over-time measures; (b) to discriminate between better and worse explanations about print current in the extant literature; and (c) to see that to accommodate societies with populations of increasingly diverse beliefs and interests, the argument for allowing a similarly diverse stream of texts—in the form of first amendment principles—can in fact be an argument about the limit for the ultimate stability and convergence of society.

Finally, and no less importantly, we can learn a great deal about the directions inquiry needs to take by considering what these simulations do not but might cover. In the simulations run for this chapter, all texts were completely available; there were no constraints on availability. Future work could explore this simplifying assumption by including as a landscape variable what we call sociocultural opportunities to read. Such opportunities include increasing the size of editions, adding libraries, dropping the prices of books, increasing disposable income and leisure in literate settings—anything that can (and has) happened since the 18th century to tilt the individual's probability of interaction toward literate interaction. Within the constructural framework, such landscape variables can be examined by manipulating the availability of texts or at least an individual's ability to access them. According to the theoretical model we outline in chapter 5, availability, as well as relative similarity, determine whether a potential reader actually chooses a particular text as an interaction partner. But with the ability to restrict availability, we could simulate the effects of individuals being primed for literate interaction but still deprived of it. Clearly, in an era when we are beginning to understand that the child's path to literacy may have as much to do with home and family history as with formal schooling (see Rose 1989, for some elegant examples), we need better ways to represent how opportunities to read are culturally expressed, and the cultural effects that result when these opportunities are restricted.

Professions

The role of the cultural contributor is to overcome [the] inertia of mass culture and routine thinking.
—Raymond Williams (1962, p. 100)

[W]riting is an empirical art, which can only be learned by doing it. . . . There is no formal way of graduating in authorship and no way of enumerating its practitioners. . . . The price of that independence is the lack of identity in the public mind.
—Richard Findlater (cited in Bonham-Carter, 1978)

These passages speak about some of the tensions between the general market "Man of Letters" of the 18th century and the rising professional class of authors created by the industrial revolution of the 19th. The movement known as Romanticism might be seen, at least in part, as an atavistic attempt within the industrialization of letters to step back from an increasingly mass-produced culture and to create new meanings from stale, habitual ways of seeing and interpreting the surrounding reality. The Romantics lionized the author as a cultural contributor (in William's sense), but with the proviso that culture stood apart from and in opposition to technological materialism. Yet, even as Romanticism tried to shield the image of the author from the industrial revolution, the revolution was quietly creating its own indigenous image of the author, whose role was well integrated with mechanization: the professional author. Professions came to the fore to address the manifold problems brought on by urban industrialization; a new specialist class was needed to pose the problems in a public forum and to communicate solutions. Unlike the

297

Romantic author, whose tool was language and the imagination, the rising professional class of writers took as tools of the trade the specialized knowledge required of the increasingly scientific and technology-based occupations. Professions and the writing they sponsored promised to surpass "lay" thinking in the pursuit of solutions toward societal problems. Professionals attributed their comparative advantage to their group identity and to the training protocols and practices furnished by the group. By contrast, authors on the open market during industrialization had no group or professional credentials to speak of. They were on their own and they were achieving more and more independence from the culture at the expense of a cultural identity. Dillard (1989) described the highs and lows of this freedom in stark terms:

> Your freedom as a writer is . . . life at its most free, if you are fortunate enough to be able to try it, because you select your materials, invent your task, and pace yourself. In the democracies, you may write and publish anything you please about any governments or institutions, even if what you write is demonstrably false. The obverse of this freedom, of course, is that your work is so meaningless, so fully for yourself alone, and so worthless to the world, that no one except you cares whether you do it well, or ever. You are free to make several thousand close judgment calls a day. Your freedom is a by-product of your day's triviality. (p. 11)

The symbolic rift between an older authorial and a newer professional culture is a theme that has played itself out in many contexts since the industrial revolution. It played out in 1850s London—the decade that Turner (1953, pp. 100–101) called the best in history for the budding writer to enter journalism—when the bohemians of Grubb Street debated whether to abandon their "art" for a career on Fleet Street (Cross, 1985); it played out among the American progressive writers who often turned to muckraking when their fiction did not sell (Schudson, 1978; Wilson, 1985); it played out among young aspiring American and European writers in the 1920s who debated whether to matriculate to the university or to seek their "education" in the cafes of Paris, where they hoped to mingle with the likes of Hemingway, Fitzgerald, Stein, and Macleish; and, finally, it continues to be played out in modern day American departments of English, which debate whether their mission is compromised when they "train" student writers for the world of work.

The traditional image of the amateur author testing an uncertain print market became increasingly estranged and out of place in the age of professionalism, so much so that, to this day, it remains unclear how or even whether the authorial role is an appropriate one to include in a standard roster of professions (doctors, lawyers, scientists). Historians of letters often dichotomize the free market culture of imaginative authors and the culture of professional writers. West (1988, pp. 19–21), for example, insisted that authoring has survived as a "craft" and a "cottage industry" in a hostile world of professionalism. Bonham-Carter (1978, pp. 5–7) maintained that authors shun the professional role and are less likely to undergo formal training than "their brethren in the creative arts—composers, choreographers, painters, sculptors, and actors." Echoing a similar theme, Findlater (1966; cited in Bonham-Carter, 1978, Vol. II, p. 15) remarked that for authors, "independence is of the essence, and this includes the freedom to practice without formal qualification, without regimentation, without the pressure of collective action."

Bellow (1977, p. 192) lamented bitterly that too many writers have ceded their "independent ground" to institutions; he contrasted the "knowledge" of the expert with the "imaginative insight" of the author. Conversely, members of the professional class who happen to write are inclined toward the same dichotomies. Accountants who write formal auditing reports would be reluctant to categorize their writing as "literature." Physicists, who readily confess to having a hand in writing dozens of technical reports and grant proposals annually, will nonetheless deny the charge "author" if the charge is pressed too vigorously.

For our purposes, the distinction between the amateur (general market) and the professional author is an interesting one only because it distinguishes print-based transactions under different conditions. Taken rigidly, the distinction begs more questions than it answers, especially when it portrays authors and professionals in necessarily antagonistic roles. Viewed nonrelationally and prejudicially, the distinction does much harm and no discernable good. A comprehensive theory of print-based transactions must account for assumptions obtaining within as well as outside of professional contexts. At the very least, it would seem, investigating the authorial role within professionalism can only increase our understanding and appreciation of the role the author has fulfilled without. We cannot make headway on the author in professional contexts, it seems, without clarifying the nature of professions and the process by which individuals are socialized into them.

WHAT IS A PROFESSION?

From a constructural perspective, a profession is a pocket of individuals who are more culturally integrated than the population at large and who have access to information that is not generally shared by outsiders.[1]

---

[1]This definition is not meant to lessen the importance of factors such as dues paying and accreditation in the characterization of a profession and the determination of its membership. Rather, this definition suggests that such factors are of secondary importance in understanding how professions work.

From this vantage, we see that a profession is not a discrete and static category but a continuous and dynamic one. Members of a profession, like nonprofessionals, engage in a variety of communicative transactions across different technological conditions: speech, writing, print, of course, and more recently, all forms of electronic communication. Being a member of a profession, it appears, has less to do with the specific way communication is transacted and more to do with the position of the professional membership within the sociocultural landscape. A profession's sociocultural position can be characterized by two variables— cultural integration and specialization. The first variable, cultural integration, was introduced in chapter 7. Applied to a profession, this variable means the extent to which individuals within a group share knowledge among themselves (and thus how likely they are to interact with each other as a consequence of relative similarity). The second variable, one we have not yet considered, is specialization, or the extent to which members of the group have information not shared by other individuals in the society.[2] A highly specialized group has little overlap with individuals outside the group. A group low in specialization, in turn, has little knowledge peculiar to its members.

Prototypical professions are groups high in both cultural integration and specialization. For prototypical professions, the information that integrates them is the knowledge that makes them specialized. Prototypical professions are ideal types and they should not be confused with the spectrum of de facto groups whose members happen to refer to the group to which they belong as a profession. We call attention to this common confusion not to demean groups who call themselves professions yet fall outside the prototype, but to point out that some groups, whether or not they call themselves a profession, are better or worse instances of a prototypical profession. Further, the prototype normally invoked to

---

[2]The notion of specialization is ambiguous. In its broadest sense, specialization means knowledge—of any kind—that is disproportionately associated with particular groups in the society. In this sense, the specialized knowledge need not be rare, but only nonuniform in its distribution. Thus, mothers in this broad sense have a specialized knowledge of childbirth. Another sense of specialization includes the notion of nonuniform but limited distribution, knowledge that expresses itself only in relatively small groups in the society. It is this second sense of specialization—in terms of limited numbers—that some authors evoke when they point out that increased specialization restricts the size of the group claiming it (chap. 9, this volume; Garvey, 1979, pp. 1–2; Meadows, 1973, pp. 18–28). In a related but slightly different sense, specialization includes the idea of professionalized knowledge, which, rare or not, is cognitively and socially valorized as prestige information because of its implications for problem solving. In this book, we regard specialization as the degree to which the knowledge between groups does not overlap. This definition allows us to incorporate many of these senses, while maintaining a certain level of precision that is not available in these other renderings.

characterize professions does not perfectly characterize the wide assortment of professional groups within a society. Professions vary widely in how well they approximate the prototype; it seems like useless question begging to use the prototype as an inflexible standard for defining a profession—the kind of question begging that results when we try to make robins the inflexible standard for defining birds. Such definition making from rigid prototypes imposes a discrete categorization on professions, which require a fuzzier definition based on a more continuous logic. Viewed from a fuzzy set vantage, professions do not fill in a single discrete niche in a sociocultural landscape but are a set of niches that bear a family resemblance to one another.

Figure 8.1 depicts a continuum of professions relative to cultural integration and specialization. Professions a through d, like politicians, are more culturally integrated than specialized. Professions e through h, like many academic groups, are more specialized than culturally integrated. A group may call itself a profession regardless of where it lies on these

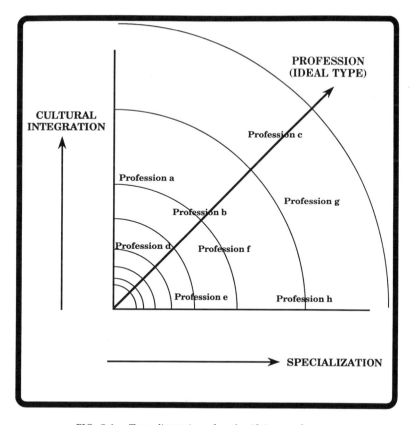

FIG. 8.1.   Two dimensions for classifying professions.

dimensions. However, the higher its level on both dimensions, the more exemplary it is of the prototype. Professions c and g, like lawyers, exemplify the prototypical profession more than the others depicted. Finally, groups that are low on both dimensions (e.g., professions d and e) are "nominal" professions, perhaps making noises for professional standing more in their official rhetoric than in their everyday reality.

When professions are viewed as a fuzzy set, it becomes evident that the boundary between members and nonmembers is ambiguous, which suggests the added importance of boundary setting and gate keeping procedures in maintaining a profession. In their public posturing, members of a profession may organize themselves to make a difference to the larger society. Their legitimation typically depends on contracts (in the forms of licenses and accreditations) made with the larger society. Yet, as members of the profession follow up on the implications of these contracts by becoming more specialized, they can also become less cognitively similar, in relative terms, to the public they claim to serve. The decrease in relative similarity can and often does lead to diminished interaction between members of the profession and the larger public. This is especially true for professions whose aim is prototypical status, to become highly integrated on a base of knowledge not shared by the public. A logical consequence of a profession attaining prototypical status may be anonymity from the public, both socially and cognitively. One might argue that sects like the Masons and Rosicrucians fill this role. This anonymity can in turn evoke distrust among the very citizens who entrusted the profession in the first place.

Buried in the principle of professional development, it seems, is a mild principle of monasticism, the notion that as a profession becomes more prototypic, more internally integrated and specialized, the boundaries between it and the outside society become less permeable. The literature on the professions tends to overlook the issue of permeability between the professional group and the larger society.[3] Rather, the literature tends to be divided between work that looks only at the internal workings of a profession and work that looks only at its external relations. The first literature investigates the workings of the insider language and sociocultural structure of a profession (Garfinkel, Lynch, & Livingston, 1981; Gilbert & Mulkay, 1984; Hempel & Oppenheim, 1948; Latour & Woolgar, 1979; Merton, 1938, and 1938/1970; and much of the sociological literature on professions, cited later). The second literature investigates the accountability of this language and structure to a

---

[3]Recent research in communication, however, has examined the permeability of professional groups (Rice & Crawford, in press). Rice and Crawford demonstrated that such permeability is measurable, and that it may be asymmetric, with one profession more likely than the other to permeate the other's boundaries.

larger public (Bender, 1984; Fisher, 1987; Kucklick, 1977). These different faces of a profession have seldom been integrated (but cf. Abbott, 1988; Geisler, 1990; Myers, 1985).

The schism in the literatures on professions is unfortunate because, ultimately, the external accountabilities of a profession devolve on its internal communicative transactions. Conversely, the profession's internal transactions place limits on the profession's obligations for its external transactions, when it is called upon to account for itself in public forums. As evidence for the importance of this permeability on maintaining professions both from within and without, Myers (1985) found that the work of the biologists he studied was profoundly influenced by the reviews of government funding agencies who, in turn, were interested in justifying the importance of the work to their superiors. Without a conduit from the inside to the outside, professions are often held to unrealistic expectations by a public unable to distill the profession's realistic promises from the public's own unrealistic hopes. Without a conduit from the outside in, the public may be forever unable to make the distillation for itself, and the concerns of the profession may become increasingly remote from social life, thus diminishing its capacity to recruit new members. Issues of permeability are thus vital to the social maintenance and growth of professions because as insiders keep it afloat, so do the priorities of the taxpayers and the politicians whom they keep in office. Issues of permeability are also essential to the cognitive maintenance of the professions. Advances in many, if not most, professions are related to advances in related fields. The allure of specialization is that it keeps a profession focused and intact around a few major questions. The handicap of specialization is that it can close off a profession from the ideas needed to keep it fresh and invigorated.

For social (Blau, 1967; Turner, 1984), cognitive (Berger & Luckman, 1966; Feldman & March, 1981; March & Simon, 1958), and institutional reasons (Etzioni, 1964; Powell & DiMaggio, 1991; Simmel, 1955), as well as for reasons supporting environments of innovation, it is important to study communicative transactions within a professional group concurrently with the communicative transactions of the larger society.[4] The institutional claim of all professions is that reciprocity between the group's change (i.e., change within the profession) and the change within the larger society will prove beneficial for both the profession and the society. This claim, unpacked in terms of the theory we are developing, means that the more stable and consensual the profession is allowed to become,

---

[4]This comment is, of course, commensurate with the idea that organizations are open systems and must be studied relative to the larger environment. See, for example, Aldrich (1979).

the more stable and consensual the society that has had the good sense to entrust it will become. The rhetoric of the military—that a strong military is a strong society—is the most dramatic illustration of this claim at work, but it applies, in quieter tones, to every profession. We need to distinguish between the claim qua claim and the sociocultural reality to which the claim pertains. For any given profession, it is conceivable that the claim is false, that what is good for the profession is decidedly not good for the society. The possibility of this mismatch has caused many to approach the professions with an air of suspicion, wondering whether a profession's rhetoric has anything to do with its reality. Indeed, government decision making in funding or offering support or inducements to a profession often hinges on whether government review panels see the profession's rhetoric and reality in alignment.

THE REALITY AND THE RHETORIC
OF A PROFESSION

Despite the importance of rhetoric in defining the reality of a profession, we can distinguish a profession's rhetoric from its reality. The rhetoric of a profession pertains to a group's official discourse about its professional status. The reality of a profession is characterized by its actual levels of integration and specialization. These levels are measured by sociohistorical methodologies designed to monitor what information the members of the profession share, how much they share, and how much of what they share is peculiar to it (i.e., whether a profession is more like Profession a, Profession b, and so on). Professional rhetoric and reality are related concepts, but they have been pursued by separate traditions with separate histories. In the following sections, we briefly recount each of these traditions.

Professional Reality

For the past 40 years, sociologists have been concerned with isolating the sociocultural variables that track the development of professions. Caplow (1954) offered a formal model of professional development and argued that professions move through a series of universal stages, from group identification to formalized training, to licensing, and finally to internal regulation. Wilensky (1964) conducted a detailed survey of individual professions and tracked important milestones in the history of their development. Finding much more individual variation than Caplow had reported, Wilensky concluded that there was no single sequence of development through which professions evolved. Millerson (1964) reported on the individual case histories of a cross section of professions and concluded that professions seem as unique as their histories—some professions decide to become a profession long before they exist as a group; others maintain ties as a group long before they realize or announce themselves as a profession. Larson (1977) concluded that professions do not develop in abstract time or logical stages but ideologically, in patterns that are sensitive to the particular historical and economic conditions.

Even longer than sociologists have wondered how professions develop, they have wondered what professions are. Early sociological theory on professions aimed at defining professions in terms of the knowledge, training, certificates, codes, and altruistic intentions of their members (Carr-Saunders & Wilson, 1933). Later theorists proposed definitions highlighting the more relational and self-interested aspects of professions, associating professions with groups whose members could claim knowledge considered precious, in high demand, and a source of upward mobility (Ben-David, 1963; Bledstein, 1976). Still another tradition of theorists since the 1960s has placed greater emphasis on the capacity of professions to dominate an economic market (Berlant, 1975; Freidson, 1976, 1986; Johnson, 1967; Larson, 1977). For example, Johnson argued that professionals do not pursue "objective" societal needs but collude to create a market for the needs they claim to fulfill. Freidson maintained that the self-interested goals of professions, autonomy and hegemony, exceed their altruistic goals of internal collegiality and the trust of their clients. Berlant described professions as enclaves within the economy seeking monopolistic control over their work. Larson defined a profession as a group that has achieved this market dominance. On her account, less powerful, often female-dominated institutional groups (e.g., nurses, social workers) have yet to attain "professional" standing because they have yet to attain economic autonomy over the conditions of their work. Collins (1979) offered an interesting consumer-based understanding of the professions. He observes that 20th-century technocracies require only a limited core of knowledge specialists but a much larger consumer class to buy the goods and services put out in abundance through technologies. According to Collins, the white-collar professions drawn from the middle class developed primarily in order to regulate entry into this consumer class. The American educational system was used as the principal gateway for entry. As the influx of immigrants to America created more competition for jobs, the educational requirements for entry into white-collar jobs became increasingly inflated, requiring undergraduate and even graduate degrees for the work that had been done in previous generations with barely a high school diploma. The steady ascendancy of what Collins called a "credential society" insured a professional class that remained predominantly White, male, and middle class, but insured little else about training. Abbott (1988, p. 19) viewed professions as a historical concept that groups use to adjudicate and resolve jurisdictional claims about work: "It is control of work that brings the professions into conflict with each other and makes their histories interdependent. It is differentiation in types of work that often leads to serious differentiation within the professions." Abbott's observations are interesting because he sees the life of a profession as determined by the historical/linguistic practices through which it lays claim to a field of work and protects its turf from competing groups. His observations begin to bridge a sociology of the professional reality with a rhetoric of the professions.

Professional Rhetoric

Since the late 19th century, the terms *profession* and *professional* have been transformed into powerful tropes. A group now routinely appeals to its professionalism to dismiss its potential for corruptibility and bias and to justify informational, educational, economic, and political monopolies of which it can take advantage. American scientists frequently find themselves having to lobby on behalf of their professionalism in order to dodge or discredit the competing arguments of religious sects and the occult (Gieryn, Bevins, & Zehr, 1985). Top-level corporate management has learned to use the symbol of the professional against employee groups to restrict their interests and perogatives. They have learned, for example, that by describing the various occupations (nurses, police, air traffic controllers) with whom they deal as a professional class, they can thwart the occupation's efforts to unionize and to receive special benefits, compensation, and overtime.

Although sociologists have played a large role in defining and tracking the development of professions through analytic schemes, the history of the rhetoric of professions was not written by sociological researchers. Instead, as much as to any other single source, it owes a debt to Lippman and his classic 1922 defense of a writing trade he hoped to make into a profession—journalism. Lippman's defense was the culmination of a century-long struggle between journalism on one hand and advertising and public relations on the other. The question of who should determine the balance of news and advertising haunted the newspaper industry in America and England since the 1840s, when James Gordon Bennett, editor of the *New York Herald*, insisted that advertising was itself a form of news that needed to change in order to sustain reader interest. Before Bennett, advertisers often ran the same colorless ad for years at a time, hidden in small type on the back page. Bennett ordered that ads be changed every 2 weeks and, eventually, daily (Turner, 1953, p. 100).

Making the ad a kind of "news" had a positive effect on circulation but also imposed a reciprocal pressure on the editorial staff to maintain the newspaper as an outlet attractive to advertisers. The problem was that advertisers wanted to reach either the richest or largest markets. The richest markets were politically conservative and the largest markets were politically diverse. The newspaper risked losing readers from one or both markets by taking political slants that were either too liberal or too specific. Consequently, as the newspaper become more dependent on advertising revenue, editors came under increasing pressure to keep their reporting neutral in content (Schudson, 1978).

Despite the growing cross influence between news and advertising, the marriage between editors and advertisers was not happy. In the 19th century, it was typical for editors to look upon the advertiser as a pariah to be tolerated only for the money (Cross, 1985, pp. 95–103). They united against granting space other than the back page to advertisers. They imposed severe typographical and layout constraints on advertising copy (i.e., small type without white space, visuals, or variations in layout) so that readers would not be fooled into thinking that advertising was anything other than it was. Throughout the last half of the 19th century, advertisers tried to get around these restrictions by submitting ads with large type and pictures of voluptuous women or other allurements (Dyer, 1982, p. 31). Yet such submissions were consistently rejected by editors (Williams, 1980). Bennett, for example, refused all advertising copy with illustrations, believing they were unfairly biased in favor of the well-to-do merchant who could afford to run them (Turner, 1953, p. 101).

By the turn of the century, the brief skirmishes between editors and advertisers intensified into more open conflicts as the economic stakes increased. Before this, the manufacturing sector of the economy had not been a player in newspaper advertising nor had it sought a visible identity among the reading public. Sponsors for newspaper ads were small, often seedy, businesses: snuff sellers, undertakers, abortionists, and miracle healers (Turner, 1953). By the 1890s, however, the large manufacturing industries aligned themselves with the new industries of retailing and finance, and manufacturers now saw that they needed greater public visibility in order to push their inventories. New products—iceboxes, furnaces, water closets, and washing machines—and retailing services—department stores, installment buying, and brand names—came on the market. Trans-Atlantic trade was becoming more competitive and manufacturers, as never before, had to fight for a market (Turner, 1953, pp. 140). Financial service industries also appeared, seeking out individuals in need of financing, capitalization, and the sale of credit. For the first time, the reading public could become common investors in stocks and securities (Schudson, 1978). Although retail and service industries had previously ignored the general reading public, they now actively sought markets within it. A new profession, public relations, evolved to do just that. Public relations was an outgrowth of journalism, with the mindset of advertising rather than news gathering.

As manufacturing, retailing, and finance gradually rose to public visibility, the advertising and public relations clients of the newspaper became more corporate and respectable, as did the agencies which sought to represent them to the newspapers. As early as 1870, some advertising agencies rivaled newspapers in internal organization, having their own editorial and design departments and, by the 1890s, their own "creative" departments (Atwan, 1979, pp. 18–22). The increased clout of the advertising and public relations industries exerted greater leverage on newspaper editors who decided on the content of the newspaper. Because greater revenues were at stake, the advertising and public relations agencies were able to insist on a more effective integration of the editorial and advertising/promotional content of the paper. Ads, which had formerly relied on unabashed huckstering and monotonous repetition, were reworked into more sophisticated narratives that included reasons for buying a product, molded around problem–solution scenarios. Ads told stories in their own right and, as such, became items of news with large layout, type, and visuals (Dyer, 1982). Public relation releases became so well masked that editors and readers alike would often mistake them for news. The phenomenon of disguising a dramatically produced saga as news to elevate its immediacy and reach was not at all peculiar to print media or even advertising; it infiltrated radio in the 1930s with the original broadcast of H. G. Wells' *War of the Worlds*.

The public relations agencies representing corporations and the prominent people who ran them prided themselves on tricking editors into such misclassifications. By all accounts, public relations writers in the first few decades of the century had reason to be proud. By the 1930s, an employee of J. Walter Thompson estimated that some 60% of the stories in *The New York Times* were the "plants" of public relation agents. This applied to some 50% of all journalistic stories in the American press. The appeal of promotional copy for editors, among other things, was that it helped to fill dead space in the newspaper each day. In the 1930s, Crawford estimated that each day a large paper routinely received 150,000 words of unsolicited public relations text. Walker estimated that in New York City in the 1930s, more individuals were employed to write public relations copy than to write the news (Schudson, 1978, pp. 138–144). Reporters from the old school of journalism increasingly began to see their work and the work of public relations writers on a collision course. The job of the reporter was to report the news without bias, yet the job of the public relations writer was to guarantee that the news came out with the "correct" spin or bias.[5]

The work of one profession seemed to undercut the work of the other, and the status of both was threatened. Abbott (1988) argued that such historical clashes and the attempts to win them by getting the powers-that-be to accept jurisdictional claims about turf are part and parcel of what it means for groups to professionalize themselves. Such claims to turf require a public discourse, a rhetoric designed to circumscribe and protect an area of work for a group. The rhetoric most effective in doing so was one that claimed prototypical profession for the group, whether it had it or not. To be strategically effective, in other words, such a discourse had to indicate the group's internal integration and specialization around an area of work. The group had to show it was not only organized from within through common training, but that its training uniquely positioned it to render its services. Lippman's *Public Opinion* (1922) was perhaps the first, and certainly the most influential, book-length treatment of a rhetoric seeking to carve out a professional identity for a group under siege. The group was, of course, journalists, and the group's antagonist was the new public relations writer who cut into the market demand for journalists. *Public Opinion* created a model rhetoric, often imitated, on how to go about claiming professional standing for a group. Lippman's model offered three strategic arguments on behalf of a group's claim to a professional identity: (a) historical legacy; (b) unique basis in science; and (c) unique value to the public. All these arguments center on the profession's information-based relationship to the larger society.

The first argument, historical legacy, is important because a profession, to be rhetorically viable, must be seen as performing a longstanding good or fighting a longstanding evil. Its work cannot be seen as invented from within but rather as growing out of ongoing historical needs that, in many cases, predate the responses of any particular group. The profession, in other words, is not isolated but shares some information with the outside world. Viewed this way, the claim to professional status is a claim by a group that seeks legitimation to organize itself in response to historical forces. Lippman argued, for instance, that journalists have been responding to recurring problems that are endemic in trying to make modern democracies work. Democracies require an informed citizenry; journalism, in an earlier era, responded to that need through the circulation of news. Yet the founding fathers had never envisioned the consequences of the industrial revolution—a society inundated by

---

[5]For a fictional account of this headlong battle, see Hubard's decology *Mission Earth*.

information of varying accuracy. Lippman claimed a new, scientific journalist is needed to help the public remain accurately informed in an environment where there is too much (not too little) information in circulation.

The second and third arguments, variations on uniqueness, are also important for a rhetoric of professions because they attest to the cognitive authority and unique social positioning that must typically be claimed by individuals within a profession. The profession, that is, grounds itself in specialized information. Science and technology were both benefactors and beneficiaries of the industrial revolution; most of the problems professions have addressed since that watershed event have included science and technology, either in their understanding of the problem, the solution, or both. It is thus not surprising that postindustrial professionals began, like Lippman, to base their cognitive authority in science. Lippman maintained, for example, that the new journalistic profession can rely on the emergent sciences of the mind and the social sciences for help in understanding how individuals and groups can sometimes be herded into adopting stereotypical[6] beliefs and attitudes from information that they would not accept when thinking rationally. He claimed that only the new profession of journalism he was trying to define renders this service to the public. Significantly, Lippman's argument relies on, but does not make explicit, the cultural integration of members of the new journalistic profession over and above their willingness to study the new science of mind. As a consequence, while "all" members of the profession could be relied on to serve rather than persuade the public, no member of the public who is willing to study the human mind is barred from the new journalism, or from any other profession willing to ground itself in the new study of mind.

Whether Lippman's image of the new professional journalist was ever successfully launched or taken to heart by later generations of journalists is a disputable point in the history of 20th-century journalism. What is not disputable has been the power and resilience of his rhetoric in guiding others, belonging to other groups, when they have penned professional manifestos for their groups. In a quirky, though not entirely unpredictable, twist given the loopholes in Lippman's own definition, Bernays, a public relations consultant and Lippman's nemesis, lifted Lippman's exact themes from *Public Opinion*, and within a year of the publication of that book, released his own book-length manifesto, *Crystallizing Public Opinion*, 1923, titled to play off of Lippman's title. Lippman's book was intended to inaugurate the new professional journalist; Bernays' was

---

[6]Lippman (1922) was the first writer to use the word "stereotype" to convey its current perjorative meaning. See Ashmore & Del Boca (1981).

intended to inaugurate the new public relations professional. True to Lippman's format, Bernays methodically detailed the ongoing historical problems to which public relations experts have continued to respond. He traced the public relations professional back to the ancient city–states and the constant efforts of their rulers to keep its citizens informed of the commercial culture around them. Like Lippman, Bernays also cited a modern crisis resulting from the explosion of information. The crisis is the widening gap between the commercial institutions of society and the stream of accurate information the public needs in order to maintain faith in them, both as citizens and investors. To deal with this widening gap, Bernays continued, the new public relations professional must be schooled in the same sciences that Lippman commended to the new journalist. Lippman's professional needs scientific training to understand why readers are believing what they should not believe; Bernay's professional must study science to understand why readers are not believing what they should. Bernay's rhetoric is thus opposite in purpose but playfully imitative of Lippman's, suggesting a deep flattery in the imitation. On reflection, Lippman's rhetoric is hard not to imitate, because of the way it captures the lines of argument needed for a group to inaugurate a professional identity for itself in industrialized society. Whether there are rhetorics of professional inauguration markedly different from Lippman's model is an interesting project for further research. But the point we draw is that Lippman's rhetoric relied on the two dimensions we see as central to being professional—integration and specialization—and any other rhetoric inaugurating a profession would, in principle, need to do the same.

PRINT AND PROFESSIONS: WHAT IS THE RELATIONSHIP?

Unlike guilds, crafts, trades, and occupations that have been structured around local apprenticeships from time immemorial, professions, it has been argued, need to be structured around printed texts, especially as professions grew in size and diversity. Print, in this sense, determined the modern profession. There is, of course, no doubt that print, the telegraph, and the phone coincided with an explosion in professional culture in the late 19th century. Between 1876 and 1900, the number of telephones soared from 3,000 to 1.3 million. Between 1870 and 1900, daily newspaper circulation jumped by a factor of 7; the number of post offices, by a factor of 3; the number of telegraphs communications, by a factor of 9; the number of copyrights, by a factor of 8; and the number of patents, by a factor of 2. Between 1880 and 1900, publishers book lists rose by a factor of 3 (Bledstein, 1976, pp. 47–48). Occupations became organized into more tightly circumscribed "knowledge niches," each developing its own specialized vocabulary. As Bledstein (1976) described it:

> Confined in its space, every serious activity found a literary expression, including a distinct vocabulary that sympathetic persons could share. . . . [there were now] magazines for each demographic group . . . bicyclists, sports, gardening. The kindergarten and primary school movement established three professional journals in the 1870s alone. . . . Legitimate authority now resided in special spaces, like the courtroom, the classroom and the hospital and it resided in special words shared only by experts. (pp. 65, 79–81)

While society was dividing itself into knowledge niches, groups within the society formed to claim niches for themselves. Between 1870 and 1890 alone, at least 200 learned societies were formed, including the American Chemical Society, the American Society for Chemical Engineers, the American Forestry Association, the American Ornithologists Union, the American Society of Naturalists, the American Climatological Society, the American Institute of Electrical Engineers, the Geological Society of America, the National Statistics Association, the American Mathematical Society, and the American Physical Society (Bledstein, 1976, pp. 70–75). The effect of specializing language within many narrow groups was to filter, intensify, and regularize the bands of relative-similarity interaction between author and reader. What had been a single diffuse print market splintered into many thin specialized markets.

The case seems plausible for positing some structural dependence between print and the expansion of the professions. But, as we previously argued, the idea of a profession depends on the specific characteristics of a group and not on a specific communication technology through which it conducts its transactions. Technologies may enhance the capacity of groups to become professions (either in reality or in rhetoric), but the mere existence of professions was not determined by print alone. It is fair to say, perhaps, that before print, professions had to rely exclusively on writing in order to break assumptions of proximity (i.e., proximity with persons) and that writing could not violate these assumptions without loss. Goody (1986, pp. 130–142) argued, for example, that the markings of a professional legal system were visible in 13th-century England when customs of behavior were written down and could be evenly applied across local districts. But the evenness of the application is suspect, given the variability in written copies and the difficulty of maintaining single copies that needed to be used on a continuing basis. By enhancing the fixity and durability of communications within a profession, print, arguably, gave professionals a more reliable means for working at a distance.

Print, or for that matter any communication technology, may support the work of professionals at a distance. Yet any such technologies, no matter how sophisticated, may effect the loss of some important advantages taken for granted in face-to-face or oral communication. Recent research suggests that face-to-face communication is qualitatively different from communication at a distance. A number of studies (Carley with Wendt, 1991; Crane, 1971; Egido, 1990; Fish, Kraut, Root, & Rice, 1992; Galegher, 1990; Kraut, Egido, & Galegher, 1990; Kraut, Galegher, & Egido, 1988) have found that some aspects of professional work are accomplished only through face-to-face proximity. Crane (1971), for example, found that scientists as a profession rely on regular face-to-face interaction to maintain their invisible college. Kraut, Galegher, and their collaborators found that professionals typically rely on face-to-face contact to get acquainted with one another and to build the base of shared knowledge that is necessary to form working relationships. They also reported that no current telecommunications equipment (e.g., video links across remote sites) has yet to provide a context as rich and supportive for initiating (not conducting) working relationships as face-to-face contexts. They explained their results by noting what equation 6.2 (in chap. 6) indicates—that proximity can heighten the probability of social interaction even in the absence of shared knowledge. Kraut, Galegher, and their associates confirmed this assumption through a number of interview, survey, and archival studies. They reported that physical proximity seems to be the best indicator for explaining the formation of professional working groups in the university. They conjectured that face-to-face proximity affords opportunities for interaction with minimal advanced planning and low personal risk. It allows people the freedom to explore a variety of topics over the lunch table without the worry that they have to get to the point. It allows individuals immediate feedback and the ability to adjust their meanings quickly in order to maximize their shared understandings:

One reason for the powerful effect of proximity is that it enables people to solve the primary relationship-level concern of this stage—establishing compatibility—easily and at low personal cost. They can exchange ideas, comments, news of their own activities and interests casually over lunch or a cup of coffee. If both individuals find the conversations and each other stimulating and enjoyable, they may discuss the possibilities for joint research more seriously and directly. But the casual conversation implies no commitment, and if a research collaboration does not develop, neither participant has lost face. . . . In the development of collaborations . . . people are more likely to feel confident about making commitments to work together when they have had the opportunity to size up each other face to face than if they learn about each other in an indirect way such as by reading each other's prior publications. (Kraut et al., 1988, p. 37)

The same research group also found that once professionals have built a base of shared understandings and are committed to work together, they are much more likely to entrust serious work to communication technologies to help them execute the project at a distance. After the initial phases of negotiating a collaboration face-to-face, professionals appear to require less frequent personal proximity, less sustained face-to-face support, less direct contact. They rely decreasingly on their personal proximity and increasingly on communication technologies to accomplish significant work with satisfactory outcomes. This same point was corroborated by Carley with Wendt (1991).

These findings qualify possible relationships between the expansion of professions in the 19th century and print. Unlike face-to-face interaction, print did not provide a rich medium that encouraged new and intense collaborations across professionals. Unlike the aims, if not the achievements, of many of the new computer-based collaboration technologies, print, because of its asynchronicity, did little to revolutionize the initiation of work relationships between professionals. Yet print did much, arguably, to revolutionize the extent to which professionals were distributed. Like electronic mail and later technologies, print allowed for a much wider geographical distribution of individuals within a profession. Moreover, print seemed to do more than allow peers who trained together to keep in touch. It also seemed to confer to strangers a sense of belonging to the same organization. Print made it possible, in other words, for individuals to size up relative-similarity relationships with others of similar background and training whom they had never met outside a text. This made it possible, in turn, for otherwise strangers to feel a sense of belonging to common organizations of regional and even national scope. This speculation can be examined formally using the model in chapter 6. Such an examination may help explain why so many professional organizations were able and inclined to charter themselves at the national level in the generation just following the adoption of the steam press.

This analysis does not yet address the dynamics through which print could increase the range of ties among members of the profession. For the sake of pursuing this question through a thought experiment, imagine that the 200-odd professional societies that established national charters in the late 19th century had tried to do so without print, using only sustained face-to-face interaction and simple written communications. It seems absurd to think history could have happened that way, but conceiving of such an alternative universe forces us to be precise about the kind of contribution print might have made to the long-distance relationships between professionals. We assume that for a profession to maintain itself across a broad geographical space, it must maintain a certain (homogenizing) stability and consensus; it must be able to counteract, in a timely fashion, challenges to homogeneity that arise as new members (from different regions) and their new ideas funnel into the profession, increasing its membership and intellectual diversity. How a profession responds to these challenges may have something to do with its level of prototypicality, the degree to which it is culturally integrated and specialized, and the technological conditions under which it operates. We address the relationship between technology, prototypicality, and the development of professional homogeneity and consensus using the model in chapter 6, which is the direction to which we now turn.

SOCIOCULTURAL LANDSCAPES

To get some logical perspective on these relationships, we construct two sets of simulations. In each set, societies consist of two groups. We call one group the profession or the professional group. We refer to the other group by various names: the nonprofessionals, the outsiders, or the remaining individuals in the society. In both sets of simulations, we run societies under two different technological conditions. In one technological condition, there are no texts and only one-to-one proximate communication—the oral condition. This condition roughly represents the condition available to professions prior to industrialized print. In the other technological condition, all individuals (whether they are part of the professional group or not) have wide access to print and can routinely shift between one-to-many and one-to-one communicative transactions—the print condition. Across both sets of simulations, we monitor the prototypicality of the professional group. We simulate each society 100 times for 500 time periods, relying on the same Monte Carlo techniques described in chapter 6. In the following analyses, we are interested in how the technological conditions and the manipulated features of the sociocultural landscape impact the time-to-stability and the time-to-consensus for each of the simulated societies and professional groups.

Technology, Absolute Size, and the Diversity of Ideas

How does technology affect the speed of consensus and stability within a profession when its membership rolls are increasing/decreasing in absolute numbers and when the population around it is increasing or decreasing at a comparable rate? How does technology matter to professional consensus and stability when the ideas the professional needs to learn are growing/shrinking in absolute terms and the ideas to be learned in the enveloping culture are growing/shrinking as well? We use the first set of simulations to explore these questions by varying the technological condition, the absolute size of professional and nonprofessional groups, and the cultural complexity.

For every society, regardless of its technological condition, we vary the population (6, 12, or 18 individuals) and the cultural complexity (10, 20, or 40 ideas). Across all the societies in this first set of simulations, we control—by holding constant—the relative size of the profession with respect to the group of nonprofessionals. We assign membership in the professional group to 50% of the individuals in the society. Consequently, the absolute size of the profession varies between 3, 6, or 9 individuals, depending on the society's overall population. The absolute size of the professional culture, in turn, varies between 5, 10, and 20 ideas. This simulation set makes it possible to examine professional organization and change in 9 societies under each of the technological conditions, oral and print.

To make sure that the possible effects of these variations are not confounded by the particular status of the profession in terms of prototypicality, the profession's initial level of cultural integration and specialization are held constant. The professional group in every society is designed to be a highly prototypical profession (i.e., high in its initial levels of internal integration and specialization). To assure high specialization, we assign half (50%) of the ideas in the society only to members of the professional group. This assignment created a professional culture, highly specialized (i.e., nonoverlapping) compared to the culture of the society at large. On average, individuals within the profession shared but 4% of all their ideas with individuals outside the profession. To assure high cultural integration within the profession, we assign every member of the profession a high percentage of the profession's culture—64% of the ideas. By contrast, we design our individuals outside the profession to be much less culturally integrated and specialized. Outsiders initially share, on average, only 4% of their ideas with one another, and because we allow the professionals (as a group) to know pretty much everything that nonprofessionals (as a group) know, the nonprofessionals have no specialized "outsider" culture to contrast with the very specialized professional culture.

Technology, Relative Size, and the Prototypicality of the Profession

How does technology matter to the speed of consensus and stability within a profession when the profession itself is becoming more or less prototypical (i.e., more or less internally integrated or specialized) and when its membership is increasing/decreasing in relative terms with respect to the larger population? We design a second set of simulations to explore these questions by varying the technological condition, the status of the profession relative to prototypicality, and its relative size compared to the group of nonprofessionals. The second set of simulations, in other words, vary many of the landscape variables that the first set controlled for, and vice versa. In the second set of simulations, societies vary by technology in the manner of the first set. The professions in the societies vary markedly in their degree of prototypicality. Some professions are highly integrated and highly specialized, as is the case for all professions in the first set of simulations. But other professions in the second set are (a) low in their initial level of cultural integration relative to the cultural integration of the nonprofessionals; (b) low in their initial level of specialization relative to the group of nonprofessionals; or (c) are relatively low in initial levels of both integration and specialization (making them nominal in their professional status). More specifically, we allow the initial percentage of the profession's cultural integration to vary among 4%, 16%, or 64%. We allowed the degree of specialization of each profession to range among 1%, 4%, or 16%. These variations define a set of 9 professions, varying in their prototypicality. Figure 8.2 plots the 9 professions we simulate, relative to the possibilities illustrated in Fig. 8.1.

Unlike the first set of simulations, where we varied the absolute size of the groups (and societies) and controlled for their relative size, in the second set of simulations, the relative size of the groups is varied within a society of fixed absolute size. We hold constant the absolute population of every society (12 individuals). We then vary the relative size of the profession by letting the number of professionals in each society be either 6 (50% of the society), 4 (33% of the society), or 3 (25% of the society). We also hold the level of cultural complexity (20 ideas) constant across each society. We initially assign half (10) of the ideas only to individuals in the professional group. This does not entail a specialized professional culture, however, as the distribution of these ideas within in the professional group could be very skewed (with one professional knowing all 10 of these ideas and everyone else knowing only 2 of them). This simulation set includes a total of 27 societies, each simulated under the oral and print conditions.

RESULTS

We present the results of these two sets of simulations in conjunction with a series of hypotheses that they have led us to generate.

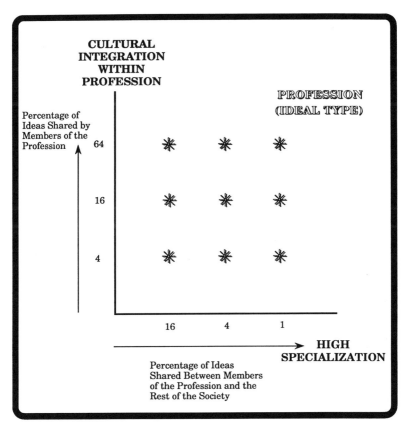

FIG. 8.2.   Characteristics of professions simulated in second set of simulations.

Efficiency Hypothesis: Print Speeds Things Up

One can argue, as we do in chapter 7, that print speeds things up. Because of the multiplicity, print can move information faster and effect more rapid stability and consensus. We call this the Efficiency Hypothesis. This hypothesis is distinct from, and should not be confused with, the Strong Print Hypothesis (chap. 7). The Strong Print Hypothesis states that print immediately (or in some timely, if not timed, interval) creates stability and consensus. The Efficiency Hypothesis is weaker, simply allowing that print speeds things up; it does not make things happen immediately but just makes them happen sooner (whether sooner is soon enough is another matter!). The Strong Print Hypothesis fashions print into a kind of stability and consensus mechanism and, as a result, conflates the technological conditions through which communication is trans-acted and the social outcomes of these transactions. The Efficiency Hypothesis, instead, makes specific claims about the enhanced perfor-mance of individuals who are able to communicate through print. Spe-cifically, the Efficiency Hypothesis suggests that print makes any individual more efficient in spreading cultural information, independent of the amount of cultural information there is to spread. Print makes it possible, in other words, to move larger quantities of information without having to increase, in direct proportion, the quantity of individuals needed to move it. Under oral conditions, when communication is one-to-one, the more ideas to be moved, the greater the number of people needed to move them. An oral culture with many stories to pass down will re-quire more story-tellers as the number of stories themselves increase. Con-versely, print is useful to a sociocultural organization—including profes-sional organizations—because it enables fewer individuals to spread larger amounts of information throughout a group or a society within a shorter interval of time.

These simulations give logical support to and provide an impetus for the Efficiency Hypothesis. Consider Tables 8.1 and 8.2 and Fig. 8.3 through 8.8. These tables and figures indicate that the technological con-dition exerts a strong effect on the speed of stability and consensus with-in the profession. Stability and consensus occur much faster under print than under oral conditions. As a way of teasing out the Efficiency Hypothesis from this data, compare the degree to which additional in-dividuals are required to gain the same speed up in time-to-stability and time-to-consensus under different technological conditions. Under the oral condition (Table 8.1), a profession of 9 individuals and 20 ideas will reach stability 24 time periods faster (viz., 87, 111) than a profession of 3 individuals and 20 ideas. Adding more individuals to an oral profes-sion, it seems, makes a sizeable difference in speeding stability within it. Yet with print (Table 8.1), the advantage gained by adding more in-dividuals at the same rate is less sizeable, speeding stability within the profession by only 11 time periods (viz., 66, 77).

These trends become even more striking for consensus (Table 8.2). The value added for consensus by adding 6 new individuals (from 3 to 9 in-dividuals) in a profession under print conditions is only 11 time periods (viz., 188, 199), compared to an added value of 50 time periods (viz., 299, 349) under oral conditions. With print, so few persons can move so much information so quickly that there is much less added value, rela-tive to an oral profession, to recruit people to move it. Ironically, from a stability and consensual standpoint, print decreases the need for authors.

Under oral conditions, individuals in professions cannot begin to dupli-cate the efficiency of print without confronting the horns of an unhappy

TABLE 8.1
Stability as the Size and Cultural Complexity of the Profession Varies
by Technological Condition

ORAL	*Number of Individuals in the Profession*		
Number of Ideas Specific to the Profession	*3*	*6*	*9*
5	30(0.66)	30(0.42)	28(0.40)
10	57(0.96)	50(0.65)	48(0.51)
20	111(1.25)	96(0.93)	87(0.72)
PRINT	*Number of Individuals in the Profession*		
Number of Ideas Specific to the Profession	*3*	*6*	*9*
5	22(0.39)	20(0.33)	20(0.26)
10	41(0.52)	37(0.43)	35(0.32)
20	77(0.75)	69(0.63)	66(0.47)

Comment: This table reports the time-to-stability when the technological condition is print for the first set of simulation experiments. Each cell contains the average—and the standard deviation, in parentheses—of the number of time periods that lapse before the members of the profession reach 90% of the stability that will be reached at the 500th time period. This average is computed across 100 societies of the same type run to 500 time periods.

Note. Table is based on data in Tables 8.5 and 8.6 in Appendix B.

dilemma—either radically increase the number of individuals or radically decrease the body of knowledge that needs to be conveyed in professional communications. Either horn brings its own set of difficulties to professional organization. Increasing the number of individuals raises difficulties of logistics and coordination for an oral profession. As the number of individuals increase, it becomes harder, on a practical basis, to insure that all the different communications that need to be passed to maintain ties are uniformly circulated. Imagine spreading a new tax law to a specialty of 1,000 tax lawyers. Let us say the law contains 100 sentences. Under print conditions, we can mail 1,000 printed pamphlets of the law to each lawyer, which each professional can then read (and reread) at his or her leisure. Under print conditions, our coordination problems are over, if we can assume that the lawyers are careful readers and rereaders. Under oral conditions, things are not so easy. Even if we send out one informed emissary to each lawyer (an improbable allocation of resources), we may still fail to reach any or all the lawyers in a complete sense. We have to insure that each emissary has been "com-

TABLE 8.2
Consensus as the Size and Cultural Complexity of the Profession Varies
by Technological Condition

ORAL	*Number of Individuals in the Profession*		
Total Number of Ideas Specific to the Profession	*3*	*6*	*9*
10	75(0.29)	65(0.63)	78(0.88)
20	160(0.27)	157(0.63)	145(0.89)
40	349(0.33)	286(0.63)	299(0.92)
PRINT	*Number of Individuals in the Profession*		
Total Number of Ideas Specific to the Profession	*3*	*6*	*9*
5	48(0.29)	44(0.59)	42(0.83)
10	85(0.29)	93(0.59)	81(0.83)
20	199(0.29)	199(0.64)	188(0.84)

Comment: This table reports the time-to-consensus when the technological condition is print for the first set of simulation experiments. Each cell contains the average—and the standard deviation, in parentheses—of the number of time periods that lapse before the members of the profession reach 90% of the consensus that will be reached at the 500th time period. This average is computed across 100 societies of the same type run to 500 time periods.

Note. Table is based on data in Tables 8.7 and 8.8 in Appendix B.

plete" in his or her communication (i.e., completeness of reach, chapter 4) and has made a full presentation of the law (all 100 sentences). These are difficult conditions to meet for many reasons. Without additional technology, oral communications:

- do not leave a visible trace;
- are difficult to archive;
- are more difficult to plan and reliably deliver in toto;
- are more likely to be stated incorrectly and with corruptions;
- are more likely to be confused with other information known to the emissary;
- are more likely to be forgotten.

The logistical problems compound when oral professions try to increase their size and range by increasing the number of individuals conscripted to keep members up-to-date.

Things fare no better should professions, under oral conditions, seek to increase their size and range by decreasing the body of professional knowledge required to maintain ties. Decreasing the body of professional knowledge makes it easier for outsiders to become professionals, as they need to know less to gain entry. This, in turn, blunts the profession's advantage in trying to evolve toward prototypical status. The acquisition of high levels of cultural integration and specialization, after all, is a much less impressive achievement when there is only a relatively small body of knowledge to be integrated and only a relatively small body of knowledge to set the profession apart from the rest of the society. With ceilings imposed on the complexity or diversity of its professional culture, a group's efforts to make itself distinct from other groups will, in all likelihood, make it more "isolated" without making it more "specialized" in the prototypical sense. It will become more of a specialty club, holding out-of-the-way beliefs (e.g., dipping into cold ponds in the middle of winter) rather than a profession.

We may conclude from the Efficiency Hypothesis that print offers certain efficiencies to professional life that oral professions cannot duplicate without foundering. This is not the same as concluding that print is indispensable to professions, which seem perfectly capable of existing without print. Indeed, according to our previous definition of a prototype profession—a group with relatively high levels of integration and specialization—we have no good reason for excluding 13th-century written law or, for that matter, an urban gang, as a profession. A profession without print is simply more likely to lack the resilience to reconstitute itself across spatio-temporal distances. We can acknowledge that 13th century written law is a profession, but it is one that may have "broken" under the strain had too many jurists been required to spread it one person at a time. We can declare urban gangs a profession of sorts, but it is one that is likely to splinter if its members extend beyond the range of a few urban neighborhoods (a key distinction between a gang and organized crime is that the latter references an organization that has "professionalized" itself enough to maintain itself across a network of cities and countries). Print is by no means essential to a definition of a profession. But without print, a profession cannot preserve its identity at a distance without facing huge problems of education or without imposing severe artificial restrictions on the level of cultural complexity it can attain. Print may not be essential to a profession, but in making arbitrary writers more efficient in reaching other members, print became essential to a profession's principled growth, both culturally and socially. The Efficiency Hypothesis explains, in part, how the growth of industrial print in the late 19th century coincided with an explosion of professions.

The Efficiency Hypothesis merits further examination in terms of the changes in written styles that began to take place within the professions of the late 19th century and gradually evolved into what we now know as the plain language standards of professional discourse (Steinberg, 1991). Print helped professional organization and professional organization exerted a reciprocal influence on print. Professional organization, bolstered by print, regularized an author's reach in a way that had been unknown since the decline of the patronage markets and the beginning of free-market authoring (chap. 3). By making arbitrary writers in a profession more efficient in reaching other members, print, in the service of professional organizations, harnessed the free-market author's notion of "fame." The free-market author after fame did not take relative similarity with readers for granted but saw relative similarity as an uncertain variable that could mean boom or bust for a book. Free-market authors, then as now, competed for the time and money individuals spent in leisure, and the publishing industry that backed them knew that people would not invest in their leisure without a personal, emotional, and intellectual payoff. Free-market authors had to be specific enough to engage a reader's emotions but not so specific as to risk offending or (perhaps worse) causing indifference; they sought a style that made themselves appear, through the language and the history revealed by that language (chap. 5), like the special persons with whom the target class of readers wanted to identify.

The situation was different, however, for the new professional writer of the late 19th century. The new professionals were after competence, and because their economic ties to ordinary readers differed from authors in the free market, professional writers did not have to put their personal language experiences or histories on the line. Professional writers were competing not in the leisure market but in the work market; their job was to document the goods and services supplied to an expanding middle class. As the 19th century wore on, the professional writer could increasingly address readers from the historically constructed and shared persona of the professional worker, committed to efficiency, conciseness, directness, a cheerful attitude toward work, and a single-minded focus on the needs of the customer or client. The result of this new demand for professional writing was an adoption of language standards that made little, explicitly, of the personal histories of the language user and everything, explicitly, of the historicized persona of the professional. As the professional persona became a more widely shared set of historicized defaults from which to compose professional discourse, the professional style was able to take better advantage of the built-in efficiencies of print.

Expansion Hypotheses

When one considers the relationship between membership in a profession, culture, and the technological condition, two hypotheses can be formulated relative to the expansion of membership and culture. These are the Expanding Member Hypothesis and the Expanding Culture Hypothesis.

Expanding Member Hypothesis

One might argue that, as a consequence of efficiency, print made the growth of membership in professions possible. This Expanding Member Hypothesis can be formulated in stronger or weaker terms. The stronger form argues that, with print, a profession can have more members yet still reach stability and consensus in the same (or less) time than it could without print and with a smaller membership. The weaker form argues that, with print, a profession, as its membership grows, increases at least its relative, if not absolute, advantage over a profession lacking print. Under either formulation, the Expanding Member Hypothesis suggests that, with print, a profession can expand in membership yet emulate some of the environmental advantages of smaller professions working under oral conditions.

Expanding Culture Hypothesis

As a profession grows in cultural complexity (things to know), it takes longer for members of the profession to learn this body of knowledge (or simply to learn of its existence), simply because there is more to learn. One might argue that print made the rapid emergence of stability and consensus possible, in spite of this ever-widening body of knowledge. We call this argument the Expanding Culture Hypothesis, which can also be formulated in stronger (absolute) and weaker (relative) terms. The strong form argues that, with print, a profession can have a larger culture yet still reach stability and consensus in the same (or less) time than a profession working without print and with a smaller body of knowledge. The weaker form argues that, with print, a profession, as its body of knowledge grows, can steadily increase (at least) its relative advantage in stability and consensus over a profession lacking print. Under either formulation, the Expanding Culture Hypothesis suggests that, with print, a profession can expand its knowledge base while continuing to emulate some of the environmental advantages of less culturally complex professions working under oral conditions.

Implications of the Expansion Hypotheses for Stability

Let us now consider in more detail the logical implications of these Expansion Hypotheses for stability. As Table 8.1 indicates, regardless of the technological condition, the more individuals in a profession, the less time it (usually) takes for the profession to achieve stability; conversely, the more ideas in the profession, the more time it takes to achieve stability. Table 8.1 demonstrates the basic Efficiency Hypothesis—the increase in individuals in a profession with print should have a smaller added value than an increase in individuals in a profession without print. This table also demonstrates the basic trend of the strong version of the Expanding Member Hypothesis: Larger professions with print at their disposal consistently attain stability faster than smaller professions without. This table further demonstrates the weak version of the Expanding Culture Hypothesis: As the cultural complexity of a profession increases, the relative advantage of professions working with print also increases.

In addition, this table demonstrates that adding ideas to a profession slows its time to stability even more than adding members. The comparative advantage of print in developing ties within groups becomes even more pronounced when a group is expanding its ideas and not simply its membership.

Print offers a curious advantage to professions that are both culturally complex and small. A culturally complex profession working under oral conditions reaches stability 24 time periods slower with 3 individuals than with 9 (viz., 111, 87; Table 8.1). Yet the same profession with print reaches stability only 11 time periods slower with 3 individuals than with 9 (viz., 77, 66; Table 8.1). For some reason, then, print is increasingly beneficial in developing ties within professions that have many ideas but few members. Why might that be? When professions are high in cultural complexity, their members must be engaged in constant interaction to develop ties because there is a great deal of information that members can potentially share. Their ties can be stronger in an absolute sense than in a less complex culture. Yet, all things being equal, when professions are small, the opportunities for communicative transactions are seriously diminished. If there are fewer group members with whom to interact, the competition among the existing members to find their peers and to find them available for interaction increases. Members, on average, will find other members committed elsewhere, and they will need to spend more of their social interaction time with nonmembers and themselves. Print, however, suspends this "all things being equal" clause; it always makes in-house members available through a written text. One historical implication is that it became much easier, after print, for members of a profession to disperse and to work on their own in isolated cities and towns. A town could have a single doctor or plumber with few or no proximate professional contacts; yet the professional could still keep up with changes in the profession through texts. This implication merits further investigation from historians and demographers.

Different results are forthcoming when we consider not the absolute but the relative size of a profession and its effect on stability. In Fig. 8.3, each dot is the average of 9 sociocultural landscapes, each simulated 100 times. Regardless of the technological condition, a profession reaches stability sooner as its size relative to the group of nonprofessionals decreases. However, the speed up in stability is much faster, in absolute terms, under print than under oral conditions across any relative size of the profession (57–69 time periods to reach stability in the case of oral transactions;

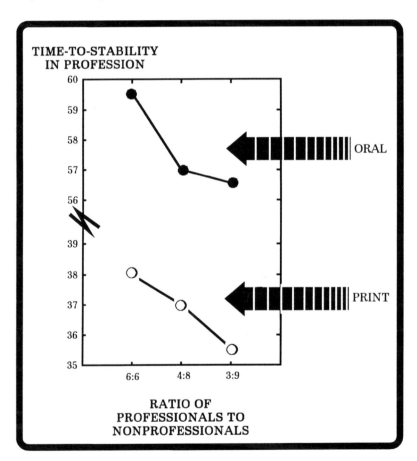

FIG. 8.3.   Relative group size and time-to-stability within a profession by technological condition.
Note. Based on comparison of aspects of Tables 8.1 and 8.2 in Appendix B.

35–38 time periods in the case of print). These results suggest that print allows a profession to grow arbitrarily large, with its relative size exerting only a minimal effect on stability.

Implications of the Expansion Hypothesis for Consensus

Let us turn to the logical implications of the Expansion Hypotheses for consensus. Table 8.2 shows that, regardless of the technological condition, the more ideas in a profession, the more time it takes it to achieve consensus. This agrees with our previous finding for stability. However, as the number of individuals increases, consensus may or may not speed up. This mixed trend for consensus represents a departure from stability, where an increase in individuals almost always leads to a speed up in stability.

To explain this discrepancy between stability and consensus, we recall an important difference between consensus and stability (chap. 4, 6). Stability, or shared knowledge, consistently increases simply by increasing the amount of knowledge shared across individuals, even if this sharing takes place in a context with wide discrepancies in what people know. For example, the stability between two individuals increases as long as the amount of their shared knowledge is increasing, whether or not the amount of knowledge they are learning and do not share is increasing. Consensus, agreements based on weighted knowledge, behaves differently. Consensus consistently increases only when the discrepancies in what people know continue to close. The more people exchanging knowledge, the more shared knowledge within the profession will increase and the faster the profession will reach stability. But that is no guarantee that the profession will also reach consensus faster. That depends on whether increasing the overall amount of shared knowledge also *decreases* the overall amount of knowledge that is not shared. The communicative transactions within a group or society can actually create, in the short run, greater nonuniformities in how knowledge is distributed, speeding stability but retarding consensus. Unlike stability, consensus is not always expedited in the short run as the number of individuals in a profession increases. Through their communicative transactions, the influx of people creates information discrepancies faster than they can be eliminated. Consensus is like stability, however, in almost always being slowed down as the cultural complexity of the profession increases. Both the Expanding Member (strong version) and the Expanding Culture (weak version) Hypotheses apply to consensus. Large and culturally complex professions with print are able to achieve consensus faster (at least relatively) than smaller or less culturally complex professions without print.

These results confirm the logic of the Expansion Hypotheses for consensus. Table 8.2 suggests additional refinements. The technological condition has an interesting effect on the optimal size required for a profession to reach consensus most speedily. On average, professions without print reach consensus fastest if they are moderately sized (i.e., six individuals). On average, professions with print reach consensus slowest when they are moderately sized. Why might moderate size be a good thing for a profession under oral conditions and a disaster for professions with print? The answer is partly due to how consensus is measured (i.e., using all information in the culture). For their eventual consensus, professions must rely on information that may initially be found only among outsiders. This is a plausible situation, as professions are not impermeable enclaves that can afford to insulate themselves from other knowledge in the culture. Within these simulations, any profession would perform nonoptimally if its members tried to act too monastically, interacting only among themselves. Optimum performance requires some communicative transactions within the group and some without. Under oral conditions, this balance of insider and outsider communication is best achieved when the profession is moderately sized. If the profession is too small and the competition for internal transactions too intense, then communication within the profession loses its regularity and consensus is delayed. If the profession is too large, and the competition for transactions with outsiders too intense, then consensus is also delayed. Thus, the size of the group makes a big difference to a profession operating under oral conditions.

In a profession employing print, the size of its membership proves a much less important consideration when it comes to building consensus. True, a moderate size is not optimal for a print profession, but it is only slightly worse than being small. And, generally speaking, the size of a print profession has a much smaller overall (positive or negative) effect on consensus than the size of an oral profession has on its consensus. Why might this be? Because of multiplicity, print offers members of a profession unrestricted access to both members and outsiders, as persons encapsulated in texts. The multiplicity of print offers a profession some of the same ecological advantages that an oral profession must try to capture strategically through physical size. Furthermore, as the cultural complexity of a profession increases, its physical size becomes increasingly less relevant, either as an advantage or a disadvantage, as long as it can rely on print (Table 8.2).

Now consider the relative rather than the absolute size of the profession and its effect on consensus (Fig. 8.4). In this figure, each dot is the average for nine sociocultural configurations containing a profession of that particular relative size, each simulated 100 times. The larger the rela-

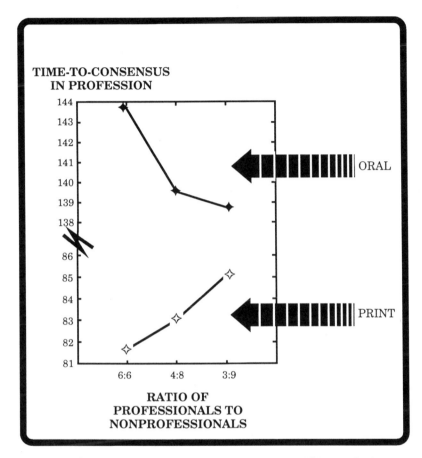

FIG. 8.4.   Relative group size and time-to-consensus within a profession
by technological condition.
Note. Based on comparison of aspects of Tables 8.3 and 8.4 in Appendix B.

tive size of the profession, the faster it reaches consensus if it has print,
and the slower it reaches consensus if it does not. If the profession is
relatively large and relies on what is initially outsider knowledge for its
internal consensus, professionals, under face-to-face conditions, will regularly interact with one another, but their interaction with outsiders will
be too irregular to facilitate rapid consensus. Under print conditions, being relatively large encourages within-group transactions but does nothing to discourage transactions with nonmembers, in light of the unrestricted access to textually encapsulated individuals made possible by
print. Being relatively large gives a print profession the best of both worlds
in terms of consensus.

Weak Integration Hypothesis: Print Reduces the Need
for a Profession to Be Integrated

The more culturally integrated the society, the faster the individuals within it reach stability and consensus (chap. 7). Arguably, the same should be true for groups in the society, such as professions. As we have just seen, print speeds consensus and stability within a profession. Putting these findings together suggests that as a profession becomes more integrated, print should promote the rapid emergence of both stability and consensus. These hypotheses, which we term the Integration Hypotheses, can be explored through these simulations by considering the effect of varying levels of initial cultural integration under both oral and print conditions on stability and consensus. The results are displayed in Fig. 8.5 and 8.6. In both figures, each dot is the average behavior of all nine sociocultural landscapes with that level of cultural integration within the profession each simulated 100 times.

We see that, regardless of the technological condition, the more highly integrated the profession, the faster it reaches stability and consensus. However, contrary to the suggestion that the effect of print is greatest for highly integrated professions, these results suggest that the less initially integrated the profession, the more it benefits from print (the slope of the line for the oral profession drops more steeply than the slope for the print profession at high levels of cultural integration). The advantage of the print, relative to the oral, condition is thus greatest at low levels of initial cultural integration and tails off as initial cultural integration increases. Whereas print increases the cultural integration of a group through the rapid dissemination of information, the rapidity of print also mitigates the otherwise undesirable consequences of being minimally integrated at the start. The boost that print can give to a profession is demonstrable, but it appears to give an even stronger boost to a profession that has minimal initial cultural integration. Print, in sum, may help compensate a profession for lacking one very important feature of prototypicality—integration. We call this finding the Weak Integration Hypothesis and suggest that it merits further empirical and historical investigation.

Strong Specialization Hypothesis: Print Increases
the Ability of a Profession to be Specialized

Few professions are so highly specialized that their knowledge base is completely unique (i.e., known only by members of the profession). Rather, as we observed earlier, many professions rely on knowledge that is not only indigenous but also imported from individuals in the larger

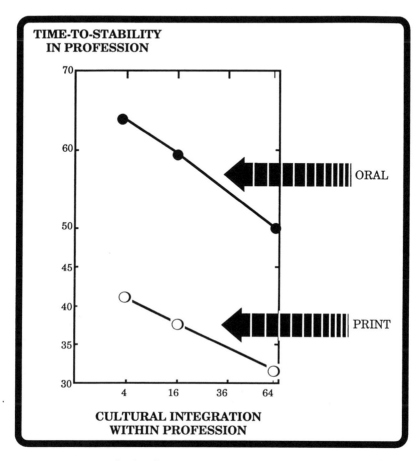

FIG. 8.5.   Initial cultural integration and time-to-stability within a profession by technological condition.
Note. Based on comparison of aspects of Tables 8.1 and 8.2 in Appendix B.

society who have, initially at least, only weak ties with members of the profession. Because of the general need for professions to remain open to outside streams of thinking, professions can become too specialized for their own good. If this occurs, members of a profession may fail to interact with people and texts on the outside from whom they can import indispensable knowledge. Literary historians may fail to interact with historiographers designing new historical methods. Social scientists may fail to interact with the statisticians paving the foundations for new statistical procedures. All professions rely on imported ideas, but they may do so to different degrees and thus vary in their level of specialization. The

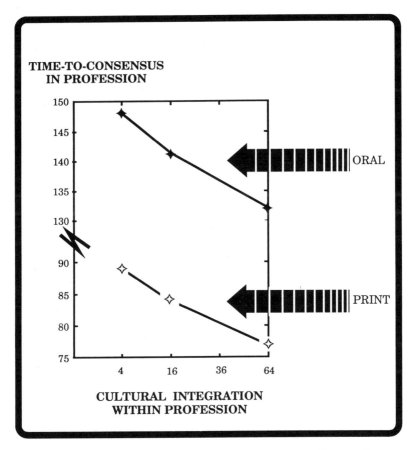

FIG. 8.6.   Initial cultural integration and time-to-consensus within a profession by technological condition.
Note. Based on comparison of aspects of Tables 8.3 and 8.4 in Appendix B.

less specialized the profession, the more it relies on outsides streams of ideas to organize itself internally. Print facilitates the rapid movement of information and should increase the rate at which the stream of ideas from outside the profession move inside, thus encouraging, in theory, a greater breadth of knowledge among members. With print, professionals can acquire outsider information more efficiently by reading. They need not rely on personal contact with outside experts or contend for the expert's limited availability to tap into his or her knowledge. They can rely on the expert as encapsulated in a text. Because print makes the borders of a profession less rigid and more permeable, print offers a greater advantage to professions as they become less specialized and need to rely more on this permeability. From these observations, one might hypothesize that the less specialized the profession, the more print, relative to oral conditions, should facilitate the emergence of stability and consensus within it. We call this the Weak Specialization Hypothesis. Figures 8.7 and 8.8 refer to this hypothesis. In both figures, each dot is the average of all 9 societies given a profession with that level of specialization, each simulated 100 times.

The results for stability (Fig. 8.7) indicate that the Weak Specialization Hypothesis does not logically follow. We do see that, regardless of the technological condition, less specialized professions tend to reach stability sooner. But, in relationship to oral conditions, print actually tends

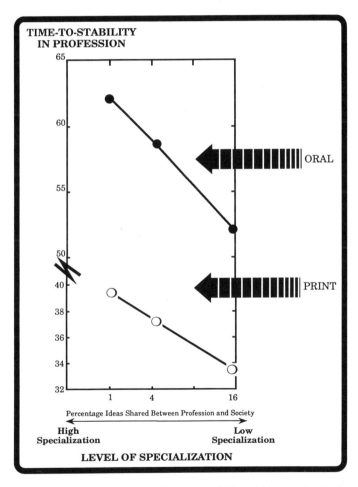

FIG. 8.7. Initial specialization and time-to-stability within a profession by technological condition.
Note. Based on comparison of aspects of Tables 8.1 and 8.2 in Appendix B.

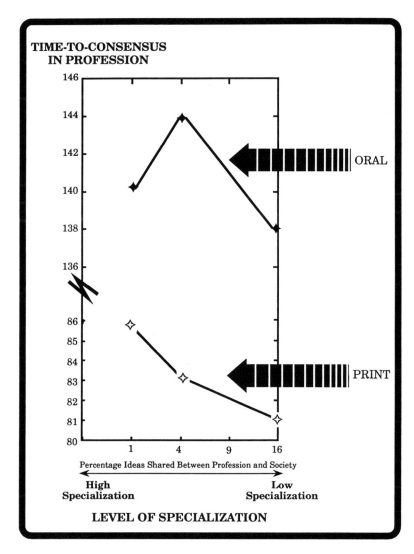

FIG. 8.8. Initial specialization and time-to-consensus within a profession
by technological condition.
Note. Based on comparison of aspects of Tables 8.3 and 8.4 in Appendix B.

to encourage, not discourage, specialization. Print, that is, benefits professions more as their level of specialization increases. The advantage of print
(for stability) over oral conditions is greatest at high levels of specialization and diminishes as the level of specialization decreases. Too much
specialization can still be damaging to the stability of a profession, but
it is relatively less damaging in a print than in an oral condition. Print

attenuates the negative outcomes of high specialization and allows a profession to become more specialized without suffering, as severely, the insularity that is typically associated with high specialization.

The results for consensus (Fig. 8.8) are different. We see, as before, the trend that a profession with print speeds up (now in consensus) as it becomes less specialized. But this trend does not apply in the oral condition. In relation to oral conditions, print seems to confer the greatest advantage to professions that are moderately specialized. Why would that be? To answer this question, we need to explain the forces behind oral professions with either high (viz., 1% overlap) or low (viz., 16% overlap) specialization rapidly attaining consensus and to discuss why oral professions with moderate specialization benefit from neither of these forces. Professions under oral conditions that are highly specialized achieve consensus fairly rapidly (i.e., rapid for oral conditions) because all group members remain tightly clustered interaction partners, spreading their knowledge to one another rather quickly. Strong in-group ties and weak out-group ties promote consensus. By exchanging knowledge rapidly among themselves and only among themselves, members reach an insular consensus, a consensus of the ignorant as it were, that results because there is almost exact uniformity in what they do not know and are not aware of on the outside. A profession, under oral conditions, whose specialization is very low will also reach consensus relatively quickly. In this case, consensus forms relatively rapidly because frequent contact with outsiders encourages all members of the profession to learn all that outsiders know in rather uniform fashion. Weak group ties and stronger out-group ties promote consensus. We call this a consensus of the informed, a process that is relatively quick but not as quick as a consensus of the ignorant (as Fig. 8.8 indicates), though less likely to change once it is formed. As that figure also demonstrates, the moderately specialized profession under oral conditions has trouble reaching consensus— period. This is because neither of the forces that make the members' knowledge uniform (i.e., the consensus of the ignorant; the consensus of the informed) and bring them to consensus are available to professions of moderate specialization. Members of such a profession do not interact frequently enough among themselves to standardize what they know; nor do they interact frequently enough with outsiders to standardize what they are learning from the outside. Moderate in-group and out-group ties simply do not promote rapid consensus. In contrast, print, because of its multiplicity, makes everyone available to everyone else, decreasing the effect of initial tie strength. Print prevents the consensus of the ignorant within a profession, and promotes a more rapid consensus of the informed; it does so increasingly effectively as the profession becomes increasingly less specialized.

PRINT AND VIRTUAL ORGANIZATION

Modern communication technologies are often credited with creating the notion of a "virtual" organization, the capacity of groups to form at a distance through electronic mail, electronic bulletin boards, and shared national databases (Meadows, 1973). The hypotheses suggested by these simulation data indicate that the credit was awarded at least a century too late and, in all likelihood, probably needed to be awarded many millennia earlier, when writing was used to organize the virtual group known as government (Goody, 1986). We see that professions without print are, on average, more sensitive to sociocultural fluctuations in their level of integration and specialization than professions with print. Professions without print, for example, are helped more when their cultural integration increases; they tend to be hurt more when their specialization increases. Print, by contrast, makes a profession less sensitive to the fluctuations in the very group variables that define its proximate boundaries from the rest of the society. Print enables a profession to maintain ties (and reach stability and consensus in timely fashion) even at low levels of integration and high levels of specialization. The rapidity and permeability of print information, it would appear, compensates for suboptimal sociocultural conditions that, if left to their own devices, would have destroyed a group's existence or never allowed it to form in the first place. It is the same rapidity and permeability of information that people now associate with electronic communication when they credit it with creating virtual groups working in virtual institutions. The hypotheses we have formulated, if further developed and tested, might indicate the profound mistake in seeing the computer revolution as an antithetical split and rupture from the print revolution. It may be more accurate to see the computer revolution, as far as professional communication is concerned, as an extension of the revolution in virtual organization begun by print.

SUPERSPECIALIZATION AND THE MAINTENANCE OF ORALITY

In the foregoing analysis, we did not consider superspecialization. Superspecialization occurs when a profession shares no professional information with those outside its ranks and little, if any, other information with outsiders. Instead, the profession relies on knowledge produced from within for its reach and consensus. The foregoing analysis suggests that professions that are superspecialized are likely to maintain their edge largely through oral conditions. As previously noted, highly specialized and highly integrated professions, which would be characteristic of superspecialized groups, have relatively less to gain from print than less prototypical professions. If the communicative transactions of a super-speciality remain oral, the speciality should remain relatively small in order to accrue the maximum benefits of orality. For superspecialties, small group size, impermeable membership restrictions, and oral rituals to socialize members should be the norm. For example, in the medical profession, superspecialists like liver-transplant surgeons are few, have many constraints placed on their membership (cost, board certification, extra study), and have a battery of oral membership rituals to pass at one of only a few selected hospitals throughout the world. Other reasons why superspecialties may retain a preference for oral interaction have been suggested: (a) limited external audiences; (b) increased bandwidth of face-to-face communication (that is, increased visual, auditory, and other sensory cues); and (c) greater fidelity of the communication. Although these may be true, we consider such explanations largely second order.

From an institutional control perspective, a profession, superspecialized or not, may enforce oral conditions in its basic communication transactions because it wants to retain a cohesive identity that print tends to blur. Print, we have seen, diminishes a group's sense of being a distinctive group with distinctive boundaries between members and outsiders. Crane (1971) found that even in large science professions that use print to convey official results, smaller, oral networks (i.e., invisible colleges) are maintained within which members feel a greater sense of cohesion. As we mentioned earlier, in field studies of collaborative work relationships, Kraut et al. (1990) found that, in general, working professionals rely on physical proximity at least in the early phases of their projects. Oral conditions also play a dominant role in education that stresses the accomplishment of actual work in a profession. In scientific professions like biochemistry, for example, students may learn their profession through master–apprentice relationships in labs rather than through textbooks (Garfinkel, Lynch, & Livingston, 1981).

SUMMARY AND IMPLICATIONS

We examined individual authors as members of a profession and reasons for and against viewing the authorial role as a survivor of professional life. We suggest that there is no reason to privilege the author either within or outside the role of the professional. We define professions as a group whose members vary along the dimensions of cultural integration and specialization, with prototypical professions being high on both dimensions. From this vantage, the reality of a profession can be distilled from its rhetoric. We do not imply that a profession's rhetoric is necessarily false or misleading about the sociocultural reality of its members. We simply suggest that a profession's rhetoric and reality yield distinct and not necessarily convergent information about the profession. One tells us about the profession's official discourse, the triumph of its public relations. The other tells us about its knowledge and interaction, the triumph of its history. To the extent that the writing of a profession's history is colored by its official discourse over time, reality and rhetoric are never fully distinct. It is preferable, we believe, to make this concession than to collapse, indiscriminately, professional reality and rhetoric. This collapse is the inevitable result of researchers seeking definitions that were discrete and categorical rather than continuous and variable. When one tries to define a profession in categorical terms, one always stumbles upon counterexamples that seem no less compelling than the confirming cases. As skepticism regarding the discrete reality of professions grows, it becomes easy to assume that their reality is their rhetoric. The problem with this argument is its premise of discreteness. A fuzzy approach to professions allows us to measure the reality of a profession in continuous and variable terms, making the study of professional rhetoric and its correspondence to this reality all the more interesting.

Using simulations based on a constructural model, we have explored, in systematic terms, some relationships between print and professions. The result was a series of hypotheses:

- the Efficiency Hypothesis
- the Expanding Member Hypothesis
- the Expanding Culture Hypothesis
- the Weak Integration Hypothesis
- the Strong Specialization Hypothesis

Only future research can confirm or reject these hypotheses on empirical grounds. We have demonstrated that they follow logically from constructuralism and the features of the communicative mode (e.g., asynchronicity, fixity, multiplicity, durability) associated with print.

These simulation results are consistent with the Efficiency Hypothesis in terms of both stability and consensus, suggesting that print makes any individual more efficient in spreading cultural information (speeding stability and consensus), independent of the amount of cultural information there is to spread. These data are also consistent with the Expanding Member and Expanding Culture Hypotheses, for both stability and consensus. These hypotheses state that print helps a large and complex profession emulate some of the ecological characteristics of a smaller and simpler profession without print. In addition to these larger trends, we identify smaller trends as well. As far as stability is concerned, print helps a profession maintain itself when its members are few or isolated, even if it is culturally complex and a good deal of information needs to pass between members to keep everyone up-to-date. Print also makes the growth and stability of a profession less dependent on its relative size. As far as consensus is concerned, print makes the consensus of a profession less dependent on absolute size and confers a decided advantage to professions that are relatively large. Print's advantage in increasing tie strength seems to increase as the profession stretches itself out to include larger proportions of the society.

This last observation furnishes some intriguing speculation about the correspondence between the proliferation of print and the proliferation of professions. Print encourages professional expansion because the same information can reach more individuals in less time. The results we discussed, especially the Efficiency Hypothesis, indicate the plausibility of this conventional wisdom. However, there is a complementary explanation as well. Print facilitated the growth of large professions not only because it allowed faster communication through multiplicity but also because it may have sabotaged groups that tried to remain relatively small. In the face of the rapid access to outside information which print provided by loosening the hard boundaries between members and outsiders, professions that tried to resist the relative expansion of their membership and to avoid strategies to absorb larger and more diverse constituencies may have been less able to maintain coalitions among existing members. Print may have initiated a principle that we now associate with global economies and advanced communication technologies: "expand or die."

Regardless of the fate of these hypotheses, it is fairly clear that future research will need to entertain the interaction of these or alternative hypotheses with a striking historical fact—the correspondence between an increase in the number and size of professions and advances in industrialized print in the late 19th century. Our analysis leaves us with a good deal to say about this correspondence. For example, envisioning industrialized print as the most effective cultural facilitator to date of "virtual" organization, we argue that print may have allowed professions to grow larger than ever before, even in the absence of high cultural integration. It may have allowed professions to become more specialized than ever before without paying the price of cultural isolation. By making society more knowledgeable about more things, print may have pressured professions to grow larger, relative to the rest of society, in order to reflect and build coalitions based on this growing diversity. Print may be perceived as a threat to moderate specialties and to working relationships of professionals, groups that require intense and focused interaction. One response to this threat would be to grow larger and rely increasingly on print; a second would be to become superspecialized and smaller, and to maintain orality as the technological condition. Most importantly, perhaps, because print loosened the boundaries between proximate organizations and virtual organizations, print may have effected a flexibility in the very idea of what a profession could be. Print made it possible for professions to realize a range of possibilities beyond the monastic prototype (e.g., high integration, high specialization) that had described professional life before the industrial revolution. This increased flexibility may have led, in the late 19th and early 20th centuries, to a new emergent rhetoric of professions, popularized by Lippman. Print made it possible, in other words, for an increasing number of socioculturally differentiated groups to call themselves professions and to compete for the benefits conferred by that title.

CHAPTER NINE

Academia

Disciplines are composed of people . . . communities of scholars who share a domain of inquiry or discourse. A discipline has form, pattern, structure. The concepts must be classified and interrelated . . . each discipline has a domain of inquiry and specialized methods by which knowledge is created and validated . . . has its own specialized vocabulary which serves as a medium of communication and a thesaurus mapping out a domain of study.
—K. J. McGarry (1981, pp. 107–108)

Academic disciplines have managed to institutionalize the role of author as authority. Individuals within a discipline belong not only to a profession propagating knowledge, but to a more abstract intellectual community under whose auspices they author—not just propagate—knowledge for the discipline's use, formulating new ideas and, through those ideas, seeking the authority to change, in small ways and large, the discipline's landscape. Disciplines not only encourage this discovery authorship and the generation of new ideas, but make it a requirement for membership. They impose a regimen, teaching aspiring members how to (a) generate and present new knowledge; (b) expand the common culture, and (c) cultivate and protect an authorial signature and handle (chap. 4) through these expansions.

Following the exponential growth of the knowledge industry over the past 250 years, particularly since World War II (Price, 1963), authors within academe have felt an increasing sense of internal competition because much is at stake economically, politically, and institutionally. At least three important factors set the stakes of the competition:

341

1. The diffusion of an academic author's texts can influence the discipline's sociocultural structure with their personal stamp.

2. The author's success or influence is, to a large extent, metered both by the extent of his or her reach (i.e., the citation history of texts, or the number of readers who found the texts useful enough to influence their own texts) and the sociocultural elaboration of the authorial handle (i.e., the reputation garnered among members of the discipline).

3. The influence of authors is heavily stratified (Cole & Cole, 1973), with a few authors exerting a disproportionate influence and the majority of authors exerting little or none.

Academic authoring and the effect of print can be examined within the constructural framework we have been using. However, we make one important qualification from the outset: We restrict our attention to authoring in science, where reach and recognition have been most regularly fused in practice through the mechanism of citation (Nelson & Pollack, 1970; Price, 1970). Writing in the humanities has an authoritative history in allusion and critical authority (chap. 2). This tradition calls upon the author to assert authority by seeking to preserve a cultural past and to transfer the positive values belonging to this past to the young. Whereas the writing in the humanities involves the discovery of new knowledge, the stress on new knowledge as revenue (i.e., earning citation points and stalking even bigger game, like patents) tends to be muted in favor of republican arguments about "humane" writing, offering wide access to the best (and worst) ideas in circulation so a citizenry can remain informed and free. In many cases, humanists who practice an intellectual mercantilism by seeking a cash equivalent for their new ideas are often put on the defensive by their colleagues elsewhere on campus. They may be asked to explain how metaphors can solve social and technical problems and merit the kind of compensation awarded to those who make breakthroughs in science and technology (see Graff, 1987, for the tensions between English departments and the mission of the research university).

This caveat aside, there is much that we can apply to academic organization. By modeling concepts like reach, diffusion, consensus, and stability, the simulation model captures some abstractions that are central to academic authorship, such as (a) owning an idea, (b) receiving societal recognition for an idea as its owner, (c) claiming priority for discovery, and (d) establishing an accredited community of authors and readers. Notions of ownership, recognition, and priority are, in our view, second-order concepts that relate directly to the first-order notions of reach and diffusion.[1] Accreditation can also be understood as a second-order concept relating to our first-order notions of (disciplinary) consensus and stability. Government and other accrediting organizations stick the label of accreditation on a profession (including a discipline) that can meet at least the presumption (if not the reality) of mechanisms for establishing high levels of stability and consensus. In sum, constructuralism and the extended model we use throughout Part II offer a useful if incomplete mapping of some important features of print in academe. We will, in future work, examine how the mapping can be extended and improved.

THE ETIOLOGY OF ACADEMIC WRITING

To understand academic organization and its effect on print interaction, we first consider its historical roots. As a historical concept, the organizing principles behind academic writing remain an ideal type, principles standing above any concrete embodiment. Strands of the ideal seem to originate with Renaissance Humanism and the Humanist's optimism in logic, rationality, individualism, action, and progress. The Renaissance Humanists were propelled by the belief that human agents, through individuating logic and rational action, could effect progress on their environment. One key word here is *individuating*, which is a synonym for local consistency (chap. 6). This is the idea that individuals with the same knowledge will act on their environment in the same way. Without local consistency, individual action cannot be rationally tied to individual characteristics. The second key word is *progress*. According to Giddens (1987), there was no strong notion of an agent making history through consistently individuating actions, prior to Humanism. Giddens called the Renaissance writer Vico the first to link local consistency with histor-

---

[1]There are many complexities we would have to add to the present model in order to handle recognition and priority as first-order concepts in their own right. As Simonton (1988) noted, the lag between discovery and the social recognition of discovery (chap. 2) often depends on cultural bias and historical contingency, if discontinuities exist in the trajectory between the cognition of discovery and the social acceptance of a discovery. As we mention in chapter 2, there are obviously continuities between these processes as well. An important goal of this chapter is to explore the relationship between discovery and its social acceptance. We do so from the idealizing assumption that there are only continuities between an original idea and its acceptance as original. Put another way, we assume that the only parameter providing a barrier to the social recognition of a new idea is its positioning in the sociocultural landscape. We thus leave out the modulations (chap. 7) of politics and bias that may lead to further barriers. Future, more complex, models need to explore the effects of these modulations.

ical agency when he observed that, "Men did it with intelligence; it was not fate, for they did it by choice; not chance, for the results of their always so acting are perpetually the same" (p. 203).

For the Humanists, the agent, invigorated by the possibility of historical importance through local consistency, could embark on projects resulting in progress and the perfection of logical thought. In addition to this Renaissance contribution, the French Enlightenment was to play its part. Eisenstein (1979) made much of the ideal of standardizing and "fixing" knowledge through the fixity of print at the time of the Renaissance. Yet the truly significant technological breakthrough in fixity began only with the Enlightenment at the dawn of industrialization. It was, in fact, some 300 years into the age of print, in the late 18th century, that fixity became a goal that technologies of print could begin to achieve seriously.

The Enlightenment and the Technological Standardization of Print

Academic writing depends on the clear demarcation of assimilated and new knowledge (chap. 2). Reliable archiving requires that this demarcation be discernible across scholars, indexers, and librarians. The demarcation must be fixed across time and space; this cannot happen unless there are also reliable standards for fixing information in print. A major purpose of the Enlightenment project was to organize and advance knowledge; this required archiving which, in turn, required fixing information in print. Not surprisingly, fixing information in print became an obsession for Enlightenment thinkers and the new specialist printers of the 18th century. Ong (1971, p. 261) observed: "[T]he enterprise of fixing knowledge in space reached a peak some three hundred years after the development of alphabetic letterpress print as, for example, in the *Encyclopedia*."

Until the mid- to late-18th century, master printers did not begin to make serious progress on technical issues concerning fixity. Prior to that time, printing shops were not profitable enough and high quality paper was not abundant and cheap enough for printers to start imposing common standards on paper. Typographic fonts varied from one print shop to the next, as did the size of the letters within a font. A printer who tried to incorporate two fonts within a manuscript had to file the letters of one to fit the size of the other. There were no systematic standards across print shops for the metal alloys needed to produce fonts and font sizes of a uniform look and readability. The fidelity of a letter on the page depended on the combination of metals used for letter punching. The printer needed alloys porous enough to accept ink yet tough enough not to damage the letter punch when struck. Although work on these alloys proceeded from the introduction of the printing press, the search for better alloys had yet to be systematized through focused experiments. In the mid-18th century, Fournier and Didot established more uniform typographic standards by adopting the convention of the "point," measured as 144th the size of the King's foot. Over a 30-year career, Fournier conducted experiments on the many alloys used by print shops for letter punching, charted their strengths and weaknesses, and experimented with new combinations of alloys, carefully documenting their effects on the fixity of the printed page (Febvre & Martin, 1976, pp. 60–65).

During the Enlightenment era, Fertel established important standards for compositing the printed page. From the early days of movable type, printers sat in front of a case of letters, removing them one at a time and placing them in a slotted receptacle called a "stick." The printer deposited each line of type in the stick into a small tray called a "galley" with a "lead" between each line. The printer would then group the lines into pages and secure the pages with wooden wedges. The speed and accuracy of this process depended on the arrangement of letters in the case. Like an expert typist, the printer could acquire great speed and accuracy with practice, as long as the letters on the keyboard did not change position. Prior to the 18th century, however, there were no standards regulating the layout of letters in the case. Different print shops had their own arrangements, and a printer moving from one shop to another had to unlearn old reflexes and start from scratch. In the 18th century, Fertel proposed a set of conventions for compositors. He suggested that large and small capitals be placed in the upper cases in alphabetical order. He further suggested that the lower case letters be stored in slots of varying size according to their frequency of use. Diderot and D'Alembert's *Encyclopedia* was successfully composited according to these conventions, which were eventually adopted across Europe (Febvre & Martin, 1976, pp. 56–71).

Enlightenment Ideals of the Distributed Intellectual Community

Standardizing print was essential for assuring the fixity of knowledge at a distance. In turn, fixing knowledge at a distance may have been a requirement for supporting, through print, the maintenance and growth of a widely distributed intellectual community. Constantly learning, all individuals acquire new information and seek more. Ancient schools of learning like Plato's Academy made this knowledge acquisition process a basis for social organization in face-to-face interaction. The abstraction of a distributed intellectual community posed the further challenge of maintaining this social organization at one level removed, through the limited expressive space of a two-dimensional text. Without a way to socially coordinate the demarcation between assimilated and new information within such a limited expressive space, the reality of a distributed intellectual community may not have gotten off the ground. The social coordination required to engineer such distributed intellectual communities was at play in both the early print cultures of the Renaissance and the more mature print cultures of the Enlightenment.

Eisenstein (1979) is at her best studying the conditions of this early social planning at the time of the Renaissance. To make a print-based intellectual community even minimally possible, she suggested, there had to be (a) enough texts to make an archive, (b) enough copies to make common archives, and (c) enough of both to make the widespread availability of a common archive a shared presumption across authors and readers (Eisenstein, 1979, Vol. 1, p. 74). To suppport this presumption, Eisenstein noted that a student living in the late Renaissance could access a larger corpus of reading material in a year than an ancient scholar could in a lifetime. Every morning, Montaigne could glance at more books in his personal study than earlier scholars would see after years of travel. Increased personal access to texts, Eisenstein observed, led to a changing consciousness about the possibility of reading across texts, of intertextuality. As readers could increasingly move across texts, authors could increasingly make this cross movement a central part of their own composing decisions and conventions for writing. Authors found it both possible and desirable to include in their written texts an assembled summary of previous sources, in the form of a progress chart called a ''literature review.'' The literature review as we know it began as an 18th-century convention, initiated by Priestley in his *History and Present State of Electricity* (Bazerman, 1991).

The literature review held two distinct advantages for the distributed scholarly community (and a third we mention later):

1. It taught readers the sources they should be reading if they had not yet done so. It thus served the purpose of acculturation between writer and reader and helped to build a common corpus for learning what an educated person was supposed to learn.

2. Perhaps more important, the literature review furnished a representation of the virtual intellectual community. Prior to the literature review, intellectual communities had mainly proximate identities. There was no stable or authoritative representation of such communities spreading themselves across time, space, and culture, across the realm of the living and the dead. The literature review ushered in the abstraction of a literate

conversation, perhaps one-sided, taking place between individuals at a distance. It brought the idea that, to address the ages, a scholarly author had to construct a literate conversation to provide an immediate warrant for the occasion of his or her writing and then had to use that manufactured occasion to "take a turn" in it.

Through empirical studies of academic writers, Geisler (1990, in press) carefully documented the abstractive skills of academically literate writers (PhDs) as they engage literate conversations through texts. She documented the many subtle, but profound, differences between engaging in a literate conversation as opposed to engaging in a face-to-face context for conversation. As human beings, we learn to manage the dynamics of opening and closing discussion topics in face-to-face settings through years of socialization and feedback. More specifically, we learn to respond to one another by controlling or monitoring the topic that is currently open for discussion and then responding to it. In the long-distance interactions of print, however, there are no facial cues or years of everyday socialization on how to open a discussion context for one's new ideas. To make matters worse, the conversational turn intellectuals wanted to take often meant a lifetime of internal reflection in relative isolation. It was a challenge in the extreme for academics to propound a body of ideas that could be suitably connected to what geographically dispersed readers would already know and want to know more about. More precisely, it was a challenge for the academic writer to compose a text satisfying the requirements of both immediate comprehension and relative similarity for an anonymous and widely dispersed readership.

One function of the literature review, incorporated as an official part of the composed text, was to improve the writer's chances of satisfying immediate comprehension and relative similarity with readers. The literature review built into the text its own contextual warrant for existing. It granted the intellectual a limited fiction-making license, for it offered the opportunity to construct an idealized conversation among writers from the near and distant past, who often did not even know of one another's existence. This constructed conversation, employing well-known authors with well-known ideas, furnished the "initializations" needed to raise the potential of the text in terms of immediate comprehension and relative similarity. It made the text more accountable to what came before; these accountabilities, in turn, made it easier for readers to be drawn to and to follow what was new in the text (Kaufer & Geisler, 1989). By considering the texts assembled in a prior literature as a progress chart on a subject matter, the intellectual could represent a new text as an attempt to etch another notch on this chart, to borrow on the previous accumulations of knowledge in an attempt to accumulate more.

The growing recognition that knowledge could be accumulated steadily through continuous acts of writing gave rise to a new metaphor for knowledge as a fragmented corpus of texts seeking metamorphosis into a single seamless one. More specifically, it led to the idea of knowledge itself comprising a written record. This was an idealization of the collective texts that would result once the gaps, biases, misconceptions, inconsistencies, and errors in the living archive were finally expurgated. As an idealization, the written record represented an ambitious hermeneutic challenge. Biblical scholars had subordinated the interpretation of different passages under the goal of revealing the singular voice of God. Similarly, the academic writer learned to subordinate the interpretation of prior, seamed texts under the goal of producing a more seamless story from them, a story around which the writer hoped to gain a consensus. Working in collusion with this idealization was the state of the actual written record, which retained the very seams and disjunctures necessary for the impetus to write (Eisenstein, 1979, pp. 74–76). The extant archive posed a challenge just by being there, open for further and better understanding. Inspired by Bacon's vision of the tree of knowledge, the Encyclopedists sought to bridge the actual and ideal in experiments to commit the written record to print, to transform the abstraction of a written record into a single bounded text (D'Alembert, 1963; Darnton, 1979, p. 254).

Two further presumptions about author–reader relationships evolved from the Enlightenment understanding of academic writing.

1. Authors and readers share enough knowledge about the living record and its imperfections that readers can follow an author's proposal for change.

2. Authors and readers share enough standards of evidence so that readers, having followed the author's proposals to change the written record, can grant them.

Although these presumptions are very useful for normative pedagogy (teaching academic writing to novices), we see later that they conceal some fundamental instabilities.

Tensions Between Cultural Expansion and Stability

Two conditions must be met to maintain academic writing as an ongoing and over-time system of authors and readers. These conditions are cultural expansion and societal recognition.

Cultural expansion occurs when scientists discover new ideas. Scientists do not proceed merely by passing along or handing down existing cultural information. Through the discovery of new ideas which, through sociocognitive processes, become signature ideas, scientists expand the overall amount of knowledge. All things being equal, then, scientific discovery leads to cultural complexity. To be technically precise, whether the scientific culture actually does expand following such discoveries is a function not only of the discovery process but also of the processes of forgetting, communication, and acceptance. Forgetting can take place at the individual level, when a person loses information once known, or at the societal level, after all the persons who retained a particular piece of cultural information (e.g., using a slide rule) either leave the society or die. Processes of forgetting decrease cultural complexity. Technically speaking, scientific discoveries increase cultural complexity but only if the rate of discovery outpaces the rate of forgetting and all discoveries are communicated and accepted.

Societal recognition occurs when scientists gain authority because their "name" becomes associated with their signature ideas. Scientists consider themselves effective agents for cultural expansion if their signature ideas elaborate a widely known handle that becomes associated with the new knowledge offered in their texts. To become an effective agent of change, in other words, it is not sufficient for the scientist simply to put out a new idea. The scientist must also forge a handle that becomes associated with those ideas, a phrase or name that, through simple mention, evokes a wealth of ideas known by many. Harkening back to chapter 5, the scientist's handle, in order to become highly authoritative, must become a standard symbol for the ideas the scientist is credited with discovering. In the annals of science, the mere names of the most famous scientists have become eponyms (i.e., factoids, chap. 5) for the ideas they are credited with discovering (e.g., Ohm, Watt). Even when the tie between the author and the idea is less explicit and consensual, specialists can often link names to ideas within their mental model of the field (Small, 1978).

When the continuous writings of scientists are characterized as an ideal type (as they are in normative pedagogy), cultural expansion, societal recognition, and a third factor—sociocultural stability—function without internal tension. Normative accounts of science writing assume that there is some adequate process by which priority claims can be submitted, adjudicated, and accepted while the overall stability of the system of scientific authors and their readers maintains itself over time (Bazerman, 1988, Holmes, 1987). In the ideal case, scientists fashion and circulate their distinctive contributions to peers, receive the recognition due them and, in turn, read and recognize the scientific contributions of others. This process repeats itself, with an ever-expanding culture within which everyone may work. All the while, the system of authors and readers who are busily expanding this common culture are also maintaining, or even increasing, their level of stability as a group over time.

Unfortunately, even at this general level of description, the writings of scientists cannot be sustained by a logically consistent social system. To understand why, consider that societal recognition relies on cultural expansion. Without cultural expansion, scientists would not be able to claim new ideas for which to be recognized. Societal recognition also depends on sociocultural stability, high levels of shared knowledge across the community of scientists. Without such shared knowledge, the new ideas of the scientist would evaporate in the air, having no solid target to effect and change. Stability, for example, is threatened in a scientific community when a specialty undergoes widescale and abrupt migration, when many members suddenly leave the field and many new members come in. Stability can also be threatened without turnover, when members shift their cognitive interests and their decisions about with whom (i.e., other scientists and scientific texts) to interact. In either case, without reasonable levels of sociocultural stability, scientists can find the sociocultural system within which they seek recognition a moving target, too evasive for a text to hit cleanly.

Another threat to stability is cultural expansion itself. In the terms of Kuhn (1970), stability is threatened by a crisis in an accepted paradigm, a crisis brought about by the very cultural expansion scientists are working toward. Although a scientific community relies on cultural expansion through both new ideas and stability, these forces are inversely related. New ideas—cultural expansions—are the lifeblood of the intellectual community; without additional checks, however, they have a destabilizing effect on a group. As we saw in chapters 4 and 7, an effective way to decrease the proportion of shared knowledge in a group is to introduce new ideas that some members have and others do not (see also Carley, 1991b). Cultural expansion, through new ideas, is the lifeblood of intellectual communities but the bane of their long-term stability.

Efforts to Maintain Stability in the Face of New Ideas

Scientific communities do not necessarily falter under the pressure of these competing forces. However, they would falter without additional checks to harness stability in the face of an influx of new ideas. They could, of course, insure stability by banning innovation, but that would also destroy the possibility of an individual achieving societal recognition; they could insure innovation by throwing away stability as a constraint, but that would create anarchy and destroy, for an entirely different reason, the possibility of societal recognition. On the basis of these observations,

it is useful to think of academic enclaves of writers as radically destabilizing yet reconstitutive professions. They are professions in which every
member seeks to exert authority on the sociocultural landscape and to
alter the body of knowledge associated with it so that it comes to resem-
ble their own mental models more closely. At the same time, they are
professions that have adopted many social conventions to assure that the
change proposed by any one member will conform to the principle of
immediate comprehension and so enforce a certain degree of orderliness
in the changes proposed. Such social conventions include the processes
by which written texts are reviewed (i.e., gatekeeping), as well as the
way texts have to be written (i.e., tying the new ideas to a review of previously assimilated texts). Among academics, it is a matter of conventional
wisdom that journals and the conventions of the academic text promote
the expression and circulation of new ideas. The conventional wisdom
here is not entirely correct. Academic conventions tend to ensure a profession's stability in the face of the many new ideas its members are generating that would, left unchecked, tear the profession apart. The issues
in the trade-off between innovation and stability and a second important trade-off, speed versus durability, become clearer when we turn to
actual historical systems of science.

HISTORICAL SYSTEMS OF SCIENCE WRITING

The Royal Society Moves to Print

Book writing has been an honored mode of scientific communication
since ancient times (Bazerman, 1988). Nonetheless, the book did little
to further the emerging perception in 17th-century Europe that science
needed to be a cooperative enterprise. The Royal Society of London,
founded in 1660, represented one of the first attempts to incorporate
science as an organized activity. Charles II, an enthusiast about the positive role of science on civic life, conferred a chapter of incorporation
to the Society. A charter of this type was conferred to any company expected to elect a President, Council, and Fellows and holding a public
trust. In this regard, the Society marked a shift away from patron-
sponsored science. The Society considered itself a radical departure from
the university system, whose main function in the 17th century and up
through the late 19th (Vesey, 1965) remained the preservation rather than
the expansion of culture. The Royal Society further distinguished itself
from "Professional" societies of its day—such as the College of Physicians or the College of Arms—whose chief role was accrediting practitioners rather than furthering the performance and promotion of research.

Politically, the Society saw itself as a positive change from party politics, recruiting reasonable men of various political persuasions and convening them to produce irrefutable knowledge (Crowther, 1941; Hunter, 1989). Moving science toward a cooperative organization meant moving it increasingly away from the communication channel of the book. Readers of science books could not continue to shape the body of knowledge presented in books—nor were they expected to. With the book, the formal channels of scientific communication were closed off from the informal and often collaborative channels of scientific activity. In the 17th century, the Royal Society and other scientific societies throughout Europe were trying to make their channels of formal communication closer and more responsive to the informal activities of science.

The incorporation of the Royal Society and other branch societies of science says more about the founders' urgency to find alternative organizations for science than it says about their prescience of how science was to evolve. The Royal Society began as a proximate working group. Its initial plan was to restrict membership to less than 100 and to hold weekly meetings at Gresham College in London (Hunter, 1989). Despite these lofty ideals, the Royal Society turned into a culturally diffuse group of individuals, more in search of a stable sociocultural structure than in possession of one. Plans for an elite and restricted membership were scrapped, in part, because the relatively small hard core of scientists in England could not support research without an endowment, and neither the government nor the crown made one available. The Society had to recruit prosperous nonscientists as members (Lyons, 1968, p. ix). Consequently, the early membership lists included a motley assortment of persons—a few government clerks, journalists, physicians, and apothecaries with a small interest in science, as well as aristocrats and bishops with even less interest. In addition, there were many scientists and scientific aspirants located outside London and throughout Europe who regularly corresponded with the Society, with postage subsidized by the Society itself. Long-distance correspondences with nonmembers increasingly occupied the time of the core membership in London. Some members stopped going to the regular meetings in London but remained in touch with members and nonmembers through the mail (Hunter, 1981, p. 53).

Merton (1938/1970) proposed a variety of explanations for the emergence of a trend toward cooperative science in 17th-century Europe. He cited such factors as population size and density, an unprecedented concentration of interactive opportunities among innovators, as well as an unprecedented belief in utility and progress. Meadows (1973) offered a compatible but different explanation of the aspiration toward cooperation, tied to the changing reporting system of science. He believed that the public reporting of science—eventually through journals, such as *Philosophical Transactions*, started in 1665—was a gradual replacement for the antiquated anagram system practiced earlier in the 17th century. In the anagram system, a scientist would encrypt the statement of an intended discovery into an anagram to disguise the original meaning. The anagram was then entrusted to an official witness, a council or some other trustee. The scientist could then retire to the laboratory to establish its certainty at leisure. Should any competitor publicly claim the same discovery, the original scientist could appeal to the trustee to unscramble the anagram and, that done, the scientist could reclaim priority. Meadows (1973, pp. 50–57) told how, in 1610, Galileo wrote Kepler a letter in Latin, containing a jumble of letters which when translated read, "I have seen the uppermost planet triple." However, the anagram system proved brittle in resolving priority disputes and maintaining societal stability. It did not resolve priority conflicts smoothly because, like the statements of the Delphic Oracle, anagrams could be so vague that judges had difficulty deciding whether and how much one statement of discovery overlapped with another. Moreover, by accepting the claim of discovery apart from the work to support it, questions arose about the appropriate locus of discovery. Did it rest with the claim or with the work? One can imagine that the original motivation was to suppress competition by discouraging the "gentleman" scientist from pursuing the same course of work already underway by another. Finally, the anagram system did nothing for the stability of science and the diffusion of scientific information because the chief mode of interaction it supported was one-to-one (i.e., the interaction between the scientist and the trustee of the priority claim). Although the anagram might, at times, settle a local priority dispute, there was nothing to insure that news of this settlement would receive wide reach. Thus, the anagram system, tailored for one-to-one communication, was a brutally slow method for establishing priority, particularly as the number of scientists and potentially overlapping discoveries to be adjudicated increased. The anagram system, it seems, could not have grown with science. Scientists, therefore, had to seek a different organization for staking priority.

The Scientific Journal: Merging Speed with Durability

Although it has roots in many earlier genres, the scientific journal merged two primary ones—the science book and the newspaper (Kronick, 1962). The early science journal and the newspaper were actually contemporaneous forms, emerging in the 17th century when roads and postal service made regional mailing more than a random event (Meadows, 1973). The scientific book, as we have mentioned, was the time-honored way of communicating science before the 17th century, and the journal did not displace it. The Royal Society put its imprimatur on books as well as journals, and the success of the journal trade only accelerated the market for scientific books. As Bazerman (1988, p. 80) observes "books and [the] article have a complex dialectical history," and it is misleading to pit one genre against the other.

Nonetheless, for the author, the scientific book and the newspaper offered a set of complementary and well-known trade-offs for science that found a compromise in the scientific journal. Consider first the trade-offs of the science book. On the plus side of the ledger, scientific books disseminated scientific information in prestige markets and promised a potential reach at least large enough to establish an author with a known handle among readers of science. On the negative side, books were expensive to produce, and publishers were reluctant to publish them when their market potential seemed low. Books were also slow to come to market. The publication of a scientific book was a relatively rare event, and books were often expected to report a lifetime of research (Roediger, 1987). Consequently, books were not the medium of choice to communicate timely information and, by the 17th century, scientific information was increasingly perceived as timely (Hall, 1965). Because of their cost, moreover, scientific books had a relatively low immediate reach; publishers were fortunate to sell out an edition of 500 copies, despite the growing number of readers with an interest in science. Thus, even before the scientific journal, the most common way to communicate scientific information and receive acknowledgement was through informal channels, such as personal correspondence among circles of scientists (Bazerman, 1988). In contrast to the 17th-century book, which was slow and expensive but had a circulation in prestige markets, the 17th century newspaper featured the reverse set of benefits and costs. The newspaper was more timely than the book but came with far fewer quality control assurances. The newspaper reported new information in timely fashion but often anonymously, leaving the handle of the newswriter invisible. On the other hand, the newspaper had incredible speed, wide reach, and relatively inexpensive production and circulation costs. A single newspaper was commonly read by dozens of patrons in taverns and town halls (Altick, 1957), and in a single week it could often exceed the lifetime circulation of most books.

Against these trade-offs, the scientific journal was an experiment to husband the very disparate advantages of books and newspapers while avoiding their separate disadvantages. It was the best compromise one could expect for a science that wanted to be both durable and timely (chap. 2). The compromise represented by the scientific journal took on a heavy burden; as a literary form it sought to present truth for all time in rapid time. Kronick (1962, p. 240) noted that by forcing the periodical "to play [this] double role . . . it is possible that we have forced upon it an impossible task."

An early roadblock was to have readers identify the journal's contents with prestige information, paralleling the information available in the book market. This challenge, arguably, was met around 1750. Prior to that date, the book market had remained the legitimate venue for establishing the priority of an idea for all time (Meadows, 1973, pp. 56–57). By the middle of the 18th century, however, certain journals came to rival the prestige of the book market, allowing an author to establish virtual universal priority through journal publication (Houghton, 1975). Nevertheless, the relative merits of books and journal articles are debated to this day. Books are still often viewed as archives of great and timeless ideas; articles present what is fashionable and in vogue. Nonetheless, with the identification of some journals with a prestige market, two hopes seemed attainable: (a) speeding the scientific enterprise without reducing its quality; and (b) maintaining the quality of the book at the speed of the periodical press.

Yet there were bound to be tensions in collapsing different types of content, such as durable information and news, into a single channel. Until the 18th century, these types of content had been routed through contextually diverse channels. Pressures moving the journal content closer toward the book encouraged articles that were longer, more specialized, and well documented (Bazerman, 1988, chap. 5). Maintaining the journal content within the counterpressure created by periodical print encouraged the writing of articles that were short, general, and underdocumented. The result of this tension was a journal article that, until the 19th century, often retained the informal characteristics of letters of correspondence. Quality control standards were not enforced in the early journal and it was not until the 1700s that scientific societies began to rely on editorial review and to classify published work as either "reviewed" or "not reviewed" (Roediger, 1987, p. 227). Throughout the 17th and 18th centuries, the majority of scientific journals did not present original results but were designed (a) to spread known results, (b) to translate science conducted from abroad, (c) to adapt scientific results to popular audiences, and (d) to archive information previously published in scattered tracts and pamphlets (Bazerman, 1988). In many cases, these functions were carried out under anonymous authorship. During this period, most scientific societies and their journals were nonspecialized. For example, until 1820 the nonscientific members of the Royal Society grew more rapidly than the scientific members. Until 1860, the nonscientific fellows held a majority over the scientific ones (Lyons, 1968, p. 233). With this lack of specialization, the boundaries between a general interest journal containing scientific information and a specialized journal appealing to the lay reader were thin and, in some cases, invisible (Kronick, 1962). Authors of most 17th and 18th century scientific journal articles were more interested in promoting science than in extending the reach of original findings under an authorial handle (Houghton, 1975; Kronick, 1962).[2]

By the mid-19th century, science was becoming increasingly specialized, professionalized, and university centered. As scientific authors came to think of themselves as building a "career" based on their new ideas, the need to index new ideas through further stabilizing conventions increased as well. More uniform quality control standards were introduced to make the journal article an "official" record of priority staking in science (Ravetz, 1971, p. 300). Before the mid-19th century, scientists still feared that a journal publication could be plagiarized with impunity. After that time, submission rates rose as the journal article became the central repository of scientific knowledge (Roediger, 1987). Document conventions required to legitimate the scientific text as an official record were also established. Well through the 19th century, it was common for articles to appear without citations or references[3] (Meadows, 1973). Articles often presented only scant evidence for their assertions (Bazerman, 1988) and did not require strict demarcations between assimilated knowledge and original results (Hunter, 1989; Kronick, 1962; Lyons, 1968). Between the late 19th and early 20th centuries, the contents of the scientific article became more structured, requiring abstracts, citations, references, and other conventions to coordinate, socially and culturally, the boundaries between assimilated and new information with greater precision. Personal references to previous authors were dropped, making the journal content conform to a more professional standard. Citations became more frequent and more uniform in format. By 1850, the majority of journal articles used citation (Bazerman, 1988). By 1880, there were barely any journals that failed to require them (Meadows, 1973).

---

[2]In the 16th and 17th centuries, not all scientific societies thought a journal was necessary. Kronick (1962, p. 236) reported that of the 220 science societies in existence by 1790, over 50 operated with no written proceedings. Unlike contemporary science, whose journals exert institutional control over the choices of authors who write for them, the journal in 1700, when collaborative editing was becoming commonplace, was still a relatively weak and inchoate institution. Journal editors in the 1700s were as likely to conform to the decisions of authors as authors to them (Barnes, 1936, pp. 157–162).

[3]In this chapter, we use the term *references* to indicate any information about a text that links it to previous texts. We use the term *citation* to indicate a specific type of reference, one where a previous text is explicitly referenced through a specific type of citing convention.

An increasingly formal concept of the "scientific paper" developed, and an increasingly homogeneous and abbreviated set of conventions for the efficient transmission of "results" claiming priority evolved (Cronin, 1984, pp. 5–12).[4]

By World War I, the association of a scientific author with published results (and thus the elaboration of an authorial handle culturally tied to these results) became the accepted path for a scientist building a career (Bledstein, 1976). Besides competition, the emergence of different research styles and institutional affiliations and the need for researchers to legitimate their own styles and affiliations were factors leading to the emergence of new specialties and new journals to organize them. As the pressure on the scientific author to address a distinctive "cutting edge" increased, the odds of an existing journal circumscribing exactly this territory decreased. This trend led to the proliferation of specialized journals with smaller and more focused readerships. Price (1963) calculated that, since the 18th century, the number of journals has increased tenfold every 50 years.

Is the Scientific Journal Too Fast or Too Slow For Science?

As we saw in chapters 7 and 8, the first order effect of print on the diffusion of new ideas relative to a face-to-face society is to increase the speed with which ideas diffuse. Within the scientific community, there seems little question that journal publication increased the speed with which new ideas diffused at a distance, particularly when compared to face-to-face interaction and the book market. At the same time, increased gatekeeping has made the content of the science journal a more constrained—and slower—form when compared to the regular newspaper. Given forces that tend to both speed and slow the diffusion of new ideas, a recurring issue for the scientific community has been whether journal publication proceeds at the right rate to support science. The body of scientific knowledge must grow, but without careful gatekeeping, too many spurious results can destroy the enterprise. Although scrupulous gatekeeping is necessary for quality control, without disseminating one's results in a timely fashion science is no less threatened.

Prior to World War II, there was widespread concern that periodical print was too fast a medium for science to conduct its business. According to Meadows (1973), a scientist could still afford to rely on:

---

[4]These standards are still in evolution, however. Even today there is no standard citation practice within many disciplines, let alone across all journals of science.

[T]he accumulation and slow digestion of a broad basis of observational and theoretical facts discovered by his elders; only after this would a new idea, more or less suddenly, occur to him; that he would then test this idea by all possible means and certainly not announce it publicly until he had done so; and that if observational data were lacking or were insufficient to supply the test, he would forget the idea or postpone it until some later time. (pp. 58–59)

By contrast, the majority of scientists today appear to believe that journals are too slow to support science. According to Cronin (1984), as competition intensifies the urgency to be first to press, the relative slowness of journal publication is widely perceived as its principle shortcoming. Consequently, different scientific communities have experimented with alternatives, such as the preprint or conference proceeding, that promise to disseminate results faster than the formal periodical. One experiment allowed authors to circulate abstracts even before the formal paper was written or the official results determined. This convention, like the anagram system, established priority as a promissory note rather than as a completed transaction. Some specialities have even created weekly or bimonthly journals that publish short-form research on this basis. In 1960, the prestigious *Physical Review* created a sister publication *Physical Review Letters* designed for the rapid transmission of research in physics (Blakeslee, 1991b). The editor of the new journal justified its creation as follows:

Because of the rapid development and the intense competition, we have found it necessary to relax our standards and accept some papers that present new ideas without full analysis, relatively crude experiments that indicate how one can obtain valuable results by more careful and complete work, etc., in short papers which under less hot conditions would be returned to authors with the recommendation that further work be done before publication. . . . We realize that thereby we penalize some physicists who, working along the same lines, want to do a more complete job before publishing. (cited in Meadows, 1973, p. 63)

Other specialties have experimented with microfilm or microfiche, encouraging its members to record and circulate their research through these storage devices. Although these media are easier to archive than print, they are harder to access and have not gained wide acceptance. Still other societies, like the American Society of Civil Engineers and the Chemical and Physical Societies of London, experimented for a time with central abstracting services, which disseminate abstracts and then make fuller papers available upon request. This experiment was abandoned by these societies, but is still an ongoing practice for papers presented at annual meetings of the American Sociological Association. This association once proposed to establish a multimillion dollar computerized system to coordinate the exchange of preprints, but this was never implemented (Garvey, 1979). Cronin (1982) reported that to date, virtually all computer networks designed to rival print in disseminating results have not worked. Nonetheless, many schemes for the diffusion of information via electronic journals are currently underway (Schatz, 1991).

There is, of course, nothing faster than the public press. Some scientists have sought to establish priority directly through newspapers, radio, television, and even electronic mail and fax communication. Utah scientists announced their "discovery" of cold fusion to the world press, only to have their experimental write-up rejected from *Nature* for lack of detail. Most members of the scientific community acknowledge that the formal journal is too slow, but this community tends to close ranks around the belief that the public press is too fast and does not provide sufficient disciplinary controls (Crane, 1974). Editors of established journals hold that scientists who leak to the press subvert the accepted system for establishing priority. Franz Ingelfinger, editor of the *New England Journal of Medicine*, announced he would publish no articles whose content had been furnished in advance to the popular press (Garvey, 1979, p. 75). These events indicate that science has not completed its search for the appropriate scales for weighing durability against timeliness, cultural expansion against stability.

PRINT AND THE DISSEMINATION OF NEW IDEAS WITHIN ACADEMIC SPECIALTIES

We assume an academic specialty is essentially a group of individuals with strong professional ties. That is to say, such individuals have a high degree of relative similarity with one another vis-a-vis their similarity to individuals outside the specialty. Such individuals, as a group, are highly integrated and specialized. We further assume that individuals in the specialty inhabit a society where print is widely available to everyone. These assumptions define the academic specialist exactly as we defined the professional in chapter 8. We now make an additional assumption that distinguishes the ordinary professional from the academic specialist. That is the relation of the academic to innovation or the generation and diffusion of new ideas. From the constructural perspective, we are concerned with the diffusion of the discovery and not with the act of discovery.

In the model (chap. 6), individuals communicate information, which can include new discoveries. The individual authors have a unique cognitive relationship to their discoveries, but the model in chapter 6 does not itself embody a cognitive theory of discovery. There are, of course, many theories now in the literature about how scientists discover new information (see Langley, Simon, Bradshaw, & Zytkow, 1987, for an example); yet the model we employ hovers above these theories and simply assumes that discovery (i.e., generating an idea that is previously unknown to the society) has occurred. The model starts with a sociocultural landscape in which a certain number of discoveries have been made, with no concern for the details underlying their generation (cf. Simonton, 1988)—and then traces their diffusion throughout the society. The focus of the model, and our focus, is not authorial discovery per se, but the nature of author–reader interaction that falls out as a consequence of discovery. We explore author–reader interaction when an author has something new to say to intellectual peers and wishes to gain disciplinary recognition for disseminating these new ideas. We should add that gaining recognition for disseminating new ideas is not always the same as discovering them (Kaufer & Geisler, 1989). An individual can be new simply by communicating information that is new to a particular group, even if it is not new to the society overall. Intellectual migrants (chap. 10), for example, are authors who commonly gain recognition as much for the ideas they are the first to impart as for those they are the first to have. Yet, for our purposes in this chapter, these types of newness are indistinguishable.

As a final caveat, the model we use is not sensitive enough to capture the various sociopolitical rites, rituals, and conventions of discourse that must be learned to gain entry into a particular discipline. These rites and rituals are domain specific and are acquired over years of practice or apprenticeship in the chosen field. Their effective use determines whether a writer can produce a persuasive argument for insiders. Toulmin (1958) called these "field-dependent" arguments. McCloskey (1987) detailed the intricate field-dependent moves required by economists when they want to persuade their peers. Geisler (1991) and Blakeslee (1991a) did the same for ethical philosophers and physicists, respectively. Although these domain specific studies are essential for a theory of acquiring writing prowess in a particular discipline, the model we use does not discriminate domain-specific features of disciplines and ignores variations from one discipline to the next, other than the variations expressed as patterns of knowledge and interaction.

These caveats aside, we consider, for the remainder of this chapter, the relationship between discovery and diffusion. In chapter 8, we paid no attention to diffusion. We considered the impact of transactions (and the various technological conditions under which such transactions occurred) on a profession's stability and consensus. We considered the role that professional communication can play in building professional community. Yet we did not consider the individual reach of a particular professional. We ignored the question of a single professional's reach because individuals in many professions never think of generating or disseminating knowledge under a personal signature or handle. Rather, they can reasonably be considered a nonunique representative of a particular body of knowledge. Because such individuals represent a body of knowledge that they do not author, one need not assume that any one individual's reach is distinctive from anyone else's. In the case of professionals, what one wants to measure are the effects of professional communication, technological conditions, and various sociocultural landscapes on the average reach of an individual's communications across a society. Stability and consensus are affected by the average reach of individuals within a society, so average reach (as measured by stability and consensus) is our focus in chapter 8.

In an academic specialty, however, being the first to generate and diffuse new ideas with a personal signature and handle is the name of the game. The differential rates of diffusion across authors is arguably, particularly from the scientist's standpoint, the most important measure of communication within academic specialties. If professions are important in the ways they make individuals alike, academics are professionals who seek importance, over and above their professional ties, by discriminating their reach as authors from the reach of their peers. Since scientific specialties are also professions, all the results of chapter 8 apply. Because scientific specialties are a special type of profession whose business is to expand culture, it is valuable to consider the impact of a specialty's professional structure (from a prototypical to a nonprototypical profession) on the diffusion of new ideas. Thus, we employ the same simulated societies we examined in chapter 8 but now we focus on diffusion.

Recall that we conduct two sets of simulations. The first set vary absolute characteristics of the society. In this set, we vary the population of the whole society (6, 12, 18 individuals) and cultural complexity (10, 20, 40 ideas). Regardless of the population size, we assign half the individuals in the society to the group designating the scientific specialty. In the second set of simulations, we vary the prototypical status of the specialty (its level of initial cultural integration and specialization) as well as its relative size. We assign all societies 12 individuals and 20 ideas. We allow the degree of initial cultural integration to vary so that individual specialists share either 4%, 16%, or 64% of all the available ideas, respectively. We allow the degree of specialization within the specialty to vary so that its members initially share 1%, 4%, or 16% of its knowledge with those outside the speciality. Finally, we allow the relative size of the specialty to vary so that the specialty is either 100%, 50%, or 33% as large as the outside group.

In both sets of simulations, we now trace the diffusion of a particular scientist's new idea. These simulations afford us a closer look at the time required for a discovery to diffuse throughout the specialty. As in chapter 8, we contrast two technological conditions, face-to-face and print interaction.

SPEED AND THE LIMITS OF GROWTH

Efficiency Hypothesis Adapted to the Academic Specialty

The overwhelming effect of print is simply to increase the rapidity with which ideas diffuse (chap. 6) and, consequently, to decrease the time required to achieve social stability and consensus (chap. 8). In the context of professions, we further identify the speed of print with the Efficiency Hypothesis which shows how print enhances the overall performance of individuals. Print, according to this hypothesis, allows the same individual to put out more communications in less time than face-to-face interaction. One suspects that a correlate of the Efficiency Hypothesis applies to academic specialities as well. The correlate states that for any new idea developed within or related to a specialty (assuming the quasi-uniqueness of the specialty and its partial reliance on imported ideas for an internal consensus), print makes everyone, within and without the specialty, more efficient in passing along the existence of this new idea, and decreases the time it takes for the idea to diffuse to a critical mass of members in the specialty.

This correlate of the Efficiency Hypothesis is consistent with the results for diffusion across all sociocultural landscapes (Tables 9.1 through 9.5 in Appendix C). Regardless of the sociocultural configuration of the society in which the specialty resides, print markedly reduces the time required for new information to diffuse within the specialty group. The reader can visually inspect these simulation results by examining Fig. 9.1 through 9.5, where in all cases the time-to-diffusion of a new idea within specialties residing in societies with print is markedly faster than the time-to-diffusion within specialities residing in societies whose technological condition is restricted to face-to-face transactions. These results illustrate that print, as cast in the terms of the constructural model, is much more efficient than face-to-face communication.

Expansion Hypotheses Adapted
to the Academic Specialty

The Expanding Member Hypothesis

One might argue that print fostered the growth of science by making it possible for more new information to get to more people faster. Put in slightly different terms, with print, new ideas could reach a larger population in the same or less time than it would take them to reach a smaller population with face-to-face interaction. Let us call this a correlate of the Expanding Member Hypothesis, now applied to diffusion. Figure 9.1 illustrates that such behavior is consistent with the constructural model. In this figure, each dot is the average of 300 cases (three societies with that size population, each simulated 100 times). Notice that whether the technological condition is face-to-face or print, the larger the membership of the specialty, the more time it takes a single piece of new information to diffuse to all its members. Nonetheless, in any given interval of time, print will carry a new idea to more members of the specialty than face-to-face interaction. Print's advantage steadily increases, furthermore, as the size of the specialty increases.

These logical confirmations of the Expanding Member Hypothesis occur only when we consider the absolute size of the specialty (Fig. 9.1). When we consider its relative size (i.e., the size of the specialty relative to the larger society), print's advantage does not increase proportionally to the size of the specialty (Fig. 9.2). Each dot in that figure is the average of 900 cases (nine societies with that ratio of groups, each simulated 100 times). In fact, the relationship of relative size to the rate of diffusion under an oral condition is negative, which is the same relationship that it had on the rate of stability (chap. 8). That is to say, the larger the relative size of the specialty, the longer it takes ideas to diffuse to everyone. This negative relationship makes intuitive sense. When everyone in the specialty is the target audience for a new idea, then the larger the target audience (relative to all possible audiences), the more time it will take for the new idea to reach the whole target. Print disrupts this process. With print, new information within a specialty diffuses fastest when the group is moderately sized, relative to the rest of society (Fig. 9.2).

Diffusion can occur directly, from the discovering scientist to the audience, or indirectly, from other scientists (beyond the original discoverer) passing on the discovery through word of mouth or referencing the new idea in written papers. Should a specialty be too small or too large in relative terms, then print inhibits indirect diffusion. Why does print have this effect when the specialty is relatively small? When everyone has access to print and the specialty is small, relative to the rest of society, the scientist finds it difficult to diffuse a new idea rapidly to members of the specialty. This is because, through the multiplicity of print, the boundaries of the specialty are highly permeable, putting the scientist's new idea in stiff competition with the ideas of those originating outside the specialty. Further, the smallness of the discipline works against the scientist because, being few in number relative to everyone else, the members of the scientist's specialty have more opportunities for external contact. This is essentially Blau's (1977) structural hypothesis, explaining why minorities in a society are forced to interact with majority members more than the other way around. Print enhances this structural effect of small relative size by enabling those outside the specialty to bombard those inside with ideas of their own.

Why does print inhibit indirect diffusion when the specialty is too large? In this case, the ability of print to permeate group boundaries is

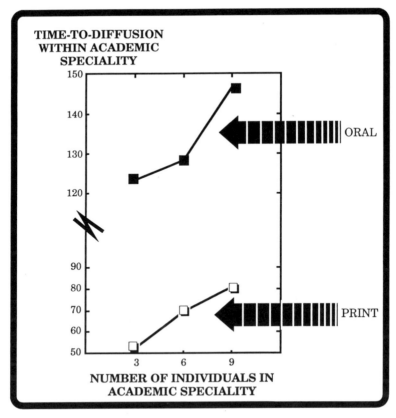

FIG. 9.1. Population size and time-to-diffusion within the academic specialty by technological condition.
Note. Based on comparison of aspects of Tables 9.3 and 9.4 in Appendix C.

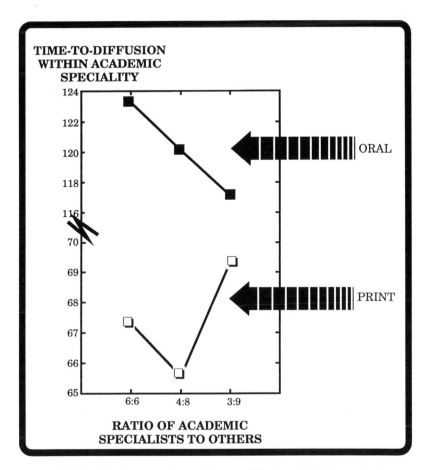

FIG. 9.2. Relative group size and time-to-diffusion within the academic specialty by technological condition.
Note. Based on comparison of aspects of Tables 9.1 and 9.2 in Appendix C.

not the controlling factor. Rather, through its multiplicity, print enables all members of the specialty to reach each other rapidly and increases the internal competition for the reception of ideas. In a relatively large specialty with print, members are bombarding one another with ideas and, for any single scientist, competition for the reading time and attention of other members becomes steep. Moderate size specialties, on the other hand, have the comparative advantage of being neither so large as to steepen competition for the reading time of insiders nor so small as to keep insiders distracted with the ideas of outsiders. Indirect diffusion works to the scientist's advantage in the moderate-size specialty more than in specialties of other relative sizes.

Taken together, these results furnish insights into the optimal development strategies of the Royal Society and other early scientific enclaves seeking to carve out a niche for themselves within a larger society. To optimize the diffusion of new information across its membership, it was advantageous for the Royal Society to grow in absolute numbers, yet reduce itself in relative size. Internal growth in absolute numbers made it possible to take advantage of print. This growth could slow down rates of diffusion, but this slowdown itself could be offset by moving to print. Reduction in relative size was also necessary, however, to keep the diffusion problem manageable, and to insure that the number of people to whom new ideas had to spread to maintain steady growth within the specialty remained a target that could be reached in timely fashion. The historical record is, of course, much more complicated than these simulation results, but for the most part it is consistent with them. In particular, the Royal Society was actively engaged in a two-pronged strategy that was consistent with increasing its absolute size but decreasing its relative size. It actively recruited members, actual scientists, to a central core which grew in absolute numbers; but it also actively recruited a much broader base of nonscientists to serve as part of the intelligentsia. These nonscientists could promote and support specific scientists, keeping the relative size of the emergent subdisciplines desirably small.

Expanding Culture Hypothesis

One might argue that print fostered the growth of science because it facilitated the diffusion of new ideas within a specialty, even as the complexity of the specialty continued to increase. To formulate the argument slightly differently, as a specialization increased the body of knowledge it needed to maintain, print continued to allow authors in the specialty to diffuse their new ideas to members in the same or even shorter intervals of time. We call this the Expanding Culture Hypothesis as applied to diffusion. Figure 9.3 illustrates that this hypothesis is consistent with the constructural model. Each dot in that figure is the average of 300 cases (three societies with that level of cultural complexity, each simulated 100 times). Regardless of the technological condition, the more ideas there are to know within the specialty (i.e., the more complex its culture), the longer it takes for new ideas to diffuse among its members. Yet, in any given interval of time, print technologies enable a new idea to be carried to more people than oral technologies. Print's advantage only increases, furthermore, as the number of ideas within the specialty increases. Conversely, as the accumulated body of ideas within a specialty decreases, the effect of the technological condition (face-to-face or print) on the diffusion of new ideas narrows, and print loses its advantage.

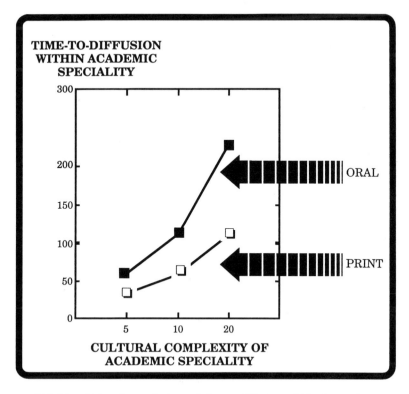

FIG. 9.3. Cultural complexity and time-to-diffusion within the academic specialty by technological condition.
Note. Based on comparison of aspects of Tables 9.3 and 9.4 in Appendix C.

These results inform our understanding of the early specialities of science and their conditions of communication. Historians of scientific communication widely agree that the scientific journals of the 17th and 18th century carried predominantly general articles, popularizations, and translations. Historians explain this occurrence by pointing out that the authors of these articles were more interested in promoting science than in advancing new ideas (Houghton, 1975; Kronick, 1962), and that the editors, faced with a paucity of papers submitted, had to accept anything (Garfield, 1980). These explanations are surely part of the story, but our results suggest an altogether independent benefit of keeping the early journals highly general. In relation to the body of scientific knowledge available today, the body of scientific knowledge in the 17th and 18th century was comparatively small. As these results indicate, print loses its advantage over oral conditions, relative to the diffusion of new ideas, when a specialty has a small body of knowledge. With a small body of accumulated knowledge, oral conditions were sufficient to diffuse new ideas to fellow scientists. As the body of scientific knowledge grew, however, print became an increasing necessity.

As we have seen, print's advantage for diffusing new ideas is greatest when the absolute number of specialists is large and the relative number of specialists is moderate with respect to the larger society. We speculated earlier that members of the Royal Society may have acted in an optimal way to increase print's advantage by recruiting committed scientists while also recruiting a large body of general interest members. (Such actions could have been fortuitous rather than calculated, at least with respect to print.) The addition of members to the early societies of science increased and diversified the culture of the group. This cultural broadening made the group's shared knowledge more general and diverse, but it also created a cultural environment conducive to the rapid diffusion of new ideas through print. Designed to reach a culturally more diversified audience, generalist journals may have been the price early scientists paid so that, when the occasion arose, they could take advantage of the benefits of print to spread ideas quickly to that central core of scientists who could make the most use of their results.

The growth of both members within a specialty and accumulated ideas slows down the diffusion of new ideas within the specialty. However, adding a new idea has an even greater retarding effect on diffusion than adding a new member (compare Fig. 9.1 and 9.3). This comparison suggests that the scientific journal would probably have been necessary even if scientific societies promoted the generation of new ideas within a fixed list of members. The business of scientists, whatever their absolute numbers, has been to expand the body of scientific knowledge through research. Working in the absence of a journal, even a small number of efficient scientists might well have found their new results getting lost as the body of accumulated knowledge grew. Conversely, had only the membership rolls of scientists increased, without a corresponding increase in the accumulated body of scientific ideas, the need for science to turn to print may have been significantly reduced. Imagine, for example, that science had expanded its membership, keeping strict limits on the mass of scientific information allowed to develop. This would have patterned science more after religion. Membership increases would have caused less of a threat to the diffusion of new ideas (when new ideas were allowed to diffuse) because these new ideas would be a larger proportion of all the ideas available for members to discuss and so more likely to become objects of discussion. Timely print became essential to science when scientists decided to organize themselves into unlimited idea factories, where the generation and spread of new ideas became part of the organizational routine.

Weak Cohesion Hypothesis

In chapter 8, we proposed the Weak Integration Hypothesis, the idea that the relative advantage of print over face-to-face conditions increases as a profession is less initially integrated. We also find logical confirmation for the Strong Specialization Hypothesis, the idea that the advantage of print increases as a profession's level of specialization increases. Taken together, these results say nothing unambiguous about the relationship between print and the prototypicalness of a profession, its initial level of cultural integration and specialization. The Strong Specialization Hypothesis suggests that print benefits groups that are highly specialized, like the prototypical profession. The Weak Integration Hypothesis suggests that print benefits groups that are unlike the prototypical profession because they are low in initial levels of cultural integration.

We consider these hypotheses in conjunction with the diffusion of new ideas within science. The results are displayed in Fig. 9.4 and 9.5. The results suggest that print offers the greatest relative benefit to specialties that fall somewhere below the prototypical profession. That is, print offers the most help in spreading new ideas to specialties that are only moderately (initially) integrated (Fig. 9.4) and moderately specialized (Fig. 9.5). The reader can see this effect by noticing that the distance between the oral and print conditions in both figures is greatest when the level of cultural integration or specialization is moderate. In Fig. 9.4 and 9.5, each dot is the average of 900 cases (nine societies with that level of specialization, each simulated 100 times). Print allows, in other words, the most rapid relative diffusion within specialties that lack the characteristics of a prototypical, cohesive profession. We refer to this prediction of the model as the Weak Cohesion Hypothesis.

It is important to note that the Weak Cohesion Hypothesis does not describe oral conditions. Under oral and print conditions (Fig. 9.4), discoveries diffuse most rapidly in highly prototypical professions. However, the relative speedup afforded by print is highest for slightly nonprototypical professions. This result suggests that a highly integrated, superspecialty might get along quite well with word of mouth, electronic mail, letters, phone, or other one-to-one channels. Under print conditions, by contrast, diffusion is not hurt and is even helped, in relative terms, when the initial level of cultural integration within a specialty is lower. In relative terms, print is most beneficial to diffusion when the group is moderately integrated. One implication is that a specialty whose profile does not quite fit the professional prototype has the most to gain by turning to print. Another implication is that a specialty employing print can tolerate less integration and still achieve rapid diffusion of new ideas.

Consider this prediction in the context of early scientific enclaves. The

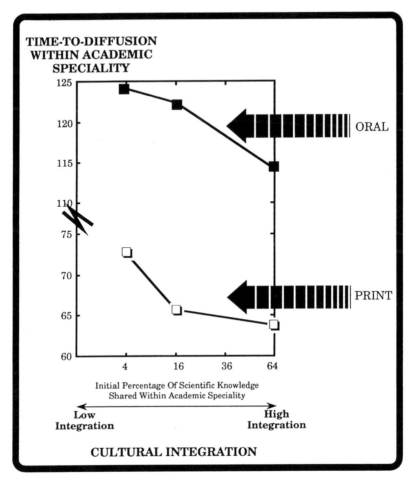

FIG. 9.4. Cultural integration and time-to-diffusion within the academic
specialty by technological condition.
Note. Based on comparison of aspects of Tables 9.1 and 9.2 in Appendix C.

early scientific community was highly dispersed, both geographically and
intellectually. Many scientists had perhaps one or two colleagues with
whom they could easily share ideas. As laypersons were encouraged to
join the scientific societies, they came to outnumber actual, knowledge-
generating, scientists. The resultant picture is one of a moderately integrated group. Thus, even without the various benefits print provided on the
basis of availability, efficiency, durability, and archivability, early science
benefited from print simply because it encouraged rapid diffusion in a
moderately cohesive group. For Meadows (1973, pp. 32–33), in order
for 17th-century science to gain autonomy, scientists had to provide a
"common language" with lay readers and the generalist journal was a
vehicle for making this move. Our analysis simply suggests that a gener-

alist journal proved exceptionally useful in rapidly diffusing even arcane results, and so facilitating the growth of a specialized science. In comparison to oral conditions, print most benefits the diffusion of new ideas when a specialty is moderately specialized (Fig. 9.5). This result follows because, given an oral condition, information diffuses the most slowly when the group is moderately specialized. High specialization aids diffusion under oral conditions because, due to the lack of multiplicity, members of the specialty (including the person with the new idea) are likely to keep their communications "in-house." Everyone in the group can learn the idea directly from the discoverer (direct diffusion), from someone who has talked to the discoverer, or from someone who has talked to someone who has talked to the discoverer, and so on (indirect diffusion). Under oral conditions and high specialization, the discoverer within a specialty benefits most from high internal, indirect diffusion. Low specialization aids indirect diffusion under oral conditions because scientists (including the discoverer) interact fluidly with outsiders as well as among themselves. Outsiders acquire the discoverer's new idea and recirculate it back to the discoverer's home specialty. Under oral conditions and low specialization, therefore, the discoverer within a specialty benefits from high external, indirect diffusion. Lacking the capacity to take advantage of indirect diffusion, either internal or external, the moderately specialized group places the greatest impediments on the speed with which ideas diffuse under oral conditions.

By guaranteeing everyone direct access to the communication partner of choice, even if the partner is only encapsulated within a text, print reduces the value and functional importance of indirect diffusion and overcomes the structural limitations of moderate specialization on diffusion speed. Recall that, in general, members of a specialty have more in common with each other than they do with outsiders and they prefer, all things equal, to interact with fellow members. This is, of course, a preference that strengthens or weakens with the level of specialization. Under oral conditions, an individual's partner of choice is not always the partner with whom an individual ends up, because of the limited availability of human interaction partners. Because of the limited availability in one-to-one interaction, individuals, under oral conditions, often need to draw upon their second, third, or perhaps even lower choices to find an available interaction partner. In a moderately specialized group, these second and third choices will often be individuals outside the group, persons who can only delay the time it takes for the new ideas generated from within the specialty to find their way back in. Print alters these dynamics. Texts are always available for interaction. As long as individuals are committed to interacting with texts, they can usually be assured of getting their first preference for interaction. Getting this first preference—which is what print conditions guarantee—makes a big difference in speeding the diffusion of new information (directly) within a moderately

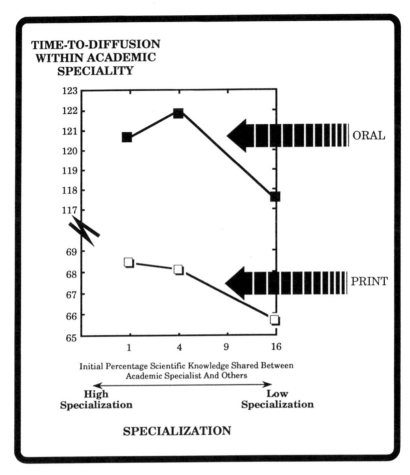

FIG. 9.5. Specialization and time-to-diffusion within the academic specialty by technological condition.
Note. Based on comparison of aspects of Tables 9.1 and 9.2 in Appendix C.

specialized group (Fig. 9.5). One implication of these results is that print allows a group to increase in specialization while still achieving rapid diffusion.

The early scientific journal, despite its general nature, served to increase the distance between the scientific community and the world. It increased the specialization of the community, even though the community was not well integrated (due to the inclusion of large numbers of interested laypersons). The foregoing results suggest that by using a generalist journal to increase the effective specialization of the scientific community at large, the knowledge-generating scientists were able to take advantage of print. These scientists could achieve faster diffusion of their highly specialized ideas through nonspecialized print outlets than they could through more specialized print outlets or without print. The early scientific societies of the 17th century had a core of specialists with arcane expertise in science (e.g., Newton, Boyle, Hooke). This group of specialists was relatively small in comparison to the larger numbers of individuals who had a general interest in science and subscribed to the scientific journals of the day. Information about science, including arcane information of predominant interest to these specialists, would reach the specialists faster in an unspecialized journal than if the specialists were to resort to one-to-one communication with one another or to start their own specialized journal. The specialists, even if few in number, would still be large enough in absolute numbers to make one-to-one communication inefficient. Furthermore, to address all the logistical problems of sustaining a journal only among specialists might require that the specialists fall back upon one-to-one interaction. Given these problems, the reasonable solution for exchanging information and priority claims rapidly among the few specialists would be to work through generalist journals.

It may be too simple to assume, on the basis of level of specialization alone, that the unspecialized journals of early science reflected less advanced intellectual communities than the highly specialized scientific journals of today. We suggest a rival hypothesis, that small pockets of early scientists achieved high levels of cultural integration and specialization, yet rationally worked through less specialized outlets, including books, simply because their relative numbers and the relative supply of high quality papers available to publish remained low. This interpretation does not violate the factual history of the scientific journal. Yet it does make the startling suggestion that publication in unspecialized journals may well have been, given the sociocultural milieu of 17th- and 18th-century science, a rational response to the specialized aims of science. To rapidly diffuse ideas to the few, they may have been written for the masses. Today, despite the larger number of scientists, there is greater division among types of science. Thus, publishing in a generalist outlet may still be a rational response that may diffuse the ideas of the discovering scientist more rapidly within the home discipline than publishing within a more specialized outlet.

SCIENTIFIC TEXTS AND THE SCIENTIST'S REACH

Thus far we have only minimally considered the effect of the content of the academic text on its diffusion. In chapter 7, we see that the nature of textual content can affect diffusion, and that (complex) texts that contain

assimilated as well as new ideas diffuse more quickly than (simple) texts
with new but no assimilated ideas. In chapter 5, we consider a networked
representation of knowledge that can underlie the content of texts and
the author's projected elaborations of this network to like-minded audiences. In chapter 2, we consider the relationship between the ratio of
assimilated and new information within texts and the prospects of these
different ratios for exerting authority, thereby creating sociocultural
change. In this section, we expand upon some of these ideas as they per-
tain to the content of the scientific article and its trail of diffusion throughout a specialty.

We begin by rehearsing some uncommon truisms about a printed text.
The printed text is a cultural artifact. Authors can, and often do, design
it strategically to influence the sociocultural structure. Their design typically takes into account the axiom of relative similarity, the principle of
immediate comprehension, and information about the extant culture and
social structure. Authors can employ this information to gauge the assimilated information to be included in the text in order to maximize the
number of readers who will grasp the new ideas it puts forward. Using
principles derived from the linear essay, the author of the scientific report
moves from assimilated information (a literature review) to a sustained
presentation of connected assimilated and new ideas (methods, results,
discussion) that are the payoff for the reader's attentive engagement. The
new ideas in the text, moreover, are bound by the fact that the text has
no innate ability to learn (has fixity; chap. 4 and 6) and cannot grow more
complex, apart from the complexity brought to it by readers. The fixity
of the text means that its complexity is unchangeable over time. Consequently, readers can, after many rereadings, harbor the illusion of learning all the knowledge that a text has to surrender. In contrast, we find
it impractical to imagine the implications of learning all the information
in an individual's mental models, particularly because mental models continue to adapt over time.

Literate readers schooled in the linear conventions of the academic
essay and journal report (Kaufer & Geisler, 1989) understand the fixity
of texts. They understand that such texts are composites of both assimilated and new information (chap. 2) and that their reading is not complete until they have followed the trail from the assimilated to the new
ideas in the text. Consequently, within academically literate communities, the general presumption is that a text has new things to say and that
these new ideas can become the focal concepts around which readers
can mentally index the text and future writers can cite and reference it.
A further presumption among academic literates is that how a text gets
publicly indexed (across the minds of readers) can affect the larger sociocultural structure within which it circulates. The content of the text

can help determine not only what the text has to say, but who will be interested in reading it and how the sociocultural environment might reconstitute itself once it has been read.

The Power of Print and the Power of Being Central

The power of individual scientists to shape the intellectual climate of their specialization through the circulation of their texts has ambivalent consequences for a specialty. With increasing reward comes increasing uncertainty. When individual scientists are doing their jobs correctly, they are creating uncertainty for their peers because their success means moving their own signature ideas closer to the center of consensus in the field and displacing others from that cultural center. Central scientists are able to diffuse more information to the field more quickly and have the additional structural advantage that their ideas become part of the field that everyone else must learn. Both veterans and newcomers are encouraged to remain abreast of the latest central authors and texts, if only to maintain the field's level of stability and consensus. This is an enormous structural advantage for the central scientists, especially as a field increases in population size and cultural complexity. As the relative number of scientists and (in particular) ideas increase, the chances of any single text becoming a "needle lost in a haystack" also increases. The needle in a haystack phenomenon does not disappear with print—for, even with print, new ideas on average diffuse more slowly as the relative number of scientists and (especially) the number of scientific ideas (Fig. 9.3 and 9.4) increases. At the same time, all ideas can potentially diffuse in a more timely fashion with print. Thus, print may work to mitigate the structural advantage of central scientists and make such sociocultural centrality a property that oscillates across authors fairly rapidly. Eventually, a theory of scientific diffusion needs to reflect the extent to which print causes centrality (a liberal theory of enfranchisement) or allows centrality to dampen the efforts of more peripheral scientists to join the center (a structural theory of disenfranchisement). Despite the importance of the relationship between centrality and print, it is beyond the scope of this book to pursue it further. We simply raise the issue as one deserving of further attention, and we return to how the content and context of a scientific text affect its diffusion within a sociocultural landscape of readers.

The Authorial Handle and Cultural Expansion

According to Ravetz (1971), the reward system of writing in academic science rests on a simple exchange theory: the author shares new ideas with the community in exchange for recognized ownership and property rights to them. Comprehending the terms of this idealized exchange is no small feat; there are no physical records to document its precise terms. Moreover, the objects putatively under exchange are themselves hard to pin down. The author's signature discovery is not a precise fingerprint but a diffuse set of cognitive explorations supported by the social interactions which the author distills into a text (Gilbert & Mulkay, 1984; Latour & Bastide, 1982; Woolgar, 1980). The accounts of these historical goings-on, prior to their distillation into a text reporting the discovery, are virtually always suppressed from the main text of a formal article (Geisler, 1992) and viewed as appropriate to disclose only, if at all, in an acknowledgment section of an article or book. For example, when Dretske (1988) inscribed in the acknowledgments to his book,

> I am, as always, grateful to my colleagues and good friends . . . for their criticisms, their encouragement, and (since I am sure I stole some of them) their ideas. After many years of fruitful exchange, it is sometimes hard to know who thought of something first. So I apologize, in advance, for inadvertent thefts. (p. xi)

he was baring both a truth and a taboo for formal academic reporting while deflecting it with humor (see Derrida, 1988, on the issue of authors and acknowledgments). A central idealization of academic cultures is that discoveries are texts and, despite its diffuse history, the discovery is seen as the author's and the author's alone to barter. The text represents what the author has to offer. In return, the author receives an authorial handle elaborated in the minds of readers, updated to include his or her most recent cultural expansions. This symbolic exchange is what is usually meant by "communicating and establishing priority." What more convenient way to clarify priority than to represent discovery as a single textual product and to make the authorial handle the focal concept around which the author's various texts/discoveries accumulate? Through these complex idealizations and sociocultural alignments, the author's handle becomes a condensation symbol (chap. 5) for cultural expansions.

Most people asked to describe "the author" relate the authorial handle to the significant cultural expansions of only a few luminaries (e.g., Shakespeare, Defoe, and other canonized authors). Within academia, the links between an authorial handle and the new ideas elaborated by the author's text are taken for granted as simple fact. Yet the simple fact is anything but. How does this type of fusion work? We must not take too lightly the remarkable mechanisms of social engineering required to "hard wire" authorial handles to the new ideas in texts. We need only remind ourselves of the thousands of free market authors for whom the most salient information attached to their handle is "died in obscurity" or "wrote three novels." None of these have anything whatever to do with the content of their texts, much less their novel ideas or cultural expansions. Although only a small fraction of academic work is ever actually cited (Cole & Cole, 1973), the linkage between the authorial handle and cultural expansion remains a central assumption of academic writing.

Given the salience of this assumption, we might well ask: What in the organization of academic science determines the extent to which the authorial handle fuses with the author's new ideas as proposed in a text? The answer to this question seems profoundly linked to both the structure of the academic text and the characteristics of the extant sociocultural environment. When a scientist generates a text, that text contains both the new idea and other information, such as (a) the author's name, (b) the name of the journal, (c) citations, (d) assimilated knowledge known generally, and (e) specific elaborations of other scientists' ideas. Other scientists, the intended readers of the text, can learn the new idea as it is related to information they already know via the principle of immediate comprehension. The scientific author, working from this principle, tries to make sure that all non-new or assimilated information in the text helps readers connect with the new and then tie this nexus of new information to the authorial handle.

The distribution of who knows what is culture and who interacts with whom is social structure (chap. 4). It stands to reason, therefore, that the author will better service new ideas by connecting them with assimilated information that is socioculturally central. By making the text appear as a continuation of ideas that are already central, the author puts an onus on readers to interact with the text or risk losing their own current hold on or aspiration to centrality. The trick is engineering the content of the text so that it carries this onus. From this perspective, the genre of the scientific text can be viewed as a piece of knowledge engineering designed to give sociocultural centrality to new ideas. One convention devised to confer this centrality to new ideas is the reference to previous work. Such referencing can be done through a variety of mechanisms (including citations such as "Jones, 1968" and elaborations that detail a previous writer's ideas in the body of the text). By referencing central authors, an author can convey the impression that the cultural expansions proposed in a text are a continuation of both the ideas and people currently central in the field.

Curiously, only a fraction of the literature on text referencing, including citation, featured this highly important function of the textual reference. From the 1960s onward, the majority of the citation literature in information science started in quite a different direction (Garfield, 1955; Price, 1963; see Cronin, 1984, for a history). The original interest in textual reference and citation began with the assumption that commonly cited and elaborated references cast a trail of the intellectual and historical mileposts and achievements of an academic specialty.[5] According to these early theorists of textual referencing, the trail of dominant texts reflected the shared cognitive structure of a discipline. Moreover, making a reference was considered a rational action (e.g., building on an earlier assimilated idea) based on a necessarily true implication (i.e., the author making the reference is cognitively related to the author being referenced). Reference patterns were used to represent a discipline as layers of cognitive bricks mortared together to produce a common intellectual culture (Cronin, 1984; McInnis & Symes, 1989, p. 391; Price, 1963; Weinstock, 1971).

The research on referencing since the mid-1970s steadily eroded the view of references as disciplinary bricklaying. There was a suspicion that, rather than emblematizing the cognitive bricks of a field, frequently cited and elaborated texts are more often placeholders, simply lending an academic specialty the appearance of being built from related bricks. Instead of reflecting common cognition and culture, Moravscik and Murugesan (1975) and Chubin and Moitra (1975) conducted research suggesting that frequently cited and elaborated references reflect more about the discourse and social structure of a field than about its pure cognitive structure. For example, they found that the majority of scientific citations in their sample have perfunctory rather than substantive value. Authors included them to fulfill the requirements of the literature review more than to represent their intellectual precursors. In a couple of influential articles, Gilbert (1976, 1977) suggested that authors used citations as two-way persuasive resources, elevating the work into scientific knowledge by citing it, and then using the elevated authority of the cited source to boost the authority of one's own work. In further support of the social function of citations, MacRoberts and MacRoberts (1986) documented many citation practices that have social but negligible intellectual and historical value, including:

- hat-tipping citations (acknowledgment of eminent figures),
- overdetailed references,
- overelaborate reporting,
- evidentiary validity (references can support any view),
- citing currently popular research trends (for funding purposes),
- conspiratorial crossreferencing,

---

[5]This assumption is currently called into question by work that examines intraspecialty citation and its relationship to the emergence of scientific specialties (Carley, Hummon, & Harty, 1991; Hummon & Carley, in press).

- pandering to pressure (citing work only because it's expected),
- nonrecognition of new authors (overlooking),
- intraprofessional feuding,
- obsolete citations,
- political considerations (citing the party line), or
- citing work in preparation (or just planned).

To a large extent, such research has overthrown the purely cognitive model of references, or at least the idea that the practice of frequently citing and elaborating references is itself evidence of a high level of cultural integration within an academic discipline. The social theory coming to replace it averred that the function of references is to reflect high levels of social interaction within a discipline, even if that interaction has little to do with cumulative science (Morman, 1981). In support of this view of references, Carley, Hummon, and Harty (1991) and Hummon and Carley (in press) found that scientific accumulation had more to do with patterns of citation across texts than with the citation frequency of individual texts.

Yet a lingering problem with both the older (cognitive) and the newer (social) view of references is that both views underrepresent the role of reference as action tying together rhetorical design with sociocultural reach. Theorists in both the old and new traditions of textual reference start with the premise that references reflect something about an academic specialty (i.e., intellectual history or social structure). But they do not focus on how an author employs references in order to do something that matters to the reach of the referencing text and that can exert increased authority based upon this reach. In brief, references have been viewed mainly as a device reflecting an existing cognitive or social order rather than as a device for helping the referencing text (and the author designing it) to gain authority over that order.

One of the few investigators to view references from the special vantage of sociocultural reach was Small (1978). Small hypothesized that in some scientific specialties, textual references allow authors to reference the cultural expansions of (prominent) authors simply by citing their texts. To test this hypothesis, Small identified 52 of the most highly referenced articles in a specialty of chemistry over a period of a few years. He further identified some 600 articles that referenced these 52 articles over a slightly longer period of time. Small measured how often the site of the reference in the referencing text included a mention of the new idea(s) for which the author was widely known. For example, for the highly referenced author Stewart, who was well known for his work on the hydrogen scattering factor, Small calculated the percentage of the texts referencing Stewart's paper that also included the exact or approximate elaboration "hydrogen scattering factor" at the site of the reference. Across all the referencing and referenced texts, Small calculated the overall consistency of mentions for referenced ideas in this specialty to be very high—87%. Small's results indicated that, for some disciplines and some prominent (highly referenced) texts, referencing authors can use their references to these texts as efficient standard symbols or terms of art (chap. 5) for culturally central ideas. Small referred to such standard symbols as *concept symbols*.

Small's work provided empirical confirmation that authorial handles can become fused to cultural expansions in scientific specialties in the minds of the specialists and that referencing authors can take advantage of the fusion for efficient reference. Small, however, did not provide a developmental or rhetorical explanation of this fusion; he did not explain how it was possible for less prominent authors to evolve such a fusion over time. Lacking a developmental or rhetorical account, Small did not explain how the fusion of the authorial handle and the author's new ideas could be a dynamic achievement of an author seeking authority within an academic specialty, not simply a static fact about a specialty. Small further missed opportunities, beyond the obvious and important factor of quality, to explain how individuals might be differentially successful, over time, in implementing the fusion of their handle with their new ideas across a culture of their peers. He saw the referencing and referenced texts as sociocultural realities reflecting reach, but he did not link these realities or this reach to the rhetorical designs and aspirations of the referencing author. We now turn to an original developmental/rhetorical account of textual reference that makes these links more explicit.

Toward a Theory of Engineered Reach

A developmental/rhetorical theory and model of textual reference, consistent with the constructural framework, is explicable within a larger theory of the academic text. The theory is based on four complementary assumptions:

1. Textual reference is not an autonomous phenomenon but one of several tactics an author of an academic text can use to assist in the communication and establishment of priority claims.

2. The problem of communicating and establishing priority is foremost a problem of diffusion. The author has a text (whose content reports a discovery) and the author's problem is to get the text in the hands of the "right" readers, those most culturally and socially central within the

profession, to speed its diffusion to the whole discipline. The author disposes of this concern by insuring that the text meets the criterion of relative similarity with preferred readers and by insuring that the text is similar enough to these readers (relative to other texts) for them to want to learn about it and to continue to talk or write about it or (if they are an editor) to publish it.

3. The author can encourage diffusion by exploiting the principle of immediate comprehension to maximum personal advantage when constructing a text. According to the principle of immediate comprehension, readers can assimilate new information only if they can integrate it with information they already know. From the author's standpoint, this principle suggests that, as much as possible, the author should link the new ideas in the text with assimilated ideas readers already know. The greater the linkage the author is able to effect when composing the text, the greater the chances the text will diffuse to readers in general, including preferred ones. We do not suggest that scientists consciously explore the space of all textual choices to maximize the text's expected diffusion potential. Rather, we suggest that the text's diffusion potential is a function of the text's content as well as the particular sociocultural landscape through which the text circulates. If scientific authors are rhetorically minded, they can influence at least certain aspects of this function by monitoring their composing choices.

4. The author of the academic text has four resources to draw upon when composing a text that can be used to create linkages between assimilated and new ideas. The first two resources—citation and elaboration—represent content-based and highly specialized types of assimilated knowledge, designed to help the author adjust the textual content to maximize its linkage to a known literature. Citations are references that increase the diffusion potential of a text because they relate the textual content to the new ideas of other authors in the field. Elaborations are sentences within a text that expand more fully than citations upon the new ideas of prior texts. Elaborations work to increase diffusion potential, much as citations do. Elaborations, however, are more complete descriptions of what is contained in a referenced text than a simple citation itself. If every citation site (e.g., Chomsky, 1959) functioned as a standard symbol—or concept symbol in Small's (1978) sense, a concept that readers could elaborate in much the same way (e.g., the work to introduce transformational grammar)—then authors, in principle, would not need to elaborate their references to other texts when they cited them. However, few citations are standard symbols in this strong sense. Thus, when authors want to control the linkages between their text and a previous author's text, they often need to rely on elaborations as well as citations to strengthen the linkage. The author's third and

fourth resources are context resources. These include the author's level of prominence in the field and the prominence of the journal in which the author's manuscript is printed. When an author is prominent in a scientific discipline, readers in that and related subdisciplines are likely to know about him or her through the author's ideas, name, or both. The expected reach of a text can increase based solely on the author's prior prominence. Finally, journals can themselves be prominent, having wide or important readerships if their readers are geographically well dispersed or centrally connected to a specialty. Prominence of both the author and the journal combine with citation and elaboration to increase the diffusion potential of the text.

Given these four assumptions, we now consider the relationship between a text's content and its diffusion potential. Every scientific article contains the name of the author, the journal, a set of citations and elaborations, and the author's new idea(s), that is, the proposed cultural expansions within the specialty. On the strength of the principle of immediate comprehension, readers can latch onto and acquire these new ideas on the minimal assumption that they can also recognize something in the author's name, the name of the journal in which the text is published, at least one of the citations, or at least one of the elaborations included in the text. Diffusion of the new ideas in the text simply will not happen for readers who hold none of these pieces of assimilated knowledge. We have parlayed this basic observation into a simple mathematical (not a simulation) model predicting the expected reach of a scientific text within a specialty. This model, which we refer to as a model of engineered reach, is presented and examined in detail in Carley and Kaufer (1990) and we review it in somewhat less detail here.

Let K be the probability that individuals in an academic specialty are familiar with any given idea. We can think of K as a measure of cultural integration within the specialty. The greater K is, the more likely it is that the average reader in the specialty will recognize some arbitrary idea elaborated in the author's text that originates in the work of a previous author. Conversely, the probability that a reader will not recognize some arbitrary idea elaborated from a previous author's work is $1-K$. Let E be the number of elaborations in the text. If we hypothesize that not knowing one idea is independent of not knowing another, then $(1-K)^E$ is the probability that the reader will not recognize any of the elaborations of other authors' work in the text.

Similarly, let S be the probability that individuals in an academic specialty are familiar with one another by name. We can think of S as a measure of the degree of social interaction and social homogeneity within the specialty. The greater S is, the more likely it is that the average reader in the specialty will recognize some author whose work is referenced in the text. The probability that a reader will not recognize some arbitrary referenced author is $1 - S$. Let us further assume, for simplicity, that referencing a prominent author is like referencing multiple nonprominent authors. If we treat prominence as a linear ranking (such as 1,2,3,4, . . .), then this assumption suggests that referencing an author with a prominence of 5 is, in terms of expected reach, comparable to citing 5 authors with a prominence of 1.

Let C be the sum of the prominence of the authors cited in the text (if no authors are prominent, then C is just the number of citations in the text). If we then hypothesize that not knowing one person is independent of not knowing another, then $(1 - S)^C$ is the probability that the reader will not recognize any of the authors whose work is cited in the text.

Let P be the probability that the reader knows the author and J the probability that the reader knows the journal. We can think of P and J as indicating the author's current level of prominence and the current prominence of the journal, respectively.

Let R be the probability that the reader will acquire the new ideas in a text, given that all the necessary connections between assimilated ideas and these new ideas have been established.

Given these definitions, we can say that the reader within the specialty will not acquire an author's new idea just in case the reader does not know any of the elaborations $(1 - K)^E$, does not know any of the authors cited $(1 - S)^C$, does not know the author $(1 - P)$, and does not know of the journal $(1 - J)$. The probability of acquiring the new idea, in turn, is one minus this probability, or:

$$R = 1 - [(1 - K)^E * (1 - S)^C * (1 - P) * (1 - J)] \qquad (9.1)$$

Equation 9.1 clarifies the complementary roles citation and elaboration play in influencing diffusion. Consider the extreme cases where citing authors (citations) as a rhetorical tactic clearly enhances diffusion more than citing ideas (elaborations), and vice versa. Imagine an intellectual community whose members are culturally integrated but socially diffuse (i.e., high K, low S). This is a common occurrence in a field with a substantive intellectual agenda but practitioners that are geographically and institutionally dispersed across many fields and subfields, who attend few common conventions. This is the field we imagined writing to when we sat down to compose this book. Our field consists of mathematical theorists of diffusion, communication theorists, sociologists and historians of science, rhetorical theorists, sociologists of professions, social and cultural theorists, composition theorists, and literary postmodernists! This field is deeply related at the ideational level (as we have suggested from the preface) but not at all related as a social entity of interacting persons.

In such a case, the writers are more likely to see their ideas reaching more readers by elaborating them in depth than by trying to drop "key" names in citations.

Now imagine the mirror image environment, one with little overlap in ideas but high in its level of social interaction (i.e., low K, high S). This is a common occurrence in fields that are institutionally but not intellectually integrated. Members of such fields regularly attend the same conferences and know one another by name; but they often have little intellectual overlap and think and write in different styles for entirely different journals. In such an environment, dropping highly recognized names through citation is likely to remain a more effective tactic for circulating a document with wide expected reach than trying to elaborate ideas across deep intellectual chasms.

These examples, drawn from Equation 9.1, indicate that exploiting shared ideas through many elaborations (i.e., high E) can compensate for the loss of expected reach incurred by a text when its author faces an environment of readers who know little about one another (i.e., low S). Moreover, exploiting social ties through brief but multiple citations (i.e., high C) can compensate for the loss of expected reach incurred by a text when its author faces an environment of readers who share few ideas in common (i.e., low K). Of course, in most of the environments scientific authors face, K and S will have nonextreme values and both will play a part in contributing to a text's expected reach, as Equation 9.1 predicts. Equation 9.1 makes a series of further predictions about the expected reach of a text within a specialty of readers. We mention only a few to illustrate the new perspective offered by this model. Such predictions include:

1. The greater the cultural integration, the more internal elaborations in the text will help extend its reach to readers.

2. The greater the social homogeneity, the more citations in the text will help extend its reach to readers, regardless of the textual content.

3. Authors with low prominence need to expend more rhetorical effort, in terms of the number of citations and elaborations, in constructing the text to get the same reach as authors with high prominence expending less effort.

In an exploratory study, Carley and Kaufer (1990) tested the validity of this model. They investigated the relative diffusion of seven different texts produced by scientists in the specialty of "social networks" in sociology. They chose this specialty because an earlier survey, to which they had access, contained data that could be used to estimate the degree of cultural integration (K), social homogeneity (S), and author prominence

(*P*). In the survey questionnaire, respondents were asked, among other things, to indicate, for each of the "official"[6] members of specialty, whether or not they had heard of that person, what journals they read, and which members of the specialty they considered prominent, both in the early 1970s (when social network theory was emerging as a discrete specialization within sociology) and in the late 1980s (when the survey was administered) and was settling into the stage of normal science (Hummon & Carley, in press). There were 109 respondents to the questionnaire.

Carley and Kaufer (1990) estimated the level of cultural integration, *K*, as the proportion of the respondents who read the key journal of the specialty—*Social Networks*. Although not ideal, perhaps, this measure is nonetheless indicative of shared knowledge (i.e., individuals who read the same journal are more likely to share the same knowledge). Using this measure, they calculated *K* as .29. They estimated the level of social homogeneity, *S*, as the average number of respondents who had heard of an official member of the specialty, divided by the number of respondents. Using this measure, *S* is .08. In calculating prominence scores, they used the proportion of respondents who listed this person as important in the specialty of social networks in the early 1970s.

From the list of official members, they selected six authors who had published papers in the social network specialty in the early 1970s. These authors were chosen because their prominence rankings varied and each of the six had authored at least one article in the early 1970s. For one author, Burt, they chose two articles published in the early 1970's. They chose two texts from a single author to compare how well their model could discriminate the diffusion of an article independent of its author. For the remaining five authors, a single article was examined. The authors and their texts were:

Alba, R. (1973). A graph-theoretic definition of a sociometric clique. *Journal of Mathematical Sociology*, 113–126.

Burt, R. S. (1973a). Confirmatory factor-analytic structures and the theory construction process. *Sociological Methods and Research*, *2*(2), 131–190.

Burt, R. S. (1973b). The differential impact of social integration on participation in the diffusion of innovation. *Social Science Research*, *2*, 125–144.

---

[6]Official members are defined as the 450 individuals who were paid members of the International Network for Social Network Analysis (INSNA) mailing list or had been at one of the two Sunbelt Social network conferences prior to the administration of the questionnaire.

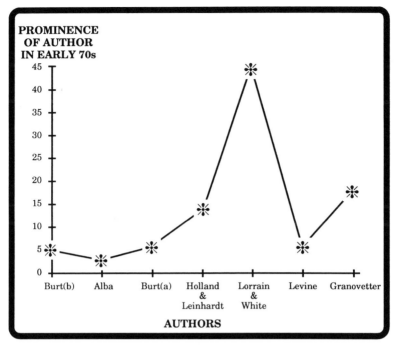

FIG. 9.6.   Prominence rankings of authors in the early 1970s.

Granovetter, M. S. (1973). The strength of weak ties. *American Journal of Sociology*, *78*, 1360–1378.

Holland, P. W. & Leinhardt, S. (1970). A method for detecting structure in sociometric data, *American Journal of Sociology*, *76*(3), 492–513.

Levine, J. H. (1972). The sphere of influence. *American Sociological Review*, *37*, 14–27.

Lorrain, F. & White, H. (1971). Structural equivalence of individuals in social networks, *Journal of Mathematical Sociology*, *1*, 49–80.

We begin by displaying the parameters of the model for each author in the Carley and Kaufer (1990) study in Fig. 9.6 through 9.9. In Fig. 9.6, we display the prominence rankings of these authors in the early 1970s. The number on the Y axis refers to the number of researchers in the specialty who judged the individual prominent as of 1971. These numbers, divided by 109, fill in the P values in Equation 9.1. When there are multiple authors, author prominence is defined as the sum of the prominence of the co-authors. In Fig. 9.7, we display the journal's prominence. The number on the Y axis refers to the scaled ranking of the journal, based on the published ranking of journals in sociology as calculated by Burt

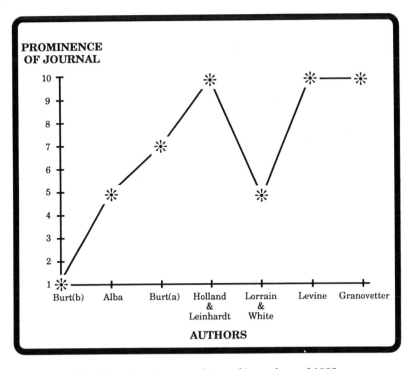

FIG. 9.7. Prominence rankings of journals as of 1982.

(1982). The journal rankings by Burt were spread out across a scale of 1 to 10. The prominence of the text was then defined as that rank divided by 20. The value 20 was chosen on the assumption that the probability of reading a journal article merely because it occurred in the most prominent of journals was about one half (.5). These numbers, divided by 20, fill in the J values in Equation 9.1. In Fig. 9.8, effort rankings for each of the authors in the sample are shown.[7] For each text, the number of citations (circles) and elaborations (stars) are plotted separately. Effort (circled star) is the sum of the number of citations and elaborations. The number of elaborations fill in the E values in Equation 9.1. In Fig. 9.9, the cumulative prominence of all cited authors is displayed. The citation prominence score for a text is computed by summing the prominence scores of all authors cited in each text. This number fills in the C value in Equation 9.1. Figure 9.10 shows the cumulative diffusion or reach of the authors as measured by the Social Science Citation Index. The final cumulative citation value as of 1983 is used to test Equation 9.1. Granovetter would be number 1 in this rank, having the largest

_____

[7]The length of the journal (in numbers of pages) was also added to the overall effort rating.

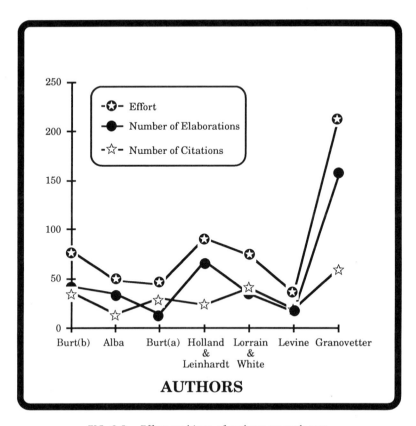

FIG. 9.8.   Effort rankings of authors on each text.

cumulative reach, and Burt (1973b), number 7, with the least. These figures demonstrate that the texts vary in content and reach.

In Fig. 9.6, 9.8, and 9.9, the authoring scientists are ordered by their actual reach in 1983, so that Burt (1973b) had the least reach (i.e., least cited) and Granovetter, the greatest reach (i.e., most cited). The ordering in these figures indicates that none of the following, taken alone, predict the reach of an author's text: (a) the level of an author's prominence, (b) the journal's prominence, (c) the sheer volume of citations or elaborations in the author's text, or (d) the author's citations weighted by the prominence of the authors cited.

To test the plausibility of the engineered reach model (Equation 9.1) we estimate the predicted diffusion, given the values in Fig. 8.6 through 8.9, and the estimates of K and S. This generates a rank order in terms of which text was expected to have the greatest/least reach. Based on the actual diffusion data (Fig. 8.10), the actual rank order is calculated.

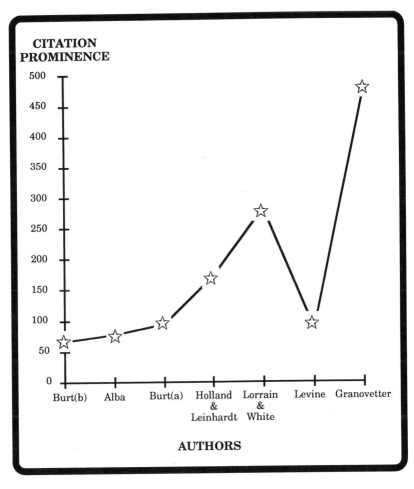

FIG. 9.9.   Prominence of citation scores for each text.

Figure 9.11 plots the difference between the actual rank of the articles (based on their cumulative diffusion or citation rate as of 1983) and the predicted rank (based on Equation 9.1). There are several points of importance: 1. The predicted rank is very robust. Wide variations in either, or both, K and S (which are the variables with the weakest measures) result in the same ranking. 2. The distance in the vertical dimension, Y, in Fig. 9.11 corresponds to the relative level of actual or predicted ranking. 3. As a result, Fig. 9.11 indicates more than that the model correctly predicts the absolute rankings of the diffusion (citation) level for five of the seven cases.

The model also captures many of the observed differences in diffu-

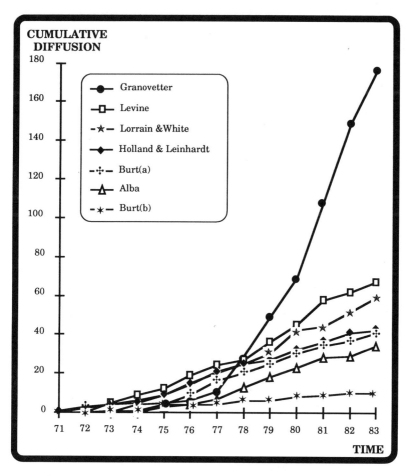

FIG. 9.10.   Cumulative actual reach of each text from 1971 to 1983 as
measured through citations.

sion (citation) levels between any two articles. For example, the model
correctly predicts that Granovetter is the author/article that will achieve
the highest diffusion; it also correctly predicts that his article will exceed
the reach of any other author/article by a very wide spread. Similarly,
the model correctly predicts that the Holland and Leinhardt article will
achieve greater diffusion than the Burt(a) article. Moreover, it correctly
predicts that there will be a very narrow spread in the diffusion (citation) rates of these articles. We should note that the two cases that are
not correctly predicted (Alba and Levine) are underpredicted. Carley and
Kaufer (1990) elaborated reasons for these mispredictions and we need
only mention them in a cursory way here. In brief, underpredictions of

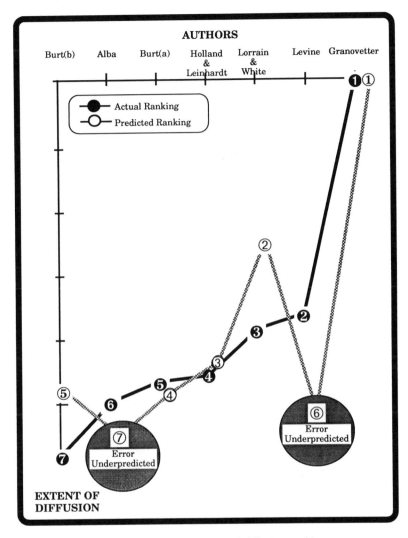

FIG. 9.11.   Predicted and actual diffusion rankings.

a text's reach (like Levine and Alba's) suggest that there may be content features not captured by Equation 9.1. For want of a better word, we might think of these unspecified content factors as having to do with "quality," but this category obviously needs to be broken down further. Finally, we should note that the reach of Alba, although underpredicted, is still in the right ballpark. In contrast, Levine's reach is grossly underpredicted.

This study, though exploratory, suggests that the model of engineered reach in a scientific specialty may have predictive power, at least for the single domain in which it is applied. Needless to say, more refined models must be developed on much larger samples and across many specialities before any firm generalizations can be made.

Nonetheless, we feel that the basic direction taken by this model, aligning information about the prominence of a scientific author, the author's rhetorical design of a text, and the sociocultural reach of that text within a specialty area, is fundamentally sound and provides a more complete understanding of the role of textual reference and citation in scientific specialities than previous approaches to reference and citation.

IMPLICATIONS

The study of science as a social system cut through its portrait as a purely cognitive, rational, and blissful enterprise long ago. Science is none of that, but then, neither is it wholly random, irrational, or based in opportunistic politics. Rather, like other aspects of social life, science is rooted in mechanisms determining the co-evolution of cognition and sociocultural interaction. Because of inherent uncertainties and tensions in this co-evolution, scientific organization is heavily dependent on the content of scientific texts to construct new realities. Despite new technologies, the scientific text has remained fairly stable as the preferred medium for establishing priority since the 17th century. Part of the reason clearly lies in the fact that texts are unalterable and archivable documents. Based on the simulation results on professions (chap. 8) and the historical record, we see further that textual conventions can help enforce stability in the academic profession in the face of new ideas that would otherwise make scientists less alike and loosen their sense of belonging to a common enterprise.

The simulation results in this chapter as well as the historical record indicate two additional reasons, both centered on the timely diffusion of new ideas, that written texts have remained a medium of choice for scientific communication:

1. Changing conditions in science (whether by choice or accident) created an environment where scientists could benefit from the rapid diffusion of discoveries afforded by print. Science itself has grown more "virtual" in its organizational structure. Scientific enclaves have become less prototypical and cohesive in their make-up. The body of scientific knowledge has grown. Science has come to claim more members in absolute terms while fragmenting into more complex and differentiated subcultures, leaving each subculture smaller relative to the whole than it was

before. All of these factors helped science attain the type of sociocultural configuration in which print (and newer electronic technologies) could have maximum relative effect in insuring that new ideas reach the greatest number of the right people in the most timely fashion. These sociocultural conditions, further, reduce the possibility that new ideas will reach the right people in timely fashion by simply relying on proximity and word of mouth. One research area to pursue, based on this result, is how much electronically aided print (e.g., electronic mail and bulletin boards) benefits the diffusion of new ideas to the right people, over print alone.

2. The scientific text has evolved, through conventions of prominence, elaboration, and citation, to a form that allows authors to engineer the diffusion of their ideas to the scientific community. Engineering a text enables the new idea not simply to diffuse (and establish priority) but to diffuse to the right people and establish prominence. The story of science becomes not only the story of new ideas but the story of the development of rhetorical behaviors and social structures conducive to carrying these ideas as far as possible and to elevating the stature of their author by carrying them to the right people. Future research along these lines might consider the extent to which scientists consciously engineer their texts and the implications of such conscious engineering for social and cultural change within science.

CHAPTER TEN

Migration and
Authority

*In science, a strong interest in disciplines outside one's specialty
correlates with distinction as a researcher. At best, a certain rather
high minimum is needed [to achieve in science] but once over that
hump the chance of becoming a scientist of high achievement
seems almost random. Of noted quality is a certain gift of
mavericity, [a] property of making unusual associations.*
—D. K. Simonton (1988, p. 43)

In the lore of the sociology of knowledge, the authors traditionally associated with the most authority and change are not rooted within a single intellectual community. Instead, they are authors on the move, the
maverick, the eccentric, the outsider, the intellectual migrant, trained in
one community and rising to fame after finding their way to another.
Travel has become a shibboleth for the authors who are supposed to exert the most authority in intellectual communities. The lore of the migrant
arises from the mystique of the nomad, itinerant, or stranger in the strange
land—Mr. Smith in Washington—who, innocent and guileless, stumbles
into a new locale and ends up amazing the local sophisticates by cutting
through the paralyzing assumptions to which they had long been re-
signed. Some sociologists have offered reasons why migrants are better
equipped than locals to revolutionize an intellectual community. Simmel
(1950, p. 402; also cited in Gieryn & Hirsch, 1983, p. 87), for example,
argued that the stranger is better equipped because he or she is not en-
slaved by the community's local biases, stereotypes, and narrow habits
of inference.

394

MIGRANCY AND INNOVATION

In *The Social Process of Innovation*, Mulkay (1973) elevated the lore of the migrant to theory. He argued that the basic condition of scientific innovation was one not so much of new ideas moving within networks of scientists but rather of scientists themselves moving into new networks. According to Mulkay, innovation in science results from the inherent instability of local scientific networks. Such networks are inherently unstable, he observed, for a variety of reasons: as scientists begin to solve their problems, they see that the problems they are pursuing are not solvable; or they lose interest as new problems appear on the horizon. Eventually the focal concerns holding together a network of scientists erode, the cultural and social ties in the old network weaken, and scientists form new networks based on new foci. Mulkay suggested that the large "disjunctures" or "revolutions" in scientific work arise not because new ideas overwhelm a resistant orthodoxy (as Kuhn (1970) maintained) but because new people are pursuing those ideas, people with different backgrounds, a different intellectual outlook, and a way of seeing problems that differs from their predecessors:

> [M]any instances of scientific innovation are marked not by arduous intellectual redefinition but by intellectual migration followed by the modified application of existing techniques and theories within a different area. Similarly, many innovations take the form of a discovery of a new area of ignorance which has not previously been defined at all and [within which], consequently, there is no clearly established orthodoxy and little resistance to the emergence of new ideas. (p. 35)

Following upon Mulkay's insights, Edge and Mulkay (1976) published the most substantive contribution to date on the importance of migrancy to intellectual innovation and authority. Their subject was the historical rise of radio astronomy. As early as 1873, based on Maxwell and Hertz's equations, physicists had been aware of the possibility that radio waves were emitted from extraterrestrial objects. In the absence of a broad theory and the technical apparatus to pursue further work in the area, the problem was ignored in physics and astronomy. The problem was, however, pursued fortuitously by a "stranger," Karl Jansky, an engineer who in 1930 was employed by the Bell System to troubleshoot the static and interfering noises that were degrading the performance of Bell's transoceanic radio–telephone circuits. In 1932, Jansky tracked the source of the noise to outer space and published his finding in a journal read by radio engineers who had little appreciation of the importance of the discovery to academic astronomy. According to Edge and Mulkay's history, Jansky was one of many outsiders to push radio astronomy to a mature subspecialty within astronomy. Edge and Mulkay conclude that migrants had been at the forefront of innovative work in that specialty throughout. In the final chapter of their book, Edge and Mulkay explored, in a larger context, the relationship of migrancy to intellectual authority. They reviewed a set of previous studies which traced the rise of a specific scientific specialty. These prior studies included:

- Gilbert's (1976) study of the rise of radar meteor research;
- Fisher's (1967) study of the rise of mathematical logic in the late 19th century;
- Mullins' (1972; 1980) study of the rise of microbiology in the 1930s;
- Ben-David's (1960) study of bacteriology and psychoanalysis;
- Ben-David and Collins' (1966) study of experimental psychology;
- Zloczower's (1966) study of scientific medicine in Germany;
- Dolby's (1975) study of physical chemistry;
- Law's (1973) study of x-ray protein crystallography.

Edge and Mulkay (1976, p. 382) defined several dimensions along one or more of which the development of these specialties vary. For example, these specialties:

1. Developed in an applied setting removed from academic discussion (radio astronomy, radar meteor research).
2. Congealed into proximate working groups immediately following the discovery context (radio astronomy, experimental psychology, microbiology, physical chemistry.
3. Exchanged information with an orthodoxy about the discovery context (radio astronomy).
4. Continued to perceive a cognitive overlap between themselves and the orthodoxy (radio astronomy).
5. Found themselves in a conflictual situation with the orthodoxy (physiology, experimental psychology, microbiology, physical chemistry, x-ray crystallography.
6. Initiated a new journal immediately following the discovery context (physiology, microbiology, physical chemistry).
7. Saw themselves as an "integral" specialty comprising a self-contained audience for their work (experimental psychology, microbiology).
8. Had established themselves as a specialty prior to establishing their specialty as "scientific" (experimental psychology).

9. Congealed into a specialty because career mobility in a parent discipline had been blocked (experimental psychology—which, in the 19th century, consisted of immigrants from philosophy who retooled in physiology and experimental science).

Despite this range of variation, Edge and Mulkay (1976) identified three factors that always seemed to attend the rise of the new specialization. Two of these factors involved (1) an eventual, if not immediate, academic home to legitimize the work and (2) the graduate students to perpetuate the work. A third constant they found was mobility and migrancy. Edge and Mulkay reported that in every case, the innovators, the authors responsible for the most change from the old order to the new, enjoyed mobility across networks, which enabled them to view the network of innovation from an outsider's, as well as an insider's, vantage.

Given the apparent robustness of Edge and Mulkay's (1976) finding for the relationship between migrancy and innovation, it is not surprising that others have sought to extend it beyond the sociology of scientific innovation. Citing Edge and Mulkay's work, Archer (1988, p. 220) claimed that migration is essential to political innovation and attributed the prominence and peculiar modern appearance of political leaders like Peter the Great and Catherine I—who toured the centers of Europe to bring home the latest information about military equipment, ship design, and education—to their early understanding of the importance of travel to leadership. Simonton (1988, p. 43) adapted a variant of the migrant thesis to explain the cognition of scientific creativity. He did not speak of migration (travel) per se as much as the "strange" frame of mind— mavericity—typically associated with the innovative migrant. More specifically, as indicated in the epitaph of this chapter, he claimed that innovation requires a "certain gift of mavericity, [a] property of making unusual associations" that is usually found by diversifying one's experiences.

DEFINITIONAL PROBLEMS OF MIGRANCY

As the migrant thesis broadened, its lack of definitional coherence has also become apparent. One can cynically predict, even before overturning the stones of an innovator's past, a record of travel to be reported and a compelling migration yarn waiting to be spun. The cynic wonders how innovation can be milked from migrancy. Everyone's past includes travel. No one, after all, is born an insider. If youth and callowness are characteristics of migrancy and marginality, the cynic wonders, on the strength of the migrant thesis, why the gift of cultural innovativeness does not grace us all. The cynicism is brought to the fore in Gieryn and Hirsh's (1983) critique of the migrant thesis or what they called the Marginalization Hypothesis. They pointed out (pp. 100–106) that if "marginal" is as broadly defined as "outsider" (meaning, variously, "a recent member of the community," "having extraneous or unusual training," "located at a peripheral or out of the way research site," "located outside the university"), then marginal status is too vague a concept to be a reliable predictor of innovative behavior.

To test this observation empirically, Gieryn and Hirsch (1983) collected a sample of 97 researchers in the field of x-ray astronomy. Using measures of innovativeness defended in their research, they classified 34 of these scientists as highly innovative and the remaining 64 as noninnovative. They then applied multiple-criteria measures of marginal status to each of these scientists to determine the extent to which marginal status, taken as a single variable or pooled across many variables, affected their status as innovators. Their first finding indicated few correlations among the measures they had initially used to operationalize the term marginal. They further found that all scientists in their sample were marginal on some factors (e.g., "young" and "recent member of the intellectual community") but nonmarginal (e.g., "published," "at a major school") on others. Their second finding was that, even when pooled, the various measures for marginal status contributed to only 20% of the variance in innovation. Gieryn and Hirsch concluded that marginals are no more likely to arrive at important innovations than nonmarginals—due in no small part to the fact that marginal is itself not an internally consistent designation.

In a reply to their article, Simonton (1984, p. 621) argued that accounting for 20% of the variance in innovation through migration factors was an impressive showing: "When one considers all the factors that probably influence scientific creativity, to have marginality explain this amount verges on the astonishing." In a second reply, Handberg (1984, p. 623) criticized Gieryn and Hirsh's measures, claiming that marginal status is a psychological concept (more closely approximating mavericity) and is better tapped through survey research than bibliometric data. In response to their critics, Gieryn and Hirsh (1984, p. 624) stand by their original results: "The hypothesis that marginality causes scientific innovation becomes trivially true [since] the biography of any innovative scientist is almost certain to include at least one attribute that indicates marginality."

Taken on their own terms, Gieryn and Hirsh (1983) are certainly right. Migration and marginality are not well-defined concepts; nor is innovation, for that matter. A thesis that causally relates one to the other is hardly as informative as one would like. But while the finding that the marginality—or migration—thesis is ill-formed has bite, it still misses what has been interesting all along about linking marginality (or, as we prefer, migration) to innovation. What makes the thesis so alluring is precisely that we know it is not universally true, yet it is probably more than coincidental. All of us travel, but for some the journey has a "magic chemistry" that leads to cultural productions that would not have been possible without the trip. The challenge underlying the migration thesis is to elicit the interplay of factors that turn travel into innovation, that turn authorial migration into visible authorial authority and change. We need to ask under what conditions the author's travel to a new intellectual community might weight the odds in favor of increased authority. There are possible answers not optimally framed within a constructural framework. Many conditions of intellectual migrancy are market driven and not easily captured by the primitives of knowledge and interaction. For example, there was cognitive overlap and proximity between 19th-century philosophy and the migrant field of experimental psychology, but no market structure within philosophy to keep the new experimentalists from splitting apart (Zloczower, 1966). Nonetheless, a surprisingly large number of migrant cases can be investigated as outcomes of the co-evolution of knowledge diffusion and social interaction. Dividing the sociocultural landscape into the migrant's source and target fields, we examine the conditions which do or do not contribute to the migrant's ability to effect change. Although many researchers acknowledge the importance of sociocultural variables to the diffusion of new information and its impacts on changing networks of interaction (Rapoport, 1953), few have actually examined the relationship (Rogers, 1982, p. 25; Katz, Levin & Hamilton, 1963). Research has demonstrated that the sociocultural integration of the adopter affects when the adoption of new ideas occurs (Becker, 1970; Burt, 1980; Coleman, Katz, & Menzel, 1966; Johnson, 1986; Lin & Burt, 1975; Menzel, 1960), but few have examined whether the overall sociocultural landscape and the relative position of the innovator make a difference to innovation. Even fewer have considered the role of the communication technology in the diffusion process and its interrelationship with the structure of the sociocultural landscape (Carley, with Wendt, 1991; Freeman, 1984; Rice, 1987; Rice & Case, 1983).

POSITIONING THE MIGRANT AUTHOR

We position the migrant author within societies composed of 12 individuals who are divided across two academic specialties. The society has a moderately complex culture of 20 ideas, of which 10 are associated with each specialty. The migrant is an individual who is culturally integrated with both specialties (i.e., the migrant shares some information with both groups). The migrant individual is a true hybrid specialist, knowing two ideas characteristic of each group and also one piece of new knowledge. This innovative piece of new knowledge is known only by the migrant. One specialty is the source specialty; the other is the target specialty, among whose members the migrant seeks increased interaction, integration, and authority.

Both the source and target specialties can vary in the level of initial integration among their members (low = 4% shared knowledge; moderate = 16%; or high = 69%). Moreover, the society may vary in terms of the overlap between the two groups. Members of the source and target specialties, other than the migrant, can share some of the other specialty's knowledge, and the degree to which such sharing occurs varies by society. Three levels of cultural overlap between specialties are explored (low = 1%; moderate = 4%; high = 16%). The lower the cultural overlap, the more specialized the two specialties vis-à-vis each other. Harkening back to chapter 8, the more integrated and specialized the specialty, the more prototypically professional. We examine three levels of integration for both specialty and target and three for overlap; there are 27 sociocultural landscapes being considered.

In addition, we examine three technological conditions:

1. The first condition is an oral society with only one-to-one interaction. This is an important condition to study because migration involves the movement of people rather than disembodied ideas. It is therefore important to consider the migrant hypothesis from the point of view of face-to-face communication.

2. The second condition is an oral society with a single printing press, belonging only to the migrant. The migrant can thus communicate through a text, but all other individuals in the source and target specialty communicate one-to-one.

3. The third condition is a universal print condition where all individuals in the society communicate through texts in one-to-many fashion.

The effect of each technological condition relative to each sociocultural landscape is considered. The various societal conditions explored through simulation are summarized in Table 10.1. We examine the effect of each technological condition in each of the 27 sociocultural landscapes.

In all cases, we focus on the length of time it takes the migrant's new idea to diffuse to members of the target specialty. This focus keeps in view the romantic allure of the migrant—the capacity of the migrant to spread new ideas to the target specialty while not being, initially at least, highly central to that specialty. By maintaining this focus across a wide

TABLE 10.1
Characteristics of Societies Examined

Sociocultural Landscape	Technological Condition		
	Oral	Migrant has print	All have print
Source specialty integration	Low	Medium	High
Target specialty integration	Low	Medium	High
Overlap between specialties	Low	Medium	High

variety of technological conditions and sociocultural landscapes, we are more likely to gain a better understanding of the conditions under which the migrant hypothesis might have logical plausibility.

An Integrated Source Specialty and the Migrant's Authority

As one might expect, the technological condition makes a difference in the time required for the migrant to diffuse a new idea to the target specialty. With only personal communication, the diffusion is slow. When the migrant has access to print, diffusion is faster; when everyone has access to print, it is faster still. Through its multiplicity, print encourages faster direct diffusion, which accounts for the more rapid diffusion of the migrant's new idea when he or she alone has access to print. More surprisingly, giving all members of both specialties access to print further increases the speed with which the migrant's message diffuses. This is because print, through multiplicity, facilitates indirect diffusion of the migrant's new idea.

Regardless of the technological condition, the greater the integration of the source specialty—the migrant's home field—the less the migrant's capacity to diffuse new information to the target specialty. In Fig. 10.1, each point represents the average final value of 900 societies (i.e., 100 replications of nine sociocultural landscapes varying in cultural integration within the target, with cultural overlap between source and target, but not the integration of the source). This effect, though slight, is reduced further by print. A highly integrated source specialty acts as a force of resistance against the migrant's interaction with members of the target specialty. Recall that the migrant is initially as cognitively similar to individuals in the source specialty (i.e., old field) as to individuals in the target (i.e., new field). This means that the more internally integrated the source field, the more the migrant will be drawn to continued inter-

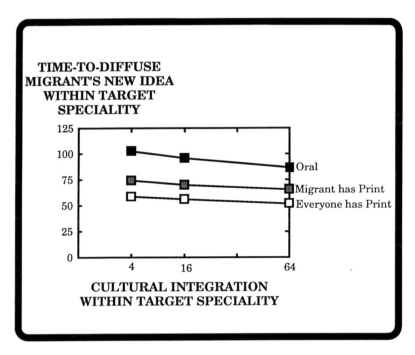

FIG. 10.1. Cultural integration within the source specialty and time-to-diffusion of the migrant's new idea to members of the target specialty by technological condition.
Note. Compiled from aspects of Tables 10.1 to 10.3 in Appendix D.

action with members of that field in preference to interaction with members of the target field.

In all cases, individuals can learn the new ideas not just from the authorial source (i.e., direct diffusion of the migrant's new idea) but also from other individuals in the society who have interacted with the migrant (i.e., indirect diffusion). Print accelerates this process by facilitating both direct and indirect diffusion. However, the more integrated the source specialty, the less likely it is that its members will interact with members of the target specialty and inform members of the target of the migrant's new idea. Thus, highly integrated source specialties prevent the migrant from being effective in a new specialty, not only because they consume the migrant's time, inhibiting direct diffusion to the target, but also because the members of the source specialty consume one another's time and indirectly inhibit the diffusion of the migrant's ideas to the target. High integration within the source specialty "contains" the migrant's innovative ideas and inhibits their dissemination to the outside.

This result is especially pronounced in oral, one-to-one interaction when the migrant's interaction with a member of the source specialty makes the migrant unavailable to act with a member of the target specialty. A corollary of this result is that any force that limits the availability of the target, such as distance, restricts migration. For example, without proximity to members of the target specialty, migrants are less likely to strike out on their own if only because they will not be aware of their full range of choices for interaction partners (see the role of proximity in the motivation phase of partner selection, chap. 6). There was, for example, substantial cognitive overlap between optical astronomers and radio astronomers but, in the 1930's, no physical proximity to make these specialties aware of one another (Edge & Mulkay, 1976).

**An Integrated Target Specialty
and the Migrant's Authority**

Let us turn to the relationship between the diffusion of the migrant's ideas and the cultural integration of the target specialty (Fig. 10.2). Across all

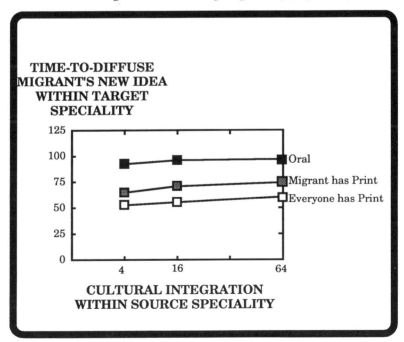

FIG. 10.2. Cultural integration within the target specialty and time-to-diffusion of the migrant's new idea to members of the target specialty by technological condition.
Note. Compiled from aspects of Tables 10.1 to 10.3 in Appendix D.

technological conditions, we see that the integration of the target specialty, in contrast to the source specialty, encourages rather than discourages migration. That is, as the level of initial integration within the target specialty increases, the time it takes the migrant's new ideas to diffuse increases. If high integration within the source field offers resistance to the migrant spreading information to the target field, high integration within the target field acts as a sponge drawing the migrant's ideas in more rapidly.

Recall from chapter 7 that in societies with oral technological conditions the higher the level of initial cultural integration, the longer it takes new ideas to diffuse. When all interactions are oral, one-to-one interactions, high cultural integration hinders diffusion because it promotes a climate of ritual interaction in which individuals repeatedly communicate known information to one another. Because individuals learn, the fraction of communicated information in any society that is ritual (assimilated) rather than new continues to grow over time.[1] This means that, over time, the individual's chance of getting any new information from another individual decreases. The higher the cultural integration to begin with, the greater the initial proportion of ritual interaction. This further suggests that societies impede the diffusion of new ideas as they become more culturally integrated. Significantly, print mitigates this effect. Unlike people, texts have a certain fixity (i.e., they cannot learn, and interaction with a text has an upper bound on the level of ritualism that it can sustain). Assuming a text has something new for a reader, the reader's chance of getting that new information from the text remains constant over time.

Although these processes are still at work in the migrant case, they do not account for the behavior we observe. Rather, high cultural integration within the target specialty means that members of the target are engaged in constant and ongoing interaction. They are exchanging information and building an assimilated web of ideas that are tied not only to their own new ideas but also to the new information coming from the outside. Formulating this observation as a more general principle, we might say that a target specialty must be culturally cohesive if it is to be receptive to new ideas that can influence it in a timely way. We see this principle at work in the development of the sciences. A level of shared belief about the importance of physics was necessary in biology for migrant physicists to move in and develop microbiology (Mullins, 1972); a similar appreciation of physics was necessary in chemistry before a specialist group of chemists (Ostwald, van't Hoff, and Arrhenius), all

---

[1]This assumes, of course, that the rate of discovering new ideas is slower than the rate of acquiring what is already known.

trained in physics, could develop the foundations of physical chemistry in the 1880s. (Servos, 1990, pp. 40–42).

Imagine the plight of the migrant without a highly integrated target specialty and with no cultural overlap between the target and the source. Such a landscape neutralizes the sociocultural advantage of a migrant, as there are initially no members of the target to take up the migrant's cause and help spread the new idea to the target community through indirect diffusion. It falls on the migrant's shoulders alone to "intrude" into the target specialty, teaching its members what they have in common with the source specialty and how the mix is valuable. Such intrusion is very costly in terms of the migrant's time (as Figs. 10.1 and 10.2 indicate from complementary perspectives).

This unhappy arrangement also illustrates when successful migration is very unlikely to occur and why successful migration is not an isolated act of the migrant but one that must be reinforced by many concurrent interactions among members of the target specialty. This result exposes the naivete of well-meaning cries for interdisciplinary cross fertilization, without the appropriate environment of social interactions to support it. Ironically, the most hardened mavericks, those most likely to be distrustful of organization and to shun the support of more orthodox colleagues, are beholden to the organization of the target community for a successful migration. Although these conclusions do not strain intuition, they are obscured in many heroic narratives of migration, which tend to romanticize the migrant's courageous break with the source specialty and to underplay the substantial help the migrant must receive from the target specialty in order to avoid the consequences of career immolation. Despite the romantic focus in migration stories on the source specialty, the success of a migrant has as much to do with locating a sanctuary to which to fly as it does with the type of home from which the migrant takes flight.

In a world with print, the migrant's ideas still diffuse more rapidly to the target, the more integrated the target. However, the effect is much less pronounced than it is when all communications are oral. Print, in this sense, reduces the migrant's dependency on a highly integrated target.

Overlap Between the Source and Target Specialities and the Migrant's Authority

The greater the overlap between a source and the target, the longer it takes the migrant's new idea to diffuse to the target specialty (Fig. 10.3). This effect is slight; it is also somewhat contrary to popular wisdom, which might suggest that the more two groups overlap and the less special-

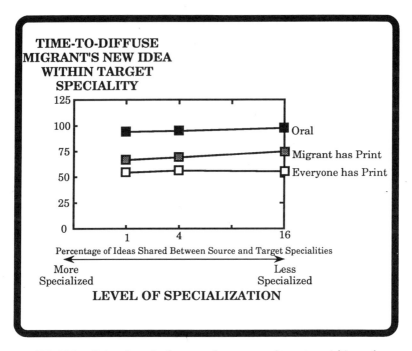

FIG. 10.3. Cultural overlap between the source and target specialties and time-to-diffusion of the migrant's new idea to members of the target specialty by technological condition.
Note. Compiled from aspects of Tables 10.1 to 10.3 in Appendix D.

ized they are in relation to each other, the easier it should be for information, and presumably migrants, to move between them. What we are seeing, in contrast, is something a bit different. We are seeing that the migrant's new idea flows faster to the target if the target specialty has less in common with the source specialty and is more specialized, relative to the source. Essentially, the higher the overlap between the source and the target, the less distinction the migrant can claim as a member of both specialties. All members of the source and target are essentially migrants as the group boundaries separating the source and the target are highly permeated. The migrant trying to push ideas from the source to the target will compete with many other members of the source trying the same thing and with many members of the target pushing in the opposite direction. In a society with only one-to-one interaction this competition is exacerbated because time spent talking with a member of the source field is necessarily time taken away from talking with a member of the target. However, when everyone has access to print, the effect of overlap is almost completely mitigated. In part this is simply because all information moves so fast under print. But print also has a more sub-tle effect. Because of its multiplicity, print enables information to move rapidly between groups regardless of their overlap. Thus print decreases the effect of high overlap because it raises the effective permeability of even highly specialized groups.

Professionalism and the Migrant's Authority

The source and target specialties vary in the degree to which they resem-ble a prototypical profession. A group high in integration and high in specialization is more prototypically professional than one low on both dimensions (chap. 8). Because of synergistic effects between integration and specialization, professionalization may have a noticeable impact on the migrant's effectiveness in diffusing new information. In particular, one might expect that the greater the professionalization of the target group, the more difficulty the migrant may have diffusing new informa-tion to that group. One might further expect that the greater the profes-sionalism of the source relative to the target, the easier it is for the migrant from the more professionalized source to infiltrate a less professional-ized target.

We examine these hypotheses by constructing a professionalism scale. We define the professionalism of a group as shown in Table 10.2. The higher the value, the more prototypically professional the group. We now consider the time it takes the migrant's idea to diffuse to the target, given the professionalism of the source and target.

First we consider the oral condition. In Fig. 10.4 we see that in con-trast to prior expectations, a highly professional source inhibits diffusion and a highly professional target encourages rapid diffusion. A highly professional source inhibits diffusion because, maintaining tight bound-aries between the profession and the outside, it keeps the migrant's ideas

TABLE 10.2
Determination of Professionalism

Integration	Overlap	Professionalism
high	low	5
high	medium	4
medium	low	4
high	high	3
medium	medium	3
low	low	3
medium	high	2
low	medium	2
low	high	1

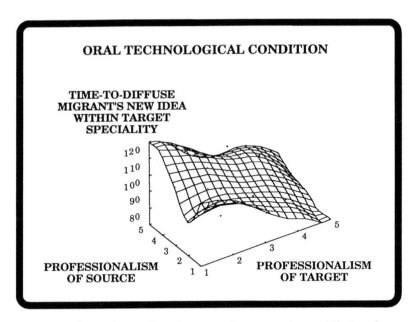

FIG. 10.4. Professionalism of source and target on time-to-diffusion of
the migrant's new idea to members of the target specialty under an oral
technological condition.
Note. This figure was created using systat plot and interpolating between
points using a negative exponential algorithm.

contained within the field and inhibits the spread of information to the
outside through indirect diffusion. Furthermore, the high integration of
the source field keeps the migrant more relatively similar to members
of the source and inhibits direct diffusion to the target. A highly professional target enhances diffusion because its high integration and specialization ensures that if the migrant's idea reaches any member of the target,
it will move rapidly, through indirect diffusion, to other members of the
target. Further, the high specialization of the target ensures that there
will be little competition for the migrant's idea from other ideas generated by members of the source. Overall, the sociocultural landscape exerts
a pronounced impact on the rate at which the migrant's idea diffuses.

When the migrant alone is given access to print, the inhibiting effect
of the source's professionalism is mitigated (Fig. 10.5). The professional
standing of the source is now an advantage for the migrant. The multiplicity of print enables the migrant, though more relatively similar to
members of the source, to reach members of the target. This is because
the medium of the text makes the migrant more available. Even when
only the migrant has print, the barriers between the highly professional

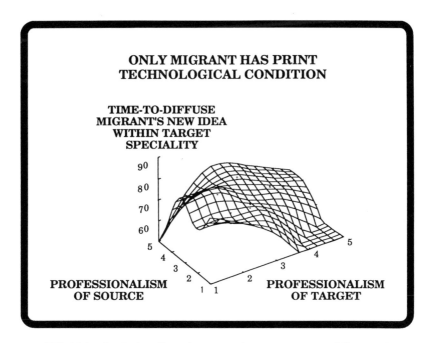

ONLY MIGRANT HAS PRINT
TECHNOLOGICAL CONDITION

TIME-TO-DIFFUSE
MIGRANT'S NEW IDEA
WITHIN TARGET
SPECIALITY

PROFESSIONALISM
OF SOURCE

PROFESSIONALISM
OF TARGET

FIG. 10.5. Professionalism of source and target on time-to-diffusion of the migrant's new idea to members of the target specialty when only the migrant has access to print.
Note. This figure was created using systat plot and interpolating between points using a negative exponential algorithm.

source and the target quickly break down because all members of the source now share more information with members of the target—specifically, the migrant's new idea. As these barriers continue to break down, members of the source will assist the migrant, through indirect diffusion, in moving the migrant's new idea to the target.

When all individuals have access to print, the professionalism of the target no longer enhances diffusion of the migrant's new idea (Fig. 10.6). In fact, the high professional status of the target now works against the migrant. Because of its multiplicity, print allows any idea to reach multiple individuals at once. The high integration of the target enables rapid diffusion of any idea, a result of all having access to print. Their high specialization will inhibit ideas from the source reaching them, but this is a factor offset by print. When all individuals have print, no idea, including the migrant's new idea, has a special advantage. The target is bombarded by new ideas, and the likelihood of the migrant's idea being picked up is reduced because of the increasing likelihood of anyone's idea being communicated.

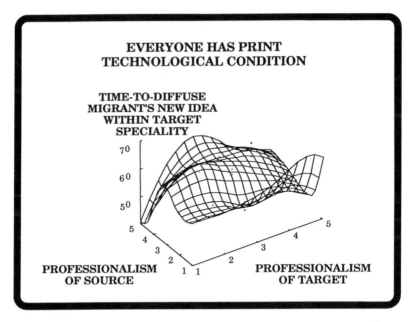

FIG. 10.6. Professionalism of source and target on time-to-diffusion of the migrant's new idea to members of the target specialty when everyone has access to print.
Note. This figure was created using systat plot and interpolating between points using a negative exponential algorithm.

IMPLICATIONS: MIGRANCY
AND COMMUNICATION TECHNOLOGY

Migrancy is foremost the movement of people and what ensues from that movement. But it is interesting to ask the theoretical question: What happens to the migrant's influence when we put the condition of print at his or her disposal? This is the question we pose in this chapter. We find that merely giving the facility of print to the migrant significantly decreases the time it takes for new ideas to diffuse to the target specialty. Print also has a slight secondary effect of altering the type of sociocultural landscape that is most conducive to successful migrancy. When the available technology is oral, minimal source integration, maximal target integration, and high specialization promote the rapid diffusion of the migrant's new idea to facilitate migrancy. Print, particularly when everyone has access to it, disrupts this picture slightly by minimizing the value of specialization.

To be sure, with print as with oral conditions, things are still worse for the migrant when there is high integration in the source specialty and low integration in the target specialty. But, in relative terms, things are much less worse for the migrant with print because the consequences of any of these "debilitating" conditions are much less pronounced. Because of its increased availability through print, the migrant's new ideas can penetrate the target specialty at a faster rate in spite of these structural obstacles. Thus, by increasing the migrant's communicative repertoire from face-to-face to print technologies, important social obstacles to the success of the migrant are lifted. The lifting of these barriers becomes even more pronounced when we give a printing press to all individuals in the society. As everyone in the source and target specialties becomes capable of communicating through texts, the migrant's capacity to get ideas to the target rapidly is enhanced through more rapid indirect diffusion. By the same token, the advantages the migrant enjoyed in an oral society as a result of a low-integrated source and a high-integrated target are diminished, in relative terms, with print. In theory at least, print serves as a great sociocultural equalizer.

Perhaps those who claim that the migrant has special innovative capacities push this point because they are impressed with the considerable sociocultural obstacles that the successful migrant in a nonprint world must overcome. The migrant, after all, is an agent who has capitalized on transactions in two or more communities of interest. We have seen in this chapter that the obstacles to migration need not be viewed as invariants of sociocultural landscapes that simply become more or less steep with changes in the technological condition. Rather, some landscapes present intrinsic obstacles to migrants and others facilitate their migration. In either case, the communication technology can exacerbate or mitigate the inherent advantages or disadvantages of a certain landscape for migration. The benefits of one type of communication technology over another, such as the various advantages of proximate communication over current communication technologies (Kraut, Egido, & Galegher, 1990; Carley, with Wendt, 1991) and electronic mail over face-to-face communication (Sproull & Kiesler, 1986; Lievrouw & Carley, 1990), will affect not only which type of sociocultural landscape is most conducive to migration but also what type of technology the migrant would be most strategic to employ in diffusing ideas.

On the other hand, given the mitigating effects of print and other communication technologies in overcoming sociocultural distance and breaking down rigid sociocultural boundaries, including professional boundaries, the migrant's seeming achievement may be less an achievement than a predictable and rather unremarkable interaction between technology and the reciprocity of knowledge and interaction (chap. 4). As technology supports relative-similarity relationships across greater distances, the reciprocity of knowledge and interaction suggests that individuals will communicate relatively more with those stationed at greater distances. Rather than a heroic victory over hostile sociocultural forces that technology tends to flatten, migrancy may simply be a pedestrian result of employing communication technologies that increase the author's potential reach, regardless of the sociocultural landscape. We can learn a good deal about the migrant hypothesis and the present and future conditions of communication technologies by holding these heroic and pedestrian images of the migrant together and searching for the grains of truth that may inform both.

Afterword

We have brought together historical information and a formal framework in an attempt to examine the impact of print systematically. Our focus has not been on what print did but on what it could possibly have done. Unlike technological determinists, we do not argue that technology alters the physical properties of the individual (mind) and is necessary for particular organizational forms such as professions and science. Rather, we maintain that communication technologies alter the physical properties of the communicative transaction and make the creation of artificial agents possible. Alterations on the communicative transaction and the creation of artificial agents are sufficient to account for, but do not necessitate, the type of social change and new, more dispersed organizational forms typically associated with industrialized print. Far from anthropomorphizing technology, conceiving of printed texts as artificial agents clarifies the sense in which print can enhance the reach of human agents. As we saw in Part II, human agents with print (like humans with any device that augments or amplifies their natural capacities) can do things, logically speaking, that agents without it cannot do. They can spread information faster and more efficiently. They can cut down on the amount of ritualized interaction and reach more people with their ideas even when they have less in common with them.

We argued that the impact of communication technologies on sociocultural organization and change can only be examined within a general framework of human interaction, shorn of special technologies, that builds social and cultural change out of the collectivity of individual changes. To understand the effect of print or any communication technology, in other words, one must understand what it adds or takes away from the face-to-face context. The framework we used is constructural theory, in which individuals adapt through the concurrent communicative transactions in which they and others are engaged. As individuals adapt over time, the larger sociocultural landscape adapts. Through the reciprocity of interaction and cognition at the individual level and the concurrency of interactions across the population, individual cognition, social structure, and culture co-evolve as part of a single ecology. As an ecological theory of communication processes, constructuralism makes the communicative transaction the centerpiece through which agents, communications, and contexts mutually influence and are mutually influenced, both concurrently and over time.

Even assuming a single communication technology, thinking through such an ecology is a difficult undertaking because of the sheer number of interactions possible. We have employed a simplified formal model to systematically explore the consequences on social and cultural organization and change as communication technologies become available to the society. Like Newtonian mechanics in physics that abstracts from physical reality, we have sought to understand some basic social properties of human communication by using simplified models that similarly abstract from social reality.

In the process of working with simplified models, we have, perforce, neglected many other interesting aspects of social life related to print. Such aspects include, but are not limited to:

- the structure of language;
- semantics;
- cross-cultural difficulties in communication;
- details of human information retrieval;
- errors in the transmission and reception of information;
- the extent to which a technology mitigates the effects of forgetting;
- the extent to which a technology, in and of itself, may foster or inhibit certain types of communications;
- the extent to which it may call attention to or suppress status cues;
- the interaction between technology and cognitive theories of discovery;
- the interaction between technology and population dynamics;
- motivations for interaction other than relative similarity.

This last omission is particularly telling, as we have yet to discuss proximity as a motivation for print. We have claimed throughout this book that print breaks the barriers of proximity and the geographic barriers to communication and social change. But we did not explore the additional boost that proximity, or opportunities for contact, can give to an agent's, or even a print author's, reach. More simply stated, just because print can compensate for distance does not prevent proximity from giving a large boost to a print relationship. Some research on what we have omitted here is already ongoing outside the constructural framework. In the future, more modules may be added to the extended model in order to explore some of these important areas within that framework.

Nonetheless, even within the model used in this book, print's ability to break down barriers of proximity is evident. Through its asynchronicity, durability, and fixity, print enables human agents to create artificial agents containing aspects of their mental models. Through texts, human agents can engage in one-to-many interactions with other agents without being physically present. This change toward print resulted in both a faster rate of information diffusion and a reduction in ritualized interactions. How much greater such effects would be, and whether there might be other effects when interaction is motivated by opportunities for contact as well as knowledge, is a matter for further research.

The value of the current study is in part methodological. For example, this study demonstrates how formal analysis can be used in conjunction with historical analysis to provide greater insight into historical events. This study further demonstrates a systematic procedure for considering the impact of print and other potential communication technologies within the framework of a dynamic model of individual and social behavior. The current study also demonstrates that the formal building block approach to theory building is particularly advantageous in understanding social systems. In this study, we add print and could examine the logical consequence of this single new addition in conjunction with the behavior predicted by a firm baseline model. Adding new building blocks to investigate features ignored in this study will increase the complexity and realism of the scenarios that can be examined within this model. At the same time, the simple incremental fashion in which building blocks can be added increases the investigator's chances of narrowing in on exactly what changes can be associated with the added block.

The value of the current study is also theoretical. Starting with a dynamic model of individual and social behavior that is consistent with a range of findings on human interaction and sociocultural change, we are able to extend that model with a print building block. Despite the relative simplicity of this additional module, it allows us to generate a great many logically plausible hypotheses about print, professions, academe, and scientific migrants and to call attention to logical inconsistencies in other, sometimes popular, hypotheses or threads of reasoning through which these hypotheses are sometimes interpreted. Additional research will be needed to test the hypotheses we have proposed in greater detail. The analyses demonstrate the importance of technological features, such as multiplicity and fixity, in speeding the rate of information diffusion, reducing ritualized interaction, and altering the impact of ties. These analyses provide us with a number of new theoretical insights.

One of the more intriguing insights to come from this analysis centers on the strength of weak ties. We have seen that whether strong or weak ties are most advantageous for the rapid diffusion of information or the development of cultural consensus depends on the communication technology. Print makes population size and the value of ties largely irrelevant. That is to say, print strengthens the value of weak ties and weakens the value of strong ties in effecting rapid information diffusion and consensus. By modulating the value of ties, print serves to equalize society. Print does not lead to instant socialization and consensus. It can even initially decrease consensus and slow down the rate of diffusion, but print does enable more homogeneous access to information.

Another intriguing theoretical result is the relationship between potential reach and the authority of the communicator (i.e., the author). Print increases the potential reach and authority of the author. We argue that the impact of a communication and the authority of the author is equally dependent on the individual's personal history, the content of the message, the extant culture and social structure, and the communication technologies available. To an extent, the individual can take actions that maximize the chances of achieving widespread authority. Such actions include the careful construction of a text's content by the author so that highly central or prominent others are cited or their work elaborated on. Through such construction, authors can help engineer their reach and authority. We have seen how academic authors can help engineer their own reach and authority in the rhetorical design of their texts. But we have also seen how the path of diffusion for even the most carefully constructed text is subject to the constraints of the sociocultural landscape. No matter how strategic, the author seeking to publish or migrate is constrained not only by a text, but by his or her own position in the landscape and by the positions of would-be readers.

As we have mentioned, print affects all these outcomes, not by altering human nature but by altering the physical nature of communicative transactions and by supporting the existence of artificial agents. As a result, print alters the conditions under which strong and weak ties promote rapid communication. Print can overcome the structural and cultural boundaries around groups normally kept intact by strong internal ties and weak external ties. Under nonprint conditions, these boundaries constrain the flow of information and help or hinder the migrant in a quest to achieve authority in a new group. But enabling greater access to information is far from guaranteeing that access. Indeed, groups may purposely choose to keep some information oral in order to maintain group boundaries. With technologies such as print that promote rapid diffusion and more homogeneous access to information, institutions, norms, and customs (e.g., scientific journals and gatekeeping) may arise simply to keep barriers in place, to regulate print's effects, and to control the achievement of authority. Indeed, the history of print can be viewed as the history of institutions, norms, and customs under construction, not because print made them possible, but because print made them necessary.[1]

---

[1]For a thorough historical discussion of the rise of social controls on information since the industrial revolution, see Beniger, 1986.

Appendix A: Simulation Data for Print (Chapter 7)

This appendix contains the simulation data for chapter 7 (print). These simulations explore the interactions of communication technologies (face-to-face vs. print interaction) and sociocultural landscapes (population size, cultural complexity, initial levels of cultural integration) on diffusion, stability, and consensus. In face-to-face simulations, all individuals communicate information according to the dynamics discussed in chapter 6. In simulations of simple print societies, individuals and societies have one text with one piece of new information (known only to one individual in the society, the author, and to no one else), which interacts with readers according to the dynamics of print-based interaction, also laid out in chapter 6. In simulations of complex print societies, individuals and societies have one text containing assimilated ideas—known to others beside the author—and a new idea, known only to the author. In order to study the effects of competition, some of the simulations involve societies with two different texts (simple or complex) in circulation.

TABLE 7.1
Diffusion in Oral Societies

Total Number of Ideas in Society	Percentage of Ideas Initially Shared	Number of Individuals in the Society		
		6	12	18
10	6%	55(1.06)	55(2.01)	53(2.32)
	25%	62(1.05)	59(1.75)	70(3.04)
	56%	63(0.97)	72(1.92)	73(2.63)
20	6%	102(1.01)	101(2.18)	106(2.82)
	25%	96(1.03)	123(2.11)	116(2.24)
	56%	124(1.15)	113(1.74)	138(2.89)
40	6%	172(1.03)	196(1.83)	193(2.19)
	25%	219(1.07)	237(1.76)	257(2.90)
	56%	208(1.05)	272(1.83)	274(2.53)

Comment: This table reports the time-to-diffusion of a single idea in oral societies in which the initial level of cultural integration, the population size, and the cultural complexity all vary. All communication is one-to-one. Each cell contains the average—and the standard deviation, in parentheses—of the number of time periods that lapse before an idea in an oral society, with that level of initial integration and that many individuals and ideas, reaches 90% of the diffusion that will be reached at the 500th time period. This average is computed across 100 societies of the same type, run to 500 time periods.

TABLE 7.2
Diffusion in Print Societies with One Simple Text

Total Number of Ideas in Society	Percentage of Ideas Initially Shared	Number of Individuals in the Society		
		6	12	18
10	6%	56(1.06)	57(1.80)	58(2.69)
	25%	60(1.04)	67(2.23)	65(2.46)
	56%	54(0.97)	64(1.64)	73(2.60)
20	6%	101(0.98)	121(1.96)	107(2.09)
	25%	117(1.09)	123(2.20)	133(3.22)
	56%	121(1.03)	125(1.96)	145(3.18)
40	6%	165(0.92)	219(2.45)	212(2.76)
	25%	183(1.06)	226(1.81)	244(2.80)
	56%	228(0.98)	240(2.02)	305(3.01)

Comment: This table reports the time-to-diffusion of a single idea in a print society that is initially known only to a single author and that is encapsulated in a single text. Initial cultural integration, population size, and cultural complexity are varied. The text interacts with readers in a one-to-many fashion. All other interaction in the society is one-to-one. Each cell contains the average—and the standard deviation, in parentheses—of the number of time periods that lapse before the single idea of the text in a single-text society, with that level of initial integration and that many individuals and ideas, reaches 90% of the diffusion that will be reached at the 500th time period. This average is computed across 100 societies of the same type, run to 500 time periods.

TABLE 7.3
Diffusion in Print Societies with One Complex Text

Total Number of Ideas in Society	Percentage of Ideas Initially Shared	Number of Individuals in the Society		
		6	12	18
10	6%	53(1.04)	48(1.09)	49(1.81)
	25%	46(0.74)	47(1.19)	49(1.67)
	56%	44(0.89)	47(1.29)	49(1.78)
20	6%	107(0.87)	90(1.15)	87(1.85)
	25%	76(0.78)	88(1.18)	92(1.77)
	56%	78(0.87)	85(1.21)	97(1.88)
40	6%	180(1.02)	171(1.41)	171(2.04)
	25%	171(0.91)	173(1.30)	187(2.13)
	56%	151(0.95)	172(1.53)	182(1.69)

Comment: This table reports the time-to-diffusion, within print societies, of multiple ideas encapsulated within a complex text (i.e., a text with both assimilated [known beyond the author] and new information [known only to the author]). The text thus encapsulates some ideas already distributed in the culture as well as an idea unique to the original author. The text interacts with readers in one-to-many fashion. All other interaction in the society is one-to-one. The initial level of cultural integration, the population size, and the cultural complexity are varied. Each cell contains the average—and the standard deviation, in parentheses—of the number of time periods that lapse before the content of the text, with that level of initial integration and that many individuals and ideas, reaches 90% of the diffusion that will be reached at the 500th time period. This average is computed across 100 societies of the same type, run to 500 time periods.

TABLE 7.4
Diffusion in Print Societies with Two Simple Texts

Total Number of Ideas in Society	Percentage of Ideas Initially Shared	Number of Individuals in the Society		
		6	12	18
10	6%	47(1.01)	55(1.55)	57(2.67)
	25%	49(1.00)	58(1.57)	63(2.05)
	56%	54(0.94)	62(2.11)	72(2.80)
20	6%	72(0.95)	93(1.94)	98(2.41)
	25%	83(1.01)	118(2.04)	116(2.46)
	56%	117(0.97)	116(1.77)	129(2.34)
40	6%	128(0.91)	173(1.68)	184(2.56)
	25%	165(1.04)	204(1.77)	245(2.56)
	56%	181(1.17)	230(1.73)	235(2.55)

Comment: This table reports the time-to-diffusion of single ideas in the content of two different (and thus competing) texts. Initial cultural integration, population size, and cultural complexity are varied. Both texts interact with readers in a one-to-many fashion. All other interaction in the society is one-to-one. Each cell contains the average—and the standard deviation, in parentheses—of the number of time periods that lapse before the single idea of the text in a single-text society, with that level of initial integration and that many individuals and ideas, reaches 90% of the diffusion that will be reached at the 500th time period. This average is computed across 100 societies of the same type, run to 500 time periods.

TABLE 7.5
Diffusion in Print Societies with Two Complex Texts

Total Number of Ideas in Society	Percentage of Ideas Initially Shared	Number of Individuals in the Society		
		6	12	18
10	6%	52(0.91)	51(1.34)	53(1.50)
	25%	49(0.96)	52(1.32)	53(1.91)
	56%	45(0.77)	51(1.30)	53(2.20)
20	6%	95(0.93)	89(1.37)	92(1.97)
	25%	80(0.74)	88(1.40)	95(1.65)
	56%	79(0.91)	96(1.51)	98(2.09)
40	6%	165(0.84)	165(1.17)	177(1.67)
	25%	155(0.78)	170(1.36)	180(1.81)
	56%	156(0.98)	172(1.65)	191(1.98)

Comment: This table reports the time-to-diffusion, within print societies, of multiple ideas encapsulated within two complex texts (i.e., different texts each with assimilated [known beyond the author] and new information [known only to the author]). Both texts encapsulate some ideas already distributed in the culture as well as an idea unique to the original author. The texts interact with readers in one-to-many fashion. All other interaction in the society is one-to-one. The initial level of cultural integration, the population size, and the cultural complexity are varied. Each cell contains the average—and the standard deviation, in parentheses—of the number of time periods that lapse before the content of the text, with that level of initial integration and that many individuals and ideas, reaches 90% of the stability that will be reached at the 500th time period. This average is computed across 100 societies of the same type, run to 500 time periods.

TABLE 7.6
Stability in Oral Societies

Total Number of Ideas in Society	Percentage of Ideas Initially Shared	Number of Individuals in the Society		
		6	12	18
10	6%	41(0.53)	38(0.31)	35(0.34)
	25%	33(0.47)	29(0.29)	29(0.27)
	56%	23(0.38)	21(0.28)	23(0.22)
20	6%	73(0.66)	66(0.50)	61(0.39)
	25%	58(0.56)	50(0.43)	47(0.35)
	56%	35(0.59)	32(0.32)	32(0.30)
40	6%	141(0.97)	125(0.67)	115(0.58)
	25%	108(0.81)	92(0.56)	86(0.47)
	56%	61(0.69)	55(0.56)	51(0.38)

Comment: This table reports the time-to-stability of a single idea in oral societies in which the initial level of cultural integration, the population size, and the cultural complexity all vary. All communication is one-to-one. Each cell contains the average—and the standard deviation, in parentheses—of the number of time periods that lapse before an idea in an oral society, with that level of initial integration and that many individuals and ideas, reaches 90% of the stability that will be reached at the 500th time period. This average is computed across 100 societies of the same type, run to 500 time periods.

TABLE 7.7
Stability in Print Societies with One Simple Text

Total Number of Ideas in Society	Percentage of Ideas Initially Shared	Number of Individuals in the Society		
		6	12	18
10	6%	41(0.53)	38(0.31)	35(0.34)
	25%	33(0.47)	29(0.29)	29(0.27)
	56%	23(0.38)	21(0.28)	23(0.22)
20	6%	73(0.66)	66(0.50)	61(0.39)
	25%	58(0.56)	50(0.43)	47(0.35)
	56%	35(0.59)	32(0.32)	32(0.30)
40	6%	141(0.97)	125(0.67)	115(0.58)
	25%	108(0.81)	92(0.56)	86(0.47)
	56%	61(0.69)	55(0.56)	51(0.38)

Comment: This table reports the time-to-stability of a single idea in a print society that is initially known only to a single author and that is encapsulated in a single text. Initial cultural integration, population size, and cultural complexity are varied. The text interacts with readers in a one-to-many fashion. All other interaction in the society is one-to-one. Each cell contains the average—and the standard deviation, in parentheses—of the number of time periods that lapse before the single idea of the text in a single-text society, with that level of initial integration and that many individuals and ideas, reaches 90% of the stability that will be reached at the 500th time period. This average is computed across 100 societies of the same type, run to 500 time periods.

TABLE 7.8
Stability in Print Societies with One Complex Text

Total Number of Ideas in Society	Percentage of Ideas Initially Shared	Number of Individuals in the Society		
		6	12	18
10	6%	40(0.46)	34(0.36)	32(0.30)
	25%	30(0.43)	26(0.31)	25(0.22)
	56%	19(0.43)	18(0.28)	19(0.23)
20	6%	75(0.61)	64(0.49)	58(0.32)
	25%	54(0.60)	48(0.46)	44(0.30)
	56%	31(0.58)	29(0.36)	29(0.31)
40	6%	140(0.84)	122(0.68)	112(0.64)
	25%	106(0.85)	88(0.58)	84(0.40)
	56%	59(0.89)	51(0.53)	49(0.42)

Comment: This table reports the time-to-stability, within print societies, of multiple ideas encapsulated within a complex text (i.e., a text with both assimilated [known beyond the author] and new information [known only to the author]). The text thus encapsulates some ideas already distributed in the culture as well as an idea unique to the original author. The texts interact with readers in one-to-many fashion. All other interaction in the society is one-to-one. The initial level of cultural integration, the population size, and the cultural complexity are varied. Each cell contains the average—and the standard deviation, in parentheses—of the number of time periods that lapse before the content of the text, with that level of initial integration and that many individuals and ideas, reaches 90% of the stability that will be reached at the 500th time period. This average is computed across 100 societies of the same type, run to 500 time periods.

TABLE 7.9
Stability in Print Societies with Two Simple Texts

Total Number of Ideas in Society	Percentage of Ideas Initially Shared	Number of Individuals in the Society		
		6	12	18
10	6%	46(0.45)	40(0.40)	38(0.37)
	25%	36(0.51)	33(0.33)	33(0.27)
	56%	27(0.49)	29(0.39)	31(0.36)
20	6%	77(0.65)	71(0.46)	63(0.42)
	25%	59(0.56)	53(0.46)	52(0.39)
	56%	40(0.58)	40(0.45)	40(0.30)
40	6%	142(0.90)	130(0.68)	117(0.59)
	25%	112(0.87)	95(0.52)	91(0.47)
	56%	65(0.80)	63(0.58)	62(0.39)

Comment: This table reports the time-to-stability of single ideas in the content of two different (and thus competing) texts. Initial cultural integration, population size, and cultural complexity are varied. Both texts interact with readers in a one-to-many fashion. All other interaction in the society is one-to-one. Each cell contains the average—and the standard deviation, in parentheses—of the number of time periods that lapse before the single idea of the text in a single-text society, with that level of initial integration and that many individuals and ideas, reaches 90% of the stability that will be reached at the 500th time period. This average is computed across 100 societies of the same type, run to 500 time periods.

TABLE 7.10
Stability in Print Societies with Two Complex Texts

Total Number of Ideas in Society	Percentage of Ideas Initially Shared	Number of Individuals in the Society		
		6	12	18
10	6%	38(0.48)	35(0.33)	34(0.26)
	25%	30(0.43)	29(0.31)	29(0.32)
	56%	21(0.40)	22(0.32)	25(0.30)
20	6%	72(0.75)	66(0.51)	60(0.36)
	25%	55(0.65)	49(0.42)	49(0.33)
	56%	36(0.63)	35(0.45)	35(0.34)
40	6%	143(0.96)	124(0.66)	114(0.55)
	25%	109(0.86)	92(0.54)	86(0.44)
	56%	60(0.82)	56(0.57)	56(0.41)

Comment: This table reports the time-to-stability, within print societies, of multiple ideas encapsulated within two complex texts (i.e., different texts each with assimilated [known beyond the author] and new information [known only to the author]). Both texts encapsulate some ideas already distributed in the culture as well as an idea unique to the original author. The texts interact with readers in one-to-many fashion. All other interaction in the society is one-to-one. The initial level of cultural integration, the population size, and the cultural complexity are varied. Each cell contains the average—and the standard deviation, in parentheses—of the number of time periods that lapse before the content of the text, with that level of initial integration and that many individuals and ideas, reaches 90% of the stability that will be reached at the 500th time period. This average is computed across 100 societies of the same type, run to 500 time periods.

TABLE 7.11
Consensus in Oral Societies

Total Number of Ideas in Society	Percentage of Ideas Initially Shared	Number of Individuals in the Society		
		6	12	18
10	6%	81(0.85)	74(1.43)	70(1.87)
	25%	80(0.89)	71(1.53)	78(2.38)
	56%	71(0.88)	79(1.56)	80(2.19)
20	6%	176(0.88)	164(1.57)	144(2.18)
	25%	144(0.89)	146(1.71)	136(2.12)
	56%	151(0.94)	137(1.51)	152(2.29)
40	6%	379(0.80)	332(1.59)	299(1.95)
	25%	344(0.91)	303(1.39)	304(2.29)
	56%	295(0.80)	318(1.75)	308(2.18)

Comment: This table reports the time-to-consensus of a single idea in oral societies in which the initial level of cultural integration, the population size, and the cultural complexity all vary. All communication is one-to-one. Each cell contains the average—and the standard deviation, in parentheses—of the number of time periods that lapse before an idea in an oral society, with that level of initial integration and that many individuals and ideas, reaches 90% of the consensus that will be reached at the 500th time period. This average is computed across 100 societies of the same type, run to 500 time periods.

TABLE 7.12
Consensus in Print Societies with One Simple Text

Total Number of Ideas in Society	Percentage of Ideas Initially Shared	Number of Individuals in the Society		
		6	12	18
10	6%	83(0.81)	78(1.42)	72(2.23)
	25%	79(0.91)	72(1.69)	75(2.35)
	56%	67(0.85)	73(1.60)	80(2.39)
20	6%	174(0.87)	160(1.57)	142(2.00)
	25%	164(0.91)	148(1.59)	148(2.12)
	56%	152(0.89)	140(1.71)	157(2.36)
40	6%	347(0.86)	333(1.53)	301(1.77)
	25%	339(0.84)	295(1.41)	301(2.23)
	56%	313(0.85)	292(1.54)	332(2.68)

Comment: This table reports the time-to-consensus of a single idea in a print society that is initially known only to a single author and that is encapsulated in a single text. Initial cultural integration, population size, and cultural complexity are varied. The text interacts with readers in a one-to-many fashion. All other interaction in the society is one-to-one. Each cell contains the average—and the standard deviation, in parentheses—of the number of time periods that lapse before the single idea of the text in a single-text society, with that level of initial integration and that many individuals and ideas, reaches 90% of the consensus that will be reached at the 500th time period. This average is computed across 100 societies of the same type, run to 500 time periods.

TABLE 7.13
Consensus in Print Societies with One Complex Text

Total Number of Ideas in Society	Percentage of Ideas Initially Shared	Number of Individuals in the Society		
		6	12	18
10	6%	83(0.91)	69(1.59)	63(2.00)
	25%	70(0.90)	57(1.36)	60(1.61)
	56%	55(0.83)	57(1.42)	58(1.85)
20	6%	171(0.89)	145(1.48)	134(1.76)
	25%	147(0.84)	123(1.34)	120(1.79)
	56%	120(0.83)	110(1.25)	119(1.74)
40	6%	367(0.91)	323(1.66)	298(1.89)
	25%	340(0.89)	274(1.23)	273(1.77)
	56%	259(0.84)	239(1.24)	241(1.53)

Comment: This table reports the time-to-consensus, within print societies, of multiple ideas encapsulated within a complex text (i.e., a text with both assimilated [known beyond the author] and new information [known only to the author]). The text thus encapsulates some ideas already distributed in the culture as well as an idea unique to the original author. The texts interact with readers in one-to-many fashion. All other interaction in the society is one-to-one. The initial level of cultural integration, the population size, and the cultural complexity are varied. Each cell contains the average—and the standard deviation, in parentheses—of the number of time periods that lapse before the content of the text, with that level of initial integration and that many individuals and ideas, reaches 90% of the consensus that will be reached at the 500th time period. This average is computed across 100 societies of the same type, run to 500 time periods.

TABLE 7.14
Consensus in Print Societies with Two Simple Texts

Total Number of Ideas in Society	Percentage of Ideas Initially Shared	Number of Individuals in the Society		
		6	12	18
10	6%	96(0.89)	78(1.39)	73(2.11)
	25%	80(0.93)	77(1.37)	70(1.95)
	56%	63(0.86)	70(1.60)	70(2.30)
20	6%	183(0.91)	167(1.38)	141(1.99)
	25%	168(0.85)	136(1.26)	141(2.14)
	56%	146(0.83)	132(1.63)	138(2.08)
40	6%	367(0.95)	328(1.46)	303(2.16)
	25%	347(0.82)	298(1.44)	291(1.86)
	56%	291(0.88)	267(1.65)	276(2.21)

Comment: This table reports the time-to-consensus of single ideas in the content of two different (and thus competing) texts. Initial cultural integration, population size, and cultural complexity are varied. Both texts interact with readers in a one-to-many fashion. All other interaction in the society is one-to-one. Each cell contains the average—and the standard deviation, in parentheses—of the number of time periods that lapse before the single idea of the text in a single-text society, with that level of initial integration and that many individuals and ideas, reaches 90% of the consensus that will be reached at the 500th time period. This average is computed across 100 societies of the same type, run to 500 time periods.

425

TABLE 7.15
Consensus in Print Societies with Two Complex Texts

Total Number of Ideas in Society	Percentage of Ideas Initially Shared	Number of Individuals in the Society		
		6	12	18
	6%	80(0.87)	72(1.53)	71(1.85)
10	25%	69(0.88)	64(1.44)	64(2.02)
	56%	57(0.90)	58(1.45)	60(2.05)
	6%	169(0.92)	154(1.50)	135(1.79)
20	25%	161(0.91)	127(1.52)	126(1.61)
	56%	122(0.84)	120(1.21)	116(2.03)
	6%	398(0.95)	343(1.51)	300(1.61)
40	25%	354(0.89)	288(1.30)	255(1.71)
	56%	286(0.84)	235(1.51)	237(1.79)

Comment: This table reports the time-to-consensus, within print societies, of multiple ideas encapsulated within two complex texts (i.e., different texts each with assimilated [known beyond the author] and new information [known only to the author]). Both texts encapsulate some ideas already distributed in the culture as well as an idea unique to the original author. The texts interact with readers in one-to-many fashion. All other interaction in the society is one-to-one. The initial level of cultural integration, the population size, and the cultural complexity are varied. Each cell contains the average—and the standard deviation, in parentheses—of the number of time periods that lapse before the content of the text, with that level of initial integration and that many individuals and ideas, reaches 90% of the consensus that will be reached at the 500th time period. This average is computed across 100 societies of the same type, run to 500 time periods.

Appendix B: Simulation Data
for Professions (Chapter 8)

This appendix includes the simulation data for chapter 8 (professions). Because professions are groups, we designed our simulations for this chapter to include groups in the society as well as individuals. Because we are interested in the collective effect of speakers vs. authors in professions rather than the diffusion of the ideas of specific individual professionals, we limit these simulations to the study of factors that affect the stability and consensus of members within the professional group. All of the societies we simulate for this chapter contain two groups: the professional group and the nonprofessional group, composed of all other individuals in the society. To study the implications of professional structure and communication on stability and consensus within the professional group, we manipulate both the levels of initial cultural integration within the professional group and the knowledge overlap (i.e., level of specialization) between the professional group and nonprofessionals. Thinking that relative size might also be a factor influencing the impact of stability and consensus within professions, we vary the size of the professional group relative to other individuals in the society. Thinking that the size of the population and the level of cultural complexity might also interact with stability and consensus within the professional group, we sometimes vary these factors as well.

The data in Tables 8.1 and 8.2 are the results for time-to-stability from simulation experiment two in chapter 8, where the societies have fixed population and complexity but vary in the ratio of group sizes and, internal cultural integration and specialization. The data in Tables 8.3 and 8.4 are the results for time-to-consensus from simulation experiment two in chapter 8, where the societies have fixed population and complexity but vary in the ratio of group sizes and internal cultural integration and specialization. The data in Tables 8.5 and 8.6 are the results for time-to-diffusion from simulation experiment one in chapter 8, where the societies differ in the size of the population and the complexity of the culture. The following simulations focus on the impact of the societal population and complexity on the diffusion of a new idea within an academic speciality. The data in Tables 8.7 and 8.8 are the results for time-to-diffusion from simulation experiment one in chapter 8, where the societies differ in the size of the population and the complexity of the culture. The following simulations focus on the impact of the societal population and societal complexity on the diffusion of a new idea within an academic speciality.

TABLE 8.1
Stability in Oral Professions in Societies of Fixed Population and Complexity

Percentage of Ideas Initially Shared by Members of the Profession (Cultural Integration)	*Percentage of Ideas Initially Shared Between Members of the Profession and Nonmembers (Specialization)*	*Ratio of Number of Individuals Within the Profession to Number Without*		
		6:6	*4:8*	*3:9*
	1%	68(0.51)	68(0.54)	69(0.52)
4%	4%	67(0.54)	65(0.47)	63(0.46)
	9%	59(0.39)	56(0.41)	57(0.48)
	1%	65(0.51)	67(0.49)	67(0.50)
16%	4%	62(0.48)	61(0.50)	63(0.48)
	9%	55(0.48)	55(0.48)	57(0.43)
	1%	61(0.46)	61(0.47)	64(0.50)
36%	4%	57(0.45)	57(0.46)	60(0.40)
	9%	51(0.39)	52(0.40)	53(0.45)

Comment: This table reports the time-to-stability within an oral profession in which the initial level of cultural integration, specialization, and relative size vary. The population of the societies in which the profession operates is fixed at 12 and the cultural complexity is fixed at 20. All communication is one-to-one. Each cell contains the average—and the standard deviation, in parentheses—of the number of time periods that lapse before the members of the profession reach 90% of the stability that will be reached at the 500th time period. This average is computed across 100 societies of the same type, run to 500 time periods.

TABLE 8.2
Stability in Print Professions in Societies
of Fixed Population and Complexity

Percentage of Ideas Initially Shared by Members of the Profession (Cultural Integration)	Percentage of Ideas Initially Shared Between Members of the Profession and Nonmembers (Specialization)	Ratio of Number of Individuals Within the Profession to Number Without		
		6:6	4:8	3:9
	1%	45(0.63)	44(0.76)	43(0.69)
4%	4%	43(0.57)	42(0.64)	40(0.73)
	9%	38(0.58)	37(0.66)	37(0.71)
	1%	41(0.55)	40(0.57)	39(0.86)
16%	4%	39(0.59)	39(0.73)	38(0.85)
	9%	36(0.57)	35(0.67)	33(0.74)
	1%	37(0.64)	34(0.66)	32(0.77)
36%	4%	34(0.65)	33(0.69)	29(0.81)
	9%	29(0.55)	29(0.72)	29(0.77)

Comment: This table reports the time-to-stability within a print profession in which the initial level of cultural integration, specialization, and relative size vary. The population of the societies in which the profession operates is fixed at 12 and the cultural complexity is fixed at 20. All communication is one-to-many. Each cell contains the average—and the standard deviation, in parentheses—of the number of time periods that lapse before the members of the profession reach 90% of the stability that will be reached at the 500th time period. This average is computed across 100 societies of the same type, run to 500 time periods.

TABLE 8.3
Consensus in Oral Professions in Societies
of Fixed Population and Complexity

Percentage of Ideas Initially Shared by Members of the Profession (Cultural Integration)	Percentage of Ideas Initially Shared Between Members of the Profession and Nonmembers (Specialization)	Ratio of Number of Individuals Within the Profession to Number Without		
		6:6	4:8	3:9
	1%	155(0.81)	149(0.62)	154(0.49)
4%	4%	139(0.91)	149(0.62)	147(0.46)
	9%	153(0.90)	143(0.60)	143(0.45)
	1%	140(0.88)	138(0.62)	137(0.46)
16%	4%	150(0.91)	145(0.62)	147(0.46)
	9%	144(0.85)	132(0.63)	139(0.46)

(Continued)

TABLE 8.3
(Continued)

Percentage of Ideas Initially Shared by Members of the Profession (Cultural Integration)	Percentage of Ideas Initially Shared Between Members of the Profession and Nonmembers (Specialization)	Ratio of Number of Individuals Within the Profession to Number Without		
		6:6	4:8	3:9
	1%	133(0.85)	129(0.64)	124(0.45)
36%	4%	135(0.90)	142(0.62)	143(0.46)
	9%	144(0.88)	129(0.60)	115(0.46)

Comment: This table reports the time-to-consensus within an oral profession in which the initial level of cultural integration, specialization, and relative size vary. The population of the societies in which the profession operates is fixed at 12 and the cultural complexity is fixed at 20. All communication is one-to-one. Each cell contains the average—and the standard deviation, in parentheses—of the number of time periods that lapse before the members of the profession reach 90% of the consensus that will be reached at the 500th time period. This average is computed across 100 societies of the same type, run to 500 time periods.

TABLE 8.4
Consensus in Print Professions in Societies
of Fixed Population and Complexity

Percentage of Ideas Initially Shared by Members of the Profession (Cultural Integration)	Percentage of Ideas Initially Shared Between Members of the Profession and Nonmembers (Specialization)	Ratio of Number of Individuals Within the Profession to Number Without		
		6:6	4:8	3:9
	1%	89(0.80)	100(0.60)	96(0.45)
4%	4%	93(0.84)	86(0.60)	86(0.46)
	9%	87(0.88)	78(0.60)	86(0.44)
	1%	82(0.78)	88(0.64)	91(0.45)
16%	4%	81(0.85)	86(0.60)	83(0.46)
	9%	82(0.84)	82(0.60)	79(0.46)
	1%	70(0.94)	75(0.59)	80(0.46)
36%	4%	73(0.92)	79(0.62)	81(0.45)
	9%	78(0.87)	73(0.59)	84(0.45)

Comment: This table reports the time-to-consensus within a print profession in which the initial level of cultural integration, specialization, and relative size vary. The population of the societies in which the profession operates is fixed at 12 and the cultural complexity is fixed at 20. All communication is one-to-many. Each cell contains the average—and the standard deviation, in parentheses—of the number of time periods that lapse before the members of the profession reach 90% of the consensus that will be reached at the 500th time period. This average is computed across 100 societies of the same type, run to 500 time periods.

TABLE 8.5
Stability in Oral Professions in Societies
of Variable Population and Complexity

Total Number of Ideas in Society	Number of Individuals in the Society		
	6	12	18
10	30(0.66)	30(0.42)	28(0.40)
20	57(0.96)	50(0.65)	48(0.51)
40	111(1.25)	96(0.93)	87(0.72)

Comment: This table reports the time-to-stability within an oral profession in which the initial level of cultural integration, specialization, and relative size is averaged out. The population of the societies in which the profession operates varies among 6, 12, and 18 individuals and the cultural complexity varies among 10, 20, and 40 ideas. All communication is one-to-one. Each cell contains the average—and the standard deviation, in parentheses—of the number of time periods that lapse before the members of the profession reach 90% of the stability that will be reached at the 500th time period. This average is computed across 100 societies of the same type, run to 500 time periods.

TABLE 8.6
Stability in Print Professions in Societies
of Variable Population and Complexity

Total Number of Ideas in Society	Number of Individuals in the Society		
	6	12	18
10	22(0.39)	20(0.33)	20(0.26)
20	41(0.52)	37(0.43)	35(0.32)
40	77(0.75)	69(0.63)	66(0.47)

Comment: This table reports the time-to-stability within a print profession in which the initial level of cultural integration, specialization, and relative size is averaged out. The population of the societies in which the profession operates varies among 6, 12, and 18 individuals and the cultural complexity varies among 10, 20, and 40 ideas. All communication is one-to-many. Each cell contains the average—and the standard deviation, in parentheses—of the number of time periods that lapse before the members of the profession reach 90% of the stability that will be reached at the 500th time period. This average is computed across 100 societies of the same type, run to 500 time periods.

431

TABLE 8.7
Consensus in Oral Professions in Societies
of Variable Population and Complexity

Total Number of Ideas in Society	Number of Individuals in the Society		
	6	12	18
10	75(0.29)	65(0.63)	78(0.88)
20	160(0.27)	157(0.63)	145(0.89)
40	349(0.33)	286(0.63)	299(0.92)

Comment: This table reports the time-to-consensus within an oral profession in which the initial level of cultural integration, specialization, and relative size is averaged out. The population of the societies in which the profession operates varies among 6, 12, and 18 individuals and the cultural complexity varies among 10, 20, and 40 ideas. All communication is one-to-one. Each cell contains the average—and the standard deviation, in parentheses—of the number of time periods that lapse before the members of the profession reach 90% of the consensus that will be reached at the 500th time period. This average is computed across 100 societies of the same type, run to 500 time periods.

TABLE 8.8
Consensus in Print Professions in Societies
of Variable Population and Complexity

Total Number of Ideas in Society	Number of Individuals in the Society		
	6	12	18
10	48(0.29)	44(0.59)	42(0.83)
20	85(0.29)	93(0.59)	81(0.83)
40	199(0.29)	199(0.64)	188(0.84)

Comment: This table reports the time-to-consensus within a print profession in which the initial level of cultural integration, specialization, and relative size is averaged out. The population of the societies in which the profession operates varies among 6, 12, and 18 individuals and the cultural complexity varies among 10, 20, and 40 ideas. All communication is one-to-many. Each cell contains the average—and the standard deviation, in parentheses—of the number of time periods that lapse before the members of the profession reach 90% of the consensus that will be reached at the 500th time period. This average is computed across 100 societies of the same type, run to 500 time periods.

Appendix C: Simulation Data
for Academia (Chapter 9)

This appendix includes the simulation data used for chapter 9 (academia). These simulations focus on how individual authors in academic specialties influence the sociocultural structure of the speciality through the diffusion of new ideas. Accordingly, these simulations focus exclusively on factors affecting the diffusion of new information, such as face-to-face communication vs. print, the initial level of cultural integration within the speciality, the degree of overlap with outsiders (i.e., specialization), and relative size.

The data in Tables 9.1 and 9.2 are the results for time-to-diffusion from simulation experiment two in chapter 9, where the societies have fixed population and complexity but vary in the ratio of group sizes and internal cultural integration and specialization.

The data in Tables 9.3 and 9.4 are the results for time-to-diffusion from simulation experiment one in chapter 9, where the societies differ in the size of the population and the complexity of the culture. The following simulations focus on the impact of the societal population and societal complexity on the diffusion of a new idea within an academic speciality.

TABLE 9.1
Diffusion in Oral Speciality in Societies
of Fixed Population and Complexity

Percentage of Ideas Initially Shared by Members of the Profession (Cultural Integration)	Percentage of Ideas Initially Shared Between Members of the Profession and Nonmembers (Specialization)	Ratio of Number of Individuals Within the Profession to Number Without		
		6:6	4:8	3:9
	1%	134(0.95)	126(0.68)	132(0.50)
4%	4%	125(0.94)	116(0.69)	129(0.53)
	9%	123(1.16)	118(0.71)	114(0.57)
	1%	114(0.93)	119(0.76)	121(0.57)
16%	4%	124(1.00)	126(0.71)	128(0.57)
	9%	123(0.99)	125(0.72)	121(0.57)
	1%	118(0.88)	118(0.78)	104(0.56)
36%	4%	119(1.08)	121(0.69)	110(0.57)
	9%	129(1.08)	112(0.58)	95(0.52)

Comment: This table reports the time-to-diffusion of a new idea within an oral speciality in which the initial level of cultural integration, specialization, and relative size vary. The population of the societies in which the profession operates is fixed at 12 and the cultural complexity is fixed at 21. All communication is one-to-one. Each cell contains the average—and the standard deviation, in parentheses—of the number of time periods that lapse before the new idea of an author in the speciality reaches 90% of the diffusion among members within the speciality that will be reached at the 500th time period. This average is computed across 100 societies of the same type, run to 500 time periods.

TABLE 9.2
Diffusion in Print Speciality in Societies
of Fixed Population and Complexity

Percentage of Ideas Initially Shared by Members of the Profession (Cultural Integration)	Percentage of Ideas Initially Shared Between Members of the Profession and Nonmembers (Specialization)	Ratio of Number of Individuals Within the Profession to Number Without		
		6:6	4:8	3:9
	6%	74(0.77)	75(0.66)	78(0.52)
4%	25%	76(0.95)	72(0.69)	70(0.51)
	56%	70(0.87)	66(0.62)	73(0.51)
	6%	65(0.86)	64(0.74)	70(0.54)
16%	25%	67(0.81)	66(0.71)	70(0.55)
	56%	66(0.87)	63(0.58)	60(0.55)

(Continued)

TABLE 9.2
(Continued)

Percentage of Ideas Initially Shared by Members of the Profession (Cultural Integration)	Percentage of Ideas Initially Shared Between Members of the Profession and Nonmembers (Specialization)	Ratio of Number of Individuals Within the Profession to Number Without		
		6:6	4:8	3:9
	6%	62(1.08)	59(0.62)	69(0.55)
64%	25%	58(1.02)	67(0.68)	67(0.57)
	56%	68(0.90)	58(0.74)	67(0.56)

Comment: This table reports the time-to-diffusion of a new idea within a print speciality in which the initial level of cultural integration, specialization, and relative size vary. The population of the societies in which the speciality operates is fixed at 12 and the cultural complexity is fixed at 21. All communication is one-to-many. Each cell contains the average—and the standard deviation, in parentheses—of the number of time periods that lapse before the new idea of an author within the speciality reaches 90% of the diffusion among members of the speciality that will be reached at the 500th time period. This average is computed across 100 societies of the same type, run to 500 time periods.

TABLE 9.3
Diffusion in Oral Speciality in Societies
of Variable Population and Complexity

Total Number of Ideas in Society	Number of Individuals in the Society		
	6	12	18
10	56(0.39)	56(0.68)	64(0.91)
20	93(0.39)	111(0.75)	130(1.01)
40	221(0.40)	218(0.67)	246(1.18)

Comment: This table reports the time-to-diffusion of a new idea within an oral speciality in which the initial level of cultural integration, specialization, and relative size is averaged out. The population of the societies in which the speciality operates varies among 6, 12, and 18 individuals and the cultural complexity varies among 10, 20, and 40 ideas. All communication is one-to-one. Each cell contains the average—and the standard deviation, in parentheses—of the number of time periods that lapse before the new idea of an author within the speciality reaches 90% of the diffusion among members of the speciality that will be reached at the 500th time period. This average is computed across 100 societies of the same type, run to 500 time periods.

435

TABLE 9.4
Diffusion in Print Speciality in Societies
of Variable Population and Complexity

Total Number of Ideas in Society	Number of Individuals in the Society		
	6	12	18
10	29(0.39)	35(0.63)	37(0.90)
20	47(0.39)	63(0.58)	65(0.95)
40	81(0.39)	111(0.71)	140(0.87)

Comment: This table reports the time-to-diffusion of a new idea within a print speciality in which the initial level of cultural integration, specialization, and relative size is averaged out. The population of the societies in which the speciality operates varies among 6, 12, and 18 individuals and the cultural complexity varies among 10, 20, and 40 ideas. All communication is one-to-many. Each cell contains the average—and the standard deviation, in parentheses—of the number of time periods that lapse before the new idea of an author within the speciality reaches 90% of the diffusion among members of the speciality that will be reached at the 500th time period. This average is computed across 100 societies of the same type, run to 500 time periods.

Appendix D: Simulation Data for Migration and Authority (Chapter 10)

Simulations for chapter 10 involve societies with two specialties: (a) a source speciality, in which the migrant is trained; and (b) a target speciality, in which the migrant seeks recognition. In all cases, we assume societies with 2 groups, 12 individuals, and 21 ideas. Both groups are composed of 6 individuals and 10 characteristic ideas at time 1. We further assume that the individual in the social position of the migrant initially has 5 ideas, 2 exclusively belonging to the source group, 2 to the target group and 1 new idea, known initially only to the migrant and to no one else. We systematically vary the initial integration within the source and the target groups. We also vary the communication scenario. We study the migrant in a face-to-face society, in a society where the migrant but no one else has print, and in a society where everyone has print. All of the simulations for chapter 10 are designed to help us isolate the conditions under which the migrant's new idea will diffuse most quickly to the target group.

TABLE 10.1
Diffusion of the Migrant's Idea Across Two Oral Specialities
in Societies of Fixed Population and Complexity

Percentage of Ideas Initially Shared by Members of the Source Speciality (Cultural Integration–Source)	Percentage of Ideas Initially Shared Between Members of the Source and Target Specialities (Specialization)	Percentage of Ideas Initially Shared by Members of the Target Speciality (Cultural Integration–Target)		
		4%	16%	64%
	1%	111(0.89)	88(0.96)	77(0.96)
4%	4%	87(0.90)	89(0.99)	83(0.96)
	16%	107(0.98)	102(0.85)	88(1.79)
	1%	110(1.88)	97(1.00)	80(0.97)
16%	4%	110(0.87)	92(0.92)	92(0.96)
	16%	90(0.88)	103(0.87)	94(0.87)
	1%	98(1.05)	98(0.96)	87(0.96)
64%	4%	112(0.88)	95(0.90)	98(1.01)
	16%	105(0.85)	97(0.90)	85(0.83)

Comment: This table reports the time-to-diffusion of a migrant author's new idea across oral specialities in which the initial level of cultural integration and specialization of both specialities varies. The population of the societies in which the migrant operates is fixed at 12 and the cultural complexity is fixed at 21. All communication is one-to-one. Each cell contains the average—and the standard deviation, in parentheses—of the number of time periods that lapse before the new idea of a migrant in the source speciality reaches 90% of the diffusion among members of the target speciality that will be reached at the 500th time period. This average is computed across 100 societies of the same type, run to 500 time periods.

TABLE 10.2
Diffusion of the Migrant's Printed Idea Across Two Oral Specialities
in Societies of Fixed Population and Complexity

Percentage of Ideas Initially Shared by Members of the Source Speciality (Cultural Integration–Source)	Percentage of Ideas Initially Shared Between Members of the Source and Target Specialities (Specialization)	Percentage of Ideas Initially Shared by Members of the Target Speciality (Cultural Integration–Target)		
		4%	16%	64%
	1%	65(0.83)	61(0.79)	56(0.96)
4%	4%	68(1.01)	67(0.92)	55(0.96)
	16%	81(0.84)	73(0.84)	62(0.79)
	1%	75(0.88)	71(0.91)	63(0.79)
16%	4%	81(0.87)	67(0.84)	70(0.94)
	16%	71(0.88)	73(0.87)	70(0.88)

(Continued)

438

TABLE 10.2
(Continued)

Percentage of Ideas Initially Shared by Members of the Source Speciality (Cultural Integration–Source)	Percentage of Ideas Initially Shared Between Members of the Source and Target Specialities (Specialization)	Percentage of Ideas Initially Shared by Members of the Target Speciality (Cultural Integration–Target)		
		4%	16%	64%
	1%	77(0.86)	70(0.85)	63(0.92)
64%	4%	74(0.92)	74(0.83)	65(0.81)
	16%	79(0.75)	77(0.91)	78(0.91)

Comment: This table reports the time-to-diffusion of a migrant author's new idea when occurring in print across oral specialties in which the initial level of cultural integration and specialization of both specialties varies. The population of the societies in which the migrant operates is fixed at 12 and the cultural complexity is fixed at 21. All communication is one-to-one, except for the migrant author in the source speciality who can communicate one-to-many through a text. Each cell contains the average—and the standard deviation, in parentheses—of the number of time periods that lapse before the new idea of the migrant author (and the author's text) in the source speciality reaches 90% of the diffusion among members of the target speciality that will be reached at the 500th time period. This average is computed across 100 societies of the same type, run to 500 time periods.

TABLE 10.3
Diffusion of the Migrant's Printed Idea Across Two Print Specialities
in Societies of Fixed Population and Complexity

Percentage of Ideas Initially Shared by Members of the Source Speciality (Cultural Integration–Source)	Percentage of Ideas Initially Shared Between Members of the Source and Target Specialities (Specialization)	Percentage of Ideas Initially Shared by Members of the Target Speciality (Cultural Integration–Target)		
		4%	16%	64%
	1%	59(0.94)	53(0.96)	47(0.96)
4%	4%	54(0.79)	48(0.90)	50(0.96)
	16%	55(0.76)	55(1.00)	57(0.79)
	1%	60(0.98)	56(0.82)	50(0.78)
16%	4%	62(1.05)	57(0.87)	55(1.06)
	16%	55(0.89)	55(0.89)	51(0.89)
	1%	64(0.99)	55(0.90)	51(0.91)
64%	4%	59(0.82)	60(0.83)	61(0.99)
	16%	61(0.82)	66(1.03)	62(1.00)

Comment: This table reports the time-to-diffusion of a migrant author's new idea across oral specialties in which the initial level of cultural integration and specialization of both specialties varies. The population of the societies in which the migrant operates is fixed at 12 and the cultural complexity is fixed at 21. All communication is one-to-many. Each cell contains the average—and the standard deviation, in parentheses—of the number of time periods that lapse before the new idea of a migrant author (and the author's text) in the source speciality reaches 90% of the diffusion among members of the target speciality that will be reached at the 500th time period. This average is computed across 100 societies of the same type, run to 500 time periods.

References

Abbott, A. (1988). *The system of professions: An essay on the division of expert labor.* Chicago: University of Chicago Press.

Adatto, K. (1990). *Sound bite democracy: Network evening news presidential campaign coverage, 1968 and 1988.* (Research Paper R-2). Cambridge, MA: The Joan Shorenstein Barone Center for Press, Politics, and Public Policy, John F. Kennedy School of Government, Harvard University.

Airaksinen, T. (1988). *The ethics of coercion and authority: A philosophical study of social life.* Pittsburgh: University of Pittsburgh Press.

Ajzen, I., & Fishbein, M. (1980). *Understanding attitudes and predicting social behavior.* Englewood Cliffs, NJ: Prentice-Hall.

Aldrich, H. (1979). *Organizations and environments.* Englewood Cliffs, NJ: Prentice-Hall.

Alexander, J. C. (Ed.). (1988). *Durkheimian sociology: Cultural studies.* New York: Cambridge University Press.

Alexander, J., Giesen, D., Munch, R., & Smelser, N. (1987). *The micro–macro link.* Berkeley: University of California Press.

Alexander, M., & Danowski, J. (1990). Analysis of an ancient network: Personal communication and the study of social structure in a past society. *Social Network, 12,* 313–336.

Allen, J. B. (1971). *The friar as critic: Literary attitudes in the latter middle ages.* Nashville: Vanderbilt University Press.

Altick, R. (1957). *The English common reader: A social history of the mass reading public 1800–1900.* Chicago: University of Chicago Press.

Altick, R. (1988). *Writers, readers, and occasions.* Columbus: Ohio State University Press.

Altick, R. D. (1962). The sociology of authorship. *New York Public Library Bulletin, 66,* 389–404.

Anderson, N. H. (1971). Integration theory and attitude change. *Psychological Review, 78,* 171–206.

Anderson, P. (1985). What survey research tells us about writing at work. In L. Odell & D. Goswami (Eds.), *Writing in nonacademic settings* (pp. 1–84). New York: Guilford.

Archer, M. (1988). *Culture and agency: The place of culture in social theory.* London: Cambridge University Press.

440

Ashmore, R. D., & Del Boca, F. K. (1981). Conceptual approaches to stereotypes and stereotyping. In D. L. Hamilton (Ed.), *Cognitive processes in stereotyping and intergroup behavior* (pp. 1–35). Hillsdale, NJ: Lawrence Erlbaum Associates.

Atkins, C. D., & Johnson, M. (Eds.). (1985). *Writing and reading differently: Deconstruction and the teaching of composition and literature.* Lawrence, KS: University of Kansas.

Atwan, R. (1979). Newspapers and the foundations of modern advertising. In J. W. Wright (Ed.), *The commercial connection* (pp. 9–23). New York: Delta.

Austin-Broos, D. (Ed.). (1987). *Creating culture.* London: Allen & Unwin.

Bakhtin, M. (1981). *The dialogic imagination: Four essays* (C. Emerson, Trans.). Austin: University of Texas Press.

Bakhtin, M. (1986). *Speech genres and other late essays* (V. W. McGee, Trans.). Austin: University of Texas Press.

Bar-Hillel, Y. (1960). The present status of the automatic translation of languages. In F. L. Alt (Ed.), *Advances in Computers I.* (pp. 92–164). New York: Academic Press.

Barnes, J. (1964). *Free trade in books: A study of the London book trade since 1800.* Oxford: Clarendon.

Barnes, J. J. (1974). *Authors, publishers, and politicians: The quest for an Anglo-American copyright agreement 1815–1854.* Columbus: Ohio State University Press.

Barnes, S. B. (1936). The editing of early learned journals. *Osiris, 1,* 155–172.

Barry, H. V. (1987). Toward a model for copyright infringement. In *Copyright Law Symposium* (Vol. 33, pp. 1–36). New York: Columbia University Press.

Barthes, R. (1981). The death of the author. In J. Caughie (Ed.), *Theories of authorship* (pp. 208–213). London: Routledge & Kegan Paul.

Barthes, R. (1982a). Authors and writers. In S. Sontag (Ed.), *A Barthes reader* (pp. 187–188). New York: Hill & Wang.

Barthes, R. (1982b). Flaubert and the sentence. In S. Sontag (Ed.), *A Barthes Reader* (pp. 208–213). New York: Hill & Wang.

Bazerman, C. (1988). *Shaping written knowledge: The rise of the experimental report.* Madison: University of Wisconsin Press.

Bazerman, C. (1991). How natural philosophers can cooperate: The literary technology of coordinated investigation in Joseph Priestley's "History and Present State of Electricity." In C. Bazerman & J. Paradis (Eds.), *Texts and the professions* (pp. 13–44). Madison: University of Wisconsin Press.

Bazerman, C., & Paradis, J. (Eds.). (1991). *Texts and the professions.* Madison: University of Wisconsin Press.

Beard, C. (1914). *Contemporary American history.* New York: Macmillan.

Becker, M. H. (1970). Sociometric location and innovativeness: Reformulation and extension of the diffusion model. *American Sociological Review, 35,* 267–282.

Belanger, T. (1982). Publishers and writers in 18th century England. In I. Rivers (Ed.), *Books and their readers in 18th century England* (pp. 3–23). Leicester: Leicester Press.

Beljame, A. (1948). *Men of letters and the English public in the 18th century, 1660–1744, Dryden, Addison, Pope.* London: Grove Press.

Bellow, S. (1977). Writers and literature in American society. In J. Ben-David & T. Clark (Eds.), *Culture and its creators* (pp. 185–192). Chicago: University of Chicago Press.

Ben-David, J. (1960). Roles and innovations in medicine. *American Journal of Sociology, 65,* 557.

Ben-David, J. (1963). Professions in the class system of present day societies. *Current Sociology, 11,* 247–298.

Ben-David, J., & Collins, J. B. (1966). Social factors in the origins of a new science: The case of psychology. *American Sociological Review, 31,* 451–465.

Bender, T. (1984). The erosion of public culture: Cities, discourses, and professional disciplines. In T. L. Haskell (Ed.), *The authority of experts: Studies in history and theory* (pp. 84–106). Bloomington: Indiana University Press.

Bengston, V. (1975). Generational and family effects in socialization. *American Sociological Review, 40*, 358–371.

Bengston, V., & Troll, L. (1978). *Youth and their parents: Feedback and intergenerational influence in socialization.* New York: Academic Press.

Beniger, J. R. (1986). *The control revolution: Technological and economic origins of the information society.* Cambridge, MA: Harvard University Press.

Bennett, W. L. (1977). The ritualistic and pragmatic bases of political campaign discourse. *Quarterly Journal of Speech, 63,* 219–238.

Bennett, W. L. (1980). *Public opinion in American politics.* New York: Harcourt, Brace, Jovanovich.

Bennett, W. L. (1985). Communication and social responsibility. *Quarterly Journal of Speech, 71,* 259–288.

Berger, P. L., & Luckman, T. (1966). *The social construction of reality.* Garden City, NY: Doubleday.

Berlant, J. L. (1975). *Profession and monopoly.* Berkeley: University of California Press.

Bernays, E. (1923). *Crystallizing public opinion.* New York: Liverwright.

Bitzer, L. (1968). The rhetorical situation. *Philosophy & Rhetoric, 1,* 1–14.

Blakeslee, A. (1991a). *Becoming a scientist: Master and apprentice.* Unpublished manuscript, Carnegie Mellon University, Department of English, Pittsburgh.

Blakeslee, A. (1991b). *Rapid dissemination of novel knowledge claims in physics.* Unpublished manuscript, Carnegie Mellon University, Department of English, Pittsburgh.

Blau, P. M. (1967). *Exchange and power in social life.* New York: Wiley.

Blau, P. M. (1977). *Inequality and heterogeneity.* New York: The Free Press of Macmillan Co.

Bledstein, B. (1976). *The culture of professionalism.* New York: Norton.

Bloom, H. (1973). *The anxiety of influence.* New York: Oxford.

Blumer, H. (1969). *Symbolic interactionism.* Englewood Cliffs, NJ: Prentice-Hall.

Bolter, J. (1991). *Writing space: The computer, hypertext, and the history of writing.* Hillsdale, NJ: Lawrence Erlbaum Associates.

Bonham-Carter, V. (1978). *Authors by profession* (Vols. 1 & 2). Los Altos: William Kauffman.

Booth, W. (1970). *Now don't try to reason with me: Essays and ironies for a credulous age.* Chicago: University of Chicago Press.

Booth, W. (1974). *Modern dogma and the rhetoric of assent.* Chicago: University of Chicago Press.

Booth, W. (1979). *Critical understanding.* Chicago: University of Chicago Press.

Booth, W. (1988). *The company we keep: An ethics of fiction.* Berkeley: University of California Press.

Boulding, K. (1956). *The image: knowledge in life and society.* Ann Arbor: University of Michigan.

Bowker, R. (1912). *Copyright: Its history and its law.* Boston: Houghton.

Boyle, J. (1991, April). *A theory of law and information: Copyright, spleens, blackmail, and insider trading.* Paper presented at the Society for Critical Exchange Conference on Intellectual Property and the Construction of Authorship, Case Western Reserve University, Cleveland, OH.

Brandt, D. (1989). The message is the massage: Orality and literacy once more. *Written Communication, 6,* 31–44.

Brandt, D. (1990). *Literacy as involvement: The acts of writers, readers, and texts.* Carbondale: Southern Illinois Press.

Brannigan, A. (1981). *The social basis of scientific discoveries.* Cambridge: Cambridge University Press.

Brooks, C., Purser, J. T., & Warren, R. P. (1967). *An approach to literature* (4th ed.). New York: Appleton-Century-Crofts.

Brooks, C., & Warren, R. P. (1959). *Understanding fiction* (2nd ed.). New York: Appleton-Century-Crofts.

Brown, P., & Levinson, S. (1987). *Politeness: Some universals in language usage.* New York: Cambridge University Press.

Bruffee, K. (1986). Social construction, language, and knowledge. *College English, 48,* 773–790.

Burke, K. (1966). *Language as symbolic action.* Berkeley: University of California Press.

Burke, K. (1969). *A rhetoric of motives.* Berkeley: University of California Press.

Burt, R. S. (1973). The differential impact of social integration on participation in the diffusion of innovations. *Social Science Research, 2,* 125–144.

Burt, R. S. (1980). Innovation as a structural interest: Rethinking the impact of network position innovation adoption. *Social Networks, 4,* 337–355.

Burt, R. S. (1982). *Toward a structural theory of action.* New York: Academic Press.

Bush, R. R., & Mosteller, F. (1955). *Stochastic models of learning.* New York: Wiley.

Callon, M., & Latour, B. (1981). Unscrewing the big Leviathan: How actors macro-structure reality and how sociologists help them to do so. In K. Knorr-Cetina & A. Cicourel (Eds.), *Advances in social theory and methodology* (pp. 277–303). London: Routledge & Kegan Paul.

Caplow, T. (1954). *The sociology of work.* Minneapolis: University of Minnesota.

Carey, J. W. (1988). *Communication as culture: Essays on media and society.* Boston: Unwin & Hyman.

Carley, K. (1984). *Constructing consensus.* Unpublished doctoral dissertation, Harvard University, Cambridge, MA.

Carley, K. (1986a). An approach for relating social structure to cognitive structure. *Journal of Mathematical Sociology, 12,* 137–189.

Carley, K. (1986b). Knowledge acquisition as a social phenomenon. *Instructional Science, 14,* 381–438.

Carley, K. (1986c). *Language: Society's chronicle* (Working paper). Department of Social and Decision Sciences, Carnegie Mellon University, Pittsburgh.

Carley, K. (1987). *Separating the effects of structure and interaction.* Presented at Sunbelt Social Network Meeting, Santa Barbara, CA.

Carley, K. (1988). Formalizing the social expert's knowledge. *Sociological Methods and Research, 17,* 165–232.

Carley, K. (1989a). *On the persistence of beliefs* (Working paper). Department of Social and Decision Sciences, Carnegie Mellon University, Pittsburgh.

Carley, K. (1989b). The value of cognitive foundations for dynamic social theory. *Journal of Mathematical Sociology, 14,* 171–208.

Carley, K. (1990a). *Computer analysis of qualitative data* [Overheads]. Washington, DC: American Sociological Association Meetings.

Carley, K. (1990b). Group stability: A socio-cognitive approach. In E. Lawler, B. Markovsky, C. Ridgeway, & H. Walker (Eds.), *Advances in group processes* (Vol. 7, pp. 1–44). Greenwich, CT: JAI.

Carley, K. (1990c). Structural constraints on communication: The diffusion of the homomorphic signal analysis technique through scientific fields. *Journal of Mathematical Sociology, 15,* 207–246.

Carley, K. (1991a). Growing up: The development and acquisition of social knowledge. In J. Howard & P. Callero (Eds.), *The self-society dynamic: Cognition, emotion, and action* (pp. 72–105). New York: Cambridge University Press.

Carley, K. (1991b). A theory of group stability. *American Sociological Review, 5-6,* 331–354.

Carley, K. (in press-a). The social construction of knowledge. In R. Lawler (Ed.), *Experiments in epistemology.* Norwood, NJ: Ablex.

Carley, K. (in press-b). Knowledge, interaction, and language. In R. Lawler (Ed.), *Experiments in epistemology.* Norwood, NJ: Ablex.

Carley, K. (in press-c). Content analysis. *The encyclopedia of language and linguistics.* Edinburgh, UK: Pergamon Press.

Carley, K. (in press-d). Coding choices for textual analysis: A comparison of content analysis and map analysis. *Sociological Methodology.*

Carley, K., Hummon, N., & Harty, M. (1991). *Scientific influence: An analysis of the main path structure in the journal of conflict resolution.* Manuscript submitted for publication.

Carley, K., & Kaufer, D. (1990, October). *Factoring the reach of a scientific paper.* Paper presented at the Society for the Social Study of Science, Minneapolis, MN.

Carley, K., & Kaufer, D. (in press). Semantic connectivity: An approach for analyzing symbols in semantic networks. *Communication Theory.*

Carley, K., & D. Krackhardt (1992). *Asymmetric friendships: A socio-cognitive examination of asymmetric relationships.* Working Paper, Heinz School of Public Policy and Management. Carnegie Mellon University, Pittsburgh.

Carley, K., & Newell, A. (1990, August). *On the nature of the social agent.* Paper presented at the American Sociological Association Annual Meeting, Washington, DC.

Carley, K., & Palmquist, M. (1992). Extracting, representing, and analyzing mental models. *Social Forces, 70*(3), 601–636.

Carley, K., with Wendt, K. (1991). Electronic mail and scientific communication: A study of the Soar extended group. *Knowledge: Creation: Diffusion: Utilization, 12,* 406–440.

Carlyle, T. (1899). On heroes, hero-worship, and the heroic in history. *Critical and miscellaneous essays* (Vols. 1–5). London: Chapman & Hall.

Carr-Saunders, A. P. & Wilson, P. (1933). *The professions.* Oxford: Oxford University Press.

Carroll, G. R. (1984). Organizational ecology. *Annual Review of Sociology, 10,* 71–93.

Cassirer, E. (1953). *The philosophy of symbolic forms.* New Haven: Yale University Press.

Chafe, W. (1970). *Meaning and the structure of language.* Chicago: University of Chicago Press.

Chase, I. D. (1974). Social process and hierarchy formation in small groups. *American Sociological Review, 45,* 905–924.

Cherry, R. (1988). Ethos versus persona: Self-representation in written discourse. *Written Communication, 5,* 251–276.

Chilcott, T. (1972). *A publisher and his circle: The life and work of John Taylor, Keats's publisher.* London: Routledge & Kegan Paul.

Christian, H. (1980). Journalists' occupational ideologies and press commercialization. In H. Christian (Ed.), *The sociology of journalism and the press* (pp. 259–306). Totowa, NJ: Rowman & Littlefield.

Chubin, D. E., & Moitra, S. D. (1975). Content analysis of references: Adjunct or alternative to citation counting? *Social Studies of Science, 5,* 423–441.

Cicourel, A. (1970). The acquisition of social structure: Toward a developmental sociology of language and meaning. In J. Douglas (Ed.), *Understanding everyday life* (pp. 136–168). Chicago: Aldine.

Cicourel, A. (1974). *Cognitive sociology.* New York: Free Press.

Cicourel, A. (1981). Notes on the integration of micro- and macro-levels of analysis. In K. Knorr-Cetina and A. Cicourel (Eds.), *Advances in social theory and methodology* (pp. 51–80). London: Routledge & Kegan Paul.

Clanchy, M. T. (1978). *From memory to written record in England, 1066–1307.* Cambridge, MA: Harvard University Press.

Clark, P., & Clark, T. (1980). Patrons, publishers, and prizes. In J. Ben-David & T. Nichols (Eds.), *Culture and its creators* (pp. 72–96). Chicago: University of Chicago Press.

Cohen, M. D., March, J., & Olsen, J. (1972). A garbage can model of organizational choice. *Administrative Science Quarterly, 17,* 1–25.

Cole, J. R., & Cole, S. (1973). *Social stratification in science.* Chicago: University of Chicago Press.

Coleman, J. S., Katz, E., & Menzel, H. (1966). *Medical innovation: A diffusion study.* New York: Bobbs-Merrill.

Collins, A. S. (1929). *The profession of letters: A study of the relation of author to patron, publisher, and public, 1780–1832.* New York: Dutton.

Collins, R. (1975). *Conflict sociology: Toward an explanatory paradigm.* New York: Academic Press.

Collins, R. (1979). *The credential society: An historical sociology of education and stratification.* New York: Academic Press.

Collins, R. (1981). Micro-translation as theory-building strategy. In K. Knorr-Cetina & A. Cicourel (Eds.), *Advances in social theory and methodology* (pp. 81–108). London: Routledge & Kegan Paul.

Conley, D. (1990). Author, user, scholar, thief: Fair use and unpublished works. *Cardozo Arts & Entertainment Journal, 9,* 15–60.

Coser, L. (1965). The profession of letters in eighteenth century England. In *Men of Ideas: A Sociologist's View* (pp. 37–49). New York: The Free Press.

Crane, D. (1971). *The invisible college.* Chicago: University of Chicago Press.

Crane, D. (1974). The gatekeepers of science: Some factors affecting the selection of articles for scientific journals. *The American Sociologist, 2,* 195–201.

Cressy, D. (1980). *Literacy and the social order: Reading and writing in Tudor and Stuart England.* London: Cambridge University Press.

Cronin, B. (1982). Invisible colleges and information transfer: A review and commentary with particular reference to the social sciences. *Journal of Documentation, 38,* 212–236.

Cronin, B. (1984). *The citation process.* London: Taylor Graham.

Cross, N. (1985). *The common writer: life in nineteenth century Grubb Street.* Cambridge: Cambridge University Press.

Crowther, J. G. (1941). *The social relations of science.* New York: Macmillan.

Cruse, A. (n.d.). *The Englishman and his books in the early nineteenth century.* New York: Thomas Crowell.

Culler, J. (1982). *On deconstruction.* Ithaca, NY: Cornell University Press.

Curran, J. (1979). *Mass communication and society.* Beverly Hills, CA: Sage.

D'Alembert, J. (1963). *Preliminary discourse to the encyclopedia of Diderot* (R.N. Schwab, Trans.). Indianapolis: Bobbs-Merrill.

Danowski, J. (1982). Organizational infographics and automated auditing: Using computers to unobtrusively gather and analyze communication. In G. Goldhaber & G. Barnett (Eds.), *Handbook of Organizational Communication* (pp. 385–433). Norwood, NJ: Ablex.

Darnton, R. (1979). *The business of the Enlightenment: A publishing history of the encyclopedia.* Cambridge: Harvard University Press.

Darnton, R. (1983). What is the history of books? In K. E. Carpenter (Ed.), *Books and society in history* (pp. 3–36). New York & London: R. R. Bowker Company.

Davis, J. A. (1966). Structural balance, mechanical solidarity, and interpersonal relations. In J. Berger, M. Zelditch, & B. Anderson (Eds.), *Sociological theories in progress* (Vol. 1, pp. 74–101). Boston: Houghton Mifflin.

Dear, P. (1985). Totius in verba: Rhetoric and authority in the early Royal Society. *Isis, 76,* 145–161.

DeGrazia, M. (1991, April). *Shakespeare in quotation.* Paper presented at the Society for Critical Exchange Conference on Intellectual Property and the Construction of Authorship, Case Western Reserve University, Cleveland, OH.

Derrida, J. (1976). *Of grammatology.* Baltimore: Johns Hopkins.

Derrida, J. (1978). *Writing and difference.* London: Routledge & Kegan Paul.

Derrida, J. (1988). *Limited, Inc.* Evanston: Northwestern University Press.

Dillard, A. (1989). *The writing life.* New York: Harper & Row.

Donaldson v. Beckett, 4 Buw. 2408, 98 Eng. Rep. 257. (1774).

Douglass, R. B., Mara, G., & Richardson, H. (1990). *Liberalism and the good.* New York & London: Routledge.

Dretske, F. (1988). *Explaining behavior.* Cambridge: MIT Press.

Duncan, H. (1968). *Symbols in society.* New York: Oxford University Press.

Durkheim, E. (1965). *The elementary forms of the religious life.* (J. W. Swain, Trans.). New York: Free Press. (Original work published 1912)

Dworkin, R. (1982). Law as interpretation. *Critical Inquiry, 9,* 179–200.

Dyer, G. (1982). *Advertising as communication.* London & New York: Methuen.

Edelman, M. (1977). *Political language.* New York: Academic Press.

Edge, D., & Mulkay, M. (1976). *Astronomy transformed: The emergence of radio astronomy.* New York: Wiley.

Egido, C. (1990). Teleconferencing as a technology to support cooperative work: Its possibilities and limitations. In J. Galegher, R. Kraut, & C. Egido (Eds.), *Intellectual teamwork: Social and technological foundations of cooperative work* (pp. 351–372). Hillsdale, NJ: Lawrence Erlbaum Associates.

Eisenstein, E. L. (1979). *The printing press as an agent of change, communications, and cultural transformations in early modern Europe* (Vols. 1–2). London: Cambridge University Press.

Eliot, P. (1978). Professional ideology and organizational change: The journalist since 1800. In J. C. B. Boyce & P. Wingate (Eds.), *Newspaper history: From the seventeenth century to the present day* (pp. 172–179). Beverly Hills, CA: Sage.

Enos, R. L. (Ed.). (1990). *Oral and written communication: Historical approaches.* Newbury Park, CA: Sage.

Erdman, D., & Fogel, E. (Eds.). (1966). *Evidence for authorship: Essays on problems of attribution, with an annotated bibliography of selected readings.* Ithaca, NY: Cornell University Press.

Etzioni, A. (1964). *Modern organizations.* Englewood Cliffs, NJ: Prentice-Hall.

Fahenstock, J., & Secor, M. (1991). The rhetoric of literary criticism. In C. Bazerman & J. Paradis (Eds.), *Texts and the professions* (pp. 76–96). Madison: University of Wisconsin Press.

Faigley, L. (1989). Judging writing, judging selves. *College Composition and Communication, 40,* 395–413.

Fararo, T. J., & Skvoretz, J. (1986). E-state structuralism. *American Sociological Review, 51,* 591–602.

Fararo, T. J., & Skvoretz, J. (1987). Unification research programs: Integrating two structural theories. *American Journal of Sociology, 92,* 1183–1209.

Fauconnier, G. (1985). *Mental spaces: Aspects of meaning construction in natural language.* Cambridge, MA: Bradford Books.

Febvre, L., & Martin, H.-J. (1976). *The coming of the book: The impact of printing 1450–1800.* (D. Gerard, Trans.). G. Nowell-Smith & D. Wooton (Eds.). London: NLB.

Feldman, M., & March, J. (1981). Information as signal and symbol. *Administrative Science Quarterly, 26,* 171–186.

Festinger, L. (1950). Informal social communication. *Psychological Review, 57,* 271–282.

Festinger, L. (1954). A theory of social comparison processes. *Human Relations, 7,* 117–140.

Festinger, L. (1957). *A theory of cognitive dissonance.* Evanston: Row Peterson.

Festinger, L., Cartwright, D., Barber, K., Fleichl, J., Gottsdanker, J., Keysen, A., & Leavitt, G. (1948). The study of a rumor: Its origin and spread. *Human Relations, 1,* 464–486.

Fish, R., Kraut, R., Root, R., & Rice, R. (1992, January). *Evaluating video as a technology of informal communication.* Human Computer Interaction Consortium workshop, Software Engineering Institute, Carnegie Mellon University, Pittsburgh.

Fish, S. (1980). *Is there a text in this class? The authority of interpretive communities.* Cambridge, MA: Harvard University Press.

Fisher, C. S. (1967). The last invariant theorists. *European Journal of Sociology, 8,* 216–244.

Fisher, W. (1987). *Human communication as narration: Toward a philosophy of reason, value, and action.* Columbia, SC: University of South Carolina Press.

Flower, L. (1988). The construction of purpose in writing and reading. *College English, 50,* 528–550.

Forkert, O. (1933). *From Gutenberg to the cuneo press: An historical sketch of the printing press.* Chicago: The Cuneo Press.

Foucault, M. (1977). What is an author? *Language, counter-memory, practice* (pp. 113–138). Oxford: Basil Blackwell.

Foucault, M. (1980). *Power/knowledge* (C. Gordon, Ed. and Trans.), New York: Pantheon.

Freeman, L. C. (1984). Impact of computer-based communication on the social structure of an emerging scientific specialty. *Social Networks, 6,* 201–221.

Freidson, E. (1970). *Professional dominance.* Chicago: Aldine.

Friedson, E. (1986). *Professional powers.* Chicago: University of Chicago Press.

Fussell, P. (1971). *Samuel Johnson and the life of writing.* New York: Harcourt Brace Jovanovich.

Galbraith, J. (1973). *Designing complex organizations.* Reading, MA: Addison-Wesley.

Galegher, J. (1990). Intellectual teamwork and information technology; The role of information systems in collaborative intellectual work. In J. S. Carroll (Ed.), *Applied social psychology in organizational settings* (pp. 193–216). Hillsdale, NJ: Lawrence Erlbaum Associates.

Garfield, E. (1955). Citation indices for science. *Science, 122,* 109–110.

Garfield, E. (1980). Has scientific communication changed in 300 years? *Current Contents, 8,* 394–400.

Garfinkel, H. (1968). *Studies in ethnomethodology.* Englewood Cliffs, NJ: Prentice-Hall.

Garfinkel, H., Lynch, M., & Livingston, E. (1981). The work of a discovering science construed with materials from the optically discovered pulsar. *Philosophy of the Social Sciences, 11,* 131–158.

Garvey, W. (1979). *Communication: The essence of science.* Oxford: Pergamon Press.

Geertz, C. (1973). *The interpretation of cultures.* New York: Basic Books.

Geisler, C. (1990). The artful conversation: Characterizing the development of advanced literacy. In R. Beach & S. Hynds (Eds.), *Developing discourse processes in adolescence and adulthood* (pp. 93–109). Norwood, NJ: Ablex.

Geisler, C. (1991). Toward a sociocognitive model of literacy: Constructing mental models in a philosophical conversation. In C. Bazerman & J. Paradis (Eds.). *Texts and the professions* (pp. 171–190). Madison: University of Wisconsin Press.

Geisler, C. (1992). Exploring academic literacy: An experiment in composing. *College Composition and Communication, 43,* 39–54.

Geisler, C. (in press). *The nature of expertise in writing.* Hillsdale, NJ: Lawrence Erlbaum Associates.

Geisler, C., & Kaufer, D. S. (1989). Making meaning in literate conversations: A teachable sequence for reflective writing. *Rhetoric Society Quarterly, 19,* 229–244.

Giddens, A. (1976). *New rules of sociological method: A positive critique of interpretive sociologies.* New York: Basic Books.

Giddens, A. (1979). *Central problems in social theory: Action, structure, and contradiction in social analysis.* Berkeley: University of California Press.

Giddens, A. (1984). *The constitution of society: Outline of the theory of structuration.* Cambridge: Polity Press.

Giddens, A. (1987). Structuralism, post-structuralism and the production of culture. In A. Giddens & J. Turner (Eds.). *Social theory today* (pp. 195–223). Palo-Alto: Stanford University.

Giere, R. N. (1988). *Explaining science: A cognitive approach.* Chicago: University of Chicago Press.

Gieryn, T., Bevins, G., & Zehr, C. (1985). The professionalization of American scientists. *American Sociological Review, 50,* 392–408.

Gieryn, T. F., & Hirsh, R. (1983). Marginality and innovation in science. *Social Studies of Science, 13,* 87–106.

Gieryn, T. F., & Hirsh, R. (1984). Marginalia: Reply to Simonton and Handberg. *Social Studies of Science, 14,* 624.

Gilbert, G. N. (1976). The development of science and scientific knowledge: The case of radar meteor research. In R. M. Lemaine, M. Mulkay, & P. Weingart (Eds.), *Perspectives on the emergence of scientific disciplines* (pp. 187–204). The Hague: Mouton.

Gilbert, N. (1976). The transformation of research findings into scientific knowledge. *Social Studies of Science, 6,* 281–306.

Gilbert, N. (1977). Referencing as persuasion. *Social Studies of Science, 7,* 113–122.

Gilbert, N., & Mulkay, M. (1984). *Opening pandora's box: A sociological analysis of scientist's discourse.* Cambridge: Cambridge University Press.

Glass, J., Bengston, V. L., & Dunham, C. C. (1986). Attitude similarity in three-generation families: Socialization, status inheritance, or reciprocal influence? *American Sociological Review, 51,* 685–698.

Glick, P. C. (1960). Intermarriage and fertility patterns among persons in major religious groups. *Eugenics Quarterly, 7,* 31–38.

Glut, D. F. (1984). *The Frankenstein catalog.* Jefferson, NC: McFarland.

Goffman, E. (1959). *The presentation of self in everyday life.* New York: Doubleday/Anchor.

Goffman, E. (1963). *Behavior in everyday places: Notes on the social organization of gatherings.* New York: Free Press.

Goffman, E. (1974). *Frame analysis: An essay on the organization of experience.* New York: Harper & Row.

Golding, P. (1974). *The mass media.* London: Longman.

Goode, J. G. (1960). Norm commitment and conformity to role-status obligations. *American Journal of Sociology, 66,* 246–258.

Goody, J. (1986). *The logic of writing and the organization of society.* Cambridge: Cambridge University Press.

Gossett, T. F. (1985). *Uncle Tom's cabin and American culture.* Dallas: Southern Methodist University.

Graber, D. (1976). *Verbal behavior and politics.* Urbana, IL: University of Illinois.

Graff, G. (1987). *Professing literature: An institutional history.* Chicago: University of Chicago Press.

Graff, G., & Warner, M. (1989). *The origins of literary studies in America.* New York: Routledge.

Granovetter, M. S. (1973). The strength of weak ties. *American Journal of Sociology, 68,* 1360–1380.

Granovetter, M. S. (1974). *Getting a job: A study of contacts and careers.* Cambridge: Harvard University Press.

Gray, H. (1981, October). *The liberal arts revisited. Eighth David D. Henry lecture.* Chicago: University of Chicago Circle Press.

Hall, M. B. (1965). Henry Oldenburg and the art of scientific communication. *British Journal for the History of Science, 2,* 277–290.

Handberg, R. (1984). Response of Gieryn and Hirsh. *Social Studies of Science, 14,* 622–624.

Hannan, M. T., & Freeman, J. (1977). The population ecology of organizations. *American Journal of Sociology, 82,* 929–940.

Harris, J. (1989). The idea of community in the study of writing. *College Composition and Communication, 40,* 11–22.

Harris, R. (1986). *The origin of writing.* La Salle, IL: Open Court.

Harvey, J. M. (1986). Social sciences. In A. J. Walford (Ed.), *Reviews and reviewing: A guide* (pp. 53–89). Phoenix: Oryx.

Heider, F. (1958). *The psychology of interpersonal relations.* New York: Wiley.

Heise, D (1977). Social action as the control of affect. *Behavioral Science, 22,* 163–177.

Hempel, J., & Oppenheim, P. (1948). Studies in the logic of explanation. *Philosophy of Science, 15,* 135–175.

Hepburn, J. (1968). *The author's empty purse and the rise of the literary agent.* London: Oxford.

Heritage, J. (1984). *Garfinkel and ethnomethodology.* Cambridge: Polity Press.

Herron, J. (1988). *Universities and the myth of cultural decline.* Detroit: Wayne State Press.

Hiltz, S. R., & Turoff, M. (1978). *The network nation: Human communication via computer.* Reading, MA: Addison-Wesley.

Hiltz, S. R. (1984). *Online communities: A case study of the office of the future.* Norwood, NJ: Ablex.

Hirsch, E. D. (1972). *Validity in interpretation.* New Haven, CT: Yale University Press.

Hirsch, E. D. (1982). Against theory? In T. Mitchell (Ed.), *Against theory: Literary studies and the new pragmaticism* (pp. 48–52). Chicago, IL: University of Chicago Press.

Hirsch, E. D. (1987). *Cultural literacy.* Boston: Houghton-Mifflin.

Hoge, D. R., Petrillo, G. H., & Smith, E. I. (1982). Transmission of religious and social values from parents to teenage children. *Journal of Marriage and the Family, 44,* 569–580.

Holmes, F. (1987). Scientific writing and scientific discovery. *Isis, 78,* 220–235.

Homans, G. C. (1950). *The human group.* New York: Harcourt, Brace.

Homans, G. C. (1961). *Social behavior: Its elementary forms.* New York: Harcourt Brace Jovanovich.

Houghton, B. (1975). *Scientific periodicals.* London: Bingley.

Houston, R. A. (1988). *Literacy in early modern Europe: Culture and education 1500–1800.* London & New York: Longman.

Hubbard, L. R. (1985). *Mission Earth Dekalogy.* Los Angeles: Bridge Publications, Inc.

Hudson, K. (1978). *The language of modern politics.* New York: Macmillan.

Hughes, G. (1989). *Words in time: Printing, the Reformation, Renaissance.* Oxford: Oxford University Press.

Hummon, N., & Carley, K. M. (in press). Social networks as normal science. *Social Networks.*

Hunter, J. E., Danes, J. E., & Cohen, S. H. (1984). *Mathematical models of attitude change.* New York: Academic Press.

Hunter, M. (1981). *Science and society in restoration England.* Cambridge: Cambridge University Press.

Hunter, M. (1989). *Establishing the new science: The experience of the early Royal Society.* Woodbridge: Boydell Press.

Innis, H. (1951). *The bias of communication.* Toronto: University of Toronto Press.

Jaeger, W (1965). The rhetoric of Isocrates and its cultural ideal. In J. Schwartz & J. Rycenga (Eds.), *The province of rhetoric* (pp. 84–110). New York: Ronald Press.

Jamieson, K. H. (1988). *Eloquence in an electronic age: The transformation of political speechmaking.* New York: Oxford University Press.

Jennings, M. K., & Niemi, R. G. (1982). *Generations and politics: A panel study of young adults and their parents.* Princeton: Princeton University Press.

Johnson, J. C. (1986). Social networks and innovation adoption: A look at Burt's use of structural equivalence. *Social Networks, 8,* 343–364.

Johnson, L. (1987). Raymond Williams: A Marxist view of culture. In D. Austin-Broos (Ed.), *Creating culture* (pp. 163–177). London: Allen & Unwin.

Johnson, T. J. (1967). *Professions and power.* London: Macmillan.

Johnson-Laird, P. N. (1983). *Mental models: Toward a cognitive science of language, inference, and consciousness.* Cambridge, MA: Harvard University Press.

Kamuf, P. (1988). *Signature pieces: On the institution of authorship.* Ithaca, NY: Cornell.

Kapferer, B. (1972). *Strategy and transaction in an African factory: African workers and Indian management in a Zambian town.* Manchester: University of Manchester Press.

Katz, E., Levin, M. L., & Hamilton, H. (1963). Traditions of research on the diffusion of innovations. *American Sociological Review, 28,* 237–253.

Kaufer, D. S., & Carley, K. (1991). *Some concepts and axioms about communication: Proximate and at a distance.* Unpublished manuscript. Pittsburgh: Carnegie Mellon University Dept. of English.

Kaufer, D. S., & Carley, K. (in press). Condensation symbols: Their variety and function in political discourse. *Philosophy and Rhetoric.*

Kaufer, D. S., & Geisler, C. (1989). Novelty in academic writing. *Written Communication, 8,* 286–311.

Kaufer, D. S., & Geisler, C. (1990). Structuring argumentation in a social constructivist framework: A pedagogy with computer support. *Argumentation, 4,* 379–396.

Kaufer, D. S., & Geisler, C. (1991). A scheme for representing written argument. *Journal of Advanced Composition, 11*(1), 107–122.

Kaufer, D. S., Geisler, C., & Neuwirth, C. (1989). *Arguing from sources: Exploring issues through reading and writing.* San Diego: Harcourt Brace Jovanovich.

Kaufer, D. S., Neuwirth, C., Chandhok, R., & Morris, J. (in press). Writing and design: A retrospective report. In D. Ferguson, S. Ehrmann & D. Bilestri (Eds.), *Learning to design, designing to learn.* Washington, DC: Hemisphere Press.

Kennedy, A. (1989, December). *The uses of literacy and the curriculum project at Carnegie Mellon.* Paper presented at the Modern Language Association session on Curriculum reform in English: Culture, rhetoric, literacy, work, Washington, DC.

Kennedy, R. (1944). Single or triple melting-pot? Intermarriage trends in New Haven 1870–1940. *American Journal of Sociology, 49,* 331–339.

Kernan, A. (1987). *Printing technology, letters, and Samuel Johnson.* Princeton: Princeton University Press.

Kernan, A. (1990). *The death of literature.* New Haven, CT: Yale University Press.

Kerr, E. B., & Hiltz, S. R. (1982). *Computer-mediated communication systems.* New York: Academic Press.

Kessler, C. (1987). Marx as cultural theorist: The prehistory of modern anthropology. In D. Austin-Broos (Ed.), *Creating culture* (pp. 35–49). London: Allen & Unwin.

Kiesler, S., Siegel, J., & McGuire, T. (1984). Social psychological aspects of computer-mediated communication. *American Psychologist, 39,* 1123–1134.

Kiesler, S., & Sproull, L. (1987). *Computing and change on campus.* New York: Cambridge University Press.

Kingston, P. W., & Cole, J. R. (1980). *The wages of writing: per word, per piece, perhaps.* New York: Columbia University Press.

Kittay, J. (1986). Utterance unmoored: The changing interpretation of the act of writing in the European middle ages. *Language in Society, 17,* 209–230.

Klancher, J. P. (1987). *The making of English reading audiences, 1790–1832.* Madison: University of Wisconsin.

Knorr-Cetina, K. (1981). The micro-sociological challenge of macrosociology. In K. Knorr-Cetina & A. Cicourel (Eds.), *Advances in social theory and methodology* (pp. 3–52). London: Routledge & Kegan Paul.

Knorr-Cetina, K., & Cicourel, A. (Eds.). (1981). *Advances in social theory and methodology.* London: Routledge & Kegan Paul.

Krackhardt, D., & Kilduff, M. (1990). Friendship patterns and culture: The control of organizational diversity. *American Anthropologist, 92,* 142–154.

Krackhardt, D., & Porter, L. W. (1986). The snowball effect: Turnover embedded in communication networks. *Journal of Applied Psychology, 71,* 50–55.

Kraut, R., Egido, C., & Galegher, J. (1990). Patterns of contact and communication in scientific research collaboration. In J. Galegher, R. Kraut, & C. Egido (Eds.), *Intellectual teamwork: Social and technological foundations of cooperative work* (pp. 149–172). Hillsdale, NJ: Lawrence Erlbaum Associates.

Kraut, R., Galegher, J., & Egido, C. (1988). Relationships and tasks in scientific research collaboration. *Human-computer interaction, 3*, 31–58.

Kronick, D. A. (1962). *A history of scientific and technical periodicals: The origins and development of the scientific and technological press 1665–1790.* New York: Scarecrow Press.

Kucklick, B. (1977). *The rise of American philosophy: Cambridge, Massachusetts 1860–1930.* New Haven, CT: Yale.

Kuhn, T. (1970). *The structure of scientific revolutions.* Chicago: University of Chicago Press.

Labov, W., & Fanshel, D. (1977). *Therapeutic discourse: Psychotherapy as conversation.* New York: Academic Press.

Laird, J., Newell, A., & Rosenbloom, P. (1987). Soar: An architecture for general intelligence. *Artificial Intelligence, 33*, 1–64.

Langer, S. (1957). *Philosophy in a new key.* (3rd ed.). Cambridge, MA: Harvard University Press.

Langley, P., Simon, H., Bradshaw, G., & Zytkow, J. M. (1987). *Scientific discovery: Computational explorations of the creative process.* Cambridge, MA: MIT Press.

Lanham, R. A. (1992). Review: From book to screen: Four recent reviews. *College English, 54*, 199–206.

Laquer, T. (1980). Toward a cultural ecology of literacy in England, 1600–1850 In D. Resnick (Ed.), *Literacy: Historical perspectives* (pp. 43–57). Washington, DC: Library of Congress.

Larmarque, P. (1991). The death of the author: An analytic autopsy. *British Journal of Aesthetics, 30*, 319–331.

Larson, M. (1977). *The rise of professionalism.* Berkeley: University of California Press.

Latour, B., & Bastide, F. (1982). Writing science—Fact and fiction. In M. Callon (Ed.), *Mapping the dynamics of science and technology: Sociology of science in the real world* (pp. 51–66). Basingstoke: Macmillan.

Latour, B., & Woolgar, S. (1979). *Laboratory life: The social construction of scientific facts.* Beverly Hills: Sage.

Laurenson, D. (1969). A sociological study of authorship. *British Journal of Sociology, 20*, 311–325.

Laurenson, D., & Swingewood, A. (1971). *The sociology of literature.* London: MacGibbon & Kee.

Law, J. (1973). The development of specialties in science: The case of x-ray protein crystallography, *Science Studies, 3*, 275–304.

Leach, E. (1976). *Culture and communication: The logic by which symbols are connected.* Cambridge: Cambridge University Press.

Lee, A. (1978). The structure, ownership, and control of the press, 1855–1914. In G. Boyce, J. Curran, & P. Wingate (Eds.), *Newspaper history: From the seventeenth century to the present day* (pp. 117–129). Beverly Hills: Sage.

Levine, K. (1986). *Th social context of literacy.* London: Routledge & Kegan Paul.

Lievrouw, L., & Carley, K. (1990). Changing patterns of communication among scientists in an era of telescience. *Technology in Society, 12*, 457–477.

Lin, N., & Burt, R. S. (1975). Differential effects of information channels in the process of innovation on diffusion. *Social Forces, 54*, 256–274.

Lippman, W. (1922). *Public opinion.* New York: Macmillan.

Litman, J. (1990). The public domain. *Emory Law Journal, 39*, 965–999.

Litman, J. (1991, April). *Copyright as myth.* Paper presented at the Society for Critical Exchange Conference on Intellectual Property and the Construction of Authorship. Case Western Reserve University, Cleveland, OH.

Lorrain, F., & White, H. (1971). Structural equivalence of individuals in social networks. *Journal of Mathematical Sociology, 1,* 49–80.

Lowenthal, M. F., Thurnher, M., & Chiriboga, D. (1975). *Four stages of life.* San Francisco: Jossey-Bass.

Lukes, S. (1974). *Power: A radical view.* New York: Macmillan.

Lyons, H. (1968). *The Royal Society 1660–1940: A history of its administration under its charters.* New York: Greenwood Press.

MacRoberts, M. H., & MacRoberts, B. R. (1986). Quantitative measures of communication in science: A study of the formal level. *Social Studies of Science, 16,* 151–172.

Madden, D. (1989). A personal view: The "Real life" fallacy. In B. Siegel (Ed.), *The American writer and the university* (pp. 182–185). Newark: University of Delaware Press.

Mailloux, S. (1989). *Rhetorical power.* Ithaca, NY: Cornell University Press.

Mallon, T. (1989). *Stolen words: Forays into the origins and ravages of plagiarism.* New York: Ticknor & Fields.

Malone, T., & Crowston, K. (1991). *Toward an interdisciplinary theory of coordination* (Tech. Rep. No. CCS TR# 120). Cambridge, MA: MIT, Sloan School of Management, Center for Coordination Science.

March, J., & Simon, H. (1958). *Organizations.* New York: Wiley.

Martin, H.-J. (1981). Printing. In R. Williams (Ed.), *Contact: Human communication and its history* (pp. 127–150). London: Thames & Hudson.

McBroom, W., Reed, W., Burns, C., Hargraves, J., & Trankel, M. (1985). Intergenerational transmission of values: A data-based reassessment. *Social Psychology Quarterly, 48,* 150–163.

McCloskey, D. (1987). *The rhetoric of economics.* Madison: University of Wisconsin Press.

McGarry, K. J. (1981). *The changing context of information.* London: Clive Bingley.

McGee, M. C. (1980). The ideograph: A link between rhetoric and ideology. *Quarterly Journal of Speech, 66,* 1–16.

McGill, M. L. (1991). *Wheaton v. Peters and the materiality of the text.* Paper presented at the Society for Critical Exchange Conference on Intellectual Property and the Construction of Authorship. Case Western Reserve University, Cleveland, OH.

McInnis, R., & Symes, D. (1988, September). David Riesman and the concept of bibliographic citation. *College and Research Libraries, 50,* 387–399.

McLuhan, M. (1962). *The Gutenberg galaxy.* Toronto: University of Toronto Press.

McMurtrie, D. (1937). *The book: The story of printing & bookmaking.* New York: Covici-Friede.

McPherson, J., & Smith-Lovin, L. (1987). Homophily in voluntary organizations: Status distance and the composition of face-to-face groups. *American Sociological Review, 52,* 370–379.

Mead, G. H. (1962). *Mind, self, and society.* Chicago: University of Chicago Press. (Original work published 1934)

Meadows, A. (1973). *Communication in science.* London: Butterworths.

Melischek, G., Rosengren, K., Stappers, J. (Eds.). (1984). *Cultural indicators: An international symposium.* Vienna: Austrian Academy of Science.

Menzel, H. (1960). *Review of studies in the flow of information among scientists.* New York: Columbia University Bureau of Applied Research.

Merod, J. (1987). *The political responsibility of the critic.* Ithaca, NY: Cornell University Press.

Merton, R. K. (1938). Science and the social order. *Philosophy of Science, 5,* 321–327.

Merton, R. K. (1970). *Science, technology, and society in seventeenth century England.* New York: Fertig. (Original work published 1938)

Merton, R. K. (1949). *Social theory and social structure.* New York: Free Press.

Millerson, G. (1964). *The qualifying associations.* London: Routledge.

Moran, J. (1973). *Printing presses: History and development from the fifteenth century to modern times.* Berkeley: University of California.

Moravscik, M. J., & Murugesan, P. (1975). Some results on the function and quality of citations. *Social Studies of Science, 5,* 86–92.

Morman, E. T. (1981). Citation analysis and the current debate over quantitative methods in the social studies of science. *Society for the Social Studies of Science Newsletter, 5,* 7–13.

Mueller, M. (1989). Yellow stripes and dead armadillos. *Profession 89, 24,* 18–24.

Mulkay, M. (1973). *The social process of innovation.* London: Macmillan.

Mullins, N. (1980). *Social networks among biological scientists.* New York: Arno Press.

Mullins, N. C. (1972). The development of a scientific specialty: The phage group and the origins of molecular biology. *Minerva, 10,* 51–82.

Mumby, F. A. (1956). *Publishing and bookselling: A history from the earliest times to the present day.* London: Jonathan Cape.

Munch, R., & Smelser, N. J. (1987). Relating the micro and the macro. In J. Alexander, F. Giesen, R. Munch, & N. Smelser (Eds.), *The micro–macro link* (pp. 356–387). Berkeley: University of California.

Myers, G. (1985). Text as knowledge claims: The social construction of two biologist's proposals. *Social Studies of Science, 15,* 593–630.

Namenwirth, J. Z., & Weber, R. P. (1987). *Dynamics of culture.* Boston: Allen & Unwin.

Nelson, C., & Pollack, P. (1970). *Communication among scientists and engineers.* Lexington, MA: Heath.

Neuwirth, C., & Kaufer, D. S. (in press). Theorizing computers and composition: Defining a mode of inquiry. In P. Leblanc & G. Hawisher (Eds.), *Reimaging composition in the virtual age.* Boston: Boynton-Cook.

Neuwirth, C., Kaufer, D. S., Chandhok, R., & Morris, J. (1990). Issues in the design of computer support for co-authoring and commenting. *Proceedings of the Conference for the Computer-Supported Cooperative work* (pp. 183–195). Los Angeles, Baltimore: Association for Computing Machinery: Special Interest Group for Computers and the Human Interface.

Newell, A. (1990). *Unified theories of cognition.* Cambridge, MA: MIT Press.

Nystrand, M. (1986). *The structure of written communication: Studies in reciprocity between writers and readers.* Orlando: Academic Press.

Nystrand, M. (1989). A social-interactive model of writing. *Written Communication, 6,* 66–85.

Nystrand, M. (1990). Sharing words: The effects of readers on developing writers. *Written Communication, 7,* 3–24.

Olson, D. R. (1977). From utterance to text: The bias of language in speech and writing. *The Harvard Educational Review, 47,* 257–281.

Olson, J., Olson, G., Mack, L., Wellner, P. (1990). Concurrent editing: The group's interface. *Human-Computer Interaction.* New York: Elsevier Science Publishers.

Ong, W. (1958). *Ramus: Method, and the decay of dialogue: From the art of discourse to the art of reason.* Cambridge: Harvard.

Ong, W. (1971). *Rhetoric, romance, and technology.* Ithaca, NY: Cornell.

Ong, W. (1975). The writer's audience is always a fiction. *PMLA 90,* 9–21.

Ong, W. (1980). Reading technology, and the nature of man: An interpretation. *Yearbook of English Studies, 10,* 1132–1149.

Ong, W. (1982). *Orality and literacy.* London: Methuen.

Oswald, J. (1928). *A history of printing: Its development through five hundred years.* New York: Appleton & Company.

Palmquist, M. (1990). *The lexicon of the classroom: Language and learning in writing classrooms.* Unpublished doctoral dissertation, Department of English, Carnegie Mellon University, Pittsburgh.

Pappas, N. (1989). Authorship and authority. *Journal of Aesthetics and Art Criticism, 47,* 325–332.

Paradis, J., Dobrin, D., & Miller, R. (1985). Writing at Exxon ITD: Notes on the writing environment of an r&d organization. In L. Odell & D. Goswami (Eds.), *Writing in nonacademic settings* (pp. 281–307). New York: Guilford Press.

Parsons, T. (1937). *The structure of social action.* New York: McGraw Hill.

Parsons, T. (1949). *Essays in sociological means and ends in a national organization.* New York: Free Press.

Patten, R. L. (1978). *Charles Dickens and his publishers.* Oxford: Clarendon.

Patterson, L. (1968). *Copyright in historical perspective.* Nashville, TN: Vanderbilt University Press.

Pfeffer, J., & Salancik, G. R. (1978). *The external control of organizations: A resource dependency perspective.* New York: Harper & Row.

Pforzheimer, W. L. (1964). Historical perspective on copyright law and fair use. In L. Hattery & G. P. Bush (Eds.), *Reprography and copyright law.* Baltimore: Port City Press.

Pocock, J. G. A. (1971). *Politics, language, and time: Essays on political thought and history.* New York: Atheneum.

Polanyi, M. P. (1962). *Personal knowledge: Towards a post-critical philosophy.* Chicago: University of Chicago Press.

Pool, I. D., & Kochen, M. (1978). Contacts and influence. *Social Networks, 1,* 5–51.

Powell, W., & DiMaggio, P. (1991). *The new institutionalism in organizational analysis.* Chicago: University of Chicago Press.

Price, D. (1963). *Little science, big science.* New York: Columbia University Press.

Price, D. J. (1965). Networks of scientific papers. *Science, 149,* 510–515.

Price, D. J. (1970). Citation among scientists, social scientists, humanists. In C. E. Nelson & D. K. Pollock (Eds.), *Communication among scientists and technologists* (pp. 3–23). Lexington, MA: Heath.

Ragan, J. (1989). A personal view: The academy and the "you know?" generation. In B. Siegel (Ed.), *The American writer and the university* (pp. 161–176). Newark: University of Delaware Press.

Rafferty, T. (1992, January). Smoke and mirrors. *New Yorker,* 73–75.

Rapoport, A. (1953). Spread of information through a population with socio-structural bias. *Bulletin of Mathematical Biophysics, 15,* 523–546.

Ravetz, J. R. (1971). *Scientific knowledge and its social problems.* Baltimore: Penguin.

Reder, W. J. (1966). *The rise of the professional classes in nineteenth century England.* London: Weidenfeld & Nicolson.

Resnick, D. (Ed.). (1983). *Literacy in historical perspective.* Washington, DC: Library of Congress.

Resnick, D. P., & Resnick, L. B. (1977). The nature of literacy: An historical exploration. *Harvard Educational Review, 47,* 370–385.

Reynolds, L. D., & Wilson, N. G. (1968). *Scribes and scholars: A guide to the transmission of Greek and Latin literature.* Oxford: Clarendon Press.

Reynolds, M. D. (1985). *Uncle Tom's Cabin and mid-nineteenth century United States.* Jefferson, NC: McFarland.

Reynolds, Q. (1955). *The fiction factory: The story of 100 years of publishing at Street & Smith.* New York: Random House.

Richards, I. A. (1936). *The philosophy of rhetoric.* New York: Oxford.

Rice, R. E. (1980). Impacts of organizational and interpersonal computer-mediated communication. In M. Williams (Ed.), *Annual review of information science* (Vol. 15, pp. 221–249). White Plains, NY: Knowledge and Industry Publications.

Rice, R. E. (1984). *The new media: Communication, research, and technology.* Beverly Hills, CA: Sage.

Rice, R. E. (1987). Computer-mediated communication systems and organizational innovation. *Journal of Communication, 37,* 65–94.

Rice, R. E., & Case, D. (1983). Electronic message systems in the university: A description of use and utility. *Journal of Communication, 33,* 131–152.

Rice, R. E., & Crawford, G. A. (in press). Analysis of citations between communication and library and information science articles. In S. Schement & B. Ruben (Eds.), *Information and behavior.* New Brunswick, NJ: Transaction Press.

Rodden, J. (1989). *The politics of literary reputation.* New York: Oxford.

Roediger, H. L. (1987). The role of journal editors in the scientific process. In D. N. Jackson & J. P. Rushton (Eds.), *Scientific excellence: Origins and assessment* (p. 227). Beverly Hills, CA: Sage.

Rogers, E. M. (1979). Network analysis of the diffusion of innovations. In P. W. Holland & S. Leinhardt (Eds.), *Perspectives on social network research* (pp. 137–164). New York: Academic Press.

Rogers, E. M. (1982). *Diffusion of innovations.* New York: Free Press.

Romney, K., Batchelder, W. H., & Weller, S. (1987). Recent applications of cultural consensus theory. *American Behavioral Scientist, 31,* 163–177.

Romney, K., Weller, S., & Batchelder, W. H. (1986). Culture as consensus: A theory of culture and informant accuracy. *American Anthropologist, 88,* 313–338.

Rorty, R. (1979). *Philosophy and the mirror of nature.* Princeton, NJ: Princeton University Press.

Rose, M. (1988). The author as proprietor: Donaldson v. Becket and the genealogy of modern authorship. *Representations, 23,* 56.

Rose, M. (1969). *Lives on the boundary: The struggles and achievements of America's underprepared.* New York: Free Press.

Rosenthal, L. (1991, April). *Disembodied Shakespeare: The author as ghost.* Paper presented at the Society for Critical Exchange Conference on Intellectual Property and the Construction of Authorship, Case Western Reserve University, Cleveland, OH.

Rouse, J. (1987). *Knowledge and power: Toward a political philosophy of science.* Ithaca, NY: Cornell.

Ruthven, K. K. (1979). *Critical assumptions.* Cambridge, MA: Cambridge University Press.

Said, E. (1983). *The world, the text, the critic.* Cambridge, MA: Harvard University Press.

Saunders, J. W. (1964). *The profession of English letters.* London: Routledge & Kegan Paul.

Schatz, B. R. (1991). Building an electronic scientific community. *Proceedings of the Twenty-Fourth Annual Hawaii International Conference on System Sciences,* pp. 739–748.

Schilb, J. (1989). Composition and poststructuralism. *College Composition and Communication, 40,* 453.

Schofield, R. S. (1981). Dimensions of illiteracy in England 1750–1850. In Harvey Graff (Ed.), *Literacy and social development in the West: A reader* (pp. 201–213). New York: Cambridge University Press.

Schudson, M. (1978). *Discovering the news: A social history of American newspapers.* New York: Basic Books.

Scott, R. W. (1981). *Organizations: Rational, natural, and open systems.* Englewood Cliffs, NJ: Prentice-Hall.

Seaton, J. C., & Curran, J. (1985). *Power without responsibility.* London: Routledge.

Servos, J. W. (1990). *Physical chemistry from Ostwald to Pauling: The making of a science in America.* Princeton: Princeton University Press.

Shulman, N. (1975). Life-cycle variations in patterns of close relationships. *Journal of Marriage and the Family, 37*, 813–821.

Siegel, B. (1989). Poets, novelists, and professors—A bittersweet mix. In B. Siegel (Ed.), *The American writer and the university* (pp. 9–35). Newark: University of Delaware Press.

Simmel, G. (1950). *The sociology of George Simmel.* New York: Free Press.

Simmel, G. (1955). *Conflict and the web of group affiliations.* (K. Wolff & R. Bendix, Trans.). New York: Free Press. (Original work published 1908)

Simon, H. A. (1976). *Administrative behavior* (3rd ed.). New York: Free Press.

Simon, H. A. (1981). *The sciences of the artificial* (2nd ed.). Cambridge, MA: MIT Press.

Simon, H. A. (1983). *Reason in human affairs.* Stanford: Stanford University Press.

Simonton, D. K. (1984). Is the marginality effect all that marginal? *Social Studies of Science, 14*, 621–622.

Simonton, D. K. (1988). *Scientific genius: A psychology of science.* New York: Cambridge University Press.

Skvoretz, J., & Fararo, T. (in press). Action programs and sociological action theory. *Journal of Mathematical Sociology.*

Skvoretz, J., Fararo, T., & Axten, N. (1980). Role-programme models and the analysis of institutional structure. *Sociology, 14*, 49–67.

Small, H. G. (1978). Cited documents as concept symbols. *Social Studies of Science, 8*, 327–340.

Smith, A. (1978). The long road to objectivity and back again: The kinds of truth we get in journalism. In G. Boyce, J. Curran, & P. Wingate (Eds.), *Newspaper history: From the seventeenth century to the present day* (pp. 153–171). Beverly Hills, CA: Sage.

Smith, A. (1979). Technology and control: The interactive dimensions of journalism. In J. Curran (Ed.), *Mass communication and society* (pp. 174–194). New York: Scarecrow.

Smith, L. P. (1971). *Words and Idioms: Studies in the English Language.* Detroit: Gale Research.

Smith, P. (1988). *Discerning the subject.* Minneapolis: University of Minnesota Press.

Smith-Lovin, L. (1988). Impression formation from events. *Journal of Mathematical Sociology, 13*, 35–70.

Sowa, J. F. (1984). *Conceptual structures.* Reading, MA: Addison-Wesley.

Speck, W. A. (1982). Politicians, peers, and publication by subscription, 1700-1750. In I. Rivers (Ed.), *Books and their readers in 18th century England* (pp. 47–68). New York: St. Martin's Press.

Sprinker, M. (1989). The current conjecture in theory. *College English, 51*, 825–832.

Sproull, L., & Kiesler, S. (1986). Reducing social context cues: Electronic mail in organizational communication. *Management Science, 32*, 1492–1512.

Stamaty, M. A. (1992, January 13). [Editorial cartoon]. *Pittsburgh Post Gazette.*

Steinberg, E. (Ed.). (1991). *Plain language: Principles and practice.* Detroit, MI: Wayne State University Press.

Stephens, M. (1988). *A history of news: From the drum to the satellite.* New York: Viking Press.

Stille, A. (1989, February). The novel as status symbol. *The Atlantic,* pp. 20–28.

Stryker, S. (1980). *Symbolic interactionism.* Menlo Park, CA: Benjamin Cummings.

Stryker, S. (1987). The vitalization of symbolic interactionism. *Social Psychology Quarterly, 50*, 83–94.

Stubbs, M. (1980). *Language and literacy: The sociolinguistics of reading and writing.* London: Routledge & Kegan Paul.

Surrey, R. (1930). *Copy technique in advertising.* New York: McGraw-Hill.

Swinnerton, F. (1932). *Authors and the book trade.* New York: Knopf.

Tannen, D. (1990). *You just don't understand.* New York: Morrow.

Tebbel, J. (1968). *A history of book publishing in the United States* (Vols. 1–4). New York & London: R. R. Bowker.

Thomas, L., & Stankiewicz, J. (1974). Family correlates of parent–child attitude congruence: Is it time to throw in the towel? *Psychological Reports, 34,* 1038.

Toulmin, S. (1958). *The uses of argument.* Cambridge: Cambridge University Press.

Tremayne, C. N. (1980). The social organization of newspaper houses. In H. Christian (Ed.), *The sociology of journalism and the press* (pp. 142–178). Totowa, NJ: Rowman & Littlefield.

Tully, J., & Skinner, Q. (1989). *Meaning and context: Quentin Skinner and his critics.* Cambridge: Cambridge University Press.

Turner, E. S. (1953). *The shocking history of advertising.* New York: E. P. Dutton.

Turner, J. H. (1988). *A theory of social interaction.* Palo Alto, CA: Stanford.

Turner, R. (1984). The role and the person. *American Journal of Sociology, 84,* 1–23.

Ulmer, G. (1989). *Teletheory: Grammatology in the age of video.* New York: Routledge.

Vachek, J. (1989). *Written language revisited.* Amsterdam: John Benjamins.

Vesey, L. (1965). *The emergence of the American university.* Chicago: University of Chicago Press.

Walford, A. J. (1986). The art of reviewing. In A. J. Walford (Ed.). *Reviews and reviewing: A guide* (pp. 14–16). London: Oryx Press.

Webb, R. K. (1955). *The British working class reader: 1790–1848,* London: Allen & Unwin.

Weber, M. (1968). *Economy and society.* New York: Bedminster Press.

Weber, S. (1987). *Institution and interpretation.* Minneapolis: University of Minnesota Press.

Weinstock, M. (1971). Citation Indices. *Encyclopedia of library and information science,* 16–40.

Weiss, T. (1989). A personal view: Poetry, pedagogy, per-versities In B. Siegel (Ed.), *The American writer and the university* (pp. 149–158). Newark: University of Delaware Press.

Wellek, R., & Warren, A. (1956). *Theory of literature.* New York: Harcourt Brace Jovanovich.

West, J. L. W. (1988). *American authors and the literary marketplace.* Philadelphia: University of Pennsylvania Press.

White, H. C., Boorman, S. A., & Brieger, R. L. (1976). Social structure from multiple networks: Blockmodels of roles and positions. *American Journal of Sociology, 81,* 730–780.

White, J. B. (1984). *When words lose their meaning: Constitutions and reconstitutions of language, character, and community.* Chicago: University of Chicago Press.

Whorf, B. L. (1956). *Language, thought and reality.* Cambridge, MA: MIT Press.

Wilensky, H. L. (1964). The professionalization of everyone? *American Journal of Sociology, 70,* 137–154.

Wiles, R. M. (1976). The relish for reading in provincial England two centuries ago. In P. Korshin (Ed.), *The widening circle: Essays on the circulation of literature in 18th century Europe* (pp. 85–115). Philadelphia: University of Pennsylvania Press.

Williams, R. (1961). *The long revolution.* New York: Columbia University Press.

Williams, R. (1962). *Communication.* Baltimore: Penguin.

Williams, R. (1976). *Keywords: A vocabulary of culture and society.* New York: Oxford.

Williams, R. (1977). *Marxism and literature.* Oxford: Oxford University Press.

Williams, R. (1980). *Problems in materialism and culture.* London: Verso.

Williams, R. (Ed.). (1981). *Contact: Human communication and its history.* London: Thames & Hudson.

Williams, R. (1982). *Writing in society.* Thetford: Thetford Press.

Wilson, C. P. (1985). *The labor of words: Literary professionalism in the progressive era.* Athens: University of Georgia Press.

Winship, G. (1968). *Gutenberg to Plantin: An outline of the early history of printing.* New York: B. Franklin.

Woodmansee, M. (1984). The genius and the copyright: Economic and legal conditions of the emergence of the "Author." *Eighteenth Century Studies, 17,* 425–448.

Woolgar, S. (1980). Discovery: Logic and sequence in a scientific text. In K. Knorr & R. Whitley (Eds.), *The social process of scientific investigation* (pp. 239–268). Boston: Reidel.

Yates, F. (1966). *The art of memory.* Chicago: University of Chicago.

Yen, A. C. (1990). Restoring the natural law: Copyright as labor and possession. *Ohio State Law Journal, 51,* 517–559.

Yinger, J. (1968). A research note on interfaith marriage statistics. *Journal for the Scientific Study of Religion, 7,* 97–103.

Young, E. (1970). Conjectures on original composition. *Edward Young's "Conjectures on Original Composition" in England and Germany.* New York: Folcroft.

Young, R. E. (1978). Paradigms and problems: Needed research in rhetorical invention. In C. Cooper & L. Odell (Eds.), *Research on composing* (pp. 29–48). Urbana, IL: National Conference of Teachers of English.

Zarefsky, D. (1990). *Lincoln, Douglas, & slavery in the crucible of public debate.* Chicago: University of Chicago Press.

Zijderveld, A. (1980). *On cliches: The superstructure of meaning by function in modernity.* London: Routledge & Kegan Paul.

Zloczower, A. (1966). Career opportunities and the growth of scientific discovery in 19th century Germany, with special reference to physiology. Unpublished masters thesis. Hebrew University of Jerusalem. Eliezer Kaplan School of Economics and Social Sciences.

Author Index

459

Subject Index

A